DAILY LIFE IN PALESTINE
AT THE TIME OF CHRIST

Daily Life in
Palestine

at the Time of Christ

Daniel-Rops

Translated from the French by Patrick O'Brian

WEIDENFELD AND NICOLSON
20 NEW BOND STREET LONDON W1

Nihil obstat Joannes M. T. Barton, S.T.D., L.S.S.
Censor deputatus.

Imprimatur E. Morrogh Bernard. Vic. Gen.

Westmonasterii, die 3 Septembris, 1962.

The Nihil obstat *and* Imprimatur *are a declaration
that a book or pamphlet is considered to be free from
doctrinal or moral error. It is not implied that those
who have granted the* Nihil obstat *and* Imprimatur
agree with the contents, opinions or statements expressed.

MADE AND PRINTED IN GREAT BRITAIN BY
MORRISON AND GIBB LIMITED LONDON AND EDINBURGH
17/6971

CONTENTS

TRANSLATOR'S NOTE

All the biblical quotations in this book come from Mgr. Knox's translation of the Vulgate; but for the names in the text, particularly the Old Testament names, I have used the more familiar forms of the Authorized Version, writing Noah, Ham and Obadiah, for example, rather than Noe, Cham and Abdias. This has led to a few inconsistencies, but I hope they are not important.

Patrick O'Brian

LIST OF ILLUSTRATIONS

1 Luxuriant vegetation along the banks of the River Jordan (*Photo: Paul Popper*)

2 The village of Malloula (*Photo: R. P. Grollenberg*)

3 The Roman road across the plains of Transjordan (*Photo: R. P. Grollenberg*)

4 The hill in Jerusalem on which the Temple was built (*Photo: Boudot-Lamotte*)

5 The barren hills of Judaea (*Photo: Chaboux*)

6 The River Jordan (*Photo: Palais de Chaillot*)

7 The Mount of Temptation (*Photo: Viollet*)

8 A Jew wearing a *tallith* (*Photo: Max Yves Bradily*)

9 Ladles used to pour wine in libation (*Photo: Petit Musée de Delphes*)

10 Biblical beasts of burden (*Photo: Dr N. Gidal Rapho*)

11 Mosaics excavated at Caesarea (*Photo: Palais de Chaillot*)

12 Stone ossuary from Jerusalem (*Photo: Viollet*)

13 Roman cooking pot (*Photo: Viollet*)

14 Women drawing water from a well (*Photo: Leinnger*)

15 Bronze sestertii and coins (*Photo: Louis Henri*)

16 Shepherds and their flocks in the shade of the walls of Jericho (*Photo: Riwkin, Stockholm*)

17 A tile stamped with the emblem of the Tenth Roman Legion (*Photo: Dr Y. Aharoni*)

18 Typical oil-burning lamps (*Photo: Viollet*)

ix

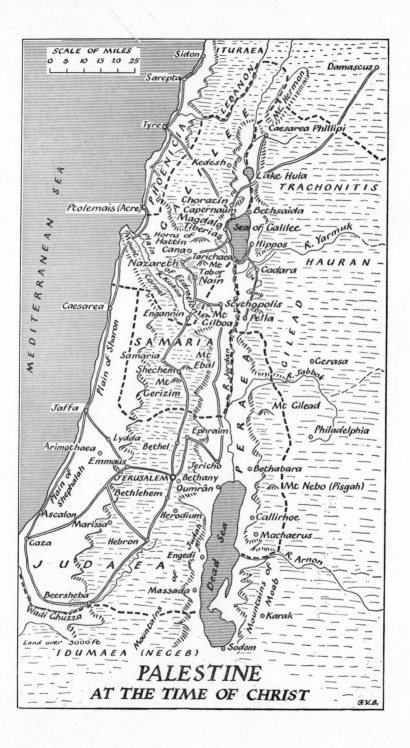

SCALE OF MILES
0 5 10 15 20 25

MEDITERRANEAN SEA

Sidon
ITURAEA
Sarepta
Damascus

Tyre
Caesarea Phillipi

Kedesh
Lake Hula
TRACHONITIS

Ptolemais (Acre)
Chorazin
Capernaum
Bethsaida
Magdala
Tiberias
Sea of Galilee
R. Yarmuk
Horns of
Hattin
Cana
Hippos
Nazareth
Tarichaea
HAURAN
Mt
Tabor
Gadara
Nain

Caesarea
Scythopolis
Engannin
Mt
Pella
Gilboa

SAMARIA
Gerasa
Samaria
Mt
Shechem
Ebal
R. Jabbok
Mt
Gerizim

Jaffa
Mt Gilead
Plain of Sharon
Ephraim
Philadelphia

Lydda
Arimathaea
Bethel
Emmaus
Jericho
Bethabara
JERUSALEM
Bethany
Mt Nebo (Pisgah)
Bethlehem
Qumrân

Ascalon
Herodium
Callirhoe
Marissa
Gaza
Hebron
Machaerus

JUDAEA
Engedi
R. Arnon

Beersheba
Massada
Karak

Wadi Ghuzza
Land over 3000 ft

IDUMAEA (NEGEB)
Sodom

PALESTINE
AT THE TIME OF CHRIST
F.V.B.

PART ONE

A Land and Its People

> Land of Chanaan, a portion allotted
> to thee and thine. (*Psalms*, 104, 11)

CHAPTER ONE

THE GEOGRAPHICAL CONTEXT

Palestine – The beauty and diversity of the Holy Land – Heat and cold: wind and rain – Trees, flowers and fruits – Imples omne animal benedictione.

PALESTINE

Palestine. To a man of our days this is a name that has a very exact meaning: it stands for a country that anyone can easily point out on the map, a country on the western edge of Asia, in that region called by Europe the Near East. A modest rectangle bounded by the 31st and 33rd parallels of north longitude and the meridians 34° 30′ and 36° East roughly contains this country. It runs from the Syrian mountains to the steppes of the Negeb; from the great Arabian desert to the shores of the Mediterranean.[1] Palestine: the name is so loaded with history, with splendour and imagery, so firmly anchored in the memory of men, that it has survived all the changes of the centuries and even today it is still current, in spite of the political decisions that have divided and cut up the Holy Land.

And yet, however surprising it may seem, the term was very far from common two thousand years ago. At all events, it would never have occurred to the people who lived there, the natives, to call their country Palestine. The Bible knows nothing of the word. Some fifteen times[2] in the Old Testament, the Bible, in its Latin version, the Vulgate, speaks of the Palaestini and the country they live in. But it is perfectly clear that this does not refer to the whole of the present Palestine nor to the people of Israel. These Palaestini are the Philistines, and that is how recent editions translate the expression. Philistines: that is, those adventurers, those pirates who appeared as the vanguard of the Aryan invasion in the twelfth century BC; those whom Pharaoh Rameses III conquered under the name of the 'Nations of the Sea'; those who settled in the coastal plain of Sharon and whom the Hebrews,

3

coming out of Egypt, had to fight with so fiercely in the time of Samson, the judge, and of the kings, Saul and David.[3] For the Israelites, therefore, the Pelescheth was merely a district of their land, one which retained the name of a conquered enemy. But the seafaring Greeks, doing business with the ports of the Philistine coast, had taken to calling the whole by the name of the part that they knew and to applying Palaistiné to the entire country: this became current usage in the Graeco-Roman world, and so it has come down to us.

If the people who lived in Palestine in Jesus' day did not call it by this name, what name did they use? In ceremonial, religious and historical contexts they said Land of Canaan. The expression is used nearly a hundred times[4] in the Bible, meaning either a nation or a country. And this too is a surprising state of affairs, for the Canaanites, the people of Canaan, had also been the Hebrews' enemies.[5] According to the biblical tradition they descended from Ham, Noah's second son, whereas the ancestor of Israel was his eldest, Shem.[6] In fact the term covered the whole comples mass of little Mediterranean, Semitic or Armenoid tribes who lived in the region 'from Sidon to Gaza and as far as Gerar and Sodom', before the coming of Joshua and his armies. The Canaanites chiefly occupied the towns, which they had fortified, and which the judges of Israel had such difficulty in besieging. Their name came from the Phoenician *kinahha*, the red-purple dye of the ancients, an important article in the trade of that time. The Israelites, therefore, in naming their country Canaan, called to mind that they had formerly won this land by main force, because God had given it to them.

In the same way they used other expressions which evoked the splendour of their past and its meaning under divine Providence. *Promised Land* was one of these, in memory of the covenant between Abraham and Yahweh, confirmed by the whole history of the Chosen People: the term is also found in the Epistle to the Hebrews.[7] *Holy Land* was another, made customary by the prophet Zechariah.[8] One might suppose that *Land of Israel* was very usual, but although Saint Matthew uses it in the Gospel when he speaks of Jesus' return as a child from Egypt,[9] this is not the case. *Land of Judah*, on the other hand, must have been quite current, for it is used more than a hundred times in the Bible, meaning not merely Judaea, but the whole of Palestine. Yet the most beautiful, the most profound, was that which is to be seen in the Talmud, particularly in those parts written by the rabbis of Babylon, far from the country of their fathers – *the Land*, the country in the highest sense of the word, the land of God.[10]

When these Israelites of two thousand years ago spoke of their country, just what extent of territory did they have in mind? What was the Land of Israel? It was not the whole country of the Bible: even without counting those parts of the Scriptures that are set in foreign parts, such as Mesopotamia, Egypt and even Persia, there are many things in the Old Testament that happen in places that the Jews of the time of Christ would never for a moment have thought of as belonging to them. The Padan-Aram, for example, the 'land of the fathers', at the foot of the Anti-Taurus mountains, where Abraham sojourned during his divinely inspired migration and where Jacob went to seek for a wife:[11] they knew very well that in those far distant times they were no more than wanderers in that land – it did not belong to them. On the other hand, they had never agreed that their own country, the Promised Land, was merely that trifling district of less than eight hundred square miles around Jerusalem, to which 'all that remained of Israel' was limited, when they returned from Babylon in the days of Zerubbabel after the terrible test of the Exile.[12] No: the Holy Land was substantially all that which had been ruled by the most powerful king in biblical history, Solomon, when, in about the year one thousand BC, his undisturbed power stretched 'from Dan to Beersheba' as the saying went – that is, from the neighbourhood of Mount Hermon to the Wadi Ghuzza, and eastwards as far as the steppes of Moab. Two centuries before Christ, after the heroic war of the Maccabees, two famous conquerors, John Hyrcanus and Alexander Jannaeus[13] had almost rebuilt the kingdom of that wise sovereign by a series of rapid victories which gained them Samaria, Galilee, the coastal plain and a large part of Idumaea and Transjordan. It was thus essentially the Palestine of our day. It had been occupied, in 63 BC, by Pompey and his legions; and the Roman administration, taking the part for the whole, called it Judaea.

Even in its utmost splendour Palestine, the land of Canaan, was still a very small country. Those rabbis of the Talmud who, in the enthusiasm of apologetics, so liberally endow it with two and a quarter million square miles[14] – Roman miles – are not to be taken literally. In fact, the area, even counting a considerable stretch of the steppes on the other side of the Jordan, did not much exceed eight thousand five hundred square miles: roughly the same as that of Wales, Belgium or Sicily. Saint Jerome, who had lived for a long time near Bethlehem and who knew the country very well indeed, reckoned its length from north to south at no more than a hundred and sixty Roman miles, which makes some hundred and forty-five English miles, about the distance from London to Exeter, or from Florence to Rome. As to its width, this same Father of the Church declined to give a measurement, so excessive did he find the disproportion between the physical smallness of the Holy Land and its spiritual significance.[15] From the Mediterranean to the Ghor of the Jordan it varies from twenty-five miles in the north to its greatest width of eighty-seven near the Dead Sea. To arrive at a true understanding of life in Palestine it is essential to remember that distances are trifling. An average walker can go from 'Dan to Beersheba' in a week; two days are enough for the journey from Nazareth to Jerusalem; and scarcely one is needed to go down from the holy city to Jericho. This explains the continual movements that the Scriptures speak of, and the relationships between district and district.

For this reason too the Israelites knew their little country well; and they loved it. They knew it in all its aspects, as a farmer knows the smallest paddock on his land. This nation, attached to the soil for at least twelve centuries, had a love for it that is expressed in a most delicate and moving way in many places in the Bible. Whole books – the Song of Songs, for example – are filled with that poetic feeling for the native land that only a deep and penetrating love can give. When they were taken from their country, the children of Israel could not find words piercing enough to express their sorrow. 'In my sad mood I will think of thee, here in this land of Jordan and Hermon, here on Misar mountain . . .'[16] And even more so, the exiled Jews by the waters of Babylon at the time of the great trial.[17] For this love of a land was greater than an earthly love for land itself: it was the sign of everlasting faith.

THE BEAUTY AND DIVERSITY OF THE HOLY LAND

How could the Israelites have failed to love their land? Palestine is a wonderful country, one whose beauty impresses itself upon the traveller even now. How much more obvious its beauty must have been before centuries of Turkish rule had caused the disappearance of so many forests and so much cultivation, and before industrial installations had reared up their pylons, their derricks, their factory chimneys, in places marked with the seal of God.

Everywhere the line of the hills is so exquisite, pure and delicate that it seems drawn by an artist's hand; there is a perfection here that only Attica can rival. Everywhere the relation of the planes, the remote distances, impress a secret harmony upon the mind and cause it to turn towards eternity. Under the hard blue sky colours blaze with an extraordinary richness – the purple of the vineyards' earth, the tender green of the orchards, the pale gold of the ripe barley, the tawny ochre of the desert; and in the sun all these contrasting tones melt into one hot glow, in the shadow into the violet shades of bronze. And, as if to make the harmony sound more clear, here and there groups of dark cypresses strike in, or suddenly the trembling surface of the olive-groves shows blue.

There are few countries that show so much diversity in so small an extent. In a few hours one can go from the shores of a lake that might be in Paradise to the frightening confusion of mountain tops, dry ravines and thistle-strewn screes where the good Samaritan went to the help of a wounded man lying at the side of the road. Five leagues off, the same depression provides the exhilarating sight of a forest worthy of the African savannahs as well as that of a dreadful place where there are no living things and where, under a burning sky, the metallic surface of the lake shines from the bottom of the naked precipices that surround it. A walk of a single hour will take one from the richest of plains to the bare hills where the sheep graze: and the caravans, toiling under the hot wind of the desert, took hope again from the sight of the snow shining on Mount Hermon.

The physical structure of Palestine at the time of Christ was obviously that with which we are acquainted today: the face of the earth does not change much in a mere fifty generations of men. At that time, however, geology and geography were still unborn: the Roman Pliny attempted both most creditably; but the Jews were unconcerned with either. And yet they must have been aware of the astonishing contrasts that exist between one region of their country and another; and however prone they were to poetic licence whenever the Promised Land was concerned they must have admitted that the well-known biblical phrase 'land flowing with milk and honey' could be only very unequally applied to the various parts of it.

The fact of the matter is that according to its geology[18] the whole of Canaan ought to be an arid region, only just good enough for feeding sheep. Apart from a few places in Samaria and Transjordan where now-extinct volcanoes have left stretches of lava, the soil lies upon a fissured white limestone, with a few narrow bands of marl interposed. From this arises the dryness of the whole country, a dryness which is made all the greater by the climate. From this too comes the characteristic appearance of the valleys, which are very deep, cañon-like gorges that isolate the stretches of high land like so many fortresses. And this again is the reason for the abundance of natural caves, which are used throughout the country for flocks and for men – caves such as those in which David hid in his flight from his rebellious son, or in which the Holy Child was born.

A geological accident, however, prevented Palestine from being like the arid chalky part of Champagne or Apulia: it was the consequence of one of those foldings whose nature was not even guessed two thousand years ago. The limestone layer, thrust from the west towards the east, first sloped in a long plane upon which alluvial deposits were able to accumulate and then rose upwards – thus allowing it to catch the clouds – while at the same time it broke apart, cracked and shattered itself into a complex series of surfaces; but above all, as if to tear itself away from the land-masses of Asia, on its eastern side it ripped itself asunder from north to south in two enormous faults which cut right down to its foundations. And between those two faults the entire surface of the ground sank down. It is this episode in geological history that has given Canaan its particular character, the four parallel stretches of its four natural regions and that striking appearance of the hills being as it were inverted, of the surface being hollowed out, which impresses one so strongly as one looks out from the heights of Jerusalem over the gulf which this great rift brought into being, and at the bottom of which the Jordan flows towards the Dead Sea.

The west was the most favoured region in Jesus' time, as it still is now. There was the straight, sandy coast, with tawny dunes running along it and only the single bay of Haifa, behind the headland formed by Mount Carmel, to provide a natural harbour; and behind this coast stretched Sharon, that splendid plain whose wealth had already been praised by the prophet Isaiah,[19] that same plain which the new Israel of our days has filled with citrus-groves. Then, after an irregular line of hills that a Frenchman would compare to the downs of Champagne, came a second alluvial plain, where wheat grew extremely well; this was the Shephalah, which no Israelite would pass without laughing at the recollection of the trick that the great Samson played on the Philistines, when he thought of tying torches to the tails of three hundred foxes and then letting them go in their crops.[20]

Three quite steep steps, intersected by very narrow gorges, lead to the region of the high country, which, running north and south and some thirty miles wide, forms the backbone of the land of Israel. This, for a pious Jew, was the true Canaan, the land holy above all others, in which the least hillock, the smallest stream or village, reminded him of some incident of his famous past. High country? This is perhaps something of an exaggeration. Ordinary language, basing itself upon the Scriptures, certainly referred to the mountains of Judah, Mount Ephraim, Mount Tabor and Mount Gerizim; but these expressions are not to be taken quite literally: after all, in Flanders the Butte du Kemmel, of some three hundred and thirty feet, is called a mountain too. These 'mountains' of Palestine are only big hills, sometimes gently rounded, sometimes weathered into striking peaks upon the horizon of the little plains. Tabor is 1,843 feet, Gerizim 2,849, the highest point of the mountains of Judah reaches 2,788 feet, and Jebel Jermak, the tallest mountain in all Palestine properly so called, does not exceed 3,934 feet. This, however, does not prevent the central region of the Holy Land from giving the traveller the impression that it consists entirely of ups and downs: to be convinced of this one has but to take the road along the ridge from Galilee to Jerusalem; that road which Jesus so often followed with His own people.

It might be supposed that all these high lands were much the same: but this is far from the case. There are three distinct regions which stand out from one another, distinguished by their relief and their climate: the men of the time of Christ were perfectly aware of this, and they were equally aware that this variety, these contrasts, corresponded to different destinies, to differing spiritual meanings. Judaea, in the south, was the stronghold, the place of decisive faith, the place where Abraham had settled, where the kings had made their capital, the place where the true God was worshipped. An arid land, where the

fields had to cling to the sides of the hills in terraces, except
where there were hollows of red silt: a land as monotonous as
the chanting in a synagogue, but beautiful with its limitless
horizons and everywhere, dispersed throughout the landscape,
that tawny colour that brings to mind the skin of a lion: heart-
rendering Judaea, which was to be the scene of Christ's passion.
To the north, beyond Bethel and Shiloh, came Samaria, a much
more variegated country, where low-lying stretches of basaltic
alluvium gave 'the promise of wheat'; where communication
between the Jordan valley and the sea, by the plain of Esdraelon,
was easy; a place of passage, where Barak, answering the call
of the prophetess Deborah, defeated Sisera and his army;[21]
a region of many contacts and also, said the Jews, who hated it,
of immorality, heresy and blasphemy. As for Galilee, composed
of a hundred hills, each with its little plain, it was a better-watered
country; and of all the provinces as far as the foot of Mount
Lebanon it was the most delightful, scattered with clumps of
trees and villages: and this too was a country that the austere
rabbis of Jerusalem distrusted, suspecting it of being soft and
easy-going, not nearly strict enough in observing the holy law.
Galilee, where Jesus was to pass His happy childhood and where
He was to arise to bring the world the good tidings of love.

The third natural region was in no way like the other two. It
was the region where the land had sunk, the *graben*, the trench,
as the geologists say. It was called the Ghor. It is astonishingly
deep. One has to go down well over three thousand feet from
the central ridge to reach its bottom. The depression is narrow –
it is never wider than thirteen miles from east to west – and it
deepens rapidly from north to south, from the foot of Mount
Hermon (which does not really belong geographically to
Palestine, as the book of Joshua had already pointed out[22])
as far as the uttermost limit, where the land of Israel becomes
Idumaea, the home of its enemies the Bedouin. It is a mysterious
wound in our planet's flesh, and geology shows that it goes on,
flanked by volcanoes, northwards into Coele-Syria and much
farther southwards through the Gulf of Aqaba and the Red Sea,
to reach the heart of Africa in the lakes Nyasa and Tanganyika:
the Chosen People had always known that it was connected with
mysterious and terrible happenings which were related in the
Bible. The accursed cities, Sodom and Gomorrah, had been
there, and where they had stood there was still the smell of the

brimstone of divine wrath. It does not appear that the Jews ever plumbed the Dead Sea and found how far down this cleavage went – it reaches 2,600 feet below the level of the Mediterranean, which is one of the lowest points to be measured within a continent. But this great cleft seemed to them so strange that there were prophecies current, according to which it was not to last for ever and that on God's own day the mountains would part and the Mediterranean would rush into the Ghor and fill the immense hollow to its brim.

Was this indeed a distant memory? For at a time within the possible recollection of mankind the entire sunken zone had been filled by a lake that has since, like those that once covered Alsace and the Limagne, been drawn off by evaporation. In the time of Christ there were still three remnants, one of which was soon to vanish, three sheets of water, unequal in size, and two of them, as Tacitus observes in an elliptical phrase 'are traversed by the waters of a river, which the third retains.'[23] This river is the Jordan, the only true river in Palestine. It was the biblical river above all others – the Holy Scripture speaks of it more than two hundred times – that Jordan which had shared in so much of Jerusalem's history and which was still to share in Christ's.

How beautiful in their variety were these 'banks of the Jordan' of which the Psalmist sang. At the northernmost end it was a delightfully wooded country, with water cascading everywhere among the oleanders, the home of the tribe of Dan, a little Switzerland in Palestine, a place where the Romans built a temple to Pan; but where Jesus, stopping with His disciples at the foot of an immense rock, was to say to the faithful Simon, 'Thou art Peter, and it is upon this rock that I will build my Church'. A level place about three miles long then held back the river in a marshy lake: this was what the Bible called Lake Huleh, known also as the Waters of Merom, and famous ever since the time Joshua defeated the allied Jebusites, Amorites and Hittites upon its shores.[24] At the time of the Gospels it was a huge lagoon surrounded by beanfields, and among its reeds, standing upon one frail leg, the stork watched for the carp. Presently, turned into a polder, it will be a Hebrew Holland with two thousand farms, where, as the only memory of the biblical lake, there will be a small zoological reservation, with a few troops of buffaloes and noisy flocks of scarlet flamingoes.

Six miles farther on the river descends rapidly. It is already six hundred and eighty-two feet below sea-level when it reaches a great lake, which it leaves after twelve miles. At the time of Christ's ministry this lake was not yet called the lake of Tiberias. Herod Antipas had only just begun to build his impious city, whose name was to recall that of his Roman protector, Tiberius. It was often called the Sea of Galilee, but this was a little pompous as in fact a boat could cross the lake in half an hour. A more poetical term was Chinnereth, which evoked its harp-like shape, and from which comes the name 'lake of Gennesaret'. Even now it is still one of the most beautiful places in the world: Como, Annecy and the lake of Geneva, the most famous in Europe, have been compared to it. Its clear water, sometimes veined with a strange marbling, varies from the blue of a sapphire to the green of jade, with great rust-red and ochre reflections at the foot of the cliffs on the eastern side. A graceful range of hills surrounds it, and they are covered with precisely divided fields. The lake was already like this at the time when Jesus called His first disciples to Him on its shores, and standing in one of the boats spoke to the crowd gathered on the bank. It may even have been more beautiful, for in our days the trees are too few. At all events it was certainly more animated: there were a great many little white towns and villages that lived by trading and fishing, and today many of these are no more than ruins. Men lived there working happily among the mimosa, the jasmin and the oleanders: this is the country where the kingdom of heaven was promised to peace-makers, the poor in spirit and the humble of heart.

Immediately after the lake the landscape changed. Beyond the barrier of lava that holds back the waters of Gennesaret, the valley grew wilder. It was no longer Paradise but the Kikkar, a strange country in which waste land and thick woods stood side by side – an almost empty steppe on the rim of the valley and a forest following the windings of the stream. Its appearance has changed a great deal in our day: irrigation has allowed *kibutzim* to be established on the dry part, and the woods along the Jordan have grown less. In Christ's time this was a region that men avoided, preferring to follow the hill-road that ran between the foot of the mountains of Judaea and the valley: along this road a series of springs had given rise to a number of oases, rich in palm-trees and adorned with balm. Jericho was the most famous of them, and there Herod the Great built a splendid palace.

Still farther down, the Jordan spreads itself out among the

reeds and the willows, and gradually it vanishes; its muddy current can still be seen for a little as it flows into the heavy grey waters of the Dead Sea, and then it is lost. At this point one is more than twelve hundred feet below the level of the Mediterranean. The air is extraordinarily heavy and quite motionless. The lake, sometimes looking like a sheet of pewter, sometimes like an opaque turquoise, exactly set among its naked rocks, stretches for forty-seven miles: it is as long as the lake of Geneva, and at its widest it is ten miles across. Its water is a strange liquid, oily to the touch and remarkably buoyant: it is filled with salts, and they give off a reek of mineral decay. Its shores are almost entirely devoid of life: there are no birds, only infuriating swarms of insects. Seasonal streams flow into it, and on their banks are a few clumps of tamarisks. In our time this dreary scene has taken on some degree of life. The soda and the potash are exploited; a *kibbutz* grows magnificent tomatoes; and there is even a petrol station and a post-office. But two thousand years ago the solitude was almost complete: no one was to be seen except hermits, dressed in white, who had fled the world in the search of God.

As for the fourth natural region which completes the country of Palestine, it scarcely belonged to it in Jesus' day – and if He went there at all, it was but in the most fleeting manner. *Abasim*, 'the mountains opposite', said the Jews, looking from the heights of Judaea towards the east and seeing there the rim of the plateau that closed their horizon. Southwards it was Idumaea, dear to the poets, the land of Edom, where the red-haired Esau went to digest his wrath after Jacob had taken his birthright,[25] which was the reason why the Bedouins who dwelt in these steppes were on bad terms with the Israelites. And this was the native land of the Herodian family, whose domination so angered the true Jews. Beyond this lay Moab, the violet range behind which Jerusalem beheld the rising of the sun: Moab was a country with great biblical associations – Mount Nebo, from which the dying Moses saw the Promised Land which he would never reach,[26] was there. And there, standing upon a wild hill, was Machaerus, one of those strongholds that the tyrannical Herod had scattered about the Holy Land: this was the ill-fated place where Herod's son, the tetrarch, had John the Baptist's head cut off, to gratify a woman's rage. Farther to the north, the plateau breaks up into abrupt, table-like masses; it has been cut into by streams subject to the most violent floods, the Yarmuk and Jabbok – that Jabbok at whose ford Jacob wrestled all night long with an angel.[27] The Jewish traders passed this way to reach the road on the plateau, the road to Damascus, the same route as that which the modern railway takes. It was a country that might have been very fertile, for the soil formed by the decomposition of basalt is often excellent; but it was scarcely exploited at all – it was no more than a pasture for nomads, crossed by the tracks of caravans. Then, little by little, these thin grazing-grounds gave way to desert.

HEAT AND COLD: WIND AND RAIN

If the look of the land has changed little in these twenty centuries, its climate appears to have altered even less. It is a typical Mediterranean climate, with subtropical characteristics that become more evident from west to east; a climate of strong contrasts in which, as it had already been pointed out in the Song of the Three Children[28] in the book of Daniel, there are in turn to be found heat and cold, fires and frosts, dew and rime, rain and wind, even snow and ice, which, indeed, are not unknown in Palestine, nor are they confined to the top of Mount Hermon.[29]

This climate, as we know it and as Christ's contemporaries knew it, has a great share in the charm of the Holy Land. Everywhere the early mornings are delightful, with all the infinity of shades that go from mauve to yellow – the rosy-fingered dawns of which Homer sang, rather that the grey-eyed mornings of Virgil. Everywhere the twilight is short, lasting moments only, for the darkness overflows the land almost as soon as the sun has dropped beneath the horizon. And everywhere the nights are of an astonishing sublimity, with their blue-black sky so sprinkled with stars that one seems to see a mist of light floating on the mountains, with their immense silence made up of a thousand tiny sounds, with their intoxicating scent of warm earth and wild plants that Ruth and Booz must have breathed long ago in the countryside of Bethlehem.[30]

Two sharply divided seasons and no more share the year between them, a long summer, and a winter of the ordinary length, the periods between them being exceedingly short. In March all vegetation bursts into growth. Even in the driest regions the ground is covered, for a few weeks, with a green carpet from which arise tulips and wild gladioli, yellow crocuses and blood-red anemones. In the fertile parts the spring is truly miraculous, well worthy of being celebrated in that most sublime of love-poems the Song of Songs – 'Winter is over now, the rain has passed by. At home, the flowers have begun to blossom; pruning-time has come; we can hear the turtle-dove cooing already there at home. There is green fruit on the fig-trees; the vines in flower are all fragrance.'

That is not to say that everything in this climate is perfect, nor that the whole country is a paradise. The average temperatures, $72\frac{1}{2}°$ F. for the year, with a monthly minimum of 59 and a maximum of 77° F., do not give a true picture. Palestine may well be a country where clothing and heating do not present very serious difficulties, but the daily and yearly variations are often great. Between midnight and noon the difference is sometimes 72° F., and the nights often so cold that the Law required the creditor to give the debtor back his cloak, taken as a pledge, at dusk. 'In *adar* – March – ' said a proverb, 'the ox shivers at dawn, but at noon he seeks the shade of the fig-trees to loosen his skin.' The contrasts are equally striking between one season and another; and naturally they are made all the greater by the conformation of the country. Thus in winter the pious worshippers in the court of the temple at Jerusalem had their faces lashed by the icy drops borne on the gale, while at Jericho the wealthy took their ease in linen robes; and on an April night, the Gospel shows us Peter coming into the high priest's courtyard for news of his Master, and trying to warm himself at a brazier.[31] On the other hand, at the bottom of the Ghor the summer is so hot – more than 122° in the shade – that even the Red Sea is less intolerable.

And there are the winds: not all of them are those wafting breezes that are held to be the breath of God. The west and the south-west winds, which bring the beneficent clouds in the autumn and which sometimes moderate the heat in the summer, are very much appreciated: but they have enemies which often prevent them from blowing. In the winter there is the *qadim*, the east wind, cold and dry, which makes the air as clear as crystal, but which lowers the temperature by 18° in one blast: it is this same *qadim* which causes 'the kind of whirlwind' that the tractate *Kilayim*[32] of the Talmud speaks of, when it blows on the Sea of Galilee, the storm that so terrified the fishermen that Simon and his companions thought their last hour had come.[33] But there is one still worse, and that is the wind from the desert, the *khamsin*, the brother of the African simoom, which takes the strength from a man's limbs, fills the sky with a thick greyness and in a single day makes the fields arid for months on end.

As to the rains, they too are far from being entirely satisfactory. They cannot be said to be wholly inadequate, for the figures show that the rainfall is better than that of many other Mediterranean regions – 16.38 inches a year, and more than 23 on the high land of Galilee; but all this rain falls in a few days, almost all of them in October and March, in those violent downpours of which the Gospel speaks,[34] storms which swell the wadis in a few minutes and which can carry away houses if their foundations are not strong enough. In short, they are rains which do not do all the good that might be hoped. Yet if they do not come, particularly the late rains, those of spring, it means ruin. So the Jews of Jesus' time would climb the hills or go up on to the rooftops on the last evening of the Feast of Tabernacles to see which way the smoke from the Temple would go, for it was believed that this would infallibly show whether the year was to be rainy or not. It goes without saying that in the Ghor, where the western winds can hardly ever blow, rain is practically non-existent, and the only water that can be used must come from the Jordan or from springs. In the Dead Sea depression not only does it never rain, but every year evaporation draws off the depth of nearly fifty feet of water, or the same amount as the river brings in – a fact that explains the high salt-content of the curious liquid that forms the sea.

The question of water, therefore, is a very serious one in this country with its dry and fissured earth; it was even more serious two thousand years ago, for then the great works that Israel has now undertaken for its solution did not exist. It is not a mere chance that the poetic aspect of water has so large a place in the Bible: 'A stream bordered with garden; water so fresh never came tumbling down from Lebanon', says the lover in the Song of Songs about his beloved; and a very old hymn, preserved in the Book of Numbers, was called, 'Let the well spring up' and it begins, 'Here is the well that was dug by princes; the chieftains of the host laid it open with the staves they carried . . .'[35] Nor is it by chance that the prophet Ezekiel, to emphasize the splendour of the time when the Messiah should come, foretold that a pure river should spring from the heart of the Temple and that it should flow towards the Dead Sea and make it wholesome;[36] nor that Christ, when He told the woman of Samaria that He was Himself the expected

Messiah, should have compared His message of salvation to 'the living water'.[37] A great many wells had had to be dug to provide the precious liquid for the people, the cattle and the fields, and it had also to be brought with the greatest care from the springs and streams to the villages. All this had already been in being for a great while in the days of Christ – from the time of the kings, indeed – and the Jews were proud of not having 'to water with their feet'[38] as Deuteronomy says, as the Egyptians did. But strict rules had had to be laid down so that the water should be used reasonably. In each village there was a 'master of the waters'; at the given hour he would open the sluices, and at once the women would come hurrying, their pitchers on their heads.

TREES, FLOWERS AND FRUITS

A question arises at this point: is the vegetation[39] that we now see in the Holy Land the same as that which Jesus knew?[40] Quite certainly, it is not. The present may give us a great deal of information about the basic aspects of the country's soil, conformation and climate as they were two thousand years ago; but this is not the case where the trees and the crops are concerned. And indeed one must take particular care to avoid the anachronisms that so many 'Eastern' painters fell into not long since in their anxiety to illustrate the Gospels in Tissot's manner, by the use of local colour.

The greatest difference lies in the tragic destruction of trees, which has affected the whole country. There where nothing is now to be seen but bare plains, ravaged soil or naked rock, the Palestine of twenty centuries ago certainly had forests. It was the Arabs and then the Turks who were chiefly answerable for this devastation; but the Frankish Crusaders and the grazing of goats also contributed to it. The former presence of trees is proved by the groves that have survived, and by many place-names and allusions in the Bible, which uses the word *sylva* some fifty times. Thus we find Esau in a 'shaggy country' which is called the Jebel Sheir, the hairy mountain, to this day, although its ridges are now completely bare. Besides, the present reafforestation undertaken by the young state of Israel (and, to a lesser extent, by Jordan) clearly shows that the country's denudation is not a natural state but one brought about by man. The replanting is successful: the soil is still perfectly capable of growing trees, providing they are of the right kind.

There are some other differences which come from the modern importation of many plants into Palestine, differences that might be thought unimportant, but which have in fact led to great changes in the appearance of the country. Obviously none of the prickly pears that are now so common was to be seen in the time of Christ, since all plants of the cactus family were brought from Mexico after the great discoveries of the fifteenth century. In the same way the agaves that now raise their elegant crests in so many Palestinian gardens were then unknown: so were the eucalyptuses that line the roads today and spread their healthy odour throughout the marshy districts; for this handsome tree is a native of Australia. The naturalized cultivated plants of recent date are even more striking: Jesus never saw those fields of majestic sunflowers that adorn the hills of Galilee; He never ate the grain that we call maize, nor did He ever eat a tomato,[41] because this cereal and this solanum, both so very much used today, are American. And if He ever picked a fruit of the orange kind, it can only have been a bitter or a Seville orange, or a citron, certainly not a sweet orange, far less a grapefruit.

With these two reservations, however, it is true that the flora of Palestine was then the same flora that we see now – exceedingly varied, fragrant and highly coloured. On the whole it belongs to the subtropical Mediterranean type, but towards the south it definitely becomes a desert flora, while in the Ghor it is more nearly that of the tropics.

The Mediterranean flora is found on the coastal plain, in the hilly districts, on the western slopes of the central highlands and in the region of Lake Gennesaret. The forests that once formed part of it had scarcely any conifers: the cedar of Lebanon, so often mentioned in the Bible and chosen as the symbol of the righteous man,[42] did not grow in Palestine proper; the Aleppo pine was rare; the cypress less so – the hard-wooded, perfumed cypress that Solomon used for the floor of the Temple and the door-panels of the Holy of Holies[43]; but these were not the thin, straight cypresses of today, the *cupressus fastigiata*, which is the result of horticultural selection. The most usual conifers were the various kinds of juniper; and they might reach a height of more than sixty-five feet. But the oaks and the terebinths were the really typical trees of the Palestinian forest; and they were also very often found standing alone or in clumps. As forests, they stretched from Carmel to the hills of Samaria and Galilee, and even as far as Bashan. They belonged to several species, the vallonia oak of at least fifty to sixty-five feet high, and the smaller evergreen kermes and gall oaks, which, however, lived for hundreds and hundreds of years – whence their names of Abraham's oak and David's oak. Still more usual were the bushy, branching terebinths or turpentine-trees, whose leaves, which gave off a penetrating scent, were not unlike those of a walnut. Both the oaks and the terebinths were part of the history of Israel: it was by the oaks of Mamre that Abraham set up his tent after he and Lot had parted,[44] and it was in the branches of a terebinth that Absalom was caught.[45] The carob was also very common, a fine tree with hanging clusters of red flowers and long pods whose sweetish flesh was used as food for cattle, and in times of scarcity, for men as well. *Johanisbrottbaum*, as the Germans say – 'tree of Saint John's bread'. These were the 'husks' with which the prodigal son 'would have been glad to fill his belly' in the parable, when he was employed as a swineherd by a stranger.[46] Oriental planes, evergreen holm-oaks, pistachio-trees and wild olives completed the sylva of Palestine – a sylva of which so little now remains.

Below the trees and in the places where there were none, stretched the fragrant seas of brushwood – myrtle, broom, lentisk, various kinds of acanthus, wormwood and the stinking asphodel – and in our time almost all that grows is everywhere reduced to this level. The wild caper of Ecclesiastes[47] produced the flower-bud that even then was used as a relish. Mustard, whose tiny seed was ground to make the seasoning, flourished everywhere; and on the shores of the sea of Tiberias the bush grew into a tree 'so that the birds of the air come and lodge in the branches thereof', as the parable has it.[48] Indeed, its growth is so striking that Jesus used the plant as a symbol for faith.[49] Hyssop, a small, quite rare shrub, was tied in a bundle and used for ritual aspersions. In the places where men had lived, there were to be found the inevitable nettles; and thistles were also very common. A great many of these heath plants were used for food or as seasoning – *aneth*, a fennel with scented seeds; mint; camomile; cummin, whose seeds were separated from it with the blows of a rod;[50] anise, which was drunk as an infusion; bitter rue – the *ruta* of the Italians – which was good for the digestion, when macerated. As for the pasture, it had the same mixture of meadow-grass, fescue, couch-grass and dandelions that one finds today. In the driest parts there grew delicate little herbs somewhat like marjoram, which, being crushed, gave perfumes, such as origan and another that imitated the very costly nard, which came from India.

As the country slopes down towards the Ghor, the vegetation becomes that of a desert: thorny plants grow more frequent, and among them there is myrrh, whose gum-resin is so valuable a scent that in the Song of Solomon the beloved compares her lover to it,[51] and the Magi brought it to the Holy Child.[52] Trees were always scarce there, except round the lake of Tiberias, where the climate was still Mediterranean. There tamarisks grew, with their charming sprays of pink flowers, and they did as well as those on the western plain. Countless laurels stood about the lake and formed hedges along the banks of the smallest wadi; for weeks and weeks they would be covered with brilliant flowers, deep red, yellow or a lively pink, scarcely outdone at all by the liturgical magnificence of the yellow jasmin on the walls. In its natural state balm is small, but it had long been cultivated: the oasis of Jericho was rich in balm, so Cleopatra persuaded Anthony to give it to her, and she carried off young shoots to plant at Heliopolis. But the nearer the river, the more dense the vegetation became, until it looked positively tropical. Acacias abounded, and there were innumerable jujube-trees, *zizyphus spina Christi*, from which the crown of thorns may have been made, and *zizyphus lotus*; but also apples of Sodom, Jericho willows, perhaps wild bananas, vast quantities of plumed reeds, *arundo donax*, sweet calamus, which was used to scent the holy oil, and, growing in the water itself, huge beds of papyrus. It was a region which, in its luxuriance of growth, contrasted strangely with the almost complete nakedness of the shores of the Dead Sea, a country of saltwort and purslane.

The Israelites were perfectly aware of the beauty of all these flowers and they were appreciative of it. No one who has read the Bible can have failed to be struck by the number of references to flowers in both the New and the Old Testaments. Many of them grew wild, and some of these were among the most beautiful. As soon as winter was over the highland forests were filled with crocuses, particularly the saffron crocus, the vivid yellow *karkom*, whose stigmas gave a powerful dye, a scent, saffron for cooking and an antispasmodic medicine. Tulips, hyacinths, gladioli and a hundred kinds of narcissus covered the hills, the plains and even the steppes, as if to fulfil Isaiah's prophecy.[53] Were there lilies in Palestine? From our Lord's praise of their splendour[55] or from the references in the Song of Solomon[54] one might suppose them to have been common: but was the lily of the Scriptures our white lily, the lovely, gentle flower that one sees in the angel's hand, presented to the Virgin Mary as a symbol of purity? That lily was certainly cultivated for the manufacture of the scented oil that Pliny speaks of,[56] but one hesitates to identify the *suson* (from which we have the name Susan) with the 'lily of the field', which may have been the crimson gladiolus, but which was much more probably the superb red anemone that covers the whole of Palestine in the spring, since it is compared to the lips of the beloved in the Song of Solomon.[57] As for the rose, which is mentioned but twice in some translations of the Old Testament,[58] it was a garden plant only, and Jericho was the place where it was most cultivated;[59] but it was so much in vogue towards the beginning of the Christian era that many girls, like Rhoda, the damsel who opened the gate to Saint Peter after his miraculous escape,[60] were named after it.

There were a great many cultivated plants: not as many, perhaps, as we have at present, but certainly more than we had a hundred or two hundred years ago, and better kept. Of all the trees that were subject to men's care, the most valuable was the olive. Its ashy grey leaves, typical of the Palestinian countryside, gave it then the same mysterious charm that they give it today. It had been there for ever; and the Hebrews, on their first coming into the land of Canaan, certainly found it there before them. Its fruit was eaten cooked or raw, and the oil that was pressed from them was used in the kitchen and for lighting, for the toilet and in medicine, and for sacred purposes, in the anointings that were part of the divine service. Its wood was so highly esteemed that Solomon made the cherubim of the Temple out of it.[61] It grew everywhere, even in stony soil fully exposed to the sun, and for this reason Judaea was particularly suitable for it: it grew slowly and patiently, but in five hundred years it would reach a height of nearly forty feet. One can understand that in the olive the Bible should have seen the tree of joy, of peace and of health, whether for the nation or the private man.[62]

The fig-tree came very near the olive in importance. In

Joatham's fable in the Book of Judges,[63] is not the fig asked to be the king of the trees, as well as the olive and the vine? It is spoken of more than fifty times in the Bible; and like the olive it had always grown in Palestine. It could easily be pruned into the form of an umbrella to give shade around the house or in the fields. Its thick foliage was favourable to meditation – just such a meditation as that from which the voice of our Lord aroused Nathanael.[64] To be 'in the shade of one's fig-tree' meant to be happy and at ease. This excellent tree gave two crops, the autumn figs,[65] which formed the chief harvest and which grew on the shoots of the year, and the immense, delicious early figs, said in the Talmud to be ready the day after the Passover,[66] which gives one a better understanding of the cursing of the fig-tree in the Gospel.[67] A hundred everyday expressions showed how much the fig was part of ordinary life. 'Do men pluck figs from thistles?'[68] asked Jesus.

As for the vine, the third of the trees that were chosen in the fable, it may almost be said to have stood for the glory and fruitfulness of Palestine: Moses' spies brought back such huge bunches of grapes that the wandering people were very much encouraged to invade Canaan.[69] Although the drink that is pressed from the grape had long been known – indeed, since Noah's day – to endanger men's steadiness, the Children of Israel loved the vine. Did not the Sacred Book, by the lyrical voice of Isaiah, list the attentions that it needed?[70] It grew freely, often festooned from tree to tree. What varieties were grown? No doubt they were grapes not unlike those very large, long, thick-skinned muscadines called *dattiers de Beyrouth*, or perhaps those round mauve grapes that are to be found (with the muscadines) in Crete and Asia Minor. Palestine was not a great exporter of wine like Gaul,[71] but it produced amply enough for its own consumption. The vine, the plant of life . . . It was not by chance that the Old Testament compared the Chosen People to it,[72] nor by hazard that Jesus likened Himself[73] to the vine, and made of wine the tangible symbol of His blood.

As well as these three kings of cultivation, there were many other trees and plants that occupied a considerable place in the life of Israel. Among the trees, the plum, the apple and the pear were indifferent; but there were others that made up for them – the magnificent Egyptian sycamore, whose fig-like fruit, nicked to hasten its ripening, was of great value to the poor; the little almond-tree, whose early flowers announced the spring[74] and whose nuts were sold as far away as Egypt; the pomegranate, so handsome that its fruits too had astonished Moses' spies, that the cheeks of the beloved were compared to them in the Song of Solomon,[75] and that they became a symbol in the liturgy.[76] Date-palms hardly grew anywhere except in the Ghor, but there they had made Jericho rich and glorious, and their heads rose more than sixty-five feet from the ground: many varieties were known – *caryotes, patetes, adelphides* and above all the *daktylos*, the *degla* of modern Tunisia, which was famous for the size and the taste of its fruit. There were no peaches and probably no apricots, and the list of the Palestinian fruit-trees closed with the citron, the mulberry, the walnut, the pistachio and the nettle-tree mentioned in Psalm 84.

Among the cereals, the most precious, the dearest to the hearts of men, was wheat. Isaac, when he was tricked into blessing Jacob, wished him abundance of it:[77] and Jesus asked that the symbol of His flesh, the flesh that He was to offer up for the salvation of the world, should be bread, the highest product of wheat.

The generic term included both true wheat and spelt. Soft wheat was rare, even in Galilee, but there were many varieties of hard wheat that were used for grist. Their culture required much care, and many customs were based upon it; for in not a few respects Israel was a nation of farmers.[78] Even older than the wheat in Palestine was the barley: it, too, was very wide-spread – it was in a field of barley, for example, that Ruth went gleaning. There were oats: but they were not cultivated. Horses, mules and asses were given barley, but this 'animals' food' as the rabbis called it, was often the food of the poor as well, for barley was half the price of wheat. Coarser still, there was a kind of millet, and also perhaps some hardy sorts of maize of a kind unlike that which the Spaniards brought from America – something of the nature of what was called *turquet* in France in the Middle Ages and which was no doubt a variety of sorghum.

The vegetables were much less varied than ours, but they provided a pleasant assortment, nevertheless. The people of Israel loved gardening, and all the villagers as well as some of the townsmen had kitchen-gardens. Jewish cookery made a great deal of use of lentils – indeed, it was for a dish of this pulse that Esau sold his birthright.[79] Lentils were ground into a flour that was mixed with that of wheat. Beans took up much more space in those gardens than haricots and peas do in ours: the pods were eaten as well as the seeds. Very great quantities of onions were grown, for this plant, which they had brought from Egypt, played a most important part in the Jewish kitchen: the variety from Ascalon, the shallot, and the leek or 'horse garlic' which also came from Egypt, were equally esteemed. There may have been no tomatoes, but they had egg-plants and red and green peppers, as well as cucumbers, pumpkins and melons, the last coming from Egypt. Lettuce, chicory, endive, cress, purslane and parsley were there for salads, and also to make the basis of those 'bitter herbs' which were to be eaten with the paschal lamb. But there were also plants grown then for food which are now no longer used, such as the arum and the iris, whose rootstocks were eaten.

Plenty, diversity, splendour and wealth . . . How could all these growing things, all these crops, have failed to awaken Israel's gratitude to Him who had given them? How could this believing people not have seen that, as Ecclesiasticus told them, here was a revelation of the wisdom of God?[80]

IMPLES OMNE ANIMAL BENEDICTIONE

The differences between Jesus' day and ours are much less marked as regards the fauna than as regards the flora. There is only one really decided change, and that is that the wild animals were formerly much more common. There are still wild boars in Palestine, porcupines, martins and foxes, and at the edge of the desert, antelopes, gazelles and the Sinai ibex; and at night one hears the howling of jackals and the harsh laugh of the hyena. An odd little creature about the size of a rabbit which is spoken of in the Bible[81] still thrives; it is rather like a marmot, but naturalists say that it is related to the elephant or the rhinoceros. The Jews called it the *daman*, 'he who hides himself', because they are gregarious animals who always post sentinels to guard them, and they vanish at the least alarm. Unlike the Arabs, the Jews did not eat them, because the Law forbids the eating of a ruminant whose hoofs are not cloven.[82] Some other animals which were certainly common two thousand years ago are now on their way to extinction: the wolves, the leopards, the lynx and the bears that are mentioned in the Bible are now only to be seen in the zoo at Jerusalem. The lion, described by Saint Peter in his epistle as 'roaring and seeking his prey',[83] has completely disappeared. In the same way the rivers and lakes of Palestine no longer shelter the hippopotamus, or the crocodile, which were perhaps the Behemoth and the Leviathan of the Scriptures.[84] In Christ's time it was quite usual for sheep to be carried off by wild beasts; and it was not pleasant to go through the hanging forests of the Ghor by night, with their thickets so well adapted for leopards and their kind.

Generally speaking, the Palestinian fauna is the same as that of all the other Mediterranean countries: the Ghor, however, has some species that are Ethiopian, some that are Indian, and some that are peculiar to itself.

There are many birds. In the Holy Land it is rare to walk about in the country without hearing their song or the sound of the white wings of a dove: and everywhere, motionless in the hard blue sky as if hanging from an invisible thread, one sees some dark bird of prey. Thus the Gospels very frequently refer to birds, to their nests and their habits. Jesus mentions them several times in His parables. Before this time the pious Job had already praised the wisdom of the ibis and the cock.[85] People were very fond of taming them, particularly certain kinds of pigeon (which, according to the tractate *Shabbath*, had been introduced by Herod the Great) and crows, which was rather less charming.[86]

The fish were, and still are, very unlike those which are to be found in our waters. Out of forty-three species only eight belong to those common to the Mediterranean rivers. In the Jordan basin, but there only, are several kinds that resemble the fish of central Africa. The most usual fishes belong to the genus *chromis* or to the carps, and a scaleless catfish is common. The lake of Tiberias has a great many fish – the Gospel shows how fishing flourished there – and the most curious among them is Saint Peter's fish, *hemichromis sacra* or *paterfamilias*, which, like the tilapia of Siam, keeps its young in its mouth: when the little fishes grow too big it expels them, taking a pebble in their place – though indeed it may be a coin instead of a stone, as we see in Saint Matthew's Gospel,[87] where Saint Peter took one that had a piece of silver in its mouth.

Many kinds of reptile live in Palestine, and two thousand years ago there were certainly more; but comparatively few of them are poisonous. Everyone knows the part that the serpent plays in the Bible; yet we do not find a marked distinction in the Scriptures between those snakes that may fairly be regarded as diabolic and

25

those which are the peasants' useful allies. However, the asp – that is, the cobra – the horned viper and the adder are mentioned, and the Bible makes many references to their bite, their tongue, their poison and their cunning. Apart from the vipers, of which there are four kinds, the horned being the most dangerous, these enemies of mankind were found chiefly in the forest of the Ghor. The harmless colubrine snakes, on the other hand, were to be found everywhere; they were protected, and almost tamed. The saurians were represented by the green lizard, the Judah lizard, the white or grey gecko (now much rarer) and the immense lizard of the Ghor called the *ouaran*, or monitor.

Until the invention of DDT Palestine pullulated with mosquitoes and flies; and it cannot be absolutely stated that they have entirely disappeared. It was not by chance that one of the names of the devil was Beelzebub, *ba'alz'bub*, the lord of the flies. Had not the fourth plague of Egypt been an invasion of these insects?[88] The rabbis, it is true, asserted that no single fly ever settled on the burnt offerings. There are hundreds of kinds of butterflies, beetles and wasps, without mentioning the scorpions and centipedes which one finds among the ruins, nor the fleas and lice that do so well among the nomads. The locust was both very useful and very dangerous: as we shall see, locusts were eaten,[89] but when enormous swarms of them fell upon the fields – a disaster that still occurs – then they were a plague in the full meaning of the word, worthy of that which Moses inflicted upon Egypt. The prophet Joel gives a most striking description of these invasions, and anyone can test the truth of what he says.[90]

As for the domestic animals, they were exactly the same as those one finds today: the introduction of new races and selective breeding dates only from the coming of the Zionists. On the whole they were all small. On the steppes and the bare hills lived sheep very like the fat-tailed sheep of Libya – the tail may weigh more than 20 lbs – and lop-eared goats. These formed one of Palestine's principal resources, and one can readily understand that the sheep should play an important part in the metaphors of the prophets and of Jesus, as well as in the sacrificial ritual. The ass and the ox, which by apocryphal tradition were present at our Saviour's birth, were also considered indispensable.

'Who among you,' asked Jesus, 'if his sheep, his ass or his ox fell into a ditch upon the Sabbath day, would not hurry to pull it out?'[91] There had always been cattle in the land of Canaan:

Abraham's people must have found them there, some two thousand years before our epoch. They may also have brought some with them from Ur of the Chaldees. There was even a wild member of the race, the *reem* that Job speaks of,[92] which was no doubt a kind of aurochs. The buffalo had been introduced from India in the time of the Persians. Cows and calves were usual inmates of a Palestinian farm, and they were often manger-fed in the byre with a mixture of chaff, barley and vetch. The red heifer, without a mark, was a symbol of purity, and her ashes had extraordinary virtues, as we see in the Holy Scriptures.[93] The swine, on the other hand, was unclean: the Bible repeated it often enough,[94] and exalted the heroism of the faithful who, in the time of the Maccabees, chose death rather than eat of the impure flesh.[95] The herds of swine mentioned in the Gospel[96] can only have belonged to pagans or to utterly unscrupulous Jews – impious men.

The ass was an integral part of Palestinian life. It was to be seen everywhere. There was no family, however poor, that did not own one of these long-eared servants. If one could not buy a donkey one hired it, at the price of three denarii a month, or about eighteen gold francs. This was not the ass of our country-side, still less the tiny, pathetic donkey of Morocco, but the Muscat ass, big and strong, able to go his five and twenty miles a day quite happily, an ass whose coat is sometimes of so pale a grey that it might almost be called white – a beautiful creature, upon which Christ could make a noble entry into Jerusalem. For draught and for carrying the ass had no rival, except its half-brother the mule: the ass was never offered in sacrifice. The horse was a much less useful animal. In the caravan that brought the Chosen People back from their exile there were only 736 horses as against 6,720 donkeys,[97] and this must still have been the proportion in the time of Christ. Furthermore, the prophets had displayed much distrust of the horse, as a symbol of luxury, force and violence: the New Testament scarcely mentions it.[98] It was used between shafts, but it was rarely mounted. The only horsemen that Jesus saw would have been Roman soldiers. The camel, so common now, was then rare: there were only 435 in the caravan that came back from exile. This was the two-humped camel to be seen in the Persian bas-reliefs. It cost a good deal, but it was sready and able to carry ten hundredweight for more than thirty miles; and it might be seen, coming in from the desert with the merchandise of distant Asia. Jesus mentions it on two well-known occasions, the one where He speaks of 'the eye of a needle' through which a camel cannot pass,[99] and the other when He reproaches the 'blind leaders' who have a strainer for the gnat and then swallow the camel.[100]

As in our time, the farms had poultry – cocks and hens, pigeons, ducks and geese, but neither guinea-fowl nor turkeys – and they were even to be found right in the city of Jerusalem, as Saint Peter so unhappily discovered upon that tragic night when the cock crowed thrice. The domestic cat, so usual and so much revered in Egypt, was rare in Palestine: there is no word for it at all in biblical Hebrew. It was perhaps for this reason that there were so very many rats, mice and jerboas. As for the dog, which is mentioned more than forty times in the Bible, it was not the friendly inmate of the home as it is in the West but a half-wild animal, with some mixture of jackal or wolf, thin from want of food and ill-natured, which roamed the streets and performed the office of scavenger by eating carrion and filth. Bread was not thrown to them, as the Gospel says,[101] and they scarcely had even the crumbs; and 'to give that which is holy to dogs', as Jesus said,[102] was the ultimate desecration.

This, however, was not to say that the poor dogs had not their share too in the divine scheme of things: in the twelfth chapter of his book Job had stated that all animals, wild and tame, had been created by God and that they bore witness to His glory. In spite of the prayer in Psalm 144, not all creatures had been equally filled with blessings by the Lord.[103] But all of them had their life from Him and all were to praise His glory, as they were required to do by the three in the fiery furnace in Daniel – all, even the whales, which are named in the hymn, though they are scarcely to be seen on the shores of the land of Canaan.[104]

CHAPTER TWO

THE HUMAN CONTEXT

The people of the covenant – Nomen numen – *A nation or a religion?* – *The curious position of the Samaritans* – *The Greek cities* – *So small and so great* – *The great dispersion of the Jews.*

THE PEOPLE OF THE COVENANT

The divine scheme of things . . . More striking than all other wonderful proofs of it was the existence, in this country like none other, of a people which thought of itself as different from all. The men who dwelt in Palestine two thousand years ago, those who made up, if not the entirety of the population, then at least the greater part of it, were convinced, or what is even better, were certain, that they were not there by chance: they were certain that their presence in this place had a meaning under Providence and that God Himself had set them in this land.

This is the basic fact, the essential idea, without which the history, the spiritual life and even the everyday existence of Israel is incomprehensible. A national pride, in comparison with which our most frantic chauvinism is as nothing, filled the heart of the humblest Jew when he remembered that he belonged to the chosen race, to the people of the covenant. What did it matter that his personal lot should be commonplace, that life should treat him roughly or that the occupying Romans should trample the holy ground beneath their feet? He might be despised, but he knew very well that in common with his whole nation he had a privilege that no power on earth could take from him, the 'unchanging priestly office' of which the Epistle to the Hebrews speaks.[1]

This certainly arose from a revelation that was already of great antiquity, no less than twenty centuries old, but which was always present in the pious hearts of Israel. A man named Abram,

29

living at Ur, a regional capital on the lower Euphrates, had received a visitation of God and had heard His command, 'Leave thy country behind thee, thy kinsfolk, and thy father's home, and come away into a land I will show thee. Then I will make a great people of thee; I will bless thee, and make thy name renowned.'² Abram had obeyed. He went out along the desert tracks, taking his old father Terah, his nephews, his cattle and all his people, willing to run the risks of a long wandering journey because of the Lord's command. This obedience had its reward. On reaching the place that had been pointed out to him, Abram several times had mystical communication with God, receiving His admonitions and His promises. The land in which he was then a wanderer would be his inheritance and his descendants would possess it. As a pledge of what was to come his name had been changed from Abram to Abraham, 'the father of a throng': and miraculously his old wife had borne him a son.

Such was the beginning of that covenant which had always existed since those distant times between the Almighty and those who proclaimed themselves His servants. A physical mark of this covenant had been established, a sign in the very flesh of man; and this was circumcision.³

But why had God spoken to Abram? Why had He chosen the little wandering clan of Terahites to serve Him? The Bible answered these questions in the Book of *Judith*, 'They came of Chaldean stock, but they made their abode in Mesopotamia, because they had no mind to worship the old gods of Chaldea; gods a many their fathers' worship owned, but they forsook it, to worship one God only, the God of heaven.'⁴ Had the nomadic Terahites therefore escaped from the astral and totemistic polytheism of the settled Mesopotamians, some two thousand years before Christ and in conditions that are still historically very obscure? And had they raised themselves to the concept of a single, invisible, omnipotent God? 'From the distant past', says Renan, 'the Semitic shepherd has carried the seal of the absolute God upon his forehead.'⁵

This was something extraordinarily original, something that made Abraham's descendants a nation truly unique in the world, the recipients of an incomparable revelation and thus the Chosen People, the People of the Covenant. The pride of the humblest Jew had no other cause than this: he knew that he was the ally of God.

If he had been capable of doubting it, the history of his race, written in the Holy Book, would have proved it to him. Everything in this strange and troubled destiny bore the visible mark of the divine will. It is striking to observe that the first Christians, who stated that they were faithful Jews, all insisted, to show their fellow-countrymen that Jesus' revelation perfected that of the ancient tradition, upon the fact that the new *berith* was only the accomplishment of the old. This was what Stephen the Protomartyr did in the speech that he addressed to those who were about to stone him, and this was the conviction of Saint Peter[6] and Saint Paul.[7]

However, if the covenant had been established once and for all, the conditions of its application had changed in the course of the centuries: the obligations had grown heavier and more profound. And the spectacle of the People of the Covenant climbing step by step up the gradations of spiritual experience to end by defining the characteristics of the purest, most noble religion in all antiquity, is not the least of the reasons one has for admiring them.

At the beginning, in the time of the patriarchs, the conditions were extremely simple. To keep faith, it was enough to believe in the only God, in Him who was referred to by the word El, or better still by Elohim, that strange plural which was used as a singular. This single God required almost no worship, no priesthood, no temple and little more than a few sacrifices from time to time. He imposed no ethics upon his servants, and the metaphysics which this religion founded were rudimentary.

A second stage was passed five or six hundred years after Abraham, when the Chosen People rightly interpreted the Exodus, that astonishing event, as one of the most striking possible proofs of the covenant. An outstanding man was chosen by God to liberate His people from the Egyptian slavery and to bring them back to the Promised Land. Under Moses' leadership the escaping Israelites miraculously crossed the Red Sea and then were preserved from death by starvation in the desert: here were two proofs of divine protection. At this time the covenant was not only renewed but rendered more exact: God gave His people a new pledge by revealing to them His ineffable name, Yahweh, the mark of His omnipotence – Yahweh, 'He who is'. In exchange, in a kind of reciprocal contract[8] He imposed commandments upon them, the famous laws, the

Decalogue; and basing himself upon these Moses could subsequently turn his genius to the development of an entire moral
and religious code, a code of political and social organization.

The covenant thus confirmed and made explicit allowed the
tribes to seize the land of Canaan, in the days of Joshua and of
the judges. It was the covenant again that set up King David and
his dynasty in their glory, the covenant having even been solemnly
renewed in their favour.[9] Yet in spite of all these many proofs
of His infinite goodness that God had given them, the Chosen
People had often broken the covenant, had yielded to the
temptations of idolatry and had indulged in heathen practices;
and in the name of Yahweh the fiery voices of the great prophets –
Amos, Hosea and so many others – had rebuked them for it.[10]
A terrible punishment fell upon the faithless nation: they were
taken away to Babylon: it was the Exile. But His mercy was still
greater than His justice: Yahweh permitted that this punishment
should have an end, and that the exiled flock should come back
to this land blessed above all others.

It had been a fruitful trial. Thanks to the Exile the Chosen
People passed a third stage in their spiritual development. In
the light of suffering the prophets, particularly the greatest
among them, men like Isaiah, Ezekiel or Jeremiah, had shown
their brethren that all that comes from God is to be worshipped
and that all works towards the perfection of man. It had already
been said long ago by Amos, that what God loved was not
sacrifices but righteous behaviour, brotherly love, justice and
moral worth. The covenant took on a still deeper meaning: it
had become the basis of a more inward, more spiritual religion.
The mission with which the Chosen People knew that they were
charged was therefore no longer merely that of asserting that
there was but one God and of proclaiming His commandments,
but rather of teaching mankind to reach towards the divine
by personal effort, moral purification and the thrust of the soul.
Circumcision, 'the mark of the covenant in the flesh', was still
obligatory, but everyone knew that, as Saint Paul was to say later,
the true circumcision was inward, something achieved within
man's heart.[11]

Everything, then, was related to the Chosen People's certainty
that they were unique, different from all others and superior
to them: everything, their monotheistic faith, love of their country,
submission to moral laws, desire to order their social and political

lives according to given principles, and their feeling for the highest kind of mystical experience. It was, therefore, theology rather than ethnology that determined their racial characteristics. If one wishes to form an idea of the world in which Jesus lived it is essential never to forget this most particular concept of the destiny of the individual and the nation.

NOMEN NUMEN

We are therefore continually coming across the strong link that existed between historical and spiritual theory and reality; we find it in all the characteristic features of the Chosen People. This begins with the very names they used for themselves. The three most usual alluded with great precision to certain great happenings in their sacred history: they were Hebrews, Israelites and Jews. If ever there was a case where one could apply the Latin tag *nomen numen* it is surely this, for each of these names has a direct application to a given aspect of their destiny.

It must be observed, however, that one of the expressions that we now use, with a restrictive meaning (and sometimes not without a shade of contempt), for the nation of Abraham, of Moses and of the prophets when we speak, for example, of *anti-Semitism*, had not then the least currency. Obviously Jesus' contemporaries knew that they were Semites, since they descended from Shem, or Sem, Noah's eldest son. They had not forgotten the tenth chapter of Genesis and its list of the generations after Noah's family came out of the ark: still less had they forgotten the ninth, which told how Shem, together with his descendants, was granted the highest place because of his righteous behaviour towards his father when Noah was drunk. But the word Semite was unknown: it is not to be found in the Bible. It was invented as a term in linguistics by Schlözer in 1781. A Palestinian of two thousand years ago was aware that the Bedouins of the desert were his cousins, since they descended from Abraham and his concubine Hagar; but they would have been very much surprised to find themselves classed in the 'Semitic race' along with the Chaldees and the Assyrians.

The most usual words, in educated or literary usage, were Hebrew and Israelite. There is the famous passage in the second Epistle to the Corinthians in which Saint Paul, to defend himself against his enemies' accusations, cries, 'Are they Hebrews? So am I. Are they Israelites? So am I. Are they descended from Abraham? So am I.'[12] A son of Abraham, a true, legitimate member of the People of the Covenant, thus proclaimed himself both Hebrew and Israelite. The two expressions were not synonymous: they corresponded to different historical and spiritual data.

The word 'Hebrew' in the Bible was related to a man named Eber, who was Shem's great-grandson.[13] It is derived from *abar*, to cross over, a root that is found again in Mesopotamia as *habiru* and in Egypt as *Apiru*, the term for the marauders who came from the steppes. The Hebrew, then, is 'he who crosses over', the man of great wanderings: the word recalls those prodigious journeys from Ur to Canaan in the days of Abraham, and from the country of the Nile to that of the Jordan in the days of Moses, during which the Chosen People had come to a knowledge of itself and of its destiny. The truly faithful had retained a longing for that time: the desert was still the place where as 'a wanderer upon the earth', as Jesus was to say, a man might come nearer to God. For the believers the nomad's tent remained so beautiful a symbol of spiritual life that it was set up again at the Feast of Tabernacles.[14] And all this was implied when a man of Saint Paul's time said that he was a Hebrew.

When he said that he was an Israelite he implied even more, perhaps. We know that Jacob was given the name of Israel by the angel of the Lord – which no doubt means the divine power – at the end of the extraordinary night when he had wrestled in the strangest of combats by the ford of Jabbok.[15] Shattered, and with his hip out of joint, but proud of having fought without giving in until daylight, the patriarch had received this name as a reward and as a pledge. The spiritual struggle, 'as furious as a battle between men', as the poet has it,[16] the hand-to-hand war with the power of fate that every man must wage, in his flesh and in his soul, had been fought by Israel both for himself and for his descendants. To be an Israelite was to be one of a nation that stood face to face with God.

As for the term 'Jew', which is found only in the New Testament and in two of the books of Maccabees,[17] it is that which the Roman administration adopted and made usual, and that which is most current today, with that wholly inappropriate and disagreeable undertone that anti-Semitic writings have given it. This name too had an admirable historical and spiritual meaning. It

34

dates from the time of the return from exile. The chief tribe whose members had been deported by Nebuchadnezzar to Babylon was (together with that of Benjamin) Judah. It was the sons of Judah, therefore, who had preserved the treasure of the faith and the ancestral traditions intact, while in Palestine the remnants of the ten other tribes had more or less given way to the temptations of paganism. Returning, they settled in Judaea, which had been named after them, about the holy city of Jerusalem; and there they re-established the religion upon the surest foundations. Jacob, dying in the land of Egypt, had foretold that the sceptre would not be taken away from Judah; and a particular blessing had been upon that tribe, from century to century.[18] The derivation was itself a symbol: the men of Judah, of Judaea, the Jews, were the men of abiding faith.

A NATION OR A RELIGION?

Another name is mentioned in the Bible and set in direct relationship with the origins of the People of the Covenant – the Syrians. The law of Moses required each believer who came to make an offering at Yahweh's altar to say, 'A wandering Syrian was my father . . .'[19]* Who, then, were these Syrians or Aramaeans? A Semitic people without any doubt, much given to a wandering life, who, at the beginning of the second millenary moved into upper Mesopotamia, at the foot of the Anti-Taurus mountains, with their flocks. This region, which makes up the northern end of the 'fertile crescent', is called Padan-Aram in the Bible, the land of the fathers. Its chief town was Haran, an important centre for caravans, on the Balikh, a tributary of the Euphrates. It was there that Abraham had paused in his divinely inspired journey, that his brother Nahor had settled and that Jacob had gone to seek his wife Rachel; and it was from there also that the seer Balaam went to deliver his disturbing messages.[20] In making his people descend from a man called Aram, the youngest son of Shem,[21] the editor of the Holy Book conveyed an undoubted fact, albeit in what may have been a mythical form.

From an ethnological point of view, therefore, the people who

---

*The Knox Version here reads 'My fathers were wanderers, hunted to and fro in Syria'. The Authorized Version has, 'A Syrian ready to perish was my father'. The Vulgate reads: '*Syrus persequebatur patrem meum*', and the Douay Version: 'The Syrian pursued my father.' The French is, '*Un Araméen vagabond était mon père*'.

lived in Palestine had their origins in a group of Aramaean tribes which, some twenty centuries before our era, had more or less detached themselves from the main body. They had allied themselves with the *'ibri* or *habiru* (that is, as we have seen, Hebrew) elements that were roving from the Euphrates to the Nile across Canaan, keeping cattle or raiding as they went. It seems that the ancestors of Israel had imposed their authority upon the *habiru* bands, had given them the first rudiments of organization and had finished by amalgamating with them. But for a long time these had had to fight against the thrust of other Aramaean tribes in the direction of their grazing lands. Much later, in the ninth and eighth centuries before Christ, when Israel had become a sedentary people, settled in the Holy Land, they had again to fight against their former brothers. At that time the Syrians, under the impulse of an extraordinary resurgence of vitality, had made Damascus a capital city; they were founding principalities as far away as the Persian Gulf, and on several occasions they had invaded Palestine.[22] It is in this period that an important linguistic change had its origin: the Aramaic tongue of the Syrians became the dominant language throughout almost all the Near East, and particularly in the land of Canaan, where it penetrated all the more easily because shortly afterwards the Israelites were deported from their country by Nebuchadnezzar. When they came back from Babylon the exiles therefore found Aramaeans living in Palestine and the Aramaic language in use: they adopted it – a curious return to their beginnings.[23]

Does this mean that the Jews of Jesus' time were simply Aramaeans and nothing more? No. The Bible shows that certain small tribes were closely related to the Aramaeans of Abraham's clan, even if they were on bad terms with it. We have already seen that this was the case with the descendants of Ishmael; but there were also the people of Moab and the land of Ammon, who descended from Lot, that is to say, from his incest with his two daughters.[24] The Scriptures also speak of seven nations which Israel's distant ancestors had destroyed and more or less absorbed.[25] Among the elements thus taken in, two may be particularly pointed out. First the Canaanites, who have already been referred to – those whom Joshua's men found in Canaan when first they came, Mediterranean and Caucasian people with a strong Semitic mixture arising from that ethnic group living on the shores of Syria and known by the name of Phoenicians. Secondly, those whom the Bible calls the people of Heth, or the Hittites. They were a pre-Aryan, non-Semitic people who for a long time were only known through the Bible. Their resurrection by Hrozny, some fifty years ago, after Winkler's discovery of the extraordinary tablets at Boghaz-Keui in Turkey, was one of the great adventures of archeology. For a thousand years the Hittites ruled Anatolia and invaded all the nearby countries, including Canaan. All the efforts of the greatest of Egyptian Pharaohs, Rameses II, to expel them from it failed in the drawn battle of Qadesh in 1290 BC; and when their empire did succumb to the attacks of the great Aryan invasion,[26] a great many of their descendants remained in Palestine. In addition to the Canaanites and the Hittites there were other ingredients in the ethnic mixture that made up the people of Palestine – so very many nations had moved along this corridor. For example, there were still some *Hurrim*, the Horreans of whom we know a little from the tablets of Ras-Shamra,[27] and some of those Amorrheans whom the Bible calls Amalekites, Perizites, Gabaonites and various other names, people closely related to the Hyksos occupiers of Egypt, who were there at the time of Moses' birth.[28]

One great historical occurrence had added much to the mixtures of races in the land of Israel, or rather two – the two slave-raids conducted first by the Assyrians under Sargon II in Galilee and Samaria (722 BC) and then by the Chaldees under Nebuchadnezzar in Judaea (586 BC). All kinds of people repopulated these devastated countries – Aramaeans, Canaanites, Phoenicians, Anatolians and even Mesopotamians; and the remnants of the broken tribes of Israel mixed with them. When the exiles came back from Babylon in 538 they were obliged, whether they liked it or not, to live alongside the newcomers. Much later, between 165 and 104 B.C., the great Maccabean conquerors used the strong hand to convert the whole country to Judaism, and they were most successful. They even succeeded in converting the Bedouin of the south, the Idumaeans, the traditional enemies of the descendants of Jacob ever since the business of the pottage. It is true that in the year 40 BC, a little before the birth of Christ, the Idumaeans had had their revenge, since Herod, who was one of them, obtained the title of King of Judaea from the Roman senate, and that without renouncing Yahweh's religion.

This conversion of the whole of Palestine to Judaism did not, however, overcome the diversity of origins: this was still evident in

Jesus' time, and there were marked differences between the people of the various provinces. In the harsh country of the south the hard core of the returned exiles – that is, primarily the tribes of Judah and Benjamin – were grouped about Jerusalem, and there the race might be considered pure. On the other hand, in the rich parts of the north, formerly occupied by the tribes of Asher, Naphtali, Issachar and Zebulon, the settlement of foreigners had been so intense that not many of the Israelites had gone back. A family of ancient lineage, like that of Jesus, which descended from King David, must have been quite rare in those regions. The fact was so well known that the country had been nicknamed Galil ha-Goyim, 'the ring (or circuit) of the unbelievers': from the time of the Maccabees' Judaization it was called Galil and no more – hence Galilee. But the people of Judaea despised the Galileans as backward provincials who spoke with such an accent[29] that there was no difference between their pronunciation of *immar* (lamb), *hamar* (wine) and *hamor* (ass). They were also suspected of being far from rigid in their observation of the Law.

It is impossible, therefore, to speak of a *Jewish race*.[30] Was there a set racial or ethnic type? Something, for example, like that which is now supposed to be the most usual – large curved nose, big, very red lips, tightly curled hair, blue-grey or light brown eyes? We know nothing about it. The New Testament and the tractates of the Talmud have nothing to say upon this point. One is naturally inclined to suppose that the Jews of Jesus' time were small, but one cannot possibly say so with any certainty. The Old Testament, it is true, shows us the Israelite David in very distinct contrast with the huge Aryan Goliath; but no sort of general conclusion can be drawn from the fact that in the Gospel the publican Zacchaeus was so small that he could not see anything for the crowd,[31] nor that Saint Paul speaks of himself as 'a person lacking size or dignity'.[32]

The very concept of race was foreign to Jesus' contemporaries, the men of the Bible. Even more so, of course, was that perversion of intelligence and conscience called racism. If the Israelites had, as a people, a vast communal pride, they were not, for all that, in the least degree exclusive. For them religion was far more important than race. They belonged to the chosen race not because they descended from a given holy man – after all, were there not a great many others who descended from Abraham? – but because they were faithful to the covenant established between

God and their ancestors. Did not the Sacred Book tell (and not without a certain humour) how Jonah, for having refused to go and convert the unspeakable Ninevites, was obliged to spend three days and three nights in the belly of a whale? Wherever the Jews lived outside Palestine they made converts, as we shall see.[33] The faithful worshippers of Yahweh despised and loathed the heathen not because he belonged to a foreign race but because he practised an abominable religion. If the pagan would announce his belief in the one God, adopt the Mosaic Law and accept all the customs, particularly circumcision, the mark of the covenant in his flesh, then he became a brother.[34] On the other hand, a brother by race, an inhabitant of the Holy Land, who refused to obey the requirements of the religion was by that fact shut out from the covenant, and he did not belong to the nation of Israel.

THE CURIOUS POSITION OF THE SAMARITANS

This was exactly the case with the Samaritans. In the middle of Palestine there was this ethnic group that the Jews considered as something worse than foreigners. The Samaritans worshipped the same God as the Jews, revered the same Scriptures (or at least part of them) and thought of Moses as the supreme law-giver: and yet they did not form part of God's people.

In fact, the enmity between the men of Judah and those of Samaria dated from long before, almost from the time when, in 935 BC, at the death of the great king, Solomon's empire was cut into two parts, Samaria and Judah. From then onwards Shechem and Jerusalem were in frequent disagreement. The unclean against the clean. Thus Jeroboam's altars had been defiled by the golden calves set up against the hill of Zion; and it was against Jezebel, that old idolatrous queen of the north, that the prophet Elijah came from the south. Samaria, the capital of this province, was built, and very intelligently built, by the king Omri in about 880, and it was always considered as a rival to the holy city: few tears were shed in Jerusalem when the Assyrians destroyed it. After the exile this jealousy turned into a simmering hatred. The motley people who had settled in those parts, all heathens by origin, had more or less taken up the beliefs of the Israelites who had remained, but in doing so they had simplified them, particularly in accepting no more than the Pentateuch as Holy Writ. As they had not been able to go and pray at Jerusalem they had adopted the habit of celebrating their rites in the high places of their country. When the exiled Jews returned, the Samaritans refused to recognise the religious supremacy of the Judaeans, and even declined their request for help in the rebuilding of the Temple.[35] In Jerusalem people began to say that the Samaritans were people outside the community – excommunicated men – and the Talmud has embodied this tradition.[36] Relations between the two groups grew more and more strained, and it ended in a break. During the reign of Alexander the Great, no doubt in the year 333, Manasseh, brother of the high priest and son-in-law of the governor of Samaria, obtained from the master of the world permission to build a temple upon Mount Gerizim that would be a rival to that at Jerusalem. He made himself the high priest of it, induced a sacrificer and some Levites to join him, and allowed them to marry heathen women. The Jewish historian, Flavius Josephus, still trembles with horror as he recounts these facts.[37]

Such, then, was the origin of the savage excommunication which the Jews inflicted upon the Samaritans. Their capital, which they built up again on a smaller scale after the disaster of 722, was utterly ruined by John Hyrcanus in 128; and one of the chief complaints of the faithful against Herod, their 'king', was that he had rebuilt the impious city in a splendid manner, in about 30 BC, calling it Sebaste in honour of his protector, this being the Greek for Augusta.[38] The division between Samaria and Jerusalem continued: the Samaritans rebuilt a sanctuary upon Gerizim, and there they maintained a dissident clergy, made their sacrifices and prayed to Yahweh. They even claimed that it was they who professed the true religion of Israel: the woman of Samaria said it in so many words to Jesus – 'Well, it was our fathers' way to worship on this mountain, although you tell us that the place where men ought to worship is in Jerusalem.'[39] Was their religion more interesting, more appealing, than that of the Jews, as it has sometimes been maintained?[40] A religion that was 'not exposed to theocratic tyranny'? The ancient history of the Church readily points out the earliest heretics as Samaritans – Simon Magus, Dositheus and Menander – which does not necessarily mean, however, that this schismatic theology was very original.[41]

What is certain is that at the time of Christ there existed an extremely violent hatred between the two groups. It was a hatred that went as far as actions. Sometimes these were comic, such as that which perhaps took place in the very year of our Lord's birth, when the Samaritans threw human bones into the sanctuary of the Temple just before the Passover, so that the holy place was unclean and therefore unusable: sometimes tragic, such as that which happened in AD 52, twenty years after Jesus' death, when the Samaritans set upon the Jewish pilgrims, who counter-attacked so furiously that the legate of Syria was obliged to interfere. He subsequently crucified a considerable number of Jews. Things did not always go so far as this, however: people usually confined themselves to cutting irony and to insults. The Samaritans were called a herd, an odd collection of undesirables, and it was not allowed that they had any right to call themselves a nation.[42] The name Shechem was turned into Sychar, which means drunkenness. A widely current proverb, which is recorded in the Talmud, said that 'a piece of bread given by a Samaritan is more unclean than swine's flesh':[43] one could not say fairer than that. When He wished to make the Jews blush for their hardness of heart and their ingratitude, Jesus held up a Samaritan as an example to them. The Samaritans, at all events, did help the wounded they found beside the road; and they, at least, when they were healed knew how to express their gratitude. Who would suppose, when the 'good Samaritan' is mentioned, that that charitable man was, in the eyes of those who were listening to Christ, a heretic, a schismatic, an excommunicated person, the outcast of the nation of Israel?

THE GREEK CITIES

Within the body politic of Israel there was yet another foreign element, the Greek cities. A certain number of towns, some of them large, were Hellenic, and in no way Jewish. Some had been founded at the time when the descendants of Alexander's generals, the Ptolemies of Egypt and the Seleucids of Syria, had held Palestine. Greek municipalities had been set up and an influx of Greek settlers had arrived. These places formed the Decapolis, the league of the ten cities. There was one west of the Jordan, the former Beth-Shan, renamed Scythopolis, the town of the Scythians, because it was remembered that these terrible nomads had set up a garrison there during their great incursion in the seventh century. The others were in Transjordan, the chief being Hippos, Gerasa, Pella, Gadara and Philadelphia; and although it was far away to the north, Damascus was also part of the confederation. Pompey had recognised the municipal autonomy of all of them, and they were under the direct rule of Rome. The Judaizing activities of the Maccabees had checked the Hellenic influence, but even Alexander Jannaeus himself had not been able to subjugate the Greeks of the Decapolis: Pella had chosen rather to be destroyed than accept Judaism. Herod had got along very well with the Hellenic cities, and by the time of Christ they were playing an important political role, guided by the king of Judaea but not subordinated to him.

Other Greek cities, or cities with a strong Greek influence, had come into being along the coast, from Ptolomais, the former Akka (Acre), as far as Gaza. Caesarea, which Herod the Great had made the chief port of Palestine, was three parts a Greek city. Shechem, rebuilt by him under the name of Sebaste, also had a great share of Greeks in its population. And when Tiberias rose up on the shores of the lake, it was peopled mostly by Greeks, all the more so in that Herod had made the mistake of including a former burial-ground within it, which was a very serious uncleanliness for the Jews. In the same way, Sepphoris, the capital of Galilee, was largely a Greek town. In all these cities, although they were founded upon Palestinian soil, the Jew was just barely tolerated. At Gerasa, for example, only one synagogue has been found, and that very small. Discord between Greeks and Jews broke out on the least occasion, quarrels and even riots, which often ended in violence. Caesarea was the scene of many of these, particularly since the Romans, on succeeding Herod the Great in the control of the town, cunningly stationed the troops they raised in Samaria there.

SO SMALL AND SO GREAT

Summing up all these elements, what figure can one reach for the population of Palestine at the time of Christ? This is an exceedingly difficult question, as the best historians of Israel acknowledge.[44] The sources upon which an estimate may be based are scattered, not wholly reliable, and often in contradiction with one another. The rabbis of the Talmud, particularly, increased the figures for reasons connected with apologetics. And there is a misleading literary perspective which makes a people seem numerically imposing because it has played a very important historical role and has produced a great many outstanding men. In fact Israel's population has never been particularly numerous. How many people would Israel have had at the time of its utmost political importance under Solomon? Certainly not a million, and perhaps considerably less. After that time, the kingdom of Judah, which alone preserved the faith in all its strictness, did not count three hundred thousand souls. And the exiles brought back by Zerubbabel probably did not exceed twenty-five thousand. These are astonishingly modest figures, and yet it is this that brings one into immediate touch with the mystery of Israel and of its survival throughout all its trials, even to our day.

A thousand years after Solomon, when his remote descendant Jesus was born, the expansion of the Jews towards the steppes of the east and the south and the demographic increase caused by the Roman peace had brought about a distinct rise. And yet if one puts the figure at two million one is being generous; and even then half a million Samaritans, Idumaeans, Moabites, Greeks of the Decapolis and people of mixed blood in the ports must be counted in. In the same area, in 1922, the census showed the figure of just 761,796 inhabitants.

But what do figures matter? It must be reiterated that Israel's glory, the importance that Israel claimed, was no more to be measured in thousands of inhabitants than it was in thousands of square miles. The humblest Jew's certainty that he belonged to a very great people or rather to the greatest of all peoples, was based upon purely spiritual considerations. A people that bore witness, a people that God had from the earliest time 'called by its name', as Isaiah said,[45] a people that knew itself, as Paul was to say, to be 'one who leads the blind, a light to their darkness, admonishing the fool, instructing the simple,'[46] how could it fail to feel its grandeur, however physically small in comparison with the great empires of the world? Here again the religious concept took precedence over all others.

THE GREAT DISPERSION OF THE JEWS

There was, however, one fact that helped to give Israel this certainty of its greatness: there were thousands of Jews, brothers of those in Palestine, living outside the Holy Land. Every single one of Christ's contemporaries was aware of this, for did they not see distant relatives coming back at the great feasts, to pray at Jerusalem – men like that Simon, born in Cyrene in North Africa, who was to help Jesus carry His cross? They all knew that in the schools of the holy city there were a great many students who came from these scattered communities – students like that Saul, son of a tent-maker of Tarsus in Cilicia, who had come to attend the lectures of the rabbi Gamaliel and who was eventually to become the apostle Paul. There was, therefore, a Jewish emigration at that time, not unlike that with which we are acquainted now. In Greek it was called the Diaspora, the dispersion.[47]

Its origins were many, and far back in the past. Without going as far as the days of Joseph and of Moses, when it is easy to imagine some Jews staying in Egypt, we may cite the perpetual upheavals that afflicted the Chosen People from the death of Solomon until the beginning of the Christian era as a potent cause of emigration. The Assyrian and Babylonian deportations had taken a great many Jews to Mesopotamia, and when Cyrus allowed them to go back to the Holy Land some chose rather to stay in the places to which they had become accustomed. And then there were incidental causes: in the sixth century, for example, a group of Jews took service with Pharaoh for some reason that is now unknown, and with their wives and children they went to form a garrison of military colonists in the island of Elephantine, near Aswan. Three centuries later others joined Alexander's army, and he gave them lands in Mesopotamia and even in Bactria. Sometimes, too, it was defeat that was the cause of the expatriation, as in the case of Antiochus the Great's Jewish mercenaries, who were taken prisoner by the Romans and settled by them in Italy. Revolutions and *coups d'état* had the same effect: thus, in the third century, when his father, the high priest, had been assassinated, Onias IV left with a great many followers and settled *at* Leontopolis in Lower Egypt, where he even built a temple. And lastly, as Greek and above all Roman order made communications easier and more sure, more and more Jews left the country for plain commercial reasons. Many of them set themselves up as traders in the great centres; and it is from this time that we first find the Jew as a capable man of business, whereas before, in the days of the shepherds and peasants of Israel, the type was unknown.

What parts did they inhabit, these scattered members of the Chosen People? In about the year 140 BC the sibyl addressed these flattering words to the Jewish people, 'The whole earth is filled with thee, and all the ocean'.[48] This was clearly an exaggeration, but Strabo of Cappadocia, the Greek geographer (a contemporary of Christ's), asserted that 'the Jewish nation was diffused into every town, and that one could not easily find a single place upon the inhabited earth which did not shelter this race',[49] – a statement that Flavius Josephus, the Jewish historian, quotes with complacency. Another contemporary of Christ, that famous Jewish philosopher, Philo of Alexandria, is more exact, and gives among the places to which Jews had emigrated Egypt, Phoenicia, Syria, Asia Minor (particularly Cilicia and Pamphilia, but also Bithynia and Pontus), and in Europe, Thessaly, Macedonia, Aetolia, Attica, Argos and Corinth, and the Peloponnese, without forgetting the islands. 'And I do not mention the countries beyond the Euphrates,' he adds, 'nor Babylonia, where all the satrapies, with a few exceptions, have Jewish colonists.'[50] And he might have added Italy to this list, with a most particular mention of Rome.

For in fact the two chief centres of the Diaspora were Rome and Alexandria. There had been Jews settled in the great Egyptian metropolis for a very long time, thoroughly settled, since Alexander had attracted them to the town at its foundation by giving them there the same rights as the Greeks; and they had thriven in that city until they amounted to at least a fifth of the population, or, as some said, even two fifths. They had come to Rome later, but they had established themselves quickly, and a considerable share of the import trade was in their hands. Cicero had praised their solidarity, their communal feeling and their spirit of enterprise: Caesar had treated them with particular kindness, and the noise of their mourning at his death had been noticed by all. They had their underground cemeteries, the forerunners of the Christian catacombs, upon whose walls one may still see their religious symbols, the seven-branched candlestick and the chest for the Torah. Alexandria and Rome were certainly the two largest Jewish cities in the world.

How many of these dispersed Jews were there? In this case too it is difficult to make an estimate. Philo speaks of a million in Egypt alone. In Josephus we find a delegation of eight thousand in Italy coming to welcome other delegates from Palestine,[51] and he reckons the number of families of Jews that Tiberius deported to Sardinia at four thousand, which is confirmed by Tacitus and Suetonius;[52] but Dio Cassius asserts that Trajan sent 220,000 to

Cyrenaica and 240,000 to Cyprus.[53] Gathering these meagre data together we come to the conclusion[54] that about seven or eight million Jews lived in the empire, without reckoning the million outside it. One Roman in ten, therefore, was a Jew; this is already a very high proportion, but since the Jews of the Diaspora were particularly concentrated in the Near East and in Greece it may be supposed that east of Italy the proportion reached as much as some twenty Jews for every hundred inhabitants. One can appreciate the importance of this by recalling that in 1939 the Jews amounted to no more than six per cent of the population even in Central Europe, Austria, Poland and the Ukraine, where they were settled in the greatest numbers.

Wherever they were to be found, these Jewish colonies showed the same characteristics: as Cicero had observed, they were communities that held together to a remarkable degree. They generally lived close to one another, although neither the Greek nor the Roman authorities ever required them to live in a ghetto: in Rome they lived in several different districts.[55] All these communities had provided themselves with a special organization of their own, independent of the pagan administration; it was of a democratic nature and within it, of course, worldly and spiritual matters were inextricably mingled. A meeting of the people was both a gathering for prayer and a political assembly: the name for the room in which the council of elders and the chief who was to defend the group's interests, the ethnarch or exarch, were elected, was the same as that for the place in which the people sang the psalms. A meeting or gathering is in Hebrew *kinneseth* and in Greek *sunagoge*, from which comes our synagogue.

The official position of these Jewish communities was perfectly clear: they were recognized and countenanced by the Roman authorities. They had even obtained the grant of an immense privilege, that of not taking part in the worship of the state and the city, but of merely praying to their God for the pagan authorities. Either by favour or by purchase, some Israelites had acquired the title of Roman citizen, among them the father of Saul of Tarsus. It does not seem that in Jesus' time there were any Jewish imperial officials, but, particularly in Egypt, some Jews held semi-official appointments in such areas as the state bank, the farming of the taxes, the collection of the corn and its shipping. Even without taking the Herod family into consideration, they being exceptional,[56] it is clear that many Jews had exceedingly grand connexions, going as high as the people immediately in contact with the emperor, and even his family.

These Jews of the Diaspora, living within a pagan society, nevertheless did not allow themselves to be absorbed by it. Obviously the wealthy among them lived more or less in the Greek or the Roman manner, and it cannot be absolutely asserted that they all scrupulously respected the requirements of the Torah. But downright apostacies were rare, and when one of Philo of Alexandria's nephews abandoned the faith of his fathers in order to become a Roman official there was a great scandal. Yet contact with the pagan world rendered the Jews of the Diaspora different in character from those of their brothers who had remained in Palestine. There came into being a new kind of Israelite, one more open to the breath of the world, one who had an understanding of the world that was quite distinct from the ideas of the faithful of the theocratic community in Judaea: these were men destined to play a most important part in the history of religious thought. We may cite two exceedingly brilliant examples, two minds intensely faithful to the traditions of their race but at the same time imbued with other influences – Saint Paul, the little Jew of Tarsus, the pupil of the rabbis of Jerusalem, who nevertheless was to profit by his youthful experience to form a concept of the grandeur of the Roman world and of the part that the new faith could play in it that was to allow him, above all others, to apply Christ's universal teachings: and secondly Philo, the most illustrious Jewish philosopher of his day, at the same time a doctor of the Law and a zealous Platonist; a man who, with a skill bordering upon genius, was able to combine the main currents of Greek thought with those of the tradition of Israel, and to demonstrate in the Platonic logos the thought of God, the inherent connecting-matter of the world, the archetype of the Creation – in short, the immediate forerunner of Saint John's *Word made flesh*.[57]

But if the Jews did not allow themselves to be absorbed by the pagans, they had no objection to absorbing them as much as ever they could. The colonies of the Diaspora were very active centres of religious propaganda. Had not Tobias said of old, 'If He has dispersed you among heathen folk who know nothing of Him, it was so that you might tell them the story of His great deeds, convince them that He, and no other, is God all-powerful'.[58] They therefore had no hesitation in sharing the spiritual treasure that

God had entrusted to them with other men of good will, though pagan. It was with this intention that, according to a tradition which historians do not take quite literally, seventy-two rabbis of Alexandria, in the third century before Christ, translated the Bible into Greek, in seventy-two days, thus producing the famous Septuagint.[59] There seem to have been a good many conversions, and still more half-conversions, in which the proselyte agreed with the spiritual and moral principles of Israel and even with some of the observances, but not with all. These people, who were called those 'who feared God', are quite often to be found in the New Testament – the centurion of Capernaum, the centurion Cornelius in the Acts, the minister of the Queen of Ethiopia, and Sergius Paulus, the high Roman official whose name was taken by the apostle Saul, all seem to have belonged to this class. 'There is not a single Greek city,' says Josephus, 'not a single barbarous nation, in which our custom of a weekly rest, our fasts and our custom of lighting lamps as well as many of our rules about food have not spread.'[60] Women were very frequently to be found among these converts or sympathisers. Poppaea, Nero's beloved wife (whom he killed by a kick on the bottom), certainly had a connexion with Judaism. Josephus gives a striking piece of information: when a pogrom that was to rid the city of a large proportion of its Jews was being prepared in Damascus, the conspirators agreed to say nothing about it to their wives, for 'with a very few exceptions they had all been won over to the Jewish beliefs'.[61]

For there were massacres of Jews. The life of the communities of the Diaspora was not without its difficulties. There was a positive anti-Semitism throughout the Roman empire, and there are many texts which prove this. There were even specialists in anti-Semitic writing, such as that Apion, the Drumont of his day, who was nicknamed 'the cymbal of the world', and who was withstood by Josephus. But there were even some moderate writers who were hostile to the Chosen People: that reserved Stoic Seneca speaks with contempt 'of the customs of this very evil race',[62] and Cicero criticised their 'barbarous superstitions, incompatible with the glory of Rome, the dignity of the Roman name and the traditions of its forefathers'.[63] What reason did they have for blaming the Jews? It appears that it was primarily their strict monotheism and their unconcealed contempt for idols – the same reasons that caused the Christians to be hated somewhat later. A single God, without an image? What nonsense, cried the mob. They must secretly worship a god with an ass's head or a pig's snout, which was proved by their refusal to eat pork. The comparative secrecy of the Jewish meetings lent itself to the propagation of fables; and the same calumnies that were to be spread against the primitive Church were already current about the synagogues – meetings that indulged in human sacrifice. And one can readily imagine the sort of merriment at the expense of the 'skinless' that the practice of circumcision provoked. Financial reasons also helped to bring about this enmity: some Jews did too well in trade. Thus one of Martial's epigrams asserts that 'from the day of their birth the children of Israel were taught to steal'.[64]

This is why violence broke out from time to time, and why the Jewish communities of the Diaspora were persecuted: between 40 BC and AD 70 we know of no less than twenty of these pogroms, those of Alexandria being the most dreadful. The Jewish war was to start off the most shocking wave of anti-Semitic violence throughout the empire. And frequently, between these bouts, when those who were hostile to the Jews gained the ear of the authorities, there were deportations, such as those that Trajan ordered – sometimes greater, sometimes less.

In spite of these shocks, Judaism throughout the world was a power which immensely strengthened the authority of the little nation in the mere ten thousand square miles of Palestine. Everything goes to show that the imperial government did not treat its Judaean subjects as if they were any odd nation under Roman authority: the Jews had too many well-placed advocates in Rome itself. And yet the seven or eight million Israelites scattered throughout the empire were never able to build up an organization which, with all its elements acting in concert, would have exerted a very strong influence upon their rulers. There were frequent and regular communications between the different groups; and the letters that travelled between them were the origin of the famous epistles of the early Christians. But there was no settled representation of all the scattered communities to form a kind of central government. It was this that limited the power of the Diaspora: if a decision was taken in Palestine that brought about unfortunate consequences, it was the Jews abroad who paid; but they had no part in making the decisions.[65]

The true bond throughout the Jewish world was that of religion. Even if he had made a fortune in a heathen country, the Jew far from the Holy Land felt himself banished: the Diaspora was still the *Galut*, the Exile, God's curse upon His people for their sins. The Jews abroad never ceased thinking of the land of their fathers with affection. 'Mine it is to reckon the folk of Egypt, of Babylon, too, among my citizens! Philistines, Tyrians, Ethiopians, all must claim Sion as their birthplace; None was ever born, the proverb shall run, that did not take his birth from her', sang Psalm 86. And to show that one was returning to Palestine one said *Aliyah*, the going up; for it was a very high place that was spoken of. From very far away men turned towards the holy city to pray. Every Jew, from the time he was twenty years of age, paid a tax to the Temple, and a special mission, which was protected by Roman law, carried the sacred money. Jerusalem, therefore, without being the political capital of the Jews throughout the world, was their spiritual metropolis, the place where the heart of Judaism throbbed.

Such was that other Israel, the Israel of the dispersion. Its existence carried the Jewish nation's conception of its own size out to the limits of the Roman empire and even beyond. The human framework in which its fate was being accomplished was not confined to its little fatherland. This is a most important consideration; and it is impossible to form a true idea of life in Palestine without continually bearing it in mind.

CHAPTER THREE

THE POLITICAL CONTEXT

God and Caesar – Theocracy – Palestine and the Roman domination – Herod 'the Great' – Herod's successors and the procurators – The occupiers and the occupied.

GOD AND CAESAR

Everyone remembers that famous scene when Jesus, asked by His opponents about the lawfulness of paying the tribute that the Roman authorities insisted upon, replied with that peasant irony characteristic of Him, 'Give back to Caesar what is Caesar's, and to God what is God's.'[1] Everyone knows, too, that men's conduct should be spiritually regulated by this precept, but that it is quite another matter, in the ordinary course of life, to put it into practice. In the Palestine of twenty centuries ago it was even harder than it is in our modern countries. For in fact, for a Jew of Jesus' time there were a very great many cases in which it was exceedingly difficult to know the limits between the realms of God and Caesar.

The primary fact, never to be forgotten when one thinks of life in Palestine then, is that it was an occupied country. Western Europeans know from experience what the word 'occupation' means and what it implies in the way of constraint and even of bondage and coercion. The Romans held the country in the fullest sense of the term, either directly or by means of their servants. But at the same time they followed their usual custom and allowed their subject people to continue to be administered by the régime that they were used to, which meant for Palestine the organization of the Jewish community as it had grown up since the return from exile. There was, therefore, a super-imposition of authorities, a fruitful source of complication.

And indeed the situation in the province of Judaea was far more complex than it could have been elsewhere, in Gaul or in Greece, for example, because of the Jew's very special ideas about the political authority and its rights. For a Roman, as for a Greek of the Hellenistic empires, 'it was the state that represented the essential ruling principle. The city-empire or the empire took to themselves the right of imposing a rule upon their subjects' lives that was in accord with their highest interests. Religion and nationality were recognised only in so far as they were instruments of the state. Religion and religious worship, according to the form laid down by the state, were a civic duty.'[2] In short, Caesar controlled God. Exactly the contrary obtained among the Jews: God swallowed up Caesar. In itself, the state had no existence. All those things which elsewhere constituted the essentials of the state were subordinated to religion in Israel, for it was religion alone that had allowed the Chosen People to survive at a time when they possessed neither a country nor a state. 'An existence without a state, and indeed beyond any political state', as Fichte said in the last century, speaking of the German nation,[3] was an obvious characteristic of the destiny of Israel. For a Jew, as later for a Moslem, there was no distinction between civil law and religious commandment, since the one sprang only from the other, nor between political power and spiritual authority. Two systems, then, lay one upon the other, or rather overlapped one another; two systems whose philosophical bases were diametrically opposed.

The extraordinary complexity of the political and administrative framework arose from this fact: and as one follows the stages in Christ's trial one realises it very clearly, for at one time it is the Roman authority that intervenes and at another that of the Tetrarch of Galilee, a petty vassal of Rome; and each has completely different conceptions of law. There was complexity not only in the political framework but also in the political attitudes and the political parties, for every religious decision had its political consequenc and in the same way every political act had religious repercussions. From this there arose an immense variety of currents and tendencies, of political parties and religious sects, ranging from the cosmopolitanism of the Herods to the revolutionary messianic beliefs of the Zealots. Even the Third or the Fourth Republic in France could not have presented a more confused appearance.

THEOCRACY

'Some nations', says Josephus in a very well-known passage,

'have entrusted the supreme political power to monarchies, others to oligarchies and still others to the people. But our lawgiver was not led astray by any of these forms of government. He framed his constitution as what one might, risking a new word, term a theocracy. He put the entire sovereignty and all authority into the hands of God.'[4] This is a relevant observation. From the time that the disaster of the deportation had destroyed the monarchy, all authority had passed to those who represented Yahweh on earth, and who were therefore the incarnation of Israel's will to live. When the Jewish community re-formed itself after its return to the Promised Land it did so grouped about the men of God; it entrusted the rule and the responsibility of dealing in the nation's name with its successive masters to them. The theocratic form of government was the natural consequence of a historical situation in which religion, the very soul of God's people, had submerged and absorbed everything else. For a believing Jew, Yahweh alone ruled; and He did so by the medium of His representatives upon earth, primarily the Sanhedrim and the high priest.

The word 'Sanhedrim' – *sunedrion* in Greek – is an exact translation of the word 'consistory': it meant an assembly, a senate, a *boulé*, as they would have said in Athens, or perhaps even a permanent commission; and it sat at Jerusalem. Naturally Jewish tradition traced it back to Moses: 'Whereupon the Lord said to Moses, Choose out for me seventy Israelites known to thee as elders and officers of the people, bring them to the door of the tabernacle that bears record of my covenant, and let them stand there at thy side.'[5] In fact, neither in the time of the kings nor even in the time of Ezra did there exist any assembly which in any way resembled the Sanhedrim of the later centuries. The first trace of it is to be found in the days of Antiochus III (223–187 BC): Josephus[6] speaks of a senate that was set up at that time. But it is under John Hyrcanus (134–104), the great Maccabean leader, that we see this assembly in action, it being then a kind of representative body of the great families.[7] After him, in the reign of his daughter-in-law Salome Alexandra, members of the priestly class were added to the assembly. When the Romans seized Palestine they did not do away with it, but indeed recognised it and gave it a *de facto* official existence. It is at this period that we first come across the word *sunedrion*, Sanhedrim, in the apocryphal Jewish Psalms of Solomon;[8]

and here the word has rather the meaning of a tribunal than of a governing council.

Its members were co-opted, and by tradition their number was seventy, with the president making the seventy-first, as there had been seventy elders together with Moses.[9] The Sanhedrim was made up, in almost equal parts, of the 'princes of the priests' (those who had served the office of high priest and the representatives of the twenty-four priestly classes); of the scribes and the doctors of the Law; and lastly of the elders of the people, outstanding laymen chosen from the heads of the chief families, those 'whose daughters had the right to marry priests'.[10] The two great parties, the Pharisees and the Sadducees, were represented in the Sanhedrim; but the latter had considerably more influence there. A duumvirate presided: the Nassi was the titular president, but the Abet Bethdin at his side was more than a vice-president, since he was the chairman when the assembly sat as a court of law. Who was the Nassi? That is to say, who did in fact preside? Was it an elected rabbi, or was this an office that was held by the high priest together with his other attributes? The question has been much discussed. Josephus[11] and the New Testament[12] seem to say that the high priest was automatically the Nassi, and this appears to have been the case in Jesus' day; but Talmudic literature, on the other hand, seems to incline towards the other hypothesis.[13]

In the Gospel, and particularly at the time of Christ's trial, we see the Sanhedrim solely as a tribunal, as the supreme court, which in fact it was, as we shall see later.[14] But it was not only a court of law. It also played the part of a pontifical college, charged with the study of religious questions, and that of a political council. It has even been asked whether the Sanhedrim was not divided into sections, like the modern French *Conseil d'Etat*, each having a given competence, with plenary meetings for the most serious decisions.[15] There is no possible doubt that it had a political function: it voted the laws; it had its own police, men like lictors, 'who beat those who behaved amiss'; and it intervened in relations with the occupying Romans. It controlled everything that had to do with religion, and as in fact everything in the Jewish community had to do with religion, it may be said that the Sanhedrim controlled everything. This did not please everybody. When Herod the Great was young he was called before the Sanhedrim on the charge of exceeding his powers; but when, after some time, he became the complete master he took a cruel revenge, and decimated that august body.

Whether he was the president of the Sanhedrim by right or not, the high priest represented an authority different from that of the assembly. In the first place, obviously, he derived this authority from his sacred character: he was the head of the priestly caste, anointed with the holy oil as once the kings had been; he was bound by exceedingly strict rules to ensure his ritual cleanliness and his holiness; he was attired in a manner that made him recognisable at the first glance, and he was truly a being apart, God's witness and the spiritual guide of the Chosen People. And this primacy had been made even stronger by political circumstances. A hundred and fifty years before the Christian era, Jonathan and Simon Maccabaeus, the heroes of the war of liberation, followed one another in the high priesthood, and after them the title remained hereditary in their family. John Hyrcanus and particularly Alexander Jannaeus, the first to take the title of king again, both held the religious authority together with the political power. Throughout the bloody struggles that followed the death of Jannaeus in 76 BC the office remained in the Asmonean family,[16] but it was kept more and more to its purely religious aspect and removed from political power. In 37 BC the last descendant of the Maccabean high priest died, beheaded by Herod, and the title was lost to that famous dynasty. But by reason of the long association of the two kinds of power something of it persisted in the minds of the people, and although officially he was only charged with his priestly functions, the high priest retained an authority that was something more than merely spiritual. In a way, it would not be improper to speak of him as a sovereign pontiff.

His, then, was a curious position. His appointment was in fact subject to the decision of the political masters of the country: intrigue, threats, and often money, had their part in his choice. If he ceased to give satisfaction he was deposed, in spite of his unalterably sacred character. At the time of Christ the office was filled by members of a priestly family whose chief merit was a remarkable skill in political creeping: a family that had managed to retain the title during fifty years. Annas was invested with the office by Quirinius, the legate of Syria, in AD 7, and he held it until the accession of the emperor Tiberius, in 14. He retained so much influence that a year after his deposition he was able to

55

bring about the appointment of Eleazar, one of his sons, and then that of his son-in-law, the insignificant Caiaphas, who beat all records and kept himself in office for eighteen years, that is to say, until 36, when the legate of Syria, Vitellius, deposed him. But he was replaced by his brothers-in-law, Annas' sons; first by Jonathan and then by Annas, who bore the additional Greek name of Theophilus.

The high priesthood, although it was so much weakened, and even in a way so much cried down, nevertheless retained a very real standing. The common people saw the high priest as the living incarnation of the Law. They surrounded him with worshipful respect. They marvelled at the sight of him living in one of the most splendid palaces in Jerusalem, attended by an almost royal household. A call by this spiritual leader could perfectly well begin an uprising, or calm it. The political masters of the country therefore preferred to be on good terms with this highly placed personage, so that in the Gospels we see the procurator, Pontius Pilate, obviously treating him with particular consideration. There was a subtle interplay between the occupying authorities and this man, who, in spite of having no official political powers, was nevertheless a real power in the land; and when this was directed by a man with an exceptionally able mind, such as Annas, it could be of great importance in Israel's political life.

PALESTINE AND THE ROMAN DOMINATION

The supreme authority belonged no less to those who, for the last half century and more, had imposed their rule upon Palestine. The conditions under which they had first established and then exercised this rule explain the Jewish people's attitude towards them. It is a little-known piece of history – the Bible says nothing of it – and it is extremely complicated, a web of intrigues, revolts, civil wars and assassinations – a series of complexities made still more difficult by the repercussions of Roman politics, which at that time, as everybody knows, were themselves far from simple.

To understand it one must go back to the beginning of the first century before Christ, to the reign of Alexander Jannaeus (106–73), the son of the great Asmonean John Hyrcanus. He was as active and as authoritarian as his father, and he had continued his policy of expansion: he restored, in his own favour, the title of king; but his opponents claimed that this was an usurpation, since he did not belong to the family of David. The zealous and pious stood out against him – all those who claimed descent from the *hasidim*, the heroes of the resistance against the Greeks, the men who were called the Pharisees. They reproached this curious high priest with being continually at war, with allying himself with the uncircumcised, and, which was much more serious, with having married a widow, which the Law forbade to members of the priesthood.[17] When the opposition of the Pharisees broke out in a revolt Jannaeus put it down according to his way of doing things, which was not gentle, and which involved the death of fifty thousand men. One might then have beheld the spiritual leader of Israel banqueting with his concubines while eight hundred prisoners were crucified and while their wives and children were slaughtered in front of them as they died.[18]

This tragedy had the most serious consequences. In the first place, it cut the nation in two, the one side being favourable to the Pharisees and the other approving of these violent methods: this was the origin of that confusion between religious and political attitudes that is so clearly to be seen in Jesus' time.[19] But above all it led a great many Israelites to hope that someone might intervene to prevent any repetition of these horrors; and they hoped it all the more in that the troubles went on after the death of Jannaeus. The reign of his widow, Salome Alexandra (76–67) was marked by the reaction of the Pharisees: it was then that they packed the Sanhedrim with their friends, doctors of the Law, who in their gratitude handed down a picture of the reign of this easy-going, half-pagan beauty as a golden age in which 'the grains of barley were the size of olive-stones and the lentils as big as gold pieces'.[20] This happy time was followed by a mortal struggle between Alexandra's sons, Hyrcanus II and Aristobulus II. The latter, a hot-headed, intelligent man, could not forgive his stupid and inept elder brother for being high priest and king. The situation, which was still further complicated by the interference of the Bedouin of Idumaea and the Nabataean Arabs from Petra, became atrocious. Civil war, devastating raids: the country sweated blood.

It was at this time that many Jews began to think of appealing to an arbiter. A 'third force' had come into existence, and it sent a delegation to that powerful stranger who was then, in the spring of 63 BC, at Damascus. Somewhat later both of the rival brothers approached him to secure his support in exchange for ready cash. The stranger to whom these frogs were so naïvely offering a sceptre was none other than Pompey.

In her irresistible eastward expansion, Rome had just reached and passed a decisive stage. Mithridates, the last of the Hellenistic princes who still possessed something of Alexander's courage, had been pursued as far as the Crimea, and there he had killed himself. In 65 BC Syria had become a Roman province. Pompey was not indifferent to the Jews' invitations, and after some months of confusion he decided to put an end to the troubles: he upheld the inept Hyrcanus and marched upon Jerusalem to deal with Aristobulus. Aristobulus and his supporters took refuge in the Temple, and there held out for three months. At last an officer – the son of Sulla the dictator – forced his way in through a breach with a handful of legionaries. This was the time of that famous scene in which Pompey, wishing to know the secret of the Jewish religion, penetrated into the Holy of Holies, with his naked sword in his hand, expecting to find there some astonishing idol, and was amazed to find nothing, nothing whatever but the *vacuum sedem et inania arcana*, as Tacitus puts it.[21]

The Romans came into Palestine, then, as peace-makers, almost as saviours; and this explains why, three-quarters of a century later, there were Jews who were in favour of their rule, or at least resigned to it as a lesser evil. Anything rather than civil war! But the Romans were unable to retain this privileged position of arbiters unchanged. Their Palestinian policy was confused and even contradictory. One has the impression that the level-headed realism for which they have so often been praised let them down when they were brought into contact with the Jewish nation's infinite reserves of guile and the startling ease with which their leaders changed sides.

The régime set up by Pompey was that of a protectorate. The Jewish state, deprived of its maritime region and the Greek cities of the interior, continued to exist, as a tribute-paying vassal of Rome. Hyrcanus II was confirmed in his office as high priest and he was even awarded the title of ethnarch, in default of that of king. His brother and enemy, Aristobulus, was taken away as a prisoner to Rome, together with his sons Alexander and Antigonus. But Hyrcanus' ineptitude prevented him from keeping a firm grasp on his power. The sons of Aristobulus escaped from their Roman prisons one after another; so did Aristobulus himself; they appeared in Palestine and raised troops. Civil war had begun again. The Romans continually had to intervene, trying to find some kind of régime that would be suitable to this singular nation.

It was in the middle of this confused turmoil that another power entered upon the scene.

A sheik of the southern steppes, called by the Greek name of Antipater, had been appointed governor of Idumaea, his own country, by John Hyrcanus. His son of the same name had acquired such power by his wealth and his connection with the Nabataean kingdom of Petra that Pompey had placed him as a kind of mayor of the palace to the unfortunate Hyrcanus II and as an overseer. This was the beginning of a truly remarkable dynastic rise. These Idumaeans, who had been converted to Judaism, longed to become masters in Israel; and to accomplish their ambitions they very skilfully ingratiated themselves with the Romans. This was by no means simple, since it was scarcely possible, in that troubled time, to tell who represented the legitimate power in Rome. Antipater II played this dangerous game with great ability. He was a friend of Pompey's, but he had managed to become even more of a friend of Caesar's after Caesar, having crossed the Rubicon on January 12th, 49, had liquidated his rival – so much of a friend, indeed, that he gained for himself the title of procurator, and for his sons, Phasael and Herod, two military commands. Herod, Strategus of Galilee, showed his capacity and power of decision in putting down a nationalist rising led by one Hezekiah: this was the occasion upon which the Sanhedrim in its anger had vainly tried to punish him. When, on the Ides of March, 44, Caesar fell under the twenty-three stabs of Cassius and the republican conspirators, Antipater and his sons succeeded in turning their coats again, and the new proconsul of Syria, who was none other than Cassius himself, had no better friends in the world. A revolt against the Romans broke out, because of the burden of the tribute, and Herod repressed it firmly: his father then died, poisoned by a traitor, and Herod inherited his wealth, his ambition and his ability.

Roman politics once more turned upside-down, and Antony, that potential dictator, found Herod and his brother quite as devoted to his cause as they had been to that of the republican Cassius. It was in vain that the Jews cried out in protest and sent embassies to their new master. The two Idumaeans received the title of tetrarch, which might be fairly translated as kinglet, and the poor Hyrcanus II was confined more and more to his priestly tasks. It seemed that now Antipater's sons had no more to do than to guess which of the triumvirate, Antony, Octavian or Lepidus, would win so that they might back him, when a new drama broke out.

Antony, whose attention was much taken up by Cleopatra, had not checked an invasion by the Parthians early enough, and under the cover of it Antigonus, the younger son of Aristobulus II, returned. Supported by many patriotic Jews and also by those who had been maddened by the Roman levies, the last of the Maccabees marched on Jerusalem: he had come to an agreement with the invaders and had promised them a thousand talents and five hundred women – a curious tribute from a claimant to the high priesthood. The Romans were busy elsewhere, and for months a savage civil war once more poured out the country's blood. In the end Antigonus took the holy city and announced that in his own person he renewed the double title of high priest and king. He had the elderly Hyrcanus delivered up to him and he bit his ears, lacerating them; for this rendered him incapable of the priesthood, which could be exercised only by those with no physical defect. As for Phasael, he had killed himself by dashing out his brains against a stone rather than be taken.

But there was still Herod, and he was a man of iron. He had succeeded in reaching the impregnable fortress of Masada on the Dead Sea. Learning of the victory of Antigonus and the death of his brother he once more unhesitatingly played the right card. He left for Rome in midwinter, and he arrived just at the moment when Octavian and Antony had patched up their quarrel. The two Romans were far too occupied to trouble with Palestine, and the young Herod – he was then twenty-three – an intelligent, capable man, whose father had been one of Caesar's friends, seemed to them the right person to put an end to the Jewish turmoil. And he was all the more qualified so to do since he had just became engaged to Mariamne, the Asmonean princess, which gave him some sort of a legitimate claim. By a decree of the senate, therefore, he was named King of Judaea: this was in the autumn of the year 40. After three years in which the supporters of Herod and the supporters of the Asmoneans cut one another's throats in a furious war, eleven legions and six thousand cavalry took Jerusalem in 37. As usual great massacres followed the capture, and at Herod's urgent request Antony had Antigonus beheaded. As for the Sanhedrim, which refused to recognise the young conqueror's kingly status, it was decimated.

This was why, at the time of Jesus' birth, Palestine had been governed for some thirty-odd years as a Roman protectorate by the 'Idumaean slave'.[22]

HEROD 'THE GREAT'

From 37 to 4 BC, then, the throne of Judaea was occupied by Herod. It is a name that has a tragic echo in history: in the Gospels it evokes memories of horror. Yet it would be unjust to judge the man solely by his well-earned reputation as a pitiless executioner. In many respects he appears to have been worthy of admiration: he was a man who never lost his courage when fortune seemed to have deserted him; as a diplomat he was extraordinarily skilful in reversing an unfavourable state of affairs; as an administrator he had immense ideas and far-reaching views; and he was a tireless builder: in all these things he was of more than common stature. His contemporaries called him 'the Great'; and this was fair enough, so long as there was not too much investigation into the sources of the greatness. In any case, he was the last great ruler of Israel.[23]

His policy rested upon little more than a single maxim, which was to be on good terms with Rome; that is to say, with the man who ruled in Rome. But who was this man, and who would he be? This was a vital question for Herod, as it had been for his father, when on September 2nd, 31, Octavian's fleet defeated Antony's at Actium. Herod had been Antony's friend: was all lost for him? No. He saved himself by his address, and that not without nobility: he said to the victor, 'I was a faithful friend to Antony. I tried to hold him back from the disastrous course that Cleopatra urged upon him. If you trust in me, I will be a most faithful friend to you.' He was able to persuade the suspicious Octavian of his sincerity, and from that time until his death, in spite of a few brief disturbances, there was an excellent understanding between the emperor and his protégé, the little *rex socius*.

We may therefore consider the master of Palestine at the time of Jesus' birth as one of those vassal princes whom the very great powers tolerate and make use of; a maharajah of Victorian times, or an Aga Khan. Herod was busy to serve the conqueror's interests, and always ready to protect them by armed intervention; he was more than a little of a flatterer, and in short his opponents were right when they said that he was merely Augustus' serving-man. His fortress was named Antonia, after Antony; but in his palace there was also to be seen a hall named after Caesar and another after Agrippa. On the other hand, he had acquired all the appearance of sovereignty over a territory only a little less than Solomon's kingdom, and this he enlarged on the other side of the Jordan. Immediately after the capture of Jerusalem he had arranged, with the help of ready cash, for the withdrawal of the legions, which were stationed in Syria, ready to intervene in case of necessity, but discreet. He had his own personal army made up of Germanic, Gaulish and Thracian mercenaries; and his bodyguard, all young men from Galatia, was splendid. He raised tribute-money for Rome, but he also had the right to levy taxes for himself, and he did not hesitate to use it. All in all, he seemed quite as independent as the Sultan of Morocco or the Bey of Tunis of a little while ago, when they were under French protection.

But he had not presumed to take upon himself the office of high priest, for he knew very well that his Jewish subjects would have regarded this as an unbearable usurpation. He limited himself to appointing the holders of the office, taking care to choose them from priestly families of sufficiently modest standing that he would not need to fear their influence. He caused seven or eight to succeed one another, and not one has left a mark in history. The only one who might have played a considerable part, his little brother-in-law the Asmonean Aristobulus, very conveniently died after six months in office. As for Hyrcanus II, Herod indulged in the gesture of reinstating him in Jerusalem, with all the marks of great respect; but with his torn ears what could the poor old man do?

Yet one must not put too much credit in the firm and splendid show of Herod's power, for in fact its foundations were far from secure, and he knew it. A considerable proportion of Jewish opinion was hostile to him, because he was an Idumaean, a barely circumcized man, a son of Esau; because he had been thrust upon them by the Roman conqueror; and because only too often his behaviour was contrary to the commandments of the Law and to Mosaic morality. This continual hostility explains the harshness of Herod's rule over the Jews, and, to some degree, his crimes. His police were everywhere: everything was under their supervision. It is said that he did not scorn to make his own investigations: walking unknown through the streets one day he asked a passer-by what the people of his quarter thought of King

Herod; the man, a knowing fellow, replied by quoting Ecclesiastes, 'Of the king, no treasonable thought . . . the very birds in heaven will catch the echoes of it, and fly off to betray thy secret'.

Furthermore, precautions never had the effect of preventing plots from being devised or crises from bursting out. Conspirators found accomplices in the tyrant's own family, or thought they found them, which was quite as serious in Herod's eyes. For this reason he struck harder and harder still. All the last descendants of the Asmoneans were dealt with: the little Aristobulus, a charming youth of seventeen, whom he had mistakenly agreed to appoint high priest, was most politically drowned by the Galatian guards in a swimming-pool in the palace at Jericho; the adored Mariamne, the only one of his ten successive wives whom Herod appears to have loved, was taken off to execution because he suspected her of having plotted against his life. Her sons followed her to the grave: so did five others, born of various unions. 'It is better to be Herod's pig than his son,' said Augustus, by way of a joke; for, obedient to at least this biblical precept, the master of the Jews would not eat pork.

For the forty-one years of Herod's reign, therefore, the political life of Israel was surrounded by the suspicious atmosphere of a police-state, with the continual possibility of a palace revolution and with spectacular purges. At one moment the people heard that some hundreds of Pharisees had been hanged for criticizing the master a little too loudly; at another that three hundred officers, suspected of plotting in Samaria, had been lynched by a mob egged on by the police; or again that the young men who had tried to wrench off the gold eagle that the tyrant had had placed on the gate of the Temple had been burnt alive or stoned. In such a climate of violence the Massacre of the Innocents in the Gospel fits in quite naturally: it is perfectly in keeping. And yet the man was not all of a piece, for on several occasions this savage tyrant showed himself as a humane being, as, for example, when he remedied a dreadful famine in the year 25 by selling his gold plate to buy corn in Egypt.

Moreover, the Jewish nation did put up with him for some forty years. There is no kind of doubt that this was because of the peace that he gave them and the real prosperity that he brought about. Yet this peace and this prosperity were paid for very dearly, and Josephus even reproaches Herod with having reduced his people to destitution,[24] which seems highly exaggerated. What is certain is that Palestine was filled with monuments during his reign, that public works were undertaken with great energy and that there were innumerable festivities, celebrated with an unheard-of splendour. It is common knowledge that this is the usual way for dictators to try to make their people forget the loss of their freedom. Intelligently-placed fortresses were built or repaired: there was Machaerus, on the Dead Sea, and Herodium, which was to be its master's tomb. Ruined cities like Samaria were rebuilt; and the port of Caesarea became the finest in the country, the rival of the Piraeus. At Jerusalem itself he built a theatre, an amphitheatre and a hippodrome; and in spite of the pious Jew's hatred for heathen spectacles, they drew great crowds. Palaces rose up, more splendid than anything that had been seen. The lowering Antonia fortress was built next to the Temple, to overlook it. And above all, upon an immense base of enormous blocks of stone – some nearly forty feet long and six feet high – a completely new Temple began to rise, so huge that a hundred years would be needed to finish it and so rich that even Solomon's was less magnificent.[25]

All this explains why, in spite of so much against him, Herod was able to hold on and, in the end, to die a natural death. Before he was forty his health began to leave him. Typhoid fever brought him to the edge of death, and the psychological and physical consequences of it remained with him. It was then that a kind of persecution-mania seized him, that he saw a murderer in each of his relatives and that his orders for execution so increased in number. It was then, too, that he went out of his mind with the pain of the thought that it was he himself who had killed Mariamne, and that he was heard shouting her name to all the echoes in the palace, as if she might come back. He continually invented new tortures for his victims:[26] the silence of a graveyard surrounded him, broken only by the chanting of the workers on the Temple and by the shrieks of the condemned. A terrible disease took possession of him – most probably an intestinal cancer – and maggots and a purulent discharge escaped from his body. He had himself carried to the waters of Calirrhoe, near the Dead Sea, hoping that the hot sulphurous baths would ease his pain; but at the first of them he fainted away. He lay dying, with his mind astray, haunted by the ghosts of his victims, in an atrocious delirium; and he commanded that after his death all the most important men of the kingdom should be executed, so that there would be at least some tears upon his grave. At last he died, this being in the year 4 BC: Jesus was then two years old.

Let us move on for a quarter of a century. During the winter of AD 27–28 a man rose up on the banks of the Jordan, at the ford of Bethabara; he spoke, drew crowds to himself and gave those who listened to him the baptism of penitence: he was soon to see Him of whom he was to say that he was not worthy to bend down and untie the strap of His shoes. The man's name was John.

At this time the position in Palestine was not at all like that of the days of Herod. It is set down for us very exactly by Saint Luke in the well-known beginning of the third chapter of his Gospel – 'It was in the fifteenth year of the emperor Tiberius' reign, when Pontius Pilate was governor of Judaea, when Herod was prince in Galilee, his brother Philip in the Ituraean and Trachonitid region, and Lysanias in Abilina, in the high priesthood of Annas and Caiphas, that the word of God came upon John, the son of Zachary, in the desert'. The kingdom of Herod the Great had therefore been divided, and the Romans had taken the most important part of it under their direct administration.

By his will Herod himself had cut his realm into three. No doubt he considered that as no one of his heirs would be capable of holding it, a division of authority and a subordination within the frame of family co-operation would be a good solution. Archelaus, the son of the Samaritan Malthace, had, together with the promise of the royal succession, the centre of the country, Idumaea, Judaea and Samaria. His younger brothers were established in somewhat subordinate positions: Antipas was given Galilee, increased by a southward extension on the other side of the Jordan; and Philip, the son of a Graeco-Egyptian from Jerusalem, had the region beyond Lake Gennesaret, extending as far as the mountainous country that the Bible calls Bashan and including it. The Jews, who had seen a fortunate omen in the fact that the tyrant had finally given up the ghost on the very day of the Passover, were very soon undeceived. They were rid of Herod, but they were no better off.

The splendid funeral, in which Herod's mortal remains were taken right up to the fortress of Herodium in a golden litter

HEROD THE GREAT AND HIS DESCENDANTS

Herod the Great (b. 73; d. 4 BC)

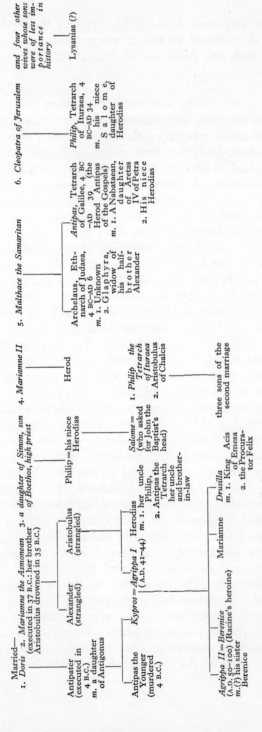

Married—
1. Doris
2. Mariamne the Asmonean (executed in 37 B.C.: her brother Aristobulus drowned in 35 B.C.)
3. a daughter of Simon, son of Boethos, high priest
4. Mariamne II
5. Malthace the Samaritan
6. Cleopatra of Jerusalem
and four other wives whose sons were of less importance in history

Antipater (executed in 4 B.C.) m. a daughter of Antigonus
— Antipas the Younger (murdered 4 B.C.)

Alexander (strangled)
Aristobulus (strangled)

Herodias m. 1. her uncle Philip, 2. Antipas the Tetrarch her uncle and brother-in-law
— *Salome* = 1. *Philip the Tetrarch of Ituraea* 2. Aristobulus of Chalcis (who asked for John the Baptist's head)

Kypros = *Agrippa I* (A.D. 41-44)
— *Agrippa II = Berenice* (A.D. 50-100) (Racine's heroine) m.(?) his sister Berenice
— Mariamne
— Drusilla m. 1. King Acis of Emesa 2. the Procurator Felix

three sons of the second marriage

Philip = his niece Herodias
Herod

Archelaus, Ethnarch of Judaea, 4 BC-AD 6 m. 1. Unknown 2. Glaphyra, widow of his half-brother Alexander

Antipas, Tetrarch of Galilee, 4 BC-AD 39 (the Herod Antipas of the Gospels) m. 1. A Nabataean, daughter of Aretas IV of Petra 2. His niece Herodias

Philip, Tetrarch of Ituraea, 4 BC-AD 34, m. his niece Salome, daughter of Herodias

Lysanias (?)

[The names of those who reigned are in italics.]

studded with precious stones, while an army of slaves followed after, carrying aromatic scents, was hardly over before Archelaus announced his intention of leaving for Rome to see Augustus and to be confirmed in the royal title. But in his very first movements he made a tactical error: he asked the immense crowd which at that season filled Jerusalem to overflowing what could be done to please them. Some called for a remission of taxes, some for the punishment of Herod's advisers: Archelaus refused and a riot broke out. The court of the Temple had to be taken by storm, and it was strewn with three thousand corpses. A fine beginning for a reign. As soon as the new ruler had embarked the troubles began again, and they were made all the worse by the extreme rapacity of a Roman tax-gatherer: the legions marched in twice, but still order was not restored. The whole of Palestine was filled with bands of resistants; the royal palace at Jericho went up in flames; two thousand deserters from Herod's army attacked the royal troops; in Judaea the gigantic shepherd Athronges proclaimed himself governor, while in Galilee Judas, son of that Hezekiah whom Herod had put to death, assumed the crown. Varus, the governor of Syria, was obliged to take the field in person: he crucified two thousand Jews. All this made the moderates decide upon an embassy to Rome to beg the emperor to put an end to the dynasty of the Herods and to include their country within the Syrian province.[27] It would have been sensible, but Augustus did not agree with this solution. On the whole he ratified Herod's will, but he only gave Archelaus the modest title of ethnarch: he might be made king later on, if he were good.

Archelaus was not. He was scarcely settled on his throne before he was at odds with almost all his subjects. He deposed two high priests one after another. He angered the Pharisees by marrying Glaphyra, his sister-in-law and the widow of the Asmonean Alexander – a marriage that was contrary to the Law. And the Jews were finally irritated beyond all bearing by the way he taxed them to rebuild the palace at Jericho in a splendid fashion and to raise up a city to be called after himself. The troubles began again and at the same time police-rule and repression. Perhaps the strong hand was the only possible method at this time when the Chosen People were in such a volcanic mood, so stirred up by agitators and filled with apocalyptic dreams of liberation and revenge; but still some intelligence in the application of force was called for. In the year 6 another delegation set off for

Rome to beg Augustus to call the petty tyrant to account. The accusations must have been overwhelming, for Archelaus was banished to Vienne, in Gaul, where according to Strabo he died.[28] His country became a Roman province.

The two tetrarchs were more fortunate, or perhaps more capable. Naturally both the one and the other followed the policy of submission to Rome to the ultimate degree as well as that of flattery. If one built a new town he named it Tiberias; and not to be outdone the other at once renamed the northern Bethsaida Julias: and if one restored Livias the other built Caesarea Philippi. Over and above this, these two neighbours on the shore of the lake had the sense to remain on good terms with one another – an occurrence sufficiently rare in the Herod family to deserve being recorded.

Herod Antipas was the one whom the Gospels call simply Herod. It was he whom Jesus termed 'that fox' when the Pharisees, hoping to make Him leave Galilee, told Him that the tetrarch wished to kill Him;[29] and it is clear that the word (which should perhaps be translated 'jackal') was loaded with contempt. It was he too who caused such a scandal by the seduction of Herodias, the wife of one of his half-brothers. And as everyone knows it was for having dared to cry out against the despot's wickedness in public that John the Baptist[30] was imprisoned in the fortress of Machaerus and that he was put to death during that banquet at which Herodias' daughter Salome asked for his head. And it was to Herod Antipas (he being at Jerusalem for the Passover) that Pontius Pilate sent the accused Christ during His trial, upon the pretext that as He was a Galilean the responsibility lay with the Tetrarch of Galilee, and hoping, no doubt, to be rid of the affair.[31] It is also known that although this princeling led a very heathenish kind of a life, he nevertheless took care to send presents to the Temple and to abstain from setting his likeness upon his coins – he even joined in the Jews' protest against the placing of votive shields by Pontius Pilate in the sanctuary of the Temple. What were his secret intentions? Did he dream of setting up his father's realm again for himself? Whatever the truth, he was accused of this ambition by his grand-nephew Herod Agrippa I, in 37, after that young man had obtained Caligula's permission to succeed the tetrarch Philip, who had died in 34, and when he wanted to gain possession of Galilee. Antipas was unable to deny having built up stores of arms, and Rome did not believe him when he said that they were only meant to be used against the threatening Arabs. He was banished to Lyons, where Herodias had the decency to follow him; and while his accuser received his lands, he was probably put to death.[32]

His half-brother Philip played an even more modest part in the politics of Palestine. He was established in the hilly northern parts of the country and provided with a little state made up of bits and pieces, whose inhabitants, according to Strabo, lived solely by crime and banditry;[33] and he clearly saw that, as Tetrarch of Ituraea, he had nothing to do with grandiose designs. He was a wise man, and learned; the gentleness of his manners was in marked contrast to all that one knows of the Herod family; he loved the arts, and letters and the sciences, particularly geography, in which his acquisitions allowed him to resolve the mystery of the sources of the Jordan. Yet can this man who spoke nothing but Greek, who lived like a Greek and who had his portrait on his coins like any other Hellenistic prince, still be called a Jew?[34]

Palestine, then, at the time when Jesus arose to bring His message, was in fact administered by two men, the tetrarch Herod in Galilee and a Roman official in Judaea and Samaria. The territory that had been taken away from Archelaus had been made into a procuratorial province of the second class, that is to say one inferior in extent and standing to those provinces that the emperor entrusted to legates. It may even be that the neighbouring legate of Syria had the right to supervise Palestine. The procurators who were sent to administer the province were recruited from the equestrian and not from the senatorial order: nevertheless, they had the *jus gladii*, that is, full powers of criminal justice; which shows that Rome gave them genuine autonomy. The then procurator was the fifth the Jews had seen arrive[35] since the year AD 6, when their rule began; he had been there since 26, and he was to be in office ten years or so: his name was Pontius Pilate.

Christian tradition has always dealt very harshly with this man, to whom it has attributed a large share in the responsibility for Christ's death: for quite other reasons the Jews Philo and Josephus are almost equally severe. Did the procurator of Judaea really deserve so much animosity? An open-minded reading of the Bible – the Gospel according to Saint John – gives one the impression not of an evil man but of a weak one, a weak man willing to act decently, with a mind not indifferent to the idea of justice, though exceedingly sceptical; a reasonably honest man, but dreadfully afraid of being denounced in Rome – an understandable dread, when one considers that the emperor was then Tiberius. Little is known of his origins: he was certainly of the knightly order, but it is not known where he came from or what his background was. Some say that his name may have been a contraction of Pileatus, that is, red-capped, in the sense of manumitted or freed from a servile state; others say that it means that he was the son of an officer who had been decorated with the *pilum*, or javelin, of honour. It has been said that he was the son of Marcus Pontius, a general in Spain during Agrippa's war against the Cantabri, that he had been a friend of Germanicus, and even that his wife, who is called Claudia Procula in the apocryphal gospel of Nicodemus, was a daughter of that notorious Claudia, Augustus' daughter, whose conduct supplied so much of Rome's gossip in her day – this would explain her husband's career and the reason for her own presence in Jerusalem, against the regulations.

No doubt all this is fabulous: but what appears to be quite clear is that Pontius Pilate was not extraordinarily able in his government of Judaea, which in any case must have been the most unrewarding and the most difficult post that existed at the time. Once he put votive shields and standards bearing the portrait of the emperor into the Temple by night: the Jewish Law prohibited all representation of the human form, and this set off such a tumult that he was at once obliged to yield. On another occasion, when he needed money to build an aqueduct he took it from the Temple's treasure, and this provoked another outbreak which he endeavoured to quell by sending his men, dressed as Jews, into the crowd to attack the demonstrators. On still another, when some Galileans made a somewhat too noisy scene in the Temple he caused them to be charged by his police with such ferocity that, as we see in Saint Luke,[36] 'their blood was shed in the midst of their sacrifices'.[37] His attitude during Christ's trial is very well known: it shows that he despised the Jews (a contempt made evident by the inscription that he had placed on the Cross, 'The King of the Jews') but that he was also afraid of them. The crowd had only to shout, 'You are not Caesar's friend', to make him give in. Six years later a crowning blunder ended his career. A 'prophet' had appeared in Samaria and had asserted that Moses' tabernacle and holy vessels were buried on the top of Mount Gerizim: he said that he was going to dig them up. On the appointed day a crowd gathered at the foot of the mountain and climbed up it, singing psalms: but Pilate had sent his troops to occupy the summit and had given them orders to disperse the people: this they did, but the dispersal turned into a massacre. Pilate was denounced to the legate of Syria, Vitellius; he was removed from office, and when he was called to Rome the procurator of Judaea was unable to escape the responsibility. Caligula banished him to Gaul. Eusebius states that he there killed himself, either by order or from despair.[38]

The rule of the procurators continued for thirty years after Pilate's time. Yet there was a gap in this succession of Roman officials, and it happened between 37 and 44, when the imperial administration, as in the days of Herod the Great, made use of a vassal prince. It is strange, but it must be admitted that this last King of Judaea, who united in himself the blood of the Idumaean rulers and that of the Maccabean high priests, showed himself to be a good sovereign, although Christian tradition has been very much against him. This Herod Agrippa I was the grandson of Mariamne, the Asmonean wife whom Herod had put to death. He had been brought up in Rome, in the imperial household, and he had had an uneasy, troubled youth; but at least it had had the fortunate result of attaching him closely to one of his boon-companions, Caligula, the heir to the throne. When Tiberius died and the handsome young madman became emperor one of the first things he did was to liberate his friend from the prison in which he was confined by reason of his debts, and also, perhaps, because he had wished a little too obviously for the accession of 'Little Boots'.[39] The procurator Marcellus, who had just been appointed, was recalled, and the new king arrived in Palestine with such splendour that one might have been back in the days of Herod the Great. A little later he had himself given the territories of his uncle Antipas, and thus practically re-formed the kingdom of his grandfather. He was as sharp-witted as Herod, and being in Rome in 41 just at the moment when Caligula was assassinated, he played a decisive part in the military intervention that brought Claudius to the throne; which very naturally induced the new emperor to confirm him in all his rights.

This last king was to leave a happy memory of himself among the Jews. Not only was his reign peaceful, but he behaved like a faithful follower of Yahweh, 'omitting nothing that the Law required', as Josephus says,[40] making a grant to the Temple, going there openly every day to pray, and even causing his police to prosecute the young pagans who had put a statue of the emperor into a synagogue. To please the Sanhedrim he 'exerted his authority to persecute some of those who belonged to the Church. James, the brother of John, he beheaded, and then, finding that this was acceptable to the Jews, he went further, and laid hands on Peter too.'[41] It was he, too, who built the third city-wall, to the north of Jerusalem, that enclosed the suburbs; and he may have undertaken a fourth. This show of zealous fidelity was in fact only one aspect of a two-faced part that he played with great skill. Agrippa I was a Jew in Jerusalem; but in Caesarea he was a pagan, living in the Greek manner, having statues of his daughters and himself set up, and striking money with his portrait upon it. One of these coins bears the word *philoromaios*, friend of the Romans: a very truthful inscription, for in fact the last of the Maccabees was the emperor's executive agent.

Yet when he died in 44 his kingdom did not descend in its entirety to his son, Herod Agrippa II. The Romans may have been made uneasy by the building of the wall; and perhaps, as the social and political situation was rapidly deteriorating in Palestine, they thought that the firm grip of a procurator was essential. At first, therefore, Agrippa's son had no more than the little kingdom of Chalcis, a modest inheritance held by an uncle and brother-in-law of his; but later Nero's friendship allowed him to exchange it for Philip's former tetrarchate and then add Galilee to it. For this kindness he renamed Caesarea Neronias. He was an intelligent and a capable man, and like his father he was able to keep on good terms with his people while at the same time he remained devotedly attached to the Romans. But it is clear that his loyalty to Rome was greater than his solidarity with the Jews, for in the final rising he joined the winning side without a moment's hesitation.

All the characteristics of these last, three-parts-Romanized Idumaeans are to be seen summed up in the person of the companion of this petty king of Galilee – Berenice. Immortal verse has stamped the image of a tender, passionately loving woman upon our minds: but in fact she was a formidable, calculating, cunning creature, born to play an important part upon the stage of politics and quite untroubled about the means she used. In 48 she lost her husband, Herod of Chalcis. She came to live with her brother, Agrippa II, and presently the rumour of their incestuous relations reached as far as Rome, where it excited the mirth of Juvenal.[42] She was with her fraternal lover at Caesarea when Saint Paul was brought before the procurator Porcius Festus: this happened in their presence, and Saint Paul cried, 'Dost thou believe the prophets, king Agrippa?'[43] Everyone knows how her love-affair with Titus made her famous, and how she dreamt of reigning beside the master of her people like a new Esther, and how at last Titus, for reasons of state, made her go away from Rome – *invitus invitam*, in Suetonius' lapidary phrase[44] – thus providing Racine with the most beautiful theme of tragic love.

After the death of Agrippa I the last members of the Herodian dynasty counted for nothing.[45] The emperor's procurator was the one and only true master of Palestine; he was the man whose decisions were to be feared, and year by year his yoke became heavier. All the procurators, Marulus, Cuspius Fadus, Cumanus, Felix the brother of Pallas, Claudius' well-known freedman, who had Saint Paul kept in prison, Porcius Festus, Albinus and Gessius Florus left Israel the memory of severe, unindulgent rulers: even Tiberius Alexander, Philo's nephew, who apostasized from Judaism to become a Roman official, did not hesitate to drown a revolt in blood. It is true that the situation in Palestine was continually getting worse and that it was very often on the point of an outbreak. The Jewish nation had always been difficult to govern, and at this particular period it had become literally ungovernable. With its mind inflamed by the lessons of history, that 'dangerous article', as Paul Valéry calls it, the nation had no other ambition but to raise the cry of the Maccabees again and to attack Rome. But this was neither the day nor the hour. And the emperor who was now reigning over the world had nothing in common with the undistinguished Antiochus Epiphanes.

THE OCCUPIERS AND THE OCCUPIED

Is the Roman administration to bear the blame for these troubles and crises which were to end so catastrophically? The emperor sent procurators only to those recently annexed provinces in which trouble was to be expected. The officials who came to Judaea therefore already knew that they were going to have to deal with a difficult people, full of incomprehensible prejudices, divided into factions and past-masters at intrigue. They were prepared.

And for the very reason that they were well acquainted with the Jews, the Roman administrators took particular precautions with them. The procurator, for example, did not live in Jerusalem, possibly with the idea of sparing the followers of Yahweh the sight of completely pagan life in the middle of their holy city, and possibly, too, because he did not trust them. He and his officials were established at Caesarea, the former Turris Stratonis, which Herod the Great had turned into a thriving port and a splendid Graeco-Roman city. He only went up to Jerusalem for the great feasts, in order to supervise the great and potentially dangerous gatherings that then took place; and while he was there he lived in what had been Herod's palace, while the Antonia tower acted as military headquarters and barracks.

Furthermore, there were few troops stationed actually in Palestine. The legions, which were composed of Roman citizens, mostly Gauls and Spaniards, had their stations in Syria, conveniently near to intervene in case of necessity, but out of sight. On the territory of Judaea itself there were only auxiliaries, Greeks, Syrians or Samaritans; for the Jews were exempt from any form of military service.[46] These formations did not amount to more than five cohorts of infantry and one wing of cavalry, each consisting of between five and six hundred men. When the troubles grew worse, between 44 and 65, Jerusalem was garrisoned by one cohort; but it is not clear whether it was there in the days of Jesus.

The procurators had direct orders to humour Jewish susceptibilities as much as possible, above all in matters of religion. It is true that there were exceptions to this rule, but they were comparatively rare. The imperial family often sent rich gifts to the Temple; and it is even stated in Philo that Augustus ordered an ox and two lambs to be offered every day 'for Caesar and the Roman people'.[47] Troops entering Jerusalem were ordered to cover the standards that had the emperor's portrait upon them; and the coins struck in Judaea (bronze only, as we shall see[48]) did not carry his head either, but only his name and some Judaic symbol. And of course the Jews of Palestine, like all the other Jewish subjects of the empire, were excused from the worship of the emperor, which was a duty rigorously insisted upon from all other communities. When Caligula, who was particularly anxious to be a god, wanted to have himself worshipped in Jerusalem, the legate of Syria and Agrippa I combined to circumvent the young maniac's command.

Clearly, this mild rule also had another aspect. It does not seem that the well-disciplined Roman troops usually behaved badly in

Palestine, nor that they often indulged in violence or looting: Philo's remarks do not appear to have been well founded. It is very probable that when an outbreak occurred and order had to be restored, the soldiers may have got out of hand; but this would have been quite exceptional. The taxes, on the other hand, did infuriate the Jews. It was not that they were heavier than in the other provinces subject to imperial tribute: the taxes, direct and indirect, were more or less the same everywhere; and everywhere they were collected by the same very bad system, that of the tax-farmers, the notorious 'publicans' of the Gospel, who made fortunes upon the back of the taxpayers. But the Jews were enraged because all this money went off for the *fiscus*, the imperial treasury, and even more so because most of these state taxes had parallel religious taxes for the Temple and the priests, and the doubled burden was overwhelming.[49]

Another cause of vexation undoubtedly resided in the precise and even niggling measures that the Roman administration took for the thorough establishment of its authority and the assessment of its taxes. One is very well known, the census that Saint Luke speaks of in the beginning of his Gospel, when he shows us Jesus' parents going to Bethlehem to give in their names.[50] It is quite certain that the Roman administration often made use of this most valuable administrative tool: the famous Augustan monument found at Ankara shows that the first emperor caused three censuses to be made, one in 28 BC, another in AD 8 and the third in AD 14. It is known that there was a thorough census of the Gauls in 28 BC. Registration at the family's place of origin was traditional throughout the east: in AD 104 we find a prefect of Egypt ordering all those under his administration to go back to their *nomos*, the district of their birth, to be counted there.[51] It goes without saying that all this caused a great deal of inconvenience; and the Jews found these censuses an extraordinarily unpleasant mark of their subjection. They were numbered like beasts in a market. 'We are of Abraham's breed, nobody ever enslaved us yet.' 'Everyone who acts sinfully is the slave of sin,' replied Christ.[52]

In the final analysis, what they could not bear was the fact that they were no longer masters of their own fate and that they were subject to the rule of foreigners. No proud nation has ever suffered subjection patiently; how much more wounding, therefore, must it have been for this people which cherished the legitimate pride of having brought spiritual truth to the world and of being

God's own ally. Israel had not been free for these five hundred years and more, but the nation had never resigned itself to this lack of liberty. In our days the coloured nations have been lifted on a great wave of freedom, and the sight of this should help one to understand the Jewish psychology of that time and its hatred for all foreign rule. But in Israel this hatred was not based solely upon patriotic reasons: its roots were religious. The Roman was not only the occupier but also the impious and abominable heathen. No fusion of his race with that of Israel could be allowed for a moment: there could be none of that blending which was to be so fruitful in Gaul, for example; none of that amalgamation of occupier and occupied which happened elsewhere. The mere sight of a Roman horseman in his red cloak and his cuirass was, for a Jew, an insult to his most deeply held beliefs.

A strange and difficult situation! A Jewish subject, if he were to conform to the precepts of the rabbis in all their strictness – and on this point they were far more rigid than Moses himself[53] – might not have any relations whatever with those who administered his country. Every Roman, being a heathen, was according to the Law unclean. This is why, in the account of Jesus' trial, we see Pilate obliged to come out of the praetorium to speak to the Jews, because 'they would not enter the palace themselves; there was the paschal meat to be eaten, and they must not incur defilement'.[54] And in the Acts of the Apostles Saint Peter emphasises that in going into the house of Cornelius the centurion he was doing something against the Law, something almost revolutionary.[55] Tacitus accuses the Jews of feeling 'hatred against all other men', and in this he is mistaken; but he is not mistaken when he describes them as being 'apart'.[56] It must be admitted that this was an attitude that did not facilitate the work of the Roman administrators. On the other hand, it was one that made the agitator's task easy and did the work of the extremists for them. We may read what Israel really thought of the Romans in the Alexandrine Jews' insertions into the Sibylline books, those collections of allegedly oracular remarks which the heathens attributed to various prophetesses: *incestuous sodomites, murderers and parricides*, were among the least of their civilities. And this hope-filled theme continually recurs: the rule of these accursed people will only last a while; 'the virgin covered with gold and drunk with shameless dissipation shall be covered with infamy'; and soon 'the Vestals will no longer light the fire'.[57]

It was not all Jews, however, who shared in these violent feelings. The more reasonable among them realised that the presence of the Romans in Palestine brought with it great benefits, preventing disorder and foreign invasion. The orderly people were on their side: thus we may read in two of Saint Paul's epistles, 'Every soul must be submissive to its lawful superiors', as well as invitations to pray 'for the kings and those who are in authority'.[58] And indeed one often has the impression that Saint Paul saw the Roman empire as a historical realisation brought about by Providence, something that formed part of the divine plan and which should be used for the good of the cause in its beneficial aspects, such as the *pax Romana*, the roads, the ships and even the police. No doubt there were but few who had the foresight of genius, however; and many more would merely have accepted Rome out of prudence or resignation.

Here again we come across that essentially religious outlook which is inseparable from all human activity in Israel. For a Jew to take up a political attitude meant that at the same time he also took up a religious attitude, placing himself very exactly in relation to doctrine and practice. Those who interpreted the Law in the most rigorous manner almost automatically set themselves among the nationalists, those who formed the 'resistance' to the pagan occupation; on the other hand, those who were more easy-going in religious matters were also less difficult with regard to the Romans.[59] It may therefore be said, in a very general fashion, that the religious sects[60] into which the Jews were divided corresponded more or less to what we term political parties. The Sadducees, who were drawn from the old aristocratic families, the wealthy, the priests and the officials of the Temple, were on principle in favour of the established order; and ever since the Hellenistic period they had been considered as people who were resigned to the occupation: this made their opponents regard them as traitors and as half-infidels, demi-pagans, although they might have said that their attitude had a firm religious basis in the concept of Jewish universalism.[61] The Pharisees, who plumed themselves on being more pious than all others, more zealous, better versed in religious matters and the most rigid interpreters of tradition, considered themselves the heirs of the Maccabees and the true guardians of their heroic nationalism. Politically, therefore, they were most bitterly opposed to Rome.

A little before the birth of Christ an extremist party had

emerged from the body of the Pharisees: these were the Zealots, which is clearly derived from zeal, or rather from *zelos*, its Greek original.[62] From the point of view of religion they were in no way different from the Pharisees; in spite of what Josephus says,[63] they did not in the least break away to form a 'fourth tendency', but were rather what might be called the militant wing of Pharisaism: 'they acknowledged no master but God, and they were ready to suffer the most appalling torments rather than recognize the authority of a man'. Theirs was already a considerable movement by the year AD 6, when Judas of Gamala, called the Galilean, and Sadduk, a Pharisee, led their followers against the Romans when a census was being taken.[64] The revolt was crushed, but like all extremists the Zealots had the sympathy of the common people. They were no longer able to bring out great numbers in a rising, so they turned to terrorism, a terrorism directed against individuals. They used that short dagger which is called *sica* in Latin, and they struck those whom they counted as faithless or treacherous even more than they struck the occupying Romans: Saint Paul only just escaped them.[65] It was these *sicarii* who continually worked up the passions of the Jewish people and who provoked those risings and revolts that went on so continually and so vainly until they ended in the catastrophe of the year 70.

For it was indeed a catastrophe that ended the Roman occupation in Palestine and what may roughly be called the time of Jesus. Signs of it were already to be seen in Christ's day, and there were even more in the last years of Pontius Pilate's administration. After that, it may really be said that Palestine's history was no more than a series of risings, harshly put down, but continually starting again. Every procurator in turn had this perpetual unrest to deal with: under Tiberius Alexander twenty thousand Zealots were crucified in Judaea; under Felix a false messiah came from Egypt, stirred up the people and gathered thirty thousand fanatics on the Mount of Olives, where the army cut them to pieces.[66] Not that this man was alone: there were false messiahs in all parts, continually rising up. The Temple had been finished; but the ending of the work had thrown ten thousand men out of employ and this caused a shocking degree of poverty. Whenever some hot-headed man announced the coming of Israel's avenger there would at once be a spontaneous uprising. The last procurator could hardly tell which way to turn: one day it would be the Jews of the neighbourhood of

Caesarea; the next, those of Jerusalem . . . And so it went on until the year 66, when the whole of Palestine was in revolt and throughout the empire, by way of reprisals, Jews were being slaughtered in tens of thousands. The time had come when Rome was to take great and terrible measures to deal with the situation. It was to mean nothing less than the end of the holy city, as Jesus had foretold in His dreadful revelation on the Mount of Olives.[67] It was to mean Titus besieging Jerusalem for a hundred days, the unspeakable horrors of the famine, the fall of the city and a massacre such as history has rarely known.

It is upon this horrifying vision that the Roman period of Jewish history closes; and with it the sacred community, the state of Israel, ends for ever. A pall of smoke rises from the blazing Temple; a desperate cry comes from out of the ruins. 'Jerusalem, city of God, what divine punishments thy own ill deeds have brought on thee!' And how long was the city to be no more than a cemetery, or even worse, a heathen town, Aelia Capitolina – that Jerusalem which had 'rejoiced generations without number', as the elder Tobit said, and whose name 'would last for the ages to come'?[68]

CHAPTER FOUR

JERUSALEM

The city of God's rejoicing – Its position and its site – A thousand years of history – 'Hole in the corner' or metropolis? – 'The nonpareil of beauty, the pride of the whole earth' – Life in Jerusalem.

THE CITY OF GOD'S REJOICING

Jerusalem . . . It is impossible to speak of the framework within which the Jews led their lives without stopping to consider this unique city, to which the fate of Israel had been so firmly bound for a thousand years. It was the capital of the country, the unrivalled, unquestioned queen of the Holy Land, the living heart of the People of the Covenant: to the Jews, Jerusalem meant even more than Paris means to the French or London to the people of the Commonwealth. The echoes that a Catholic hears when he says 'Rome', the powerful emotions that the word evokes – all this was felt by every Jew when he uttered the syllables (so often repeated in his daily prayer) of the splendid name, 'as sounding as the cry of trumpets yet also as sweet as a shepherd's pipe'.

Jerusalem . . . The pilgrims who travelled towards its holy courts honoured its glory in those 'songs of ascents', those psalms that they chanted in chorus as they went along. 'Welcome sound, when I heard them saying, We will go into the Lord's house! Within thy gates, Jerusalem, our feet stand at last; Jerusalem, built as a city should be built that is one in fellowship. There the tribes meet, the Lord's own tribes . . .'[1] The dearest dream of all the Jews scattered to the four corners of the world was to see it, to visit it at least once in their life. The famous expression 'Next year in Jerusalem' comes down from the remotest centuries. Those who could not realize their dream thought of the holy city as a place of happiness and splendour, where everything was beautiful, rich and surrounded by a supernatural glory. And so, 'by the waters of Babylon', in the dark days of the exile the Jews far from home wept when they remembered Zion and sang this hymn which still tears one's heart – 'Jerusalem, if I forget thee, perish the skill of my right hand! Let my tongue stick fast to the roof of my mouth if I cease to remember thee, if I love not Jerusalem dearer than heart's content!'[2]

For in fact, to the Jews, Jerusalem was something quite other than a mere earthly city, a town among all the other towns. It was an integral part of the working of salvation: it could not be separated from the revealed words of God. The prophet Isaiah had told them that God Himself had said, 'Joy of yours, pride of yours, this new creation shall be; joy of mine, pride of mine, Jerusalem and her folk, created anew. I will rejoice in Jerusalem, take pride in my people . . .'[3] It was God, too, who had called the town by its name, when His 'voice bade Jerusalem grow populous'.[4] He Himself had chosen the city, in order that He might be worshipped there.[5] And it had been said in Ezra that the only true God was He who was worshipped at Jerusalem.[6] The holy city had been linked with every happening in biblical history; and so it was to be again, at the end of time, when the whole assembled people should see the prophecies accomplished. Then 'sapphire and emerald Jerusalem's gates shall be, of precious stones the wall that rings her round; shining white and clean the pavements of her streets; no quarter of her but shall echo the Alleluia-chant of praise. Blessed be the Lord, that has set her on the heights; may He reign there for ever, reign for ever as her king.'[7]

ITS POSITION AND ITS SITE

Jerusalem, standing in the heart of those Judaean high lands which are Palestine's moral as well as its physical bastion, stood there because of certain geographical facts: and, to a certain degree, geography was also at the base of its splendid destiny. The whole region was one in which the settled people of the plain came into contact with the nomads of the steppes; yet the little district in which the town grew up was even more particularly a zone of contact and a place of passage. The most southerly track by which one can cross the Ghor before the way is blocked by the Dead Sea, leads to its gates, where it is joined by the ridge-road from Samaria and Galilee, which follows the backbone of the country. And from Jerusalem, too, the roads to Gaza, Jaffa, Jericho and Shechem radiate like the arms of a star. Twelve hours of walking bring one to the Mediterranean, six to the Jordan. Jerusalem's role as capital, fortress and market is therefore quite understandable.

At the point where the city was built the central chain of the Palestinian mountains resolves itself into a kind of plateau, which stands at an altitude of some two thousand five hundred feet and which has been cut by the erosion of violent torrents into two raised parts running from the north to the south-south-east and separated by a shallow valley that was called the Valley of the Cheesemakers, the Tyropoeon. It was on the southern part of these that Jerusalem was built, a citadel protected by the deep ravine of Hinnom on the west and that of the Kidron on the east, both wadis or seasonal streams which were often dry, but which turned into furious torrents when they were swelled by the winter floods – so furious that one of them was called 'the cloudy stream'.[8] The western hill, the higher of the two, which reaches 2,580 feet, is made up of the Gareb and of what the Christians have called the district of Zion: this is not the Zion of the Hebrews, but the upper town, where the wealthy had their palaces. The narrower eastern hill is divided into three smaller plateaux; the highest (2,581 feet) was called the Moriah, and upon it, covering it completely, stood the Temple: the two lower plains, which stood one to the north and the other to the south, were called Bezetha (2,411 feet) and Ophel (2,132 feet). Biblical study and archeology situate the original Jerusalem, David's Zion, upon Ophel; and even more precisely, by the side of the Fountain of the Virgin, *Ain Sitti Mariam* or Gihon, whose waters were stopped up by Hezekiah in the seventh century BC and led through a tunnel nearly two thousand feet long to the pool of Siloam, to serve as a supply in case of siege.[9] On the other side of the ravine of the Kidron rises a long hill whose name speaks to every Christian heart: it is the Mount of Olives, where the risen Christ vanished from His disciples' sight.[10] Its continuation towards the south is called the Mount of Scandal, because it was there that Solomon, Solomon himself, the anointed of the Lord, permitted altars to be set up to the gods of his heathen wives.[11] At the end of this hill the three valleys of Jerusalem join one another to form the Wad En-Nar, whose bed runs down towards the Dead Sea.

Such is the topography of Jerusalem, and such it was at the time of Christ. Standing there upon that site it gives the curious impression, as one comes nearer to it by the road, of being a fortress, a 'city of the high place' as the Scriptures so often put it; and yet at the same time, when one sees it from far off or nowadays when one flies over it, the impression of being a town that is surrounded by hills, a town at the bottom of a hollow. The single break in the ring of hills, the edge of the hollow, is that of the Wad En-Nar: by this breach Jerusalem is in touch with the desert and with Asia; and it is by this breach that the dreaded *khamsin* blows in from the burning sands. Yet Jerusalem's altitude does give it peach-coloured evenings after the sky has lowered over it all the day, and nights of a delightful freshness. It also brings the city those rains from the west which are so looked forward to, and which come borne by great armies of clouds: and sometimes snow comes with them too, for winter is not a meaningless word in Jerusalem.

A THOUSAND YEARS OF HISTORY

The site of Jerusalem has been occupied by men for a very long time indeed. According to the Psalmist, the holy city must first have been called Salem; for he says, 'There in Salem He makes His abode, dwells in Zion'.[12] That, in any case, is the name by which it is called in Genesis,[13] in that strange passage where Melchisedech 'the king of Salem and priest of the most high God' brings Abraham bread and wine and blesses him. Even before the days of the patriarch the true God must have been known there. The rabbinical explanation of the change in the city's name is this:[14] well before the birth of Abraham, Shem, the son of Noah, had already called it Salem, perhaps because this word means safety; but the patriarch wanted to call it Jeru or Jireh, and Yahweh, so as to disappoint neither the one nor the other, cried, 'Then I shall give it both of the names!'

Archeology, however, is more informative than this artless tale.[15] It shows that the site was inhabited as early as the third millennium by people who lived in caves near Mary's Well. By about the second millennium the village had become an oppidum not unlike those which the Ligurians were building in the West: defensive moats have been discovered, and a primitive sanctuary with a rock carved in cup-shaped hollows. By the fifteenth century BC it was a formidable city, surrounded by an immense wall with a great many towers; and a tunnel called the *sinnor* gave access to the spring – a tunnel which was therefore nearly a thousand years older than the underground canal dug in the days of King Hezekiah. This powerful town was known as far away as Mesopotamia, where it was mentioned in documents under the name of Urusalim, which has a curious likeness to the name of Ur, the Chaldean city from which Abraham began his divinely-inspired journey.[16] The men who then lived there were Canaanites, part of that people whom the Jewish armies were to meet in so many hard-fought battles after Moses had brought them out of Egypt to the conquest of the Promised Land. These Canaanites were experts in fortification: wherever traces of their work have been found – in Jericho, for example – its technical efficiency has been admired by specialists: it therefore took the invading Israelites close on two hundred years to overcome their resistance, in spite of the protection of Yahweh and of His miracles. Urusalim was one of the last places to stand out against them. The Canaanites who held it – they were called Jebusites – were so confident of the strength of their walls that they had a common saying, 'Blind men and cripples are all that is needed to defend this city'.[17]

It was King David who, in about the year 1000, had the glory of taking the impregnable stronghold. He directed the siege in person, and at first he concentrated his attack upon the fortress of Zion, upon Ophel, which protected the town built upon the Moriah from the south. He promised that the first man to enter would be given the command of his army, and it was Joab who accomplished the feat, by creeping along the passage that led the water in and thus taking the garrison by surprise. The king left Hebron, Israel's former capital, as being too far from the centre, and at once installed himself in the town he had just taken. The 'city of David' rose up on Zion, and under the guidance of Phoenician architects a first royal palace took shape. What splendour! But all this was God's will: it was His power that had given His people the victory, according to His promise. David did not forget it and he gave thanks in the most fervent of his psalms.[18] And to show his gratitude thoroughly he caused the ark of the covenant, the tabernacle that the Israelites carried with them in the desert, the holy receptacle for the Tables of the Law, to be brought to Jerusalem; and there, upon the hill Moriah, was built a place for it, made of masoned stone and cedar-wood, the

first Temple. Upon the glorious day that the ark came in, David himself was to be seen 'dancing with all his might, there in the Lord's presence; clad in the sacred mantle, he must dance too'.

By the time of Christ, then, Jerusalem had been the holy centre of God's people for ten centuries. The sacred writings carefully noted the city's enlargements, one after another: they recorded how the illustrious Solomon, the son of David, had linked his father's stronghold with the Moriah and its palace and its Temple,[19] by a great earth-platform; how he protected his capital by a wall built upon the western hill,[20] the 'first wall', whose northern face had Ephraim's Gate and the Corner Gate;[21] and above all (a subject upon which the inspired writer was not sparing of detail) how, with the help of his friend, the Phoenician King Hiram of Tyre, he had undertaken the building of the Temple, the greatest, the most beautiful, the most splendidly adorned temple that ever was, the work of the hands of a hundred and fifty-three thousand men.[22]

From that time onwards the city of the Almighty had never ceased to grow. Suburbs were formed outside the walls, that new trading town of which Zephaniah spoke so fiercely;[23] and in the eighth century, under the kings Ozias and Hezekiah, a second wall was built, which is remembered by the Fish Gate.

The *sinnor* was by that time no longer usable, and it was then the underground canal was made, to bring the water to the pool of Siloam; it was then that the fortifications of Ophel were strengthened by a great round tower, whose base has been discovered by the archaeologists; and it was then that the royal tombs were constructed at the foot of the walls. All this made a beautiful whole, and the book of Nehemiah gives a precise idea of it as he tells how everything had to be rebuilt after the disaster.[24]

For the city of God had known a disaster; and even after five centuries had gone by the memory of it was painful to all the Jews. Had Yahweh then forgotten the covenant and broken His promise? No: not Yahweh, but His people. In the time of the last kings of Judah abominations had been done in Jerusalem itself. The prophets had cried out against them, but in vain.[25] Altars to false gods had arisen, even in the very Temple of the Single One: that whoredom which the Babylonians called sacred prostitution had flourished in all the courts; and even the king himself, Manasseh, the anointed of the Lord, had burnt children to the greater honour of the Phoenician Baal-Moloch in the hollow, called from that time on the Valley of the Slain.[26]

It was therefore as a divine punishment that Nebuchadnezzar and his Chaldees surrounded the town, and that after an appalling siege the defenders, decimated by starvation and the plague, had to yield. 'Never a woman in Sion, never a maid in all Juda's cities, but has met with dishonour; merciless hands hurry our princes to the gallows; reverence is none for grey hairs.'²⁷ The whole town had been burnt, including the palace and the Temple. It was with this appalling spectacle in their eyes that the Israelites had had to leave their sacred city, as they were led away into captivity in Babylon.²⁸

So after the exile, when the benevolent Cyrus, the Persian King of Kings, allowed them to go back to their home in 538, the 'saved remnant' of the Chosen People could think of no action more urgently called for nor more holy than the rebuilding of Jerusalem. This was a wonderful undertaking, filled with faith and energy; and the book of Nehemiah was to hand it down to posterity.²⁹ Exactly where the city of their fathers had stood they built a new city: and at the same time Ezra rebuilt the city of the spirit, the Law of God. The walls thrown down half a century before were raised up again. The whole nation was called upon to help. Guarded by sentinels and with 'one hand to work with, and one closing still on a javelin', some thousands of men accomplished the holy task in forty-two days. At the beginning of the fifth century, therefore, Jerusalem was once more a beautiful and splendid town: it was certainly a more modest capital than Solomon's had been, but one still worthy of Yahweh.

It had continually increased since then. The rule of the Seleucids, those Graeco-Syrian princes, brought great prosperity to Jerusalem: it became more and more important as a market and a centre for caravans, and all the merchandise of the Hellenistic world and the Orient flowed in. New districts were built, particularly on the plateau of Bezetha, to the north of the Temple – the district that Herod Agrippa I was to enclose by a third wall, but this was very much later, well after Jesus' death. Of course, the development had not all been smooth or easy: the extraordinary Antiochus Epiphanes, commonly called Epimanes, or the Crazed, destroyed Nehemiah's walls and built, probably upon a jutting spur of the western hill, a fortress called the Acra, intended to command the town.³⁰ At the same time he began that persecution which provoked the liberating fury of the Maccabees. The victorious rebels at once tore down the Acra, rebuilt the walls and even made another for the better protection of the citadel from the town side.[31]

It was Herod who added the last touches to Jerusalem as it was in the time of Christ. He was a great builder, and as soon as he became king he undertook the protection of the upper town by raising up a powerful palace-citadel, crowned by three enormous towers, and to strengthen the Temple by the great Antonia fortress. And above all he determined, in spite of a certain hanging-back on the part of the Pharisees and the priests, to rebuild the Temple, doubling the surface of the Moriah by prodigious retaining walls and terraces. He set some ten thousand men to work, and then eighteen thousand; and he gave the building all the splendour that Hellenistic art could provide. The impressive remains that are still to be seen at the base of the present 'tower of David', a part of the royal palace, and at the foundations of the great terrace of the Temple – the present Wailing Wall – give a splendid idea of Herod's architecture. Many palaces were also built in the upper town; streets and wide squares were opened; the Tyropoeon had its middle part covered over; and new districts appeared in Bezetha and Gareb and even on the Mount of Olives and the Mount of Scandal. Such was the Jerusalem that Jesus knew.[32]

'HOLE IN THE CORNER' OR METROPOLIS?

Was Jerusalem really a great city? It is exceedingly difficult to form an exact idea of its population. The results of the Roman censuses have not come down to us, and even if they had, they would have to be used with caution, for like all eastern peoples the Jews distrusted and disliked these countings, and many of them certainly escaped being numbered. The population of eastern towns remained but vaguely known until a very recent period; and even at the beginning of this century one guide-book to Cairo gave the figure of two hundred thousand, while another gave four hundred thousand.

Cicero speaks of Jerusalem with contempt as 'a hole in the corner',[33] but Josephus in *Contra Apionem*[34] quotes a passage from Hecataeus of Abdera in which the Greek geographer asserts that in Alexander's time it had a hundred and twenty thousand inhabitants. As Jerusalem continually expanded during the Hellenistic and then the Roman periods, it may then be supposed that by the time of Christ its population would have been a hundred and fifty thousand. This would be a maximum. In 1875 no more than fifteen thousand inhabitants were counted in the area limited by the 'second wall': taking into account the expansion of the town under Herod and the procurators, this figure should be multiplied by four, which brings one to sixty thousand. This roughly agrees with Renan's figure of fifty thousand. It may therefore be allowed that the true number lies somewhere between fifty and a hundred and fifty thousand, that is, in the neighbourhood of a hundred thousand. But all this is conjectural: and one ought certainly to reckon with the Orientals' wonderful ability at crowding a great many people into a very small space.

In any case, this figure ensured Jerusalem of an honourable place among the cities of the empire, though not indeed a position in the first rank. It was not to be compared to the great metropolitan cities of the time, Rome and Alexandria. Augustus states in his *Res Gestae* that when he was consul for the twelfth time, that is to say, in 5 BC, he gave sixty denarii to each of the three hundred and twenty thousand citizens of his capital: counting the women and children and the great numbers of slaves, this leads one to the conclusion that Rome had more than a million inhabitants;[35] and this is exactly the same figure which is to be assumed for Alexandria, since Diodorus Siculus,[36] who wrote in the middle of the first century BC, says that the great Egyptian city had three hundred thousand free men in it. Jerusalem was not even the greatest Jewish city in the world, for as we have seen,[37] the Jewish colonies in Alexandria and Rome outnumbered it considerably, the first having perhaps twice or even three times its population.

The paradoxical position of the Holy Land and its people, both so small according to ordinary reckonings and yet so great in history, standing and influence, was not repeated in the capital of this land and this people. Jerusalem was certainly no hole in the corner but a medium-sized city, like many others in Europe; and at the same time it was a great spiritual metropolis.

'THE NONPAREIL OF BEAUTY, THE PRIDE OF THE WHOLE EARTH'
But however moderate in size, the Jews admired it. 'The nonpareil of beauty, the pride of the whole earth!' cried the prophet Jeremiah,[38] and a rabbinical aphorism said: 'He who has not seen Jerusalem has never seen a beautiful city.'[39]

Taken as a whole and seen from some distance, Jerusalem

certainly had a noble appearance. Even visitors of our time can see this: until the most recent times, when modern buildings have spoilt a good deal of it, it still had much of the look that it must have had twenty centuries before, the Crusaders' walls being very like those of Herod, no doubt, and the mosque of Omar playing a more modest version of the part the Temple played in the composition of the landscape. When the pilgrims from the north reached the top of Mount Scopus and stopped to gaze at the city, they saw it 'like a stag lying among the hills', tawny and dun – for this was the colour of the sun-baked limestone – and flecked with white patches, which were the marble palaces. The town undulated gently, curving from the upper town down to the hollow along the middle and then rising again to the walls of the sanctuary.

But the incomparable view, the most splendid of them all, was that from the east, when, coming from Bethany, one stopped on the top of the Mount of Olives, there where Jesus had looked out over Jerusalem and wept for the town. It was a most striking, arresting impression and it is still: Jerusalem looked like a fortress, an impregnable fortress, and yet at the same time like a vast jewel upon a setting of bronze. Beyond the ravine of the Kidron a wall reared up two hundred and fifty feet and more, and it was topped by towers, of which one, the corner-tower in the south-east, the famous pinnacle to which the Tempter carried Jesus,[40] mounted no less than two hundred and ten feet higher still. Resting upon its foundation of cyclopean masonry the Temple rose up in its splendour, stretching its gilded spires towards the blue sky; and upon its northern flank stood the immense cube of the Antonia tower. Behind, in the old town, the houses huddled together in an ochre mosaic, enclosed by lines of shade. Far back to the westwards the palaces of the Asmoneans, of Herod and of the high priests showed their white roofs and their colonnades, and beyond there was to be seen the dark line of the city wall climbing towards the top of Mount Gareb, mounting in great steps and crowded with towers.

To reach the city, unless one were coming from the north, from Caesarea or Samaria, it was necessary to cross one or other of the ravines that bounded it. These were unlovely places, and they made a strong contrast with the suburbs full of gardens that mounted, particularly on the east, to meet the hills, with their olives and their fig-trees. A great part of the valley of the Kidron was a cemetery, that famous cemetery of Jehoshaphat in which every pious Jew longed to be buried, because the prophet Joel had said that it was there that men would be gathered on the Day of Judgment.[41] Here there were shown the tombs of some of the great men of Israel, such as Absalom: and according to an apocryphal tradition it was here, among the tombs, that some of the apostles hid on the evening of Good Friday. As for the other ravine, the valley of Hinnom, the *Ge Hinnom*, it was the only too-well-known Gehenna, of evil memory. Ever since the holy King Josiah had been outraged by the sight of human sacrifices to Moloch in this infamous place and had ordered it to be the town midden,[42] filth and dead animals had been thrown into it, and there was a perpetual fire kept up to burn the city's rubbish. This horrible place was an image of hell, and from the time of Isaiah[43] onwards its flames were the symbol of the eternal fire.[44] Nobody would venture there after nightfall.

To get into the town one had to pass the famous walls. They ringed it round without a break, running for more than two and three-quarter miles. Beginning at the Temple, where it merged into the retaining-wall of the court, the wall enclosed the mound of Zion, turned above the junction of the Hinnom and the Kidron, climbed the heights as far as the palace-fortress of Herod, made a right-angle, with the Hippicus tower at its corner, seemed to go into the town by two redans, of which the second bordered Golgotha, the 'place of the skull', where men were put to death, and then ran on straight to reach the Temple again or, to be more exact, the massive base of the Antonia fortress. This wall was built by Herod, partly upon the foundations of Hezekiah's wall, and it was, in the most exact meaning of the word, formidable. It was far better made than the 'third wall' which was put up hurriedly by Herod Agrippa I in 44, and of course even more so than the 'fourth wall' which was discovered, far to the north of the city in 1925 – a wall that Titus' legionaries must have laughed at. Herod's wall was built of enormous blocks (the smallest weighs a ton) laid irregularly, 'full of cleverly arranged projections and depressions', says Tacitus,[45] crenellated, strengthened by towers at every two hundred cubits – or something less than a hundred yards, a spear's throw. It was thought to be impregnable, and in fact it took fifteen thousand Roman soldiers a hundred days to overcome it.

All of the gates were fortified. The wall was enlarged to two or three times its ordinary width, and an arched passage, closed at each end by heavy doors, was made through it. Above the arch there was a guardroom to shelter the defenders. The Bible very often speaks of the strength and the splendour of these gates: how many of them were there, and just where were they placed? There were most probably seven or eight chief gates, without counting the posterns. On the east the Golden Gate, now walled up, led directly to the Temple. To the south of this, the Fountain Gate also opened on to the valley of the Kidron: the Gate of Ephraim and the Corner Gate, also called the Gate of the Gardens, were to the west: on the south there was the Dung Gate, giving on Gehenna: and roads from Samaria, Jericho and the coast all met at the Fish Gate in the north. As to the Sheep Gate, to which Our Lord compared Himself,[46] it was no doubt that which is now called after Saint Stephen: it was here that the herds intended for the sacrifice came in, and it stood to the north of the Golden Gate. Jesus must very often have entered the city and have left it during the Holy Week by the Sheep Gate.

Once through the gates, one found oneself in a maze of narrow streets that zigzagged between blocks of houses without any apparent plan, as they do in Venice or the Casbah of Algiers. Many of them were cut into steps, which made it easier for men and asses: some of these stepped streets have been found, particularly the one that led down to the district of Siloam, and, in the land belonging to the Assumptionists, that which Jesus no doubt took on the evening of Good Friday to go to the Mount of Olives. There were scarcely any wide avenues or considerable open spaces. The central hollow of the Tyropoeon was crossed by a broad causeway, however, and by a bridge which linked the Temple and the upper town; and below it stretched a great paved square, surrounded by colonnades and bounded on the north by the old palace of the Asmoneans. It was Herod who had caused this to be laid out to serve as an agora or a forum in the Graeco-Roman way, and it was called the Xystus, meaning the flat place. Other smaller squares are referred to in the Talmudic treatises, and they were called after certain trades – the Square of the Butchers, the Wool-weavers, the Fullers, the Fishmongers – or simply termed the Upper Market and the Lower Market. The streets, too, or at least those that had a name, were often called in the same way after a trade, for the men of one calling all kept together in the same district, as they did in Europe in the Middle Ages. This explains the extraordinary

number of synagogues, where the people met to pray, or sometimes to debate: there were no less than four hundred and eighty.
Each guild, each block of houses had its own, as well as each of
the bodies of strangers who came up to Jerusalem at the time
of the feasts.[47]

'A beautiful city', said Jeremiah: but was this really the case?
'One should not imagine any kind of luxury in the building:
the whole body of recovered evidence for this period denies it.'[48]
Only rich men's houses were roofed with tiles: the poor made
do with that covering of reeds and beaten earth to which Saint
Mark refers.[49] There were great differences between the various
districts. Zion, the oldest, was a casbah in the native manner;
the upper town housed the rich and the powerful, and the suburb
of Bezetha the merchants. Dressed stone was unusual, and the
walls of rough, mortared blocks were far from elegant: the Jews,
unlike the Romans, were not born masons.

Yet quite apart from the Temple, whose splendours were
beyond all comparison, Jerusalem had palaces, grand houses
and public works. Of the last, the most esteemed were those that
supplied the town with its water, that precious substance. There
were a few wells, among them the Well of the Fullers which the
Book of Kings refers to,[50] but much more important were the
great reservoirs and pools to which the water had been brought
with immense labour. In the lower part of the town there was
the one which was fed by Hezekiah's famous canal and which
was called Siloam, a word which means 'sent out', a name heavy
with mystical significance, which John the Evangelist obviously
had in mind when he set down his account of the blind man whom
Jesus healed by sending him to wash there.[51] It was at that time
a basin surrounded by a noble Herodian portico. 'In the service
of the Feast of Tabernacles there was a procession thither to
draw water which was carried up again to the Temple.' At the
time of Christ the other pool was still outside the walls, and
perhaps this was one of the reasons that induced Herod Agrippa I
to build the third wall: it was the famous pool with five porches,
where, as Saint John says,[52] a crowd of blind, crippled and
disabled men came to bathe themselves, because it was held
that from time to time an angel came and stirred the water,
and the first man who stepped into the pool after the stirring of
the water was healed. Possibly it was confused with the 'pool
of the test' which, in former times, had served to wash the

sacrificial animals. In any case, it was a fine building – the
archaeologists have rediscovered it – about a hundred and thirty
yards long and sixty-five wide, surrounded by an arcaded gallery;
it was divided in the middle by a barrier upon which stood a
fifth gallery with a colonnade: the pool was a public bathing place.

Several palaces were the pride of the city. The palace of the
Asmoneans was the oldest: it probably dated from John Hyrcanus.
Herod Antipas would have stayed there when he came to
Jerusalem for the feasts, and no doubt it was there that Jesus
was brought before him.[54] The splendid fortified palace that
Herod built at the corner of the upper town was the Roman
procurator's residence when he too came to Jerusalem. 'Magnificent beyond all words', says Josephus, who was somewhat
given to strong expressions.[55] It was said to have been built
exactly on the place where David sang his psalms, and it then
formed part of the city wall. Massive four-sided towers protected
it; and Herod the Great had given these the names of people he
had loved, his friend Hippicus, his ill-fated brother Phasael, the
victim of the Parthians, and that beloved wife, Mariamne, whom
he had had put to death. The last was the tallest of them all,
and it reached a height of ninety-two feet. By night there was a
watch-fire on the top of the Phasael tower. But the inside of the
palace had none of this warlike appearance. It was built of marble;
its floors were paved with rare stones or mosaics; it had a hundred
rooms and in the banqueting halls there was space enough for a
hundred couches for the guests. Its furniture and decoration
astonished all beholders, but even more the beauty of its gardens,
where delightful pools were filled by the water of many aqueducts.
The high priest in office had a more modest palace, but one
which was still quite imposing, since on the tragic night of
Christ's trial we find a whole group of servants sitting round a
fire in the courtyard: and there seems to be no doubt that the
deposed high priest, Annas, had another.[56]

The Antonia tower was not a residence but a barracks. At
this point, where the rise of Bezetha makes attack comparatively
easy, generation after generation had built up defences upon the
emplacement of a fortification of Solomon's time; and after
the return from exile the Hananeel tower was built, the tower
whose Greek nickname was Baris, the citadel above all others.
The Asmoneans had increased this, making a castle of it, and
Herod had given it its final shape. It was a long rectangle of

about a hundred and ten yards by fifty-five, and each of its corners had an immense square tower nearly a hundred feet high: it was the true key of the holy city and the guardian of the Temple. The Roman garrison therefore occupied it, and by night the cries of the sentinels could be heard, answering one another from tower to tower. Stairways led down into the sacred courts, and in case of need the soldiers would hurry down them with a clatter of army boots;[57] and secret passages led under the Temple terrace into the heart of the town. The middle of the rectangle made one vast courtyard, and within it the painstaking work of the Dames de Sion and the Dominicans of the School of Biblical Studies have succeeded in identifying the flat paved space, the famous Lithostrotos upon which Pilate set up his judgment-seat to sentence Jesus, as we read in Saint John:[58] and it is very moving to see these great foot-worn slabs with their various inscriptions, stones which Christ undoubtedly walked upon.[59] They are in the underground part of the convent of the Dames de Sion.

Of the Temple little more need be said than that it outweighed all the other glories of the city, and that the pious Jew coming to Jerusalem had eyes for nothing else. This was the Temple of Herod the Great, the building that the magnificent tyrant had begun in 20 BC in exactly the same place as Solomon's, which had been destroyed by Nebuchadnezzar, and the far smaller one of the time of Ezra and Nehemiah; the place which is now occupied by the blue-domed mosque of Omar, standing upon the Hassam esh Sherif. Although the Idumaean had celebrated the feast of dedication ten years after the beginning of the work, upon the anniversary of his accession, and although a thousand priests and more than ten thousand workmen had laboured upon it for forty-six years (Saint John gives the period in the second chapter of his Gospel) it was far from being finished when Jesus knew it. The work was not really terminated until between 62 and 64, that is to say, a very short time before its destruction by Titus. It was therefore completely new; its marble was white and the gold shone brilliantly upon its façade. Like a diadem of stone crowning the stone-built, stone-surrounded city of Jerusalem the vast mass of the Temple stood there at the summit, with its walls, its courts and its sanctuaries one behind another in an arrangement full of symbolic significance.[60] It was worthy of being the 'house of God', this great building for which nothing was too fine, nothing too splendid, this 'holy place' to which 'as with some rich feast . . . in joyful accents, singing thy praise',[61] the devoted pilgrims mounted up.

LIFE IN JERUSALEM

Without falling into that sin of anachronism which Lucien Febvre has called the worst of all for a historian, is it possible to form some kind of an idea of what life was like two thousand years ago in that city whose topography we now know so well? It cannot be very far wrong to employ the analogy of those eastern cities whose old quarters are still to be seen; the ancient parts of Jerusalem as we see them now, for example, or old Cairo or the Damascus of the Caliphs. One's general impression would have been that of a tightly packed mass, with every inch of space in use. The houses clung to one another, overlapping and even interpenetrating. There were no gardens, except for Herod's and that walled garden of roses which, according to the Talmud,[62] dated from the time of the prophets; and only here and there was a fig-tree to be seen, rising from a courtyard. It was only after Herod Agrippa I enclosed the Gareb with his wall that there were to be many beautiful gardens. There were no statues at the street corners, whereas in the pagan towns it was impossible to move any distance without being obliged to acknowledge some god or other. Most of the streets were exceedingly narrow, so narrow that two asses, bearing the panniers that they usually carried, could scarcely pass: even people on foot would jostle one another, and this caused a great deal of shouting and dispute. The traders' stalls, lining the streets in an open-air market, were scarcely calculated to make the traffic easier. And there was a maze of alleys and lanes and inner courts where only the locals could find their way. The most animated places were the gates and the two markets, that of the upper town being frequented by the better sort of people. There were no carriages, and only a few rich men's litters; but there were a great many asses, and their hooves could be heard everywhere, tapping on the cobbled steps – steps, since it was impossible to walk for a quarter of an hour in Jerusalem without either climbing up or going down. And there were great numbers of sheep and cattle: so very many were needed for the sacrifices. From time to time there might pass scornful troopers of the Gaulish or Numidian auxiliaries, wearing the crested helmet and the cuirass, with a red cloak on

95

their shoulders, and mounted on horses that negotiated all these steps with great difficulty.

The whole city, more or less, was filled with a strong smell, made up of many elements. There was a police regulation forbidding 'open-air ovens, because of the smoke'[63] and another which forbade the use of manure for trees and flowers.[64] But their existence was surprising, for the smell of the hot grease of cooking mingled with the sharp stench of the rubbish that, according to the Talmud,[65] was swept away from the open places every day, but which was no doubt scarcely ever disturbed in the alleys. Furthermore, if the wind blew only a little from the east the smoke from the altar of sacrifices would turn back not only into the courts but over the whole city, bringing a mixture of the horrible reek of burning flesh and the heady smell of incense. The Jewish crowd had the reputation of smelling unpleasant, and indeed this was one of the stock jokes of Roman heavy comedy; yet the women used a great deal of scent, and it was said that they went to great extremes to surround themselves with a sensuous perfume when they thought that this was called for. In vain the rabbis said, 'The incense of the Temple ought to be enough for you'. The upper market, where myrrh and nard and costly balm were sold, was always crowded.

The town was not only rich in odours; it was also rich in noise. Except at night and during the very hot hours of the siesta or in winter when the west wind brought its piercing blasts of rain, the whole city was filled with a confused din. Everything was mingled to form this general sound, the shouting of the tradesmen trying to attract custom, the cry of the water-carriers bearing their skins on their backs and offering their services, the public criers who called for silence to make an official announcement, and sometimes the shouting of the guards making way for some condemned man who was being taken to 'the place of the skull', carrying the beam of his cross upon his back. The animals being driven towards the Temple bleated and lowed; sometimes the asses brayed, but more rarely, since they had learnt patience. A group of pilgrims would pass, singing a psalm in chorus to the tune of *The Doe of the Morning* or *The Dove of the Far-away Terebinths*. In the fullers' quarter might be heard the dull, monotonous noise of fulling; in that of the coppersmiths' the rhythmic din of hammering. And then, four times a day, at the hour of sacrifice and at the three ritual pauses, the triple blast of the seven silver trumpets rang out from the gate of the men's court in the Temple and imposed a comparative silence, during which the pious prostrated themselves.

This was the activity of ordinary days; but at certain times of the year the city's animation increased enormously. These were the periods of the great feasts, the Passover, the Feast of Weeks, the Day of Atonement and that happiest of them all, the Feast of Tabernacles: and how many days did they amount to, all these between them? During these seasons prodigious crowds of pilgrims filled the city; and even if one divides Josephus' millions by ten one still wonders how Jerusalem can have held them all. As it was, a great many had to sleep outside the town in the suburbs, on the hills, in tents or in huts made of branches, or just under the open sky, as Jesus and His disciples did in the Garden of Gethsemane. The crowding was unbelievable – vast throngs of men and of animals too, for at a single Passover it could happen that two hundred thousand lambs would be brought. This was the time when the inhabitants of Jerusalem might see their brothers from the whole of the Diaspora, Jews from Babylon with their trailing black robes, Jews from Phoenicia in tunics and striped drawers, Jews from the plateaux of Anatolia dressed in goat's-hair cloaks, Persian Jews gleaming in silk brocaded with gold and silver. All these people crowded into the court of the Temple: the sellers of sacrificial animals and the money-changers made their scandalous fortunes, to the indignation of pure minds, such as Christ's. Men jostled to take their turn in the queues of those who offered a lamb to the priests. It was a fair, yet a pious fair, an astonishing hurly-burly: the spectacle of Mecca, at the height of the great pilgrimages of Islam, gives some idea of what it must have been.

We may imagine one of the most solemn of these days, when as the evening fell, before the ninth hour the *shofar*, the ram's horn, would utter its long sad note followed by the six ritual trumpet-blasts to announce the day holy above all others, the Sabbath of the Passover: and then the moon of Nisan would glide through the great calm sky over a Jerusalem at last fallen into quietness.

PART TWO

Days and Nights that Bless the Lord

> Bless him they should, ice and snow, day-time and night-time, light and darkness . . . (*Daniel* 3, 71).

CHAPTER ONE

A CHILD OF ISRAEL

---

*'To our race a son is given' – Marked with the seal of God –
The name – The education of the young – Coming of age.*

'TO OUR RACE A SON IS GIVEN'
The birth of a child in a Jewish family was the most welcome
of all events, one that caused the parents the utmost joy. The
news was sent round the village or the quarter and the neighbours
were told that presently, according to the ancient custom, there
would be a feast, and that all the relations and friends and people
near at hand would be invited to come and rejoice. The most
humble of couples took as their own Isaiah's great cry, all loaded
with messianic implications, 'For our sakes a child is born, to
our race a son is given'.[1]

For the Jews, children had always been considered as a blessing
and as the highest form of wealth. One psalm said 'Fatherhood
itself is the Lord's gift, the fruitful womb is a reward that comes
from Him', and another compared the father of a large family
to a man whose table is surrounded by young olives.[2] A common
pun turned the word *banim*, children, into *bonim*, builders.
Barrenness, then, was a standing shame, as Elizabeth, John the
Baptist's mother, said in so many words;[3] and the rabbis went
further, stating 'that a childless man should be thought of as
dead'.[4] As for voluntary sterility, it was so grave a sin that the
prophet Isaiah came to call the king Hezekiah to account for it,
telling him that death was the just penalty for such a crime.[5]
The desire for children was so great that in the early times a
legitimate wife would agree to her husband's begetting them
with one of her maids, as Abraham did, and Jacob after him.[6]
But it is not known whether this polygamous practice was still
in use at the time of Christ.[7]

So a child was born. And usually it was born without great
difficulty. The women of Israel prided themselves upon having

their babies quickly and easily – not like the Egyptians, they said.[8] Not that this prevented them from suffering, which they did, according to the sentence that God had pronounced. They were helped by midwives, who are mentioned as far back as the time of the patriarchs,[9] and who made use of delivery seats. But Jewish women could perfectly well do without midwives, as Mary did in the stable at Bethlehem.[10] The wish to see children born was so great that the rabbis allowed an exception to the holy law of Sabbath rest: it was licit to help a woman in labour, to bring a midwife to her, to tie the baby's umbilical cord and even, asserts the tractate *Shabbath*, to cut it.[11] If there were danger to the mother, contraceptive practices were not only allowed but even recommended.[12] In no circumstances was the father to help at the birth; he was to wait until someone came to announce it to him: this, at any rate, is the conclusion that is drawn from a verse in Jeremiah.[13]

The moment the father was told he came and took the child upon his knee: this was the official recognition of the baby's legitimacy. If one of the child's ancestors was present, he was sometimes given this privilege, as we see in the case of the patriarch Joseph, whose great-grandchildren 'he took on his knees'.[14] The child was washed, rubbed with salt to harden its skin and swaddled;[15] it could then be shown to the company. The congratulations were particularly warm in the case of a son; if it were a daughter they were less enthusiastic, so little enthusiastic, indeed, that sometimes they were more like expressions of sympathy. Daughters were no addition to the family fortunes, since as soon as they were married they belonged to other families. 'Girls are but an illusory treasure,' observes the Talmud; and then adds, 'besides, they have to be watched continually.'[16]

But – and this should be emphasised, for it is very much to Israel's credit – the horrible pagan custom of exposing babies, common in Egypt, Greece and Rome, was, if not unknown to the Jews,[17] at least absolutely forbidden. An Egyptian father could write to his wife on the point of having a baby, 'If it is a boy, bring it up; if it is a girl, kill it'.[18] But at the same period Philo was writing against this dreadful practice in a particularly admirable passage.[19] It was possible, in Israel, to show no very great delight at the birth of a girl, but whatever happened she was kept.

The greatest pleasure of all was when the first child born to a family was a boy. Hebrew had a special word, *bekor*, for the first-born son, and it was this word that Saint Luke translated and applied to Our Lady's child.[20] He did not necessarily mean that this 'first-born son' was to be followed by others, as the sceptical Lucian[21] and the other adversaries of Mary's perpetual virginity should have remembered, but only that as 'the pride and first-fruits of His Father'[22] He was the future head of His family, with all the duties that that implied but also all the high standing,[23] and that His was the right of primogeniture, that is to say at least a double share in the inheritance.[24] If twins were born great care was taken to note which of the two was delivered first, sometimes by tying a red thread to the baby's hand, as in the case of the children that Tamar had by Judah:[25] this was, as it happens, an error, for modern obstetrics have shown that the elder, the first conceived, is the second to emerge.

Son or daughter, eldest or not, the baby was always suckled by its own mother: this was a duty, and the rabbis reminded the women of Israel of it.[26] It was only very occasionally that the wives of great men might indulge themselves in the luxury of a wet-nurse. The child was suckled for a long time, for two or even for three years when it was feasible, in order to spare the child the diseases of the climate, dysentery being the chief of them. When the child was at last weaned there was a feast and a sacrifice, in memory of Abraham's celebration of the time Sarah stopped suckling Isaac.[27] But by that time the child had long before been solemnly made a member of the religious community and marked by the seal of God.

MARKED WITH THE SEAL OF GOD

The Law stated with utter finality that every male child must be circumcised.[28] At the time of Christ it had to be done eight days after the birth. The obligation was so absolute that the little operation of cutting off the foreskin had to be done even if the day fell upon a Sabbath.[29] The rabbis had carefully laid down what, in violation of the commandments of the Law, might be done – 'The making of the cut, the tearing of the skin, the sucking of the wound and the placing of a plaster of oil, wine and cummin upon the wound'.[30] No Jew, therefore, was able to avoid the obligation. The *Book of Jubilees*, an apocryphal work of the second century BC, goes so far as to declare solemnly that the angels themselves are circumcised.[31]

How did this duty arise? The Jews had no hesitation in replying that it originated in God Himself, who ordered Abraham to perform it, both for himself and his descendants. 'This is the covenant you shall keep with me, thee and thine; every male child of yours shall be circumcised; you shall circumcise the flesh of your foreskins, in token of the covenant between me and you'.[32] It is of little importance that the analysis of texts may have raised the question of whether the rite might not have been taken by Moses from the Midianites[33] or perhaps by Joshua upon the Hill of the Foreskins when he entered into the Promised Land with his people:[34] what is sure is that this was a custom of the greatest antiquity, which is borne out by the persistent use of flint knives for the operation.[35] In the time of Christ it was thought of both as a physical mark of the covenant and as an act of ritual purification. Men like Herod might say that it was merely an act of cleanliness; but they were heterodox. It is possible that at one time it may have been a rite which adolescents went through at puberty, a rite not unlike those which are practised today among certain African Negroes; but ever since it was applied to the newborn, it stood for the admission of the child to the tribe and its incorporation into the community of the faithful. In the same way a ceremony, a purely religious ceremony in this case, had been devised for the little girls, to mark their entry, too, into the people of God.

The operation was thought of as little enough in itself; yet the tractate *Shabbath* observes that it may be painful, particularly on the third day. In the early days it was the father of the family who undertook it, as Abraham himself had done;[36] the mother might not do it except in very serious cases, as, for example; in the extremely dangerous days in which the mother of the Maccabees lived.[37] At the time of Christ each town had a *mohel*, a man who specialised in this delicate operation. It had to be very well done, for if the prepuce were not properly removed the man would not be admitted to 'eat the Terumah', that is to say, the first-fruits offering that the faithful made to the priests.[38]

The Jews held by this rite more than anything in the world, more even than their lives, as was seen in the time of the Maccabees when Jewish mothers chose rather to be killed than to give up circumcising their sons.[39] For in circumcision they saw the mark of their true belonging to the people of God. Not to be circumcised, said the *Book of Jubilees*, was to belong 'not to the

sons of the covenant but to the children of destruction'. To call
any man uncircumcised was the most wounding of all possible
insults. Did the Jews not know that other nations had practised
the same rite, the Egyptians, for example, and even their
neighbouring enemies the Midianites, Edomites, Canaanites and
Phoenicians? (Among the Phoenicians, however, it was tending to
die out.) Undoubtedly they did know: but it was their circumcision that had marked them off from the Greeks and which
marked them off still from the Romans. In the days of the
impious kings, very few indeed had 'grown themselves a new
foreskin' so that they could go into the heathen gymnasia without
blushing.[40] It was for this reason that the truly faithful were so
much attached to the rite – a rite which Jesus certainly had to
undergo. Yet the Law and the Prophets had said that the mere
fact was nothing unless there was a spiritual intention there as
well, and that the true circumcision was that of the heart:[41] this
was a great teaching that our Lord was often to repeat, in various
forms.

Circumcision was not the only religious ceremony which
accompanied a birth in Israel: there was another which had to do
with the woman who had borne the child. Every woman who had
borne a child was by the Law unclean, like a man who had touched
a dead body: it was clearly the remains of a taboo far older than
Moses, but his law had confirmed it. The period of uncleanness
was twice as long for the birth of a girl as for the birth of a boy:
eighty days instead of forty. During this time she must 'touch
nothing that is hallowed, never entering the sanctuary. . . . When
the days needed for her purification, after the birth of boy or
girl, have run out, she must bring a lamb of one year old as a
burnt-sacrifice, and a young pigeon or turtle-dove by way of
amends, to the tabernacle door. . . . If she cannot lay her hand on
a lamb fit to be offered, she must bring two turtle-doves or two
young pigeons, one as a burnt-sacrifice and one by way of amends;
these will suffice, and at the priest's intercession she will be
purified.'[42] Christian tradition has kept the memory of this rite
in the ceremony of churching.

When the child was a first-born son, his parents had a particular
duty. This was part of a general law, for in Israel all the first-born
of all living things, as well as the first-fruits, belonged to Yahweh.[43]
The Almighty, speaking to Moses, had commanded that all the
first-born of men or of beasts should be dedicated to Him. In the

Gospel Saint Luke even uses the Greek word *hagion*, which means holy, the child becoming a holy thing, given to God and apart from the ordinary world of men. Where did this custom come from? Reading the commandments in Deuteronomy one has the impression that it was derived from a reaction against the 'abominations' of the neighbouring peoples who burnt their children as offerings to their idols:[44] Yahweh Himself had stopped the faithful Abraham just as he was about to sacrifice his son Isaac to Him. Instead of killing the newborn child, then, they dedicated it in a wholly spiritual manner and then ransomed it, that is to say they gave a sacrifice in its stead, or a sum of money: this was what Yahweh Himself had required of them,[45] in memory of the mercy He had shown His people on that night when His angel had struck all the first-born in Egypt but had spared those of Israel, being satisfied with a lamb instead.[46] At the time of Christ this duty had to be fulfilled within a month:[47] a burnt-sacrifice of two pigeons or two turtle-doves had to be offered, which was little enough; but the parents also had to give five shekels of silver, which was twenty gold francs or three pounds sterling or about nine dollars, quite a serious sum for poor people. But no Jewish family would have presumed to avoid this pious burden: and Saint Luke shows us the most dedicated, the most holy of the children of men 'ransomed' by His parents in that moving scene of the presentation at the Temple, where the inspired voices of the aged Simeon and the prophetess Anna gave Joseph and Mary their mysterious intimations of glory and pain.[48]

THE NAME

It was also during the first weeks, and probably on the day of his circumcision, that the child received his name. The choice of it was of the greatest importance, for the Jews, like all the inhabitants of the ancient world, attributed a numinous influence to names. In the Egyptian legend of Isis we find the wonder-working goddess refusing to heal the god Ra from the bite of a serpent until he tells her his name, in which the secret of his power resides. In the same way, in the story of Moses, God gives him the highest mark of His confidence by revealing to him His ineffable name.[49] It was believed that the name was an integral part of the person, that it had a bearing upon his character and even upon his fate. This was so firmly held that a rabbi said, 'The sentence of heaven can be diverted by a change of name'.[50] Remnants of these beliefs have certainly come down to us: there are many people today who are convinced that a Christian name has its influence; and there are novelists like Balzac, who choose their characters' names according to their nature.

The right of choosing the name of his son, therefore, belonged to the father, the head of the family. There are many instances of fathers naming their sons in Holy Scripture:[51] in the account of John the Baptist's miraculous birth in the Gospel we find Zacharias insisting upon this right, although he was dumb.[52] However, there are also a good many mothers who named their children in the Bible; and the first was Eve, the mother of us all.[53] It may fairly be concluded that the choice was usually made in agreement by both the father and the mother.

The name which was chosen corresponded to our Christian name: the Jews had no surname – it did not exist. This does not mean that the sense of family was not very highly developed among them: it was. A son necessarily bore his father's name, as among the Arabs of today. A man was called 'son of so-and-so', *ben* in Hebrew and *bar* in Aramaic: for example, John ben Zacharias, Jonathan ben Hannan, or Yeshua ben Joseph. An eldest son was very often given his grandfather's name to carry on the onomastic tradition of the family and also to distinguish him from his father.[54]

Some of these names, or rather of these praenomina, were in the nature of nicknames, recalling the circumstances in which the child was born or begotten. Some were very pious indeed: the Baptist, for example, was called Yochanan (John), because he had been 'wished by God'. There were also less agreeable names of this kind. A case is quoted in which a mother, exasperated at having borne nothing but daughters, called the fourth Zaoulé and the eighth Tamam, which may be translated as 'the nuisance' and 'that is enough'. Other names were chosen to bring the child good luck, and some rabbis even advised consulting the stars, a practice to which others were opposed. The names of animals were quite usual: Rachel, a ewe; Deborah, a bee; Yona, a dove; and Akbor, a mouse. And there were trees: Tamar, a palm; Elon, an oak; Zeitan, an olive. A very great number of names were taken from the Bible – the patriarchs and prophets, the saints and the heroes. There were therefore a great many Jacobs and Josephs, Elijahs and Daniels, Sauls and Davids, and a great many boys named after Simon and Judas, the glorious Maccabees. Many were theophorous, that is, they evoked the name of God, or rather one of His names. Thus Jesus, Yeshua, meant 'Yah (i.e. Yahweh) is salvation'. The names with the termination -el recalled the exceedingly ancient biblical name for the One God, El, Elohim. But very often these names had lost their historical or sacred meaning with use, and their signification was no longer thought of: some had even been deformed, and one of these was the very usual Myriam, which scarcely called Moses' sister to mind any longer, and whose original meaning of 'the beloved of Yah' was forgotten: under the influence of the Aramaic word *mary* it was no doubt pronounced Mariam, the Greek and Latin form of which was Maria, and it meant 'the lady' – and curiously enough this turns into Italian as Madonna, to French as Notre Dame and English as Our Lady.[55]

All these Jewish names had foreign competitors, and that to a continually increasing extent. These might be Aramaic, such as Marta, Tabita or Bar-Tolomai (Bartholomew); or they might be Greek or Latin. Though of the two Greek was far more likely, since the *koiné*, the Greek of the people, was the empire's universal language. Since the time when the Seleucids had ruled the country there had always been some Jews ready to Hellenize their names: there was that Jesus, brother of the high priest Onias III, for example, whom the half-crazed Antiochus IV put in his brother's place, and who called himself Jason Antiochener.[56] By the time of Christ the custom was so usual that half the people in the New Testament have Greek names. Among the apostles, for example, Philip and Andrew are pure Hellenic names; Thaddaeus and Matthew are Greek deformations of Hebrew names (Matthayah, the gift of Yah, became Matthaios, as Yeshua became Jesus and Myriam Maria); James, John and even Simon appear to be Hellenized forms of old biblical names; and Judas alone is entirely Jewish. The taking of Greek names was most general among the important people, and among them it had sometimes entirely done away with the original name: in the case of the Herodian dynasty, for example, the Bedouin family from which it arose is quite lost to history, being completely masked by the Greek name meaning sons of heroes. The ancient Jewish cemetery of Beth Shearim has recently been discovered, and among the inscriptions there are a hundred and seventy-five that are Greek as against only thirty-two Hebrew or Aramaic, which shows the extent of this Hellenization.[57] Naturally it was even more developed in the Jewish communities of the Diaspora, where all the names in Yah or El had become Theodore, Theophilus, Dositheus or Dorothy. A Jewish family in Egypt, whose archives have been found at Edfou, was made up of a father named Antonius Rufus and of five sons, Nikon, Theodotos Niger, Theodoros Niger, Diophanes and Ptullis.[58] It is possible, however, that these pagan names were used for dealings with the outside world, and that among themselves the Jews continued to call themselves by their old religious names: the royal style of Herod Agrippa I was half Greek and half Roman, but as high priest he was called Mattathias, in memory of the hero who had struck the first blows of the war of liberation in killing a Greek official and an apostate Jew.

THE EDUCATION OF THE YOUNG

The child, circumcised, named, marked with the seal of God, remained for its first years entirely in its mother's care: Jewish fathers do not seem to have been much inclined to play the nurse. Furthermore, Jewish women made excellent mothers, conscientious and devoted: the Bible is full of instances of this. Daughters remained with their mothers up to the time they were married; they helped with the housework, carried water, spun wool and, in the country, took their part in the work outside – they would glean after the reapers, or keep the sheep during the daytime. It was the father who looked after his sons, and started to teach them his trade as early as possible, so that they should soon be able to be his apprentices and then his journeymen. Thus in the parable of the two sons, the Gospel shows a man with a vineyard sending his boys thither,[59] and in that of the prodigal, one of the rich man's sons working for him.[60] Jesus would certainly have learnt the carpenter's craft with Joseph.

Education was also in the father's province; and it appears from rabbinical traditions that the Jewish methods of teaching were very good. The disagreeable results of the patriarch Jacob's particular liking for Joseph had given rise to the prudent advice, 'A man should never make any difference between his children'. 'One should never threaten a child,' said another wise man, 'but either punish it or be silent.' And another, 'Never say to a child that you will give it something and then not keep your promise: this is teaching it to lie'.[61] But it must also be admitted that their methods were not unduly tender. 'Spare the rod, and thou art no friend to thy son,' say the Proverbs, countenancing our common phrase of 'Spare the rod and spoil the child'. Another verse says, 'Nor ever from child of thine withhold chastisement; he will not die under the rod; rather, the rod thou wieldest shall baulk the grave of its prey'. And again, 'Boyhood's mind is loaded with a pack of folly, that needs the rod of correction to shift it'.[62] And, as we may see, Ecclesiasticus approves of these sound principles.[63]

The true Israelites, then, attached more importance to moral education than to anything else. 'There is a proverb,' says Holy Writ, 'a boy will keep the course he has begun; even when he grows old, he will not leave it.'[64] And as moral law merged into religious law, a father's first duty was to teach his children the commandments: this in any case was the direct order that Yahweh had given, by the voice of Moses, to all the men of Israel; the order that was repeated in the morning and at night in the prayer, 'Thou shalt teach thy children My commandments'.[65] In the same way, since the practice of religion and the history of the race both formed part of the Law, fathers told their children of all the wonders that Yahweh had done for His people; they explained the meaning of the great feasts to them, and showed them how each of the customs that they observed had a holy significance. This, furthermore, was required of them by the Law. When He caused the Feast of Unleavened Bread to be begun, Yahweh had said, 'And thou shalt tell thy children in those after times all the Lord did for thee when thou madest thy escape from Egypt. This custom is to endure like a mark branded on the hand, to be kept in view like a badge worn on the forehead.'[66]

Does this mean that schooling was despised? Far from it. The rabbis said again and again that it was at the base of everything and that it was quite indispensable. 'If you have knowledge,' said a very often repeated maxim, 'you have everything: if you do not possess knowledge, you possess nothing.' There were doctors of the Law who said, 'It is better that a sanctuary should be destroyed rather than a school'.[67] And one of them, who must have been a schoolmaster by profession, went so far as to explain the divine command 'Lay no hand on them, never hurt them, servants anointed and true spokesmen of mine'[68] as referring to schoolchildren and their teachers.

There were schools, then, in the Palestine of Jesus' time. They were a comparatively recent invention, going back no more than about a hundred years. The rabbi Simon ben Shetach, brother of the queen Salome Alexandra and president of the Sanhedrim, opened the first *beth ha-sefer*, house of the book,[69] in Jerusalem. His example was followed, and little by little a whole system of public instruction came into existence. Some thirty years after the death of Christ, in about the year 64, the high priest Joshua ben Gamala promulgated what may be considered as the first educational legislation: there was nothing wanting – the parents were obliged to send their children, there were punishments for idle children and those too often absent, and there was a form of secondary education for the most intelligent pupils.[70] In His childhood, Jesus did not have the benefit of such a system; but it is probable that the rabbi Gamala was only giving a final shape to arrangements that were in existence well before his time.

The primary school was connected with the synagogue, just as it was, in the mediaeval West, with the parish church. The children, both those of the poor and of the rich, were taken there at the age of five. The master was none other than the *hazzan*, the guardian of the sacred books and the minister of the synagogue: later it was determined that whenever the number of pupils was greater than twenty-five, the special master should be appointed. The teaching profession had a very high standing; indeed, it was currently said that a schoolmaster was 'the messenger of the Almighty'. There even appear to have been inspectors charged with the oversight of the education.

The children's principal task, as they sat on the ground round the master, was to repeat by rote, and all together, the sentences that he said out loud.[71] Mnemonics, which were a necessary part of the expression and transmission of thought,[72] as we shall see, were very commonly used in teaching – parallelism, repetition, alliteration – and children clung to them even in their games, witness those in Saint Luke 'who call out to their companions in the market-place and say, You would not dance when we piped to you, you would not mourn when we wept to you'[73] which are obviously mnemonic verses.

What did they learn at the school? Primarily the Torah; or to be more exact, practically nothing but the Torah, the holy Law of God. It was said that 'a child ought to be fattened with the Torah as an ox is fattened in the stall'.[74] The maxims of the Law, learnt in childhood 'go in by the blood and come out at the lips'. It was used for everything, even for learning the alphabet: to make learning more agreeable, words were formed with each letter in turn, as they are in our ABCs, and so arranged that a child could turn them about into a little tale. The language, grammar, history and geography, or at least the rudiments of them, were all studied in the Bible. 'It is in the Bible', says Josephus, 'that the finest knowledge is to be found, and the source of happiness.'[75] He himself boasted of having known it completely at the age of fourteen; and Saint Paul reminds his disciple Timothy that he was taught the holy learning from his childhood upwards.[76]

It appears that it was this exclusive use of the Scriptures in teaching that induced many rabbis to deny girls the right to be educated. Women had no official place in religion, so why teach them the Law? 'It would be better to see the Torah burnt', said one somewhat overheated doctor, 'than to hear its words upon the lips of women.'[77] The same doctor, who was obviously a misogynist, asserted that 'teaching a girl was the same as starting her upon the road to moral depravation'. Perhaps in this may be seen a reference to the manners of the pagan world, in which the education of women set them in close contact with men, to the great detriment of good order. Yet not all rabbis were of this opinion, and the same tractate of the Talmud which shuts the little girls out of school also includes this wise man's maxim, 'Every man is required to teach his daughter the Torah'. If we may judge by the example of the little Virgin Mary, it may be supposed that many Jewish girls knew the Holy Scriptures as perfectly as their brothers; for when she spontaneously spoke the splendid words that we know as the Magnificat so many biblical echoes came to her that one can distinguish more than thirty of them.[78]

Their solemn studies did not prevent the children of Israel from playing, however. Zachariah shows us the streets of Jerusalem thronged with boys and girls at play,[79] the eternal play of children in the open. The Gospel refers to children copying grown-ups and playing at feasts and burials.[80] We see too that in the days of Job little girls played with young animals, even with 'leviathans', that is to say, with little crocodiles:[81] they also played with dolls. Excavation has brought to light small pottery creatures, particularly birds like those to which, according to the apocryphal *Gospel of the Childhood*,[82] the child Jesus gave sentient life; rattles, decorated balls and dice: no doubt in this case the Law and its prohibition of the making of the likeness of any living thing might be disregarded. And in various places, especially Megiddo, there are lines scratched on the pavements that call hopscotch to mind.

What may be termed primary education had a continuation for those who wished to specialize in religious studies – a higher level altogether. To profit by this, it was necessary to go to Jerusalem and to join one of the *beth ha-midrash*, those schools which were taught by the most famous doctors of the Law. It was thus that the young Saul, from Tarsus, came to sit at the feet of Gamaliel. But there was no notion of acquiring any knowledge other than that of religion in these schools: even the concept of a profane culture was impossible in Israel. These groups, in which casuistry was the ruling discipline, existed to produce the future doctors of the Law: the great mass of Jewish children did not go as far.[83]

COMING OF AGE

The Talmudic tractate *Pirke Aboth*, 'sayings of the fathers', whose essential parts are certainly earlier than the Christian era, laid down the following stages of a child's development: 'At five he must begin the sacred studies; at ten he must set himself to learning the tradition; at thirteen he must know the whole of the Law of Yahweh and practise its requirements; and at fifteen years begins the perfecting of his knowledge.'[84] Apart from those who wished to perfect their religious knowledge, therefore, the Jewish boys finished their schooling at thirteen. They also legally came of age: this comparatively early date is explained by the undoubted precocity of their race. At thirteen a young Israelite had certainly left childhood behind, even if he were not capable of reasoning, like the child Jesus, with the doctors of the Law gathered in the courts of the Temple.[85] From then onwards he would be required, as an adult, to recite three times every day the famous prayer *Shema Israel*, in which every believer must proclaim his faith in the One God: he was to fast regularly, on the set days, particularly at the great ceremony of the Day of Atonement. He would undertake the traditional pilgrimages, and when he went into the Temple he would be allowed into the 'court of the men'. He would be a full member of the nation of Israel.

For this reason the *Bar Mitzvah*, at which the boy, upon coming of age, was declared a 'son of the Law', was celebrated with a religious ceremony in which he was to read a passage of the Law in public and with great rejoicings. It was a date that counted for a very great deal in Jewish life; and even now in Israel, among the least practising families it has still retained a quasi-religious character; the boy is taken from the *kibbutz* to some point on the frontier where he takes his turn as one of the armed guards of the Holy Land, or else he gives some of his blood, to be used in transfusions. As it was two thousand years ago, the child of Israel, upon coming of age, must understand that he belongs to a community.

Furthermore he has a duty, one which the community requires of him: but is it no more than a duty? 'A young man is like a colt that whinnies,' says the Talmud again, 'he paces up and down, he grooms himself with care: this is because he is looking for a wife.' The realistic rabbi to whom the observation is due adds, 'But once married, he resembles an ass, quite loaded down with burdens'.[86]

CHAPTER TWO

FAMILY, 'MY OWN FLESH AND BLOOD'

'My own flesh and blood' – *Taking a wife* – *Prohibitions and obligations* – *From the engagement to the wedding* – *The father of a family* – *Women in Israel* – *Shortcomings and failures in marriage.*

'MY OWN FLESH AND BLOOD'

When the young Jacob went to his uncle Laban in Haran to find work and a wife, Laban, in acknowledging him as a member of his family, said, 'Thou art my own flesh and blood'.[1] The figure, so typical of the biblical style, was commonly used by the people of the Book, and it answered the factual reality. In Israel the family was the essential basis of society, the corner-stone of the entire building. In early times it had even, from the point of view of law, formed a distinct entity, a part of the tribe; by the time of Christ it was perhaps less strong than it had been in the days of the patriarchs, when the individual counted for nothing in comparison, but it was still exceedingly important. Its members really did feel of the same flesh and blood; and to have the same blood meant having the same soul. Legislation had taken this principle as its base, and had developed from it: the law had also multiplied its commands in order to uphold the permanence, the purity and the authority of the family. In so far as Jews wished to remain faithful to the Law (and this was almost universal) they never ceased to admit the predominant place of the family in society. Furthermore, the family was not merely a social entity but also a religious community, with its own particular feasts, in which the father was the celebrant while all the members took part. Some of the very important ceremonies which the Law required had a strong family character – the Passover, for example, had to be celebrated in the family.[2] The religious family link was so strong that in the Gospels and in the Acts we find that fathers who turned to the teachings of Christ brought with them all their household.[3]

The word 'family' had a wider meaning than: in Aramaic the term *aha*, the Hebrew *ah*, meant brother, half-brother, cousin and even near relation; so Abraham, speaking to Lot, his nephew, said, 'Are we not brethren?',[4] an expression that Laban also used referring to Jacob. In the first Book of Chronicles[5] the sons of Kish are described as the brothers of the daughters of Eleazar, whereas in fact they were their first cousins. This was undoubtedly still the usage in the time of Christ.[6]

Good fortune for one member of the family meant rejoicing for all the others, who, furthermore, quite expected to profit by it. Successful Jews practised nepotism upon a great scale, without the slightest shame, whether they were high priests like Annas, kings like the Herods or simply influential men like Philo of Alexandria. On the other hand, a misfortune which struck one made them all unhappy, and a single dishonour would darken the whole family. The teaching of the rabbis repeated that not to 'keep watch over one's brother' was in fact to behave like Cain,[7] and it praised the example of Joseph who forgave his wicked brothers for having tried to kill him, and, on becoming Pharaoh's vizir, welcomed them and established them in the land of Goshen.[8] That was how a true Israelite ought to behave. Nothing could break the tie of blood, and everybody benefited from it. It was therefore of the first importance for a man to make sure of the perpetuation of the family, that is, to marry.

TAKING A WIFE

Furthermore, this was the first order that the Eternal gave to the first man and the first woman, 'Increase and multiply'.[9] A text upon which a rabbi commented in these strong words, 'A bachelor is not truly a man at all'.[10] And celibacy was thought of as an anomaly, almost as a disgrace. However, at the time of Christ there were some men who were celibate by vocation, those to whom the Gospel refers in speaking of eunuchs who 'have made themselves so for love of the kingdom of heaven'[11]— such men as the Essenes, for example, the monks of that astonishing sect on the shores of the Dead Sea, whose library has caused such floods of ink to flow since its discovery in 1947.[12] And the Nazarites would vow celibacy or at least continence for a given length of time.[13] Saint Paul may have shown partiality for celibacy at first,[14] but it is certain that among the earliest Christians several of the apostles, Saint Paul among them, as well as many leaders of the Church, were married.[15] Yet it seems that the tendency towards celibacy had been increasing under the influence of the pagan world; and in particular many more celibate women were to be found than in former days; but there is no doubt that in most cases this was not from the high spiritual motives that Saint Paul had in mind.

To make more certain of the permanence of the race and of the family the ancient Hebrews had admitted that a man might have several wives. Polygamy had even been quite commonplace: the kings, whether they were 'saints of God' like David and Solomon or not, provided themselves with numerous harems, this being one of the signs of their power;[16] but ordinary men could not afford more than one or two wives.[17] If the first wife were barren, the husband would find himself obliged to take a second or to have a concubine. 'The wife of his youth' of whom Isaiah speaks,[18] was not repudiated, but supplemented, and this is the more comprehensible in that Eastern women age so quickly; but it could scarcely happen without many difficulties arising. Concubines, however, might be added to the household without any specific reasons: the Hebrew word for them, *pilleges*, was of foreign origin – it is *pallas* in Greek and *pellex* in Latin – which leads one to suppose that slavery may have had a great deal to do with these harem customs, at least among the rich; for the poor could scarcely take it upon themselves to feed several women.

Was this still the case at the time of Christ? It is very difficult to say. On this point there seem to have been two different trends in the tradition, and this becomes clearer when one looks into the Talmud. The tractate *Yebamoth* contains contradictory opinions: 'A man may marry as many wives as he chooses,' said one rabbi; another allowed the wife of a man who took a concubine to divorce him; still another limited the harem to four wives,[19] the number at which Mohammed also stopped.[20] But a whole web of religious traditions, reaching even farther back than the Mosaic Law, held up monogamy as the ideal union that God desired and that was in accord with nature. In the account of woman's creation[21] the mysterious play on words 'it shall be called *isha*, this thing that was taken out of *ish*' was interpreted as the charter of monogamic marriage. The first man mentioned in the Bible who had several wives was Lamech, a descendant of Cain: an indifferent authority.[32] The Book of Tobit, that family story, speaks of nothing but single marriages. In the prophetic writings we find the single marriage as a symbol of the covenant between Yahweh and Israel in Hosea, Jeremiah, Isaiah and Ezekiel.[23] The Sadoqite sect prided itself upon being strictly monogamous; and the high priest was utterly forbidden to have more than one wife,[24] which proves that the single marriage corresponded to a high ideal. It appears that at the time of Christ monogamy predominated, partly because of this tradition and partly because of the Greek and Roman examples. Although Jesus Himself did not directly pronounce against polygamy, the elevation of His words upon marriage quite does away with any possibility of the idea of a harem. In abolishing Moses' concessions to human frailty, He desired that the husband and wife should be united physically, morally and spiritually, their whole life long. Love had become a sacrament.[25]

Marriage was early in Israel: a great many rabbis held that for men the age of eighteen was the most suitable. A father was advised to marry his son 'while he still had his hand upon his neck'. The most liberal allowed that one might wait until one had reached twenty-four before taking a wife; but the most rigid asserted that 'the only Holy One – may He be blessed – cursed the man who, at twenty years, was not married'.[26] As for the girls, they were married as soon as they were physically ready for marriage, which, according to the Law, was at the age of twelve and a half. When Our Lady bore her Son she was probably no more than fourteen.

The rabbi who advised the father to marry his son 'while he still had his hand upon his neck' shows, by implication, the real state of affairs: in most cases it was the parents who married their children. No doubt it was said that marriages were decided in heaven, decided by God Himself forty days before the boy's birth; but there is no doubt either that it was the parents who referred to this tradition, in order to justify their choice. The initiative lay with the future husband's father, since it was his family that would be increased by the marriage; and this had been the custom since the time of the patriarchs and the judges. Furthermore, the wisdom of the rabbis provided the parents with excellent advice: it was not prudent to marry a young girl to an elderly man, nor a small one to a tall man.[27] It sometimes happened, however, that a young man would follow his own inclinations and choose his wife for himself, as Esau had done, to the great distress of Isaac and Rebekah.[28] Therefore the rabbis continually advised the young, 'Reflect for a long while before choosing a wife. Do not consider beauty, for it passes: think of the family.' If some young imbecile were so foolish as to bring home a wife of an inferior standing the custom was that his father should carry a barrel filled with fruit into the street and break it there, crying that he would never acknowledge the wench's offspring, and that her children would not belong to the family but would be scattered like the melons, the figs and the carobs rolling in the gutter.[29] Yet this did not prevent some rabbis from giving the advice, 'Go down one step in taking a wife'[30] for fear of being despised if one were to marry a woman of a higher rank. It is clear that the wise men of Israel had a profound knowledge of marriage and its difficulties.

PROHIBITIONS AND OBLIGATIONS

The Law did more than give advice: in some cases it pronounced interdiction and in others it required the performance of a duty. This was always, of course, in the interests of the family. In giving His people the Law, the Lord had said, speaking of foreigners, 'Nor must thou find wives for thy sons among their daughters; faithless themselves, they will make thy sons, too, faithless, and worshippers of their own gods'.[31] There was also the example of the ancients: Abraham had sent to find a bride of his own race for Isaac; and when Jacob was of an age to marry he was told to go and seek a wife among his cousins in Padan-Aram. The Israelites remained faithful to this principle of endogamy at least in theory for a very long period. After the return from exile, Nehemiah inveighed against those Jews who were allowing women 'from Azotus, or Ammon, or Moab, with children that spoke half in the Philistine dialect, not like true Jews' into their families; and in his indignation he had pulled out the culprits' hair.[32] Did this rigidity last until the time of Christ? There had been protests against the uncompromising attitude of the reformers at all periods; and when all was said and done, it was impossible to conceal the fact that Abraham's first-born was the child of an Egyptian, that Moses had had one Midianite and one Ethiopian wife, that Ruth, David's ancestress, was a Moabite, and that it was more than likely that Bath-sheba, the great king's wife (his adulterous wife) was a Hittite.[33] It is very remarkable to see that neither in the New Testament nor in any one of the tractates of the Talmud is there to be found any trace of the ancient prohibition of exogamic marriage, marriage outside the tribes of the Chosen People. Was this because the forbidding was taken for granted? Had custom and public opinion utterly condemned it? Was it included in the general horror that the Jews felt for all heathendom?

There were some marriages which the Law forbade absolutely: those that were within the prohibited degrees. The basic principle was to be read in the Law, 'No man is to betake himself to a woman who is near of kin to him, and mate with her'.[34] From this arose a scrupulously exact definition of what was to be understood by 'near of kin' – a definition which had some extraordinary omissions, however. All these were forbidden: the union of a son with his mother (yet the Law said nothing about fathers and daughters, perhaps because of the memory of Lot); of a man with one of his father's wives; of a man with his sister or his half-sister (but had not Abraham married his half-sister Sarah?); of a nephew with his aunt (but had not the mother of Moses and Aaron been their father's aunt? And there was nothing to prevent an uncle marrying his niece, which seems to have happened quite often); of a man with his grand-daughter, his daughter-in-law or his sister-in-law (except in the case of the levirate, which we will speak of in the next paragraph); and he was even forbidden to marry two sisters, no doubt because Jacob, who married Rachel and Leah, had found it so very unsuccessful.[35] These were all relationships that made any marriage completely null, and it is certain that at the time of Christ the prohibitions were still respected. The Law punished transgression in these cases with great severity: the guilty were to be put to death, and they might even be burnt alive.[36] For Yahweh had said, 'These are abominations'.

If an Israelite could not always marry where he chose, there was, on the other hand, one case in which he was obliged to marry a woman, even if he had no liking for her. When a man died without leaving a son, his brother or his heir had to marry his widow, to raise up a posterity which would be counted as the dead man's. This was the duty of the levirate – the word is derived from the Latin *levir*, a brother-in-law, which translates the Hebrew *yaham*. The Law defined the duty in the strictest terms, but the practice varied from period to period. If a man refused to fulfil his obligations, the injured widow had the right to take off one of his shoes and spit in his face, crying, 'This is for the man who would not continue his brother's line'.[37] This was, however, considerably less severe than the punishment which was meted out to the only too-well-known Onan, who, being required to marry his brother's widow, had used the simplest of contraceptive measures in order not to beget children who would not belong to him: and for this God caused him to die.[38] There is no possible doubt that the levirate was practised at the time of Christ. Everyone remembers the tendentious questions His enemies put to him about the woman who had lost seven husbands, her first and then the six brothers-in-law she married: which of the seven would be her husband when the dead rose again? The synoptic Gospels, in recounting this, show that Jesus' opponents were speaking of a legal requirement that was still quite as much in force as it had been in the days when Ruth asked Booz to cover her with his mantle, as one who was near of kin.[39] But it must be admitted that the fulfilment of this duty was so delicate a matter that no less than a whole tractate, or very nearly a whole tractate, of the Talmud was needed to lay down all the rules – the tractate *Yebamoth*.

FROM THE ENGAGEMENT TO THE WEDDING

When the future bride had been chosen, either by the parents or the young man, there began the period that preceded the marriage, the time of the betrothal. This was very important, particularly in those cases where the betrothed scarcely knew one another or even did not know one another at all. It usually lasted for a year; but curiously enough, although the Jews can hardly have known the 'widow's delay' of modern French legislation, they agreed that a widow's betrothal time need only be a month.

According to our laws it is marriage alone that has an absolute and legally binding character: breach of promise is rarely considered actionable, and then only in cases where real damage has been suffered. In Jewish Law this was not the case at all. Two conditions were clearly distinguished: betrothal and marriage. Young people who had agreed with one another with a view to marriage were betrothed, but they would not be considered as truly married until the husband, according to the words of Deuteronomy, should have 'taken her to himself'.[40] The 'taking possession', the *hakhnashah*, was really the 'uniting' of two beings for life; the word had both meanings. Thus, in Saint Matthew the angel says to Joseph, 'Do not be afraid to take thy wife Mary to thyself' – that is: 'Let her, who has been your betrothed, become your spouse.'[41]

But although these two conditions were in theory quite separate, in fact they merged into one another. The fact is that the Law recognized rights and obligations during the betrothal that were almost the same as those of marriage. A betrothed woman suspected of unfaithfulness was put to the famous trial of the bitter water laid down in the Holy Writ;[42] the *Protevangel of James*, one of the most widely spread apocryphal books in the early Church, says that Our Lady was submitted to it.[43] A fiancée who was found guilty of adultery was to be stoned, exactly as if she had been a wife. On the other hand she did have the advantage of some legal rights: she might not be rejected except by a letter of divorcement; if her fiancé should die, she was counted as a widow; and a child born during the betrothal was held to be legitimate. This preliminary state, therefore, had a very close resemblance to definitive marriage.

Before the wedding could take place an important question had to be decided: the question of the dowry. It was not really a dowry in the sense that we understand it, for it was not the father who gave his daughter money or goods, but he who received them. The custom was exceedingly ancient, and the Bible mentions it a great many times.[44] The gift that the man was to give to the father of his betrothed was called the *mohar*. Was it a purchase price? The Arabs assert that their *mahr* is only one element in an agreement allying the two families. It is still obscure. In any case, the Law called for the payment of the virgin's *mohar* if a seducer, legally obliged to marry the girl he had lain with, was refused by the father.[45] The discussion of the dowry was a long-drawn-out affair and it gave rise to interminable arguments. It was generally agreed, by reason of a text in Deuteronomy,[46] that fifty shekels of silver (about 160 gold francs or nearly £22 10s.) constituted a suitable *mohar*. Once the sum was agreed upon a contract was drawn up and signed, on a Wednesday if it were for a girl and a Tuesday for a widow, always in the middle of the month, as the full moon brought good luck. But this was not the end of the bridegroom's financial obligations: custom required him to offer his future bride a collection of gifts, which was called the *mattan*. This was not the *Morgengabe* of Germanic Law, the present due after the first night of the marriage, but rather a dower which the woman would keep if she were left a widow. It would also happen that some fathers, to increase their daughters' standing, would make them the present of a positive dowry, the *silluhim*; but Jesus the son of Sirach says, in his twenty-fifth chapter, that it is a shame for a man to be kept by his wife.

Were all these formalities still insisted upon at the time of Christ? It is not certain that they were. There were some people who had a higher notion of the status of women, and among these it is possible that the old custom of the purchase of the betrothed would have yielded place to a plain certifying of the marriage. It also appears that in some cases it was the young man who entered into the family, as Jacob had joined that of Laban,[47] where they were glad to welcome him, even without any *mohar*, because he brought with him his strength, his youth and his zeal for work: it must have been thus in those families where there were only girls and where a man who would provide descendants had the appearance of a saviour.[48] The father's words, 'Today you are my son-in-law', left no more to be said.

When everything was at last agreed, finished and signed, the time of betrothal was over. Now the marriage was to come, the wedding-day to which Jesus so often referred in the parables as being a feast-day above all others, and to which Christian tradition has given a mystic meaning when it speaks of the wedding of the Spouse. Autumn was the best time for marriages: the harvest was in, the vintage over, minds were free and hearts at rest; and then it is the season when the nights are so delightful and when it is so agreeable to sit up late. All relatives were asked, the whole village, all friends and the friends of friends; and thus we find Jesus with all His disciples invited to the wedding at Cana.[49] People might come from far away, and it was certainly worth the trouble, for the rejoicings went on for a long time.

On the eve of the great day the bridegroom, accompanied by his friends, went to fetch his betrothed from her father's house. He wore particularly splendid clothes for the occasion, and some would even put on a crown, either to follow Solomon's example[51] or because of the verse in Isaiah.[50] A procession was formed under the direction of the 'bridegroom's friend', who acted as master of the ceremonies and who remained by his side throughout, 'rejoicing too'.[52] The bride was brought in a litter, with her hair on her shoulders and a veil over her face and golden rounds on her forehead;[53] and all along the way the people sang those wedding songs that were handed down from generation to generation and which are to be seen at their finest in the Song of Songs – 'Who is this that makes her way up by the desert road, erect as a column of smoke, all myrrh and incense, and those sweet scents the perfumer knows?'[54]

So the procession reached the bridegroom's house. His parents then uttered a traditional blessing, which was taken up by all those present and which expressed their wishes for the happiness and the fruitfulness of the marriage: there were several of these blessings in the Scriptures, and people were expected to know them.[55] This was almost the only religious element in the marriage. The evening was passed in games and dancing: the bridegroom took part, but the bride withdrew with her friends, her brides-maids, into a room that was kept aside for her.

The great day came next morning, and the atmosphere was that of feast, a general rejoicing and a holiday. The young men played various games of skill and the young women, so we learn from the tractate *Taan*, danced in the vineyards, singing to draw the attention of those who might be inclined to marry. There was a meal towards the end of the day, and the men and women were served apart: this was the time for the giving of the presents. The bridesmaids stood about the bride, all dressed in white – there were usually ten of them – and, if we are to judge by the parable of the wise and the foolish virgins, with burning lamps in their hands. The bride sat under a canopy, the *huppah*, which had been part of the ritual for a very long time[56] and which gave her the air of a queen – the whole ceremony, for that matter, had something regal about it. It was no doubt at this time that she sang those beautiful hymns of love from the Song of Songs – 'A kiss from those lips! Wine cannot ravish the senses like that embrace. . . . Draw me after thee where thou wilt; see, we hasten after thee, by the very fragrance of those perfumes allured!' To which the bridegroom would reply, stepping towards her, 'Rouse thee, and come, so beautiful, so well beloved, still hiding thyself as a dove hides in a cleft rock or crannied wall'.[57]

The spouse had come at last, and happy were those wise virgins who had oil enough in their lamps to shine upon the meeting. 'How beautiful thou art, my beloved, how beautiful,' sang the bridegroom; and he praised his bride's charms one after another, using those poetic images that the Scriptures offered in such abundance – her black hair like the kids in the mountains of Gilead, her teeth as white as the sheep that come from the washing, her lips as red as the anemone and her cheeks as rosy as a halved pomegranate. Seeds were now thrown down in front of the pair or a pomegranate was crushed – both old fertility rites – and a vase full of scent was broken. Was there then some solemn promise, and a blessing given by the representative of the community? We do not know: but the present Jewish ritual leads one to suppose that this was the case and that the actual marriage was contracted 'under the canopy'. What is quite certain is that the feast began again with even more noise and energy than before. Men and women were now at the same table; everybody ate a great deal and everybody drank a great deal – so much, indeed, that sometimes the wine would run out, as it happened at Cana in Galilee: one might almost say that it did so on purpose, in order that Jesus should there perform the first and the kindest of His miracles.

The rejoicings went on for seven days, and sometimes twice as long. But on the first evening the young pair vanished and the marriage was consummated. According to a somewhat naïve custom the blood-stained linen was kept as a souvenir of the marriage-night, because the twenty-second chapter of Deuteronomy said that it was proper to have proofs against any future insinuations on the part of the husband. Having done this, the young couple did not go off for a honeymoon but returned to share in the merriment, the songs and the dancing under the star-strewn sky.

THE FATHER OF A FAMILY

Once it was brought into being, the family unit, soon made larger by children, was completely independent. In Israel the household was autonomous, whereas among the Syrians it was not, and the fellahs of the Hauran still live in kinds of clans, administered by the head of the family, the *sheikh-el-beith*, and made up of all his descendants and even his collaterals.[58] This large family group is not found in the Gospels, but only couples – Joseph and Mary, Zebedee and Salome, Zacharias and Elizabeth. Property, too, must have been upon a simple family basis.

The father really was the head of his family, and that in the strongest sense of the word 'head'. His wife even called him *baal*,

lord, or *adon*, master. The expression 'father's house' was used
for family in ordinary speech. Theoretically his sons and
daughters were his absolute property, and he could dispose of
them as he wished; if he chose he could sell them as slaves. If
they committed a serious crime he could condemn them to death.[59]
In the course of time, however, these rigours had become less
terrible: for example, it had been very early decided that the
right of life and death could only be exercised with the consent of
the elders.[60] By the time of Christ there was no longer any
question of such a thing, nor of the sale of the children. Yet
the rights of the father of the family were still far beyond anything
that any modern legislation could possibly concede: he was in
fact the *oikodespotes*, the absolute ruler of the house, and this is
the term used in the Greek of the New Testament.

Everything was under his command. The Hebrew *baith*, like
the Greek *oikia*, meant the family, the house it lived in and its
possessions. The father was responsible for all three, and over
all three he had the most extensive rights. We see the *oikodespotes*
in Christ's own words, a powerful man, solidly based, with his
sons paying him the greatest respect, a man who sees that his
land is sown with the best seed, who defends his property against
thieves, who allots their work to the labourers and gives them
their just reward: in short, someone like the Eternal Father on
a very much smaller scale.

In the same way the respect that his children owed him had a
similarity to that which they owed to God. The famous commandment in the decalogue, 'Honour thy father and thy mother;
so thou shalt live long'[61] is clearly a transposition of a more
absolute order – the son who does not honour his parents must
be put to death. And in fact the Law condemned the disobedient
son[62] or he who 'cursed his father and his mother'[63] to lose his
life. By the time of Christ this would only have been carried
out in the most serious of cases. Yet He Himself never failed to
insist upon the importance of the commandment, as, for example,
when He told the rich young man the essence of the Law.[64]
Saint Paul, writing to his friends in Ephesus, goes so far as to say
that honouring one's parents is the 'first commandment'.[65]

How is the word 'honouring' to be understood? Ecclesiasticus
had already explained this;[66] but the rabbis of Israel produced
an unending flow of commentaries upon this obligation and of
exemplary tales which showed how it was best fulfilled – the

tale, for example, of the perfect son whom his father struck with
a sandal in a moment of wrath; the sandal flew out of the angry
father's grasp; the son fetched it and gave it back, kissing his
father's hand. And there was another, who heard that his father
had been conscribed by the authorities and who went to do his
work and to suffer the overseers' blows in his place.[67]

Were all sons as worthy as this? One had but to look into the
Gospels to know that they were not: there were, to be sure,
'sons obedient to their parents', with Jesus Himself as the first
among them; but the story of the Prodigal shows clearly that in
those days, as in all other times, there were youths who followed
only their own desires. And Jesus too explained how undutiful
sons would avoid coming to the help of their old parents by
saying that they had made an offering, a *corban*, of their goods
at the Temple, a trick which the Pharisees connived at:[68] so
true it is that the best of possible laws are not enough to make
men perfect.

WOMEN IN ISRAEL

The very wide powers that a man had over everything that made
up his family extended to his wife as well, at least in a considerable
degree. Theoretically a husband had no legal rights over the
person of his wife, and no sacred text could be brought forward
to say directly that he had. But some texts lent themselves to
exegesis, and naturally enough men took advantage of this;
for example, when God gave the ten commandments He said,
'Thou shalt not covet thy neighbour's house, or set thy heart
upon thy neighbour's wife, or servant or hand-maid or ox or ass
or anything else that is his'.[69] Men concluded only too easily
from this list that their wives belonged to them like any other
chattel. It was furthermore so much the case that a woman
was considered as subjected to her husband that according to
the Law the wife of a slave was sold with him.[70] A wife was an
exceedingly valuable possession, and no one else had the right
to touch her: Pharaoh learnt this to his cost when, without knowing
it, he took away Abraham's wife; an act which brought upon him
the terrible plagues of God's punishment.[71] Did these old
commandments and these ancient warnings still have the force
of law by the time of Christ? One has the impression that the
severity of the rules about marriage had not grown much less
than it had been in former days (there is the example of the

woman taken in adultery, for instance) and that Jewish husbands were the more inclined to harshness because of the spectacle of the disturbing freedom of the Greek and Roman women.

The wife owed her husband total fidelity, but she might not claim it in return. Her husband could not sell her, but he could repudiate her without any difficulty: the cases in which the wife could ask for a divorce, on the other hand, were exceedingly rare. The rank which society assigned to her was inferior, from every point of view. A rabbinical dictum said that every man should thank God every day for not having been born a woman any more than he had been born a pagan or a proletarian.[72] Women did not eat with the men, but stood while they ate, serving them at the table. In the street and in the courts of the Temple they kept at a distance from the men. Their life was in the house, and often the windows on the street were grilled, so that they might not be seen.[73] In former times they never went out without a veil,[74] and this was still the custom among some particularly strict observers. It was most improper for an Israelite to speak to a woman in the street, even – indeed, above all – if she were his wife. When the apostles saw Jesus talking with the Samaritan women they were, as Saint John admits, perfectly astonished.[75]

In the eyes of the law a woman was considered a minor, an irresponsible person: her husband could refuse to acknowledge any engagement she entered into, and the injured party had no remedy at law. Except in the most exceptional cases her evidence was not accepted by any court: and finally, as a general rule she did not inherit, neither from her father nor from her husband.

This does not mean that she had no rights. Far from it. Because she was weak, the law protected her. One has but to read chapters twenty-one and twenty-two of Deuteronomy to realize this: the Bible protected the girl whom a man had seduced and even more so the one he had raped, and the woman whose honour had been traduced, and even the captive whom the conqueror sought to enjoy. Naturally the whole of the wife's maintenance fell to the husband, who was to house, feed and clothe[76] her according to his status and his means: if she were not properly looked after she might ask for her father's help and protection, and he would rebuke his son-in-law. But generally speaking there was no need for this: Jewish husbands liked to see their wives well dressed, adorned with pendants, rings and brooches, and to let it be known that in their houses the fine wheat flour, the honey and the oil were to be found in abundance; for thus Yahweh treated his spouse, the Chosen Race, in the famous passage of Ezekiel.[77] The respect that the children owed their parents obviously included the mother; and in Leviticus she is even mentioned first in the commandment 'You must reverence mother and father'.[78]* And if, strictly speaking, the husband was the sole guardian of the household's common property, it appears that the wife was not prevented from using her personal earnings as she thought fit: speaking of the perfect wife one of the Proverbs says, 'Ground must be examined, and bought, and planted out as a vineyard, with the earnings of her toil'.[79] Those who spun at home and who made more thread than the family needed, kept the product of their sales.

The position of the Jewish woman from the religious point of view was defined by a statement preserved in the Talmud: 'Women are excused from the duties that begin *Thou shalt*, and from all those that must be fulfilled at a given time.'[80] That is to say, they were not required to recite the *Shema*, to be present at the reading of the Law, to wear phylacteries and fringed clothes, to live in a tent at the Feast of Tabernacles, and so on. But these things were not forbidden to them; and, said the rabbis, 'Before all the commandments of the Torah, men and women are upon the same footing'.[81] They were even advised to know the Law well so that they might instruct their sons and urge their husbands to the fulfilment of their religious obligations.

It goes without saying that in the small kingdom that is the home the wife was queen; and then, as in all other periods, she was aware of it. Her importance was all the greater since among the Jews, as among most of the nations of antiquity, a great many things that we buy made in shops or factories were produced at home: cloth, for instance, was spun and woven in the house. It was the wife who made the bread: she ground the corn between the stones of the little mill that every household owned, kneaded the dough with her hands, carried the risen dough in its sloping-sided wooden trough on her head, and cooked it, either by putting

*The Knox Version actually reads: 'You must reverence father and mother.' (Lev. 19, 3.) The Authorized Version reads: 'Ye shall fear every man his mother, and his father', but the Vulgate again has: '*Unusquisque patrem suum, et matrem suam timeat.*'

it in an oven or by spreading the dough on a hot metal plate to make flat cakes; and all this work called for as much skill as it did strength. Naturally it was also the woman who fetched the water at the fountain, and a man in the street carrying a pitcher for water was an uncommon spectacle.[82] Providing the oil was also a woman's duty, a duty held to be symbolic; and she had particularly to take care of the very pure oil for the Sabbath lamp, which she was to tend so that it should not go out on the holy day: the tractate *Shabbath* avers that those who forget to provide the oil or fail to keep the flame alight die in childbirth.[83]

The woman, then, was quite as necessary to the man of Israel as she is and always has been to men of all other times and nations. And as men have always done, everywhere, those of Israel took their revenge for being so bound to the weaker sex, and so dependent upon them, by loading them with abuse. It would not be at all difficult to compile a most edifying anthology of remarks against women from the Old Testament: the prophets are particularly outstanding for their misogyny – women are ridiculously vain, says Isaiah; voluptuous and froward, he adds; cruel, says Amos; two-faced, say Jeremiah and Ezekiel.[84] The apocryphal books go further: the *Testament of the Patriarchs* scarcely sees them as anything but the occasion of fornication.[85] As for the rabbis, their sayings upon the subject of women are not to be counted, and many of them are far from tender. 'The Lord gave ten measures of words for the whole of humanity; the women seized upon nine of them.' 'Greedy and idle, jealous and quarrelsome, that describes women: they also listen behind doors.' ' "From which part of the man shall I take the woman?" the Almighty asked Himself. "From the head? She would be too proud. From the eye? She would be too inquisitive. From the ear? She would eavesdrop. From the mouth? She would be garrulous. From the hand? She would be wasteful." In the end He took a very obscure, well-hidden part of the body, in the hope of making her modest.'[86]

Not all the doctors of the Law shared this misogynic attitude however. A charming fable is attributed to the most illustrious of them, the rabbi Gamaliel, Saint Paul's master. 'An emperor said to the Wise Man, "Thy God is a thief; to make the woman he had to steal a rib from the sleeping Adam." The doctor did not know what to answer, but his daughter said, "Let me take care of this." She went to see the emperor and said to him,

"We call for justice." "Indeed? What for?" "Thieves got into our house in the night: they have taken away a silver ewer and they have left a gold one in its place." "Ha, ha," said the emperor, "I wish I could have burglars like that every night." "Well," said the girl, "that is what our God did: He took a mere rib from the first man, but in exchange He gave him a wife." ' [87] Other rabbis praised women's penetrating intelligence, their ardour for work, their steadfastness and their kind hearts. In any case, did not the Holy Scriptures advocate respect for women? Had not the first man cried, at the sight of the first woman, 'Here, at last, is bone that comes from mine, flesh that comes from mine'?[88] Had not God commanded that a man should leave his father and mother and cling to his wife instead, so that the two become one flesh?[89] Did not the Proverbs state that 'a good wife is treasure found' and show Wisdom in the form of a woman?[90] Did not the Bible offer a great many examples of women admirable for their courage, their magnanimity, their long-suffering fortitude and their greatness of spirit? From Deborah to the mother of the Maccabees, from Ruth to Judith and Esther, what a splendid array of women might be found. And lastly, with the Messiah in mind, was it not possible to imagine a new Eve, a spotless maiden of Zion, who would redeem the first Eve's sin of tempting Adam and so help to accomplish the divine plan?[91]

These were splendid examples and splendid images: they helped to give the Israelite woman a higher moral status, a greater degree of esteem, than those of Greece or Rome. She was set a very high and indeed a noble standard: for example, there are those verses that Ecclesiasticus devoted to women – 'Happy the man that has a faithful wife; his span of days is doubled. A wife industrious is the joy of her husband, and crowns all his years with peace. He best thrives that best wives; where men fear God this is the reward of their service, good cheer given to rich and poor alike; day in, day out, never a mournful look.' And further on, 'Great content an industrious wife brings to her husband; health to every bone of his body is that good sense of hers. No better gift of God to man than a prudent woman that can hold her tongue; a soul well disciplined is beyond all price. Grace so gracious is none as woman's faithfulness and woman's modesty; woman's continence there is no valuing.'[92] And everybody knows the poetical description of the good woman before God, with which the Book of Proverbs ends, the woman whose price is beyond pearls, and who brings her husband happiness and knows how to gain his love, who spins, cooks, watches the lamp, works day and night and yet dresses well and helps her husband in his social duties.

It is a wonderful picture; and it is admirable that Israel should have conceived it and set it up as a model for the nation's women. It is admirable in spite of the fact that one must admit that the whole ideal exists only in reference to man, his happiness and his welfare, and in reference to the interests of the family. One of the very important contributions of the Christian message was to be the promotion of women to the status of human beings in their own right, no longer merely as mothers of many children, good house-keepers, their husbands' subordinates; and this change was to take place when the love of men for women became a sacrament.[93]

SHORTCOMINGS AND FAILURES IN MARRIAGE

Alas, not all women were like the industrious wife of the Bible: nor were all husbands kind, faithful and open-handed. In Israel, as much as anywhere else, there were unhappy marriages. As the Bible was drawn up, or written down, by men, it naturally emphasizes those womanly faults that spoil a marriage and speaks little of those which are to be found in men. Ecclesiasticus glides primly past the unpleasant, stupid, avaricious, vain, lying and adulterous husband, but dwells long upon the ill-natured wife, the kind of woman whose husband has to seek refuge among his neighbours, to whom he bitterly recounts his misery. Was the son of Sirach speaking from experience? One would think so, judging from the convinced ring of his voice. 'A man will endure any wound but the heart's wound, and any malice but a woman's. . . . No head so venomous as a viper's, nor any anger like a woman's. Better share thy home with lion and serpent both, than with an ill woman's company.'[94] Poor husband: how understandable it is that his face should be 'as grim as a bear's'. Since comparisons have taken a zoological turn, it would be better for him 'to hold a snake between his hands'. The rabbis held that among the men 'who would not behold Gehenna' ranked those who had had a bad wife upon earth: they had served their term of Purgatory in advance. And when a man married his friends would ask him, by way of a joke, 'Will it be for *matza* or for *motze*?' For if the Proverb said, 'A man who has found (*matza*) a vigorous wife has found a rare treasure,' Ecclesiasticus replied, 'I find (*motze*) woman more bitter than death'.[95]

Yet there was one worse than the shrew, and that was the adulterous wife. The Law, the protector of the family, was exceedingly severe upon her; even more severe than it was towards the man; and this, in view of the principles upon which marriage was based in Israel, is understandable. The teaching was that all adultery was forbidden: Yahweh's commandment was absolute, 'Thou shalt not commit adultery'.[96] The rabbis even ranked it with the supreme crime of atheism, for Job had described how the adulterer waited for nightfall, saying within himself, 'No one sees me';[97] whereas God sees all. Some of them taught that to keep down adultery it was necessary to condemn not only the act but also the look and the wicked thought,[98] that 'casting of the eye on a woman so as to lust after her' which Jesus was to speak of with so much force.

But the definition of adultery in a woman was not the same as that for a man. Every unfaithful woman was held to be an adultress because, says Ecclesiasticus, she breaks the law of the Most High, she plays her husband false, giving him for heir a child that is no son of his, and she defiles herself.[99] The interests of the family called for the severest punishment of adultery in a woman; but fidelity in a husband, on the other hand, was not insisted upon, since his ill-conduct had no effect upon his family. A man's adultery was a crime only if he seduced a married or a betrothed woman, because then he injured the family of another.

The woman suspected of adultery was put to that same ordeal of bitter water that fiancées had to suffer, as we have already seen. It is described very exactly in the Book of Numbers:[100] she had to drink a horrible mixture, in which the chief ingredient was dust from the Temple floor, and if she vomited or felt unwell her guilt was taken as certain. If she were taken in the act itself she was condemned to death.[101] They dragged her 'by the neck of her gown' before the people and killed her. Death by stoning was laid down by Deuteronomy only in the case of unfaithful fiancées: at a later period strangling was introduced for adultresses in the more exact sense of the word.[102] Yet it appears, by the very well-known example of the woman taken in adultery, in Saint John's Gospel, that unfaithful wives were certainly stoned by the people at the time of Christ. Were the other punishments set down in the Law[103] also still carried out in all their rigour?

That is to say, were the children examined so that their illegitimacy might be established and they themselves thrust out of the community? Ecclesiasticus was still at the stage of the old biblical idea of collective responsibility: but from the time of the prophets Jeremiah and Ezekiel that of individual responsibility had been gaining ground, and it is doubtful that this penalty would still have been enforced.

As for the man taken with a married woman or with one betrothed to another, he was put to death, together with her. Yet if violence had preceded the act, if he had dragged his victim to a lonely spot where no call for help would have been heard,[104] he alone was killed. If the woman were a slave that he had lain with, the penalty of death was not carried out, but the man had to pay compensation to the owner and offer an expiatory sacrifice at the Temple.[105] It is clear that these massive precautions were taken to safeguard the rights and the purity of blood: but it was from quite another point of view that Jesus was to condemn adultery – adultery considered as a defilement of the soul and an injury to the inner life far more than as something harmful to family interests.

Adultery was one of the causes which could bring about a dissolution of marriage: it was a reason for divorce; which seems to prove that not all betrayed husbands sent their wives to their death. Commenting upon the verse of Deuteronomy in which it is said that a man may repudiate his wife 'if he find some taint of defilement in her',[106] most of the rabbis laid down that 'the woman who has committed adultery must be repudiated':[107] some even held that this was a religious duty. But adultery was far from being the only cause. In so far as the wife belonged to her husband (and this was the case to a very large extent, as we have seen) he could get rid of her without any trial. Further-more the doctors of the Law were not in agreement as to the reasons that could authorize repudiation. Some understood the expression 'taint of defilement' in Deuteronomy as meaning repugnant, or disagreeable; which was going rather far. A more liberal school held that unfaithfulness alone was to be understood; but another school again said that if a wife regularly spoilt the dishes that she cooked, that was quite sufficient to establish that she was disagreeable and repugnant. The rabbi Akkiba even thought the finding of a better-looking woman a sufficient reason for the repudiation of his wife.[108] It must be observed, however, that a man could not repudiate a wife he had been compelled to marry for having seduced her as a virgin, and that madness was not a basis for divorce, but that sterility, established as having lasted for ten years, was.

In theory the woman had no right to seek a divorce: her only means of bringing it about was to make herself so disagreeable that her husband would take the initiative. However, rabbinical doctrine allowed that the Assembly might 'bring strong pressure to bear' on the husband to induce him to repudiate his wife in a certain number of cases – duly established impotence; refusal to carry out matrimonial duties properly; habitual cruelty; a repulsive and incurable disease, such as leprosy; a change of trade and the adoption of a disgusting kind of work by the husband, such as the collection of dogs' dung for tanners; or the decision to leave Palestine and live far away.[109]

There was no need to appear before a court to be divorced. Judging by what Hosea says,[110] in the early times, when a husband expelled his unfaithful wife he accused her in front of her children, crying, 'She is no true wife of mine, nor I any longer her lord'. And if she refused to go he stripped her and left her naked as the day she was born. These very forceful methods were no longer customary by the time of Christ. For a very long time – it is mentioned as early as Isaiah and Jeremiah – the husband had been required to give his wife a letter of divorcement, a writ of separation, the same that is referred to in Saint Matthew; and the legal basis of this usage was a verse of Deuteronomy.[111] Many tractates of the Talmud, particularly the tractate *Gittin*, gave models of these writs of separation, in which the husband was to state directly that it was his express intention to send his wife away, and no less absolutely that she was from that time on free to live as she chose and to remarry.

The lot of a repudiated wife was not in fact very pleasant; as Isaiah had said in his time, she usually lived in affliction.[112] In most cases she had to go back to her parents' house. Yet unless she had been turned away for infidelity she kept the children, the sons until they were six and the daughters until they were married. The husband had to pay a kind of indemnity called the *kethubah*, and this bore a relation to the dowry that the wife had been given and to the family's status. The rabbis had drawn up a whole list of circumstances in which the payment of the *kethubah* could be avoided, but there were still cases enough in which it was compulsory to act as an effective hindrance to over-hasty divorce. If a husband had an unbearable wife but was unable to find the *kethubah*, it was a very usual piece of wit was to apply to him that verse in the first chapter of the Lamentations of Jeremiah, 'The Lord has given me up a prisoner to duress there is no escaping'.

For this reason and for some others, divorce was not so usual in Israel as one might have supposed. A mere passing rage was not enough to lead to the writing of a letter of repudiation which was subsequently to be officially produced before the whole community: nor to the amassing of the indemnity. Furthermore, a man had to think of the money he had paid to his wife's father at the time of the betrothal – a sum which was quite lost in the event of divorce. And still further, he had to reflect that he would bring upon himself the anger and perhaps the vengeance of his wife's family. Strangely enough, the Law did not allow any second thoughts: a man was not permitted to take his former wife back again if at a later time she became free once more.[113]

And more than all this, public opinion was set against divorce: Israel was very unlike Rome at this time, for in Rome, as Jérôme Carcopino[114] says, there was to be seen 'an epidemic of broken marriages, in spite of the laws of Augustus, or even indeed because of them'. In Israel, they had never 'debased the dignity of marriage'. It was clear that the biblical ideal of marriage was opposed to divorce, and it was only accepted as a last resource, when nothing better offered. The last of the canonical prophets, Malachi, damned the whole practice in a shattering passage in which he compared it to treason against God – 'The Lord bears witness to her wrongs, that wife of thy manhood's age, whom now thou spurnest, thy partner, thy covenanted bride'.[115] And the rabbi Shammai uttered a similar dictum, 'The altar itself weeps over the husband who repudiates his wife'.

No one is likely to forget the famous dialogue in Saint Matthew, which is confirmed by the two other synoptic Gospels: 'Then the Pharisees came to him, and put him to the test by asking, Is it right for a man to put away his wife, for whatever cause? He answered, Have you never read, how He who created them, when they first came to be, created them male and female; and how He said, A man, therefore, will leave his father and mother and will cling to his wife, and the two will become one flesh? And so they are no longer two, they are one flesh; what God, then, has joined, let not man put asunder. Why then, they said, did Moses enjoin that a man might give his wife a writ of separation, and then he might put her away? He told them, it was to suit your hard hearts that Moses allowed you to put your wives away; it was not so at the beginning of things. And I tell you that he who puts away his wife, not for any unfaithfulness of hers, and so marries another, commits adultery.'[116] A new and decisive step had been taken. The sacred character of marriage had been proclaimed more strongly than it had ever been before; and the little parenthetical phrase *not for any unfaithfulness of hers*, helped to assert its indissolubility. This was to be the essence of the Christian teaching on marriage, and Saint Paul was later to make the doctrine more exact.[117] It was a teaching that went beyond the old Mosaic rules, and it made them obsolete; as indeed the charity of Christ made others, such as the 'eye for an eye, tooth for a tooth'. And yet did not the highest and the purest elements of the traditional view of the family in Israel in some degree contain the germ of the Christian doctrine?

CHAPTER THREE

HIGH AND LOW, RICH AND POOR

From tribe to social class – Slavery in Israel – 'At toil repine not' – Who were the am-ha-arez? *– Beati* possedentes *– A class apart: the scribes – Relations between the classes.*

FROM TRIBE TO SOCIAL CLASS

Did the family unit make part of any larger formations? It certainly did in the early times: there were then those enlarged families, those groups, which were called houses and which were named after their real or supposed founder – groups that were essentially the same as clans. The Bible often mentions them, as for example when it speaks of Elkanah, the father of the inspired holy man Samuel, going up to Shiloh 'to offer the Lord due sacrifice, and pay his vow, taking all his household with him'.[1] And above all there were the tribes, those typical formations of a nomadic period, groups of clans theoretically linked by blood and historically bound to one another by more or less legendary traditions; mystically bound by ceremonies, commensal feasts and intermarriage; militarily and administratively bound by obedience to a single chief. This famous division into the twelve tribes was traced back to Jacob's blessing of his twelve sons,[2] and every Israelite knew the list of them by heart – Reuben, Simeon, Levi, Judah, Zebulun, Issachar, Dan, Gad, Asher, Naphtali, Joseph and Benjamin. It was agreed that this division had been the Chosen People's administrative basis ever since Moses' great work of organization, although it was practically impossible to draw a coherent history of each of the tribes from the Bible or even to prove that twelve tribes had ever had an official existence all at the same time.

These traditional concepts had scarcely any importance left by the time of Christ: they had almost faded out of existence. The 'house' was still used as an expression showing illustrious descent, however, and the evangelist does not fail to point out that

Jesus belonged to 'the house of David'. Families preserved genealogies which went very far back, sometimes even as far as Abraham. As for the tribe to which a man belonged, this only had a meaning for those who belonged to the tribe of Levi, for they had the privilege of providing the Temple with its servants, the Levites.[3] Yet people also took a certain pride in claiming to belong to Judah or Benjamin, those tribes which had repopulated the Holy Land with true followers of God after the exile. Apart from these cases, however, when 'the people of the twelve tribes' were spoken of, it was either as a reference to history or to the end of time, to that day of glory when, as Saint Paul told King Herod Agrippa, 'the promise should be attained',[4] and when, according to the Apocalypse, there would be the great counting of the chosen, while the seven trumpets gave their terrifying blast.[5]

When the horizontal separation disappeared it was replaced by a series of vertical distinctions, a social stratification or differentiation by class – replaced, that is to say, if we may assume that differentiation by class had not always existed. This differentiation, however, had nothing in common with that which existed in Rome; for there the division depended upon money, the *humiliores* being the humble people without any real, visible capital, and the *honestiores* the tradesmen made respectable by the possession of five thousand sesterces; the members of the noble orders also owed their position to their fortunes, since those of the equestrian order had to have four hundred thousand sesterces, and the senators, those splendid people who supplied the legates and proconsuls of wealthy provinces and the commanders of legions, no less than a million. In Israel one class alone could claim precedence, and that because it had a religious dignity: this was the priestly class. 'For as much as some are accustomed to draw the ground of their nobility, the one from this man, the other from that,' says Josephus, 'so among our nation the mark of true nobility is, to derive a man's pedigree from the priesthood.'[6] Theoretically, then, the high nobility consisted of the heads of the eight families which had the honour of supplying the wood for the burnt-offerings at the Temple and from which the high priest was chosen. But in practice the priestly class had lost a very great deal of its standing ever since it had let the scribes, whose importance we shall speak of later, set themselves up as specialists in the holy Law and as the defenders of traditional values; and above all since the Romans and the Herodian princes had tamed the leaders of the class.[7]

What then was the basis of social stratification? In fact it was based upon money, as it was in the Roman empire. It is a striking fact that nowhere in the New Testament is there a reference to a distinction as between what we would call gentle and simple, or nobles and commoners; but on the other hand one continually finds rich and poor. How many of Christ's parables have to do with status based upon wealth, that distinction which our modern society knows so well. The ruling class (unlike that of the West at the height of the Middle Ages) asserted itself not because of the services that it gave but because of the wealth it possessed and of the political connections that its wealth provided.

But what sets Israel completely apart from the other nations of the ancient world is its attitude towards this social inequality and towards the privileges of wealth. The religious principle was absolute: apart from the priestly class, which was held to possess a special grace, all Jewish laymen were most strictly equal among themselves. Saint Paul's famous exclamation was founded upon this: 'Are they Hebrews? So am I. Are they Israelites? So am I. Are they descended from Abraham? So am I.'[8] That is, we are equals; I am as good as they are. A Roman *humilior* meeting a wealthy patrician in his purple-striped toga on his way to the senate with all his clients about him, did not feel his equal; but the most wretched of the faithful, standing in the court of the Temple with his arms raised towards heaven in prayer, knew that in the eyes of Yahweh he was as good as Herod.

In the tradition of Israel, then, there was a current of egalitarian feeling, and this is borne out by a very great many biblical texts; or rather it might almost be called a revolutionary current, one which tended, upon the spiritual plane, to overturn all earthly hierarchies. Holy Writ not only told the rich man, 'Wilt thou look round at ill-gotten gains, and tell thyself thou hast enough for all thy needs? Trust me, when vengeance finds thee out, all this shall nothing avail thee.'[9] It did not only bid him, 'Do not steel thy heart and shut thy purse against him [a fellow-citizen fallen upon evil days]: be generous to his poverty, and lend him what thou seest he stands in need of'.[10] It went further, and announced that the poor man should be raised from the dust, the beggar raised from the dung-hill and set among the princes,[11] and that

God would 'give the friendless redress',[12] that is to say, that He would punish the man who 'persecuted the helpless, the destitute, the grief-stricken'.[13] Throughout His teaching Jesus applied Himself to overturning the order of classes, particularly in the Beatitudes, the most sublime of His words:[14] for Him, clearly, the rich and powerful man was an unfortunate creature, one who could no more enter the kingdom of heaven than a camel could go through the eye of a needle, whereas the poor man and the outcast won favour for all eternity. But this was a doctrine that was already so current in Israel that a young maiden like the Virgin Mary, improvising the splendid words of the Magnificat before her cousin Elizabeth, praised the Lord for having 'put down the mighty from their seat, and exalted the lowly'.[15] Even though the principles of equality upon the spiritual plane may not have overcome the hardness of men's hearts in the hurly-burly of every day, they had an influence upon Jewish social life that can very often be detected.

SLAVERY IN ISRAEL

The most striking example of its influence is the attitude of the Jews towards the existence of slavery, that shocking and essential element in all the societies of the ancient world. There were undoubtedly slaves in Israel at the time of Christ. He Himself brings them into a great number of His parables, for instance that of the unmerciful servant, that of the wheat and the tares, of the prodigal son and many others;[16] for wherever the recent translations use the modest word servant it seems certain that in fact slaves, *servi*, were meant. And yet, as one reads the New Testament or Josephus, one does not get the impression that among the Jews there was an immense servile class representing a quarter of the population or even more, as it did in some great Greek and Roman cities, and creating a permanent state of social insecurity. The free workmen were paid very low wages, and this alone made the purchase of slaves, who had to be kept, a poor investment. An official document of the year AD 71 shows that in one region where the fiscal authorities counted three hundred and eighty-five tax-payers, all these people together owned no more than forty-four slaves, that is to say, one slave between nine of them.[17] The situation was therefore in no way comparable to that in the pagan world.

Nor was the behaviour of the Jews towards their slaves. It

would be a platitude to speak of the cruelty of the Romans towards theirs, to quote the well-known passage in which Juvenal shows a Roman matron asking, 'Is a slave a man?' or to remind the reader that legally the slave belonged to the class of things, *res*, and that he was, in Varro's words, 'a kind of tool that can speak': and in any case this reputation for cruelty seems very often to have been belied by the facts, for literature has many examples of the kindness of Roman masters towards their slaves.[18] Yet although it may be true that the Romans' behaviour was almost always better than their laws, among the Jews the laws on slavery were far superior to the Roman or the Greek legislation, and these laws, being religious, dominated behaviour.

This does not mean that there are not horrible words upon slavery to be found in the Bible or the Talmud. Ecclesiasticus, who was clearly no sentimentalist, gives advice that the elder Cato would have approved: 'Fodder thy ass must have, and the whip, and a pack to bear; thy slave, too, needs food and discipline and hard work. Under duress he toils, what marvel if ease should tempt him? Leave his hands idle, and he will seek to be his own master. The stubborn ox yoke and rein will subdue; slave held to his task is slave bowed to thy will; keep rack and stocks for one that is bent on mischief.'[19] There were rabbis at the time of Christ whose views were quite as savage. They accused the slaves of being idle, debauched and thievish; they suspected them of all the vices, even that of hating their masters.[20] It appears that this was commonplace gossip – slaves were spoken of then as servants are now by some of the women who employ them.

Yet in the Bible and in the teachings of the doctors of the Law there was also another tradition, and it is certain that this was predominant at the time of Christ. The same passage of Ecclesiasticus, whose brutality we have just seen, goes on, 'Yet do not burden flesh and blood more than it can bear, nor inflict more than lawful punishment while the plea is still unheard. Faithful slave if thou hast, make much of him as thy own self; treat him as if he were thy brother.'[21] The holy man Job spoke more deeply when he said, 'How shall I meet His scrutiny, Who fashioned in the womb this one and that, man and master alike?'[22] Many times the Bible reminded the Israelites that they had been slaves in Egypt, and told them that this memory should urge them to be merciful. Besides, the Law protected the slave, punished the master who put him to death, provided for the liberation of the slave whose master maimed him or chased him away with blows, and even of the slave who was notoriously ill-used. Most of the rabbis insisted upon the most generous understanding of the precepts of the Law. The rabbi Jochanan never ate meat or drank wine without giving some to his slave; and the rabbi Gamaliel's reply to a person who expressed surprise at seeing him sad for the death of his slave Tobit was often quoted: 'My slave Tobit was a man; he was an honest and a pious man.'[23]

But the Law made a considerable difference between the pagan and the Hebrew slaves. The first, who were bought in the market in the usual fashion, were less protected than the second. They could not be killed, however, nor maimed nor ill-treated; they had a right to a day of rest,[24] and, in opposition to the Roman usage, if they escaped they were not to be given back to their master.[25] As they belonged to an Israelite, they were subjected to certain biblical requirements, but they could not be circumcised against their will, and if a slave refused to agree to this requirement for more than twelve months, he was to be sold back to the pagans.[26] On the other hand, if he acquiesced, from that moment on he was considered a member of the family – so much so, indeed, that a circumcised slave belonging to a priest had the right to eat the 'holy food', the hallowed offerings.[27]

And yet even if he were circumcised, the slave of pagan origin did not have the same religious obligations as a Hebrew slave, nor the same civil rights. There can have been very few Hebrew slaves bought in Palestine: the Law forbade the keeping of an Israelite in slavery against his will unless he were a guilty man,[28] and this must have made the slave-merchants send their human cattle, when the slaves were Jews, to other countries and other markets. But a savage legal provision reduced the bankrupt debtor to slavery[29] as well as the thief who was unable to make good his theft.[30] There were also poor people who, rather than starve, would make slaves of themselves, and in this case their masters would pierce through the lobe of their right ear as a mark of their servile state.[31] The Law strictly regulated the conditions in which an Israelite might become a slave in this manner, and most particularly the circumstances in which he was to be kept: the principle was that he was to be treated exactly like a free worker, a hired servant;[32] he was not to work more than ten hours a day; he was to work only by day, and not at night; he was not to be used for work serving the public, such as being a tailor, a bath-attendant or a barber; and he was to be made to do nothing that might humiliate him.[33] These requirements were so scrupulously laid down that there was a common saying, 'Whoever buys a Hebrew slave gives himself a master'. And then there was the famous law of the sabbatical year,[34] that extraordinary measure so typical of all that was most noble in the Jewish tradition, which regularly restored the balance of society, wiped out debts, gave everything rest, even the cattle and the earth, and which laid down, 'If thou dost buy a slave that is a Hebrew by race, he shall do thee six years' service, and in the seventh year, without any ransome paid, he shall go free'.[35] The immediate result of this was that the Hebrew slave was worth less than a twentieth part of the price of a pagan slave, who, in theory, was only to be liberated in the years of jubilee, that is to say, every fifty years.[36] It seems quite clear that by the time of Christ custom and legal measures had between them almost completely done away with Hebrew slaves in Palestine, even in the case of insolvent debtors: only the sale of thieves was still commonplace. If an Israelite were bought by a pagan master or by another Jew who intended to take him away from the Holy Land, the community would redeem him, if his family could not. Philo, after all, was not mistaken when he said, 'Even those who were called slaves were in fact workers'.[37]

It need scarcely be said that the position of a woman-slave, whether she were Hebrew or pagan, was quite different from that of a man. If she were married to a slave she shared his lot if he were set free or re-sold, unless she had belonged to the master before her marriage, in which case he could keep her and her children – a proceeding that was frowned upon by the rabbis, however. But the chief difference was that many of them became concubines to their masters or their master's sons. In this case the manumission of the sabbatical year came into operation only if the woman required it. But these slave-concubines were protected by the Law, which would not have them sold out of the family when they no longer gave pleasure, which automatically freed those who were married in a regular manner, and which forbade their children to be taken from them. Rabbinical doctrine, furthermore, was hostile to the enslavement of women. 'He who increases the number of men-slaves in his household increases theft,' said the rabbi Hillel, 'but he who increases the number of women-slaves increases lechery.'

Apart from the obligatory manumission of the Hebrew slave on the seventh year, many slaves were given their freedom by their masters; some because they had succeeded in scraping together the price of their redemption, others because their families helped them, and others again because of their masters' generosity. The rabbis laid down several cases in which the slave had a right to liberty: the slave was free if his master mutilated him, if he allowed him to marry a free woman or vice versa, or if he made him his heir. The ceremony of liberation had a religious character: the slave, in his master's presence, bound on the phylacteries, those little leather cases holding four passages of the Law which were worn on the forehead and the left arm during prayer. After this the freedman, if he were a Hebrew, belonged to the Jewish community with all the rights of the other Jews: if he were a circumcised pagan he belonged too, but with diminished rights. These *hofsim* do not seem to have occupied the same place in Israel that the freedmen did in the Roman empire, where they are often to be found in the highest rank of power and prestige.

The comparative mildness of the servile condition goes some way to explain why Jesus should not have been particularly preoccupied with it. Besides, it is clear that He was far more concerned with moral slavery, the slavery that sin inflicts upon every man. 'The truth that makes men free' is that which liberates them from their vices. Jesus was perfectly well acquainted with the servile condition, on the material plane,[38] and He permitted it because it has little importance from the spiritual point of view, since the true life is not of this earth. But His whole teaching tends towards the abolition of distinction between master and slave, all difference being lost in universal love. Saint Paul, on several occasions, gives masters excellent advice, counselling generosity; and in the same way he bids slaves be obedient.[39] There is also his most moving short epistle to Philemon, in which he speaks so generously of a fugitive slave. Within the communities of the primitive Church, with their new view of the world, there were no more to be 'either masters or slaves' (as there were not, by the way, among the Essenes); and this feeling was in evidence long before the institutions that arose from Christianity slowly succeeded in making an end of the plague of the heathen world.[40]

'AT TOIL REPINE NOT'

The small number of slaves in Israel and also, as we shall see, the want of a middle class comparable to our bourgeoisie, brought about the strengthening of the workers as a social category, both those who worked on the land and those who worked at the various trades. One has but to look into the Gospels to see how great a place they occupied in the Jewish world; the ploughman and the sower, the cattle-breeder, the lake fisherman, the carpenter and the mason, and a great many others, continually appear. Jesus came from this class, and He speaks of those who belonged to it as of men He met every day and with whose lives He was perfectly familiar.

This fact, as well as some exact religious reasons, explains why the Jewish attitude towards manual labour and the workers was so wholly different from that of the Greeks and the Romans. At Athens there was the saying, 'You cannot make a citizen out of a workman'; and that master of irony, Lucian, speaks contemptuously of 'the wretched artisan compelled to gain his bread by the work of his hands'. But Ecclesiasticus had said, 'At toil repine not'.[41] God Himself had commanded the first man to earn his bread with the sweat of his brow, as a consequence of his sin and as a sign of his condition.[42] But the rabbinical exegesis suggested a very satisfactory explanation of this stern requirement: it was said that Adam, on hearing the Almighty say that 'thorns and thistles it shall yield thee, this ground from which thou dost win thy food' (verse 18), burst into tears. 'Lord,' he cried, 'am I to eat the same food as my ass, then?' To which God replied by verse 19, 'Thou shalt earn thy bread with the sweat of thy brow'. Which was as much as to say, 'Your labour raises you above the level of the beasts'.[43]

All the teaching of the Holy Scriptures, then, and all the rabbinical development of it, showed the necessity of work and the dignity of work: in the Old Testament alone we find more than thirty passages which express these two ideas, and more than a hundred could be drawn from the Talmud. On the other hand, neither the one nor the other has a single word in favour of idleness, nor one which shows the least contempt for work. Work was obligatory: Saint Paul's well-known words, 'The man who refuses to work must be left to starve'[44] (words that were to be taken up by Lenin, by the by), sum up the unchanging opinion of the Jewish world. The dignity of labour: commenting upon that verse of Deuteronomy, 'Wilt thou not choose life?'[45] a rabbi made this admirable remark, 'The Almighty meant by this, choose to labour'.

The highest gave the example: had not the patriarchs, the prophets and the first kings of Israel all worked? And the rabbis averred that Adam himself, while he was still in Paradise, already tilled the ground, from delight in the wonderful garden. All the doctors of the Law worked to gain their livelihood: the rabbi Akiba was a woodcutter, the rabbi Joshua a charcoal-burner, the rabbi Meir a public writer, the rabbi Jochanan a shoe-maker, the rabbi Saul a grave-digger, and the great rabbi Hillel himself was in so modest a station (from the mundane point of view) that he earned no more than half a denarius a day as a labourer – about eighteen pence. It is scarcely necessary to recall that Jesus and all the apostles were workers, artisans or fishermen or clerks: and there are the proud assertions of Saint Paul, the son of a tent-maker and himself a worker at that trade in the course of his apostolic journeys – 'We would not even be indebted to you for our daily bread, we earned it in weariness and toil, working with our hands, night and day, so as not to be a burden to any of you,' and 'These hands of mine have sufficed for all that I and my companions needed'.[46]

This does not mean that there was not an order of esteem among the trades. The goldsmiths, the sandal-makers and the wood-workers, for example, were thought of as being better than the rest: whereas shearers and tanners, who were always smelly, were counted as inferior, and the scent-sellers, whose trade brought them into continual contact with loose women, were lower still. Popular opinion held that some trades were even worse, trades in which highway robbery was commonplace: and this civil list included sailors, the leaders of caravans and the shopkeepers. But these remarks, behind which one feels some degree of jealousy or ill-will, in no way invalidated the general principle, 'Work is great: it honours those who perform it'.[47]

From this principle Israel derived rules to regulate the relations between the masters and the men. The first social legislation in all human history is Jewish, and this fact, which reflects the greatest honour upon the Chosen People, is too little known. It dates from remote antiquity, from Moses himself. In Deuteronomy we find, 'And if thou hast a hired servant that lives from hand to mouth, be he thy fellow-Israelite, or some alien that shares thy land and city, do not withhold his wages; pay him his day's wages before set of sun. It is all he has, in his poverty, to support life with; cries he to the Lord, thou art a sinner manifest.'[48] The principle was therefore established, and it was applied to the humblest of the workers, the general day-labourers who were to be found in such numbers and of whom our Lord speaks in the famous parable of the labourers of the eleventh hour.[49] To be sure, admirable legal enactments do not necessarily ensure the reign of justice upon earth, and Malachi, in the long-past days of the return from exile, had been obliged to cry out furiously against the injustice of the masters towards their men and to denounce it as the nation's crime.[50] But by the time of Christ the rabbis had done a great deal of work upon the question: they had scrupulously laid down the conditions under which the workers were to be fed, housed and clothed; they had set the hours of work and the forms of payment for those who were hired by the hour or the half-day, and they had always stressed the fact that any man who injured a wage-earner transgressed 'five commandments of the Torah'.[51]

The workers did not only have rights: religious doctrine imposed duties upon them too. The Bible required, as Saint Paul reminded them, that they should respect their masters, obey them and serve them faithfully. The rabbis had some excellent moral tales in which exemplary workmen were held up to be admired. One day the rabbi Joseph, who was a mason, was on his scaffolding when a man below called up to him, asking for advice upon a religious question. 'Wait until this evening,' replied the doctor of the Law, 'I cannot come down: I am paid by the day and I may not give away a minute that belongs to my master.' And the rabbi Hilkia, who was a surveyor, gave the same answer to some people who came and importuned him to teach them a prayer that would make the rain fall. We cannot say that all Jewish workmen necessarily had such delicate consciences; but it was already something that the men who commanded the widest attention in Israel should have given such admirable examples.

There seems to be no doubt that at the time of Christ some trades had formed themselves into bodies like guilds, or even trade-unions.[52] In reading the Gospel one gathers that the fishermen of the sea of Galilee had a corporative organization, based upon the working team, the same men working under the direction of a team-leader: Saint Peter was one of these.[53] Professional associations have been traced as far back as the period just after the return from exile, among the potters, weavers, metal-workers, dyers and bakers, and it is more than likely that the evolution in this direction should have been accelerated by the example of the Roman *collegia*, which were very wide-spread in the first century. In Alexandria, the Jewish guilds possessed, in their famous 'house of labour', the *diplostoon*, such splendid offices and warehouses that when the rabbi Judah returned from a visit to Egypt he said, 'No one who has not seen the *diplostoon* of Alexandria has any idea of the glory of Israel'. The workers' associations were undoubtedly less powerful in Palestine, but they were nevertheless strong enough to make sure that their members' hours of work were properly respected, and to insist upon compensation for a man who, bringing his ass for the purposes of his work, lost it.

It does not appear that these beginnings of trade-unionism resulted in strikes. The only one that is spoken of in the Talmud was that of the Temple servants, who refused to prepare the shew-bread and the incense or to teach the faithful to sing. On the other hand – but this is no doubt the real reason for the absence of strikes – unemployment was a constant evil. The Talmud often speaks of the *pollim bethelim*, or as one would say in Italian, the *disoccupati*. During this last period Israel was in the grip of an agricultural crisis, varying in severity, but continual; and parallel to this there was a general economic crisis brought about by the finishing of the work upon the Temple a little after Jesus' death, and by the lessening of the great undertakings of the Herods. In the parable of the workers of the eleventh hour, we find the master of the vineyard speaking to a group of men in the market-place at a time when the day was almost over. 'How is it, he said to them, that you are standing here, and have done nothing all the day? They told him, It is because nobody has hired us.'[54] A sceptical mind might think that perhaps they had hurried but gently in search of work, and that they must have spent the day strolling about, gossiping and drowsing in the shade. But many Christians feel themselves too much 'workers of the eleventh hour' to throw a stone at those to whom, after all, the master was to pay an unhoped-for wage.

WHO WERE THE *AM-HA-AREZ?*

There was one class of workers, however, whom the doctors of the Law to a man detested, and against whom they preached a horrified hatred. They were called the *am-ha-arez*. A very curious anthology could be made from all those Talmudic texts in which the fury of the rabbis (a far from violent or bloody-minded class of men) bursts out against these people. The gentle rabbi Hillel asserted, 'They have no conscience, and they are anything but human'. Rabbi Jonathan hoped that every one of these wretches might be split in two: yes, in two, like a fish. 'A Jew must not marry the daughter of an *am-ha-arez*,' it was said. Why? Because the sacred book of Deuteronomy said, in its twenty-seventh chapter, 'Cursed be the man who mates with any beast'. As for the rabbi Eleazar, he said, 'It is allowable to quarter an *am-ha-arez* on the Sabbath day, and even upon the Day of Atonement'. And when his disciples, somewhat astonished, suggested that perhaps the word 'slaughter' might be better, he replied, 'The slaughtering of an animal calls for a blessing: quartering does not'. No doubt one must take these civilities with a grain of salt, but even so they are the evidence of a remarkable state of mind.

Who, then, were these *am-ha-arez*? The word means 'the people of the land' or 'the people of the earth'; but in the course of time it had, in fact, covered a wide variety of human groups.[54] In the first place they were the rich Canaanites like that man from whom Abraham was obliged to buy the field and the cave of Machpelah,[55] then the Israelite landed proprietors who had sometimes played a quasi-official role during the time of the kings,[56] but who were despised by the soldiers and the priests. Then immediately after the exile the expression became totally insulting, and this for a very simple reason: during the Jews' absence in Babylon the lands of Palestine had, as we have seen,[57] been occupied by people of various races, Samaritans, Aramaeans, Philistines and even Mesopotamians; and the returning Jews had never forgiven them this usurpation.

To this very natural feeling of resentment there was added the contempt, or indeed the hatred of the practising Jew for those who, although they were circumcised, did not observe the Law. That was the great reproach, and it was still to be heard on the lips of those Pharisees in Saint John, 'As for these common folk who have no knowledge of the Law, a curse is on them'.[58] As the doctors of the Law had acquired more and more influence in the Jewish community the contempt for the *am-ha-arez* had increased; and it was now reinforced by the contempt of the learned man for the illiterate. The formal definition of the *am-ha-arez* in the Talmud is, 'He who does not eat his bread in a state of ritual cleanliness',[59] that is to say, he who plays fast and loose with the Torah. It was not a mere chance that Galilee was thought of as the chief centre of the *am-ha-arez* and that it was so much abused by the rabbis of Judaea; for it was in this province that the mixture of races had been greatest, to such a degree, indeed, that the very name of the place, as we have seen, meant 'the circle of the unbelievers'.[60] A little before the disaster of the year 70, that is to say, at a time when the rabbis had very strong reasons to mistrust the class and the region from which the chief ring-leaders of the Christian sect had sprung, the rabbi Jochanan ben Zakai wrote, 'Galilee, Galilee, thou hast always hated the Law'. There seems to be no doubt that the hatred of the *am-ha-arez* was based far more on religion than upon any social reasons. But the *Encyclopaedia Judaica*, in the article that it devotes to the *am-ha-arez*, judiciously observes, 'This attitude contributed a great deal to the strengthening of the new sect of Christians. Among them, the 'people of the land' found a loving welcome, whereas on the part of the learned they met with nothing but the most violent repulsion. Christianity did not receive those who came to it with the Pharisees' rigid requirements as to the faithful observation of the Law, but it had a greater understanding of the people's way of life.'

'BEATI POSSEDENTES'

The great mass of the people of Israel, then, was made up of the workers on the land and the workers at the various trades, the *am-ha-arez* and the slaves. In spite of the natural wealth of Palestine these people, as a whole, were poor, and even very poor: S. W. Baron goes so far as to say 'of a horrifying poverty', but perhaps this may be a little too strong. And yet in reading the Gospels one has the impression of great economic stringency: the woman who has lost a piece of silver spends hours searching the house for it;[61] the sum of a hundred pieces of silver seems enormous,[62] although the denarius was worth less than one gold franc* – yet a denarius was a day-labourer's wage,[63] the ordinary cost of a day's living.[64] The poverty of the Jews was even a stock subject for mirth in the pagan comedies, in which they were shown as beggars, with only one shirt apiece, obliged to feed themselves on carobs. 'The daughters of Israel are beautiful,' said one rabbi sadly, 'it is a pity that they should be made ugly by poverty.'[65]

*About 2s. 10d.

One also gains the impression from the New Testament, the Talmud and Josephus that the middle class had no existence, or almost none. The bourgeoisie, as we understand it, is a recent phenomenon; but at Rome and in Greece there were people of intermediate standing, somewhere between the rich and the poor. In Palestine they would only have been found in the Greek cities, which did not belong to the Chosen People. The great majority of the traders were small shopkeepers, practically the same as artisans who sold their own products. Men of what we would call the liberal professions were ranked either among the artisans (the medical man is listed next to the weaver and the carpenter) or in the religious categories. A Jewish bourgeois would have been found only in the Diaspora.

However, there were certainly rich people – that wealthy young man who came to see Jesus, for instance, or the evil rich man of the parable whom we find in Saint Luke 'clothed in purple and lawn, and feasting sumptuously every day',[66] or that one of whom Saint James speaks, with a gold ring on his finger.[67] Everything goes to show that at the time of Christ there was, in Israel, a more than moderately wealthy class of men, that they were often hard to the poor, and that they led a luxurious kind of life, spending in one day more than a labourer could earn in a year. Their wives dressed splendidly and ruined themselves in jewels and scent. This was nothing new. Long before, Amos, the prophetic shepherd, had thundered against rich women, whom he had termed 'kine of Bashan',* accusing them of ill-treating their servants and warning them that in the day of God's wrath they would be 'trussed on spears'.[68] It seems plain that the species had not died out, or rather that it had come into being again after the catastrophe of the exile. Yet not all the rich were necessarily evil: there were good men among them, like Joseph of Arimathaea, who gave his new tomb to the disciples after the crucifixion, or that open-handed Nicanor who gave the Temple the famous bronze door which needed twenty men to open it.[69]

Yet one must not fall into exaggeration: this class of wealthy Jews cannot have been numerous, particularly in Palestine. And if some fortunes, such as that of the Herods, were indeed remarkable, many others would only have seemed so by the contrast

*The Knox Version has: 'pampered cattle that dwell at Samaria'. 'Ye fat kine' is the Douay Version, and the Vulgate: '*Vaccae pingues, quae estis in monte Samariae.*'

with the surrounding poverty. What was the source of this wealth? It appears to have come primarily from the land: there was a class of great landed proprietors who had been able to acquire and to increase vast domains, men like those whom Isaiah had already in his day accused of 'acquiring house after house, field after neighbouring field, till all the world goes wanting',[70] those monopolists upon whom the prophet Micah had called down the curse of God.[71] Judging by the Gospel, it seems that many of these capitalists thought of land only as a form of investment; they did not exploit it themselves, but entrusted it to a steward, a *vilicus* or *oikonomos*, who was certainly a freeman and who at least in theory took care of everything; though as the parables say, the dishonest steward would often cheat his master.[72] But in spite of our very faulty documentation upon land-holding in Israel the impression remains that the small farmers far out-numbered the great capitalist proprietors: in any case there is no evidence for the existence of latifundia, those immense holdings so usual in Italy.

Another source of wealth was trade, above all wholesale trade; and since the return from exile the Jews had acquired a certain ability in this,[73] although Josephus asserts that they had no taste for it.[74] Wholesale trade, import and export, banking: at the time of Christ, as in our days, big business brought in big returns – a hundred times more than investment in land, according to the Talmud.[75] There must have been a good many business-men among the Jews; and there were even some among the earliest Christians, for Saint James gives them a grave warning.[76] Their way of doing business was not widely different from ours.[77] There were no doubt very rich men among them, and also among those who farmed the taxes, according to the pernicious fiscal system of the time.[78]

To these must be added (though perhaps they form a class hardly distinguishable from the great landed proprietors, the big business-men and the bankers) the members of that small group near the seat of power who associated with the Romans. The descendants of the ancient biblical kings may no longer have had wealth or importance (Joseph and Mary descended from David), but the Herods lived in the grandest manner; so did the remaining Asmoneans and the families of the high priests. They owned immense landed fortunes and they had shares in trading concerns. When the Jews sent a delegation to complain of

Herod to Augustus one of their chief grievances was that he had engrossed real estate beyond all reckoning. Josephus states that he had a thousand talents of gold (a hundred and fifty million gold francs or about twenty-one million pounds sterling), and his taxes, duties and levies must have added greatly to this. All his descendants appear to have lived in the utmost wealth – palaces in Palestine, palaces at Rome, splendour in their court and their travels. The high officials of these wealthy rulers made their own fortunes by the age-old means of bribery, as Josephus[79] tells us angrily. The relatives of the high priests, who, as we have seen, were very closely connected with the supreme power,[80] took advantage of their amenability and also lived in a high state of splendour. One of these was that Martha, the daughter of Boethos, who bought the office of high priest for her second husband, Simon ben Gamala, at the price of three *qabs*, or about a gallon and a half, of gold pieces; she insisted upon having a carpet unrolled for her every time she went to the Temple, and she died, during the siege of 70, not from a Roman arrow, but from having to eat a coarser fare than she was accustomed to. But it goes without saying that not all the eighteen thousand priests and Levites who made up the priestly class were men of wealth.

A CLASS APART: THE SCRIBES

In any case, the priestly class, which was increasingly torn between rich and poor (with eighteenth-century France in mind one might almost say between the high and the low clergy), had little remaining importance. It was confined now to its purely religious functions, and it was no longer what it had formerly been, particularly during the exile – the people's guide, its living conscience and the guardian of the traditions of Israel. By a very strange phenomenon, the priests of Yahweh had brought into being a new class which was presently to enter into competition with them, and this exactly in proportion to the zeal with which they had upheld faithfulness to the Law. The Torah was Israel's safeguard: all Israel's hopes lay in it. Therefore it was essential to scrutinize it, to magnify it, to probe all its teachings and to make it in fact the spiritual nourishment of the Chosen People. It was thus that the class of scribes came into existence, even during the Babylonian exile: and it was a class that was to have a very remarkable growth.[81]

The scribes were theoretically divided into *mebhinim*, jurists, and *soferim*, writers or actual scribes, the first settling the religious law and the second handing it on, but in fact the same man might have both functions; and they were charged with uttering the commandments of Yahweh.[82] It was the scribes who, under Ezra and then Hezekiah and Josiah, undertook that great work of organisation of the Holy Scriptures after the exile which resulted in the Old Testament, almost as we know it now. They were acknowledged as being 'learned in the Law', and little by little they set themselves up in contrast to that class of priests whose competence extended no further than the offering of sacrifices and the burning of incense. Ezra, who was of priestly birth, is typical of their development, their state of mind and their manner of life: the Bible, furthermore, never calls him anything but 'scribe'.[83] The circumstances had all been in their favour: the Chosen People having become an entirely religious community and nothing else, those who were profoundly versed in theology necessarily took on a very great importance. As we have seen,[84] they had succeeded in gaining entry to the Sanhedrim, and once there, they very soon began to play a considerable part.

By the time of Christ they had gained the upper hand. The coming of the synagogue, that meeting house in which the Scriptures were expounded but in which no sacrifice was made,[85] had given them a great advantage over the priests; and there were synagogues everywhere. The most eminent scribes had the flattering title of doctor of the Law,[86] and in speaking they were called rabbi, master.[87] It was these high-ranking scribes who taught in those schools to which the pick of the young men came for their learning,[88] and some of them – the rabbis Hillel, Shammai and Gamaliel, for example – drew crowds of students. As law was essentially a religious matter, they had necessarily to be consulted whenever it was a question of meting out justice; and it may be said, indeed, that they laid down the philosophy of human law. They were not all Pharisees, as one might be led to suppose by seeing how often the scribes and the Pharisees are mentioned together in the Gospels, how often they are treated as birds of a feather; but they were all passionately given to biblical study and to textual exposition, and they were all fertile commentators, rich in subtle deductions. It was the teachings of their leaders that made up the Talmud.[89]

It is undeniable that they formed a class apart, or more exactly, a caste. Their recruits came from the most varied backgrounds, many being, as we have seen, men of the people, working with their hands. Others, like the rabbi Jochanan ben Zakkai, had been traders. But the fact of having pursued the same studies, of having thought deeply over the same problems and of having the same interests, created exceedingly powerful bonds between them all, even when they spoke violently against one another in public controversy. Jesus acknowledged their learning[90] and would even dispute with them, but he reproached them with having immobilized tradition instead of obeying the living voice of God and with having become so obsessed by the letter of the Law that in the end they had forgotten its spirit. Yet their importance is evident from the manner in which the evangelists speak of them: there were not a great many in the provinces, though Saint Luke mentions some in Galilee,[91] but they abounded in Jerusalem. Their class was so tightly organized, so coherent, that a great many of them succeeded in escaping at the time of the disaster in the year 70; and after the ruin of Jerusalem they reassembled in the little town of Jamnia, to the south of the Sea of Galilee, which they made into a religious centre, and here the greater part of the Talmud was compiled.

RELATIONS BETWEEN THE CLASSES

It may be asked whether this Jewish society, whose constituent parts have just been passed in review, was a well-balanced community. Were its classes in harmony with one another? Truth compels us to say that it appears that they were not. Obviously there are some invectives and polemics that must not be taken at their face-value any more than in our day we are to accept the recriminations of the extremist papers as being literally true; but nevertheless, one has the impression that in Israel there was a considerable amount of disagreement between the classes. One disillusioned rabbi wrote, 'God created humanity in a single specimen, undoubtedly in order that all the families who were to descend from this one man should not quarrel among themselves. But when one now sees so much disagreement one may well ask oneself, What would it have been like if God had made two Adams?'[92] There was nothing new about this situation in the time of Christ. Jesus the son of Sirach, that patrician who in about 175 B.C. wrote Ecclesiasticus, his famous treatise on wisdom, had already observed, 'Pot and kettle are ill matched; it is the pot breaks when they come together; rich man, that has seized all he can, frets and fumes for more; poor man robbed may not so much as speak'.[93]

There is a wealth of documents that show a lively enmity between the classes. The *Assumption of Moses*, one of those apocalyptic writings which flourished at that time,[94] is full of bitter indictments of the wealthy, 'who eat the goods of the poor, who think of nothing but feasting, who bear themselves like princes';[95] and the man who wrote these avenging pages extends the limits of the wealthy class very wide indeed, for he includes all the Pharisees. The great priestly families were particular marks for dislike. A wide-spread complaint against them, which is to be found in two places in the Talmud,[96] tells us what the common people thought of the great men of the Temple: 'House of Boethus? Woe upon us, beware their whip! House of Cantharos? Woe upon us, beware their pen![97] House of Annas? Woe upon us, beware their adder's hiss! House of Ishmael ben Phali? Woe upon us, beware their blows! They themselves are high priests and their sons treasurers and their fathers-in-law great men of the Temple. As for their servants, they fall upon us with cudgels.' The scribes were equally disliked. The rabbi Akiba said to his disciples, 'Before I became a scribe myself, I thought, "Ah, if only I had one in my grasp, I would bite him like an ass." ' 'Master,' said a disciple, 'would it not have been enough to bite him like a dog?' 'No, like an ass,' replied the sage, 'For an ass bites better: he crushes the very bones.'[98] The *am-ha-arez*, and no wonder, were thought to be particularly strong in their hatred for all other classes and especially the scribes and the doctors of the Law, who despised them so. 'They hate us,' said the rabbi Eliezer, 'even more than the pagans hate Israel. If they did not need us to buy their produce from them, they would kill us.'[99]

It appears that the society's equilibrium was uncertain, its solidity precarious. The hostility between the classes was continually breaking out on slight pretexts, and it took on the colour of political and social reasons. The common people, being wretched, clung desperately to what hope they had and to any men who, while upholding the faith, would offer them a happier future: it was this that gave the Pharisees and even the extremist Zealots their influence. It was easy to say that the rich and the powerful had sold themselves to the Romans and that they were more than half paganized, for it was very largely true. The inequality of fortunes and the disparity between the different ways of life was too great: even within the priestly class there was a genuine proletariate, ready to make common cause with the rebels. A crushing system of taxation helped to keep the country in misery – a country which should ordinarily have lived in modest but certain comfort. If a drought came, or an invasion of locusts, it meant famine and the sound of the people's fury.

This is one of the sides of daily life in Palestine at the time of Christ that is very rarely considered; yet it had considerable importance in history. One should never forget that in Israel at that period there existed a proletariate, and even a class below that, made up of ill-paid workers (one denarius a day: four or five at the very most), day-labourers with unemployment hanging over their heads, downtrodden *am-ha-arez*, more or less circumcised slaves, freedmen whose masters would not always give them that little sum that the Law desired them to give, beggars, poverty-stricken in the streets, and, it must be remembered, lepers and cripples for whom there was no hospital.[100] It was among these despised people, these outcasts, that Christ's message first spread, and that it went on spreading. And in the same way, when the economic crisis of the first century had made the misery even worse, it was among them that the uprising was prepared, the insurrection, as much social as it was religious and political, which brought the Chosen People to the great disaster of the year 70.

CHAPTER FOUR

SOCIETY'S IMPERATIVE COMMANDS

An obligation unknown to the Jews – The heavy burden of taxes – Human justice a dirty rag – Judges and courts – Civil law – Crimes and misdemeanours; punishments and penalties.

AN OBLIGATION UNKNOWN TO THE JEWS

Ever since organized societies came into being the individual has always been obliged, however little he may like it, to obey three imperative requirements of the collective authority: he has always had to bear arms, to pay taxes, in one shape or another, and, more generally, to obey the laws enforced by the judicial power. The Jews were spared one of these three obligations. Josephus states[1] that they had obtained, in their own country, a complete exemption from military service. Was this prudence on the part of the Roman authorities? Probably it was, but in any case there was the fact; and it was very much appreciated by the followers of Yahweh, who would have been most uneasy at having to fight in the ranks of the pagans.

This nation, therefore, which had formerly held the art of war in such high esteem, was now disarmed; the Bible had praised its heroes from the song of Deborah[2] to the epic of the Maccabees, but now the people of David, that warrior-king, had no army. The last leader of Israel who still had any claims to being a soldier was the Idumaean Herod, who had studded the country with fortifications, Alexandrium, Hyrcanium, Masada, Machaerus, and above all the two most famous, the Antonia tower, which guarded (and supervised) the Temple, and the Herodium, which was destined to be his tomb. But although his army was excellent it was made up solely of Idumaean cavalry, Thracian archers, and Germanic, Gaulish or Galatian infantry. His descendants were only able to keep a very few troops in their provincial tetrarchies; and Herod Agrippa himself, the builder of Jerusalem's new wall, might only have a few centuries of hired foreign soldiers. At the time of Christ no Jew carried arms, except for the guards of the Temple, who were something between porters and policemen, and the Samaritans, those false Jews, those outcasts, who would gladly engage in the Roman army, so as to do the opposite of what a true Jew would do.

The soldiers and the officers one finds in the New Testament were therefore certainly not Jews; nor would they have belonged to the Roman legions, which were, as we have seen, stationed in Syria, but to the auxiliary formations, few in number, that remained in Palestine.[3] The centurions, those company-commanders who all play such sympathetic parts in the Gospels and the Acts, were of course pagans: the centurion of Capernaum, for example, an officer in the service of Herod Antipas, the tetrarch of Galilee; the centurion named Cornelius, at Caesarea, 'who belonged to what is called the Italian cohort', as the Bible says,[4] and who was probably a Roman officer, of Italian birth, sent to command Samaritan or Thracian troops; or Julius, the centurion charged with taking Saint Paul to Rome, and who was perhaps one of those *evocati Augusti* who were detached from the praetorian guard for police or liaison duties.[5]

The fact that there were no Jewish soldiers does not mean that the Jews had no weapons, however. Among the modern Arabs it would be impossible to think of life without a rifle: it must have been much the same in Israel two thousand years ago. Quite apart from the curved scimitars which the great men carried as ornamental weapons, it is clear from well-known texts that the people were possessed of arms: among others there are those in which all four evangelists show us the worthy Saint Peter, on the evening of Christ's arrest, drawing his sword and cutting off the ear of Malchus, the high priest's servant.[6] In Jewish households there would also have been hunting-weapons that could be turned to other purposes: hardwood bows with gut strings, and slings exactly like that with which the young David slew Goliath or those which the Benjaminites wielded so well that they 'could sling a stone without missing their aim by a hair's breadth'.[7]

Only the existence of household arms can explain the fact that whenever the many revolts broke out against the Herods, or later against the Romans, it was always easy to bring considerable bodies of combatants into the field. But their existence would not have been enough if there had not at the same time been an ideal among the people, if the soul of Israel had been disarmed. Many signs showed that the Jews had not lost their warlike spirit; for although they were glad not to serve in the pagan Roman army, many of them dreamed of a war of liberation. There was even a recrudescence of the ancient idea of a holy war, not in the sense of the *jihad* of the Koran, for the concept of a war of religion, of conversion by force of arms, had always been foreign to the Jewish tradition, but in the sense of a war desired by Yahweh and directed by Him and in which His people would join as an act of faith. In the time of the kings war had taken on altogether too much of a political and a conquering character, but the idea had come to life again with the Maccabees, when Judas and his brothers 'fought Israel's battle'[8] and when God Himself sent His angel on the road to Bethsura.[9] Were these times not to return? Would not Yahweh launch the final struggle, the supreme attack? Among the Dead Sea scrolls[10] there is an extraordinary manuscript of apparently a little before the time of Christ which gives an account of the battle between the Sons of Light and the Sons of Darkness, which was to take place at the end of time. No doubt for those who wrote it down it had an essentially spiritual meaning. It is a call to a holy war, one in which the Lord of Battles is to lead His faithful troops and His angels against Belial and his empire; and on the standards will be written *The Right Hand of God*, the *Moment of God*, and *God's Slaughter*.[11] This document was certainly widely known in Israel; and it may be that Christ Himself refers to it when He speaks of 'the children of light'.[12] But from a wordly point of view, did it not also interpret the deep longings of the now disarmed 'conquerors in the name of the Lord'?[13]

THE HEAVY BURDEN OF TAXES

In being excused military service, the Jews were spared the payment of the tax of blood; but the taxes that they did have to pay in money and in kind were exceedingly heavy, and they were all the heavier in that two forms of taxation ran side by side for them, civil taxes and religious taxes; and neither was light.

The first were of great antiquity in Israel. They were at least as old as Solomon, who had ingeniously divided his realm into twelve districts, each of which in turn had to supply his needs.[14] This system, naturally, had been kept and improved upon. At times of great crisis there had even been capital levies, as for example under Menahem to pay the Assyrian tribute[15] and under Jehoiakim of Judah to pay the sum required by the Pharaoh Nechoh.[16] Yet these were still taxes raised by the government of Israel for the glory or the safety of the Chosen People. But after the return from exile the taxation became far more bitter to the people, since the taxes were to be paid to pagans, Persians,[17] Greeks from Egypt and then from Syria, and then Romans or Roman vassals. Herod the Great, particularly, made himself so unpopular by the severity of the impositions that he laid on the people to finance his immense undertakings and his ostentatious policy that on several occasions he was forced to grant a remission in order to prevent an outbreak of rage. His heirs the tetrarchs modestly followed his example: in direct taxes alone Archelaus raised six hundred talents (somewhat more than three million gold francs or £450,000) in Judaea and Samaria; and Galilee brought in two hundred for Antipas.

In that part of Palestine which was incorporated into the Roman empire after the year AD 6, the Roman system of taxation was established; and it was the same rapacious system that was known everywhere else. Even Tacitus, who is so hostile to the Jews, lets it be understood that it was this taxation that was the immediate cause of the great rising.[18] There were then, as there are in our modern states, direct taxes and indirect taxes: Saint Paul refers explicitly to both. [19] The first, which were collected by agents of the imperial treasury, included on the one hand a tax on real property, affecting all producers, especially land-owners, which was paid in kind and which is estimated to have amounted to between twenty and twenty-five per cent of the product; and on the other hand a capitation or poll-tax, which was perhaps in proportion to the payer's wealth: it was about the lawfulness of this last tax that the Pharisees questioned Jesus one day, trying to draw Him into an embarrassing position.[20] The indirect taxes were more like the import duties and internal customs of some European countries than our sales-tax: they were collected at certain bridges, fords, important crossroads, the entries into towns and the market-places; and thus we find Matthew 'sitting at work in the customs-house' at Capernaum.[21]

These indirect taxes were made far heavier by their manner of collection. They were farmed, as the salt-tax and the aids were in France as late as the eighteenth century. Under the supreme control of a financial procurator, who had to be a Roman knight, the farmers-general (they might be individuals or groups) signed a contract, usually for five years, by which they agreed to pay the state a fixed sum in return for being allowed to reimburse themselves by collecting the dues as they saw fit. For this they raised a whole army of tax-gatherers, with officers (Luke speaks of the small-statured Zacchaeus as 'the chief publican'[22]), gaugers and inferior minions. It need scarcely be said that under such a system every form of dishonesty was possible, and as Jesus Himself implies, the tax-gatherers would claim 'more than their right'.[23] The employees of the revenue department were therefore cordially hated and despised; partly because they stole and partly because they served the pagans. These men were the notorious publicans who are to be met with so often in the Gospels, and whose very name was synonymous with public sinner, contemptible creature, outcast of society. Everywhere they were seen, with their stick in their hand and their brass plate on their chest, peering in their grasping and rapacious manner into bales and containers. The Talmud[24] says that they formed a positive caste; and when one member of a family became a publican, all the rest followed him. The example of Zacchaeus proves that there were good and generous men among them, that excellent little Zacchaeus who gave 'half of what he had to the poor, and if he had wronged anyone in any way, made restitution of it fourfold'. And it is quite certain that there were admirable souls, like that publican who stood 'afar off' and humbly in the Temple and prayed so well to God.[25] But on the whole, it is comprehensible that this breed of men was not widely popular.

The civil taxes were not the only ones: the religious taxes were to be paid as well as those that the Romans collected. They went back to the remotest antiquity: had not Abraham 'given the tithes of all he had won' to the Almighty?[26] But since then the system had been much improved: the rabbis listed no less than twenty-four dues that were owing to the religious authorities, and they exhorted the faithful to pay them with the greatest care. It may be supposed, however, from the repetition of the homilies upon this theme, that the Jews were not always over-eager with their payments. These religious taxes were recognised by the Romans and they had an official character: the Temple authorities were given great facilities for the collection of the money, and its transport was protected by the imperial troops.[27]

In a general manner, these religious taxes fell into two categories. The Temple tax, or rather the true Temple offering, was intended for the upkeep of the sanctuary and the costs of the officiating priests. It was collected everywhere, in Palestine as well as in the Jewish communities of the Diaspora, from the fifteenth day of Adar onwards, that is to say, during the month which preceded the feast of the Passover. Every adult Israelite, by which was meant every Israelite of over thirteen, had to pay it, whether he was rich or poor. Traditionally it was half a shekel, as Yahweh Himself had stated to Moses that that was the amount.[28] We know from a very exact verse in Saint Matthew[29] that at the time of Christ it was a didrachma, or about five shillings.

This was very little, in comparison with the tithes. In principle the payment of tithes meant the payment of a tenth part of everything that the soil produced, and it was the very type of religious obligation. For was not Yahweh the owner of the earth, and was it not thanks to Him that the fruits of the earth were to be had? It was therefore but right to offer a share to Him, the 'first-fruits of all the crops' which as far back as the days of the desert were put in a basket and carried to the sanctuary 'with rejoicings in all the good things that He had given His people'.[30] These first-fruits were now taken by the priests, and not returned to the producer as they had been in early times, and they had become a due which the priests insisted upon most strictly, sending out Levites to collect it and insisting that everything, however small, should be tithed. The rabbis had laid down the principle that all untithed products of the soil were unclean and that the eating of them was an exceedingly grave sin. The sheep of a flock were to be tithed just as much as the eggs from the poultry-yard or even, as we see in the Gospel,[31] the humblest plants used in the kitchen, such as mint, dill and cummin. It was only during the sabbatical year that the tithe was not due, for in that year, at least in theory, both the land and its workers were to rest.

However onerous the tithes may have been, particularly when they were added to all the other taxes, they were still paid more willingly than the dues that had to be given to the occupying authorities. Indeed, the getting ready of the carts that were to take the first-fruits to the Temple was something of a rural holiday. There was a proper and accepted way of preparing the carts: the barley had to be put in first, at the bottom, then the wheat and the dates, then the pomegranates, the figs and the olives, and at the very top, the grapes. Properly loaded and decorated with branches and flowers, the carts met at one of the twenty-four centres,[32] then they were led off in picturesque processions to the sound of psalms as far as Jerusalem, where they were joyfully welcomed by the priestly dignitaries and by crowds of the ordinary people. It would be pleasant to think that these rejoicings made the burden of taxes, dues and payments seem less overwhelming.

HUMAN JUSTICE A DIRTY RAG

The third obligation that society imposes upon the individual, that of obeying the laws and of being punished in case of infraction, was made heavier and more complex by the fact of the Roman occupation. Judaea, being an annexed country, came under the justice of the emperor: his *edicta*, *mandata*, *decreta* and *rescripta* were law, as they were in all other imperial provinces; the master's representative, the procurator, was therefore the supreme judge in all cases except those in which Jews who were also Roman citizens were involved, for they had the right of appeal to Caesar – the right that Saint Paul was to exercise.[33] It is exceedingly probable that the Romans supervised justice even in the little tetrarchies of the descendants of Herod. Yet according to their invariable practice the Romans left the people of the country a wide autonomy in legal and in administrative affairs: they saw no harm in cases being settled according to Jewish Law, outside their courts. They did not interfere except to calm excessive excitement, and they reserved to themselves only the most serious decisions, as we see from Pilate's role in the trial of Christ.

Law, among the Jews, was of the greatest antiquity, and it was very highly developed; which is the same as saying that its essence was religious. The Bible supplied Israel with all the fundamental legal data, just as today the Koran acts as both penal and civil code for the world of Islam. This had always been so among the Chosen People; at least it was certainly held to have been the case ever since the time when Moses said, 'Some dispute arises among them, and they come to me so that I may make a just award between them telling them of the decrees which God issues, and of his law'.[34] In fact the Bible contained three codes; the oldest, which was based upon the extremely ancient customary law and which was no doubt drawn up a thousand years before our era, was contained in what is termed the Book of the Covenant, that is to say, chapters twenty to twenty-three of Exodus; the second, later and more highly developed, forms the heart of Deuteronomy, chapters twenty-one to twenty-six, and it must have been laid down in about 622 BC, being the inspiration of Josiah's reforms; and lastly the third, which was brought into existence by a whole school of priestly lawyers during the Babylonian exile, and which was put into force immediately after the return by Esdras:[35] this code forms the essence of Levitivus. And from the fifth century BC onwards the scribes and the doctors of the Law had continually meditated upon this *corpus juris divini*, making glosses upon it and multiplying those statements upon jurisprudence which were to be incorporated bodily into the tractates of the Talmud and which made Jewish Law so remarkable a jungle. These origins explain the essential nature of the whole system: the Law, in its penal as in its civil aspect, was not really concerned with compensating an injured party nor making an example, still less with reclaiming a transgressor, but solely with satisfying a God angered by wrong-doing. The one fundamental command of Jewish Law was summed up in the admirable formula of Leviticus, 'Be holy as I am holy',[36] and the purpose of human law was to realize this ideal on earth. 'The spirit of God', said the tractate *Makkoth*, 'must shine upon the *Beth Din*, the house of judgment.'[37] But the followers of Yahweh knew only too well how great a chasm sinful human nature sets between the ideal and its application, and they had a contempt for all merely human justice, a contempt that Isaiah splendidly expressed in likening it to 'a clout a woman casts away'.[38]

JUDGES AND COURTS

The constitution of the law-courts shows the union of law and religion very clearly. The Great Sanhedrim was a court of law as well as a political council and, as we have seen,[39] a theological academy. Indeed, we know it best in this aspect, because of the trial of Jesus, and, later, of Saint Paul.[40] As a court of law it was the highest of them all, being both the final court of appeal and a kind of supreme court which could take cognisance of cases of the utmost gravity, above all, that is to say, those which concerned religion. When this court was in plenary session, with the *Ab Beth Din* as president, it sat in the *Liscat Haggazith*, the hall of polished stones, which dated from the time of King Jannaeus. This was part of the Temple and it was within the sacred enclosure, but it opened outwards on to the Court of the Gentiles, into which anyone might go: the judges came in from the Temple end and the accused from the other. For the less important matters it was not necessary to assemble all seventy members of the Sanhedrim; twenty-three were enough to make a *halakha*, a deliberation, valid, but it was laid down that the judge might leave only if he had made sure that the quorum would still be complete after his departure. The sittings took place on Mondays and Thursdays: there were none on the Sabbath or any great feast day. It sometimes happened that the Great Sanhedrim would sit at night, but in that case it was not allowed to pass a sentence of death. It appears that the power of the court declined very much shortly after Christ's death, for Herod Agrippa and after him the procurators distrusted it on political grounds: it was even prevented from sitting in the hall of polished stones. Nevertheless, it survived the fall of Jerusalem, and moving from place to place, it lasted until the end of the fourth century. The quarter of the strictly practising Jews, Bet Shearim, now prides itself on having been one of its last seats.

But well before this it had lost its territorial jurisdiction in a decentralization that Josephus attributes to the legate Gabinius.[41] Four 'courts of twenty-three judges' (that is to say, bodies not unlike the parliaments of pre-revolutionary France) were set up at Jericho, Sepphoris in Galilee, Amath and Gadara. Yet for a great while there had been local courts, 'little sanhedrims'. Every regularly constituted community had its own, which judged minor cases; but its penal sentences could not exceed scourging, and only thirty-nine strokes, at that.[42] It was ordinarily composed of three members, at least in theory; for the rabbis taught that no being may judge alone except the Almighty';[43] yet as competent people were sometimes hard to be found in the country districts, it was allowed that 'a single man might decide without colleagues or assessors, if the parties publicly declared that they would accept his decision'.[44]

There were very strict rules as to the qualities required in a judge. 'In civil matters, any Israelite is qualified to judge,' said the rabbis, 'but in criminal cases, only priests, Levites and members of those families who may marry their daughters to priests,[45] are to be chosen as judges.' There is a passage in the tractate *Sanhedrin* which shows the ideal judge, a great and dignified man, able to speak 'the seventy languages' so that he never has need of an interpreter, acquainted with the magic arts so as to be prepared for the cunning of sorcerers and other necromancers:[46] he was not to be too young nor too old, nor a eunuch; nor must he be a hard-hearted man, added the rabbi Judah.[47] The judges were not paid. 'The judgments of any man who has received fees are invalid.'[48]

About the judges there naturally swarmed a whole army of secretaries, ushers, men charged with carrying out the court's orders and those whom the Greeks ironically termed *hyperetes*, secondary rowers, or wholly useless people. The best known of these was the *hazzam*, so often spoken of in Talmudic literature: he was an important man, combining in his person beadle, usher, clerk of the court, official scourger and gaoler. Saint Matthew's Gospel shows how formidable he was.[49]

Procedure, too, was carefully regulated. Scores and even hundreds of verses in the Bible lay down the rules for it, and the doctors of the Law had studied them so profoundly that no doubt there was no single detail that had not been provided for. The tractate *Sanhedrin* contains a collection of a great number of these precepts: their scrupulousness does honour to the rabbis' juridical sense and to their feeling for equity.[50] A case was never initiated by what we would term the public prosecutor. In a civil case the initiative belonged to the parties concerned; in a criminal, an accuser was required. It was therefore for the injured person or for the victim's relatives, or even for any person who had knowledge or suspicion of a crime to tell the judges and indeed to sue. An adultress, for instance, might be denounced by her husband or by popular outcry. This way of proceeding was less dangerous than one might suppose, for the accusers were severely punished if they had brought their charges against an innocent person. The disgusting elders who had falsely accused the chaste Susanna were put to death when she was saved at the last moment by the young Daniel; and in memory of this the false accuser always suffered the penalty that the innocent victim would have incurred.[51]

It appears that an enquiry was required to be held before the day of the trial, and that the results of this were gathered together and given to two secretaries. When the time came, each secretary had in his possession the documents concerning one of the sides if it were a civil matter, and if it were a criminal case then one secretary had the papers of the defence and the other those of the accusation. Some doctors, like the rabbi Judah, insisted upon a third secretary in cases where a man's life was at stake, to make sure that the voting was carried out properly.

The sittings, and particularly those of the Great Sanhedrim, were of a most solemn nature. The president, the *Ab Beth Din* in the case of the supreme court, sat in the middle of a wide semi-circle; to his right and his left the seventy judges were ranged in order of seniority. The public, consisting mostly of the disciples of the rabbis who were members of the council, sat facing them. Behind them stood a quantity of servants, ushers, beadles and guards. The *Shema Israel* was recited before the cases were begun. Even a scamped session, hurried along in a most irregular way, like that in which Jesus was tried, still gives the impression of solemnity.

A very curious point in the Jewish procedure was that circumstantial evidence, however strong, was inadmissible; there had to be witnesses, best of all eye-witnesses, for those who had heard but not seen were not believed. When it was desired to disconcert a suspect, it was usual to hide two witnesses behind a curtain, so arranged that they might see the prisoner, who had two lights put by him. Two witnesses were required:[52] it was the same in Roman law, which had the axiom of *testis unus* – 'a single witness is never to be believed'. The witnesses' responsibility was therefore exceedingly heavy, so heavy that it was they who were obliged 'to throw the first stone' at the culprit whose condemnation they had brought about.[53] It was this custom that suggested to Jesus the terrible lesson that He gave to those who denounced the woman taken in adultery – 'Whichever of you is free from sin shall cast the first stone . . .' On the other hand, when false witnesses were discovered, they, like the false accusers, were, in theory, to suffer the same punishment that they had wished to bring upon the accused.[54] For this reason witnesses were chosen with the greatest care: women, minors, slaves, the deaf, the dumb and the blind were all set aside as people who lied too easily; the near relations of the accused were also objected to. Did this do away with false witnessing? The reading of the Psalms and the Proverbs and even the Ten Commandments is enough to make one doubt this, quite apart from the famous trials like those of Jesus and of Stephen.[55]

But to avoid it, a very scrupulous interrogation was insisted upon: in what year, on what day, in what hour had the witness seen the crime committed? Did he know the accused? Had he warned him that he was about to break the Law? Any variation in detail – the difference between the mastic-tree and the holm-oak in Susanna's trial – was to be interpreted as favourable to the accused; so was any change of opinion or retraction of an earlier statement. Lastly, the court had the right to require the witness to take an exceedingly solemn oath: there were a very great many of these – by God, by Heaven, by Jerusalem, by the Temple, by the consolation of Israel, by my children, by my share in Paradise. In the Sermon on the Mount,[56] the Gospel plainly says that these oaths did not prevent false witness, and that to false witness they added perjury as well. But the innumerable counsels of prudence and sincerity that the rabbis gave to those who were about to give evidence in court nevertheless did them great honour.

When the accusers and the witnesses had been heard, the accused made his own defence: it does not appear that there were true advocates in Israel as there were in Rome; and yet no doubt certain 'witnesses' would have acted in that capacity, after this the court deliberated and pronounced its sentence. Very great legal precautions were taken so that the verdict should be entirely just, above all in criminal proceedings. During the deliberation, for example, a judge might produce an argument in favour of the accused, but not one against him. The youngest members of the tribunal voted first, as the lowest in rank do in our councils of war. For an acquittal a relative majority was enough; for a sentence of death, two more than the absolute majority of votes was required. If the Sanhedrim was unanimous in condemnation, the sentence was 'deferred', an expression that some rabbis interpreted as meaning 'acquittal because of pre-judice', others as meaning 'to be reflected upon' for at least one night. Finally, the verdict was carried out at once if it meant the liberation of the accused, but postponed for twenty-four hours if it were against him.

It must be granted that all these requirements were most praiseworthy. Were they always carried out? This may be doubted. In troubled times, or when men's minds were disturbed by violent passions, were not these fine principles disregarded? In the trial of Jesus the illegality is so flagrant that in our days commissions of Jewish theologians and lawyers have repeatedly re-tried the case; and that the periodical *Jerusalem* has said that the condemnation was 'one of the most terrible mistakes that men have ever committed'.[57] But in *The Wars of the Jews* Josephus reports the truly abominable trial of one Zachariah ben Baris before the Sanhedrim in the year 67, who, being found innocent, was nevertheless put to death in the Temple itself.[58] The best laws have never been enough to make human justice perfect: Isaiah's 'dirty rags' are always with us.

CIVIL LAW

The three codes in the Bible contain less of civil than of criminal justice. But upon these somewhat fragmentary bases the rabbis were able to build up a whole legal system. For example, there are no less than three whole tractates of the Talmud devoted to damages and compensation and the like; they are the three *Baba*, or gates – the *Baba Kamma*, *Baba Mesia* and *Baba Bathra*. In abiding by fundamental principles one would suppose that they might have produced a concise civil code; but in fact it was, in certain aspects, exceedingly detailed and even curiously minute.

We have already seen the essence of the civil law in as far as it affected the personal rights and marriage,[59] both the one and the other being based upon the religious concept of society and the defence of the family as the social unit. The free adult man was the only person who was a complete civil entity with all civil rights. The head of the family had authority over his wife, his minor son, his unmarried daughter and his slave: the Law or custom set limits to this authority, however, in denying the man the power of life and death and in protecting the wife and the Israelite slave. Particular enactments laid down the law with regard to the foreigner, the sojourner, the *guer*. The Book of the Covenant had already reminded the Israelites that they themselves had been *guers* in Egypt[60] and that remembering their own misery they should be kind to strangers. Deuteronomy had stated that anyone who did not give the *guer* his rights was accursed.[61] Leviticus went further still in commanding, 'Your award must be the same, whether it was citizen or stranger that did the wrong'.[62] This is one of the points in which Jewish law was far more generous than Roman law, and Josephus is right in praising the 'justice of the lawgiver of Israel towards foreigners', which is all the more remarkable, he aptly observes, 'in that no people have

ever taken more care than us to keep our traditional rites unaltered'.[63] There is here a striking contrast between Jewish
exclusiveness, their refusal to make any contact with the unclean
pagans, and this generosity in their Law. Saint Paul was the heir
of the finest, most humane of the traditions of his people when he
cried, 'There is no distinction made here between Jew and
Gentile; all alike have one Lord'.[64]

We have little information about the law of inheritance, although
this forms a considerable part of the legislation of well-organized
societies. The relevant texts are scattered about the Pentateuch,
but some are also to be found in Job, Joshua and the historical
books of the Kings. It appears to have been developed after the
return from exile under the influence of Hellenic law: there was,
for instance, the custom of 'making a will in due and proper form'
referred to by Saint Paul in writing to his Galatian friends;[65] and
this was certainly something new. The rabbis had studied the
question with great earnestness, and they had carefully regulated
the conditions in which a will was valid. Ordinary inheritance,
apart from that which was affected by wills, ran as follows: the
sons or the nearest male relations succeeded, but not the widow;
and the daughters had no right to a share unless they married
within the family, although on the other hand they had to be
maintained by their brothers until they came of age. The first-
born among the sons had a favoured position laid down in
Deuteronomy[66] and certainly still maintained at the time of
Christ, as may be seen by the parable of the Prodigal Son:[67] the
patrimony was divided into equal parts, and of these parts the
eldest son had two. The parable also shows that anticipation of
inheritance was already practised.

As to that side of the Law which concerns civil duties or obligations, it is limited in the Bible to a few rulings upon ownership,
buying and selling, loans, pledges and debts; but the rabbis had
built up a great body of detailed legislation upon this. They had,
for example, established the ownership of lost property subsequently found and the difference between a loan and a deposit;
they had laid down rules for the letting of real and personal
property, not forgetting the cases of the year of thirteen months;[68]
they had settled the time that might elapse between sale and
delivery; and as accurately as the Romans they had fixed the law of
title-deeds and prescriptive ownership. But their scrupulous,
unquenchable zeal was to be seen at its best in their development

of the rules laid down in Exodus upon the subject of damages.[69] The law was based upon the excellent principle that every man is responsible for any injury done by anything that is his; responsible for his ox or his cistern, or the harm that his sheep might do or for a fire passing from his property to his neighbour's. In some cases the responsibility was greater, as for example if a man persisted in keeping an ox known to have the habit of goring people or if he entrusted his sheep to a shepherd who was half-witted, purblind or deaf and dumb.

CRIMES AND MISDEMEANOURS; PUNISHMENTS AND PENALTIES

If the Holy Scriptures are not a systematic and orderly code of civil law, drawn up as neatly as the Code Napoléon, no more are they a complete body of criminal legislation: yet they do provide a great many precepts of penal law scattered in various books; and from these it was not very difficult to form a system. Here again rabbinical teaching added a mass of commentaries and explanations to the biblical texts, and these are to be found in at least a score of Talmudical tractates.

The difference between crimes and misdemeanours was not very well defined: indeed, is it very clear even today? All misdeeds might roughly be classed under five main headings: killing, with an exact distinction between murder and manslaughter; physical violence, with a careful listing in order of seriousness of the various wounds and blows; conduct prejudicial to the family or to morality (thought of as particularly heinous in a society which was, as we have seen, so very much based upon the family as its essential unit) which ranged from marriage within the prohibited degrees to unnatural practices and bestiality, and from the rape of a betrothed girl to the public cursing of a father by his own son; and wrongs done to the property of others, which, in the case of armed or nocturnal robbery, were crimes, as were also the wilful removing of landmarks and the use of false weights. The biblical precepts and the decisions of the rabbis on all these matters show a great deal of thoughtfulness, juridical sense and feeling for justice. It was not murder, for example, to kill a thief who had broken in by night, but killing him by daylight was, for in daylight he might have been seized alive.[70]

But of all kinds of wickedness, the worst in the eyes of the Law and the least pardonable, were crimes against religion. This, given the sacred nature of all Jewish institutions, was perfectly natural: for God's own people there could be no worse fault than rebelling against God, and in a way such an act was very like that which our profane codes term high treason. These shocking crimes had always been punished in Israel: the Covenant itself provided for this. But it must be admitted that the list of them had been considerably lengthened over the centuries, and in the most recent period those specialists, the doctors of the Law, had much enlarged the area within which these crimes could be committed. Idolatry, of course, was a crime; so was the practice of magic, necromancy and even divination; so was blasphemy, and blasphemy stretched as far as the plain wrong use of the Holy But breaking the Sabbath was also a crime worthy of death; and Name: and it may be granted that all this was perfectly in order. refusing to have one's son circumcised or failing to celebrate the Passover were so grave that the culprit was to be outlawed. In the early days, under the influence of primitive taboos, the man who masturbated or lay with a menstruating woman was treated as a criminal: but at the later period the tendency of the priests and the scribes was to consider all men who disobeyed the least ecclesiastical law, above all those concerning the payment of the Temple offering and the tithes,[71] as atheists and rebels against God. There is no sort of doubt that at the time of Christ, the increasing influence of the Pharisees had provided the practising Jew, the ordinary Jew, with a very great number of occasions for crime and misdemeanour.

Punishment was harsh. There was only one penalty for all crimes against religion, and that was death. This was the indictment upon which our Lord was to be condemned. The same applied to a great many other crimes that modern law treats more mildly: among them (under certain conditions, as we have seen) was adultery.[72] Death was also the penalty for any man who made a slave of a Jewish freeman, for any man who used false weights, for the priest's daughter turned whore, for the woman who married concealing her unchastity. But at the time of Christ the harshness of the Jewish system was mitigated by a decision that the Romans had made a little earlier. 'Forty years before the destruction of the Temple,' says the tractate *Sanhedrin*, 'trials involving the death-penalty were taken away from the court.'[73] Other writers think that the Jewish authorities still had the right to examine these cases, but that the Roman procurator reserved the right to authorize or quash the sentence.

The very ancient tribal laws concerning crimes and injuries were still in theory valid. The *lex talionis*, the most famous of these, is to be found no less than three times in the Bible: 'An eye for an eye, a tooth for a tooth, a hand for a hand, a foot for a foot, burning for burning, wound for wound, bruise for bruise'; and, of course, 'life must pay for life.'[74] It seems a shocking commandment: but perhaps in fact its aim was to limit the excess of revenge in ancient times, to prevent 'Cain being avenged seven times over and Lamech seventy times as much', or 'a man being killed for a wound and a stripling for a blow'.[75] The centuries had lessened its severity by allowing that the literal retaliation should be applied only in the case of wilful murder or of wounding so grave that the man could never work again. It is very unlikely that by the time of Christ the *lex talionis* was much enforced: compensation in money had taken its place. This is very far from saying that the people were capable of accepting the great lesson of the Gospel that flatly condemned the old custom of an eye for an eye and a tooth for a tooth and asked men to forgive everything, bidding them 'turn the other cheek also'.[76]

The *lex talionis* was part of the general principle of revenge: vengeance on the part of the community, vengeance on the part of the family, in a word, the vengeance of God. A crime upset the divine order of things: a counterbalancing punishment restored this order. And this, by the way, is the sole justification for the death-penalty, which has been shown a hundred times over to be useless as an example and which can obviously provide the injured with no sort of reparation other than just this psychological satisfaction of revenge. The Bible was therefore absolute on the matter: 'Whoever sheds a man's blood must shed his own blood in return.'[77] Revenge was a sacred duty for the whole family. The nearest relation of a murdered man was to constitute himself the *goel*, the avenger of blood. But here again the Law did its best to limit the effects of this disastrous system: revenge was not to be the same in a case of deliberate murder and in a case of unpremeditated killing;[78] and it was not to reach to the innocent members of the guilty man's family.[79] Was there a 'blood-price', a list of the payments that the criminal or his family could pay to avoid the punishment, as later there was in the Germanic laws? It is sure that there was as far as wounds and injuries were concerned, and it existed too in the case of the death of a slave, when the sum to be paid was thirty pieces of silver, those too-famous thirty pieces that Judas had for betraying Jesus; but it is very doubtful that such a payment could be made when the victim was a freeman. It seems most unlikely, in any case, that the orderly Romans would have let any kind of self-perpetuating vendetta continue in a country occupied by them.

The criminal law was severe, and its punishments and penalties were very stern. The fines for blows and injuries, for culpable negligence (for having dug a ditch or a cistern without warning people, for example), for slander and calumny, for the seduction of maidens and for theft were all carefully fixed: the man who stole an ox, for instance, had to give back two.[80] The physical punishments to be carried out in virtue of the *lex talionis* are not exactly stated in the Bible, but the rabbis speak of the certain number. The only mutilation that the Scripture provides for is the cutting-off of a woman's hand should she have helped her husband in a fight by seizing his opponent in an indelicate manner.[81] The bastinado would have been quite usual, perhaps as a mere police-measure without any order from a judge, thus differing from the terrible scourging: this happened in Egypt, to unwilling taxpayers. For the early Hebrews, prisons were there only to make sure that the accused did not escape,[82] or, under the kings, to serve as instruments of policy;[83] but in the time of Ezra and Nehemiah imprisonment became a form of punishment,[84] particularly for insolvent debtors. The New Testament often refers to this.[85] It was made even more unpleasant, sometimes, by setting the prisoners' feet in stocks, which happened to Paul and his disciple Silas at Philippi.[86] It appears, too, that the frequently reiterated formula in the Bible 'He shall be cut off from among his people' or 'He shall be lost to his people' did not mean death but rather banishment, which in itself implied religious excommunication.[87]

The forms of execution were many and various. The tractate *Sanhedrin* speaks of four: stoning, burning, beheading and strangling. This order of seriousness seems odd, particularly when one remembers that burning was carried out by the condemned person being thrust into a dunghill as far as his waist while his upper half was surrounded with tow and two executioners forced open his mouth to thrust a lighted stick into it: this was the death for a man who had lain with both a mother and her daughter or for the daughter of a priest who had turned prostitute. A son who had struck his father was strangled; so was a false prophet; and this was done with a garrotte.

The most usual punishments and the best-known were scourging and stoning. The first was either a punishment complete in itself or else an addition to the death-penalty. It seems most probable that it was the Romans who brought the custom of flogging condemned men to Palestine.[88] In ordinary flogging it sometimes happened that the wretched man would die under the blows, and for this reason the Jewish Law set the greatest number of lashes at forty and commanded that the flogging should stop at the thirty-ninth, for fear that it might be the fortieth itself that would prove fatal:[89] Roman law knew nothing of this humane measure. At the same time the whips that the Jewish executioner used, which were plain, tripled or quadrupled lashes, were much less cruel than those of the Romans, loaded as they were with lead or the knuckle-bones of sheep, which took off the skin at every blow. It was no doubt the second kind of scourging that our Lord had to undergo, tied to a low column and given over to the brutality of the lictors.[90]

Stoning was a capital punishment and nothing else. It was the typical Hebrew execution: it was of great antiquity and it is continually mentioned in the Bible. This was the punishment that the accusers of the woman taken in adultery wished to inflict upon her, and that under which Stephen died, the first of the Christian martyrs. Deuteronomy plainly states that it is the punishment inflicted by the whole community: the accusers and the prosecuting witnesses were to throw the first stones and after them the whole people.[91] In the tractate *Sanhedrin* there is a piece of further information which makes this form of execution seem a little less barbarous: the condemned man was to be taken to a cliff 'the height of two men' and one of the accusers was to throw him down backwards, obviously to stun him by the fall or to break his back; it was only after this that the stones were to be thrown, and the first was to be aimed at his heart.

One might be tempted to think, because of the death of Jesus, that crucifixion was a usual punishment in Israel; but in fact it was imported by the Greeks and the Romans. Originally the Israelites did not crucify or hang those who were condemned to death: their bodies were 'to be hung on the gibbet'.[92] Crucifixion, that most hideous kind of execution – *crudellissimum taeterri-mumque*, as Cicero puts it – probably came from Phoenicia, and to begin with it was no doubt only used upon rebellious slaves. It spread throughout the whole of the ancient world, and it was said to have reached Rome in the time of Tarquinius Superbus. Alexander Jannaeus used it on a very large scale in Judaea, for the execution of the defeated Pharisees.[93] The place of crucifixion was outside the city gates,[94] and there the upright posts stood permanently fixed: the condemned man was brought out and tied or nailed by the hands to a smaller cross-piece which was hauled up by ropes either to the top of the upright or until it reached a slot cut in it. Men were crucified with their backs to the cross, facing the spectators: women the other way. A sort of horn or rest between the legs prevented the body from sagging, so that death should not come too quickly; and indeed it did not come for hours and hours, being caused in the end by an increasing asphyxia, the tetanic state of the muscles, hunger and above all thirst, to say nothing of the wounds made by the loathsome birds that always haunted the place. There was a commandment in Deuteronomy that forbade the leaving of corpses on the gibbet by night,[95] so if death were too slow in coming, they broke the crucified man's legs or else thrust a sword or a spear into his side.

All this is hideous enough, in all conscience: but although the guillotine and the electric chair may be held to be less cruel, are they much less ugly? In any case, there was a tendency against the death-penalty in Jewish opinion: the Talmud mentions it.[96] And the Jewish Law even provided for some services to the condemned that most of the modern codes entirely lack; it was ordered, for instance, that there should be a mounted guard by the place of execution, with relays, so that if the judicial authorities wished to stop the proceedings they could do so up to the last moment. The condemned man was also obligatorily given a 'strong drink' as the Proverbs call it,[97] apparently a hypnotic made of incense or myrrh dissolved in wine or vinegar – the same that was offered to Jesus. There were associations of religious women, not unlike the confraternities of penitents in the Middle Ages, who took care of this duty: in default of them, it was incumbent upon the authorities of the town to do so.[98] Such was the last mark of kindness that the community of Israel showed the most wretched of its members.

CHAPTER FIVE

THE TABLETS OF HEAVEN AND
HUMAN CALCULATIONS

---

*The year and the months – The week of seven days – The
day and the hours – Weights and measures – Money in
Palestine.*

THE YEAR AND THE MONTHS

Everybody in Israel was more or less familiar with the splendid
stories in the *Book of Enoch*, that strange work which some rabbis
thought inspired but which was not included in the canon;[1]
everybody knew, therefore, that the archangel Uriel had showed
Enoch the tablets of heaven and had taught him how to measure
the time that the Lord had made, and how to reckon the years,
the months and the days, by attending to the angels who ruled
the courses of the stars. For like everything else in the world and
in life, the measurement of time was of divine origin, being the
mathematical frame of all events and all men's deeds.

The basis of this reckoning was the year; and the year, together
with the day, was the most often-mentioned measurement of
time, continually referred to in the Bible. It was a lunar year;
and this, too, says Ecclesiasticus, was of divine origin: 'The
moon, too, that keeps tryst so faithfully, ever marking how the
seasons change, and giving the signal when feast days come round!
. . . the month its name-child; cresset of watch-fire that lights up
the high vault of heaven with its radiant glow.'[2] Yet another
book, the *Book of Jubilees*, which was also very widely read
although it did not form part of the Holy Scriptures, asserted that
God, after the Flood, had laid down that men 'were to observe
a year of 364 days', and went on to say that men's misfortunes
had come upon them because they had forgotten this commandment.[3] Why was this? Perhaps because in very early times there
was competition between the Egyptians' solar year and the lunar
year which was much more used throughout the Near East and

even in the Mediterranean countries – the Romans, for example, had a lunar year until Caesar made his revolutionary changes in the calendar in 46 BC. Certain passages in the Bible seem to hint that in Moses' time the year may have been solar: for instance, when he died in the land of Moab, the official mourning lasted for thirty days.[4] But at the time of Christ it is quite certain that the lunar year of 354 days was in use and that it was so completely habitual that the very word that was used in Hebrew for 'month' also meant 'lunation'.

As everyone knows, the lunar year has the serious disadvantage of lagging some eleven days behind the solar year, which quickly brings about a want of correspondence between the seasons and the months. From time to time, then, the difference had to be caught up; otherwise the summer months would have opened in mid-winter. It was just for this reason that Caesar, observing that the legal year was sixty-seven days out, decreed that the year 45 BC should have 445 days and that every following year should have 365. The Egyptians, whose solar year had twelve months of thirty days, dealt with the same problem by adding five movable days; but the Jews could not do this, because the eleven days of their error could not be fitted into any lunation. They therefore waited until the error amounted to about a whole month and then inserted an extra month, *Veadar*, between the two spring months of *Adar* and *Nisan*. This embolismic year had nearly four hundred days.[5] The intercalation was made in an entirely empirical manner, and it was based upon farming activities, the principle being that the earliest ears of barley must be ready for the Passover. 'The lambs are still too young and the chickens too small,' wrote a rabbi to a Jewish community of the Diaspora, 'and the corn is not ripe. So we have decided to add a month to this year.'[6] It was a *Beth Din*, a court of three doctors of the Law, which initiated the case of the month as if it were a trial; a court of five members debated the case, and lastly one of seven gave the judgment.[7] When everything had been thoroughly considered the intercalation was ordered to be made: 'the *Veadar* was consecrated', as the formula put it.

In early times, the autumnal equinox and the harvest feast marked the end of one year and the beginning of another, as we find in Exodus.[8] But during the Babylonian exile the Jews had adopted the calendar named after Nippur, according to which the year began at the spring equinox, and this they retained, because of international relationships, after their return to the Holy Land. There were therefore two years, each with a legal existence: the religious year, which began in autumn, on the first of *Tisri*; and the civil year, which began seven months earlier. But the new year that was feasted with so much joy was that which began on the first of *Tisri*.[9]

The dating of the years set more difficult problems, not only for the Jews, but for all the people of the ancient world. The Roman system of dating by the names of the consuls called for great accuracy of memory, even when the date from the legendary foundation of the city, 753 BC, was added: the Greek manner of counting by the olympiads was no better. The Egyptian and Assyrian systems, with their lists of dynasties and their eponymous kings, were equally inconvenient. In the earliest times the Jews dated very simply by some outstanding occurrence. 'It was two years before the earthquake,' says Amos.[10] Under the kings the years were counted from the accession of the reigning sovereign, which could lead to a certain amount of confusion. The situation was made somewhat clearer, however, when the Seleucids inherited Syria from Alexander in 312–311 BC and began their counting from that date – a system that is still retained by certain Syrian religious communities. But at the time of Christ it was not all Jews who would use it. The ardent nationalists wanted a national era after the style spoken of in Maccabees – 'In the first year of Simon's high priesthood, chief paramount and governor of the Jews',[11] that is to say, 142 BC. Some cities had been well treated by Pompey, and they decided to date from the Roman conquest, or 63 BC. The doctors of the Law, and particularly those of the Diaspora, had worked out that according to the information in the Bible, the world began in 3761, a date still accepted by the Synagogue. The whole situation was confused.

The year was divided into months. The object that we call a calendar and which shows the months, weeks and days at a glance does not seem to have been known to the Jews. Yet there has been found, in a Jewish grave, one of those little tablets with rows of holes for pegs which were perhaps used by the Egyptians for the same purpose.[12] As for the mosaic zodiacs which have been discovered in several Palestinian and Syrian synagogues, they date from many centuries after the Christian era and they are quite certainly based on Graeco-Roman models. The division into months was also decided by a *Beth Din*, according to a complex procedure. Witnesses were examined, and the most important among them was asked with scrupulous exactitude just where he had seen the moon, the size of its crescent and its height above the horizon. The month began on the evening of the twenty-ninth day at the moment when the thin sliver of the new moon appeared in the sky: if it did not appear, then necessarily the month had thirty days. Once the court of seven members had duly established the fact, fires were lit on the hilltops and all along the roads messengers announced that the month had legally begun.

Ordinarily there were twelve of them, and each had a name. In very early times these names were based on the work in the fields and upon the weather, like those of the French Revolutionary calendar. For instance, there was the month of ears of corn, the month of the dry streams, the month of fruitfulness, and *Ziv*, the delightful month of the opening of flowers, in which Solomon began the building of the Temple.[13] Yet perhaps because these delightful old names were originally Canaanite, that is to say pagan, many biblical authors merely gave the months their ordinal numbers; this is to be found in Paralipomena or Chronicles, for example, and Ezekiel. But at the same time as they adopted the calendar of Nippur, the exiled Jews also took to naming the months in the Babylonian manner, which was useful in business. These names were strongly suspected of paganism: *Tamuz*, for example, commemorated the Babylonian god of growth, and *Yiar* was connected with that fruitful goddess Ishtar. Yet the habit became so rooted that even the men who wrote down the Bible used these names, no more thinking of the Mesopotamian gods than we think of the god of war at the beginning of March or of Janus in celebrating New Year's day. Roughly speaking these months span ours – *Nisan*, for example, goes from the middle of March to the middle of April – and their names (all names that Jesus must have used) are *Nisan, Yiar, Sivan, Tamuz, Ab, Elul, Tisri* (which means the beginning), *Hesvan, Kislev, Tebet, Sebat* and *Adar*, the last being duplicated by *Veadar* in the years of thirteen months.

The division of the year into months was the only important one: the division into seasons, which means a good deal to us, did not to the Israelites, for the very understandable reason that their climate only separated the year into a wet, cold period and a dry, hot one, with very short intermediate stages. The learned certainly divided the year into four parts, basing them upon the equinoxes and the solstices, but they named these parts only by the months that began them, for example, *tequfath Nisan* and *tequfath Tamuz*, the three months' period beginning with *Nisan* or *Tamuz*. It was also usual to speak of the rainy season and of the dry season. But above all the chief points of the year were known in relation to the feasts: no Israelite hearing that something happened at 'the time of the Passover' or 'the season of Tabernacles' or that of the Day of Atonement could possibly mistake the exact period of the year in which the event took place.

Matters were much complicated, however, by the fact that by no means all the inhabitants of Palestine used the official calendar of the Jewish community. There were a great many who would not, quite apart from the Roman civil servants and soldiers, who naturally used the Roman system. The Samaritans, in the first place, refused to recognize the intercalary month determined in Jerusalem: they fixed upon another, whenever they thought fit. The Greek cities had the Macedonian calendar which Alexander had brought with him, a calendar of twelve lunar months with a thirteenth intercalated; but this did not coincide with the calendar of Jerusalem. Some Herodian princes followed this – Philip the Tetrarch and Queen Berenice, for example, who dated not by *Yiar* and *Tisri* but by *Artemisios* and *Dios*, that is to say by Artemis and Zeus. It was the same in the Diaspora, and Philo of Alexandria uses the Graeco-Macedonian reckoning. But as the Syrians and the Egyptians had each adopted Alexander's calendar in their own way, this led to still further confusion; and in a Greek city of the Decapolis there might perfectly well be three concurrent calendars, the Jewish, the Syrian and the Egyptian, quite apart from the Roman.

And lastly it now seems quite certain, since the discovery of the Dead Sea scrolls, that some religious groups who were faithful to the tradition of the *Book of Jubilees* still used the ancient calendar of 364 days, which had four terms of ninety-one days each, and which were each made up of thirteen weeks. This had the advantage of making the great feasts, such as the Passover, fall on a given date. The Essenes of the monastery of Qumrân undoubtedly used it. And it is possible that Jesus and His disciples followed it too.[14]

THE WEEK OF SEVEN DAYS

It appears that the seven-day week, now so universally adopted, has its origin in the Hebrew calendar. Nobody in Israel doubted its great antiquity, nor, of course, its divine beginnings. To convince oneself of this one needed do no more than start the Bible at the first page and read the noble opening of Genesis, where the inspired writer tells how, from the vast emptiness of the original chaos, God in turn made first the lifeless things and then the living creatures in an order of rising excellence that finished in man, 'made in His own image'. The seven days of the creation were therefore the archetypes of the seven days of the week.

This account of the birth of the world in the first chapter of Genesis belongs in fact to what the exegetists term the priestly source as opposed to the Yahwist source, which provides the account of man's creation in Chapter II. When this tradition was reduced to writing, probably in the sixth or fifth century before Christ, the learned of Israel had long been accustomed to theological and scientific labours; they therefore associated a division of time that was no doubt of immemorial antiquity with the divine work.

At the beginning of the second millennium, when the future patriarch Abraham (then still Abram) was wandering with his clan in the plains of lower Mesopotamia, his neighbours in Ur of the Chaldees were already acquainted with the week, the fourth part of the lunar month. It corresponded to each of the moon's phases as they were seen one by one in the clear nights of the Euphrates. In *Enuma Elis*, the Babylonian poem of the creation, Marduk tells the moon what part she is to play: 'At the beginning of the month, to shine upon the earth, thou shalt show horns; and so six days shall be reckoned. On the seventh day thou shalt divide thy crown in two . . . On the fourteenth thou shalt set thyself in full view . . .'[15] In Babylonian the day of the full moon was called *sabbattu*. It seems clear that it was Moses, that most gifted founder of almost all Israel's institutions, who gave the week its final shape and, by linking its days with those of the creation and the seventh with the Lord's day of rest, its religious significance. A kind of play upon words helped this connection: the root *s b*, which was read as *sabua* and which corresponded to the figure seven and thus meant week, was very like the root *s b t*, which meant to stop or to cease work; and this was read *sabbat*. The week, then, was essentially the space of time between two Sabbaths, for as Ezekiel said, the Sabbaths were from the Lord, 'a token between me and them, a token that they were divinely set apart'.[16] Sometimes, indeed, in Holy Writ the Sabbath stands for the entire week.[17]

Thus one single day in the week had its own particular name, the day above all others, the Sabbath – which corresponded, by the way, to our Saturday. Sometimes the day before it was given a name meaning 'the eve of the Sabbath'[18] or 'the day of preparation'.[19] The other days were named simply by their order, and thus Saint Matthew begins his account of the discovery of the empty tomb on the morning of Christ's resurrection, in his twenty-eighth chapter, with the words, 'On the night after the Sabbath, at the hour when dawn broke on the first day of the week . . .' This was the practising Jews' method of reckoning the days, and it was that used by Jesus and His disciples.

But there is no doubt that in the Palestine of their day other systems were in use. The Roman administration would certainly have named the days according to its own fashion – a very awkward one, however traditional and legal, which was based on the calends, ides and nones. And all those who believed in astrology, a very numerous body indeed at that time, perhaps including a good many Jews, had the habit of naming the days of the week after the heavenly bodies that protected them – the moon, Mars, Mercury and so on. Dio Cassius thought this a specifically Roman usage,[20] and as we know, it was to survive the collapse of the astrologers and the triumph of Christianity, with the one difference that the 'day of the sun' (the Germans' *Sonntag* and the Sunday of the English) was changed to the 'Lord's day', Domenica, which was none other than the Jewish Sabbath moved on twenty-four hours.

THE DAY AND THE HOURS

The word day had two meanings for the Israelites, as it has for Most Western people. It meant both the astronomic, legal day, corresponding to one complete revolution of the earth (or rather to one apparent revolution of the sun), and the natural day, the time of daylight as opposed to the time of darkness.

Nations have always found it difficult to make up their minds exactly when the legal day ought to begin. Some have said dawn, others noon: officially we say midnight; but when one wakes up at two in the morning and thinks of something that is going to happen at noon on the same day it is scarcely possible not to think of it as belonging to tomorrow. In Israel the immemorial custom was to make the day finish and the next begin at the moment of sunset. Work is done, and this is a natural pause; the weary body knows that a natural period of time has come to an end. The Bible has a great many passages which refer to this custom[21] and to the dignity and holiness of the evening. This was the hour at which the paschal lamb was to be offered up, the hour at which every day the 'second sacrifice' was made, the 'evening offering', the hour of the last prayer, the raising of the arms in supplication.[22] At Jerusalem the ending of the day was announced by the sound of trumpets, and for the great feasts by the sad cry of the *shofar*, the ram's horn.

The natural day, of course, began with sunrise and finished with sunset. It was sometimes even called 'dawn-dusk' to distinguish it from the legal day. At Jerusalem, as soon as the sun had risen up from behind the black line of the mountains of Moab, there was to be heard the thundering of bronze as the team of Levites on duty for that day opened the famous double gate of the Temple, the Nicanor Gate. Then the sound of trumpets announced the first prayer, and from the courts of the Temple and from the houses of the faithful there arose the chanting of the holy words of the *Shema Israel*.

The division of the day into hours was comparatively recent in Israel. The very word 'hour' is not to be found in the Old Testament except in the Book of Daniel, and even there it is taken in so wide a sense that some modern translations render it 'moment'.[23] Noon, *sohoraim* (which evokes 'two halves') was used, and the other landmarks were the hours of the morning and the evening sacrifice.[24] But by the time of Christ the division of the day into twelve hours was commonly accepted. The New Testament gives many proofs of this: there is the parable of the labourers of the eleventh hour,[25] for example, and Saint John's statement that our Lord sat by the Samaritan woman's well 'at the sixth hour',[26] and Saint Mark's that He was crucified at the third hour and that He died at the ninth.[27] This means that the custom, which was no doubt of Babylonian origin, had become general since the return from exile, under the influence of Graeco-Roman civilization.

The twelve-hour system then in use throughout the Roman empire had of course no relation to ours. Our hours are each the twenty-fourth part of a legal day, calculated mathematically: the Roman system was based upon the duration of the sun's presence in the sky: on December 25th, therefore, the winter solstice, when there were but eight hours and fifty-four minutes of possible sunlight in the day, the daytime hour shrank to less than forty-five of our minutes, while each of the night-hours drew out to an hour and a quarter of our time.[28] It would be exceedingly difficult to say exactly what duration was meant when the disciples were reproached at Gethsemane for not having had the strength 'to watch even an hour'.[29] As to the division of the hour into minutes and seconds, known to the mathematicians of Egypt and Chaldaea from far earlier times, the ordinary people had either never heard of it, or took no notice if they had.

This general vagueness in the reckoning of the time of day reveals much of the character of daily life in Israel at that time; and for that matter it is still characteristic of all Eastern countries, to say nothing of some on the European side of the Mediterranean. Our care, even our mania, for promptness, was utterly unknown. No man with a workshop would ever have dreamt of reproving his men as they arrived 'at the fifth hour'; nor would anyone have imagined the possible existence of a timetable for the departure of caravans or ships. It would have been meaningless to give an appointment for half-past ten or six o'clock: an invitation would be limited to a suggestion of the evening, which was the most favoured time, the time when people loved to talk, talk interminably while the sky turned from mauve to dove-grey and then to dark blue sprinkled with stars. This was not perhaps the most convenient of all arrangements, but life was slower then, and people were rarely in a hurry.

Were there instruments to tell the time? We know that the Greeks and the Romans had at least two, the sundial and the water-clock. The Athenians had invented the first – Meton's gnomon – and its use spread rapidly throughout the Hellenic world: the Romans, prompted by the intelligent Valerius Messala, then consul, adopted it at the beginning of the second Punic war, in 263 BC. The second, which was technically more advanced, was perfected by the Alexandrians in 159 BC: they used the sundial to provide a graduated scale of hours on the water-clock, and the diminishing level of the water showed the passage of time. These *horologia ex aqua* grew fashionable, and some were known which threw a pebble or an egg into the air at each hour, or which even whistled. Did the Jews possess these ingenious machines? Strangely enough, the Bible does not allude to them at all. It certainly tells how the prophet Isaiah asked God to give a sign to Hezekiah the king, and how the 'shadow had gone back ten degrees',[30] but this might mean ten steps of a flight of stairs just as well as ten hours on a sundial. Archaeology has not yet found a Jewish sundial in Palestine: not that this necessarily implies that the rich men of that time may not have had them set up on the walls of their houses, nor that they were unable to send to Alexandria or Rome for one of those clepsydras which so astonished all beholders.

The division of the night-hours, when obviously no gnomon could function and when even the water-clocks could only give a general notion of the time, was even vaguer than that of the day. From the earliest period the night had always been divided into watches, those lengths of time which a sentinel was to stand guard over a camp or a shepherd over the flock. The period always seemed long, particularly as the relief could not very well have come at an exactly given moment; and yet, as the Bible said, 'a thousand years were but as one of the night-watches' in the eyes of God.[31] Ever since the Romans came to Palestine their custom of having four watches had been adopted; and each of these had roughly four hours. There are many allusions to them in the New Testament: Saint Matthew, for example, states that it was the fourth watch of the night when our Lord walked upon the water to join His disciples in the middle of the lake.[32] And Saint Mark[33] shows that these four watches were part of everyday usage and that they were perfectly distinct one from another. There was the evening watch, when the yellow light of the oil lamps shone upon the awnings and the striped carpets on the flat roofs of the city; the sombre midnight watch, vaguely anxious even under the moon and the stars, when, as Psalm 129, the *De profundis*, says, the watchers look for the day; the cock-crow watch, when Jesus, coming from the high priest, looked at Peter with a glance that pierced the unhappy man to the soul; and the dawn watch, when at last marvellous colours appeared on the horizon little by little, and men and beasts woke up, and life began again on earth.

WEIGHTS AND MEASURES

Telling the date and the time may not have been easy in Israel; but that was nothing in comparison with the complexity of the weights and measures – the complexity for us, that is, for the Jews of two thousand years ago must obviously have been used to it; and they may even have considered their system normal and efficient, as the English consider theirs, however much the Europeans of the Continent may find it difficult and illogical. Ancient Palestine did not possess the admirable system of measurements that the great Mesopotamian empires had worked out some three thousand years before our era. Solomon established one, no doubt with the Babylonian standards in his mind; and he had even required the Levites to see to the measures of capacity and length.[34] But naturally this system evolved in nine centuries, and the same words no longer meant the same measurements that they had in the time of the great king. Lengths and volumes varied even from province to province, for the exiles had brought the ways they had learnt in Babylon back to Judaea. In addition to this the Greek and Roman occupations had superimposed completely different systems, to which the people attempted, more or less successfully, to adjust the Jewish measures. It is clear that the archaeologists and historians who have to grapple with this problem have their work cut out for them. And everything is made more difficult by the fact that nothing is more unreliable than the translation of a measurement into another language: for example, the *zereth* and the *tofah*, the span and the hand (or palm), are both translated *palmus* in the Vulgate, although there are three *tofahs* in one *zereth*. And by a most unhappy chance no archaeological digging has yet turned up a single unbroken standard of length or capacity.

With these reservations, and with the clear understanding that all conversions of ancient measurements into modern measurements are merely conjectural, we may attempt to give an outline of the Jewish system. For the measurement of short lengths they used standards based on parts of the human body: the cubit was reckoned from the elbow to the end of the second finger, and it was the same as two spans, the span being the space between outstretched thumb and little finger; the span was three palms, three hands' widths; and the palm consisted of four fingers. This was plain enough; but there were two sorts of cubits, the weak and the strong, the latter containing seven palms instead of six; and this, it appears, was the cubit used by architects. When the Gospel says that no man can add a cubit's growth to his height,[35] only the general bearing of the words is exactly understood. Learned calculations[36] have worked out that the weak cubit was about 17·7 inches (which would show the Jews as a short people), and the strong 21·25 inches.

For longer distances, for roads and the like, the Israelites had long used, and no doubt were still using, measurements taken from everyday life, such as a bow-shot[37] or a day's journey.[38] Another usual expression was the 'Sabbath day's journey', the distance one might go without violating the law of rest; in the Acts this is said to be the distance from the Mount of Olives to Jerusalem.[39] No doubt the peasants and the common people counted in paces or in thousands of paces, as Jesus did when He said that if a man compelled one to attend upon him for a journey of a thousand paces, one should go two thousand of one's own accord.[40] But other measurements had been brought in at the time of the Greek conquest, and the Hellenic manner of counting in stadia was usual.[41] According to the rabbis the Sabbath day's journey was six stadia; and the stadium was 600 feet (606 of our feet, or 202 yards). It was also eighty of the fathoms then in use, though this was even then more a measurement of depth, and we find the sailors of Saint Paul's ship casting the lead and finding first twenty fathoms and then fifteen.[42] And of course the Romans had introduced their mile of 1,618 yards into Palestine; their milestones have been found in the Holy Land and all the surrounding regions.

They measured areas on the same principle that we use when we speak of square yards and square miles. For small expanses surveyors used the qaneh, the 'measuring reed', the rod with which the man of bronze in Ezekiel's vision measured the future Temple:[43] it must have been a little longer than three yards and therefore the area that it measured would have been in the neighbourhood of ten square yards. For larger surfaces the 'cord' was used, and it was so usual to count in 'cords', that is to say in square cords, that the word 'cords' in ordinary language meant a piece of land.[44] Most unfortunately, however, we do not know exactly how long the cord was. Yet the common measurement of area, the measurement that the Jewish peasants used, was the yoke, the surface that a pair of oxen could plough in a day, the Latin *jugerum* of 3,200 square yards (about two-thirds of an acre), which is quite close to the old French *arpent*, or the *journal*, which is still used in some parts – Dauphiné and Savoy, for example – for measuring land.

But although the Jews had long been familiar with the idea of measuring area by the square of a given length, they knew nothing of measuring capacity by its cube. In this they resembled the other nations of antiquity, all of whom confused by the difference between a given volume and the quantity of goods that it could hold – a quantity which, when weighed, varied immensely from one commodity to another. Furthermore, the Jews did not have exactly the same system for indicating the measures by volume for solids and for liquids; for solids they reckoned by the *log, kab, seah, epha* and *homer*, for liquids *log, kab, hin, bath* and *kor*. Strangely enough both the decimal and the duodecimal systems were to be found, mixed together; thus the *bath* of water consisted of six *hin* or eighteen *kab*: but ten *bath* made one *kor*, and four *log* one *kab*. It is generally held that both the liquid and the solid *log* amounted to about thirty-two cubic inches.

We gather from the New Testament, however, that the most usual measurement was that which is usually translated 'bushel'. This was none other than the Roman *modius*, which contained 8.65 litres, or about a little less than a peck; but at the time of Christ the heavy *seah*, holding nearly three gallons, was preferred. There was some container in every Jewish house, whether of wood, metal or earthenware, which would serve to measure out the bushel of barley or wheat needed for the family's bread; and among the poor people this bushel was used as a low table – that is why Christ said, 'Nobody lights a lamp, and then puts it away in a cellar or under a bushel measure'.[45] There were larger units, both for corn and for liquids: Saint John, speaking of the jars which held the water at the time of the miracle at Cana, says that they were of two or three measures apiece:[46] two or three firkins, say the translations. Perhaps these were the Greek *metretes* of nearly nine gallons, or three Roman *urnae* of 825 cubic inches.

This mingling of Jewish and pagan measures, then, appears to have been perfectly commonplace in Palestine at the time of Christ. It was even more marked in the matter of weights, which is understandable, since weighing is at the very basis of all commercial transactions. Just as in most Mediterranean ports of today ship's coal is reckoned in English tons and fuel oil in American gallons, so then the Jewish traders in the import and export business were obliged to use pagan standards of weight. The Sephalah excavations have shown that the Alexandrian system was in use; but even more important was the pound, the *libra* of about eleven of our ounces, which the Romans brought with them, this being the standard of weight for the whole empire. It was in pounds that Saint John gauged the amount of the 'pure spikenard ointment' that Mary of Bethany poured upon our Lord's feet[47] and the myrrh and aloes that Nicodemus brought to prepare Him for burial.[48]

Yet the Roman pound certainly did not supersede the old weights, the talent, the mina and the shekel, which are often mentioned in the New Testament. These were ancient Babylonian measures, and there were sixty shekels in a mina, and sixty minas made a talent. Whether or not the talent ever was used as a weight (and since it came to between seventy and a hundred and thirty-two pounds it would scarcely have been very manageable) it was certainly not employed as such in the time of Christ: yet it was used as a money of account, a reckoning for quantities of gold and silver; because of this it acquired a figurative sense, and to say that a man had a thousand talents was to say that he was enormously rich. This also applied to the mina. Israel's real unit of weight was the shekel, which was divided into halves, quarters and twentieths: it is very often mentioned in the earlier books of the Old Testament, but not in the later, and it is not spoken of once in the New Testament. This leads one to suppose that the ancient weight-shekel (for the money-shekel still existed) had been linked with the pound, perhaps in the proportion of four or five pounds to the shekel.

How did weighing actually take place? Either with a steel-yard (a very ancient example has been found at Megiddo) or with scales and weights, which were made of stone, sometimes very hard stone such as basalt or porphyry, bronze or lead. Weights in the shape of lions, ducks, frogs and beetles have been found, but it is not sure that these were Jewish, because of the prohibition against the likeness of any living creature. Weights were stamped by a controller, just as our bank-notes carry a signature. There are many to be seen in the museum at Jerusalem with inscriptions such as 'Timinnios the Cretan' or 'Agathocles, inspector of weights and measures'. These are Greek names, but the custom was certainly general.

MONEY IN PALESTINE

Exactness of weight was important not only for dealings in corn and other goods, but also as a guarantee of the soundness of the currency. The Proverb 'Scale and balance are emblems of the Lord's own justice; no weight in the merchant's wallet but is of divine fashioning'[49] refers both to honest weight and to good money. Long before money in the sense of coins struck with a symbol or a likeness existed in Israel, men had settled their debts by producing a given weight of precious metal: it was in this way that Abraham at Ephron weighed out four hundred shekels of silver, warranted silver, to buy the field and the cave where his wife Sarah was buried.[50] The word 'shekel' was derived from the root *sekel*, which in both Assyrian and Hebrew conveyed the notion of counting as well as weighing. The practice of weighing money rather than counting it was still general in the Palestine of Jesus' day, as it was all round the Mediterranean. The scales also served to ensure that the coins were of the true metal and that they had neither been filed nor clipped; indeed, this inspection was one of the banker's and money-changer's chief tasks. It must have been far from easy, when one thinks of the variety of coins current in Palestine at the time.

It was when they were in Babylonia that the Jews had discovered how much more convenient it was to use money guaranteed and struck by a recognized authority than to barter, or to weigh out metal for the smallest purchase. But since their country, since the return from exile, had practically never been out of the control of foreigners, every kind of coinage had spread among them. Palestine may not have had coins of Croesus, that fabulously wealthy king of Lydia, who invented money, but it did receive, as its first coins, the famous darics, those gold pieces of Darius, the king of kings, mentioned in Ezra.[51] And how many others followed! On the beautifully minted Hellenistic coins there were to be seen Antiochus of Seleucia, the Egyptian Ptolemies and Cleopatra; and of course the Romans, in occupying the country, imposed their financial system upon it and insisted that the direct tax, the capitation,[52] should be paid in Roman money; and those who rendered under Caesar what was Caesar's did so in coins bearing his own imperial head. But the Roman *denarius* had a rival, which trade brought into Palestine; this was the *zuz*, a silver piece of similar value which was struck by the Phoenician bankers of Tyre and which was so much appreciated that the doctors of the Law allowed, and even desired, that the Temple offering should be paid in *zuzim*, as if they were Jewish coins.

Anyone who reads the New Testament will see something of the diversity of the coins that circulated in Palestine: it speaks of drachmas (in the parable of the lost coin[53]), of *denarii*, as in the dialogue between Jesus and His opponents upon the subject of Caesar's tribute,[54] as well as on ten other occasions, of *asses*, those exceedingly small coins with which two sparrows could be bought,[55] of shekels, minas, talents and many others. Now the drachma was Greek, the *as* and the *denarius* Roman, and the mina, whose name recalled its Sumerian original, *mna*, was the Phoenician money of account, current throughout the whole of the Mediterranean East.

But this is not all, for there were also Jewish issues.[56] They were quite recent in Israel: it was Simon Maccabaeus who was granted the right to mint bronze and copper by Antiochus VII in about 150 BC. This flattered Jewish national pride, and he chose specifically Jewish symbols for his coins, the citron and the palm-frond, the *ethrog* and the *lulab*, used in certain Temple ceremonies, with such inscriptions as 'Zion delivered' or 'The high priest and the community' ... The Romans had continued this authorization with the same limitations: that is to say they allowed the Jewish mints to strike only the bronze coins, the small change that women used in shopping, and either sent the silver from Rome or minted it themselves upon the spot. Jewish money continued to differ from pagan money by the exclusive use of plants and symbols in the design, for all human likeness and even all animal forms were forbidden by the Bible: 'Thou shalt not carve images or fashion the likeness of anything in heaven above, or on earth beneath, or in the waters under the earth.'[57] Nobody would have dared disobey this commandment. Even Herod the Great, with all his pride, never put his head on his coins, but only 'Herod king', and on the other side a cornucopia, or flowers and fruit, or even a helmet and a shield. All his descendants did the same except for one, Philip, whose realm was up by the Syrian frontier and who therefore did not scruple to put the heads of Augustus and Tiberius on his coins, and even his own. As for Herod Agrippa, as king of Judaea, he remained faithful to the sacred custom and if he went so far as to put a parasol, a royal symbol upon his coins, he stopped short at his own head or the heads of Caligula and Claudius; but at the great cosmopolitan port of Caesarea, where he loved to reside, he did not hesitate to issue sacrilegious money, and the Jews saw his sudden death as a well deserved punishment for this crime. The Romans themselve

paid attention to the Jews' extreme susceptibility in this respect:
the small coins that they struck in Judaea bore only the name of
the reigning emperor, with a laurel crown and Jewish emblems or
symbols of prosperity. Their silver pieces with the emperor's
head were so unusual among the common people that they did not
cause much scandal. Jesus, replying to the Pharisees, asked to be
shown one: He did not possess such a thing. It was laid down by
the doctors of the Law that the only money in which the Temple
taxes could be paid was Jewish money: if a pilgrim from the
Diaspora or the provinces came with pagan coins he could
neither pay the tax nor buy a victim for the sacrifice without first
going to the money-changers, who ranged their tables in the
Temple courts – a fact that enraged our Lord, who one day
thrust them out.

It must be admitted that with all this confusion of currencies the
money-changer's trade would certainly have been very profitable,
and that it would have allowed all kinds of knavery. Was the
denarius worth exactly the same as the drachma? Was the shekel
the same as the stater, and was that the same as the tetradrachm?
What proportions did the *as*, the *quadrans* and the *lepton* bear to
one another? It is easy to imagine that a worthy Galilean peasant
coming to Jerusalem for the Passover and wanting to buy a lamb
would not have been able to follow these calculations very well.
In a general manner, and allowing comparisons that were by no
means exact in practice, it may be said that the basic unit, the
shekel of silver, was divided into four silver *denarii* or drachmas
(or two didrachms), and that the *denarius* or drachma consisted of
sixteen *asses* or sixty-four *quadrantes* or a hundred and twenty-
eight *lepta*. As for the talent and the mina, these were only
moneys of account, the mina being one hundred *denarii* and the
talent six thousand. It goes without saying that any conversion
into modern terms must be entirely arbitrary, for the prices of
gold and of silver have enormously varied in the course of the
centuries, and the purchasing-power of money in a rural society
like that of Israel cannot be compared with its purchasing-power
in an excessively industrialized society like our own. We may
give an estimate of the various coins' gold-equivalent, which
would make the shekel come to 15.53 grains of gold, now worth
about 8s. 1d. or $1.14; the drachma 4.32 grains at 2s. 3d. or
32 cents; and the *as* a quarter of a grain at about three halfpence,
or rather less than two cents; but this does not give a true idea of

their value. Nor does it help much to point out that the ordinary rural labourer's daily wage was a *denarius* or a drachma, as the parable of the workers of the eleventh hour demonstrates; for as we have seen,[58] wages were low in Palestine, and the daily bread was hard to earn.

CHAPTER SIX

BED AND BOARD

'Give us this day . . .' – *'. . . our daily bread'* – 'Vinum laetificat cor hominis' – *Meals* – *'The cloak and the coat'* – *The house.*

'GIVE US THIS DAY . . .'

One of the particular marks of the Jewish religion, a characteristic that it has handed on to Christianity, was its sturdy realism, its concern with the everyday realities of ordinary men. Nothing could be more remote from it than the Hindu doctrine of all-pervading illusion, nor than that Persian dualism which held creation to be the work of the evil principle. For the Jews the whole created world was the work of a good and a righteous God: was it not clear enough from the book of Genesis? From a hundred places in the Bible there arises a sublime hymn of thanksgiving to the Creator for having surrounded men with such valuable things, to Him who 'dost prepare it [the land], watering the furrow, loosening the clods, multiplying, with soft showers, the grain',[1] to Him who clothes and shelters His people. 'And all look to thee to send them their food at the appointed time; it is through thy gift they find it, thy hand opens, and all are filled with content,'[2] said the Psalmist.

From both the Old and the New Testament a kind of 'theology of things'[3] might be compiled: the most ordinary actions in life, such as eating and drinking, were hallowed because they were part of the divine plan; indeed, they were almost godlike. In the earliest days of the sacred history of the Chosen People that most mysterious figure Melchizedek, the king and 'priest of the most high God' in whom Psalm 109 was to see a prefiguration of the Messiah, offered Abraham bread and wine;[4] that same bread and that same wine (the most usual form of food and drink) of which Christ was to make symbols in the Eucharist, the most holy of symbols, since therein God Himself would be present.

In Israel, then, everything that was useful in man's ordinary
life, everything that helped to keep him in house and food, was
consecrated. Food itself was a holy thing, and the Law required a
man to say a prayer every time he had eaten[5] – a pious custom
that we find our Lord obeying, giving thanks after His meals.
The rabbis maintained that a meal without a prayer was a meal
that was accursed.[6] Our grace is a survival of this usage. Man's
dwelling was also consecrated, for Deuteronomy also said, 'Thou
wilt build thyself fair houses to dwell in . . . beware lest thy heart
should swell with pride, and forget the Lord thy God'. In two
places the Scriptures require the holy words to be 'inscribed on
door and gate-post',[7] and in fact all Jewish houses had, and still
have in the state of Israel, a little cylindrical case, the *mezuzah*,
holding the commandments of God, fixed at the right-hand side
of the door. Clothes, too, were consecrated, for in the same text
the Law said that the commandments were to be 'bound close to
thy hand as a remembrancer', a rule from which arose the use of
phylacteries in which the words of God were kept; and the
wearing of the *tzitzith*, the fringed garment – for fringes were
necessary, and without them the *talith*, the shawl worn over the
head in prayer, was unfit for its function.[9]

The pious Jew acknowledged the hand of God in all the things
that were needed for daily life; and therefore it was permissible to
ask Him for them. The asking-prayer, then, was exceedingly
ancient. 'Give us this day our daily bread,' said Jesus in the most
sublime of prayers, and this is almost exactly the same as a verse
in the Proverbs:[10] and a great many of the prayers of the learned
of Israel, which are to be found in the Talmud, particularly in the
tractate *Berakoth*, contain the touching plea, 'Lord, provide us
with what we need'. The rabbis did not reduce prayer to a
blunt request for material objects; they were perfectly aware
that prayer should raise a man above himself, direct his life toward
its true end, bring him into a loving relationship with God and
generally cause his soul to overcome all that is earthly and
material. Yet one must not forget, in reflecting upon the daily life
of the Jews, that even these earthly and material aspects of life
had been blessed by God.

'. . . OUR DAILY BREAD'

It is not very difficult to form an idea of how the Jews ate at the
time of Christ: one has but to open the Bible to find that both

the New and the Old Testaments are filled with references to food, drink, cooking and meals. In His parables, our Lord very often alluded to things to do with eating and drinking, and to table-customs. All this information in the Scriptures can be confirmed and enlarged by the study of the present resources of the country in animals and plants, although one must take care not to fall into anachronism of supposing that two thousand years ago Palestine had such things as tomatoes, maize, sunflowers, apples, pears and bananas; for they, like the guinea-fowl and the turkey, are of recent introduction.[11]

Generally speaking, the Israelites of the time of Christ were frugal eaters, as most of the nations of the East are to this day. Bread was the essential, basic food: 'to eat bread' in Hebrew meant 'to have a meal', exactly in the same way that in the *Iliad* and the *Odyssey* Homer says 'a bread-eater' to mean 'a man'. Bread, then, was to be treated with respect: it was forbidden to put raw meat on top of a loaf, to set a pitcher of water upon it or a hot plate against it, and it was forbidden to throw away the crumbs, which, if they were 'as large as an olive' were to be gathered up. And bread was not to be cut, but broken.[12]

The poor ate barley-bread, the rich the bread of wheat.[13] The corn was ground between two millstones, almost always by the women, and at home: more than usually careful work produced the particularly fine flour that was used for cakes and certain liturgical purposes. The dough was worked in kneading-troughs, and these homely objects are to be found as early as Exodus.[14] Then, except when the unleavened bread was to be made for the Passover, yeast was put in to make it rise: it was important to have fresh, brisk yeast, not a sour ferment like that 'leaven of the Pharisees' in our Lord's figure of speech.[15] To make the heavy barley-bread rise, the women used a very strong millet and barley yeast, but a 'fig of wheat-yeast' was enough to make the good white bread's dough fill its basin overnight. The loaves were so usually made round that the common expression was 'a round of bread' or just 'a round'. Then it was baked, and baked in that small household oven that Leviticus speaks of[16] and which is still to be seen in Palestine: it was put directly on to the embers, with great care that it should be neither overcooked nor underdone. But how-much care ever was taken the bread went mouldy very soon, particularly in summer, and it had to be made fresh every two or three days.

Corn was also used in other ways. The Bible often speaks of roast wheat:[17] this was used in time of war or during voyages or at harvest-time, and it was also served with the meat, as maize is now. Coarsely ground, it provided a meal that made a kind of porridge something between Italian *polenta*, the *couscous* of the Arabs and that dish of the Franche-Comté called *gaudes*. The women would also make cakes, large cakes of the best flour, well kneaded with oil and flavoured with mint, cumin, cinnamon and, as we shall see, locusts. There were also confections resembling honey-doughnuts fried in a pan, like those which are served throughout the Near East, for the gentle sickening of Western palates. For banquets these delicacies were shaped into animals or palaces, by means of a technique that the Hebrews may have learnt in Egypt.[18] And they already knew how to make starch and how to mix it with honey and flavour it with rose, jasmin or pistachio to make a sweetmeat almost exactly the same as that which we know under the name of Turkish delight.

Was Palestine the land flowing with milk and honey of the ancient poetic phrase?[19] Both the one and the other were much appreciated by the wandering Hebrews of former days, and they were still very much in use among the Jews. Cow's milk was rare, and in any case it was not so much liked as ewe's and goat's milk. It tended to turn very quickly, because of the heat; but this 'hardened milk' was eaten. They understood 'the wringing of milk for butter' as the Proverb puts it (adding, very strangely, that the wringing of one's nose will also produce blood).[20] In the country it was made in a skin bag, hung up by three sticks and strongly shaken. They also made cheese, and the Tyropoeon,[21] the 'valley of the cheese-makers', at Jerusalem perhaps owed its name to a former cheese-market.

Honey was even more widely used than milk, and indeed it was quite indispensable, for at that time the making of cane sugar was unknown. The Holy Land produced a great deal, so much that some was exported. But it was not only the honey of wild or domestic bees, scented honey taken from hollow trees or rocks: the thickened juice of grapes and dates passed under the same name. The Jews were very fond of them all. The 'juice of the comb', that is to say the unpressed virgin honey, was a treat for children: all the things that were called honey were used by the pastry-cooks, and the curative virtues of true honey, praised in the Bible,[22] were known to medicine.

On the other hand very few eggs were eaten: they are never mentioned once in the Old Testament, and in the New only Saint Luke (not Saint Matthew) shows us our Lord using the word.[23] Now as we know, Luke was from the Diaspora, not from Palestine. Poultry had only been brought into Palestine since the exile, and hen's eggs (which the Romans knew how to prepare in so many different ways) would only have been found upon the tables of the reasonably well-to-do.

The diet of the ordinary people certainly included a great many vegetables. Beans and lentils came first on the list (Esau's famous dish of lentils shows how old the use of them was); and there were cucumbers too, so very much esteemed that whole fields full were grown—fields that had to be guarded against the jackals, who also appreciated cucumbers;[24] onions, which the Chosen People had first met in Egypt and which they regretted so during the Exodus, when they had none;[25] they now used them in immense quantities, as it were to make up for lost time; and then as green stuff they had lettuces and chicory, which they ate either in salads or cooked. There were also some roots not unlike salsify and artichokes, and others, that we do not use at all, which were produced by certain kinds of iris.

Very little meat. This was the food of luxury, and the wealthy ate a great deal of it, quite as much for show as from liking. The poorer people never slaughtered an animal for their own eating except when there was a family feast; but when there was one, the fatted calf, the proverbial fatted calf of the parable, was a most appropriate victim. Though generally a kid or a lamb was made to do. The animal was usually roasted at a wood fire, as in the *méchoui* of the Arabs; but there were also made-dishes or stews, lentils and mutton being a very usual combination. Chickens were scarcely to be had, but pigeons were cheap. Game was much sought after, and all the kings, from Solomon to Herod, had been great game-eaters. The deer and the gazelle were the true kingly dishes; but the partridge and the quail were not despised, any more than our mediaevals despised that elegant fowl the Indian peacock, which was reckoned a great delicacy.

But for the common people, fish was more important than

meat: bread and fish, that was a most usual meal. This is evident from our Lord's words, 'If any one of yourselves is asked by his son for bread, will he give him a stone? If he is asked for a fish, will he give him a serpent instead?'[26] On the day of the miracle of the loaves of bread, the only provisions that the disciples found among the people there were fish, 'a few small fishes', presumably dried. And the risen Christ, to show His disciples that He was not an illusion, ate fish with them, grilled over a charcoal fire.[27] In the tractate *Berakoth* it is asserted that fish makes a man prolific. The Sea of Galilee had quantities of fish in it, and many fishermen also lived on the Mediterranean shore. As fish soon turned bad, it was often salted; and at Magdala the people made *muries*, a preparation of salt fish whose fame reached as far as Rome. It appears that the consumption of fish was so great that some had to be imported: the tractate *Shabbath* speaks of salt herrings and 'Spanish tunny', which might not be set to un-salt itself in warm water on the holy day of rest.[28]

One of the most surprising forms of food was the locust: though indeed it is hard to see why this should surprise anyone who esteems the frogs and snails of the French cuisine. Everone knows that John the Baptist lived in the desert upon 'locusts and wild honey'.[29] But he was not the only one to appreciate this delicacy. The tractate *Taanith* goes so far as to claim that there are eight hundred kinds of edible locust, all belonging to the migratory race;[30] but it does not specify their names. But in any case there were four in current use. Sometimes they were cooked rapidly in salt water, and then they had a shrimp-like taste and some a shrimp-like colour; and sometimes their heads and legs were taken off and they were dried in the sun. Once dry, they were either put up with honey or vinegar, or else ground to powder. This locust-powder, which tasted rather bitter, was mixed with wheat-flour to make a much prized kind of biscuit, rather like those which the Chinese cooks produce under the name of 'shrimp-bread'.

This whole cuisine was of course based upon oil: butter was the rare exception. Palestine had a very great many olive-trees, so many that the excellent, strongly flavoured oil was exported. The olives themselves were eaten, too, either in brine or in oil, as we see them today. The oil was very often made in a little press at home, but there were also much larger concerns, real mills, in which men or asses turned an upright grinder in a tank.

There were various qualities of oil; the best, the virgin oil, was kept for liturgical purposes and for the most delicate pastries. How could men have lived without oil? For it was not only used in cookery but also in pharmacy and medicine. It is not surprising that at least thirty passages of the Bible hold it up as a symbol of strength and health.

Lastly, fruit had an important place in the people's food. They ate a great many melons, figs, both ordinary figs and sycamore figs, and pomegranates, and they were also fond of walnuts, almonds and pistachios, which were split and gently roasted; and of course there were blackberries in the hedges. Dates, and particularly the dates from Jericho, were much esteemed. Some fruits were dried and pressed into cakes; perhaps apricots, but certainly figs, for the expression 'cake of figs' is found several times in the Bible. The dried Palestinian fruits were sold even in Rome.

Unfortunately it is very difficult to make out much of the actual manner in which the Jews of two thousand years ago cooked their food: the cookery-books of the Hittite and Egyptian housewives have been found, but no Israelite *cordon bleu* has left us her secrets. Apart from joints roasted on the spit and ragouts like that for which Esau sold his birthright, they had fricassees '*à la mode d'Ascalon*', that is, presumably, with shallots; and stuffed fish and wine and honey sauces. One thing that is certain, is that they liked their food strongly seasoned. They did not merely put salt (which came, very appropriately, from Sodom, to the south-west of the Dead Sea, where until very lately the deposits of the Jebel Usdum were still exploited) but many other condiments: mustard, capers, cumin, rue, saffron, coriander, mint, dill and *jeezer*, a kind of wild rosemary; all these were continually used, as well as garlic, of course, and onions and shallots. Pepper was scarce and dear: it came in the caravans from the distant India. The 'scented cassia' of the Revelation[31] was probably cinnamon, a spice that was also brought from a great way off, from Ceylon or China; and it is clear from the Bible that it was often the object of speculation.

It would have been surprising if religion, which entered into all other Jewish activities, had had nothing to do with their cookery. Quite apart from the obligation of tithing the slightest thing that made part of any meal, so that the Almighty's priests should have their due share, there were a great many rules governing the preparation of various dishes. Lamb, for example, had to be roasted over wood from the vine. *Halmé*, a kind of aromatic pickle, used for preserving fish, was so carefully regulated that a whole paragraph of the fourteenth chapter of the tractate *Shabbath* is devoted to it. But above all there were the laws concerning what might and what might not be eaten, and it was exceedingly dangerous to disobey them. Pork was absolutely forbidden: the Bible repeated this four times.[32] The hare also appeared on the list of unclean animals,[33] which was a great pity, for it was very good. The rabbis were not in agreement about the camel, and some forbade its milk as being unclean. There was a very rigorous prohibition against the eating of the flesh of any animal, even one killed hunting, that had not been bled; for the blood 'animates all living things',[34] it is the soul of the flesh and it would have been a terrible thing to have swallowed the soul of an animal. This is the reason for the existence of the kosher butcher's shops that are still to be seen in any Jewish community. James Frazer of course considered this to be an ancient taboo that had survived from exceedingly remote times: however that may be, it is generally accepted that the author of the *Golden Bough* was right when he said that another well-known prohibition in the Bible, which states in three different places, 'Seething a kid in its dam's milk is a rite forbidden thee',[35] was a surviving taboo; unless indeed it was a precaution against stopping the goat's milk if the kid had been taken too soon, or even a sentimental objection.

'*VINUM LAETIFICAT COR HOMINIS*'

There was another subject upon which the Law had a great deal to say: that of drink. There were certainly drinks other than wine for slaking one's thirst; there was the pure water of wells and springs, to begin with, and very good it is in hot weather after a long walk; then milk, vinegar much diluted with water (the *posca* of the Romans), the more or less fermented juice of pomegranates or dates, or *shechar*, a kind of light beer made from barley and millet, rather like the Latins' *cervisio*. In order to astonish their guests, very rich men would offer them beer from Media. But none of these was anything in comparison with wine, the drink above all others.

There was no possible doubt that wine was part of the religious scheme of the world: everybody knew that it was God Himself who had first shown Noah how it was made. Palestine prided itself on producing a great deal of very good wine, and there were popular wine-stories (the tractate *Kethuboth* has preserved some) like Tartarin of Tarascon's hunting-stories: 'As for me,' said one man, 'each of my bunches produces a whole barrel.' 'For my part,' said the other, 'I have pressed so much that for several stadia all round you walk in a sea of wine up to your ankles.' What is more, the Bible (which speaks of wine a hundred and forty-one times) spoke of the juice of the grape in the most cordial possible terms. The famous *'vinum laetificat cor hominis'* is verse fifteen of Psalm 103. But the author of Ecclesiasticus was more enthusiastic still, in saying that wine was a man's life, and asking what kind of a life would one lead without it.[36] It was for this reason that the Proverbs said that there should be 'wine for the afflicted heart'.[37] Since the vine was the symbol of Israel and since a golden vine was to be seen in the Temple, was not wine a holy drink? Therefore it had its ritual laws. Like meat, it had to be kosher, and it had to be made entirely by Jewish hands. When Jesus spoke of Himself as the vine, and when He consecrated wine to that high point of saying, 'This is my blood', He was speaking like a son of Israel – He was entirely in the tradition of His people.

It was certainly red wine that they drank: the Old Testament speaks of the redness of wine many times,[38] and there is not a single mention of white. Some kinds were better than others, and the account of the marriage at Cana in the Gospel shows that the best was served at the beginning of the meal and the inferior wine later, when the guests had already drunk a great deal. Generally speaking it was a very full-bodied deep purple wine, rich in both alcohol and tannin, and it was drunk mixed with water, not neat. The Jews were familiar with the practice of blending, that is, of improving a small wine by the addition of a more fruity one. They kept their wine either in great tall jars or in wine-skins: the skins were made of carefully tanned goat's hide, and they had wooden stoppers. The best were to be had at Hebron; and with them there was no risk of seeing the new wine suddenly burst out and spill during the fermentation.[39]

They always filtered their wine before they drank it: the rabbi Eliezar held that filtering was permissible even on the Sabbath, but other learned men insisted that the Law was infringed, the rest broken, unless the filter were placed over the jug the day

205

before. The Greeks and the Romans had a way of scenting their wine with thyme, cinnamon, roses and jasmin flowers, and this habit had spread to the richer classes among the Jews: but the common people preferred theirs in its natural state. The rabbis allowed that the preparation of honeyed wine on the Sabbath was licit, which shows that the sweetened drink was fairly common.

They drank their wine out of metal goblets or earthenware mugs, for although glass was known it was scarce and expensive. The Song of Songs says that these goblets were shaped 'like a maiden's navel';[40] which is perhaps a little less than precise. Some are to be seen on the coins of the Asmoneans, and they mostly have a handle. They were very large; and in this lay the root of the trouble. For although nothing could be better for a man than wine 'drunk in moderation' as Ecclesiasticus says, the Jews well aware that it could also be exceedingly dangerous; and Yahweh knew how much they drank when there was a celebration. Indeed, in Aramaic, which was the language of the people, the word for wedding was *mistitha*, a carouse, or drinking-party. The Bible is therefore full of warnings, and in the same passage in Ecclesiasticus which praises wine so highly there is also this: 'Never challenge a hard drinker to a drinking-bout; wine has been the ruin of many... To the drunkard, life is no life at all; wine is death, when it so deprives a man of life ... Wine drunk in excess brings anger and quarrelling and calamities a many; it is the poison of a man's life.' Chapter 23 of Proverbs shows the disadvantages of drinking in the person of a red-eyed drunkard fighting with his neighbours, his mind confused, his steps wandering and himself 'as helpless as a mariner asleep in mid ocean'. And there are a score of equally categorical passages in the Bible. In any case, the Israelite had but to remember Noah and Balthazar and Holofernes to realise the treachery of the delightful drink. A piece of apocryphal Hebrew literature of the first century before Christ, the *Testament of the Twelve Patriarchs*, says very pertinently, 'The spirit of whoredom has wine for its servant'; and here whoredom has not only its blunt literal sense but also the figurative meaning of apostasy. For all these reasons judges engaged in a trial were forbidden to drink; so were officiating priests and Nazarites[41] – those who were under particular vows. There were even teetotallers, who never touched wine at all: these were the descendants of those wild nomadic Rechabites of the time of Jeremiah; but there were not many of them.

MEALS

The Jews liked eating in the open air, and would often take their meals in the courtyard; but in the winter they had to be indoors, usually in the one large room which was also the kitchen. Only the quite well-to-do people, who built their houses in the Roman manner, had a *triclinium*, a dining-room. The table and chairs were ordinarily set afresh for every meal: those fixed 'dining-room suites' that one sees at Pompeii, either in the houses or in a sheltered corner outside, have not been found in Palestine.

The times of meals were less rigidly fixed than they are in England or France – more like Spain or Sicily. 'Eat when you are hungry, drink when you are thirsty,' said the tractate *Berakoth*. The great majority of the people had only two meals a day; the one very early, before going off to work, and the other when work was done, in the evening; at noon they made do with a snack and then a siesta: this is the rhythm that many Americans follow at present. On the Sabbath day, the mid-day meal was larger; and generally speaking those who were not manual workers ate more for lunch than the others. The rabbis had a saying that to eat a great deal at noon was 'to throw a stone into a wine-skin'; and there was a proverb, 'If you have lunched very early, sixty runners will not be able to catch you up'.

Men of all nations, and at all times, have asked their friends to eat with them – the table is a place for the meeting of friends. The Jews were very open-handed with their invitations: had not Abraham asked God Himself to eat with him at Mamre?[42] The invitations were usually for the evening, so that there would be more time, and particularly for Friday evening, when the Sabbath had just begun: but there were sometimes invitations to breakfast, too. Again and again in the Gospels we see our Lord asked to a meal – to a Pharisee's house, to Zacchaeus the publican, to the loving home of Lazarus, Martha and Mary: we even see Him, after the Resurrection, seated at table with the disciples at Emmaus.

When there was a particularly important banquet, a wedding, for example, or a circumcision, the invitations were taken round by slaves or servants, as we see from the parable of the wedding-feast;[43] and for these parties it was essential to put on ceremonial clothes[44] – evening-dress, as we should say. The host received his guests, giving them the kiss of peace[45] and seeing to it that their feet were washed, as if they had come a great way to reach the house.[46] The guest, for his part, was to wash his hands[47] – or rather one hand, the right hand, which was used for eating. Some even went so far as to bathe entirely before sitting down; this was customary among the Essenes[48] and those rigorous men who were to be found scattered all over the country, living in the Essenian manner. Perhaps that Pharisee who, having invited Jesus, was astonished that He did not go through the ceremonial ablutions,[49] was one of these. At great feasts it was thought suitable to pour scented oil upon the heads of distinguished guests: this was a custom coming from remote antiquity; the Gospel mentions it several times.[50] Sometimes the guests were also crowned with wreaths; but this was really a heathen practice, more suitable for a Roman orgy, and the doctors of the Law condemned it. And of course no meal, however humble, began without a blessing. 'The man who eats without having blessed his food', said the rabbis, 'desecrates a holy thing'.

No one ever ate standing up. Our fork dinners, the Russian *zakouskis* and the Scandinavian *smörgåsbord* would have seemed repugnant and absurd to the Jews. 'Eating or drinking upright upsets a man's whole body,' said the learned.[51] In former times it had been customary to eat sitting, either on chairs or cross-legged on the ground: 'They sat down together and ate', as the Bible says so many times.[52] But even in the strictest circles of the Chosen People the Graeco-Roman habit of eating stretched on a couch or a kind of divan furnished with cushions had become general; and Jesus Himself must often have taken His meals in this manner, for how otherwise could the 'sinful woman' have poured the ointment on His feet and dried them with her hair, or Saint John have sat 'with his head upon Jesus' breast'?[53] The correct way was to lean upon one's left elbow, using the right hand for the food.[54]

Precedence was exactly observed at table, and in several places the Gospel shows that the Jews were punctilious over such matters: if a man were to take a higher place than was his due the master of the house would soon require him to move down again. The most honourable table was in the middle, facing the open space left for the servants. It never held more than three people, and the place of honour was at the 'upper part' of the table, that is to say, at the right of the master, who reclined in the middle. The side tables where there might be as many as six or seven guests, were of less importance.[55]

During the meal the guests were to behave decently: the Bible has a particularly telling passage on party-manners – 'Sit thou at a rich man's table, be not quick to remark upon it; it is ill done to cry out, Here is a table well spread! Be sure a covetous eye shall do thee no good . . . take sparingly the good things set before thee, nor court ill-will by thy gluttony. For manners' sake, leave off eating betimes, or thy greed shall give offence. When there are many about thee, do not be quick to stretch out thy hand, quick to call out for wine.' It is clear that Jesus the son of Sirach was full of wisdom; and in his excellent advice he carried plain-speaking very far, for he adds, 'Though thou have been constrained to eat beyond thy wont, thou hast but to leave the table and vomit, and thou shalt find relief, nor come to any bodily harm'.[56]

The master of the house himself served his guests in turn, choosing the helpings according to the rank of each. Thus at the Last Supper we see Jesus dipping a piece of bread and giving it to Judas.[57] Anyone who has travelled in Mohammedan countries is familiar with the somewhat depressing honour of being offered a kidney, dripping with fat, or even an eye, which must be accepted or the host will be most cruelly hurt. In ordinary meals it was permissible to put one's hand into the dish, but never to put it at the same time as another guest – that would be quite excessively rude, as Ecclesiasticus had already pointed out. In our time the Arabs believe that this brings bad luck.

The implements of eating must have been most rudimentary among the poor. There is very little information in the Bible, which mentions a knife once, but never spoons, nor of course forks, which only became usual in the West, and then not before the Renaissance. A kind of flat, broad cup made of tinned metal served instead of a plate – metal, because of the ritual uncleanliness of earthenware – or else a flat cake of hard bread. Things were much more luxurious, naturally, among the rich and the powerful: they had cloths on the table, gold and silver plate, knives of various sizes, spoons made of ivory or of rare and decorated wood, like those which the Egyptians used for cosmetics, or simpler spoons made of bone or terracotta – there were some with pointed ends, specially for eating boiled eggs and shellfish. The Romans had also brought in the use of ladles, *trullae*, so that sauce could be served out and the guests spared sopping it all up out of the dish with their bread.

It remains to be seen how the meal was arranged. Among

the poor it was reduced to its simplest terms – barley-bread, olives, fruit and locusts with no other dressing than salt. In the tractate *Berakoth* we even read of a poor man who, coming home from his day's work, ate no more than bread and salt. It is true that in the same part of the Talmud we find that then, as now, there were men and women who, in order not to grow fat and to keep healthy, confined themselves to water and dry bread in the morning. Fish was very usual in somewhat less restricted but still modest diets, and it must often have formed part of our Lord's meals. In a moderately well-to-do family an ordinary meal would have consisted of fish or kid, vegetables (particularly onions) and cakes, with local wine to wash it all down.

But there were also feasts and banquets. The Jews were very fond of them, and it was considered that there was nothing better for strengthening the ties of family or the sense of community. Holy Writ, therefore, has a great many accounts of ceremonial banquets in favour of friendship or alliance; and it was not at all by chance that Jesus uses the figure of a banquet to give a notion of the brotherhood that the righteous will know in heaven.[58] 'Blessed are those who shall have a place at the feast in the kingdom of God,' He said. And it was during a banquet that He Himself gave His people the supreme pledge, the most lofty of all messages, in bringing the Eucharist into being. And it was a feast too, in imitation of the Last Supper, that constituted the essence of the early Christians' agapes, those feasts of brotherly love which are constantly mentioned in the literature of the primitive Church, and about which Saint Paul gave the faithful such excellent advice.[59]

Some feasts, indeed, were obligatory under the Law, which laid down even the smallest details – the Passover, for instance.[60] But it was not all banquets that had so religious a character or such an air of solemnity: one given for a marriage or the circumcision of a first-born son would obviously be much more cheerful and gay. They went on for a very long time, at least five or six hours; and they were enlivened with music, songs and dancing. 'Music and wine, carbuncle set in gold, music and wine, signet ring of gold and emerald, so the wine be good,' said the unfailing Ben Sirach. There was nothing surprising in the appearance of the dancing Salome at the banquet during which John the Baptist's death was decided: there were always dancing-girls at the more splendid feasts.

At these feasts people ate a very great deal: they ate enormously. Wherever they went, the Romans brought with them their extraordinary gluttony,[61] and there is nothing improbable in the 'bull's kidneys, dormice and minced nightingales in vine-leaves' that Flaubert makes Herod Antipas offer to Vitellius in *Hérodias*: indeed, if the tetrarch's guests had no more than that they might very well have thought themselves hardly done by. Trimalchio, in Macrobius' *Saturnalia*,[62] did things far better with his soft-boiled eggs stuffed with ortolans, his crayfish, his young sows' vulvas, his braised joints of beef, his hares made to look like Pegasus and his whole sucking-pig with its belly bursting with black-puddings. Naturally, it cannot be asserted that all wealthy Jews indulged in gastronomic flights of this kind; but it is certain, from the unimpeachable evidence of the Bible,[63] that they delighted in 'the fat of the tail of the sheep' – and this does not sound as impressive as it is in fact, for the tails in question were the prodigiously large tails of the fat-tailed sheep, tails so heavy that a kind of bucket or wheeled case was fitted to them so that the precious fat should not be spoilt. Indeed, in chapter five of the tractate *Shabbath* it is forbidden to let out the rams 'with the little cart' on the day of rest.

The delights of the table, then, were not unknown to the Jews. But here too the Law made itself heard, and the rabbis often commented upon its wise counsels of moderation. The tractate *Gittin* said, 'There are eight things in which excess is harmful, and in which moderation is to be observed: travelling; sexual relations; wealth; labour; food and drink; sleep; hot baths and letting blood'. Over-long banquets with too much to eat and drink degenerated into orgies, as everyone knew: besides, there was the memory of that great banquet that their forefathers had held about the Golden Calf – a feast that could not have ended worse. It was far more prudent to listen to the advice of the wise Ben Sirach once more: 'Do not fall upon all the meats thou seest; much feasting breeds infirmity, gluttony the bile, and many have died of surfeiting . . . Wakeful nights come of excess and bile and griping pains.'[64] Which is an excellent word to end on.

'THE CLOAK AND THE COAT'

We remember Christ's words, 'If a man would take away thy cloak, do not grudge him thy coat along with it'.[65] Leaving aside all interpretation of the mystery of this precept and all analysis of the excellent reasons that men have invariably found for not following it, let us observe, from a strictly pragmatic point of view, that at the time of Christ the coat (or tunic) and the cloak appear to have been the two essential pieces of clothing.

But what were they really like? How were they shaped? Were there other garments usually worn with them? These are difficult questions to answer. Cloth is above all things perishable, and archaeology almost never finds any trace of it. And then again, as the Jews never represented human figures, we have nothing comparable to the Egyptian frescoes of the Pharaohs' tombs, which have given such wonderful information about the costume of that country. Finally, in trying to form an idea of how Christ's contemporaries dressed, we have to take into account two opposing trends, the strong conservatism of the Chosen People on the one hand, which was made all the stronger by the religious character which certain garments might possess,[66] and on the other the foreign influences that made themselves felt, particularly those from Greece and Rome. In any case, all the archaeologists are agreed[67] that the 'Eastern' costume in which the nineteenth century clad the figures of the Gospel, garments based upon Arab or Bedouin models, could not possibly be right. Jesus and His apostles did not wear the burnous or the gandoura.

In very early times, when the nation that was to be the Chosen People still wandered as nomads in lower Chaldaea, and even later, when installed in the land of Goshen they worked so hard for Pharaoh until their liberation by Moses, they would commonly have worn the loincloth that we see in the sculpture and paintings that have come down to us from Mesopotamia and Egypt. Only a very little while ago there were still Semitic tribes in Syria who wore a little skirt with coloured patterns on it. In the Israel of the time of Christ a relic of the ancient loincloth survived: this was the *saq*, translated sometimes as 'sack', which had led to confusion. It was made of linen, and it was the undergarment of the ordinary people – presumably that which Jesus kept on when He washed the disciples' feet like a servant.[68] On days of mourning and repentance men and women would put one on that was made of a very coarse stuff, a positive sackcloth; and the more zealous wore it directly against their skin, like a kind of hair-shirt. The prophets had formerly worn the *saq* as a sign of protest against luxury: in the Revelations it is said that just

before the Day of Judgment God 'will give the power of prophecy
to my two witnesses; for twelve hundred and sixty days they shall
prophesy, dressed in sackcloth'.[69]

The wearing of a coat and a cloak was also of great antiquity.
To be persuaded of this it is only necessary to remember the
'cloak of Noah' which the ninth chapter of Genesis speaks about,
that cloak with which his two good sons Shem and Japheth
covered his nakedness when the juice of the grape had played
him false, and Joseph's coat, in the thirty-seventh chapter, the
'long, embroidered coat' which his evil brothers sent to their
father, dabbled in blood, to make him believe in an accident.
At the time of Christ both these garments were in everyday
use: they are frequently mentioned in the Gospels.

The coat or tunic or *chalouk* must have been very like the
chiton of the Greeks, but longer: it came down well below the
knees, and the rabbi's coat had necessarily to appear for a good
hand's-breadth below the cloak. The ritual tassels, which were
usually very deep blue, hung from the bottom. For ceremonies,
the coat was made of embroidered silk or decorated with coloured
stripes. Most coats were cut out and then sewn together, but
there were some made of woven wool that were all in one piece,
and these were very much esteemed – it was such a coat the
soldiers took from Christ, the coat for which they drew lots, so
that it should not be torn.[70] The coat was kept on for work,
but at night, in going to bed, it was taken off.

The cloak, the *talith*, took the place both of our suit and of
our overcoat. It was so necessary a garment that the Law required
a creditor who had seized his debtor's cloak as a pledge to give
it up at nightfall.[71] It was also a dignifying garment, without
which it would have been improper to appear at the Temple
or before a superior. Nevertheless, it was used for all kinds of
purposes – a blanket, even a bed if one had to sleep in the open,
a saddle-cloth and even as a carpet to welcome great men, as
we see in the account of Christ's entry into Jerusalem on Palm
Sunday.[72] It is by no means sure how these cloaks were made.
Perhaps some were a simple piece of cloth with a hole for the
head and others two blankets sewn together; but there must
also have been some of a better cut, with separate sleeves, probably
not unlike our barristers' and graduates' gowns.

The indefinite, billowing shape of the coat made the use of a
belt quite essential, otherwise it would have been exceedingly

awkward to work or even to walk. As may be seen in Daniel and the Revelation,[73] even the angels wore belts: they were golden belts, it is true; for a splendid belt was a mark of standing. There were all kinds – rope for the long-haired hermits and prophets, leather for the soldiers and labourers; and the latter had a way of tucking their coat into their belt to leave their legs freer -- this was the 'girding of the loins' that one reads of so often. Many were made of a length of cloth, sometimes highly decorated, sometimes not at all, which went several times round the waist: the folds in these could be used as purses or for holding a dagger, or even a quantity of corn or a small lamb[74] – the biblical expression 'in the bosom' refers to this space. A handsome present for a woman at that time was not a handbag but a belt; which, after all, was much the same thing.

The influence of foreign ways had brought other garments into use. Formerly there had been the Canaanite shirt, like those which Samson had promised to the thirty Philistines at his wedding if they could answer his riddle, 'Out of strength sweetness' within a week.[75] It was a particularly grand piece of clothing, no doubt worn for banquets. At the time of Christ wealthy men wore a fine linen shirt as an undergarment; but at unusually elegant parties they followed the Roman fashion which, like that of ancient Canaan, called for the shirt on top, a light, decorated shirt, embroidered and even shining with gold. There were also special clothes for the great ceremonies, and these were Asiatic garments like vast greatcoats, magnificently decorated, which the Hellenistic Levantines had brought from Persia: only the great men and princes might wear them. Herod the Great had quantities of them, and the high priest's liturgical robes were of much the same kind.

Of course, those who were obliged by their trade or their calling to be out in all weathers paid no attention to the refinement of dress. John the Baptist's well-known clothing, which Saint Matthew describes in the third chapter of his Gospel, was the same as that which the prophets had worn; it was that of the hermits and most probably of the Essenian monks: a single garment, serving for both cloak and coat, made of woven camel hair, and a leather belt round the waist – though some say that this was a leather loincloth, a *saq*. Travellers wore woollen coats and often crossing bands of cloth round their legs in the fashion that the Roman soldiers had brought with them from Gaul.

but above all they wore a special kind of cloak, made of the hair of camels or goats, very thick, and waterproof. The best were made in Anatolia and Cilicia; and Saint Paul wore one in his travels – it was a cloak of this kind that he asked his dear disciple Timothy to send him when he was a prisoner at Rome. The shepherds of the Turkish plateaux still wear this invaluable garment: it is so heavy and stiff that when it is put down it will stand up of its own.

All these clothes were for men: what of those for women? It is difficult to give any exact idea, for the same words, coat, cloak, belt, are used indifferently for male and for female garments; and yet there must have been a difference, since the Law utterly forbade men to wear women's clothes and women to wear men's,[76] and since it is clear from the Talmud that doing so gave rise to the suspicion of homosexuality. Most probably the distinction would have been in the greater fineness of the stuff used for women's clothes, and their more ample cut. We learn from the tractate *Shabbath*, so valuable for information upon costume, that women also wore ribbons made of wool and silk, shawls tied over their shoulders, 'plaited strands' and a variety of ornaments whose utility seems no more evident than that of some of the objects worn at present by our bedfellows. Hellenistic fashions had certainly influenced women's clothes as well, and a great many women would have worn that pleated dress, with or without sleeves, that was so much favoured in Alexandria, as well as the *himation*, which was wound elegantly round the body, with a length remaining to go over the top of the head.

The usual head-covering for both men and women was a piece of cloth tied at the forehead, like the modern *couffieh*, and falling over the shoulders. This is still the liturgical headwear of the Jews, and the tractate *Shabbath* states exactly how many strips of cloth may be bound round the head upon the day of rest. In the same tractate there is an allusion to another head-covering, one of rolls of cloth, which seems to refer to something like a turban; and as the putting-on of head-gear of this kind is slow and delicate, as we may see from the Mohammedans of today, this would explain the unchanged Jewish custom of keeping the head continually covered, even in a holy place like the synagogue.

The cloths from which all these clothes were made were those cloths which alone were to be found in the East until the recent invasion of synthetic textiles. The technique of cloth-making

had changed so little that the herring-bone weave of the famou
Sindon, the holy shroud, at Turin might very well be of the time
of Christ or three or four centuries before His birth or fourteen
after it. However, the Law forbade the wearing of cloth made of
two different materials, as, for example, a mixture of wool and
linen.[77] Wool was the most usual fibre, and it was so carefully
washed and whitened that the prophets used its virginal cleanliness
as a figure for the purity of the soul. Most woollens came from
Judaea: Galilee chiefly produced linen, and flax had been grown
there time out of mind. The finest linen was called *byssus*, from
the Greek *byssos*, and it was much preferred to that imported from
Egypt, which had a reputation for coarseness. Silk was used, but
not very much: it was brought in by the caravans, and it was dear
Silk was one of the marks of insensate luxury in the 'great
Babylon' of the Apocalypse;[78] but no doubt the *mestri* from which
the veil of the Temple was woven was of this material. Since
their return from exile the Israelites had grown acquainted with
cotton, but it was still far from widely used.

All these cloths might be left their natural colour or bleached
but dyeing was also very general. The dyes were all natural
animal or vegetable products: Levites' clothes were dyed with the
yellow of the saffron crocus. Blue and brown were common
colours, and cloaks were often striped with white and brown
Pomegranate bark gave a very pleasant pink. Crimson was
produced by a little scale-insect that lives on the dwarf kermes-oak
But the most esteemed of all dyes was the purple, which was
obtained from a shellfish, the *murex*, which the Phoenicians had
fished for for centuries all round the coasts of the eastern
Mediterranean. Purple, in Israel as in Rome and Carthage, was a
sign of power: the evil rich man in the parable was dressed 'in
purple and lawn',[79] and the faithful were warned by their teachers
against this pagan colour – this, however, did not make it any the
less fashionable.

Apart from dyes, clothes were also ornamented with embroidery
The Jews had first acquired the taste for it in Babylon, for all the
great men of Mesopotamia had embroidered clothes, and from
there they brought it back to Palestine. The priests' robes were
embroidered and also the fashionable garments of both sexes
The Jews also understood the weaving of brocades and quilting
this means that needles had been known for a great while, and
indeed the archaeologists have found them in their excavations

At the time of Christ they were commonplace, although the Gospel only mentions the word once, in the well-known parable of the camel – 'it is easier for a camel to pass through a needle's eye, than for a man to enter the kingdom of heaven when he is rich'.[80] For fastening a cloak, a belt or a shawl there were also buckles or brooches and pins quite remarkably like our safety-pins: archaeological digging has turned up a great many specimens. When they were made of precious metals, as they often were for women, they were to be classed as jewels.

Both women and men wore a great many jewels. They were made of gold and silver and pearls and gems: Berenice's diamond, when she arrived in Rome, caused a great sensation. A circle of gold, as a ring or an ear-ring, was so much appreciated that the Proverbs liken it to wise reproof given to a wise listener.[81] In the same book we find, 'A woman fair and fond, a sow ringed with gold'.[82] This might allow one to suppose that the women of Palestine wore rings in their noses: they certainly wore them in their ears. But the Law forbade all mutilation of the body and so they could not pierce either nose or ears to hold the ornaments. Rings had always been known, and they were worn not only on the fingers but also on the toes; and the rings that men wore often had a seal to them. Yet as vanity induced them to have these rings exceedingly large and heavy they were often obliged to carry them on a chain hung round their neck. At grand gatherings women took pride in wearing what the tractate *Shabbath* calls a 'city of gold', a diadem more or less resembling the fortifications of a town. Loops of gold thread, shoulder-knots like the aglets of some of our officers' uniforms, and little cases with amulets in them made up the list of these ornaments, which were all, of course, for the rich alone. The use of them was a luxury against which the austere rabbis cried out, and the teaching of the New Testament condemned all this finery even more severely still. Saint Paul, in his first epistle to Timothy, warns good Christian women against gold ornaments, pearls and rich clothes:[83] in his view, no doubt, it was far better to cast them before the swine.

As for footwear, there were two kinds: the shoe, made of soft leather, and the sandal, which was hard. Both were worn without socks, except by a few dandies who loved extraordinary foreign fashions. Everyday shoes were made of camel's hide; the better ones of jackal or hyena. The soles were very rarely made of leather but of palm-bark or rush. It appears from the tractate

Shabbath that some sandals were hobnailed, to make them stand up to long journeys; and for this reason they were forbidden to be worn on the day of rest, when no long journey might be undertaken. Half-boots had been introduced from Mesopotamia, those same half-boots that the terrible Assyrian warriors had worn. And the Romans had brought in their *calceus*, with its four bands, the light *solea* for indoors and the *soccus*, which was much the same as our bedroom-slipper. But in holy places, as, for example, in the sanctuary of the Temple, no one was to walk but with bare feet.

THE HOUSE

'House' is a word that the Bible uses hundreds of times. Sometimes it means a group of families as a social entity,[84] sometimes the Temple, the house of God: using the word in its figurative sense, it links it to spiritual reality – the 'house of the Father' is heaven. All this is significant: it shows that the Jewish nation, settled now for hundreds of years, had nothing of the wanderer left – by the time of Christ the tent was no more than a faintly nostalgic memory and a figure for the pure austerity of former times. And the Jews had never been a seafaring race. The house was the centre about which life revolved; and although people did not live indoors a great deal except in the winter, the courtyard or the garden formed part of the home, the place where one had one's being and where one loved to receive one's friends. To understand the emotional significance of the house in the daily life of the Jews of two thousand years ago, one has but to think of that home in Bethany where Lazarus, Martha and Mary welcomed their friend Jesus.

Yet the ordinary Palestinian dwelling was neither large nor splendid. Most of the people of the Holy Land were country-men and the majority of them lived in villages, often very small villages – hamlets scattered about wherever the presence of water allowed them to exist. In the arid Judaea the houses were necessarily more concentrated round the few springs and wells. For a long time the difference between the village and the town was that the latter had a wall behind which the peasants of the neighbouring villages took shelter in time of danger: by the time of Christ the difference was chiefly administrative – the town had its court of law and its judges. The evangelists make it quite clear that Capernaum, Nain and Nazareth were towns, whereas Bethlehem and Emmaus were not.

Yet it would be mistaken to think of Capernaum or Nazareth as in any way resembling our great modern cities. Apart from Jerusalem and four or five other places the Palestinian towns were all very small; and archaeologists are astonished, when they dig out some 'city' whose name rings so loud in the Bible, to find a village that could all be fitted into the Place de la Concorde in Paris. The planning was rudimentary, particularly in the case of the truly native towns: at Marissa, which was built where the Judaean mountains come down to the maritime plain, 'the streets form a very irregular chequered pattern with wide areas between, each of which contains an utterly confusing maze of little houses and courtyards'.[85] The Hellenistic cities, such as Samaria, which was rebuilt a hundred and fifty years before Christ, or the towns of the Decapolis, like Gerasa (Jerash), were built according to a far more carefully studied plan, with a rectangularity almost worthy of New York; but there was not a single one in all Palestine that could show a street two thousand yards long like that famous 'street that is called straight' in Damascus, where Saint Paul took up his lodging,[86] nor the mathematical regularity of Dura or Europus in Syria. The cities built in the Greek or the Roman manner had a centre for public life, an agora or a forum, and Jerusalem had its Xystus; but the small, purely Jewish cities had nothing of the kind, at least none within the walls. It was before the gates that there was the open space for the market, and this was where justice was meted out and where men came to hire day-labourers or merely to gossip. It was a very noisy place, except in the heat of the day or the middle of the night, and the main streets of the town were scarcely less so; but in the alleys, courts, passages and lanes everything was quiet in the cool shade. Many of the townsmen went out every morning to work in the fields, and they came back at nightfall: the gates were closed behind them, and sentries mounted guard.

The individual Jewish house had nothing more remarkable or artistic about it than had the group of which it formed a part. The Jews had never been great architects: Solomon even had been obliged to have recourse to the knowledge of the Phoenicians in order to build the Temple of his God. Furthermore, how could a country continually overwhelmed by invasions and occupied for five hundred years have avoided coming under foreign influence in architecture? And yet nothing could be more mistaken than thinking of the typical Jewish house as something one might perhaps have seen at Pompeii. To be sure, there were splendid houses built in the Roman manner in Palestine, but they were very, very far from being in the majority. It is most unlikely that any of those blocks of flats, with each family having its own dwelling, were built even in Jerusalem, although there were so many of them in the less agreeable districts of Rome. No doubt the best idea of the Jewish dwelling of those days is to be formed by looking at a village or the poorer quarter of a town in the Near East.

In the country – at Nazareth, for example, when Joseph and Mary were bringing up Jesus as a child – the usual house was a rudimentary affair, a whitewashed cube with few openings, perhaps none except the door, and a single room inside, divided into two, one half for the animals, the other for the family. Some houses were partly cave-dwellings, built up against a limestone rock-face that was either naturally or artificially hollowed out: the crypt of the basilica of the Annunciation, which stands in the place of that which Saint Marcarius built at Constantine's command upon the traditional site of the angel's coming to Our Lady, is a little converted cave.

A rather better sort of house was that which was built round a central court with little rooms opening on to it. This kind of building has the advantage of needing only short beams for its roof and by its shape it retains the coolness: it was known in Mesopotamia two thousand years before Christ, and in Palestine it began to be used after the return from exile; at the time of Christ it would have been very usual. There had even been a considerable development of the type, for Lakish in Judaea was only a very little town, and yet the archaeologists have found a house of this kind there, dating from at least the third century BC which measures no less than thirty-eight yards by fifty-five, with a score of rooms round its central court, some of them raised to the height of several steps and connected to the court by a loggia - these were quite obviously the private rooms of the house, seeing that a bathroom with its underground water-pipes has been discovered among them.

People who had houses of the middling sort did not content themselves with the poor man's single room which served as kitchen, dining-room and bedroom all at the same time. Yet there were no separate kitchens properly so called except in the houses of the very rich: the cooking was ordinarily done in the courtyard, or, in case of rain, under a lean-to.

The roof was of real importance in everyday life. It was a flat roof, with just enough slope to carry off the rain into the gutters – those gutters whose flow the Proverbs compare to the words of a scold[87] – and surrounded by a parapet, which was commanded by the Law,[88] for otherwise 'if anyone should lose his footing and fall to the ground, thy house is polluted with blood, and the guilt is thine'. There was a staircase up to it, usually on the outside of the house. People kept tools on the roof and spread the washing out to dry; in the evening they sat there for the coolness, and on summer nights they slept there too. Some even put up tents. It was also a place to which men would retire to pray and to meditate. It is clear from the Proverbs[89] that to live 'in a corner of the housetop' was to be in a poor way. Our Lord refers to this habit of frequenting the roof when He speaks of the great tribulation at the end of the world: '. . . those who are in Judaea must take refuge in the mountains; not going down to carry away anything from the house, if they are on the housetop'.[90] And again when He orders, 'What has been whispered in your ears, you are to proclaim on the housetops'.[91]

Among the wealthier people there had sprung up the habit of setting a light building upon the roof, instead of a tent, and this gradually turned into another storey. And sometimes, to light it from above, they surmounted it with a square lantern. This building was the 'upper room' which is mentioned so often in the Gospels.[92] Guests who were staying overnight were put there – the outside stairs left them perfectly free – and if several people were asked to a meal, if it were inconvenient to serve it in the courtyard, the party was held up there. It was in one of these upper chambers, these *cenacula*, that Jesus, on the evening of Maundy Thursday, held the Last Supper; and according to the tradition it was in just such a room that the disciples gathered after the Resurrection, particularly on the day of Pentecost.[93] As well as this addition on the roof, some houses had others over the street – balconies, sometimes of considerable size, like the *moucharabieh* of the Turks. The tractate *Shabbath*[94] distinctly lays down that balconies are private places, although they may be above the public highway. Women were very fond of sitting on these balconies, to watch what was going on; and it may well have been from a balcony that the temptress of the Proverbs uttered her 'honey-sweet words'.[95]

In the towns it was rare that even a small garden could be annexed to the house; the number within Jerusalem could easily be counted;[96] at the most there might be a corner of the court with a sweet-scented jasmin growing in it. Yet there were gardens outside the walls, such as that which lay next to the place where Christ was entombed, and where Mary Magdalen thought she saw a gardener on Easter day.[97] But in the country everyone had a garden where they would grow flowers and lie in the shade of their fig-tree.[98] In one corner of the house there would be a storeroom for provisions, and where it was possible it was often dug into the rock, or an existing cave was used, so that the wine should keep well in the coolness. In the fields and the vineyards there were often little huts or cabins, lightly built, but very useful for resting in the heat of the day or keeping tools.

All this concerns the houses of the ordinary people, and perhaps those of the moderately rich. But the really wealthy, the great and powerful men of the world, they had what can only be described as palaces. As we have seen,[99] there were some particularly fine ones in Jerusalem, above all the palace of Herod, where the Roman procurator was staying at the time of Jesus' trial. The finest of them all was certainly the wonderful retreat that Herod the Great had built for himself at Jericho: the archaeologists have discovered its ruins, and they are still immensely impressive. Its pattern was the Hellenistic house, and it was not unlike the most beautiful buildings in Pompeii with its two colonnaded courts, its rooms at various levels, its loggias and even a little theatre, the whole resting upon enormous vaulted foundations. It was surrounded by delightful terraced gardens, with sheets of clear water and fountains, as well as that famous swimming-pool in which the tyrant had his little brother-in-law Aristobulus drowned by his guards.[100] Archelaus enlarged it; but this earthly paradise, which his cruelty had turned into a hell, was destroyed during the troubles at the end of the hateful ethnarch's rule.[101] When He went from Jericho to Jerusalem, our Lord must have passed by these ruins, which the local peasants used as a stone-quarry; and He might well have bade His followers reflect upon the vanity of temporal possessions. There were other palaces to be seen elsewhere in Palestine, not quite as splendid, perhaps, but certainly comparable; and in several of these the Graeco-Roman style gave way to that of the fortress-palace, capable of withstanding a seige – Machaerus, near the Dead Sea, that stronghold where John the Baptist was martyred, was one of these, and so was Malatha in the north, where Berenice passed her childhood so sadly, yet with her mind already filled with ambitious dreams.

What were these various buildings, from palaces to hovels, made of? The mass of the people, the poor peasants, built in wattle and daub or at the best in clay bricks, which they pressed by foot, mixed with straw and baked more or less efficiently in an oven. In either case the houses were easily broken into by thieves; and when our Lord referred to this[102] He would have been understood by everybody. Rich men's houses were made of stone. The limestone of Palestine provided excellent building material, and it was quarried by driving wooden wedges into the natural cracks and then soaking them to make them swell. They made the walls exceedingly thick and solid, and the corner-stone – Christ speaks of the corner-stone in an allusion to a passage in the Psalms[103] – must have been a piece of cut masonry: it is possible that it was blessed. But since the coming of the Romans people had taken to building in their manner – two thin walls of *opus reticulatum* made of pebbles and bricks with the space between filled with puddled clay and gravel: some of the palace of Jericho was built like this. Foundations were dug with the greatest care, the aim being 'to build upon rock', as the Gospel so happily puts it, lest the wind and the rain should come and carry the house away.[104] They used a mortar of tempered clay mixed with shells and ground potsherds. They had long been acquainted with lime (Isaiah refers to it[105]) and they used it chiefly for rendering or coating walls and as a whitewash: Jesus alludes to this second use when He calls the Pharisees 'whitened sepulchres';[106] so does Saint Paul in saying to the high priest 'whitened wall that thou art'.[107] Among the poorer people the floor was beaten earth, among the richer, pebbles or baked clay tiles: only princely houses had floors of cedar or cypress; and the Roman way of covering the floor with mosaics does not seem to have reached Palestine by the time of Christ. The arch was hardly used at all, except in fortresses; and as what arches there were were most indifferently made of flat corbelled stones, roofs were held up by beams. These roofs, these flat roofs, were occasionally made of bricks or tiles, but much more often they consisted of wattling covered over with beaten earth, and they had to be looked to and repaired every year before the rainy season; they were so thin that an opening could be made in a moment – a hole wide enough, for example, to pass the palsied man of the Gospel[108] through, or, as we read in the Talmud, the body of that rabbi Honna,[109] which could not be got out by the door.

The doors, indeed, were often very narrow, and the 'narrow gate' by which our Lord tells us to make our way in,[110] was not a fanciful figure at all: they were not only often very narrow, but they were low as well, and the expression 'to heighten the door' meant 'to try to be clever' or 'to show off'.[111] The only comparatively wide and tall door was the main entrance of the house, the door whose posts were adorned with the *mezuzah* containing the commandments of God. The Jews had hinges, and the Proverbs, speaking of idleness, say, 'Sloth turns about, but keeps his bed, true as the door to its hinge'.[112] The lower pin usually turned in a hollowed stone.

Keys had been known for a very long while, as far back as the time of the Judges; but these early keys must have been very simple affairs, adapted only for raising a latch, like those which are still used in monasteries as a *passe-partout*. The modern key was invented in the Hellenistic cities by men who moved bolts by means of nails fixed in a turning stem: the Romans improved the system, and made their keys of metal. The Jewish keys were of a considerable size, and they were carried with some ostentation, hung on the bosom, as they were until very recently in Turkey: a key was a mark of standing. And when Jesus said to Simon called Peter, 'I will give thee the keys of the kingdom of heaven'[113] everyone there must have known that He made him thereby the leader and the guide of the disciples; for a great landowner would confide the keys to his steward as a particular mark and outward sign of his confidence.

It may be asked whether life was comfortable in these houses. In the first place it must be observed that the notion of what constitutes comfort varies remarkably with the century and the place. The climate of Palestine did not make the same demands as that of Norway, for example. People lived in the open air a great deal. Most of our Western twentieth-century conveniences were obviously unknown then. Water, so exceedingly important, as we have seen,[114] was piped into but very few houses, and they the most splendid: ordinary people went to the fountain for theirs when the water-warden gave the signal, or else to the well or the stream, with skins, jars and all kinds of pitchers. Some cities, however, had a system of distribution by conduits: there were also sewers, particularly in the district of the Temple at Jerusalem, and drains for carrying the sewage to the sea have also been found at Caesarea. The 'secert place' to which our Lord refers when He says that a man is not made unclean by unclean food but by unclean thoughts, was generally known; the Talmud even asserts 'that to stay for a long while therein lengthens a man's life', and it quotes with approval the case of a rabbi who, in going from his house to the school in which he taught, would stop no less than twenty-four times in suitable spots that he had discovered.[115]

There was no great difficulty about heating in Palestine, and in many regions it was not necessary at all. Most of the houses, therefore, had no fireplaces. If it grew too cold, they lit charcoal braziers, like those which the servants of the high priest were keeping up on the night between Maundy Thursday and Good Friday, which Saint Paul came to warm himself by:[116] one has been dug up at Theanac. A fire in the open air was often considered good enough for cooking: the custom was to hollow out a place and border it with two stones – indeed, the Hebrew word for a cooking-fire comes from the same root as 'to hollow'. There were also little portable stoves with two holes; and the tractate Shabbath[117] shows that straw and grass were burnt in these: only rich houses had a wood- or turf-fired oven, but every village had at least one which everybody could use.

Lighting was not very abundant, either; nor was it complicated. 'No lamp like thy word to guide my feet, to shew light on my path,' sings Psalm 118. Were the Jews content to put up with God's light alone? Not quite. Their houses were very dark and they had great need of physical illumination – in the parable of the lost piece of silver: the woman had to light the lamp to find the coin.[118] It would have been a lamp of the same form that was known throughout the whole of the East in ancient times – a very well-known object, which has been found again and again in diggings. It was either round or oval, tolerably flat, and with two holes in it, one for the flax of hemp wick and the other for filling it by; and the whole was prolonged by a kind of ear or handle, which allowed it to be picked up and carried about. When it was made of clay an ornamental pattern was often cut into it. The most handsome lamps had several holes, some as many as seven, by way of imitating the seven-branched candlestick. Wealthy people had bronze lamps, and those who lived in the pagan manner did not scruple to have them with finely chiselled handles in the shape of an animal – a galloping antelope, for example. But whatever their form, all these lamps spread a sweetish smell of somewhat rancid olive-oil throughout the room: this was the typical odour of the house of the ancient world, as that of rancid butter is of the Tibetan dwelling. Oil was expensive, and the humbler houses had but one lamp. Jesus always speaks of *the* lamp. It was either set in a hole in the wall, or as the Gospel makes it clear,[119] on a stand made of metal or earthenware – a kind of lamp-holder. And, so that there should always be fire in the house, the lamp burnt day and night. All this seems very rudimentary; but did the inhabitants of Palestine live in a markedly different manner as recently as a hundred years ago?

Furniture was extremely simple, and the chief object was the chest – there were chests for provisions and chests for clothes – and even among the wealthy it was very much in use. Very poor people ate on the chest, or on the bushel, the grain-measure, turned upside down.[120] But moderately well-to-do households had tables, and these are very often referred to in the Gospels – there is the table of the rich man, from which the crumbs would have made Lazarus happy.[121] The old nomadic way of sitting on the ground to eat and to talk had not been lost, and many people followed it; but seats in the form of stools, chairs and armchairs were known. They were made of wood frames with stretched cloth or woven straw, and there were also divans for use during the more formal meals. Far removed from feasts were the splendid special chairs such as that of the high priest or the tall seats upon which the doctors of the Law sat in order to teach.

At least among the richer people, the furniture that was used at night was more comfortable than the rest. Sleep was thought to have many virtues: the rabbis had laid down that one ought to sleep at night, and had even decided that those who did not, or could not, would be punished.[122] The bed of our time, mounted on feet, was only to be found among the wealthy, but the influence of the Romans was making it more usual, and some were even to be seen – a most damnable sight – whose wooden frame was in the shape of a pair of immensely drawn-out beasts, with their carved heads forming the foot of the bed. There were cushions and blankets in plenty to make the bed comfortable; and the Proverbs tell us that women who received gentlemen by night scented their beds abundantly.[123] In the summer, the bed was there for the siesta, and it was usual to lie with the back of one's neck in an alabaster head-rest. As for poor people, they put up with mats put on top of one another as a bed, and these they set out in the evening on the floor of the living-room or upon the flat roof: when it was cold they rolled themselves in their cloaks or in a blanket, if they had one. For pillow they had a piece of wood or even a stone, and it is to this that Jesus refers when He says the Son of Man has not a stone upon which to rest His head. Yet the rich man's fine wool blankets as well as the harsh camel-hair covering of the poor were but temporary. Sleep, said the rabbis, was a little death, the 'sixth part of death'. And the terrible Isaiah had proclaimed the eternal lesson, 'There thy corpse lies, with the moth for its shroud, worms for its cerecloth'.[124]

CHAPTER SEVEN

'BY THE SWEAT OF THY BROW'

---

*The divine institution of labour – The 'good shepherd's' life –
The workers in the fields – 'Cast your nets' – The craftsmen.*

THE DIVINE INSTITUTION OF LABOUR

The ancient obligation to 'earn his bread by the sweat of his brow'
which God had laid upon man as a punishment for his fall, was
seen, as we know,[1] by the Jewish tradition as a sign of human
greatness. It was equally regarded by the Law as an imperative
duty which no one had a right to avoid; even the study of the Torah
did not excuse a man from winning his bread.[2] Idleness was
despised and condemned in many places in the Holy Scriptures,
and in the Proverbs alone the idle man, a useless, maleficent
public danger, is furiously blamed no less than thirty times. A
Jew had to have a calling.

But among these callings there seems to be one sort for which
the Chosen People had a particular love – all those kinds of work
that had to do with the earth. Ben Sirach states that 'the farmer's
trade is of divine appointment'.[3] The rabbis pointed out that
Yahweh, to make the kind of work that His people were to do in the
Promised Land quite clear, had said, that they would have 'a
harvest of wheat, and wine, and oil'.[4] One of them, meditating
upon Adam's fate, observed, 'Before he could eat he had to plough
to sow, to reap, to set the corn up in stooks, thresh it, winnow it
and grind it, knead the dough and make the bread'.[5] And his
descendants had to do the same.

One must therefore think of Israel at the time of Christ as an
essentially agricultural and pastoral nation, a people whose
economy was based upon the land. Country matters take up a
surprisingly large proportion of the Scriptures: there is a very
great deal concerning rules for fields, fallow ground, stolen sheep
and fired crops. The festivals of the corn-harvest and the gathering
of the other crops were exceedingly popular among the religious

feasts. In their tireless commentaries upon biblical precepts the doctors of the Law built up no less than four whole tractates of the Talmud to do with agricultural matters, *Peah*, *Dammai*, *Kilayim* and *Sebiith*; and a large proportion of at least ten more also had to do with farming. The Gospels exhale the good smell of ploughed earth, the dry scent of ripened ears of corn and the marvellous odour of the burgeoning vine and the fig-tree. Jesus was a countryman's son: the people and the things of the countryside were very near at hand. And so we find that in most of His parables and His sayings the images are taken directly from the life of those who live on the land. There is the sower, 'the sower gone out to sow' whose seed falls on to different kinds of ground; there is the field of wheat with the tares in it; there are the labourers in the vineyard, the shepherd going off to search for a lost sheep. It is a positive 'Theatre of Agriculture', as Olivier de Serres put it; and its scenes come to life before our eyes.

THE 'GOOD SHEPHERD'S' LIFE

The oldest of all the country callings in Israel was that of the stock-breeder and sheep or cattle herd: long before they had settled as farmers, the Chosen People had wandered from place to place, living in tents and driving their animals from one pasturage to another. This was still a very important occupation at the time of Christ, and in Judaea, particularly, there were immense herds, either on the western heights, from which they could come down in the autumn towards the valleys which still remained green, or in the *midbar*, the waste or 'desert' of Judaea, or in the Jordan valley, where grazing-rights had to be paid, or lastly in the *darom*, the south, towards Idumaea, where the young David had driven his flocks. Samaria and Galilee, too, were not without their herds; nor, on the other side of Jordan, Moab and Peraea. These numerous flocks were made up of sheep and goats; for the cattle were raised in the farms, where they were fed through the winter on a mixture of chaff and barley – green fodder was only just beginning to make its appearance, lucerne, which the Romans (who had it from the Persians) had brought in, being the chief of these crops.

It might be supposed that looking after sheep would be an easy, peaceable trade; and no doubt when there were only a dozen of them they might well be entrusted to a child. But it is clear from many statements in the Bible that some herds consisted of

thousands, even of tens of thousands, and these bleating armie
could only be entrusted to highly skilled men. Shepherds wer
not looked upon with unmixed confidence: there was even a
popular saying that included theirs among those 'brigand'
trades' that no true Jew should ever teach his son. But on
the other hand there were many who praised the excellence of the
shepherd, standing alone there in the vast open spaces under th
sky, leaning on his crook and, like Amos, revolving prophecies
or, like David, poems. Evil minds might hint that many shepherd
'rested quiet among the sheep-folds'[6] instead of looking afte
their charges, but the Book of Proverbs[7] lavishes excellent advic
upon the shepherd and also praises the happiness of the well
conducted pastoral life.[8]

In fact, it was not at all an easy calling. The flocks had t
spend the greater part of the year in the open air: they were le
out the week before the Passover, and they did not come bac
again until half-way through November, at the first rains o
Hesvan. They passed the winter under cover; and from this alon
it may be seen that the traditional date for Christmas, in th
winter, is unlikely to be right, since the Gospel says that th
shepherds were in the fields. Wool shorn at the end of the summe
was better than that of the spring, because the keeping of the shee
indoors matted and soiled their fleeces. Watching over thes
immense flocks called for a very great deal of care and attentior
although the sheep often had one leg fastened to their tail t
prevent them from straying,[9] there would always be some wh
would wander off so far that the dogs could not bring them back
and then the shepherd would have to go himself. Hyenas, jackal
wolves and even bears were fairly common, and it was not unusu
for a shepherd to have to do battle with wild beasts: for this reaso
they were all armed with a solid, iron-bound cudgel and a larg
knife. The 'good shepherd who gives his life for his sheep'[10] wa
no myth: two thousand years ago he was a fact of Palestinian lif
It was a rough living. 'Burning heat by day, and biting frost b
night,' said Jacob, Laban's shepherd.[11] In March and Apri
October and November, there must have been bitterly cold night
on the high plateaux, in spite of the shepherds' thick woolle
cloak. There could be little sleep; yet sometimes a number o
shepherds would agree among themselves and bring thei
different flocks to the same place in the evening, so that eac
shepherd might watch in turn, which would allow the others t

et some sleep in the tent. To make the watching easier, it was usual to make huge sheep-folds with dry-stone walls, high enough o be difficult to get over. Some pasture-grounds even had towers ike those which were built in the vineyards – they exist to this lay – and from the top the watchers could keep a look-out for he approach of robbers, whether they had four legs or two. In he morning, leading the creatures out to drink, the shepherds vould utter piercing cries[12] (as they do to this day) which the sheep new so well that, as the Gospel says, they never mistook one for nother. Shepherds would also play upon a pipe or a flute as they valked along with their sheep.

It is plain that this job was not a sinecure by any means: the hepherd also had to look after the sick sheep and those that were urt, take care of the gravid ewes and the new-born lambs, make vethers of the male lambs that were not to be kept for rams, and ithe the flock according to the Law, which was done by making ll the animals pass through a narrow gate, every tenth beast eing set aside for the priests. The sheep and their shepherds ontinually lived together, and this bred up a real affection, just s one sees today in the Alpine flocks.[13] The famous parables in vhich Christ uses the images of pastoral life were exceedingly vocative for the Palestinians of His time, for they were intimately vell acquainted with that life. There were tame sheep who would ome to their names:[14] shepherds loved their sheep, and the sheep oved them. For a lost ewe, a shepherd would feel the same nxiety as Christ for a soul in danger of perdition: he would be in read for it, would hurry out in search of it, and having found the we, would carry it back on his shoulders. This calling has left nen the unforgettable figure of the Good Shepherd,[15] and one annot speak of it without kindly warmth.

THE WORKERS IN THE FIELDS

s we have seen,[16] the soil of Palestine was reasonably fertile; and n the whole it was well cultivated. In Judaea the various crops vere confined to the lower parts of the little narrow valleys, while he upper slopes and the plateaux were left for grazing; but in ialilee there were more springs and more rain, and the soil, which a any case was better, was almost entirely covered with carefully ended fields; and the Jewish plains, particularly those round the ike, were known as *Jizreel*, God's own plantations. The western trip, the Shephalah, had been the country for excellent wheat

and golden barley time out of mind. The Jewish peasants were
very good at terracing their land against erosion with dry-stone
walls, like those one sees in Provence. They used cattle and sheep
manure, digging it into the fields and mulching the fruit-trees
with it – an operation that the Gospel alludes to in the parable of
the barren fig-tree.[17] And as we have also seen,[18] they had worked
very hard to solve the problem of water, with a whole network of
canals, reservoirs and dams across streams. They praised God that
they were not often forced to 'water with their feet', as they had had
to do in Egypt,[19] that is to say, with engines worked by foot-power
nor to use asses carrying water-skins. But the holdings were often
divided into very small confused plots, far apart, which meant
journeys and so loss of time, without speaking of the loss of
cultivable land, turned into stony roads and paths.

Husbandry was honoured among the Jews; at least, it was at the
time of Christ. For in the earliest times the men from the steppes
had the traditional contempt of the nomad for the settled peasant
This explains why, in the fourth chapter of Genesis, Abel was a
shepherd and Cain a tiller of the ground. Things had changed
however; and in any case the Holy Scriptures had spoken so
frequently of the miracle of the springing plant which comes out
of the earth to bear fruit and harvest that the peasant, as the human
instrument of the divine generosity, could not be despised – far
from it. And at no time did there appear any of that half-witted
superiority of the modern townsman towards the 'mere yokel'
When the Gospels speak of the ploughman, the sower, the worker
in the vineyard, they do so in a tone which acknowledges their
dignity in a way which is more easily felt than defined.

Work on the land is one of those activities that have changed
very little with the centuries. Until the very recent introduction
of the tractor, the fellah of Palestine ploughed, sowed and win
nowed on the threshing-floor just as he had done at the time of
Christ. And there are still many points in which there is no
change. Where small areas, such as kitchen gardens, were
concerned, they broke up the ground with a spade, mattock
and hoe: archeologists have found examples of all these tools
The mattock, indeed, was the proverbial, the ideal tool; did not
Isaiah speak of a time when swords should be turned into
mattocks?[20] For fields, the earth was opened up with a plough
a primitive wheel-less plough such as is still to be seen in Palestine
consisting of a curved wooden coulter with its pointed lower

end engaging in an iron ploughshare, the coulter being attached
to the sole of the plough by the piece of wood, and the sole to
the beam by a leather thong: it is a modest instrument, and it
scratches the earth rather than breaks it up. The plough was
usually drawn by oxen, less frequently by asses or camels. The
Law, in its kindness to animals, said, 'Do not plough with an ox
and an ass together'.[21] To possess a pair of oxen, a yoke, was the
dream of every Jewish peasant. 'The rich harvest tells of the ox
at work,' said the Proverb.[22] The man in the parable[23] who was
asked to the feast thought it perfectly natural that he should
refuse the invitation because, as he said, 'I have bought five pair
of oxen, and I am on my way to make trial of them'. The ploughman held the stilt of the coulter in his right hand and in his left
the *dorban*, the goad which was used to direct the beasts and to
break up the clods. Once he had set his hand to the plough
he had to keep his eyes straight ahead and not look back, as our
Lord observes.[24] It was heavy work, and although ploughing
was not done until the first rains had fallen, the earth was still
often very hard and filled with stones against which the thistle-
clogged share would grate and shriek. The ploughman would
not begin his work until he had said a prayer: 'Lord, my task is
the red, the green is Thine: we plough, but it is Thou that dost
give the crop.'[25] *Red*, for the good ploughland of Palestine is of
a warm deep purplish-red under the brilliant sky.

Once the field was well worked (and often it called for several
ploughings), they went over it with the harrow and then sowed.[26]
This usually happened during the month of *Tisri* (October) or
at some other time in the winter, but there were also spring
crops that were sown in *Adar* (March). Many people contented
themselves with sowing broadcast, with that well-known 'august
motion' of the hand, but particularly careful men would bend
down and set the seed in the furrow, especially in the case of
wheat, so that it should not be lost 'among the stones and the
briars' as the parable says.

Towards the Feast of the Passover, the fields became 'white
with the promise of harvest', in the words of Saint John;[27] and
it was in April that the apostles found and ate ripe ears of corn.[28]
The harvest began with the barley, and the wheat followed a
short month later. There were no scythes, and the reaping
(as Saint Matthew's Gospel points out in the parable of the crop
growing by itself[29]) was done with a sickle: some sickles had

233

notched blades, others were plain, but neither kind was strongly
curved. The Law gave the poor the right to glean[30] (one has
but to recall the lovely Book of Ruth) and even to pick up forgotten sheaves;[31] and it laid down that the corners of the fields were
not to be reaped, but to be left for the needy.[32] The sheaves were
stacked by the house, and the people would take advantage of
fine dry days to begin the threshing. To do this they spread the
corn out on the *goren*, a threshing-floor made of pounded earth
and situated some way out of the village, if possible on a height
that would catch the wind, and passed the husking-sledge over
it. This was a thick wooden slab with points in it, and a man
would stand upon it to make it heavier: the oxen that dragged it
round the floor were not to be muzzled, for they had a right to
share in the harvest.[33] Presently the threshing-floor would be
filled with a mixture of cut straw, husks and grain, the whole
making a golden mass, and the like was to be seen throughout
the Holy Land, gleaming from afar. This was the moment for
winnowing: the men, armed with three-pronged wooden forks,
would throw the mixture into the air for the wind to separate
it – the grain fell straight down, the chaff was carried away. But
as Ecclesiasticus says,[34] it was not right to winnow with every
wind: the morning or evening breeze, blowing from the Mediterranean, did not threaten to carry everything away, as the wind
from the desert certainly would. Then they 'swept the threshing
floor clean',[35] and after that there was no more to do but to
heap up the grain in the storeroom (not in the *greniers*, or attics,
since with flat roofs) there were none with all due precaution
against thievish birds or men.

All these tasks called not only for labour but also for care.
And how hazardous a business it was. The desert-wind might
parch up the young shoots; there might not be rain enough.
It was only too possible that tares might invade the field, for
when the tares and the corn were both young they could not be told
apart. The seeds of tares, mixed with corn, made the eater ill; and
however much care was taken with the cleanliness of the seed and
the sowing, an evil-minded man might always come and scatter
tare-seed in the field, as it says in the parable.[36] Again, a cloud
of locusts might come down, and these voracious creatures, tons of
them, would not leave a single green shoot standing. Yet if God
wished, the harvest might be good: not all the seeds would produce
the 'hundred for one' of the parable, but ten or twenty stems from

each plant would be quite satisfactory; and the rabbi Jose speaks of a modest five measures of corn for one of seed.[37] This must have been about the average yield in Judaea.

But clearly ploughing, sowing and harvesting did not make up the whole of the countryman's necessary work. The Palestinian economy was still somewhat primitive, and each farm had a tendency to try to produce everything it needed. There would be a kitchen garden and three or four sheep for the family's wool; and usually the women looked after both. The poorest country family would have a few vines, so that they might have grapes, and there were some to be found in the towns, growing in court-yards. But there were also real vineyards, worked in a big way; and in these there were watchtowers, like those which the shepherds built. Figs and other fruit trees, and even sometimes olives, were planted in vineyards, to enable the vines to climb up them and trail from tree to tree; but the vines were also allowed to run at ground-level. Pruning as we understood it was quite unknown; there was a little trimming after the flowering, and that was all. In any case, they did not pamper the vine at all: it did extremely well in the soil and the climate of Palestine, and at the most it was kept clear of weeds. The biblical expression 'to be under the vine and the fig-tree' meant the delight of doing nothing whatever. The real work in the vineyard started at the time of the vintage; but it was an unusually cheerful kind of work. The weather was fair and warm, and people went to camp among the vineyards; the gatherers, armed with little hooked knives, cut the full bunches and they sang and laughed as they did so. The young men took the baskets and carried them to the village press, where the grapes were thrown into the vat – not a large vat, only some six feet by six feet – and trodden by the bare-foot workers to the sound of songs and the clapping of hands. The intoxicating smell of the new wine would turn many a head.

Unending labour of the countryside: there were also the figs to be gathered, dried in the sun and pressed into cakes that every household had to have. And then twice a year the olive-trees had to be struck with long wands, the first time to see whether the olives were ready, the second to bring them down; and once down, the ripe olives had to be picked up (knee-pads were put on for this work) and crushed in the olive-press, either in a large one, with an ass turning the stone, or at home, in which case the women did the work. Some districts had special crops:

for instance, at Jericho, that wonderful oasis that hangs over the Jordan, there were the date-palms: their cultivation called for great care and some acrobatic skill for their fertilization, but the fruit sold very well. In Galilee there was the flax, which might be considered the only industrial crop in the Holy Land: in spring its sky-blue flowers covered immense areas. The peasants pulled it up and sold it dry, the leaves and seeds being removed, but the retting and scutching of the flax was the work of a specialised artisan.

All in all, was the countryman's life a happy or an arduous one? It was probably between the two, a happy medium. They did not work extraordinarily hard: in the East nobody has ever worked extraordinarily hard, except the slaves and the convicts. The average man was happy if he had enough to live on – if he could honestly come by the necessities of life he was content. At the time of Christ the economic crisis which was to grow so serious between the years 30 and 70 had hardly begun, and it did not yet affect the ordinary peasant. To be sure, there was a vast difference between the standard of living of a great landed proprietor whose estates were managed by a steward and that of the man who worked his own piece of ground himself; but although many of the countrymen were poor, real grinding poverty was exceptional.[38] The holy land which the One God had intended for His people, kept them adequately. 'Where Thy feet have passed, the stream of plenty flows . . . herds throng the fields, and the valleys stand deep in corn; the shout of joy is everywhere, everywhere the hymn of praise,' sang the Psalmist,[39] and all the Jews were ready to echo his words.

'CAST YOUR NETS'

Next to the peasant stood the fisherman. Officially, we know the two callings are still joined. These men 'had an honourable place in society, although it may not have been very lofty', in the first place because they 'supplied one of the most important items in the ordinary diet', and then because they, like the Bretons, had the reputation of being unusually pious. 'Their great piety sometimes appeared in an embarrassing form. When the fishermen of the lake of Tiberias decided not to work on the partial holidays during the Feasts of the Passover and Tabernacles this act of supererogation aroused general protests.' What would people eat?[40]

There had been fishermen in Israel beyond the memory of man. Archaeologists have dug up weights for nets, needles for repairing them, and fish-hooks. Isaiah, Jeremiah, Amos, Habakkuk and Job all speak of fishermen and their work. The Gospel is filled with scenes from the life of fishermen: Christ took his first disciples from among them, and His teaching has a great number of figures taken from their calling.[41]

It is sure that at the time of Christ the fishermen formed a well-known and well-liked body of workers. There were some who lived on the Mediterranean coast – at Jaffa there has been found the inscribed gravestone of one of them – and in imitation of the Phoenicians they sometimes went a considerable distance northwards. But it was chiefly round the Sea of Galilee that they were to be found: as we have seen,[42] this water was full of fish, and in reading the Gospel one even gets the impression that the majority of the people on its shores must have lived from fishing, some, most probably, working their fields as well. The little ports of the lake had names that support this impression – Bethsaida, 'the fishery', and Magdala, 'the fish tower' or 'the dried fishes'. Strabo speaks of Tarichaea, under its Greek name, as an important centre for preserved fish.[43]

Their manner of fishing was also of the utmost antiquity, though no doubt the ancient fish-hook made of a thorn, of which Amos speaks,[44] had given place to the copper, brass or iron hooks that the archaeologists have found. There were two sorts of nets, which is quite clear from the Bible: when Jesus says to the disciples, 'Cast your nets,' He obviously cannot be speaking of the same kind of net as that in the parable – a net that 'enclosed fish of every kind at once; when it was full the fishermen drew it up, and sat down on the beach'.[45] The first was the throwing-net, a round one of perhaps twelve feet across, with leads all round the edge, and it was designed to catch the fish by dropping over them: the second was a seine, the *sagene* of the Greeks, a band five hundred yards long and more, and twelve feet deep, with floaters above and sinkers below. It was used in this way: 'When they reach the place where they intend to fish, some of the crew go ashore, holding the end of one of the long ropes that terminate the net at either end, while the boat goes away from the bank until the rope is all paid out. Then one of the men afloat gently lowers the net into the water while the boat travels in a great semi-circle. As soon as this course has brought them in to the shore again, the men on board get into the water, carrying with them that second rope which finishes the other end of the net; and once they are on land they all haul on the two ropes, each being pulled equally and without stopping until the net is near to the shore.'[46] These nets were expensive and they needed a great deal of maintenance – the first apostles were in the very act of mending theirs at the moment when Christ called to them to follow Him. As for the boats, which are also frequently mentioned in the Gospel, they must have been very like those which are still to be seen, big, wide and solid, standing up well to the wind, but not very fast. Nothing is more slow to change than the shape of a boat that is well adapted to the conditions it has to sail in and the work it has to do: there are vessels made of papyrus on Lake Tana in Abyssinia which are exactly like those in the Egyptian hieroglyphics; and the Welsh coracle of today is that which Caesar described.

When the fishes were caught, they had to be sorted out, in the first place because the different kinds varied in worth – the fishermen of the lake of Geneva or Le Bourget carefully set aside the trout, then the pollan, then the perch and the pike, and then the rest. But the Galilean fishermen had another reason for very exact sorting, since some fish could not be sold, at least not to practising Jews – these were the unclean fish,[47] those without scales or fins, such as catfish, eels, rays and lampreys, which were thrown back,[48] unless they were hidden and sold privately to pagans, who as it happened, were particularly fond of these particular abominations.

The fishermen were obliged to club together to buy the necessary equipment; they also had to co-operate to carry out the work. They formed crews that usually numbered six or eight, with one as captain, like Simon called Peter, or Zebedee. In speaking of the members of these teams Saint Luke uses the two words *koinonoi*, associates, and *metochoi*, partakers,[49] which shows that their partnership extended to sharing the proceeds. It has even been supposed that perhaps the fishermen of the lake, or at least all those of one village, joined in a true co-operative union, in order to sell their fish to the salters and the wholesalers of Jerusalem on better terms. The yield was necessarily hazardous: fish were there or they were not there; and one could not always have the Son of Man with one to ensure a miraculous draught.

The fisherman's life strengthens his character: it is work that insists upon courage and firmness, as well as patience; and it is clear that those freshwater sailors, the fishermen of the Sea of Galilee, stood out from all the other workers who are mentioned in the Gospel. They seem to have been men of strong and ardent minds, open, hearty, enthusiastic spirits – 'Sons of thunder', as Christ called two of them, James and John, not without a kindly irony.[50] Even today one may see the Galilean fishermen skipping for joy at a good catch; and under the fierce sun they may be heard chanting at the top of their voices.[51] It is understandable that for the work He meant to undertake, Christ should have called upon these strong, brave, spirited men and upon their loyalty. He said to them, 'Come and follow me; I will make you into fishers of men'. And Simon and Andrew, and then James and John, left their nets on the ground.[52]

THE CRAFTSMEN

Most of Christ's Jewish contemporaries may have earned their living by farming or fishing, but there was nevertheless what may be called a working class. Obviously, it was relatively much less numerous than it is in our modern Western societies, in which industry is the ruling element: it bore roughly the same proportion to the rest as ours did in the Middle Ages. A great many of the products that now come from factories were then made at home. The women ground their own corn, and every day or at least every two or three days each housewife spent an hour in turning the upper millstone on the lower, which was fixed to the ground: the rumbling of the grinders was the sign of continuing life; if it were to stop, it would be the end of the world – a figure used both in Jeremiah and the Revelation.[53] When the dough was kneaded and when it had risen, it was cooked at home in a little oven or upon stones covered with a hood of fire-resisting clay: the very poor went to the town's communal oven. To a large extent the clothing was home-made, too: the excellent wife of the Proverbs 'busied herself with wool and thread', holding the distaff and the spindle. She herself 'made the coverlet on her bed and the clothes of lawn and purple that she wore'.[54] These domestic activities, then, almost entirely did away with the miller and the baker, as well as the oil-presser, and entered into competition with the weaver and the tailor, to say nothing of the cheese-maker and the man who prepared preserves and a great many other craftsmen, who had scarcely any reason for existence.

There is a noble discussion of craftsmen, their nature and

their worth, in Ecclesiasticus,[55] in which Jesus ben Sirach speaks of those who 'look to their hands for a living', the men without whom 'there is no building up a commonwealth'. There were craftsmen in Israel, then: and the Bible mentions twenty-five separate trades. They were to be recognised in the street: the carpenters and joiners had a chip behind their ear, the dyers a coloured rag, the tailors a very large bone needle stuck into their upper garment, and even the scribes carried a pen: but all were forbidden to go out on the Sabbath wearing the signs of their trade.[56] The crafts were usually hereditary, going down from father to son: there were families, whole dynasties, of sandal-makers, tent-weavers – Saint Paul comes to mind – potters and goldsmiths.

In the passage that has just been quoted, Ben Sirach picks the smith and the potter as examples of craftsmen: there is the first sitting by his anvil, intent upon his iron-work, cheeks shrivelled 'with the smoke, as he battles with the heat of the furnace, ears ringing again with the hammer's clattering', and the second 'at work, treadles flying, anxious continually over the play of his hands, over the rhythm of his craftsmanship; arms straining at the stiff clay, feet matching its strength with theirs. To finish off the glaze is his nearest concern, and long he must wake to keep his furnace clean.' In these two perfect miniatures we see village industry in action – artisans working on their own account. At the time of Christ this was the most widely spread form of production. In a society three-quarters of whose members were peasants the craftsmen worked primarily for the peasants. The smith was essential for the making and repairing of agricultural tools, mattocks, spades, ploughshares, axes; every big village had its own, and his hammer sounded through the working hours. But there were also travelling smiths who visited the hamlets. Iron came from Lebanon or from Spain, and it was sold by the Phoenicians.

No less useful was the potter, and in several places the Bible likens his work to that of God the Creator Himself.[57] It was a very old trade indeed, which the Israelites had learnt from the Canaanites, who in their turn had no doubt had it from the Egyptians. People went to the potter for a great many things: pitchers, bowls, great jars for storing grain, lamps, braziers, toys and even writing-tablets as well as a hundred other objects. The potters, almost as if they meant to help the archeologists of the future, often changed the shape and the decoration of their wares, and this allows one now to date them when they are found. At the time of Christ, saucepans with a wide, convenient lid were fashionable, as well as rounded pitchers with long necks and two handles, and little oil-lamps with longer handles for greater ease in carrying; and it had become usual to decorate surfaces with delicate ribs made on the wheel.

But before a man needed pots he had to build his house and furnish it, and here again skilled craftsmen were needed, not only the stone-quarriers who worked the limestone and the basalt, but even more the men who dug the clay in the Jordan valley – the clay that was used for pottery and for the wattle and daub of the poorer houses. (Near the Dead Sea there were also sulphur quarries, but these were not worked by individual craftsmen.) The stonecutters from whom one ordered the vats for the wine-presses (they were made from a single piece of stone) and the basalt grinders for the household mills, as well as the fine masonry for the houses of the rich, were specialists: who else would have had such tools – picks, special saws, wedges, polishers – and who else would have known how to use them? Men could do without masons when it was a question of building a dry-stone wall or making a mud and wattle partition, but for the more difficult things they had to be called in, with their special hammers, saws, lines, levels, trowels, plumb-lines and measuring rods. The wealthy brought highly skilled workmen in from the coast of Phoenicia and Greeks, but the village mason did not lack employment.

Of all the rural craftsmen's trades it appears that there was one of particular importance – Saint Joseph's trade, and undoubtedly that of Christ in His youth.[58] The word 'carpenter' in exactly the sense that we use it today, did not exist in Hebrew, but there were 'cutters' or 'workers of wood', and their part in the village was considerable. Their work was not only indispensable, but even insisted upon by the Law, for Leviticus speaks of the stones and wooden beams in the construction of a house, and Ben Sirach observes that a dwelling whose wooden framework is well made will stand up to violent shaking.[59] The carpenter would have been a familiar sight in the everyday life in Israel, as we may gather from Christ's famous words to the Pharisee: 'How is it that thou canst see the speck of dust which is in thy brother's eye, and art not aware of the beam which is in thy own?'[60] The carrying

241

of beams in those little crowded streets must have been tolerably dangerous, and one of the rabbinical discussions concerns the case of a man bearing a beam colliding with one holding a pitcher.[61] Not without irony, Christ tells the hypocrite that instead of minding his neighbour's business, he would be better advised to watch the beam that is approaching – the beam that may thrust out his eye.

The carpenter's trade properly so called was comparatively recent in Israel. In the days of Solomon and David, Tyrians had to be sent for:[62] but under Joas there were carpenters attached to the Temple,[63] and after they came back from Babylon the Jews took to the trade as a matter of course. But at that time, unless very splendid buildings were concerned (and perhaps not even then) or the Temple of Herod, the work must have been of the simplest kind – nothing in comparison with the roofing of a steeple or the calculation of a spiral staircase, as our journeymen-carpenters of today are required to do. As the roofs were flat, all that was needed was the laying of the beams and the covering of them with interwoven reeds: and the outside staircases went straight up. It is not likely that the craftsmen could have lived on this kind of work alone. But in fact the carpenter was much more than a mere layer of beams. *Naggar* in Aramaic, like *tekton* in Greek, meant both carpenter and joiner, and in a general sense 'the builder of houses'. And to this may be added cabinet-maker, carver, wheelwright and plough- and yoke-maker, as well as woodcutter, to begin at the very beginning. In short, all the crafts to do with wood – a lack of specialization quite typical of rural industry.

The prophet Isaiah shows the wood-worker going into the forest to choose the ilex and the oak and felling the pine and the cedar, both to have his raw material and wood for his fire.[64] The same thing would certainly have happened in the time of Christ. The most esteemed wood was that of the sycamore, which was proof against the worm and which, when it was properly treated, was hard enough to serve instead of iron as a ploughshare: cedar was the most costly, because its transport for the Lebanon in bulk was expensive, and scarcely less dear was the oak of Bashan. For ordinary use, people made do with olive and cypress, or, for small things, old vine trunks.

The workshop of the carpenter, of the *naggar* – a workshop like Saint Joseph's, for example, at Nazareth – had to be equipped for all the kinds of work that would be ordered. One man would come to have the stilt or the coulter of his plough repaired; another would ask for a pergola to be set up along the side of his house; a woman might come to buy a chest or possibly a bushel to measure her wheat, another a kneading-trough, and still another a support for straw pallets; or a mason would come to order jambs and lintels for doors. What a variety of things! The tools were very much the same as those which our modern wood-workers use: axe, hatchet, saw, knives, adze (the *ascia* of the Romans, which the Christians made one of their secret symbols, meaning the Cross[65]), plane, the square and the cramp: the hammer, of course, was well known, as well as nails, which were often made of bronze. The archeologists have turned up a good many of them. At an early date the drill had been introduced from Egypt: it was a bow-drill, turned with great rapidity. Clearly, then, the carpenter of Palestine was a man of parts: he was uncommonly useful, and he was very much esteemed.

This village craftsmanship was all that Israel had until the exile; but new kinds of work grew up with the growth of the towns. The townsmen, even those who still had pieces of land outside the walls, could not produce all they needed in the way of food and clothing, and obviously it was no longer possible for them to build their own houses. And on the other hand, as the peasant became better off, he was no longer content with his rustic products, and when he came in to sell his vegetables, eggs and oil at the market, he hoped at the same time to buy something that would increase his comfort at home. This evolution towards the development of an urban class of artisans and workers became apparent in Jerusalem after the return from exile, and it became very much more pronounced throughout all the cities of Israel in the century that preceded Christ's birth. Thus the Greeks and the Samaritans competed for the milling trade, both in corn and oil:[66] the butcher, pointless in the village, prospered in the city, under the inspection of the priests, who saw to it that the meat was 'clean', that is, that the animals had been properly bled: the clothing trade also grew up, and there were carders, weavers, tailors, tanners, leather-workers and sandal-makers. Tailors are never mentioned in the Old Testament, but they appear in the Talmud.[67] The growing towns, then, had brought into being real industries that catered for the needs of all, the comfort of the well-to-do and the luxury of the rich. Goldsmiths

flourished, all the more so in that men too wore jewels – ther
was the gold ring that the Prodigal's father put on his hand, fo
example – and that women delighted in bracelets, necklaces
gorgets, ear-rings and diadems: the apocalyptic writers cried ou
against this shameless luxury, but in vain.[68] It was the sam
with the use of scent, which had been customary from ver
ancient times in Israel but which in the last few hundred year
had grown in an extraordinary manner: scents for the womer
scents for the guests invited to a feast, and also, it should not b
forgotten, scents for the ceremonies of religion and for th
embalming of the dead. All this amounted to a very considerabl
clientele.

In addition to these callings which produced the peoples
necessaries or their luxuries, there were those which provide
services – the little trades like that of the water-carrier, fc
example, a very much needed person, seeing that almost n
houses had their own water. There were also barbers and hair
dressers, who looked after women's hair, cut it and oiled it, a
well as caring for the beards of men; all the people employe
in the public baths, stokers, masseurs and servants; and th
'fullers', who were none other than our laundrymen, as tha
verse in Saint Mark proves which, in the account of the Trans
figuration of our Lord, reads: 'His garments became white
dazzling white like snow, white as no fuller here on earth coul
have made them.'[69]

Men of the same trade tended to live together. Sometime
there were technical reasons for this: for example, it was con
venient for the weavers to live at Sapphoris in Galilee, in the middl
of the flax country. At Magdala and Tarichaea, on the shore
of the lake, there were the fish-salters; at Hebron, Maresa, Zep
and Soccoh, where there was clay that moulded well, there wer
the potters. And affinity brought them together in the town:
so that at Jerusalem there was the street of the butchers, that c
the smiths and that of the bakers; which seems to prove th
existence of trade-guilds like those of Europe in the Middle Age:
But in any case there is a reference in a text as early as the Boo
of Nehemiah to a corporation of apothecaries and to Uzzi
the son of Harhaiah the chief of the goldsmiths:[70] they gathere
together for mutual assistance, and also so that they could kee
an eye upon one another. It seems that it was this system c
guilds that brought about the obligation of working only ever

The Land—its Beauty and Diversity

I

Luxuriant vegetation along the banks of the River Jordan contrasts with the severity of the surrounding country

The village of Malloula. To this
day its inhabitants speak
Aramaic, the language that
Christ spoke

3

The Romans built this road
across the plains of Transjordan

4 and 5

The hill in Jerusalem on which the Temple was built (*right*). The barren hills of Judaea, little changed since the time of Christ (*below*)

River Jordan winds its way
gh the surrounding desert
the length of the country

7
The Mount of the Temptation
in the Judean desert between,
Jerusalem and Jericho

The People, and Their Everyday Life

8

A Jew wearing the *tallith*, prayer shawl

9

Ladles used to pour wine in libation

10

The ass and the camel, two Biblical beasts of burden which are still used today

11

Mosaics excavated at the ancient
Roman port of Caesarea

12

Stone ossuary from Jerusalem,
dating from the time of Christ.
Such chests, often decorated
with chip carving resembling
woodwork, were used to house
the bones of the dead removed
from family vaults to make
room for further burials

13
Roman cooking pot found in a tomb at Hugog, Galilee. 1st – 2nd century AD

14
Women drawing water from a well

15
(1) Bronze sestertius of Tiberius, AD 15–16. (2) Bronze c of Herod of Archelaus, BC–AD 6. (3) Bronze coin Antioch in Syria, time Augustus. (4) Bronze coin Caesarea, AD 14. (5) Bro sestertius of Tiberius, w head of Tiberius, c. AD 15– (6) Bronze coin of Procur of Judaea, time of Augus c. AD 5–6

1

2

3

4

5

6

16
Shepherds, with their flocks of long-eared sheep, in the shade of the walls of Jericho

17

A tile stamped with the emblem
of the Tenth Roman Legion
—LEG (10) X FRE (TENSIS).
It was excavated at Ramat
Rahel, near Jerusalem

18

Typical oil-burning lamps.
These were found near
Jerusalem

Survivals from the Time of Christ

19
The pool of Siloe, the scen
of the healing of the man w
was born blind (John, 9)

20

Part of the original Temple walls left standing after the destruction of Jerusalem by the Romans (*right*)

21

Another tomb in Jerusalem, sealed, as was Christ's, with a large rock (*below*)

22

This tomb near the Basilica of the Holy Sepulchre in Jerusalem is traditionally that of Joseph of Arimathea

23

These steps on the eastern slope of Mount Sion, leading from the Cenacle (the place of the Last Supper) to the pool of Siloe, were probably used by Christ and the Apostles

24

The tomb of Rachel, wife of Jacob. It is near Bethlehem, on the road to Jerusalem

25

Jesus must have taken this r[
when he went from Nazaret[
Cana

26

Remains of the synagogue s[
to have been built by [
centurion whose servant [
healed by Christ at Capernar[

Religious Life

Containers in which the Dead
Sea Scrolls were found

29
Phylacteries; small leath[er]
boxes containing vellum i[n]
scribed with texts from Exod[us]
and Deuteronomy

The *shofar*, a musical strument fashioned from ram's horn, used to usher the Holy Days

other day in the callings whose trade was slow, with the consequent risk of unemployment, and that induced the rabbis to enforce it. But the disadvantage of the system was that it kept back technical advance, all the more so because the Jewish workman, in his distrust of everything pagan, was unwilling to imitate the occupiers and follow the ways of Rome.

From a technical point of view, then, the Jewish workshops must have been well behind those of Rome and the Hellenistic cities, except in the communities of the Diaspora and in those towns which were three parts paganised, like Caesarea. Obviously, there was nothing that could be compared to our modern industries. No machines, except the mill turned by asses: and one does not get the impression that the water-mill, which is described by Vitruvius, was known in Palestine. Nor did the Jews know the clothes-press which the Roman tailors used. Everything was at that early stage at which hand-power is all that is available for setting the tools in motion – sometimes feet as well, as with potters. The unit was almost always the small workshop: a master-craftsman, a few journeymen and apprentices. It was only in the making of cloth, particularly among the Galilean *byssus* weavers, that larger workshops were to be found; and even then it is not sure that the numbers went beyond fifty or so. The only very large bodies of workers of which we have any knowledge were those which the rulers brought together for their great undertakings: for example, there is the exceptional case of Herod and the ten thousand he employed in the building of the Temple.

All this was rather unimpressive; and upon the whole it appears that the peasant, the fisherman, the stockbreeder and the country craftsman were better off and more highly esteemed than the urban workers. Of course, there were those who maintained that this was not so, and some rabbis who asserted that the country callings were of no value and even 'that they were base'. But the wisest were not of this opinion, and the tractate *Yebamoth* went so far as to state that when time came to an end 'all the craftsmen would come back to the land'.[71] There is nothing new about urging people to seek the grass-roots again.

CHAPTER EIGHT

FROM TRADERS TO BRIGANDS

'Neither are we delighted in merchandise' – Big business and banking – The moral aspect of money and business – 'Where, then, does wisdom lie? . . . Not here, cries the abyss . . . and the sea echoes, Not here' – Roads and caravan-tracks – Travellers and brigands.

'NEITHER ARE WE DELIGHTED IN MERCHANDISE'

There is a remark in Josephus' *Contra Apionem* which is likely to astonish the twentieth-century reader: 'First, therefore, our nation neither inhabiteth a country bordering upon the sea, neither are we delighted in merchandise . . . But our cities are situate far from the sea in a most fertile soil, which we till with all industry.'[1] Among all the means of gaining a livelihood that are open to a man today, it seems that commerce rather than agriculture is the one in which a descendant of the Twelve Tribes is likely to excel: yet a valid reply to this is that one must not confuse acquired characteristics with those which are inherited, that the Jews' concentration upon business is more a matter of historical conditioning than any 'commercial genius', allegedly one of the chief qualities of the Chosen Race, and that in any case the success of the Zionist *kibbutzim* has given the lie to the anti-Semites' theory that the Jew is incapable of working on the land.[2]

It may well be, however, that Josephus' words had an underlying purpose: he may have wished to counter one of the anti-Semitical arguments of his day. For although it is true that when the semi-nomadic Israelites first came into the land of Canaan they were not interested in trade, which they left to the natives of the country – uninterested to such a point that in biblical Hebrew one of the words which is translated as 'merchant' is in fact 'Canaanite'[3] – and although it is true that Deuteronomy, so meticulous in all matters concerning pastoral and rural law, has not a word to say about commercial legislation, yet never-theless it is quite certain that as soon as they were firmly settled in Palestine the Israelites undoubtedly had to engage in trade, even if it were only to sell what they produced and buy essential commodities, such as iron for their tools, for example. The growth of the towns naturally quickened the increase of trade: no considerable community can live without traders. Even before the exile the prophets were speaking of merchants; and in Amos and Hosea there are unflattering portraits of traders grown rich by the use of false weights and through dishonest speculation.[4] In Babylon the exiles had no land and therefore were obliged to suit themselves to something other than a rural life. After the return from exile Palestine became a part of the Hellenistic world, which was commercial to its marrow, and whether they liked it or not the Israelites were necessarily affected by the commercial nature of the period – that is to say, they lived in the midst of business. So although it may be true that at the time of Christ the Jews 'did not delight in merchandise', it is equally true that they managed to overcome their repugnance and engage in trade.

In the first place there was the local commerce of the markets and fairs, which, among so rural a population, were very much frequented. The peasants came in to sell their corn, their figs, wine and lambs, and to buy manufactured goods, tools, shoes, jewels, scent. The tractate *Baba Kamma* in the Talmud makes it clear that the women of Judaea brought excellent woollen cloth to the market, and those of Galilee linen garments.[5] Another tractate shows that there were already positive tariffs fixing the prices for a whole region.[6] In order to deal with excessive prices and false measures the local Sanhedrim appointed market inspectors with wide powers, who could even settle the right price of an article in case of dispute.[7]

Another form of trading existed alongside this local commerce – that of the travelling merchants and pedlars. There seem to have been a good many of them, and they were very much like those who are still to be seen in the country today: they went from village to village with their heavily laden asses and offered the housewives their tempting wares: purple robes from Sidon, fine-spun linen, gold rings and gorgets, and even carpets, as the Levantines do today. They calculated their journeys so as to arrive at the great cities in time for the feasts: at the Passover they crowded round the Temple and even made their way into its courts. There are two other Hebrew words that mean 'trader': one of them, *rokel*, is literally 'he who moves about', and the other, *soher*, 'the traveller'.

But in the towns the pedlars had formidable rivals, the shop-keepers. These had been in existence for a great while: the Book of Kings shows that in the time of Ahab and Jezebel (before 850 BC) it was possible for the prosperous owner of a bazaar in Samaria to have branches in Damascus.[8] At the time of Christ, Jerusalem and the other great towns would have had *souks* like those which we see now in the East, with very small shops side by side, opening on to the narrow streets, and merchants who spread out their wares and cry their praises in the hope of attracting customers.

It is a curious fact, and one which supports Josephus, that the Jewish traders should have complained of the competition of the cunning pagan merchants, just as the Christian traders of the West used to complain (and still do, from what one hears) of the competition of the Jews. The trading Greeks had invaded Palestine, with their felt hats, their Laodicean sandals, their beautifully worked caskets, their delicate pottery; this was easy for them, since the Greek cities of Palestine[9] served as *entrepôts*. When Herod Antipas built his unclean city of Tiberias, the practising Jews would not live in it,[10] and it became a centre for Greek traders, which confirmed its evil reputation.

But in spite of the markets and the fairs, the peddling and the bazaars, all this trade did not amount to anything very consider-able. This is proved by the rarity of silver coins and by the fact that only bronze, minted in Judaea itself, had any general currency.[11] Another indication is the payment in kind, to which Christ alludes when He bids us give 'good measure, pressed down and shaken up and running over' for 'the measure you award to others is the measure that will be awarded to you'.[12] It was scarcely commerce, but rather barter.

BIG BUSINESS AND BANKING

But Jewish business certainly did not confine itself within these primitive limits. What we know as 'big business' had long been in existence. The first kings of Israel, David and even more Solomon, had also been the first big business-men: with the help of their friends the Phoenicians they devised a whole system of exchanges which brought them in wood, metals, cloth and various luxuries against their corn, oil, wine, honey, fruit and aromatic products.[13] Solomon even organized very profitable sales of horses; and he had an interest in Tyrian shipping. These royal enterprises were imitated by others, and from as early as the eighth century the traders of whom Amos and Hosea spoke would have gone beyond the modest commerce of fairs and markets. But i. was above all during the time of the exile that the Jews discovered the nature of big business, for Babylon was indeed one of the world's trading capitals. However sad they may have been because of their exile from the Holy Land, the Jews still reacted vigorously against their adverse fate, and several among them set up as traders or bankers, making their fortune thereby. The ledgers of the Rothschild of those days, one Muraschu, have been discovered; and in the records of a trading house of Nippur may be read countless Jewish names among the clients. It may even be the case that the return to the Holy Land after the decree of Cyrus was financed by the wealthy Jews of Babylonia, as Zionism is by Jewish millionaires in America today.

The Jews who came back to Palestine had therefore learnt how to handle great commercial undertakings, and they went on doing so. The extension of the Jewish colonies in the Diaspora provided them with agents of their own nation everywhere: Babylon, Damascus, Alexandria, Ephesus and later on in Rome. Their business was carried on with their cousins. Not that this prevented them from having dealings with the pagans: far from it. The Maccabees, the heroes of the war of liberation, had done their utmost to acquire a window on the Mediterranean, and this they obtained, in the form of Jaffa. Simon and then John Hyrcanus took a close interest in sea-borne trade, and their example was followed. Verses twenty-three to thirty of Psalm 106 give the liveliest description of the perils that the sea-going commercial traveller of Jewish big business had to contend with upon the deep.

At the time of Christ, Israel had its big-business world, which was in continual touch with the communities of the Diaspora and also with the pagan merchants of the entire empire: and the men in power were very close to this world. Herod the Great shared in the profitable commercial operations which were based on Caesarea, the new commercial centre that he had built. The Epistle of Saint James gives us an idea of the business practice of those times: a trader would go and settle in a distant city and spend a year there negotiating sales and then return to Palestine to execute the orders – it is not altogether unlike our system of representatives.[14]

What was the big business of that time concerned with? Chiefly with grain, import and export, and banking. Corn was dealt with by wholesale, for the peasants were very willing not to have to take their harvest and sell it in the town, and the bakers of the towns could not go out from village to village for their supplies. This brought into existence the dealer known to the Greeks as the *sitones*, who was, furthermore, very often a Greek or a Hellenized Alexandrian Jew. 'He buys the wheat wholesale to sell it retail,' says the Talmud: some acted merely as collectors; others, who were bolder, dealt as we now say in futures – they would buy the standing crop, hoping to profit by the peasant's desire to have his money quickly. Some traders dealt not only in wheat, but also in oil, salt fish and dried fruit: the Greeks called these men *monopoles*, and the word, as well as the man, was perfectly well known in Palestine.[15] Christ no doubt alludes to these people in the parable of the wise and the foolish virgins.[16] At Alexandria, the Jewish *monopolei* had pride of place; in their famous *diplostoon*, as we have seen, they had warehouses for all kinds of product, and they were thought to control the whole corn-trade of the empire.[17]

These wholesale dealings were naturally accompanied by an import and export trade. Palestine produced enough wheat, oil, meat and dates to be able to sell all these commodities, and the Greek cities and those of the coast bought them. The export of the rarer products took them much farther, as far as Egypt and Rome: among these was the balm from Jericho, which according to Strabo[18] sold for the price of gold. The scent trade was in the hands of a small group of intelligent merchants, who were conversant with the limiting of production to keep the prices up. Pliny relates[19] that during the great war the Jews tried to destroy all the growing balm, for fear that any should fall into the hands of the enemy, and that 'there were furious combats for the possession of a bush'. Palestine, on the other hand, was obliged to import a certain number of raw materials, primarily wood and iron, as well as such things as silk, spices, scents and sandalwood. Of all these importations from abroad the most necessary was incense, for the Temple services could not do without it. It came from Arabia, or to be more exact from what is now the Hadhramaut

– most probably the Queen of Sheba's realm – and the trade was entirely confined to the great organizers of caravans.

All these important dealings called for capital: that is to say, it was essential that there should be men who could dispose of and manage large sums of money. These were the bankers. They were first of all money-changers, an indispensable function in that confusion of currencies in a country traversed by so many nations and in which there were to be found Greek drachmas, Tyrian *zuzim*, Roman *denarii*, Israelite shekels and the coins of the tetrarchs; in this confusion the money-changer had the opportunity of gaining a great deal, and as we shall see, the rabbis were obliged to make laws concerning the exchange of the sacred Temple coins. The money-changers were thought of as sharp-witted, intelligent men who thoroughly understood business: Clement of Alexandria, and seventy more authors with him, quotes a saying of Jesus which does not appear in the Gospels, but which Saint Paul certainly seems to refer to: 'Be prudent money-changers, knowing how to test every coin and to separate the bad from the good.'[20]

But exchange was not the intelligent banker's only activity. There were those who specialized in making money out of money, that is to say, in lending it out at interest and in investing it. Christ Himself speaks of these operations. When the master blames the timid servant who had buried the talent entrusted to him, he reproaches him in these words: '. . . all the more was it thy part to lodge my money with the bankers, so that I might have recovered it with interest when I came'.[21] Loans at interest were made locally, of course, to the peasant or the small dealer who was in need; but they were also made on a large scale internationally. Those who fitted out ships and caravans were important customers for the banker; and from certain passages in the Talmud it appears that there may have been special associations of capitalists for the financing of maritime ventures and caravans.[22] The parable of the talents in the Gospel, which has just been mentioned, proves that wealthy peasants deposited their money in a bank. The system of letters of credit drawn by a banker upon a correspondent in a distant country, which was known in ancient Egypt and practised throughout the empire, was certainly employed by the Jews.

In short, the essential operations of modern business are to be found in the big-business dealings of the Israel of two thousand years ago. And in succeeding in this the defeated had to some degree taken a real revenge upon their pagan conquerors: whether they were tax-gatherers or bankers they went far towards fulfilling the prophecy in Deuteronomy: '. . . many nations shall be thy debtors, and none thy creditor, many thy servants, and none thy master'.[23]

THE MORAL ASPECT OF MONEY AND BUSINESS

The religious Law was obviously not indifferent to commerce. Although the Pentateuch may not, as we have pointed out, have contained any direct commercial legislation, the precepts of the Mosaic Law were clear enough to allow a whole code concerning money and business to be drawn from them, and the rabbis had not omitted to do so. The Talmud, therefore, lays down a great number of requirements upon these subjects, particularly those tractates which were drawn up at Babylon, very much a commercial centre.

Must it be owned that it was in fact quite necessary to remind the people of the Lord that Yahweh's moral law was also to be applied to commercial affairs? On reading the very many texts which speak of business and business-men, one might really think so. 'Two dangers I see that are hard to overcome,' says Ben Sirach, 'how shall a merchant be cured of careless dealing, or a huckster for his lying talk find pardon?'[24] For him, it was inevitable in their calling – a kind of professional hazard. 'Stake between two stones cannot escape; nor may sin be avoided when there is seller on this side, buyer on that.' This might almost be called encouragement. In one of his most splendid, thundering prophecies Ezekiel denounces the great merchants of Tyre;[25] but a score of other passages in the Bible force one to believe that commercial bad faith was not the exclusive property of Israel's Phoenician neighbours.[26]

But at least the Holy Writ laid down the first principles with the greatest force. In the end everything stemmed from that commandment inscribed upon the tablets of the Law: Thou shalt not steal. Since it was forbidden to take one's neighbour's goods from him, as well as his ox, his ass or his hand-maid, it would necessarily seem that it was equally forbidden to injure him in selling or buying. And yet although the Scriptures were very exact on the subject of offences against property,[27] they confined themself to generalities on commercial matters. For example, it was stated at least ten times that true weights and honest scales must be used:[28] this was a minimum requirement. But the Bible has nothing so clear to say about the various other, less obvious, means by which a dishonest merchant might make illegal profits.

It is rather in the rabbinical writings that exact statements are to be found. The tractates *Baba Mesia* and *Baba Bathra*, for example, very subtly analyse the requirements that must be fulfilled if a sale is to be legal, the circumstances in which the buyer may cancel it, the limits within which bargaining must be confined (the price might not be asked by a man with no intention of buying), the manner in which a mortgage must be written and the periods required for prescriptive rights. Other lessons concern the avoidance of forgeries, laying down what kind of papyrus and what ink should be used for an acknowledgment of indebtedness: it was forbidden to 'wipe', or as we should say to alter, documents of this kind: the exact manner of tracing the X-shaped mark which meant that the deed was annulled is also given. The teaching of the doctors of the Law was also exceedingly severe against all speculation in foodstuffs, all cornering of wheat and oil, all combination of sellers to make prices rise. The rabbis' customary scrupulousness therefore made the rules of business procedure very strict indeed; or at least it would have done so had their rules been thoroughly observed: and seeing that their repetition appeared to be quite necessary it may perhaps be presumed that they were not. Yet there were cases when their control must have been effective – in the markets, for example, where the Sanhedrim's agent might arbitrate, as we have seen, and at the gate of the Temple, where the rate of exchange was fixed at one half-obol to one half-shekel, which was, as it happens, a rate raised by ten per cent.

This brings us to a particularly delicate point, a highly controversial question. Might money breed money? The Law of the Covenant, that is, chapters twenty-one to twenty-three of Exodus, stated categorically, 'If thou dost lend money to some poorer neighbour among my people, thou shalt not drive him hard as extortioners do, or burden him with usury'. In principle, then, all lending at interest was forbidden. Deuteronomy went further and made the prohibition apply to food and anything that might be lent.[29] Could such exactness be maintained in a society more highly organized than it was in the nomadic days? It would have made all trade on a large scale impossible. Besides, it could easily be circumvented, and that in a manner that more or less complied with the Law, since the insolvent debtor might be seized together with his goods and sold; which provided a very handsome interest, of a kind. By a less legal, but also less ferocious, device, the lender might insist upon a gift before advancing the money. The rabbis had therefore built up a system of laws to cope with the situation: in theory lending on interest was forbidden, but what in fact was really condemned was usury. They worked out a doctrine of a return upon capital investment, exactly as Saint Thomas Aquinas, in the Middle Ages, found that it was allowable to hire money for use in commercial transactions. In many respects the tractate *Baba Mesia* is the forerunner of the *Secunda Pars* of the *Summa Theologiae*. On the other hand, the extortion of excessive interest from poor people hard-pressed by need was called by the Talmud 'the abomination of abominations', and the usurers who committed this abomination incurred exactly the same guilt as 'those who shed blood'.

Yet it does not appear that these outright words prevented the existence of usurers. When Christ was in the Pharisee's house and the sinful woman wept at His feet, He uttered a parable of a creditor[30]; and it certainly seems that this was a professional money-lender. There were some who were utterly unscrupulous, and they would have bonds drawn up by shady lawyers, before witnesses, for loans at high interest. In the Talmud we read of one of them who, on being reproached with breaking the Law, sarcastically replied: 'If Moses had known how much you can gain by lending money at interest, he would never have thought of forbidding it.'[31] It is difficult to say what rate was considered usurious, or how far the greed of an usurer might take him. Philo says that there were lenders in Alexandria who insisted upon a hundred per cent;[32] but he does not say whether these were Jews or pagans.

But the Law itself provided an exception. Deuteronomy said that interest might be taken from foreigners,[33] and this might be considered as a direct biblical encouragement of banking in Israel. The rabbis allowed lending to a convert so long as he was not circumcised, but, says the *Baba Mesia*, as soon as he had undergone the little operation that made him a member of the Chosen People, the creditor was to say to him, 'The money thou hast borrowed from me no longer bears any interest'. It would be interesting to know whether this really happened in practice

The doctors of the Law were very indulgent as regards all dealings with pagans. Thus, although it would be criminal in a practising Jew to eat pork – see Leviticus 11, 7 – he was in no way prevented from selling the unclean animal to unclean foreigners.[34] As far as commercial dealings with strangers went, the rabbis were sparing in both precept and prohibition. The difference between the treatment of the Jewish and the heathen slaves[35] even leads one to suppose that the business-men of Israel may not have felt above joining in the profitable slave-trade that was the speciality of the Sidonians.

This view of the morality of business and money-making was in some respects noble and elevated, in others less so: are we to contrast it with that of the Gospels? There are few points of doctrine which make one more sensible of the superiority of Christ's teaching over that of the Jewish Law, or that make one feel more clearly that He calls upon His followers to go far beyond it. Our Lord often mentions money and commercial dealings, but always to teach an entire contempt for any love of money-making. The creditor is bidden to forgive his debtor his debts as God forgives us ours: and how many times? Seventy times seven, if need be.[36] The evil rich man who has grown wealthy on the unhappiness of others goes to hell, whereas Lazarus the poor lies in Abraham's bosom.[37] In Christ's eyes, money and everything connected with it was essentially a part of the kingdom of Mammon, the master whom no servant of God could serve, since a man might have only one master at a time;[38] money was 'base wealth', whose only use was to allow the believer to heap up treasure in heaven by giving alms.[39]

'WHERE, THEN, DOES WISDOM LIE? . . . NOT HERE, CRIES THE ABYSS . . . AND THE SEA ECHOES, NOT HERE'

What routes did the profitable trade of the rich Jewish merchants follow? To a considerable extent it went by sea. Not that this means that Israel had a merchant navy to carry all its imports and exports: as we should say today it was not 'under their own flag' that the Israelites' merchandise travelled over the ocean.

They had never been a seafaring people, although they had always recognised the sea's utility: the patriarch Jacob, in blessing his sons, pointed out that Zebulun, dwelling by the coast, would have the advantage of ships,[40] and Moses, confirming this, prophesied that his tribe 'should be fostered by the wealth of the sea'.[41] In her famous song of victory the fighting prophetess Deborah said 'Dan was busy with his merchant ventures' by sea[42]. One can only say that the descendants of Jacob, Moses and Deborah do not appear to have cultivated this maritime vocation. The sea is mentioned close on two hundred times in the Bible, and several passages even display a real understanding of sea-travel; but the ships always belong to foreigners, like those 'ships of Tarshish' which are so often spoken of,[43] or those which Solomon and his friend Hiram of Tyre shared in sending to Ophir for precious things,[44] which were in both cases undoubtedly Phoenician.

From the heights of their mountains the Jews beheld the vast extent of the sea; but unlike the Greeks and the Phoenicians they were not attracted by it. Indeed, they distrusted it. 'There lies the vast ocean', said the hundred and third Psalm, 'stretching wide on every hand; this, too, is peopled with living things past number, great creatures and small; the ships pass them on their course. Leviathan himself is among them; him, too, thou hast created to roam there at his pleasure.' This was far from reassuring. And Psalm 106 gave an even more alarming description of a storm at sea. Jesus ben Sirach, that advocate of a somewhat earthbound wisdom, observed, 'Hear we what perils in the deep mariners have to tell of, and wonder at the tale'.[45] The sea was certainly one reason more for admiring the works of God in His creation; but no very close acquaintance with it was desirable. The words of Job concerning wisdom, that it did not lie in the sea,[46] were readily held to be literally exact, and it was thought better to leave the danger to the half-witted heathen. It is significant that our Lord never uses sea-terms, and that when in the parables He speaks of the sea He always means Lake Gennesaret.

This dislike was clearly based upon geographical reasons. The Palestinian coast is a bad one for shipping: the wind from Africa blows upon it with great force, moving great masses of sand, which make the sea shallow, so that vessels of a considerable draught must anchor far out to avoid the shoals. It is a straight coast, and it has but one reasonably well-situated bay, that where the coast-line curves in under the shelter of Mount Carmel and even that is dangerously exposed to the north wind. Palestine has none of those welcoming creeks, those quantities of little islands, which contributed so much to making the Greeks a

maritime people. We have it from Josephus himself[47] that the
ports which Simon Maccabaeus and then John Hyrcanus took
such pains to hold[48], such as Dor and Joppa (now Jaffa) were
but very modest roadsteads, just suitable for the small fishing-
vessels and those which were used for gathering the shellfish
that made purple dye. Ptolemais, our Acre, was entirely Greek.
A very small port called Eloth, near the present town of Aqaba,
had replaced the fine harbour of Ezion-geber, at the head of the
Gulf of Aqaba, which Solomon had constructed at great expense
for trade with the Indian Ocean.[49] The only real port was that
which Herod the Great had built up from nothing on the site of
Turris Stratonis, a Syro-Phoenician village: a mole, resting upon
immensely solid foundations, ran out two hundred feet into the
sea, protected by enormous blocks of stone from the waves;
its entrance, on the north-west, was angled, so that the wind
should not affect the harbour, and the place was thoroughly
equipped with docks and warehouses. But in spite of the number
of Jewish merchants who came there, Caesarea was a pagan town,
controlled by the Romans – it will be recalled that the procurator
resided there – and managed, from the point of view of shipping,
by Greeks and Syrians.

The sea, then, was not the province of the Jews. Before the
Chosen People would launch themselves upon the waves they
had to be obliged by imperative necessity. Josephus,[50] speaking
of the consequences of the disaster of AD 66–70, says, 'Many
Jews, no longer able to live in their devasted country, decided
to take to the sea, and they fitted out several pirate ships, with
which they raided the Syrian and Phoenician trade going to
Egypt, making all traffic impossible in these waters'. This was
not the case at the time of Christ. The wealthy Jewish business-
men, both for their own voyages and the movement of their
merchandise, hired the services of Greek, Phoenician or Roman
shippers. The Mediterranean, the *mare nostrum* of the empire,
was continually crossed in every direction by countless vessels,
particularly in the favourable seasons of the year. There were
two chief kinds: the *oneraria* or *frumentaria* of the Latins were
what we would call cargo-ships; they were slow and they were in
no way elegant, being scarcely four times as long as they were
wide; the second kind was more handsome; it had better lines,
and it was used for carrying passengers. These were all sailing
vessels, and the rig was almost invariably a single heavy square

sail, which could not be reefed in foul weather; only the best ships, and these were generally Phoenician, had something in the way of a mizzen, which would allow the vessel to lie-to in a storm. The keel was unknown: so was the rudder, and ships were steered with one or two large oars, a little forward of the poop; they broke easily, and as soon as the sea grew rough they had to to be taken in. And of course the ships always kept in sight of the coast, moving along from one landmark to another – rocks, villages, lighthouses – for to lose sight of them would have been the height of folly.

If one wishes to gain an exact idea of what a sea voyage was like at the time of Christ, of the working of shipping and of the perils that might be met with upon the sea, one has but to read the voyages of Saint Paul in the Acts, particularly those remarkable chapters twenty-seven and twenty-eight, which Lord Nelson described as having taught him his trade. Here we see the apostle first using the coasters which carried their mixed cargoes, cattle and passengers from port to port in Asia Minor, from one Greek island to another and so to Europe, just as the ships of the Grecian archipelago do to this day: then we see him being taken to Rome, to be judged by Caesar, and put aboard a coaster, then changing to a cargo-boat on the Alexandra–Pozzuoli run at Myra. Then comes a storm lasting for fourteen days, the saint's shipwreck and finally his arrival in the Bay of Naples in a Roman vessel named the *Castor and Pollux*.[51] It is quite clear, from this all-too-adventurous account, why those Jews who were urged on neither by apostolic zeal nor an overwhelming desire to make a fortune should have preferred to remain on God's dry land.

ROADS AND CARAVAN-TRACKS

The rest of the trade, and certainly the most important part of it, moved by land. Palestine, that narrow strip running north and south with the Mediterranean on one side and the desert on the other, has always been a place of passage; and to this it owes its tragic fate (as clear today as it ever has been) of a country that is continually fought for. Yet it is by no means easy to move about in Palestine. Beyond the Jordan, on the high land of what is now the Kingdom of the Jordan, the run of the chief roads and tracks is plain enough; they made the fortune of Damascus, Palmyra, Baalbek and the mysterious, rose-red Petra; and it is along the main line of travel that the railway has now been built. In Palestine proper, however, this is not at all the case. To go from the east to the west one has to go right down to the bottom of the Ghor, rise again more than two thousand feet by difficult gorges and descend once more in three stages to the maritime plain. There are three natural routes from south to north, but none is really easy: the Shephalah road is the best, but it runs up against the Carmel range; that which follows the valley of the Jordan is impossible for months on end because of the heat, and dangerous at all times by night because of the wild beasts; and the most usual, which follows the ridges of the hills (and which is very beautiful) goes up and down continually; furthermore, the middle part of this road was often avoided by strict Jews, who would rather make a detour than go through the country of the heretical Samaritans.

During the life of Christ, the main trade-route of the country was certainly that which ran the other side of the Jordan. The convoys from Cappadocia and Anatolia, having traversed the Taurus gorges, reached Padan-Aram, and there joined with those coming from Mesopotamia by the ancient route of Abraham and the patriarchs – it was unusual to cross the desert in a direct line – and so went southwards to Palestine, which they entered by the road of Caesarea Philippi, at the foot of Mount Hermon, or by those which came down from Moab. In the other direction, the same track served for the caravans coming from the south, carrying the produce of Arabia and East Africa, brought by the coasters of the Red Sea and the Gulf of Aqaba, as well as the caravans from the Persian Gulf, which reached it by the central Arabian depression. The Jewish merchants shared in this important commerce, associating themselves with the Arab traders who had a complete control over its movement – those of Palmyra in the north, and the Nabataeans in the south. The latter competed successfully with the sea-borne trade of Alexandria, never hesitating to attack their heavy cargo-ships with light pirate boats: from Petra they overlooked the three caravan-routes, quite apart from that which led to the copper-mines of Arabah. One of the chief causes of Herod the Great's fortune, both financial and political, was the fact that he had managed to make himself the ally, the friend and the controller of the Nabataeans.

Within Palestine proper there was no route comparable to this for the importance of the trade that passed along it. The chief roads, apart from those three from north to south whose short-comings have just been mentioned, were the one called the 'royal road', which went from the port of Caesarea in the north of the country by the way of Scythopolis, where it crossed the north-south ridge-road, to join the great caravan-track to Damascus near Derat; the road from Joppa to Nablus to Shechem, which passed between Mount Ebal and Gerizim; and finally the roads which set out in all directions from Jerusalem, the two to Gaza, one passing by Bethlehem, the other by the Wadi es Surar; the two to Joppa (Jaffa), the one by Emmaus, the other by Lydda; and above all the famous road to Jericho, which went on to cross the Jordan at the last place where it could be forded, the ford of Bethabara, the place of Christ's baptism, and then climbed the great hill of Moab to join the main caravan-route or else to continue to Philadelphia, which we now call Amman.

From a technical point of view, what were these roads like? It is very likely indeed that they were poor. Father Poidebard's admirable studies and his extraordinary aerial photographs[5] have shown that in the Roman province of Syria the conqueror established that system of roads which, throughout the empire was an essential part of their strength. The true *viae* have been found, with their immense paving-slabs set in concrete, some roads sixteen feet wide, others only eight, but with places arranged at intervals where carts could pass one another; there are also *viae terrenae* remaining, those roads of tamped earth covered with paving, as well as caravan-tracks with covered wells and guiding marks along them. Bridges have been found, and more frequently improved fords, with the bottom of the wadi paved with stones that have deep channels in them, so that the driver of a cart had but to set his wheels in them to be sure of getting across the water. Did the Palestinian roads join this magnificent network, which covered all the natural routes of Syria and Transjordan – did they form part of it? This is not known for sure, for Father Poidebard's system of aerial detection has only just begun; but it is not at all likely. The great work on the Syrian roads was undertaken by the Romans when the frontier, which Pompey and Augustus had fixed at the bend of the Euphrates, was carried beyond it by Trajan, and above all when the Antonines (and later Diocletian established the *limes*, the line of fortifications against the threat of a Parthian invasion. It is improbable that under Augustus and Tiberius the Roman administration should have made very

great efforts to improve the communications in a trifling, remote
sub-province, whose trade did not concern them and which was
not a part of the frontier; and it is more improbable still that the
petty tetrarchs should have spent a great deal of money upon
enterprises so very much less showy than palaces.

TRAVELLERS AND BRIGANDS

There was a great deal of traffic on these roads and tracks, all the
more so since they were, after all, relatively few. Of course, there
were not many people who travelled just for the pleasure and the
improvement of it, although in the Bible we find Ben Sirach
observing, 'I myself have seen much in my wanderings, the
customs of men more than I can tell'.[53]* and although it may be
granted that there were wealthy Jews among the tourists who
came to pass the winter in Egypt, taking advantage of their stay to
visit the colossus of Memnon, the Valley of the Kings, the temple
of Isis at Philoe, without forgetting the bull Apis at Memphis and
the sacred crocodiles at Arsinoe, which had always to be given
cakes.[54]

But there were many other reasons for travelling; and indeed,
does one not get the impression from the Gospels that the Jews
were perpetually moving about? Family relationships being what
they were, visits were very usual – visits such as that which Our
Lady paid to her cousin Elizabeth, the Visitation itself. Pilgrimages
also brought thousands and tens of thousands of people on to the
roads: at the time of the great feasts, above all that of the Passover,
there was an almost continuous stream of pilgrims who 'went up'
to Jerusalem, and who then went home after the ceremonies were
over, as we may see in that passage of Luke, where Joseph and
Mary think that their little boy is with some other members of the
caravan.[55] Lastly, there was the great reason for travelling: trade.
On the main roads one would see not only Jewish merchants
going by, but also the lean Nabataean caravan-men, the great
Babylonian dealers, dressed in silk and with heavy gold rings in
their noses, business-men from Syria, and even copper-coloured
Abyssinians and Sudanese negroes, without mentioning the

*The Knox Version does not give exactly the same meaning as the
author to the verse he quotes at this point (Eccles. 34, 9), so the
translator has substituted 5, 12. A variant of 5, 9 reads, 'A man that has
travelled knows many things . . . and the lessons he has learnt will make
him a wise talker'.

Greek chapmen and bazaar-suppliers, Roman tax-gatherers and, naturally, the peasants going to sell their produce at the market.

When a man had a considerable journey to make, he would arrange for it to begin with the beginning of the week, so that he should not be held up by the obligatory Sabbath rest, when he might not go more than about a mile.[56] He would also take care to dress properly: the nights could be cold and it was always possible that he would have to sleep in the open air; the days could also be exceedingly hot, and he had to provide against thirst. He would 'gird his loins'[57] by tucking his coat into his belt,[58] so that it would not get in his way. He would put the money for the journey into his belt, and if he were pious he might also put the book of the Law into it as well.[59] It was usual to have a spare pair of sandals or shoes – those spare shoes that our Lord said the apostles were not to take.[60] A wallet or bag for the journey was always carried, and a staff, for a man might have to defend himself. A thick cloak was necessary if it were no longer summertime or if it were necessary to go over the mountains – that thick cloak which Saint Paul prized so highly, as we have seen.[61] If the man were mounted for the journey he would take a skin of water mingled with wine or vinegar; otherwise he would make do with a flask. But he would never go without a dried, emptied gourd, with a stone in it to give it weight, so that he could draw up water from any well he might meet with,[62] and not be obliged to ask this service of some impious creature, such as a Samaritan woman, for example.

If the weather made it impossible to sleep out, wrapped in a cloak, the most usual way of finding a bed was to ask at a house. Hospitality was considered a great virtue among the Jews, as it was among all the nations of the ancient world: a man would always find somewhere to stay, except in Jerusalem at the time of the feasts, when the whole town was filled to overflowing. There were also inns: this is evident from Saint Luke, who tells how Christ was born in a stable and laid in a manger 'because there was no room in the inn'; and another is also referred to in the parable of the good Samaritan, as well as in an anecdote in the tractate *Shabbath*. There do not seem to have been many of them; and those that existed were no doubt like those caravanserais that are still to be seen in Eastern countries – nothing particular in the way of comfort: just a square surrounded by a wall, an uncovered space for the animals, a wooden loggia running round to shelter the people, and a few very small rooms for the wealthy travellers

The usual mount for a journey and the usual pack-animal was the donkey: he had no equal for the climbing, stony and often narrow paths. There were, therefore, firms which specialised in the hiring of asses and ass-drivers by contract: the tractate *Baba Mesia* lays down the clauses for these contracts, and carries precision to the point of regulating the quality of the creatures' food and the maximum weight of their loads.[63] The asses of Lycaonia were preferred for long journeys: they were uncommonly obstinate, but they were the strongest of all breeds. The Romans ordinarily travelled by horse (and the horse was the best servant of the imperial posts), but the Jews very rarely did so. Some had horses, however, since the tractate *Shabbath* found it necessary to state the conditions under which it was permissible to look after them and put a chain upon their necks on the day of rest. The same applied to camels, which might be taken out on the Sabbath with a bit in their mouths or a ring in their noses.[64] Generally speaking they were used only for the Arabian and Mesopotamian trade; that is to say, they nearly all belonged to Nabataeans. A camel would often carry a load of nearly half a ton and go twenty-five miles a day.

Wheeled vehicles were not unknown, but they were little used. the chariot was the rich man's way of travelling, as may be seen from the Ethiopian eunuch in the Acts, the minister of Queen Candace whom Philip the Deacon met on the road from Jerusalem to Gaza, reading Isaiah as he went.[65] These were of the simplest construction – a kind of lattice-work box on two wheels, drawn by two horses, asses, mules, or even oxen in the case of commercial transport. The pole rested on their withers, being attached to a yoke which was fixed to their necks by a strap; this had the disadvantage of partially throttling the creatures, which naturally diminished their drawing-power.[66] The four-wheeled chariots were the Rolls-Royces or the Cadillacs of the era: rightly speaking, they were reserved for members of the imperial family, but the lesser kings and the tetrarchs also used them. The height of luxury, for shorter distances, was the litter carried by porters.

One last point about travelling in Israel: a man would never go on any journey, unless it were very short, by himself. Every journey had its risks, and some of them are listed in Ecclesiasticus – sand-storms, sunstroke, a stumbling horse – and the traveller is advised never to set out without praying to Him who gives protection and strength. But there is no mention of another peril, which was nevertheless very general. Men travelled in groups; they formed caravans (as we see in Luke[67]) even to go on pilgrimage, entrusting themselves to a guide, 'the eye of the caravan', as the Bedouin still call him; and clearly this was not to protect themselves from sunstroke or the shying of their mounts. It was to guard against thieves and brigands.

This was one of the curses of the time. The imperial authorities had difficulty in coping with it even in Italy. It is very striking to see how important a place the risk of theft, robbery and assault upon the road had in everyday life in the Gospel. Of course there were the housebreakers, who, we read, could pierce the wall of a house as though it were child's play, and the cattle-thieves who would quickly snap up any straying beast: but when one looks again into the parable of the good Samaritan one sees that it was a question of armed robbery, a violent attack from which the victim only recovered by a miracle. It happened in so ill-looking a place that all the other travellers hurried by, without wasting any time in going to the help of the wounded man. Yet where was this place? On the road from Jerusalem to Jericho, one of the most frequented of all highways, a mere two or three hours from the capital.[68] What must it have been like farther off, above all when one reached the real desert? In the hills and the ravines of Judaea lurked a whole pack of unemployed shepherds, beggars up to any mischief, workless mercenaries and escaped slaves, as well as the resistants, the *maquisards*, the *sicarii* from the bands which rose from time to time against the Herods or the Romans; and farther to the east banditry reached an even higher point of organized perfection. There the men of those nomadic or partially nomadic nations whom King Aristobulus had compelled to accept circumcision had no hesitation in launching well-planned raids against the caravans. 'If they have no one else to rob,' said Josephus, 'they rob one another.'[69] What could be done against such people? In the time of Nero, the brigand-chief Eleazar held out for twenty years against all the forces of authority, until the procurator Felix managed to seize him.[70] Intelligent merchants would come to an agreement with the leaders of the bands and pay them a tribute to be left in peace; and some would even hire one brigand against another. These are customs which were familiar in the West in the early Middle Ages, but they are scarcely what first comes to mind when one thinks of Christ's time and His country.

CHAPTER NINE

THE SPOKEN AND THE WRITTEN WORD

What languages did Jesus speak? – Rote-learning, rhythm and antithesis – What kind of writing did Jesus read? – Writing-materials – How news was spread.

WHAT LANGUAGES DID JESUS SPEAK?

Anyone who has been to the modern state of Israel, who has looked at the newspapers there, has seen the signs at the cross-roads and heard the politicians and the speakers on the radio, might be apt to reply that the ordinary language of the Jews is Hebrew. But was this the case two thousand years ago? It was not. The living Hebrew of today is a modern language, brought into existence by the extraordinary efforts of Eliezer ben Yehuda and insisted upon first in the Zionist settlements, then in the young Jewish state, because it was very rightly considered that a common language was the best bond of national unity. But this was certainly not the case at the time of Christ.

Yet Hebrew had been long used by the Chosen People, and it still was employed. Philologists class Hebrew among the Semitic languages,[1] that is to say, in that whole group of related languages that were used in the vast region that goes from Asia Minor to the southernmost point of Arabia, and from the Mediterranean coast to Mesopotamia; and they divide them into three main sections: the north-eastern, with Accadian, Assyrian and Babylonian; the north-western, with Syriac, Phoenician and some others; and the southern, of which northern Arabic, the tongue of Mohammed, was to become the most important language. Hebrew, like the language of Canaan and Aramaic, belongs to the north-western group. But all these languages were, and still are, close to one another, quite as close as French is to the other Romance languages, Italian, Spanish, Roumanian and so on. The word 'father', for example, is *'áb* in Hebrew, *'ab* in Aramaic, *abu* in Accadian and *'ab* in Arabic.

When the nomads of Abraham's tribe reached Palestine, they must have spoken a Semitic dialect resembling the Babylonian of Lower Mesopotamia. The Canaanites spoke other dialects, more exact and better constructed. One of these Canaanite dialects was taken up by the Hebrews at the time when they settled in the land and at the same time crystallized their language – that is to say, probably after the Exodus, when they came back from Egypt. This became Hebrew. Or rather, the various kinds of Hebrew; for just as in mediaeval France there were different kinds of French, the *langue d'oc* and the *langue d'oïl*, so the people of Judaea would pronounce, for example, the *s* of the Ephraimites as *sh*,[2] and in her famous song the prophetess Deborah used a highly individual vocabulary. But the Hebrew of Judaea supplanted the others, because the Holy Scriptures were drawn up almost entirely in that dialect.

Until the Babylonian Exile, then, the ordinary language was Hebrew; and Hebrew was the language that David and Solomon spoke, as well as Athaliah and Jezebel. But after the return from Babylon the old national language fell slowly into disuse, being ousted for everyday purposes by another dialect. And since this was just the time at which the groups of learned men of Ezra's day were setting down the Scriptures in writing, Hebrew became 'the language of holiness', *leshôn ha kodesh*, or *lêshon shakamim*, 'the language of the learned', exactly like the Latin of the schools in the Middle Ages or the liturgical Latin of our time. The Law was read in Hebrew in the synagogues; prayers were said in Hebrew, both privately and in the Temple. The doctors of the Law taught in Hebrew. Apart from those prayers which were known by heart, like our *Pater* and *Ave Maria*, people would use Hebrew for those stereotyped biblical quotations which were used in ordinary conversation, rather as we use Latin tags from the back of the dictionary. Yet the manuscripts recently discovered in the Judaean desert show that a little before the Christian era there was a revival of Hebrew: it may have been spoken in the monastic community of the Essenes. There is no doubt at all that Jesus knew Hebrew thoroughly: in the Gospel of Saint Luke we see Him reading in the synagogue – 'The book given to him was the book of the prophet Isaias; so he opened it'[3] and read, apparently without the slightest difficulty.

But in ordinary life and in His teaching He would certainly

have used another language, Aramaic. Whatever has been advanced to the contrary, this was in no way at all a corrupt form of Hebrew, a kind of degenerate dialect that the Jews brought back with them from Babylon. Aramaic was just as much a true language as Hebrew: it was the language of those active, stirring tribes which moved about the Fertile Crescent from the earliest times, founding more or less ephemeral kingdoms, never uniting into one body – those tribes from which the Israelites claimed descent.[4] For reasons that cannot now be made out, when the rise of the Aramaeans was over and politically they no longer counted for anything, their language did not die away, but on the contrary it spread in the most extraordinary manner. It supplanted all the native languages of hither Asia from the sources of the Euphrates to its mouth, from the Mediterranean as far as Persia. The King of Kings, the Persian monarch himself, adopted it as the administrative language, which did a great deal to extend its use; and Israel did not escape this domination. There was a very curious reversal of values, for whereas only the great men spoke Aramaic in the eighth century, while the ordinary people used Hebrew,[5] at the time of Christ exactly the opposite obtained. Aramaic was a more highly evolved language than Hebrew, suppler and altogether more suitable for narrative in its different forms and for the expression of thought in its varying aspects and connections. The manner of speaking it varied also, and it is clear that the Galileans did not pronounce it in the accent of Jerusalem, since it was from his speech that Peter was detected as one of Christ's companions on that tragic night of Maundy Thursday.[6]

As one reads through the Gospels one sees clearly that Aramaic was the usual language of the people. There are many Aramaic words in them, and of these several are said by Christ Himself: Abba, Aceldama, Gabbatha, Golgotha, Mammon;[7] and even whole phrases, such as the *Talitha, cumi* which He said to Jairus' daughter[8] and the terrible *Eloi, Eloi, lamma sabachthani* of the supreme agony,[9] which is a translation into Aramaic of the Psalmist's words. Moreover, some parts of Ezra and Jeremiah were written in Aramaic, as well as Daniel; and Saint Matthew wrote the first draught of his Gospel in it, before translating the Aramaic into Greek.[10] The Targums (*targumim*), which now form part of the Talmudic literature, were in fact translations or paraphrases of the Hebrew text into Aramaic, with or without commentary. In each synagogue there was a *Meturgeman*, an interpreter, to make the Law comprehensible to the simple people who did not know Hebrew well. And about four hundred years before Christ it became a settled custom, even among the rabbis, to teach no longer in Hebrew, but in Aramaic.[11] Eastern Aramaic, or rather various dialects of it, has lasted until our day in Mesopotamia: liturgical Chaldean is one of its forms. And about forty miles from Damascus there is a little group of villages round Malloula (or Maamoula) where the people speak the western Aramaic that our Lord would have used. Recently the Lord's Prayer in Aramaic was recorded there.[12]

Hebrew and Aramaic were not the only languages spoken in Palestine two thousand years ago, however. This is clear from the account of Christ's trial: Pontius Pilate wrote a proclamation to be fixed on the cross, *This is the King of the Jews*, in three languages, Hebrew, Greek and Latin.[13] The Latin would have been there for official reasons, it being the language of the imperial decrees; but one has the impression that it was not much spoken in Palestine. Indeed, Josephus states that instructions sent from Rome were always accompanied by a Greek translation.[14] For Greek was in fact exceedingly widely known and generally spoken all over the Near East, and for that matter throughout the whole empire. The rabbis tried to withstand the invasion, seeing the language as a precursor of heathen ways: but in vain. 'The man who teaches his son Greek', they said, 'is as accursed as the man who eats pork.'[15] However, this did not prevent the great doctors of the Law, even Gamaliel himself, from knowing it. When Saint Paul spoke to the crowd in Jerusalem after his arrest, it pleased them (as the Acts observe) that he spoke not in Greek but in Aramaic.[16] Greek was the language of the upper sort, the rich and the powerful, the language of the Herods; but it was also the international business language. The Gospels, the Acts of the Apostles, nearly all the Epistles and the Revelation were all either written in Greek or at once translated into it. It is not quite certain whether Jesus knew it or not: there is not a single Greek quotation among His sayings, not even an allusion; whereas there are a great many in Saint Paul. But when He was questioned by Pontius Pilate, it does not seem that an interpreter was called for; and it is very unlikely that the Roman procurator would have taken the trouble to learn the language of the country he governed.

The Greek which was spoken in Palestine was that somewhat debased variety which had developed in Alexandria and which had spread throughout the Hellenistic world, displacing Attic, Ionic, Doric, Aeolic and other local dialects. This *koine* or international Greek was a simplified version of the classical language: it no longer used difficult words and it had dropped some of the complications of declension and conjugation; it used analytic constructions with prepositions rather than the synthetic forms of classical Greek, and it had also taken in quantities of foreign words, particularly from Latin, as well as some of the sounds of the Eastern languages. It was not Plato's Greek, nor that of the tragedians, but it was a useful tongue and well suited for the international part that it was to play.

ROTE-LEARNING, RHYTHM AND ANTITHESIS

No discussion of the languages spoken in Palestine at the time of Christ can fail to point out how widely both Hebrew and Aramaic differed in their nature from our Western languages, or how different were the uses to which they were put. Of course, when it was a question of conveying factual data or even ideas, the Israelites spoke as we do: it was the same when they expressed feelings or if they wished to warn, persuade or threaten. But language may have many other purposes: for example, there is that poetic function for which our matter-of-fact civilizations have so little room, but which played so great a part in Israel and all the other nations of the East, particularly the Semites; and there is that of handing down thought from generation to generation – a function inseparably linked, as we shall see, to poetry.

To understand this very special aspect of words and speech in Israel thoroughly, we must forget our paper-civilization (gramophone- and tape-recorder-civilization, we may add at this day) and its habits: for us writing and reading, that is to say, setting thought down in a lasting, material form so that it can be found again in an unaltered state, are acts that seem so natural to us that we can scarcely imagine societies that were able to do without them almost entirely. Our memories have become anaemic and impotent; our improvising abilities are far more didactic than poetic. This was not at all the case in Israel, nor indeed among the other Eastern nations. Thought was handed on, handed down in the most lasting and permanent manner, very largely by the spoken word; and this, of course, necessarily affected the spoken word, giving it some very particular characteristics.

Long before it was ever set down in writing, at first partially under Hezekiah and Josiah and then more completely in the fifth century, when the scribe Ezra is said to have 'dictated' ninety-four of the sacred books, the Old Testament existed only in the form of the spoken word. It is formally stated that the prophecies of Jeremiah were 'said' for twenty-two years before they were reduced to writing; and it is clear that the Psalms, the Proverbs and the wedding chants of the Song of Songs had their being first in speech or song and only assumed their written form at a later date.[17] This was the case with the Homeric poems, too; at Athens Peisistratus was famous for having given their text its definitive form by putting them into writing:[18] and the holy book of the Persians, the Zend Avesta, was fixed in the same way by Zarathustra. The Koran, too, existed first in oral tradition alone; and indeed its very name conveys the idea of recitation.

Even when the holy text had been fixed in writing, the habit of oral transmission of thought was not lost. There are many proofs of this: the rabbis taught by word of mouth and their sentences were handed down in the same way; the tractate *Gittin* even said that writing them was unlawful.[19] In about the year one thousand of our era, Sherira Gaon asserted that 'the learned consider it their duty to recite from memory'. Furthermore, the word 'Talmud' means 'learnt by heart'.[20] We also know that among the early Christians it was usual to hand on the 'good news', that is, the account of our Lord's life and His teaching, solely by word of mouth. The Acts of the Apostles, the Epistles and the Revelation were certainly written at their inception, but it is equally sure that the four Gospels were spoken before they became books. The men who undertook the spreading of the new teaching undoubtedly had mnemonic devices to help them, and these may be traced in the Gospels; but what was all-important for them was what they had learnt, what they knew. It only became necessary to put things down in writing when Christianity reached those Graeco-Roman circles in which reading and writing were so much more commonly practised; but even in about the year 130, when the books of the four evangelists had long been circulating, Saint Papias, bishop of Hieropolis in Phrygia, said that what he preferred above all, in matters of tradition, was 'the eternal living word'

And a little later, Saint Irenaeus at Lyons spoke of the time when he had listened to Saint Polycarp, the great bishop of Smyrna, relating what he had himself heard from the mouth of Saint John the apostle.[21]

Memory played an important part in this system, and the rabbis attached the greatest importance to its training. The rabbi Dostai, son of Janai, speaking in the name of the rabbi Meir, said, 'The man who forgets something of what he has learnt brings about his own ruin'.[22] And a disciple's highest praise was that 'he was like a well-cemented cistern, that does not lose a drop of its water'.[23] There was also a common saying: 'The man who does not recite is impious.'[24] For training their memory, then, pupils were made to learn immensely long passages by heart, and these had to be repeated without an omission, without adding or changing a single word. A visitor to a Mohammedan school of today may see that the method is still used in Islam; a score of boys, sitting on the ground, all repeat together, in a high, rhythmic voice, verse after verse of the Koran. It is the same in the traditional Talmudic schools. It must be emphasized that this systematic training of the memory was not only for specialists, theologians or professional annalists: as we have seen,[25] children were brought up to learn by rote from the earliest age. And when one thinks of the inordinate length of the prayer of the *Shemoneh 'Esreh*, the eighteen benedictions, one must admit that the Jew's memory was indeed wonderfully well trained.

This deliberate use of memorizing gave the language and its forms of expression some highly individual characteristics. In the first place, since all the texts that were learnt by heart were taken from the Scriptures, the learner's mind was stored with biblical facts, sentences and figures, which explains the innumerable scriptural echoes that were to be heard in the speech of the Jewish men and women of that time – in the speech, indeed, of Joseph and Mary themselves. But above all, the learned men of Israel, wishing both to help the memory and to imprint the learning that it was to retain and transmit as deeply as possible, had devised a whole system of rhythms, melodies, alliterations, repetitions of words and antitheses which made the recollection of the verbal elements easier; and this system was all the more important since the learner would not have either a notebook in his pocket or a dictionary upon his desk. Recent studies have proved the physiological and psychological importance of this 'rhythmic teaching'. It is exceedingly likely that the great majority of the Old Testament was composed on these lines, in double or triple rhythms. As for the Gospel, one has but to read it carefully to feel the rhythmic beat and the play of the antitheses: the characteristic technique is still clearly perceptible, although the book has been translated into Greek and from Greek into English – that is to say, into two languages whose rhythms and constructions are radically different from those of the Semitic tongues. The Sermon on the Mount is a typical example, particularly in Saint Luke's version,[26] with the beatitudes and the succeeding maledictions. But in the parables too and even the more ordinary sayings we feel what Father Jousse calls the parallel recitatives, which in either the Hebrew or the Aramaic must have been strikingly clear to everyone.

When a Jew, therefore, had to speak in a somewhat formal manner, as for example in teaching, or when he prayed, this would have been the basis of his style; and it is highly probable that something of it would have carried over into the language of every day. And a young woman of the people, like Our Lady when she spontaneously uttered her thanksgiving, the Magnificat, naturally gave it a poetic cadence which is still evident even in its English version: 'My soul magnifies the Lord; my spirit has found joy in God . . .'[27] In our modern state of mind, which is based upon the written word, words are in one place, melodies in another and rhythms in a third; in the Israelite's conception of language all these interpenetrated; they all came into play together; and the expression of thought tended naturally to become a form of art.[28]

WHAT KIND OF WRITING DID JESUS READ?

Yet however great the part of the spoken word in Israel, the written word was no less important; for these were the People of the Book, and their whole life was ruled by written texts. And we have seen[29] that among them there was a separate class, the scribes, whose entire function it was to write and to make known what was written. Generally speaking, one has the impression that the majority of the Jews knew how to read and write. We find many allusions to this ability, even looking no further than the Gospels: in the parable of the dishonest steward, the cunning fellow says to a debtor, 'Sit down and write it as fifty'. There is Zacharias, who being unable to speak writes the name of his son John, the future Baptist. Christ Himself speaks of the *jod*, the smallest letter of the alphabet; and when the woman was taken in adultery, He is shown 'writing on the ground with His finger', writing, no doubt, His answer to the accusers, 'Whichever of you is free from sin shall cast the first stone at her'.

The two national languages current in Israel at the time of Christ, Hebrew and Aramaic, had both been written since much earlier days. It was in about the twelfth century before our era that the alphabet, that inspired invention of the Phoenician merchants, had become generally used, replacing the complex Babylonian cuneiform and the Hittite or Egyptian hieroglyphics by a wonderfully clear system from which the Greek and Latin alphabets were to develop, as well as all those we now use in the West. The twelfth century BC was also roughly the date of the Exodus; it has been suggested that it was Moses who brought the alphabet into the life of Israel; and this is asserted as a fact by Eupolemus, the Hellenistic historian. In any case, there are Yahweh's frequent orders to Moses: 'Write this. Write my words.' And it so happens that it is in the very heart of Sinai, the chief place of the Mosaic revelation, that some of the oldest alphabetic inscriptions in the world have been discovered.[30]

The original Hebrew alphabet was based upon the Phoenician alphabet. The letters of this archaic Hebrew therefore had some forms that were remarkably close to the Greek, which had the same origin; but there was this essential difference: the Hebrew was written from right to left, and not from left to right. Some letters, such as delta, gamma and theta were almost exactly the same. But a little before the Christian era, after passionate discussions among the rabbis, this 'Phoenician' alphabet (which is still to be seen in some of the Dead Sea scrolls) was replaced, except among the Samaritans, by another, of Aramaean origin, which is the square character of the modern Hebrew. At the time of Christ, therefore, both languages were written in the same script.

However it was written, this alphabet had one great advantage and one great defect. The advantage was that it was clear and exact: each letter (particularly in the archaic script) was perfectly distinct, and each sound had its own letter – there were none of the absurd complications of the *gh* in English, for example. But this simplicity had another aspect that we find rather surprising: the twenty-two letters of the Hebrew alphabet consisted of nothing but consonants. An English reader might well ask what would be left if all the vowels were taken away from such a phrase as *European unity*, or how *Abednego sees an icon* could be distinguished from *Badinage uses no cane*, or even *A boding oasis in Aconaea*, with no vowels to be seen. And indeed the Israelites themselves realized that this system of writing the consonants alone was incomplete. They had therefore adopted the custom of using certain consonants to represent the chief vowel-sounds; there were just four of them, and although they did not lose their value as consonants, they might in certain cases be pronounced as vowels, rather as *y* in English can serve either purpose – a consonant in *yellow*, a vowel in *lymph*. It is the system known to linguists as that of the *matres lectionis*. It is clear from the Dead Sea scrolls that this was the system in force when they were compiled – that is to say, roughly the time of our Lord. It may seem difficult to us, but to the reader who was used to it, it recalled the current pronunciation reasonably well; it must, in any case, have been quite practical, since it is the method that the state of Israel has adopted for the writing of official Hebrew, having recourse to the masoretic system of vowel points (which was elaborated much later and which is always used for biblical Hebrew) only for particularly difficult words. We therefore have the curious fact that the Hebrew that Christ read would have been much the same as that which the modern inhabitants of Tel-Aviv see in their newspapers.[31]

WRITING-MATERIALS

It should be observed that this writing was rarely inscribed upon stone. Only one monumental inscription of a time before the Hellenistic era is known, and that (the inscription of the canal of Siloam) was not meant to be seen. 'Was this', asks Cardinal Tisserant, 'because the Jews recoiled from imitating the tables of the Law, upon which the finger of God had written the decalogue?'[32] Whatever the cause, the fact was strange in a world so filled with Egyptian, Babylonian, Greek and Roman inscriptions. By the time of Christ, however, the Jews had adopted the practice: Saint Paul refers to it in the second Epistle to the Corinthians,[33] and archaeology has discovered several inscriptions in cemeteries. Job speaks of the manner in which the letters were cut with a graver and molten lead poured into the grooves.[34]

The holy man also speaks of writings upon bronze,[35] and in fact among the most curious of all the objects found in the caves near the Dead Sea are those two copper scrolls, about two and a half feet long and a foot wide, covered with a deeply engraved text. At first it was thought they were catalogues of the manuscripts deposited there; but when they were with great difficulty unrolled (they are about a third of an inch thick) and deciphered, it was found that they had to do with a treasure hidden somewhere in the Judaean desert.

Unlike the Mesopotamians and the Hittites, the Israelites never used the clay tablet, baked in the sun after one had written what one wanted to say upon it with a stylus that made wedge-shaped marks: the Hebraic alphabets were not suitable for a cuneiform adaptation. Yet the archaeologists have found a few *ostraka*, those potsherds vaguely resembling oyster-shells which the whole ancient world of the Mediterranean used so freely for short written statements. Most of these humble documents of everyday life – notes, rough draughts, *billets doux* or voting-papers – were simply written in ink, as well as the writer could manage, upon the rough surface of the piece of broken bowl or pitcher.

Apart from these, written documents are singularly rare in Palestinian diggings: until the extraordinary discovery of the Dead Sea scrolls in 1947, scarcely more than a few dozen were known. This proves that the Jews ordinarily wrote upon perishable materials; and that as they did not imitate the Egyptians in their burial-customs, they did not place papyri in their tombs – those papyri which are to be found in such quantities in Egypt.

Their writing-materials were therefore the same as those which the rest of the Mediterranean world and the whole Roman empire employed. In the first place wooden tablets covered with wax, upon which one wrote with a bone, bronze or silver stylus; one of its ends was pointed, but the other was flattened so that one could wipe out the inscription by passing it over the raised wax and use the tablet again. The author of the Revelation alludes to this everyday practice in the passage where the chosen soul is told by the master of the seven spirits of God and the seven stars, 'His name I will never blot out of the book of life'.[36]

The wax-coated wooden tablets were not used for long texts. From very early times skin had been used for these. *Sefer*, the Hebrew word for book, comes from the same root as the word meaning 'to scrape': the oldest books of the Jews must therefore have been written on scraped skin; and this, as we read in Herodotus and Diodorus, was the usual practice in the East.[37] Goatskin or sheepskin was used, and it was specially prepared; the best came from the district of Pergamum in Asia Minor, hence the Latin *pergamena* and the English parchment. Saint Paul, writing to his dear disciple Timothy, particularly asks him to bring his rolls of parchment with him.[38] As parchment was expensive it was sometimes split into sheets of half the thickness: this was the fine, thin *duksystos* (*dischotos* in Greek) of which the outer side was better than the inner. But all the rabbis agreed in insisting that sacred texts should be written upon skin that was *gewil*, that is to say, unsplit. The use of skin for writing upon was certainly very general at the time of Christ: the *Letter of Aristeas*, a piece of apocryphal Alexandrian Jewish literature, which dates from a few decades before the time of our Lord's birth and which gives a wonderful account of the translation of the Bible into Greek by the Seventy, affirms that the text which was sent to Pharaoh to be translated was written upon scrolls of whole skin.

At this time, however, a much cheaper and handier writing-material was competing with parchment: papyrus. Some three thousand years before, the Egyptians had discovered this aquatic plant and its utility: Palestine grew a little, in the marshes along the Jordan and even in some of the damper parts of the Negeb, but Egypt was the great supplier, and ever since Rome began to buy it in large quantities the prices that those who had the virtual monopoly could ask had continually increased. The small, poorer countries like Palestine were obliged to fall back on local supplies or return to parchment. The technique of preparing papyrus was the same as that which had been perfected on the banks of the Nile even before the building of the pyramids: the stems, sometimes ten feet long, were peeled and cut into narrow strips which in their turn were pasted to one another in layers, the grain in these layers going first one way and then the other; these sheets were then beaten with a wooden mallet and finally smoothed with a scraper. As papyrus was comparatively dear it was used several times over, either by being washed or by having what was written on it scraped off. Old papyri, like our old papers, were also used for wrapping: the tractate *Shabbath* even specifies that on the day of rest it was forbidden to carry more old papyrus than would suffice to wrap up one bottle of oil.[39] It is very probable that the Epistles were written on papyrus particularly those of Saint Paul. Like the Jews, the early Christians used it to make further copies of their holy books: thus, in the famous Chester Beatty papyri of Dublin and the University of Michigan, the Ryland papyri of Manchester and some others, we may read pieces of the Old Testament and passages from the New, particularly a part of the eighteenth chapter of the Gospel according to Saint John, which can be dated at about the year 140. In a dry climate papyrus keeps exceedingly well.

A split reed was used for writing, whether on parchment or papyrus, as we see at the beginning of Psalm 44; and Saint John, ending his third Epistle to his friend Gaius, says that he has much more to tell him, but that he has no mind to convey the message 'by ink and reed'. This writing-reed was the *calamus*, which was cut in a sloping manner and then split. Our metal nibs are its direct descendants, and there have also been found some bronze *calami* which have a curious resemblance to our fountain-pens. The goose-quill, on the other hand, was quite unknown; and it only came into use among the Byzantines, in the fourth century. The ink of those times was not a liquid like ours, but a mixture of lamp-black and gum which was kept dry and only wetted to be used, in exactly the same way as Chinese ink: this allowed it to be easily washed out, but it also permitted all manner of forgeries – the parable of the dishonest steward gives some idea of them. Red ink was also known. It was made with *sikra*, a red powder that women also used for making-up their faces. Perhaps it was because ink served for such profane uses and because it allowed such a great deal of deceit that Saint Paul reminded the Christians of Corinth that the words of Christ were not merely to be written with ink, but with the Spirit of the living God, with human hearts, instead of stone, to carry them.[40]

If a man had a fairly long text to write, he would not fold the material upon which it was written (which would have been difficult in the case of parchment) but pasted or sewed the sheets one after another, so as to make a long band that was rolled round either one or two wooden cylinders. Some of these scrolls might be forty yards long and more. To be read, they were held in both hands, the right rolling up what had been read and the left unrolling: this is the attitude in which our Lord would have read a passage of the Law in a synagogue. In the Revelation there is the terrifying image, 'The sky folded up like a scroll, and disappeared'.[41]* The custom of folding the leaves of papyrus came in about a hundred years after Christ, particularly among the early Christians; and from this folding came the codex or bound book, often a *quaternio* of four sheets folded to make eight leaves and sewn, as our books are, into a volume.

Lastly, to protect the most valuable manuscripts, they were wrapped in cloth; when they were manuscripts of the sacred books, in fine linen, decorated with hyacinth-blue embroidery and fringed at the edges. They were then placed in special jars; and an important library must have looked very like a great wine-store. As everyone knows, it was in jars that the Dead Sea scrolls were discovered in 1947 and the following years. The most generally accepted hypothesis is that they formed the library of a community of Essenes, whose monastery has been found not far from the caves, at Qumrân – a library that the monks hid at the time when the Roman legionaries of Titus were ravaging the country during the great uprising of AD 66–70.[42]

In the ruins of Qumrân, too, there have been found three bronze and two clay inkwells, with dried ink still in them; and one of the rooms of the monastery is reminiscent of a Western monastery's scriptorium. It seems that these may have been monks who gave themselves up to copying, working to hand on the holy texts as our Benedictines did in former times. In any case, one of the chief functions of the scribes, whose importance we have mentioned,[43] was the copying of the Bible. The rabbis had laid down the most extraordinarily minute rules for those who devoted themselves to this task: nothing was to be copied down from memory, but every single word was to be checked, and even if the original contained an obvious fault it was to be copied, while the authorities were to be told about it, so that they might decide. The holy name of God was to be left blank, so that it might be written in another and absolutely pure ink, by a scribe who had performed ritual ablutions for the purpose. Furthermore, it was not everybody who might own the sacred books and keep them in his house (though there was an exception

---

*The word 'folded' in the Knox Version is perhaps a little unfortunate in view of the author's statement that the material was not folded: but the Vulgate reading is *sicut liber involutus*, which bears him out, without making the Knox Version in any way wrong – it is a slightly different sense of 'folded'.

made for the Book of Esther, which had to be read at home to the family at the Feast of Purim), and some doctors of the Law, with Gamaliel among them, even taught that the touch of them 'made the hands unclean', a teaching that may seem strange, but which was no doubt simply the equivalent of the prohibition that guards the holy vessels of Catholic worship. Even incorrect books or those which were suspected of heresy or which were merely different from the accepted texts were not destroyed, but placed in one of those 'book-cemeteries' which were called *ghenizah*.[44] The word 'bibliomania' has been used, and it is perhaps too harsh; but in any case the Jews had a great respect for the written word.

HOW NEWS WAS SPREAD

One of the chief functions of the written word in our society, a function so important that the invention of the telephone and the radio is far from doing away with it, is the dissemination of news: in ancient Israel, and in all the communities of the ancient world, for that matter, it can only have done this in a very much smaller degree. The wonderful ease with which we buy paper, that splendid aid to thought,[45] and buy it so cheaply, and two centuries of postal development, have made our daily post (the business-man's tyrant) into one of the essential bases of communication. Twenty centuries ago, in Palestine as in Rome, this was scarcely so.

The materials that we have just spoken of were also used for writing letters – parchment, papyrus, wax tablets. The Romans had made two-leaved tablets usual: the two leaves were attached to one another by leather bands, and they were folded wax to wax; but a slight overlap of the wood prevented the written-upon surfaces from touching one another. The man who received the letter had but to wipe out the words and he had the material for his reply at hand. Letters written on parchment or papyrus were rolled and tied with a cord. To make it clear that they were genuine, they were signed, as they are today, particularly if they had been dictated to an amanuensis – the equivalent of our typist. Sometimes the man signing it would add a more friendly, personal word: Saint Paul, for example, finishes his letter to the Colossians with a greeting, and he particularly says, 'Here is a greeting for you from Paul in his own hand'.[46]

But a signature was not enough: the letter was incomplete

without a seal. Every man of any importance had his own, with either his name upon it or a decorative pattern; and the cutting of these seals called for very highly skilled workmen – the Bible speaks of them – and they engraved the inscription with a diamond point[47] in metal or a hard stone, such as agate. The seal might be of wax or more rarely of lead; but in either case it was essential – no letter of any consequence could do without one. The seal was highly symbolic, and the Holy Scriptures make very frequent reference to its use: according to Job, God Himself had set His seal upon man;[48] circumcision was the seal of faithfulness to Yahweh;[49] for His disciples, Christ's message was marked with the seal of the truth of God;[50] and the Last Judgment, said the Revelation, was to be sealed with seven seals.[51]

When the letter had been properly signed, closed and sealed, it had in some way to be sent to its destination. This was not easy. It is true that the Roman empire had its postal service, a service that it had copied from that which the Persian Darius, the King of Kings, had perfected in the fifth century BC: it was a very considerable organisation, a positive ministry, with an army of couriers, people to look after the posting-stations and supervisors; and there was a system of priorities according to the urgency of the message.[52] But the number of those who might make use of the imperial posts was very small: and we do not get the impression that either Herod or his descendants ever set up any organization of this kind.

Private men, therefore, were obliged to use messengers: their own slaves, if they were wealthy, or those who made a trade of carrying letters. These letter carriers are mentioned in the tractate *Shabbath*:[53] they put the messages either in their belts or in wooden tubes which they hung round their necks. Those who were too poor to hire a messenger would take advantage of the departure of a friend, an official or a travelling merchant to entrust the letter to him. The important traders would club together to send a man to Alexandria or Babylon, carrying the letters of the whole group. The Great Sanhedrim and the high priest had special messengers to communicate with the provincial sanhedrims and the communities of the Diaspora, as the last chapter of the Acts makes quite clear.[54] Naturally, these were not very rapid posts: a private letter to Cicero dawdled for a hundred days between Syria and Rome, and the imperial courier took fifty-four days to go from Rome to Caesarea.

To make news publicly known or to convey official orders to the people they were written up on the walls. There were even inscriptions in the Temple, forbidding pagans to go into the courts reserved for believers. The Roman authorities used these notices, and it appears that they wrote them, like that which was put over the Cross, in three languages, of which one was either Hebrew or Aramaic. And the people of the streets, as they always have done everywhere, also made their sentiments and opinions known by writing them up on the walls. The archeologists have found a certain number of graffiti, like those which are to be seen at Pompeii or on the Palatine. One of them, on the lower wall of the Asmonean palace, states that 'Simon and all his household shall go to hell and burn there': at least, this was the view of Pampras, a displeased mason.[55]

Was there any method of distributing news more widely? Some authors have said that 'there was an attempt at circulating a kind of newspaper in Jerusalem', and that this 'fact is mentioned in the rabbinical archives'; though it is 'impossible to make out whether this was a private enterprise or whether on the other hand it was undertaken by the Roman government or the high priests'.[56] If this is true, the manuscript 'newspaper' can scarcely have been very widely read. It is better to assume that news spread verbally: it is notorious how quickly any event is known both in the East and in Africa. The pedlars and the many wandering beggars would have seen to the spreading of more or less truthful accounts of all that occurred, both important and trivial. The well or the fountain, where the women came for their water, was the village information-centre; and one may be sure that news of any importance became known throughout Palestine. Thus, in the Gospel we see 'the multitudes' flocking to be baptized by John or to hear the preaching of the new teacher, Jesus: they had needed no newspaper or radio message to be informed of these things. This completely simple way of broadcasting news had a very pretty name, 'the bird's wing'.

CHAPTER TEN

LETTERS, ARTS AND SCIENCE

A literature without 'mere letters' – The art of the spoken word – 'Non impedias musicam' – A nation without art? – Knowledge, God's secret.

A LITERATURE WITHOUT 'MERE LETTERS'

'The books amongst us, containing the history of all ages,' says Josephus,[1] contrasting the Jews with the Greeks, 'are neither infinite nor one repugnant to another: for all our chronicle is contained in twenty-two books, to which books it is impiety to deny credit.' This was one of the most marked singularities of Israel, that singular nation: they were the People of the Book, but books in the plural they did not produce: they were a people whose whole existence was ruled by a Writing, but who contemptuously rejected all that which (with Verlaine[2]) they might have termed 'mere writing'. There is not a single book known in ancient Israel that deals with a profane subject or which aims solely at giving pleasure. It is impossible to imagine a Jewish Theocritus or Catullus, still less an Ovid, Apuleius or Petronius. Josephus is not quite exact in stating that Israel had no other book than the Bible, but it is perfectly true that Israel had nothing outside its sacred literature.[3]

What, then, did the Jews read? The answer is simple: they read the Bible, that is, the Old Testament, and writings that concerned the Bible. The early Christians did the same: they never tired of reading or hearing the wonderful history of God made man, the account of the Good News and the commentaries upon it in the letters of those who had known Christ. These ideas are so very far removed from ours that it is difficult to understand them. Among the practising Jews, the rejection of all profane literature was strengthened by their hatred for idolatry – Graeco-Roman letters being a source and a vehicle of both idolatry and immorality. The same hostility is to be found in the Fathers of the Church. This explains the absence of all Jewish plays, the total absence of a Hebrew theatre: the ancient Greeks knew the sacred function of tragedy, but it was to take the Christians a thousand years to discover it again.

It is true that in the Old Testament the Jews found a wonderful diversity of matter, for it treats a great many different subjects in a great many different ways. The nature of the writing varies from place to place; the importance of this variation of style, nature and subject is emphasised in Pius XII's enlightening encyclical of 1943, *Divino afflante spiritu*, and without an appreciation of it it is impossible to understand the holy text according to the true meaning of its authors.[4] The Jews, in reading their Bible, found poetry there and history, metaphysics and ethics, fascinating exemplary stories and inexhaustible collections of maxims. They read the glorious annals of their forebears with passionate pride, Judges, Kings and Maccabees; they were profoundly moved by the Psalms and the exquisite harmonies of the Song of Songs; they gained great experience of life and the nature of man from Job, the Proverbs and Ecclesiasticus; and could the lovers of romantic adventure ask more than the stories of Jonah or Tobit or of those heroines of Israel, Judith and Esther, the admiration of every Jewish girl?

And in the Bible, or arising directly from its sacred text, there were writings of such a nature that they are almost inaccessible to the Western man of the twentieth century, or at least exceedingly difficult for him to appreciate fully. The works of the prophets, above all, which were so important to the Jews (as the formula 'the Law and the prophets' makes clear) that they were classed with those in which the will of God was laid down. Did not this will, in any case, express itself just as much by the inspired voices of those great men who, standing as it were outside time, where past, present and future joined, could show the people of Israel their mysterious destiny? It is difficult to imagine a whole nation whose literary life was lived at the spiritual level of Isaiah, Jeremiah or Ezekiel; and yet from the continual allusions in the Gospels and the Epistles alone, it is clear that all these great, splendid, violent books were known in their smallest details – and not only the great major prophets, but the minor prophets too, those whom the modern Christian scarcely knows even by name – Nahum, Micah, Zephaniah, Habakkuk.[5] The earliest Christians, however, were great readers of the Bible; they were brought up on it; and in the events and the teachings of the Holy Scriptures they recognised the prophetic and symbolic foretelling of the mystery of Christ, the accomplishment of the Law, as Saint Paul said; and in the former covenant the promise of the new.

There was indeed a literature apart from the Bible itself, but it was very closely linked to it. These were the writings that later were to be collected by the rabbis to form the Talmud.[6] We have already mentioned the Targums, which were intended to make the text plainer to all by translating it into Aramaic,[7] as, for example, that from which Saint Mark certainly took the quotation from Psalm 21 that he puts into the mouth of the dying Christ,[8] or those versions from Genesis and Job which have been found among the Dead Sea scrolls, or those again which were collected by the rabbis.[9] But above all there were the commentaries upon the texts, those innumerable commentaries which the Israelites' very close relationship with the Bible brought into being. The *midrash*, whose name was derived from the same root as the words 'to teach' and 'to investigate', was an exposition and a commentary that was intended to explain the solutions that, in a veiled or obscure form, were contained in the Torah; the vital treasures of the word of God; and it was a typical product of the Jewish mind, for which the moral and spiritual meaning of an event was of more importance than its material aspect. The *midrash* was not only the work of the learned; in the synagogues the ordinary believers might make their exegesis, and we see our Lord Himself in the act of doing so; and all these, written down, would be added to the others in this immense literature of piety. One of the most esteemed forms of the *midrash* was the *pesher*, which was intended to show the present realization of texts that were searched out in the Scriptures: this literary form was so common that the evangelists turn to it many times to emphasize that some given fact of Christ's life occurred 'so that the Scriptures might be accomplished'.[10]

Lastly there was one other class of books: these did not arise directly from the Bible, but they were very closely connected to it. In the first place it consisted of those books which were not admitted to the canon, the official list of books which the religious authorities had declared inspired, dictated by God.[11] These uncanonical books were nevertheless widely read: among them, for example, was the *Book of Jonah*, to which our Lord Himself alludes,[12] and those magnificent psalms which have been found in the Dead Sea scrolls, and which are so very near to those in the Bible.

But the great majority of this class of books was made up of works whose authors endeavoured to make use of the authority of the Scriptures, although they took the strangest liberties with them. All these come under the heading of apocryphal literature, but this is an ambiguous term, and it does not have the same meaning for the Jews and the Protestants on the one hand, and the Catholics on the other.[13] It was a literature that gave itself out as an esoteric teaching, 'to be delivered only to such as be wise among the people', said one of them,[14] and as one that revealed the secret intentions of God. One claimed to give the secrets of Enoch, the father of Methuselah, of whom Genesis says that 'he walked with God';[15] another was the *Ascension of Isaiah*, another the *Assumption of Moses*; still another, and more ambitious, was the *Life of Adam and Eve*. Several others added chapters to the biblical books of Ezra, Baruch and Maccabees, or attributed anti-Roman psalms to Solomon. These apocryphal writings were fabricated all over the place. In the Jewish colony of Alexandria someone even had the idea that it would be clever to appropriate the famous pagan prophecies of the Sibyls, and to put out a much revised and corrected edition of the Sibylline Books which would make them say just what the Jews wished the pagans to hear. This was a literature, then, that contained everything, except pro-portion and discretion: there was historical fiction, or fictional history, pious tales, legendary lives of holy men, prophecies and apocalypses. The last was a particularly numerous group. They were strange works in which some famous biblical character was supposed, in visions, to unfold the history of the world, ending by a revelation of the last days of mankind.[16] Obviously, there was a high degree of disproportion and even of nonsense in this curious world of the apocryphas – these delirious ecstasies, as Saint Jerome called them – but there is no doubt that they were very widely read by our Lord's contemporaries. Their apocalyptic violence answered only too well to the deep longings of this humiliated nation, for whom a universal cataclysm was now the only revenge to be hoped for.[17] It is significant that the Fathers of the Church quoted from some of the Jewish apocryphas, that several of the early heresies drew upon them, and that even the most authentic tradition of the Catholic Church was not un-influenced by them, as we may see from that line in the Dies Irae, *teste David cum Sibylla*.[18]

All in all, the literature of the Jews at the time of Christ was

a very strange one to us: it is as if some Christian nation of today
should confine itself exclusively to the sacred books and theological
commentaries upon them, and by way of diversion should read
either the *Golden Legend* and works of that kind or poems like
the *Divine Comedy* of Dante, Milton's *Paradise Lost* or Blake's
Marriage of Heaven and Hell. Many of the fundamental
characteristics of the Jews are explained by this, as well as many
of the happenings which, just before the time of Christ, prepared
for the vast upheaval in which the People of the Book were overwhelmed – happenings which indeed brought the upheaval about.

THE ART OF THE SPOKEN WORD

If one bears in mind the part that the spoken word had played
in the communication of thought, and the fact that the Bible
itself, for example, existed orally long before it was written,[1]
it is easy to realize that there was a necessary and strong connexion
between literature and the art of speaking. In fact the two could
not be separated. Those men whom we would call 'writers'
were first 'speakers': not 'orators', for that has different implications for us. In Israel, as in the countries of the East today
there were men who spoke in the streets and the open places
or in the Temple courts, and crowds would gather round them
What is still more striking is that those rabbis whose duty i
was to teach but who did not possess the gift of public speaking
had beside them as it were heralds, relayers or loud-speakers
who passed on what the master had to say to the listeners. Perhap
this custom throws light upon Christ's words: 'What has been
whispered in your ears, you are to proclaim on the house-tops.'[2]
There is no sort of doubt that Jesus Himself was a great master
of the art of the spoken word, commanding all the resources
using all the forms of language from the uttermost violence to
the greatest persuasiveness, from the extreme of tenderness to the
highest degree of pathos. John the Baptist was certainly another
the few words of his that have come down to us are singularl
impressive. And the achievements of Saint Paul's preaching ca
only be explained by the possession of great oratorical power.

But the Hebrew art of speaking had nothing in common with
what the Greeks and the Romans understood by eloquence
Saint Paul himself was brought to realize this at Athens, where
as we know, he was not an outstanding success.[21] The orderl
arrangement of ideas, the logical development and proof, th

whole basis, according to Cicero, of the art of speaking, was utterly foreign to the Jewish mind – as it still is, for that matter, to the Mohammedan. For the Israelites the art of speaking consisted not so much of carrying conviction by reasoning as of establishing a contact with the hearers' emotions, their sensibility. The excellent speaker was the man who possessed the technical methods of the doctors of the Law and even, as we have seen, of the schoolmasters, in their highest perfection – alliteration, echoes and parallels, rhythm. By its nature high eloquence reached up to join poetry; and although there were no fixed rules and rigid metres as there were in Greek or Roman poetry, it frequently happened that the words of the best speakers would naturally run into verse with a deliberately uneven beat, and even into stanzas with refrains.

As regards the matter of his discourse, the master of the spoken word was to be recognized by certain distinguishing marks: he was to be able to fill it with biblical quotations or allusions which his hearers would instantly recognize – when Saint John said, 'I am the voice that cries, "In the desert, prepare for the coming of the Lord" ',* he was quoting Isaiah word for word, and his audience knew it.[22] Every statement had to be supported by the word of God. The great speaker had to be able to produce a great number of developments on any given theme, as a musician improvises variations upon a melodic phrase: in the sixth chapter of the tractate *Sanhedrin* it is stated that the great rabbi Gamaliel, upon being given a theme, could produce three hundred expositions of it. But above all, the master of the spoken word had to be an expert in the *mashal*.

It is essential to understand the conception of the *mashal* in order to comprehend the nature of Jewish eloquence: its application is to be found in countless places in the written literature, the Old and New Testament; but fundamentally the *mashal* was a function of the spoken word. Hebrew, though concise and full of colour, is curiously inept when it deals with abstractions and the higher reality: it circumvents this difficulty by the use of figure, symbol and comparison. This, furthermore, is in entire conformity with the Jewish frame of mind, which is wonderfully strong in intuition, which at once seizes upon the immediate, realistic and familiar point, and which draws a lesson from it with great ability. This way of taking a particular case or situation

*This is the author's translation, not that of the Knox Version.

in real life, so that the mind and the imagination may possess it and mould it into symbol or draw a generalized question from it was in fact the *mashal*. Was this very Oriental process a kind of game? Not at all, for every *mashal* had to have a bearing upon conduct, and at least implicitly to refer to religion.

The Greek translation of the Seventy often renders *mashal* by *parabole*, but it would be a mistake to suppose that all *meshalim* were parables in the sense that we understand the word: a convincing proof is the fact that *Meshalim* is the Hebrew name for the Book of Proverbs. The root of the word contains the idea of 'collecting', or of 'comparing', but its ordinary connotation was much wider. A contemporary French writer[23] classes all his works under the heading of poetry: 'poetry of the novel', says he 'poetry of criticism' or 'poetry of the cinema'; and it is clear that by this he wishes to define a fundamental attitude of his creative thought. The fact helps one to explain that there were, in the literature and oratory of Israel, poetical, oracular, satirical and proverbial *meshalim*, as well as those in the form of moral fables.[2]

The parable in our sense of the word, that is, a little story like an apologue which provides a moral or spiritual lesson in a more or less obvious form, was certainly one aspect of the *mashal*: it was one way of making the concrete fact reveal its surprising potentialities. It was a sort that was very widely used. A hundred years before Christ, the rabbi Meir had become famous for his extraordinary powers of producing *meshalim* of this kind: his all had a fox as the chief character, and it is said that he composed three thousand of them. There are hundreds of such apologue in the Talmud, and some of them are very picturesque: to explain how it comes about that there is good and bad in the world, perfect men and evil ones, for example, one commentator upon Genesis compares God to a man who mixes boiling water with cold in a basin before filling his jug with it, for fear of cracking the earthenware. Curiously enough, some are identical with the fables of Aesop: for instance, a Talmudic gloss upon Ecclesiasticus tells how a fox, wishing to get into a place by a hole that was too small for him, fasted for several days in order to get thinner. It seems that the parable-*mashal* had been so much used by the time of Christ that among the rabbis it was beginning to grow somewhat ossified and stylized, for the same comparisons very often appear in the works of several rabbis, and very often the composition lacks both strength and life.

It is abundantly obvious that Christ was acquainted with the *mashal* and that He used it. It would have been quite impossible for a Jew of His time not to have heard one of these ingenious little tales either uttered spontaneously or repeated by someone who had heard it. In fact, the Talmud contains some parable-*meshalim* which are almost the same as His: there is one, for example, on the wedding-guests, and another about the foolish virgins. Our Lord employed the *mashal* in all its forms. The 'Physician, heal thyself' of Saint Luke's Gospel,[25] is a *mashal*; so is the apophthegm in Matthew[26] about what makes a man unclean: and among the *meshalim* parables there are several different kinds, varying much in length and nature.[27]

But when one compares the parables of the Gospels with those of the Talmudic tractates it is at once apparent that their character is new. There is nothing stereotyped or conventional about them: one feels that the comparison has sprung naturally from the mouth of the speaker; it is simple and exact, and (which is something that is not to be found in the Acts, and still less in the apocryphal Gospels) the tone is one that cannot be copied – it is a wholly personal style, the true sign of the Master. The parable of the Gospels 'starts from the humblest realities and reflects the most elevated concepts with the greatest clarity; it is to be understood by the simple and at the same time it calls for the deep reflection of the learned. From the literary point of view it is artless, and yet in its emotional power it goes far beyond the most elaborate literary artifice. It does not so much amaze as persuade; it does not merely conquer, it convinces. From the word *parabole* we have the word *parole*: may not this etymology mean that Christ's *parabole* is the *parole* or word of man raised to its highest possible elevation, and at the same time the word of God that has come down nearest to us?'[28]

'NON IMPEDIAS MUSICAM'

Music, close to this conception of the art of speech and associated with it, had a considerable place in Israel. '*Non impedias musicam*, do not break in when music is a-playing,' said Ben Sirach,[29] giving these words a more literal sense than Claudel. The Old Testament often speaks of music, musical instruments, songs and dances; and the marvellous story of God made man in the Gospel begins with the happy singing of the angels in the sky and the sound of the shepherds' flutes. Like all the men of the ancient world, the Hebrews attributed a quasi-divine origin to music: it was at mankind's very beginning, a few generations after Adam, that Jubal invented the 'flute and the *kinnor*' and became the founder of all those who play music.[30] The Bible recognised a kind of relationship between music and prayer and adoration and ecstasy: something in the nature of a dance to the rhythm of flutes and cymbals had often been necessary to the prophets so that 'the hand of God should be upon them', that is to say, so that they could accomplish their mission.[31] And everybody in Israel was aware that the young David had played the *kinnor* to ease Saul's unhappiness,[32] and that when he became king himself, he sang and danced before the Ark. The Jewish nation, then, was a nation of musicians.

There was no family feast that was unaccompanied by music. 'Today, in Palestine, the piercing melodies, the clapping of hands and the quick rhythm of dancing feet on the threshing-floor still give wedding-parties their intoxicating excitement.'[33] Banquets and other splendid meals, as we have seen,[34] were incomplete without music. The results of this 'intoxicating excitement' were not always in complete agreement with moral principles: if we are to believe Isaiah, the young ladies who played harps did not delight only the ears of the guests.[35]

If music increased the pleasure of the happy hours, it also had its part in sadness. A funeral procession necessarily had its mourners, who chanted their lamentations, and these recitatives taken up in a minor key by the rest of the people, might reach an extraordinary pitch of frenzy. A self-respecting burial had to have women who played flutes, and we see them already doing so when Christ came to raise Jairus' daughter to life, in Saint Matthew's Gospel.[36] The poorest funeral still had one mourner and two flute-players.

As to religious music, it was so important that there was not a single ceremony, not a single rite, into which it did not enter. The Psalmist said that it was where the trumpets pealed that the Lord went up, and that it was 'with the harp, with harp and psaltery' music; with trumpets of metal, and the music of the braying horn that He was to be praised.[37] From the pages of the Bible there arises a great chant, a rhythmic, modulated acclamation of the Almighty. The Sabbath and the great holidays were announced by the sound of the horn, and the hours of prayer by trumpets. Indeed, many parts of the Book itself were sung: for instance those nuptial hymns in the Song of Songs that the people chanted as they went along with the bride and bridegroom, or those psalms of the 'going up' which the long caravans of pilgrims tirelessly sang as they went towards Jerusalem. Many psalms have, as a heading, the name of the tune to which they are meant to be sung – 'The dove of the distant terebinths' or 'The lily of the Law' – or that of the instruments, strings or woodwind, that were to accompany them. The services themselves included song. The Temple had its Levitical cantors; and bearing in mind the relationship between music and mystic ecstasy, it is noteworthy that the Bible sometimes terms them seers or prophets.[38] Ever since a decision of the Persian king, they had been exempted from paying taxes,[39] and Josephus states that they claimed the right of wearing linen garments like those of the priests – a privilege that Herod Agrippa II granted them. There was singing in the synagogues, too; and this was a custom that the early Christians retained, as we learn from Saint Paul's Epistle to the Colossians: 'Now there will be psalms, and hymns, and spiritual wisdom, as you sing with gratitude in your hearts to God',[40] he says.

Song had a very important place in Jewish music, and it would appear that by the time of Christ it had become almost entirely separated from instrumental music, since this had grown out of its ancient limitations and was no longer a mere accompaniment to the human voice: musical instruments are very little spoken of in the New Testament. It was very usual to sing in choir under the leadership of that 'choirmaster' who is so often to be seen in the headings of the psalms; the singing was probably in unison, but solo parts were not unknown, and it is also quite clear that some psalms were intended to be sung antiphonally, as we do today. The services of the present traditional synagogues give one an idea of what the ancient religious music was like: that continuous flow of which Robert Aron speaks, 'now swelling at those moments when the sacred nature of the service grows more intense and now quietening as it lessens, a flow which increases as simply and as imperiously as the panting of a man's breath, to reach its height at the moment when the rolls of the Law are taken from the tabernacle'.

Israel thoroughly understood the emotional power of the human voice. Yet for all that, instruments were very much used: the Bible mentions several kinds, and there is no doubt that they were all in use at the time of Christ. The wind instruments were the flute, horn and trumpet; the strings the *kinnor*, that is, the zither or lyre, and the *nebel*, or harp; the percussion, the tambourine and the cymbals: Psalm 150, the last, speaks of them all. But there may have been still others, such as the psaltery that King David played, the Babylonian sackbut which is mentioned in Daniel, and the sistrum that was brought back from Egypt. The Israelites were considered excellent harpers and flautists, and Queen Salome Alexandra sent Cleopatra a famous harp-player in order to win her favour. They were so much attached to the flute that they had invented a great many varieties, from the simple reed-pipe to an instrument analogous to our bagpipe, as well as the side-flute and a tongued flute like our oboe. They were made of reed, wood and even bronze; and there was no Jewish house without one of some kind. Among the trumpets and the horns the best-known was the *shofar*, made from the horn of a ram: this was the liturgical instrument above all others, the one that evoked the revelation of Sinai, for when Moses went up the mountain he had gone to the blast of the ram's horn: its sound, less musical than moving, stirred men to repentance, and for this reason the *shofar* was used to announce the great holy days, particularly the Rosh Hashanah, the first day of the year, when 'the books of life and of death' were open before the Lord.

Of the actual nature of Jewish music we know nothing. In Greece the music for the *kithara* could be written down, but this was not the case in Israel: there was no doubt great liberty for improvisation. The few hints that we find in the Bible are imprecise: we read of 'over the octave' but there is no mention of key or scale. Some psalms seem to have a reference to the mode in their first verse, but it is impossible to say what modes these may have been. The Talmud, indeed, does give some information upon musical notation and upon the use of 'musical accents', but this was the work of the Masoretes, that is to say, it dates from four centuries after the time of Christ, at least.

Judging by modern Jewish and Arabic music we may reasonably suppose that it was a sort of chanting recitative, using a restricted range of notes, with half- and quarter-tones, shakes and a kind of vibrato produced by the hand on the throat, as one sees in the bas-relief of a Mesopotamian singer. It would all have been accompanied by the beating of tambourines and the clapping of hands and the rhythmic clash of cymbals: from this general mass of sound the shrill note of a flute would have emerged from time to time, with the whole punctuated by the deep sound of the horn. Rhythm was certainly the chief element, far outweighing melody and harmony: rhythm, because music almost invariably went with dancing, with marching and counter-marching, with farandoles, jigs and those to-and-fro movements with linked arms that are still to be seen in Palestine.[41] As for the dance in the fuller sense of the word, the dancing of professionals, it certainly existed: a proof of this is to be found in the Gospel, in the account of Salome's dancing before Herod. One cannot say what kind of dance it was; but perhaps it was imported from Rome: in any case it was sufficiently moving to make the tetrarch lose his head so thoroughly that he ordered the execution of John the Baptist.[42]

A NATION WITHOUT ART?

Music may have had a considerable importance in the daily life of Israel; but did the same apply to the other arts? It did not. History has not retained the name of a single artist in Israel, nor has archeology discovered a single Jewish masterpiece. Does this mean that the Chosen People had the appearance of 'a barbarous nation from the point of view of art'?[43] It has been maintained[44] that it was not 'the lack of artistic ability that prevented the Jews from creating plastic forms', and that as Semites they, like the Semites of Mesopotamia, could very well have brought works of art into being. Far from despising artists, they gave them a very high rank, which is plain from Exodus,[45] in which Moses gives high praise to Bezaleel: 'The Lord has filled this man with his divine spirit, making him wise, adroit, in every kind of craftsmanship, so that he can design and execute whatever is needed, in gold, silver, bronze and sculptured gems, and carpenter's work.'

But the development of art in Israel was always paralysed by that famous prohibition in Exodus, repeated in Deuteronomy:[46] 'Thou shalt not carve images, or fashion the likeness of anything in heaven above, or on earth beneath, or in the waters under the earth.' The uncompromising concept of an invisible God put all representation of man or beast under the heading of idolatry: if these two themes were taken away from Greek art, what would remain of its sculpture? And what would Western art be in such conditions? To this must be added the fact that except in the time of Solomon, and to a lesser degree of Herod the Great, Israel's rulers were never rich enough to set up as patrons of the arts: and if, together with these considerations, one allows for the varying, contradictory influences of the successive occupations, it becomes quite understandable that Israel should not have had a strikingly original art. It was far more important for the Jews to preserve their spiritual life than their potentialities of aesthetic creation.

At the time of Christ, Palestine was certainly not without art; but to a very large extent this art was foreign, an art brought in by the Greek occupiers, and after them by the Romans. When the architecture was genuinely Hebrew it was quite unassuming;[47] it only became splendid when it adopted the ways of the pagans, as could be seen only too well from Herod's building, his palaces at Jerusalem and Jericho, the theatre and the hippodrome that he had dared erect in the holy city, and still worse, the temples in honour of Augustus or of Roman idols that the imperfectly circumcised man had raised at Samaria and Caesarea. And was not the very Temple on the sacred hill of Zion more or less based upon those of Jupiter?

Sculpture was an even greater source of scandal. Doubtless no one had ever presumed to set up the smallest statue in the city of God, for a revolution would have broken out at once – there was the example of what happened when Herod set the gold eagles upon the gates of the Temple. But the strict Jews, when they went into the Greek cities, or to Caesarea, or even when they passed through the land of the heretical Samaritans, were unable to prevent their eyes from being defiled by the sight of idols, those 'abominations of desolation' of which the Bible spoke. There was no Jewish sculpture of living figures whatever; and it is by no means sure that the Temple of Herod contained even those wooden cherubim that had been in the Temple of Solomon. The only permitted designs were those that represented plants, palm-trees or citrons; some liturgical objects, such as the seven-branched candlestick; and scrolls and arabesques. As we have seen,[48] coins also obeyed this rule: even Herod and his descendants did not presume to infringe it, at least as far as those coins which were minted in the Holy Land and which were meant for the Jews were concerned (they took greater liberties elsewhere); and they never ventured beyond the representation of a helmet or a shield. In any case, these pieces were poorly struck and the designs indifferent.

As for painting, it was still more poverty-stricken: nothing at all dating from the time of Christ has been found. The unpretending floral or geometrical decorations that may perhaps have given the whitewashed walls of the Jewish houses a little colour have all disappeared. So have the painted and gilded decorations upon a sculptured background, such as the famous golden vine, which once glittered in the Temple. Yet at Dura Europus, a small Syrian town near the Euphrates which the Seleucids built in the fourth century BC, some extraordinary frescoes have been found in the local synagogue: they show scenes from the Bible, and particularly the resurrection of the dead as Ezekiel described it. But this is a work of a period very much later than the time of our Lord; which also applies to the paintings discovered in the tombs of Marissa in Idumaea. The Greek influence is very clear; and no one has yet been able to explain how it can have come about that the Mosaic prohibition was so deliberately disobeyed. Christ's contemporaries would have been horrified.

Our only means of forming an opinion of the artistic taste of the Jews is their pottery. These little red earthenware pitchers decorated with black circles, and these bowls of yellow clay, with a fine red underlining their delicate turned ribs, which have been found in the various excavations are not without their charm; but are they really Jewish, or are they imports from Alexandria or Cyprus? The wealthy of those times bought their fine ceramics abroad, and the poor attached no importance to profane decoration.[49]

KNOWLEDGE, GOD'S SECRET

In Israel, literature and the arts were, in their varying degrees, subjected to the requirements of religion; but it may be said that the sciences, or what took their place, were entirely absorbed by it. The Greeks and the Romans knew what pure scientific research was; they understood the search for knowledge for its own sake: this attitude of mind, from which the whole of our modern science has sprung, was completely inadmissible to the Jews. There could be no science other than theology. The word *hakhamim*, which is translated 'learned men' meant above all 'wise men', and it was applied to those who were outstanding masters of religious knowledge. Wisdom, said the Proverbs,[50] was God's 'when first he went about his work, at the birth of time, before his creation began', and all human knowledge had meaning only in so far as it was related to this wisdom. But wisdom was 'naturally identified with the Torah': scientific work, therefore, 'was not brought about by rational enquiries into the phenomena of the universe, but rather by attempts at deducing from the sacred text its teachings about the origin and the constitution of the world'. This was the cause for that distrust for all research prompted by an enquiring mind, the disturbing *libido scientiae* which had urged the first human pair towards evil. 'Do not search into things that are too difficult', said the rabbis. 'Do not probe into what is hidden.'[51] To know the whole of Israel's science, therefore, one has but to open the Bible. And it does not seem that even the Jews of the Diaspora, who were in contact with pagan science, the Jews who lived at Alexandria, for instance, that great centre of scientific research, relinquished this way of thinking.

There were some notions of astronomy to be drawn from the Book. Had not God created the stars, as He had created the sun, the moon and the earth? 'Is it at thy command the glittering bright Pleiads cluster so close, and Orion's circlet spreads so wide? Dost thou tell the day star when to shine out, the evening star when to rise over the sons of the earth?' Thus the Creator questioned Job, that holy man.[52] But directly afterwards He added, 'Is it thine to understand the motions of the heavens?'[53] The Jews therefore had an astronomy, and one by which they could establish their calendar. It was doubtless less an astronomy derived from that of the Babylonians, based upon learned calculation, than one that arose from simple, easy observations that anyone might make. It is striking to see how simply Christ speaks of the astronomical phenomena: the rising and the setting of the sun and of the moon; the presence of the stars in the sky – obviously all the things to which He refers are within the knowledge of His hearers, and they are all elementary. Yet were the learned of His day much better informed? If they were, they have left no trace of their labours: the *Pirke Aboth*, the *Sayings of the Fathers*, flatly denies astronomy the status of an independent science: it is to remain 'one of Wisdom's dependencies',[54] that is, it exists only to proclaim the glory of God.

The Jewish cosmology was not lacking in precision. For them the universe was enormous: 'One would have to live five hundred years', says the tractate *Berakoth*, 'to cover the distance between the earth and the heaven that is immediately over us; there is the same distance between that heaven and the next, and the ends of each heaven, considered in its breadth, are equally far apart.'[55] For there were seven heavens. Why? Because the Bible uses seven different words for heaven. It is from this notion that we have our expression 'in the seventh heaven'; and Saint Paul certainly seems to refer to it, though he is speaking mystically.[56] For the same reason the earth too was formed of seven successive layers – an idea which, scientifically, is not so far from the truth.[57] It was traditionally held[58] that in the Temple there might be seen the stone which the Almighty threw into the primordial sea so that the land might form about it. There was a mysterious line that went right round the universe, dividing the light from the darkness: it was held to be this line that Isaiah referred to in the strange verse: 'A land of burning pitch . . . plotted with the Lord's measuring-line, an empty void, tried with his plummet, a hanging ruin.'[59] The origin of the 'three first elements', heaven, earth and water, was also explained by learned expositions of the Book of Genesis.

Geographical knowledge had the same basis. Several Talmudic tractates concern themselves with geography, and from them one can form an idea of the information that an educated Jew of the first century possessed. The earth was round and flat,[60] and it was surrounded by water.[61] God was seated above this circle, which He Himself had drawn.[62] The earth's surface was divided into two, Israel and the rest. Israel, naturally, was in the middle, immediately under God. Some rabbis called the rest 'the countries of the sea'. But it was common knowledge that Israel was washed by seven seas: the Great Sea (the Mediterranean), the Sea of Gennesaret, the Samochonite Sea (perhaps Lake Huleh, or Merom), the Salt Sea or the Sea of Sodom, the Sea of Acco (the Gulf of Aqaba), and the Seas of Shelyath and of Apamea, these last two being perhaps some little Idumaean lakes which Diodorus Siculus speaks of, and which have since disappeared. The Holy Land had four rivers, the Jordan, the Yarmuk, the Kermion and the Pigah. (The last two have never been identified.) It is apparent that the mystic figures seven and four played an important part in this knowledge.

Natural history seems to have been quite advanced. The Israelites, a peasant nation, were interested in animals and knew their ways: our Lord alludes to them many times. The Bible, too, provided a considerable amount of information. The Book of Proverbs spoke of the ant;[63] Job, particularly interested in the subject, of the hind, the wild ass, the ostrich, the horse, the eagle and even the hippopotamus and the crocodile.[64] As early as Genesis the whales were distinguished from the other denizens of the sea.[65] The Scriptures even contained lists that separated the wild beasts from those that could be tamed, and which distinguished between those which had cloven hoofs and those which had not, between seed-giving and fruit-giving plants.[66] This was all somewhat rudimentary, of course: no Pliny seems ever to have arisen among the Jews.

Mathematics, which now form the basis of all science, did not exist; at least, not as a Jewish science, though it is likely that the Greek and Roman knowledge had seeped in to some extent. There appears to have been no abstract science of number: the Jews went no further than empirical calculation. Geometry, for example, was limited to the practical application of land-surveying. They had the decimal system of counting, together with the remains of a sexagesimal system which was dying out, no doubt because of foreign influence. Figures were written by combinations of letters, as they were among the Romans.

Naturally, Jewish arithmetic turned first towards the Bible. For example, all the letters of all the canonical books were counted (this is why the doctors of the Law were happy to be called *soferim*, counters), and it was found that the word exactly in the middle of the Old Testament was the verb 'to seek'; which was not without significance. Above all the Jews tried to establish the relation between the figures and the letters that represented them: it was thought that by adding up the numerical values of the letters that composed a word, one might penetrate to that word's secret, inner meaning; and this was particularly valuable when the word was a proper name. This kind of calculation originated in Babylon; it was also known to the Greeks and the Romans; and it was to this that the Revelation refers, particularly in those strange verses that end the thirteenth chapter: 'Let the reader, if he has the skill, cast up the sum of the figures in the beast's name, and the number will be six hundred and sixty-six.' This stood for 'Nero Caesar', the persecutor of the Christians at the time when Saint John was writing his book, for the sum of the numerical values in that name comes to six hundred and sixty-six.

Some rabbis pushed this esoteric arithmetic very far: for them, the Bible, and especially the Pentateuch, was a coded document, from which, by combining the values of all the words, one might work out equations whose solution would allow one to penetrate the divine, cosmogonic, prophetic and metaphysical secrets that a simple reading of the text did not reveal. This method, which was not peculiar to the Jews – Plato seems to speak of it in the *Republic* and the *Timaeus*[67] – was later to be much developed by the Talmudists; and from this development arose that extraordinary mixture of extravagance and profound speculation that is known under the name of the *Kabbalah*.[68] At the same time the idea of an esoteric knowledge reserved for the initiated was certainly widely held in Christ's day: some people followed two branches of study, the one according to the 'order of creation' in the first chapter of Genesis, the other according to the 'order of mystery', which was also called the 'order of the chariot', in reference to Ezekiel and his chariot of fire.[69] But it must be observed that nothing was more foreign to these speculations, these secret messages reserved for the initiated, these gnostic illuminations, than the teaching of Christ, in which everything is clear and plain, to be understood by the poor and the simple.

CHAPTER ELEVEN

HABITS AND CUSTOMS; PERSONAL CLEANLINESS; AMUSEMENTS

Everyday life – Personal cleanliness – Social relationships – Devils and the stars – Leisure and amusements – Whoredom.

EVERYDAY LIFE

There still remains a great deal to be said about the life of a human community even after its geographical and historical frame has been defined, its essential social institutions described, together with its housing, clothing and food; even when its methods of communication, its language and writing, and its intellectual and spiritual activities have been dealt with. To describe the life that a society of some given date led in its ordinary existence of every day one should also be able to pick out those innumerable little ways and customs, those usual forms of behaviour, attitudes of mind, tastes, needs, common expressions, superstitions, which all combine to make up the atmosphere of a period, and which are mostly so little noticed, so nearly automatic, that nobody troubles to record them. And yet it is these things which make the climate of the time and which distinguish one period from another, even one that is very close; for these little habits and customs are extraordinarily changeable. Even now, when we possess a whole range of tools for seizing the moment as it passes – newspapers, cinema, tape-recorders – it is difficult to convey just what it is that makes the nineteen sixties different from the nineteen fifties. This is the impalpable dust of history, the iridescent powder that the wings of a butterfly leave on one's fingers.

For the Israel of the time of Christ, the task is far more difficult. Our chief source should be the New Testament, for the Old stops more than a hundred and fifty years earlier; but it goes without saying that the evangelists and the apostles had an aim very different from that of supplying us with information upon this subject. Nevertheless, an occasional brief allusion does pin down some characteristic habit of the time: the kiss of Judas, for example, and the formula in which an unnamed woman acclaimed our Lord,[1] tell us about certain ways of greeting and addressing; but these pieces of exact information are rare.

There are of course the inexhaustible tractates of the Talmud. In their desire to apply the precepts of religion to every possible case, the rabbis specifically fixed countless little details of everyday life. But although many of the tractates were composed a little before or a little after the time of Christ, they assumed their final shape and they were gathered together a hundred or a hundred and fifty years after Him; and although at that time history was not subject to that immense acceleration of which Daniel Halévy speaks,[2] by the year AD 150 many terrible events had placed the Chosen People in conditions completely different from those in which they lived during the years 25 and 30. Furthermore, a great part of the Talmud was compiled in Babylon, that is to say, in a cultural atmosphere very unlike that of Palestine. It is entirely permissible to use the Talmudic tractates for questions concerning law and institutions, and even for certain attitudes of mind and practices to some degree governed by religion, for the great strength of tradition in Israel with regard to these matters prevented any rapid change. But can the same be said for little passing ways and customs? The tractate *Shabbath*, for example, sets down what it is forbidden to do upon the day of rest with extraordinary minuteness, and it tells us that a woman was not forbidden to go out wearing false hair;[3] but this tractate was drawn up in Babylon, most probably about AD 135. Does it then allude only to a custom of the well-dressed women of Babylon, or was this usual among those of Jerusalem a hundred years before? Historically, it cannot be held to prove that the women of Palestine wore wigs or false buns at the time of Christ.

PERSONAL CLEANLINESS

One thing is certain: the Israelites were very clean. 'Cleanliness', says the learned rabbi A. Cohen, 'is not merely a near neighbour to piety; it is an integral part of it, and a most important part, at that.'[4] Washing was among the great requirements in Leviticus: 'Keep your persons undefiled.'[5] It was literally a sin to eat without having washed one's hands. Washing thoroughly, said the rabbis, was better than all medicines. Others asserted that the dirty might go mad. And some went so far as to say: 'It is forbidden to live in a town which has no baths.'[6]

There were, therefore, many of these baths: they had increased during the Hellenistic period, and of course the Romans, who were much attached to them, had built even more: the archaeologists have found the traces of a great many. Some were no more than common bathing-pools open to all, but there were some that were very elaborate, like the Roman *thermae*, with pools of hot and cold water, sweating-rooms and rooms for resting, and a whole staff of masseurs and serving-maids. The rabbis recommended a steam-bath followed by a cold shower, so as to 'temper the body like steel', and after that a thorough rubbing with oil. Rabbi Khannina, at the age of eighty, could still 'stand on one foot while he put his slipper on the other',[7] because his mother had accustomed him to this practice from his childhood.

The ashes of soda-yielding plants together with some kind of fat were used for washing. Was it to this mixture that Job alluded?[8] His words might also refer to pumice-stone, which was well known to the Greeks and the Romans. If a man were really very dirty, he would use *natron*, that 'nitre' which, according to Jeremiah, would not suffice to wash out the sins of the faithless nation:[9] it was sodium carbonate, and it was brought from Egypt or Syria. It is significant that its name came from the same root as the word meaning 'to froth'. This soda was used by those who worked at dirty trades, the tanners and the leather-dressers, to clean themselves on Friday afternoons, before the beginning of the Sabbath. It was also usual to rub oneself with strongly scented herbs, such as rosemary and marjoram. Sponges were known – that is quite clear from the very well-known episode in the Gospel when a bystander at the Crucifixion held up a sponge filled with vinegar and water on a rod for Jesus to drink[10] – and so were brushes. Not toothbrushes, however, nor toothpaste: to make one's breath pure 'scented pepper' was used – no doubt a kind of anise.[11]

Did the men shave? The Bible mentions shaving so often that one is tempted to believe that it was a usual practice. It is stated for example, that any man who took a Nazarite's vows[12] was not to shave;[13] but on the other hand, on the day the Levites made themselves ritually clean they were to shave all over.[14] But in the first case it was the hair of the head that was meant, and in the second the hair of the body. No doubt the 'barbers' who are frequently mentioned in the Septuagint existed; but it is not known for sure whether these were not merely hairdressers. Many passages in the Bible seem to show that the Jews let their beards grow: Psalm 132 directly states that Aaron, Moses' brother, had a beard; and balm flowed down it to the very skirts of his robe. To take no care of one's beard was indeed a mark of unhappiness;[15] and in the deepest mourning one shaved it.[16] To cut off a man's beard was to insult him very deeply.[17] As the Romans were clean-shaven, it is most probable that the Jews of Christ's time would have looked upon their beards as a real part of their resistance to the conquerors. It is therefore practically certain that Jesus, as a faithful Jew, would never have chosen to incur the censure that Jeremiah uttered against those who shaved.[18] It may be that like the rabbis of today He wore that part of the beard which is as it were the continuation of a man's hair at the temples, those long curled side-locks that Leviticus made obligatory.[19]

It is an odd fact that Leviticus also directly forbade any kind of tattooing:[20] this was probably because the Phoenicians and other pagans tattooed their hands and their foreheads in honour of their idols. Perhaps the prophets alone may have had on their foreheads or their hands the 'Lord's mark' which Isaiah mentions.[21] It is conceivable that the Revelation, in speaking of 'the mark of the beast' and 'the seal of the living God',[22] meant tattooing; the first, no doubt, alluding to the heathen custom, and the second, as a metaphor, meaning a spiritual mark.

Hair was the object of much attention and care. The wealthy, without necessarily all being Absaloms[23] or fairytale princes with curling 'raven hair' like that of the Beloved in the Song of Songs,[24] were very fond of wearing it long, a practice that Saint Paul termed 'a disgrace'.[25] Depraved young men, says Josephus, would sprinkle it with gold dust to make it more brilliant. Old bucks like Herod, still according to Josephus, dyed it. The men of the people also wore their hair long, but not so long; and except on holidays they plaited it or rolled it up under their head-gear. At banquets, as we have seen[26] and as the Gospel states in many places,[27] it was very usual to have one's hair scented; the host, or one of his servants, would pour perfumed oil upon the chief guest's head. Unkempt hair, on the other hand, was a sign of sorrow; even more so a shaven head or hair torn out. To look after their hair, the Jews had gold, ivory or wooden combs, often decorated with a pattern of flowers, like those which have been found in

Egypt. The mirror, made of polished metal and provided with a handle, had been known from a very remote period; since the Egyptian period, no doubt, seeing that they are spoken of as early as the Book of Exodus.[28]

Naturally the women paid even more attention to their hair. Did not Saint Paul himself admit that a fine head of hair was 'a glory' to a woman? Though it is true that in his first Epistle to Timothy he advised Christian women not to exaggerate in this matter of dressing their hair.[29] The women of Israel were very clever at plaiting their hair, adorning it and even curling it. Among the well-dressed women, particularly those who were more or less paganized, fashion no doubt entered into consideration; and when, at Rome, this was in favour of hair piled up on the top of the head, there is little doubt that Herodias and Salome copied Claudia and Livia. Of all the prohibitions in the tractate *Shabbath* the most disagreeable to the women was certainly that which prevented them from plaiting, curling or putting ribbons and ornaments in their hair on the day of rest. In Jezebel's time it was usual for women to repair the insults of the years by dying their hair with Antioch-red or Alexandrian henna. And if the information in the Talmud is valid for Palestine, they also wore false hair made 'either with their own, or with a neighbour's or with that of some domestic animal'.

Furthermore, they made up and they scented themselves. Among the objects found in archaeological excavations there are a great many little pots and spoons for rouge, made of bone, ivory or metal, as well as spatulas for spreading it on. This was a very ancient practice: even before Abraham reached Palestine, the women of Crete and Egypt were quite as well acquainted with make-up for their eyes, faces and lips as the Parisiennes of today. This was an example that would have been followed very quickly and did not Job name his third daughter by the singularly picturesque name of Pot of Antimony?[30] For antimony, or *pouch*, was used to darken eyelashes and eyebrows: the Romans called it *stibium*, and it is known to the Arab women of today as *kohl*. For their cheeks and their lips they used *sikra*, which has already been mentioned as the colouring-matter of red ink. The leaves of a kind of privet, called *al khanna* (it is often mentioned in the Song of Songs, that catechism of love[31]), when reduced to ashes provide a reddish-yellow dye, which is used by Arab women for colouring their nails and the palms of their hands, and even, in the absence of other dyes, their hair. Did the Jewesses of Christ's time use it? Some, but not all. We may picture Mary Magdalene with blackened eyebrows, blue eyelashes, made-up face and dyed palms, at the time before our Lord took her away from sin.

As for scent, it was used a very great deal, by men as well as by women. Like all the people of the East, the Jews used it both because they liked it and because it diminished the unpleasant effects of sweating, that inconvenience of hot climates. It is proof enough to open the Old Testament: one might say of the Book what Ben Sirach said of wisdom:[32] 'Cinnamon and odorous balm have no scent like mine; the choicest myrrh has no such fragrance. Perfumed is all my dwelling-place with storax, and galbanum, and onycha, and stacte and frankincense uncrushed; the smell of me is like pure balm.'[33] The Queen of Sheba's camels brought loads of scent to Solomon; Hezekiah possessed whole cellars full; before Esther was presented to the king she was perfumed for a whole year; and the Beloved of the Song of Songs literally dripped with strongly-scented oil. The women of Israel, then, found authority and encouragement in Holy Writ for their love of scent. Those of Jerusalem had the right to spend the tenth part of their dowry upon it: some even wore very small leather vaporizers in their sandals, and they had but to move their toes to be surrounded by the most heady of all means of seduction. Some scents were particularly esteemed. First came nard, that nard with which Mary Magdalene anointed Christ's feet, and whose odour was so penetrating that it filled the house at once: it came from India, and it was exceedingly expensive; an imitation of it was therefore made from a local plant. Cassia, after which another of Job's daughters was named, was a brisk scent, a little like camphor; it was the opposite of myrrh, that very costly product imported from Arabia, and of balm, which was to be had at Jericho; for both these were heavy scents. Delightfully smelling flowers, the lily, the jasmin, the rose, were also used, macerated in oil. As for the onyx, or onycha, which is still known as 'scented nail', it was not a mineral, but the horny operculum of the shellfish of the same name. All these things were bought from specialized craftsmen and shopkeepers, men and women perfumers; they are often mentioned in the Bible, but always with a certain degree of reprobation, since obviously their best clients were loose women; but these were by no means their only customers. It was allowed that a perfectly respectable woman might be heavily scented; but those who did not resort to these charms were quite as much admired. One of the songs sung in bringing the bride to the place of the wedding said in her praise, 'Neither rouge nor powder, neither unguent nor scented oil, she has nothing artificial about her: she is as clean as a doe'.

All these points of personal hygiene and adornment give a very much more 'civilized' impression than one might have expected. And today in the East, even in the tents of the nomads, one finds refinements that the Western peasant of the Middle Ages would never have dreamed of. Yet there is one aspect that leaves one uneasy: neither the Bible nor the Talmud contains the slightest mention of the handkerchief, that modest square of linen that we think so entirely necessary. This does not mean that the Jews were unacquainted with colds in the head, but rather that they, like the Romans, coped with its outward manifestations more simply, more naturally than the Chinese, who, for their part, had known the paper handkerchief for centuries.

SOCIAL RELATIONSHIPS

The very care with which people washed and brushed and scented themselves shows how much importance they attached to social relationships; for one rarely puts on scent for one's own delight alone. The Israelites were, in fact, a very sociable nation. There were many reasons for this. The first was the climate: as in all sunny countries, the people of Palestine lived very much out of doors; although the house was greatly appreciated, it had nothing of the nature of the closed, jealously guarded home that it has in the colder parts. There were religious and social reasons, too; for the assembled people, the community, the 'synagogue', had a fundamental place in the Jews' relationship with God.

One of the marked characteristics of the Jews in the Bible is their hospitality: but this Israel had in common with all the nations of antiquity. To treat a guest well was a duty of honour to allow him to be insulted in one's house was a serious fault; to kill him was the most infamous of crimes. They were ready with their invitations to a meal: Abraham, for example, kept his unknown visitors at Mamre to eat a fine roast calf – those unknown figures who were in fact the angels of the Lord.[34] In the Gospel we often see Christ inviting Himself to the house of this person or that, without any ceremony; to the house of His friends at Bethany, as much as to a Pharisee's home or that of the good publican Zacchaeus; and it was quite natural for His disciples at Emmaus to say to their unknown travelling companion, 'Stay with us, it is towards evening, and it is far on in the day'. Besides, many places He Himself advises the generous giving of hospitality, that most urbane form of charity;[35] and He also states exactly how His disciples are to behave when they receive it.[36] Saint Paul makes the same recommendations in his Epistle to the Romans;[37] and the realistic Saint Peter adds that when one receives guests one should not grudge them what they have;[38] and the Epistle to the Hebrews reminds them that 'men have before now entertained angels unawares'.[39]

One's chief guests, of course, were one's friends. Friendship, indeed, played an important part in the life of Israel, more important than the trade-union solidarity in the life of the working-men of today. It even had its religious aspect, sealed by an oath like that which united David and Jonathan in the Bible.[40] To be sure, true friends have always been rare, friends like the one the Proverb refers to in observing, 'He is thy friend, who is thy friend at all times';[41] but how beautiful friendship can be! Ben Sirach has an admirable passage upon the subject, ending '. . . the fear of God gives friendship evenly shared, friend matched with friend'.[42] Christ uses the word 'friend' so often that it is impossible to give all the references; and what kindness He shows towards those of whom He uses the expression! It would seem that three among them, Peter, James and John, those He took with Him to behold His transfiguration, were particularly close friends, more directly associated with His mission than the other apostles. In Israel there were occasions upon which friendship assumed an official character: at the marriage ceremony there was, as we have seen,[43] the 'friend of the bridegroom', who played the part of the indispensable factotum.

Friends kissed one another, as did parents and children, brothers and sisters, cousins, and, naturally enough, husbands and wives who were on good terms. Kissing is very often spoken of in the Bible, and one could easily use it to draw up a list of all the kinds of kisses: love-kisses, kisses of affection and those kisses which were called for by civility. One was required, for example, to kiss any guest coming into one's house; a superior would show his benevolence by kissing his inferior; the inferior, on the other hand, would kiss the superior's hand or his knees, or even, if he wished to show limitless respect, his feet. A rabbi's disciples would greet him by kissing his hand: the only too-well-known kiss of Judas was no doubt a gesture of this kind rather than the kiss on the cheek that so many painters have represented. Those who belonged to the same religious group would exchange the 'kiss of peace'; this was the practice of the Essenes, and among the early Christians it was the mark of brotherly love.[44]

When kissing would have been out of place, as for example in meeting in the street, set greetings were used, after the style of our 'How are you?' or '*Bonjour*'. From the New Testament we see that two of these were very generally employed: 'Peace be with you' and 'Greetings'.[45] From the Talmud it appears that the first was the formula of the traditional true believers. *Shalom alekh hem* is still one Jew's greeting to another. But a practising Jew would have taken particular care not to address such a wish to a Samaritan or a pagan: if it were possible he would rather mutter a curse. To a friend, a fellow-countryman, on the other hand, he would readily add a blessing to his greeting, like that which a woman once called out to Jesus: 'Blessed is the womb that bore thee, the breast which thou hast sucked.'[46] This was the exact opposite of an insult that was also very widely used: 'Cursed be your mother.' And there were others designed to throw doubts upon the legitimacy of the recipient's birth. But whatever the greeting, it was never that of our days, the raising of the hat: a man would never take it off at all, even before a superior, even before a great potentate to whom he would use the expression 'your slave' in speaking of himself; he would not take it off even before God, in the Temple or the synagogue.

As we have said, life was lived much in the open, in the streets and public places; the life of the men, that is, for it was not customary for women to loiter, except at the fountains, where they would form large, noisy bands. As we have seen in the case of Jerusalem,[47] the streets were regularly swept, at least in the towns. Friends walked about together not, as they do in Italy today, with linked arms, but hand in hand. It would have been most improper to have walked like this with a woman however. There were no cafés in which the men might gossip, they sat cross-legged before a threshold, on the steps of a flight of stairs or in a shady corner. But they had to pay attention to the nature of the shade, for as the Talmud says, evil spirits were particularly fond of the shade of the caper-plant, the service bush and the fig-tree, which must have been very inconvenient

ince the garden of every house had its fig. Lying in the shade
f a boat hauled up in a harbour was even more foolhardy, for
ne ran the risk of seeing the devil in person.[48]

In the streets one often met beings who, though less alarming,
vere still sometimes a nuisance: the beggars. Their presence was
ypical of the Jewish life of the time, and there were a great many
f them. The New Testament speaks of several, from Lazarus,
vho lay covered with sores, wishing that he might be fed with
he crumbs that fell from the rich man's table, and the blind
3artimaeus whom Saint Mark shows sitting by the wayside
ust outside Jericho, to the lame man found by Peter and John
t the Beautiful Gate of the Temple.[49] Some were feckless and
tupid, no doubt, idle and shiftless, but there were also the crippled
nd the sick, for there were neither hospitals nor alms-houses to
ake them in; there were lepers, too, and there seem to have been
nany of them: altogether they made up a little world of half-
tarved ragged people, which was one of the very ugly sides of
ewish life. It was in the guise of one of these miserable men that
Christ referred to Himself when He spoke of the last judgment:
I was hungry, and you gave me food, thirsty, and you gave me
lrink; I was a stranger, and you brought me home, naked, and
ou clothed me, sick, and you cared for me.'[50]

For, though poverty was very great, alms were regularly given,
nd in abundance: religion insisted upon this. There are the
trong words of Job: 'Did I spurn the naked that were ready
o perish with cold, too poor to find clothing; did I never earn
hanks, from the back that went bare till fleece of my flock
varmed it? . . . Then let shoulder of mine hang from shoulder-
lade, every bone in my arm broken!'[51] One of the most usual
ctions in the life of a Jew was to give money or a piece of bread
o the unfortunate who begged for it in the street. Jerusalem,
articularly, at the time of the great pilgrimages, was thronged
y all the beggars in the Holy Land: they knew very well that
hose who came to pray for God's pardon would be in a charitable
rame of mind. At other times the beggars wandered along the
oads, going to the markets and the fords of the river, and profiting
oo by the permission the Law gave them to eat ears of corn in
he fields and grapes in the vineyards, providing they carried
either basket nor sickle,[52] and to pick up windfalls and gather
verlooked bunches.[53] The daily life of Israel was punctuated
y the sound of their entreaties.

DEVILS AND THE STARS

Of all those who wandered about the public places and the roads the most disturbing were not the lepers (for they, in any case could be recognised from afar by the cry of 'Unclean, unclean! that they were obliged to utter if anyone came near them) but the possessed, those who were the prey of devils. Only a carefully conducted exorcism, appropriate to the evil spirit that had taken possession of them, could cure them. There were, therefore professional exorcists among the rabbis. Our Lord obviously refers to them in His reply to those who accused Him of casting out devils 'by the power of Beelzebub'.[54] They went from town to town travelling the roads of the Holy Land in the practice o their calling.

That there were in fact cases of possession is quite certain theologically certain. The Bible gives many proofs of this, and the Gospel confirms it by speaking of seven examples of possession cured by our Lord[55] and by showing Him handing on to His disciples the power of casting out devils.[56] But this does no mean that in addition to the genuinely possessed there was no a host of madmen, of unbalanced, neurotic and hysterical peopl whose behaviour had nothing to do with Satan or his works The very notion of mental illness was foreign to the Jewish way of thinking, as it was to that of all the people of the ancient world evil spirits seemed the best explanation.

The belief in evil spirits, furthermore, was so deeply rooted among the educated and the common people that it was th subject of a great many precepts in the Talmud:[57] thus it wa permissible to light a lamp on the Sabbath in order to put a devil to flight, or, in running away from one, to cover more than the regulation distance. There were also sins that were considered to be so obviously the work of the Evil One that the sinner wa not held to be answerable for them.

What was the origin of these devils? Some were fallen angels obviously; but it was also thought that some might have com from the children that Adam may have had before he was hundred and thirty, the age at which he begot a son 'in his own image', as we learn from the fifth chapter of Genesis. The were ordinarily invisible, but if one put sifted ashes on th threshold of the house, their footprints might be seen in th morning, prints like those that a cock would leave. They wer to be found everywhere, but particularly in ruined houses marshes, the shade of certain trees, as we have seen, and in lavatories: one rabbi, in order to protect himself against them, always took a lamb with him, every time he went to the lavatory. They attacked animals as well as human beings; but among the humans those whom they most frequently attacked were chronic invalids, engaged girls and the best man, or groomsman, at a wedding: which, from a psychological point of view, is eminently sound. It was exceedingly unwise for a man to sleep all alone in a house: he would be the victim of Lilith, the she-devil, and anything at all might happen to him.

Fortunately God had appointed guardian angels for those who observed all the requirements of religion, and these beings were so powerful that when they fought against the devils 'a thousand of them would fall on one side and a thousand on the other'. Yet it was necessary to help these supernatural defenders. By prayer, in the first place: 'The person who recites the *Shema Israel* in getting into bed has as it were a double-edged sword against the demons of the night!' It was also prudent to put on *tefillin* (those little cases that are worn on the arm and forehead during prayer) as soon as an evil spirit was felt to be moving about: in the leather case of the phylactery there was a verse of the Bible that was sovereign against the devil – it is the fifth verse of Psalm 90, the same psalm that Catholics still recite at complines: 'Nothing shalt thou have to fear from nightly terrors, [nor] from the arrow that flies by daylight.'

But alas, many Israelites, even the very pious, were not content with these legitimate weapons against the onslaughts of the devil. In a more or less hidden manner they also wore amulets. This must really have been a very thoroughly established custom for the tractate *Shabbath* to think it necessary to lay down that it was licit to go out on the Sabbath with a locust's egg, a fox's tooth or a gallows-nail. In the diggings a great many little objects have been found that were certainly charms of this kind: pierced shells, animals' teeth, lunar crescents, disks with a star on them. It may even be that in breach of the law against the representation of all animal figures, some people wore those little metal serpents, gold flies and lapis-lazuli hippopotamuses that were usual among the pagans of Phoenicia and Egypt. Had not some of these heathen objects been found upon the bodies of Jewish soldiers during the wars of the Maccabees?[58] It is exceedingly likely that the descendants of these heroes retained the same custom:

and may it not be that the women's pendants and ear-rings were
also a remnant of the same practice?

In reading the Talmud, one gains the impression that supersti
tion played an important part in the Jewish life of every day
There is nothing surprising about this; for the nation was so
soaked in religion, so enclosed in a system of rigid observance
any breach of which brought serious punishment, that necessarily
among the simple people belief turned towards the setting up
of taboos and to something like fetish-worship. For reasons a
obscure as those which today make the figure thirteen so dis
agreeable, even numbers were held to be unlucky, whether it
was a question of the date of setting out on a voyage or the numbe
of glasses of wine to be drunk. If two people eating togethe
threw little balls of bread at one another they were sure to fal
ill. To put one's hand in the dish at the same time as anothe
guest also brought ill-luck. It was essential to equip one's hors
or ass with a red rag or a fox's tail, hung between the eyes
otherwise one might have a fall – the Greeks of today provid
their mounts with blue beads. But what was far worse was th
fact that there were some people who had the evil eye, and whos
mere presence brought ill-fortune: one rabbi even asserted tha
out of a hundred deaths, ninety-nine were attributable to thi
cause. There were formulas to deal with this peril, however.

This climate of superstition, so unlike the transparent, pur
atmosphere of the Gospel, naturally bred the magical arts. Ye
the Bible most vehemently forbade the practice of magic: th
eighteenth chapter of Deuteronomy carefully drew up the list o
these forbidden pursuits: 'There must be no wizard, or enchante
none who consults familiar spirits and divinations, and would
receive warnings from the dead.' One rabbi added snake
charmers and ventriloquists to the catalogue. Were thes
prohibitions strictly observed? The question certainly arises whe
one sees how insistently the Talmud promises that 'those wh
never indulge in soothsaying will have a place in heaven into which
even the officiating angels will not be allowed'. It was particularl
apocryphal *Book of Jubilees*, which was written in about 150 BC
said that it had been taught by the wicked angels; and in th
Sibylline Books it was called 'that baleful science, which has bree
every kind of misfortune'. But in that case, why did the holy tex
show that it had been practised in ancient times?[59] And why di

some rabbis tell stories that proved that astrology told the truth? The tale, for example, of King Nimrod, to whom the stars revealed that a child was about to be born whose descendants would supplant the Chaldees, so that Abraham's parents were obliged to hide him. Or again that story which explained the well-known attitude of Potiphar's wife towards the young Joseph: it appears that the stars had told her that he would give her a descendant, but without specifying whether this child would be born by her or (which, according to the rabbis, turned out to be the case) by her daughter Aseneth.[60] The Jews may not have thought divination and astrology so important as did the Romans of the same era,[61] but there is no sort of doubt that they took both into account in their everyday life and in the choice of their children's names. The disagreement among the rabbis on the matter is revealing: one stated, 'Wisdom and wealth is determined by the planet under which one is born'; another asserted, 'The stars have no influence whatever upon the fate of the Israelites'. But later, when Jerusalem lay in ruins, the compiler of the tractate *Sota* sadly wrote the words, 'It was superstition and immorality that destroyed everything'.

LEISURE AND AMUSEMENTS

It may almost be said that the Bible never mentions amusements or games: the only allusions that there are refer to the play of children. Christ, for example, repeats the chorus of that children's round-dance that has already been spoken of.[62] We have also seen[63] that the little Jewish girls, exempt in this from the law that forbade the representation of any living creature, no doubt had the dolls and pottery animals that we discussed earlier[64] and of which examples have been found in the excavations. Did the contemporaries of Christ have no free time? One thing is certain, and that is that amusements did not occupy the same place in their lives that they did in the lives of the Romans; for in Rome, as everyone knows, they were a means of government and a question of high policy. The notorious *panem et circenses*, which was to become more and more the empire's political watchword, had no equivalent among the Chosen People.

It goes without saying that many of our amusements would have been perfectly inconceivable in Israel. It would never have entered into any Jewish head to set out upon a journey merely for the pleasure of travelling. The indefatigable anglers who line all the rivers of France every Sunday, tormenting the gudgeon, would have seemed utterly ridiculous then: fishing was a trade, and a hard one; not an amusement. Did they hunt, at least? There is very little mention of this noble sport in the Bible either, and the allusions that there are in the New Testament to traps and pitfalls[65] obviously refer to a kind of hunting more in the nature of work than pleasure. It was hunting in order to kill wild beasts and to eat game, not in order to amuse oneself. Yet the Roman custom of hunting for the sake of hunting seems to have made some headway among the wealthy: Josephus assures us that Herod was, like Nimrod, a mighty hunter before the Lord. They hunted with bow, sling and sword; that is to say, with the same weapons that were used in war. Unlike the Mesopotamians, the Jews do not seem to have used hounds. The ever-watchful Law, of course, took cognizance of hunting just as it did of every other human activity: it required the immediate bleeding of all animals killed, just as if they were calves or sheep, and the covering of the blood with earth, 'because it animates all living things'.[66] But in its way the Law was kind, and it forbade the taking of the bird upon her nest, if she had eggs or chicks: she was to be made to fly, and then without guilt one might take the little birds.[67]

'Parlour games' were known, and strangely enough they were quite like ours. The archaeologists have found counters, teetotums and dice, the last exactly the same as those we now use. One, indeed, has been found that is so irregular that it might be called cogged or loaded. The rules of their games are lost, although we can tell how the Hittites played. There were some, like our game of goose, that seem to have been very ancient in Israel: in this they threw dice in order to move cone-shaped pieces on from one square to another. Little ivory tablets have also been found with holes in them rather like our game of solitaire. These were all near neighbours to those games which the Romans called *latruncula* and the Greeks *plinthrion*. In Palestine and Jordan today they still play at *mancala*, with a rack or stand with two rows of seven holes in it, into which counters are slid; and the game appears to date from long before the Mohammedan invasion.[68]

There were also some games like these played in the open air. Plutarch says that when they were not on duty soldiers played at dice or a game rather like our draughts. Those who drew lots for the cloak without a seam at the Crucifixion must have carried dice in their belts. On the paving-stones of the *lithostrotos*, the flagged court of the Antonia fortress, where Pilate set up his praetorium, one can clearly see the lines for a game like hopscotch, and that 'circle game' of which Plautus speaks. This was played with four knuckle-bones, marked with letters that were also numbers. Some moves had names, as they have in our game of chess: there was 'Alexander's move', the 'ephebe', the 'Darius', and best of all the 'move of the king', *basileus*, in Greek. Now on the flag-stones one sees the rough line of the circle perfectly well, and it runs through various figures; in several places there is the B for *basileus* and lastly there is a royal crown. May not this be at the origin of the soldiers' barbarous mockery of our Lord, and of the crown of thorns? The king's move for the King of the Jews. The sight of it wounds one's heart.[69]

There were some other open-air games which came nearer to sport. Judging from the Bible it seems that the Hebrews had always loved wrestling and those contests to which the Philistines challenged Saul's followers. They also shot at the mark[70] with bows and slings,[71] some aiming 'to within a hair's breadth'. And when Isaiah tells one Shebna, in charge of the Temple (or perhaps the palace), that he is to wait until the Lord 'tosses thee like a ball into the great open plain',[72] he seems to be referring to a game which must have been the ancestor of our football.

There is every reason to suppose that the Jews of the time of Christ played these traditional games like their ancestors; did the influence of the Greeks and the Romans add others, the games of the circus, the stadium, the hippodrome and the amphitheatre? Joshua, known as Jason ('the vile Jason', says the Second Book of Maccabees) by way of 'perverting his fellow countrymen to the Gentile way of living', introduced the pagan games into the Holy Land, although he was high priest.[73] Herod the Great, who went to watch the Olympic games, encouraged the development of Greek wrestling and above all, chariot racing: not far from his palace, he had built a hippodrome that was considered one of the most splendid of the time and also, perhaps at Jericho, an amphitheatre. There were other hippodromes and amphitheatres in certain other Palestinian cities, such as Caesarea, Tarichaea and Samaria-Sebaste. But they were heathen amusements that went on there, and the rabbis spoke out against them: the true believers did not go. It is significant that the Gospel makes no allusion whatever to any of these games. When Saint Paul spoke of the races in the stadium he was speaking to the Christians of Corinth, converted Greeks or Jews living in a pagan city.[74] It is certain that Israel turned with disgust from the vile and revolting spectacles that delighted the Roman crowds: gladiators fighting until one was killed; condemned men killed in public by wild beasts. And in this the honour and the worth of the nation appeared.

WHOREDOM

But were the Israelites not acquainted with other amusements, less avowable than hopscotch, knuckle-bones and wrestling? It must be admitted that they were: the texts leave no room for doubt. In very early times, one of the Chosen People's gravest temptations was that of growing too interested in the pagan temples of Canaan or Phoenicia, where the sacred prostitutes of either sex were to be seen. And in spite of the direct prohibition in Deuteronomy,[75] it would even appear that true Israelites, boys and young women, became what the text bluntly terms 'dogs'. There were certain high places, such as Mount Eryx in Sicily, one of the centres of religious prostitution for hundreds of years, which were known to attract packs of these dogs, as well as their followers: they were also notorious for idolatry. For a long while the trade was in the hands of the Phoenicians and the Carthaginians, before the Romans took it over. Religious prostitution vanished from Israel after the campaigns of Amos and Hosea and the measures of King Josiah, and those who wished to indulge in it had to go down to the coast, to the Syrian and Phoenician ports.

Not that prostitution did not exist in Israel at the time of Christ: the New Testament proves that it did. It is probably incorrect to attribute a very harsh meaning to the expression 'sinful woman', which the Talmud uses so widely as to include a wife who gives her husband a dish that has not been properly tithed; but still there is little doubt that this was the profession of Mary of Magdala, the most moving transgressor in history, before our Lord drew her from it. The woman who anointed the feet of Christ during His meal at the house of Simon the Pharisee, whether she was the Magdalene or not (a point that is still discussed), is formally described as 'a sinner'. In the parable of the Prodigal Son, Jesus directly states that the foolish young man had wasted his substance among whores. And the 'successive husbands' of the Samaritan women whom He met at Jacob's well, might very well have been called, in plainer language, her customers.[76] Christ speaks of harlots in several places;[77] and as we know, He refers to them with more pity than harshness, undoubtedly seeing in them victims rather than criminals – indeed, he even told the Pharisees that some whores would more easily find admittance to heaven than they. We do not know whether the brothels which are often mentioned in the Old Testament[78] still existed, but it is more than likely, seeing that the *lupanar* was one of the great and flourishing institutions of the Roman empire, and that many roadside inns had a staff of 'little she-asses' – inns like that in the *via dell' Abbondanza* in Pompeii, for example, whose alluring sign offers the services of its inmates to the passer-by. It does not appear that conversion to Christianity was enough to do away with the sad spectacle of the social pest and these evil ways: Saint Paul speaks of it with blunt severity.[79] Although the Gospel does not refer to masculine prostitution, it was certainly not unknown at the time, as we may see from Saint Paul's Epistle to the Romans (I, 27) and from the apocryphal Jewish Sibylline Books, which violently denounces 'those who have unclean relationships with young men'.[80]

It goes without saying that the whole of Israel's religious teaching was against these lewd practices. The disgust at prostitution that was felt by those who wrote down the Bible is strikingly evident from the way they use this word to mean the abomination of abominations, idolatry itself. 'To prostitute oneself', in the language of the prophets, did not necessarily mean to sell one's body; it meant even more the giving up of one's soul to false gods. Babylon, the 'great whore' of the Revelation (that is to say, Rome), was both a centre of debauchery and the symbolic capital of paganism. The Law condemned all prostitution, and it forbade fathers to prostitute their daughters;[81] yet it did not lay down any punishment, except in the case of a priest's daughter, who was to be burnt.[82] Furthermore, it was forbidden that a priest should marry a whore.[83] But more important than these enactments, there were the warnings of the prophets and the great holy men to keep the Jews from following the evil road. The finest of all these is chapter nine of Ecclesiasticus, in which Ben Sirach describes the harlot's ways with such remarkable skill and realism, as well as the degradation of the man who gives in to her and his consequent misfortunes. And yet one cannot be absolutely certain that all Jewish men were entirely convinced that 'dead men were the whore's company, no guest of hers but was guest of the dark world beneath'.[84]

CHAPTER TWELVE

WHEN THE BIRD-SONG DIES AWAY

Man's condition: suffering and death – Hygiene and health – Diseases – Medicine and medical men – Death and the grave – 'Where, then, death, is thy victory?'

MAN'S CONDITION: SUFFERING AND DEATH

In Israel there was no believer who did not know that the wages of sin was death. The constantly re-read Book of Genesis continually reminded everyone of God's terrible words to the first man: 'Dust thou art, and unto dust thou shalt return.'[1] It was not only the man who went a-whoring who 'sank towards the grave', as Isaiah and the Psalmist[2] said, but also the righteous, the man whom God loved. Man's inescapable fate was to suffer and to die; and tirelessly the Bible repeated this lesson.

In reading the Old Testament, one cannot but be struck by the important place occupied by sickness, suffering and death. A pious Jew, thoroughly accustomed to the Book, had these reminders continually before his eyes. Ben Sirach, a profoundly religious man beneath his sarcastic exterior, most earnestly told the believer of the necessity and the value of remembering death. There was also that intensely moving description of the years that were to come for each man when he should say, 'I have no pleasure in them'; the time when the strong men would grow bowed, the women no longer grind either corn or olives, and when indeed, as the poet said, the song of the birds should die away.

Yet this should not lead one to believe that biblical wisdom ended in complete despair, in *taedium vitae* and fatalism. Not at all: in many places the Bible reiterated that it was man's duty to struggle against death, to overcome sickness if he could, and to take all precautions against it. These precepts were taken up by the rabbis and commented upon with such minute care that several of the tractates of the Talmud form handbooks of hygiene, pharmacopoeias and medical encyclopaedias. Because of the

318

principle that body and soul are necessarily and entirely bound to one another, so that 'a sick body could not be the right or suitable instrument for the functioning of a pure soul',[3] treating and healing were obligations – religious obligations. It was Israel, then, which gave the pagans' *mens sana in corpore sano* its true spiritual depth.

Furthermore, one of the most significant and moving sides of Christ's personality, one which even the most rationalist critics admit, is His thaumaturgic aspect. He heals the sick, gives the paralysed back their strength and the blind their sight; and by His miracles and His example He gives mankind the hope of defeating death.

HYGIENE AND HEALTH

Generally speaking, the Israelites were a healthy and vigorous nation: Tacitus himself, who was by no means prejudiced in their favour, admits this: 'The fortunate result of a healthy climate, a frugal diet and a simple life.' It was the result, too, of hygienic measures which, although they were more primitive than ours and less careful of asepsis and prevention, were none the less of real importance. As we have seen,[4] cleanliness was general. Baths and washing, which were made necessary by the heat and dust and at the same time insisted upon by the Law, were measures whose efficacy should not be underestimated. It is said that one summer's day the great rabbi Hillel, having finished a lesson, said to his disciples, 'Now I am going to perform a religious duty'. 'What religious duty?' they asked. 'That of taking a bath,' he replied. And as the young men seemed astonished, he went on, 'Ought I not to take care of my body? Was it not created in the likeness of God?'[5] Another learned man taught that the want of cleanliness brought about every kind of disease, from stomach-ache to ulcers, from insanity to blindness.

There is no possible doubt that many of the biblical obligations were based upon hygiene. There are those, for example, in chapters eleven and twelve of Leviticus, which concern clean and unclean animals. Nothing could be wiser than prohibiting the consumption of cattle that have died from some illness instead of having been slaughtered, and even the prohibition of unbled meat, for the presence of blood in the flesh hastens its corruption. The same prudent intentions barred the flesh of vultures, kites, crows and other carrion-eaters, as well as that of snakes and frogs. It is also reasonable that when a man has handled spoilt meat he should wash his hands; and the law-giver, by ruling that any person who has touched a dead body is unclean, obliges him to do so. There are many other requirements that seem even stranger to us but which are certainly to be explained by the nature of the Israelites' life at the time. They were all certainly obeyed by the Jews at the time of Christ: Saint Peter asserts that he never ate anything but kosher meat;[6] and there is no doubt that the same would have applied to our Lord.

The Law also laid down rules for the health of the community which were by no means without wisdom and foresight: when numbers of people were gathered together, for example, the prescription of Deuteronomy[7] came into force – prescriptions concerning the cleanliness of the camp and the burying of excrement. The rabbis, carrying these prescriptions further, ruled that a cemetery must be at least fifty cubits outside the walls of a town; and the same distance was required for the place where the bodies of animals were left, and for tanneries.[8] Furthermore, they stated that the direction of the predominant wind was to be taken into account, so that evil odours should not be brought into the town. Prophylaxis has a great part in those long chapters of Leviticus which deal with leprosy.[9] All clothing which had any suspicious marks upon it was to be examined by an expert, carefully washed, and then, if the stains did not vanish, burnt. The rules about the 'leprosy of houses' are the first measures of slum-clearance known to history, and in them the Bible gives a striking description of those foul dwellings that bred disease, with their 'dents in the surface of the walls that are pale or reddish in colour', that is to say, mouldy cavities, with their fallen plaster and stones loose in the mortar: the owner was to leave his house, have its walls scraped and replastered, and naturally offer an expiatory sacrifice of two birds, one being killed so that its blood might be used to sprinkle the cleansed house and the other (a beautiful symbol) allowed to fly away.

For it need hardly be said that all measures concerning health, even the humblest and the most earthy, came under the governance of religion, which concerned itself with matters that now seem to us utterly foreign to it. We have already seen[10] that the rabbis did not think it beneath them to pay attention to the most intimate aspects of personal hygiene; and the famous tractate *Berakoth*, or Blessings, assures us that 'costiveness brings about dropsy, and the retention of urine jaundice',[11] and has a form of thanksgiving for the accomplishment of the natural functions of the body, for 'it is the Lord who has created man and all his orifices and vessels'. And if anyone should be tempted to laugh at this unexpected piety, let him remember that in a truly consecrated life there is nothing that is not related to God.

The most important of the Law's rules of health was of course that which insisted upon moderation in everything. The Bible frequently repeats it; and the Proverbs, for example, state in many places that excess of any kind is as bad for the soul as it is for the body; and the same book contains the liveliest description of a drunkard.[12] The teaching of the rabbis was most eloquent upon this subject, as one may see from the words of the wise man upon 'the eight things in which too much is an evil'.[13] The discipline that all these strict rules imposed upon the Jewish people must have done a great deal towards keeping them healthy and in a good physical condition.

DISEASES

Yet obviously this did not prevent the existence of diseases. The climate is in general healthy enough, but its sudden changes of temperature can be very dangerous. On a day when the burning khamsin blows the thermometer may rise to more than a hundred degrees in the shade, and during the night it may fall to the freezing-point: the change can bring about inflammation of the lungs, pneumonia or a plain cold. Saint Cyprian tells us that the number of sudden deaths was so great during the season of the east winds that it was necessary to give the priests special powers of absolving apostates.[14] The very hot weather, on the other hand, produced what was often a serious kind of dysentery, which was made all the more general by the great consumption of fruit: a dysentery-bacillus which seems to be peculiar to the country has recently been identified in Jerusalem. There was malaria in the marshy regions by the Jordan; and in those days there was no way of dealing with the mosquitoes. The hot summers, with their brilliant light and their all-pervading dust, caused a great deal of eye-disease; and this is still the case, for at present the ophthalmic hospital of Saint John of Jerusalem treats twenty thousand patients a day.

It is not surprising, then, that the Bible should very often speak of sickness. The Old Testament mentions some fifty diseases, from itch to apoplexy, consumption to gout, exanthema to peritonitis. The New Testament also refers to a great many: paralysis, dropsy, piles, blindness, deafness and of course leprosy and mental disease, as well as several others. Sometimes the malady is described with an almost medical precision: Saint Peter's mother-in-law suffers from 'a violent fever',[15] which brings to mind a sharp attack of malaria; the fever of the son of the nobleman of Capernaum is said to be mortal,[16] but also associated with paralysis; perhaps it was an acute form of rheumatism. In the same way the Acts state that the fever of which Saint Paul cured the father of Malta's leading citizen[17] was accompanied by dysentery. It is quite clear from the texts in which they are mentioned that the various paralytics were affected in different degrees: the man with a withered hand whom our Lord met one Sabbath[18] no doubt had but the one limb touched; the crippled man of the pool of Bethesda could still drag himself along;[19] but on the other hand the one who had to be lowered through the roof[20] and the son of the centurion[21] must have been much more seriously ill. All this gives the impression of a real understanding of disease: besides, Saint Luke was a physician.

One of the most dreaded of all diseases was leprosy. It is very frequently mentioned indeed in the Bible, and always with a strong feeling of horror. It was certainly very common. 'Today', says S. W. Baron, 'it is difficult to imagine how large a proportion of the population of the Ancient World was affected by leprosy.'[22] There is no doubt that some diseases came under this heading that were not leprosy at all; not only the purulent form of bone-tuberculosis which is still found in the East, and elephantiasis, that painful and contagious malady, but also dermatosis (which is shown by the fact that 'curable leprosies' were known, whereas the real disease was then incurable), the sequelae of serious burns, 'head-leprosy', which must have been some form of alopecia, and even ordinary baldness, which was thought suspicious as soon as red marks or wens appeared on the bare scalp. But of course the true leprosy was there as well; and there were two forms of it. The most usual was the 'white' leprosy which was also called 'mosaic' leprosy: it begins with white patches appearing on the skin, patches that are entirely devoid of feeling and for this reason it is now termed anaesthetic leprosy. The second kind was the nodular form. Both slowly ate away the tissues, attacking the limbs, as well as the face. In reading the

WHEN THE BIRD-SONG DIES AWAY

Gospel, one has a clear picture of roads of Palestine, particularly
those near the entrance of the towns, haunted by these human
wrecks who would hold out their dreadful fingerless hands to
awaken the pity of those who passed by, or the handless stumps
of their arms, but who would only succeed in terrifying them by
the horrible 'lion's mask' that the disease sets upon the sufferer's
face. Sometimes it happened that these wretched people would
go about together in troops.[23]

At present, humanity has some weapons against this true
leprosy, *zaraath*; there are medicines that check the disease and
that may even cure it. Two thousand years ago men were completely powerless. It was God alone who could heal and clean
the unfortunate sufferers, if He chose: when, in the days of
Elisha, Naaman, the leprous chief of the Syrian army, came to
ask the King of Israel to cure him, the astonished ruler cried,
'Am I God . . . that he should send a leper to me to be cured?'[24]
This was the universal opinion. The only measure was that
which our own Middle Ages were to take – the leper was cast
out and kept far away from healthy men. In chapters thirteen
and fourteen of Leviticus the Law gave scrupulous directions
concerning this, and we see in the Gospel that they were still
observed at the time of Christ: the leper was to go bare-headed,
wearing special clothes; he was to live far away from towns and
villages, and whenever he came near a healthy man he was to
call out in a loud voice '*Amê! Amê!*' – unclean, unclean. Christ's
kindness towards these poor souls, the way He received them
and often healed them, was in striking contrast to the harshness
of the Law. There is no doubt that His healing of lepers had a
great influence upon His standing. Leprosy was an uncleanliness,
because it seemed as much a spiritual as a physical disease, the
most glaring manifestation of human sin. The expression 'the
leprosy of sin', which our theologians still use, was already
current then. But there were also other diseases that made the
sufferer ritually unclean – the venereal diseases, for example.
They were all diseases that were considered, more or less, as
punishments. A vitiated body was thought to be the sign of a
vicious soul. Ben Sirach says flatly, 'Offend thou thy maker by
wrong-doing, much recourse thou shalt have to physicians'.[25]
Yahweh struck the guilty man with a disease either directly or
by means of His angels or, more frequently and more aptly,
through the wicked angels. Some things, such as corns upon

323

one's feet, were even taken as the mark of an obvious intervention by an evil spirit. It was allowed that the cause of an illness might not be sin on the part of the sufferer, but one committed by his family. This idea explains the question that Christ's disciples asked Him, when He saw a man who had been blind from his birth: 'Master, was this man guilty of sin, or was it his parents, that he should have been born blind?' To which our Lord replied, in His infinite wisdom, that neither he nor his parents were guilty.[26] The concept also explains why every truly medical form of activity was accompanied by a series of religious rites and purifications.

MEDICINE AND MEDICAL MEN

Man, then, was to take care to avoid everything that might cause illness; but if nevertheless he fell sick he was to have recourse to everything that the Creator had placed upon the earth to help him, to ease his sufferings and to combat death. Was it not wonderful that there should be plants, minerals and animal substances scattered about the world, which healed, if they were intelligently used? And men with the knowledge of these God-given remedies?

For there were physicians in Israel, and there had been for a very long while: several of the prophets refer to them. In some particularly strict circles it was held that as Yahweh was the true healer it was a want of faith to entrust oneself to a doctor;[27] but wiser minds agreed with the excellent words of Ecclesiasticus upon the subject: 'Deny not the physician his due for thy need's sake; his task is of divine appointment, since from God all healing comes . . . High rank his skill gives him; of great men he is the honoured guest . . . Thus it is that the physician cures our pain and the apothecary makes, not only perfumes to charm the sense but unguents remedial . . . Son, when thou fallest sick, do not neglect thy own needs; pray to the Lord, and thou shalt win recovery. Leave off thy sinning, thy life amend, purge thee of all thy guilt. With frankincense and rich oil make bloodless offering of meal; and so leave the physician to do his work. His task is of divine appointment, and thou hast need of him; let him be ever at thy side.'[28] Such a justification of the medical profession obviously needed no commentary. However, the rabbis did add 'The disciple of wise men should not live in a town that has no physicians'; and another saying went further: 'It is forbidden that any man should live in a town without physicians.'[29] This leads one to suppose that they must have existed all over the country. There were even official physicians, attached to the Temple for the treatment of the priests, who often caught dysentery because of their walking about barefoot upon the sacred flag-stones and their frequent cold ablutions. The common people called them by a name which may roughly be translated as 'gut-doctor'.

For then as now, people were very ready to make game of medical men, particularly when they were not unwell. The crisp statement in the tractate *Kiddushin*,[30] 'Even the best of physicians is destined for hell', was certainly written by a discontented patient: another rabbi sighed, 'Ah, may blessings fall upon the doctor who does not ask too great a fee', which seems to show that heavy payments were customary even then. The excessively busy doctor who makes people wait for ever was also known; so was his colleague who, being one of the important men of the town, takes no care of his patients; so was the man who asks no fee, but who is also perfectly incompetent. The Gospels frequently speak of physicians, and in them we find a particularly amusing little piece of medical psychology: it concerns the woman whom Christ cured of an issue of blood. Saint Mark tells of this in his fifth chapter, and he states that she had suffered from it for twelve years, 'and had undergone much from many physicians, spending all she had on them, and no better for it, but rather grown worse'. Yet Saint Luke, in reporting the same event in his eighth chapter, says no more than that 'she could not be cured by any'. Now, as we know, Saint Luke was himself a medical man.

No one will be surprised to learn that the medicine of the time was rudimentary and that in many respects it was nearer to primitive magic than science; yet it does appear that the Jewish physicians had from very early times possessed an empirical knowledge of some remedies and of the curative properties of plants. There are a great many instances of this in the Old Testament, and for their part, the Talmudic tractates overflow with medical prescriptions; some are very amusing, but some give the impression of real knowledge and experience. It was thought that an supposed Book of Solomon contained a catalogue of all the remedies in the world, and the Essenes were thought to know its secrets. Oil was one of the most frequently used medicines, being generally rubbed on with the idea of softening and calming: it was even permissible to use it on the Sabbath. It was often mixed with wine, and it was with this mixture that the good Samaritan of the Gospel treated the wounds of the man he found lying on the road to Jericho.[31] Another generally used ointment was honey, which was put on to open wounds; but it was also swallowed for sore throats, as it is today. A poultice of figs was held to be sovereign against anthrax: it was thus that Isaiah cured King Hezekiah. Purple aloes mixed with wine was also very good, however. Many plants were recommended for stomach-ache or pains in the belly: rosemary, hyssop, rue, polygonum, bignonia, and above all certain kinds of palm, from whose roots was extracted the 'water of Dekarim'. Barley soaked in curdled milk was the remedy for palpitations of the heart. 'Against tapeworms,' said one sage, 'drink maidenhair fern.' And another advised poultices of fish-brine for rheumatism, presumably as a counter-irritant. The mandrake, which is a strongly scented solanaceous plant closely related to the deadly nightshade, was considered to possess a great many virtues, as the Bible says;[32] possibly this was because of the very odd appearance of its forked, fleshy root, which has a certain resemblance to the human body, and which may have had a magic significance. This too may have applied to certain animal substances, such as that liver with which the young Tobit cured his father's cataract, and which he also used to put the fiend to flight upon his wedding-night.

The Jewish physicians also had many other forms of treatment some of which do not seem in the least ridiculous to us. They recommended bleeding 'every thirty days up to the age of forty' They practised cupping. They treated the various forms of ophthalmia with eye-salves, some of which were based upon antimony, to protect the eye from the excessive power of the sun. The benefits of thermal waters had long been recognized and baths were much used at the time of Christ: people went to El Hamma, on the shore of the Sea of Galilee, or to Calirrhoe near the Dead Sea; this was the place to which the dying Herod had himself carried. Surgery, of course, was fairly primitive because of the lack of sound knowledge of anatomy and physiology But small operations, such as cauterization, the lancing of abcesses the curetting or scraping of wounds and the reduction of fractures were usual; and even more was certainly undertaken, for the

Talmud speaks of a soporific draught given at the beginning of an abdominal operation. The Caesarian delivery, well known to the Romans, was also practised in Palestine. Some skulls found in the diggings show that the Jews were not ignorant of trepanning: but were these holes made in the course of surgical treatment or in order to expel evil spirits? The tractate *Shabbath* states that is was forbidden to go out with an artificial leg on the day of rest, which shows that they were ordinarily used. As for the dentists, they had not yet taken to their horrible but beneficent little drill, but they treated toothache with garlic or pellitory-root and pains in the gums with salt or yeast, and they drew teeth with great skill.

As one might suppose, a good many of these remedies came very near to superstition. The rabbi Cohen admits that they believed in sympathetic magic;[33] and some of the treatments remind one of the cures mentioned by Frazer in the *Golden Bough*, that vast enquiry into primitive manners. Did not the wearing of amulets have a more or less directly magical intention? Although the rabbis forbade 'treating oneself by means of quotations from the Scriptures',[34] how could a sick man be prevented from placing verse twenty-six of the fifteenth chapter of Exodus upon the seat of his pain, the verse that reads: '. . . never shall they fall on thee, the many woes brought on Egypt; I am the Lord, and it is health I bring thee'? There are countless allegedly magic remedies against all sorts of illnesses in the Talmud. Against the tertian ague one should take seven splinters from seven palms, seven shavings from seven beams, seven nails from seven bridges, seven ashes from seven ovens, without forgetting seven hairs from old dogs and hang the whole on one's bosom with a white thread: there is nothing better. If man should suffer from a corn on his foot he ought to put a piece of money under the sole of it: this will redeem the pain. How would the Jewish physicians have treated that woman whose bloody flux our Lord cured by a word? They would have made her sit at the forking of a road with a glass in her hand, and they would have given her a sudden violent fright, by suddenly bellowing just behind her, for example. Or still more decisive treatment would have been to make her eat a barleycorn found in the dung of a white mule. One could go on for ages with equally curious recipes; but we have little room to laugh, seeing that just the same kind of thing occurred in

327

our own medicine in the Middle Ages, and even as late as Molière.[35]

All medical treatment was accompanied by the prayers that are mentioned in Ecclesiasticus, and very often by religious rites as well. Every cure or healing was to be consecrated by a religious ceremony; and it is to this that Christ alludes when on several occasions He bids the lepers He has healed 'show themselves to the priests'. In the case of leprosy, the recovered patient was to offer three sacrifices, the third being a burnt-offering: for the poor they were birds, for the rich, lambs. The ritual was carefully laid down. A priest caught the blood of the sacrificed animal in the palm of his hand and went to the former sufferer in the 'lepers' room', in the corner of the court of the women in the western courtyard of the Temple; he caused him to put his head out of the room into the court, and touched him with the blood on the ear, the thumb and the foot. It was only when this ceremony was over that the man was officially recognized as healed and allowed back into the community. In other cases the touching was not done with the blood of an animal, but with the saliva of the officiating healer; but this too was to be accompanied by prayers.

For in the last resort who accomplished the healing? Was it the physicians? No. There were cases, said Ben Sirach, where the cure was in their hands; but this was by no means so in all cases. The only true healer was the Almighty. And Ecclesiasticus also said that healing came from the Lord, 'like a gift that one receives from a king'. It would have been madness to deny such evidence. He who had made man from the dust would also cause him to return to it in his due time. Life and death were between His hands.

DEATH AND THE GRAVE

A man's last hour has come: the hour that God had fixed from all eternity. 'His breath fades away', as the popular expression has it He is about to go down into Sheol: but not before the community has paid him their last duties.

The Jews had a deep respect for death, like all the nations of the ancient world; but perhaps theirs was still more profound since for them man's body was so very directly the work of God and made in His great image. The Bible laid it down rigidly that no dead body was to be left unburied, even those of the worst enemies, as Ezekiel had said,[36] nor even, according to the commandment of the Mosaic Law, those of men who had been executed.[37] In order to describe the horror of the state to which the heathen had reduced God's people, Psalm 78 uses the strongest words that were to be found: 'They have thrown the corpses of thy servants to feed all the birds of heaven; wild beasts prey on the carrion of the just.' And the worst malediction that Isaiah could hurl against the King of Babylon was: 'Thee the grave itself rejects, like a withered root, like a thing unclean. Rots thy corpse unrecognized, beneath yonder coverlet of men slain, that went down to the deep pit together.'[38]

The dead man therefore had a right to a ceremonial treatment that was laid down by the texts and by custom. As soon as he was dead, his eyes were to be closed – this appears as early as Genesis[39] – he was to be kissed with love[40] and washed,[41] aromatics and scents being used for the purpose. The tractate *Shabbath* said that it was allowable, on the day of rest, to do 'everything that is needed for the dead, to wash them and to anoint them with perfumes'.[42] This was not a true embalming, in the Egyptian manner, but rather a kind of tribute of the same nature as that which was paid to the living when scented oil was poured on their head at a banquet. Nard was the most usual of these scents: it was nard that Mary Magdalene used to anoint Christ – an action of which He said, 'She has anointed my body beforehand to prepare it for burial'. But myrrh was also used, and aloes, which clearly had nothing to do with that foul-smelling liliaceous plant which is now used in pharmacy, but was aloes-wood or lign-aloes, the present *agalacoun*, or the *alagoche* brought from India, both delightfully scented. A literal reading of Saint John's Gospel would lead one to suppose that the body was enveloped in an immense quantity of these aromatics. The evangelist says that Nicodemus brought 'a mixture of myrrh and aloes, of about a hundred pounds' weight' for the burial of Christ;[43] but no doubt it is to be understood that the aromatics were to be laid in the tomb beside the body.

In former times a dead man was dressed in his usual clothes and buried with the marks of his calling or office: the king with his crown, the soldier with his sword, the prophet with his cloak; and this custom is referred to in several passages in the Bible. But at the time of Christ this was no longer generally done. From the evangelists' detailed descriptions of the raising of

329

Lazarus from the dead and of the burial of our Lord, we learn that the body was wrapped in a shroud,[44] the face veiled with a *soudarion*,[45] and the feet and hands tied with linen strips.[46] The dead man would then be carried to the 'upper chamber' of the house, where his relatives and neighbours could come and say good-bye for the last time.

He would not be left there long. The burial usually followed eight hours after the death: in a hot climate it cannot be delayed. Coffins were rarely used: yet we read in the tractate *Gittin* that during the siege of Jerusalem by Titus the rabbi Ben Zakkai passed through the Roman lines shut in a coffin, which seems to show that they were not excessively unusual.[47] Generally the dead man was carried to his grave on a kind of litter, an open bier, and all the passers-by could see him: the funeral of the widow's son at Nain, which Jesus saw, seems to have been proceeding in this way. There was often some symbol that showed the status of the dead person: a feather or a key, for example, was put on a bachelor's bier, and a betrothed girl had a canopy. There were no professional carriers, no undertaker's men: it was the man's relatives and his friends who took it in turns to show him this last mark of affection. Very little children were carried in their people's arms.

When the funeral procession set out, the women would go in front of the bier. 'Because,' they said, 'as Eve, a woman, brought death into the world, women should lead death's victims to the grave.' Whether there was a great deal of sorrow or not, the demonstration of it was always noisy – ritually noisy. It would have been indecent not to cry out very loud, not to throw dust upon one's hair: people even hired professional mourners – they are mentioned as early as Jeremiah[48] – who uttered piercing cries the whole length of the journey, and flautists[49] who drew a sad music from their instruments. By custom the poorest of Israelites was obliged, if he lost his wife, to have at least two flute-players and one mourner.[50] It was also necessary to tear one's clothes; but the Talmud was obliged to give exact details upon how small a tear might be considered decent.

These were not religious rites properly so called. There was no ceremony equivalent to the funeral mass and the Christian prayers of intercession for the deceased. This does not mean that the relatives of the dead man did not pray as they went with him to his grave. There is a piece of Christian apocryphal literature – unfortunately the only known versions, in Coptic and Arabic, date from the third or fourth century – called *The History of Joseph the Carpenter*, which gives the text of a very beautiful prayer that Christ is said to have uttered over the body of His foster-father: 'O Lord of all mercy, seeing eye and hearing ear, hear my cry and my plea for Joseph, the old man, and send Michael, the chief of Your angels, and Gabriel, the messenger of light, and all the armies of Your angels and of Your choirs, so that they may march with the soul of my father Joseph, until they bring him to You.'[51] Another prayer, written in Aramaic, which dates from the time of Christ, is the equally beautiful *Kaddish*, which is still recited at present by orphans: following in this one of the particular characteristics of the Jewish faith, its verses glorify the Master of Life, blessing and magnifying His name, and then confine themselves to saying: 'May the prayers and the entreaties of all the people of Israel be received before their Father who is in heaven.'[52] This is the same as the Christians' manner of praying when they stand about the coffin while during the intercession for the deceased the priest silently repeats the Pater Noster.

Unlike the Romans, the Israelites did not cremate their dead; indeed, they had a horror of burning, for it seemed to them against the law of nature; and for those who believed in the resurrection of the flesh it seemed to make it impossible. This is why the penalty of burning was considered particularly terrible, even when it was not inflicted upon the living body, but only as an additional punishment that followed execution. The dead were therefore buried; yet there were no true cemeteries. It was only custom that caused several graves to be made in the same place near one another, always at the legal distance of fifty cubits from any dwellings: the valley of Jehoshaphat near Jerusalem, for example, was filled with them.[53] The only official cemeteries were for the indigent and for strangers. A man had to be very poor indeed not to make himself a tomb: the wealthy bought a well-chosen place, or had their graves on their own land.

The kind of tomb that is most usual in the West today, a simple grave with a flat stone over it, was not unknown in the Israel of the Gospels: Saint John, speaking of the raising of Lazarus, describes just such a tomb;[54] and at the Benedictine abbey that stands upon its traditional site it is a grave or vault with its mouth flush with the ground that they show. In the

331

cemetery of the Essenes that has been discovered near the ruins of Qumrân, the thousand tombs are all of this kind, neatly arranged in parallel lines, as in our Western graveyards. Yet it seems that this type of grave was not the most usual. From the findings of the archeologists, the statements in the Gospels and the details in the tractates of the Talmud we may picture the typical tomb as being a kind of cave or excavation, a vault cut into a rocky cliff, with a little vestibule before it. One had to bow one's head to go into the vault itself.[55] Sometimes the same entrance would lead to several vaults: as many as eight have been found together. The body was laid upon a bench specially cut in the rock, and no doubt surrounded and covered with aromatic herbs, often a great many of them. The tombs of the poorer people were closed by being walled-up, but the grander tombs had a more solid kind of gate, which is still to be seen in Palestine: it is a great round, like a millstone, set in a deep groove and held open by a wooden wedge; as soon as the wedge is taken away the heavy stone sinks into its place and guards the entrance from all comers, thieves or hyenas. It is this custom that explains the question that the holy women asked one another on Easter morning as they went up towards the tomb of the risen Christ: 'Who is to roll the stone away for us from the door of the tomb?'[56]

Once the tomb was closed, it was usual to raise a neatly arranged pile of stones upon it, or, if it were feasible, a monument. The fashion for these monuments (for there are certainly fashions in funerary art as in any other) was spreading just at the time of Christ, because of the influence of the Romans. Herod built a vast mausoleum for himself, the famous Herodium,[57] which was at once a fortress, a palace and a grave; but quite apart from this, it was during this period that there were erected those well-known tombs that are still to be seen in the valley of the Kidron – that which is called the tomb of Absalom and which the Arabs have nicknamed Pharaoh's hat; the tomb of the Judges with its triangular Doric pediment, obviously influenced by the pagans; the tomb of Saint James; the tomb of Zacharias; and again, at the foot of Mount Scopus, that tomb of the Kings which the Pereiras gave to France and which appears to be that of a Hellenistic princess converted to Judaism who settled in Jerusalem during the first century. The same Graeco-Roman influence brought the use of cut-stone sarcophagi into Palestine at the same period: the decoration of those that have been found is clumsy, and it consists only of foliage and geometric designs, some patterns, such as the pine-cone of Dionysus, being unconsciously pagan. The name of the dead was very rarely written upon the tomb: the Jews, as we know, did not often cut inscriptions in stone. It was only in the ossuaries or charnel-houses that the names of all whose bones were put there were written up, because as the place was used for generation after generation at times it was necessary to take out the earlier skeletons to make room.

When the sad rites were finished, the family would gather for a funeral meal. This was the 'bread of mourning' of which Hosea and Ezekiel speak.[58] There was a ritual drinking of wine as there was at the time of the Passover: but the Sanhedrim had very wisely fixed the maximum number of glasses that might be drunk, after the libations that followed the burial of a well-known rabbi had degenerated into a carouse.[59] After this the friends, particularly those who had not been able to go to the funeral, paid their visits of sympathy: the tractate *Baba Bathra* states that it is necessary, in such a call, to rise seven times from one's seat and to bow seven times to the dead person's family. Mourning lasted for thirty days: for the first three no work was done at all, and no greeting answered in the street. During this month of mourning phylacteries were not worn during prayer: the really pious went further – they did not shave or wash; they wore old and dirty clothes or even the *saq*,[60] that kind of camel's hair loincloth that still symbolizes sorrow. Faithful widows would even wear sackcloth until they died.

Afterwards, at given dates in every year, it was usual to visit the grave, particularly in the month of *Adar*, the last in the liturgical year, when the family would 'whiten the sepulchre', that is to say, whitewash the stone at the entrance and the cairn or the monument. This is the custom that Christ refers to in speaking of the Pharisees as whitened sepulchres, and again when He compares them to abandoned tombs 'which men walk over without knowing it'.[61] The Talmud speaks of the purpose of this whitewashing several times: it was done because contact with death brought about an exceedingly serious ritual uncleanliness, like that which was given by the touch of a leper; the whiteness therefore warned the living not to come near.

All peoples have and have always had burial ceremonies: did those of the Jews perhaps verge upon excess? Were not the lamentations and the cries that followed the body all too often false, mere pretence? 'Leave the dead to bury their dead':[62] Christ's famous reply to a disciple who asked permission to go and bury his father before following Him, shows clearly that He meant that life was to be found by looking beyond death. Saint Paul said, 'Make no mistake, brethren, about those who have gone to their rest; you are not to lament over them, as the rest of the world does, with no hope to live by. We believe, after all, that Jesus underwent death and rose again; just so, when Jesus comes back, God will bring back those who have found rest through him.'[63]

'WHERE, THEN, DEATH, IS THY VICTORY?'

These words of the apostle of the Gentiles defined the fundamental attitude of the followers of Christ. In the very words of his creed, a Christian must essentially 'believe in the resurrection of the flesh'. Did this also apply to the Jew of the time of Christ? It is strange to find that upon this point, which appears so all-important to us, there was no single, precise teaching: religion, so scrupulous in everything else, left each man to believe what he pleased concerning the nature of death and the hereafter. According to one's sect one either did or did not hope for an after-life.

The oldest concept, which may be traced in a hundred places in the Old Testament, was that death was the final end of life. When the angel of death of whom the Talmud speaks had put 'the drop of bitter gall' between the lips of the dying man he took his soul and carried it away. In that moment the breathing stopped, the breath of life, the *rouach*, with which the Creator had quickened the flesh on the day of its birth, was gone: and 'who has a right to tell us that the spirit of man mounts upwards, and the spirit of a beast sinks down to the depth?' asked the third chapter of Ecclesiastes. As for the body, the *bachar*, that certainly returned to the dust from which it had come, as the Scripture said. Did nothing at all remain of a man's personality, then? Yes: something was left; an immaterial presence, a shade, *repha*. The proof of this was that the shade might be called up and rendered visible for a fleeting moment, as the witch of Endor did with the shade of Samuel for Saul.[64] These shades, these *rephaim*, dwelt in a mysterious place that the Old Testament often calls Sheol. It was a place entirely unlike the world of the living: 'a place of darkness and of the shades of death', says Job; 'the dwelling of silence', says the Psalmist. It was so far from the world of men that even 'the anger of the Lord could not reach them there'.[65] Some rabbinical legends certainly maintained that this meta-physical abyss had also a concrete reality, and that one could get into it by raising the great rock that closed it and which was in the very middle of the Holy of Holies; but this was not the universal opinion. In Sheol the *rephaim* were nothing; they did nothing; they knew nothing; there was nothing that they could do: the word 'nothing' defines the only reality of that state which is the opposite of being. The prophet Isaiah even cried out to God, 'Thou hast no praise in the world beneath, death cannot honour thee'.[66] For a pious Jew not to honour God, not to fulfil his splendid duty, required indeed that he should be reduced to nothing. And naturally, since all living men were destined to come to this condition, there could be no question of punishment or reward. 'Never fear death's doom', said Ecclesiasticus.[67]

But this poverty-stricken, sad conception of the hereafter, so wanting in poetry that it is surprising to find it in a nation so preoccupied with spiritual matters,[68] was not the only one current in Palestine at the time of Christ. For by that period other doctrines were held in Israel and had been for centuries. They are to be found in the most recent parts of the Bible: Maccabees, Daniel, the Book of Wisdom. The Old Testament apocryphas, which, as we have seen, formed, together with the Bible, the literature that was read by the Israelites, were all in agreement with the new teachings, which were also collected in many of the tractates of the Talmud – a proof that many rabbis taught them. Did the exiled Jews in Babylon, bitterly tried, develop these new conceptions as a response to their unhappiness? Since God had promised His people His protection, it was necessary that the faithful should be rewarded and the unfaithful punished; and if it were not in this world, then it must be in the next. Here there is to be seen no straying from the true principles of Israel, no heathen contamination,[69] but rather a step forward, a more exact fore-knowledge of the truth, an approach towards the final Revelation. And Israel made this pace forward, as it made all those of its spiritual journey, under the stimulus of suffering: a fact that is in relation to its mystery, to its divine mystery.

Many Jews, then, at the time of Christ, did not believe that man's future, after death, was limited to the traditional Sheol. The angel of death, says a *midrash* upon Psalm 40, leads the soul to the judgment: if the dead man has lived his life according to the

335

Law, there is a cry of, 'Make ready a place for this righteous man'. If not, the soul is turned away. 'Thou wilt not leave my soul in the place of death', as Psalm 15 had phrased it. At once the concept of Sheol changed: for the *Book of Enoch* it was the place that devoured the impious, where the angels Michael, Gabriel, Raphael and Phanuel threw the wicked to undergo eternal pains.[70] Conversely there was another place where the saved souls were taken in, and this was called the Paradise of Righteousness;[71] it was compared with the Garden of Eden in which the first man lived before his fall,[72] and it was also very often referred to by a mysterious expression which comes from the central tradition of Israel, 'the bosom of Abraham'. It is this concept of an after-life in which the good are rewarded and the wicked punished that Christ invariably affirms or implies. The very words which He uses to speak of it are taken from His people's tradition: in the parable of the evil rich man, He speaks of the poor man Lazarus being 'in Abraham's bosom',[73] and on the Cross itself He promised the good thief, 'This day thou shalt be with me in Paradise'.[74] This concept, which emerged from Israel, reached its full extension and its complete development in Him; and it was He who provided the logical conclusion of the presentiment in Ecclesiasticus' 'Remember at all times what thou must come to at the last, and thou shalt never do amiss':[75] for He imposed the teaching of personal reward and retribution.

It was His teaching and His example too that gave dogmatic force to a doctrine that until then had been no more than a belief whose soundness could be questioned, at least among some of the Israelites: that of resurrection. It had its roots far back in the Jewish tradition; or rather the doctors of the Law who were teaching it at the time of Christ, found these roots for it, quoting now a verse from Deuteronomy,[76] now a passage from the prophets,[77] now the words of Job: 'Once more my skin shall clothe me, and in my flesh I shall have sight of God.' (19, 26.) The rabbi Gamaliel had provided himself with a whole armoury of proofs of this nature. In fact, it was during the exile too that Israel had made a decisive advance in this respect. 'Fresh life they shall have, Lord, that are thine in death; lost to us, they shall live again. Awake and utter your praises, you that dwell in the dust': the splendid cry of Isaiah must have echoed with tremendous force in the hearts of the exiles. Soon resurrection was formally associated with the reward of merit: 'Many shall wake', says

Daniel, 'that now lie sleeping in the dust of earth, some to enjoy life everlasting, some to be confronted for ever with their disgrace.'[78] And the Book of Wisdom developed this theme with great amplitude.

At the time of Christ, then, a whole section of the Chosen People believed in resurrection. The apocryphal writings continually revert to the subject: it is to be found in the *Testaments of the Patriarchs* and the *Psalms of Solomon* as well as the *Second Book of Baruch*.[79] In the same way there are innumerable passages in the Talmud which provide evidence for the same belief. One of the Blessings, the famous *Berakoth*, runs: 'We bless Thee, oh Eternal God, who restoreth the soul to the bodies of the dead';[80] and the rabbis were lavish with their details of the manner in which this would come about. Yet it was not all the believers of Israel who accepted this doctrine: the Gospel directly states that the Sadducees were 'men who say that there is no resurrection'.[81] According to them the tenet was not to be found in the Pentateuch; and on this point they made common cause with the Samaritans, who, for their part, officially recognized as inspired only the first five books of the Bible. But the Samaritans were heretics, and the Sadducees strict, conservative traditionalists. Among the ordinary people it seems that belief in resurrection was very general. In the Gospel according to Saint John, which the Church causes to be read at the funeral mass, Christ says to Martha, the sister of Lazarus, 'Thy brother will rise again,' and she replies, 'I know well enough that he will rise again at the resurrection, when the last day comes'.[82]

Christ, as it were, made this doctrine His own and raised it to a principle of belief, a dogma. He did this not only by His words but also by His example: He raised the dead; and still more, He Himself rose up again. He told Martha the secret of His message when He said to her, 'I am the resurrection and the life'. But it would appear that some thought of this resurrection as a mere reanimation of the body, a kind of reincarnation: and there were, of course, many pagans who held that metempsychosis was a fact. It was for this reason that our Lord answered those Sadducees who wished to embarrass Him with the ironic question about which husband a seven-times-married wife would have after the resurrection,[83] with the words, 'When the dead rise again, there is no marrying and giving in marriage; they are as the angels in heaven are'; and this mysterious statement throws much light

337

upon His reply to Lazarus' sister: 'He who believes in me, though he is dead, will live on.'

Thus this concept, which was born in Israel and developed with transcendent power by Jesus, was to become the very basis of the Christian faith. In their essence the Christians were to be, as Saint Paul continually repeated the witnesses of the Resurrection. 'If Christ has not risen, then our preaching is groundless, and your faith, too, is groundless,' as he said to the Corinthians. There is something glorious in the fact that it should have been the Jew Saul, the pupil of the rabbis of Israel, who, having become Paul, gave to the world those unparalleled words, words with which, ever since, the worldly life of every believer has ended: 'Where, then, death, is thy victory; where, death, is thy sting?'[84]

PART THREE

A People and Its God

> Who but the Lord is our God? And what
> are we, but folk of his pasturing, sheep
> that follow his beckoning hand? (*Psalm* 94, 7)

CHAPTER ONE

THE AGE OF GOD

*Israel's religious life – The consecration of the day by prayer –
The consecration of the week by the Sabbath – The consecration
of the year by the feasts – The sabbatical year and the jubilee.*

ISRAEL'S RELIGIOUS LIFE

We have seen how the daily existence of the People of God was
regulated and controlled, even in its smallest detail, by religion.
We have seen how the Torah and the commentaries upon the Law
influenced every aspect of life, how they gave a truly religious
significance to the home, for example, and men's clothing and
food; how they governed human relationships, in the family, at
work, and in the community, as well as the means by which
thought was expressed: in a word, we have seen how they placed
the individual within a frame, a setting that enclosed him from
birth to death, and from which he could not escape without being
heavily punished; for since the civil authority identified itself with
the religious authority, secular law was merely the application of
the law of God.

A Western man of the twentieth century, even if he is a believer,
finds this way of life difficult to understand; he scarcely sees its
validity. The behaviour of the mediaeval Christian was not so
very unlike it, although the nature of his submission to the
dictates of religion was far removed from the scrupulous and
rigid Jewish legalism. But since the cathedrals lost their whiteness,
and above all since the 'enlightenment' of the eighteenth century,
our society has undergone a process of secularization which by
now makes this continual intervention of religion in daily life
seem to many of us absurd, out of the question. And indeed how
many Christians practise a kind of spiritual division which leaves
religion in a specially reserved area – one in which a man is
married, has his children baptized and wishes to be buried, but
which he does not allow to impinge upon either the practical or
the moral aspects of his daily life in the least degree. For a Jew

of the time of Christ, this division would have been infamous: or, to be more exact, he would have been unable to imagine its existence.

When we come to consider the public manifestations of Israel's religious life, therefore, it must not be forgotten that the whole of Jewish life was 'religious' in the fullest sense of the word. The feasts, the religious ceremonies and the meetings in the synagogue were no more than incidents in the life of every day; they formed part of it, and they were manifestations of the same spirit as that which governed it in all its aspects. They were the more solemn, more formal, outward appearances of a faith upon which the hearts of men were set, as the Psalmist said, night and day: 'On that Law, day and night, his thoughts still dwell.'[1]

THE CONSECRATION OF THE DAY BY PRAYER

Each day, and several times each day, the practising Jew set himself to prayer. Anyone who has lived in a Mohammedan country must have admired the regularity with which at the given hour the Mohammedan, wherever he may be, lays his cloak upon the ground, puts off his shoes, sprinkles a little water on his forearms, and prays, turned towards Mecca, gravely, simply, and without any affectation. This admirable custom, which Mohammed no doubt adopted from the Jewish travelling companions who helped him to give expression to his message, provides an exact idea of what the daily prayer of the practising Jews must have been.

'God has spoken to Israel, and I have said it again to you,' said Rabbi Eleazar about a hundred years after Christ, 'when you have to pray, go and pray in the synagogue of your town if you cannot pray in the synagogue, pray in your field; if you cannot pray in your field, pray in your house; if you cannot pray in your house, pray in your bed, and there, at least, speak to God in your heart and be silent.'[2]

It was, therefore, an absolute duty for all adults, that is to say for all of thirteen and upwards: only women, children and slaves were excused. The hours of prayer had varied in the course of the centuries, but there seems little doubt that at the time of Christ men prayed in the morning and the evening, as well as at the noon of the Psalmist, which corresponds to the sixth hour the time at which the Acts show us Saint Peter, when he was at Joppa, going up on to the housetop to pray.[3]

In praying, the observant Jew was to wrap himself in his *tallith*, his prayer-shawl, and to wear the *tefillin*. This was obligatory to so high a degree that several tractates in the Talmud assert that God Himself obeys this rule. The *tallith* was – and indeed still is, since it is used today – a very large kind of scarf which, when it was thrown over the head and shoulders, came down to the waist, covering the whole upper part of the body: when possible it was made of fine white silk, often with a bunch of grapes or a pomegranate embroidered on it in deep blue. Its edges had the ritual fringes, and at the corners there were the *tsitsit*, tassels which had eight threads apiece, so that there were thirty-two altogether, which was the numerical equivalent of the word 'heart'.[4] As for the *tefillin*, which are also known as phylacteries, from the Greek, they were little square black cases, made of the skin of 'clean' animals, which contained passages from Exodus and Deuteronomy, written on parchment;[5] and they were tied to the forehead and the palm of the hand with thongs.

The Jew, in praying, would turn towards Jerusalem, following the example of the prophet Daniel during the exile:[6] if he were already in the holy city, then towards the Temple; and if he were in the Temple, towards the Holy of Holies. Generally speaking, he would not kneel: this was only done in very particular circumstances, and to entreat the Lord with uncommon earnestness. On the other hand he would often prostrate himself; sometimes merely bending his knees, sometimes with bent knees stretching out his hands, sometimes bowing his forehead as low as possible, sometimes throwing himself face down on the ground. It was also usual to hold one's hands towards heaven in prayer: 'May my raised hands be like the evening sacrifice,' said the Psalmist. This too was an attitude much favoured by the early Christians, as may be seen from the well-known *orantes* in the catacombs. Yet it was not customary to join one's hands: this seems to date only from the fifth century of our era, and to have come perhaps from Byzantium or perhaps from the Germanic tribes. The true believer prayed with his eyes down, like the publican in the Gospel, sometimes beating his breast.[7] And usually he prayed aloud.

There were two set forms that were used in daily prayer. The first, which was obligatorily recited morning and evening as well as on many other occasions, just as Catholics say the Pater Noster and the Hail Mary, was the famous *Shema*. *Shema*, listen! That is its first word. It is a profession of faith, taken from

343

Deuteronomy:[8] 'Listen then, Israel; there is no Lord but the Lord our God, and thou shalt love the Lord thy God with the love of thy whole heart, and thy whole soul, and thy whole strength. The commands I give thee this day must be written on thy heart, so that thou canst teach them to thy sons, and keep them in mind continually, at home and on thy travels, sleeping and waking; bound close to thy hand for a remembrancer, ever moving up and down before thy eyes; the legend thou dost inscribe on door and gate-post.' The prayer goes on for two more paragraphs of the same nature, repeating the same assertions of uncompromising monotheism and recalling the believers to the strict observance of their faith.

The other prayer was longer. It was to be recited three times a day, and in secret if it could not be said aloud. It was presumably this prayer that Saint Peter and Saint John were going to recite when they went to the Temple at about three o'clock, as we read in the Acts.[9] It is now called the *Shemoneh Esreh*, the Eighteen Benedictions: in its present form it is certainly not that which Christ and His disciples would have used, for in it there are allusions to the ruin of the Temple and even to the Nazarene sect; but its essential parts are very much earlier, and it expresses the religious ideal of Israel with impressive strength and often with great beauty. The *Shemoneh Esreh* is filled with insistent repetition; it has a magnificent slow, long surge, and from its opening verses it raises the soul to glorify the Almighty, the God of Abraham, of Isaac and of Jacob, the great, strong and terrible master who is also the giver of all good things, He who has breathed life into every moving thing on earth, the Being from whom proceeds all wisdom and all holiness. Although many Jews may have recited its verses mechanically, 'as if to be rid of an unwelcome task', as the tractate *Berakoth*[10] admits, it is nevertheless admirable that every believer's day should have been given its rhythm by these splendid words, and that each day should thus have been consecrated to God. And the requests that followed the opening of the prayer, requests for daily bread spiritual grace and the forgiveness of sins, the restoration of Jerusalem, the reuniting of the tribes and the advent of the kingdom of God, are no less filled with mystical significance The Pater Noster, the most beautiful of men's prayers, is, in its simplicity, a kind of purified and clarified *Shemoneh Esreh* disembarrassed of any rigidly national associations, with its range extended to cover all humanity. Yet it is certainly from the Jewish daily prayer that it takes many of its expressions, including its first two words, which are the same as those which begin the eighteenth benediction.

THE CONSECRATION OF THE WEEK BY THE SABBATH

The same intention of bringing man before his Maker at regular intervals in his life, associated no doubt with other ideas of a social and hygienic nature, brought about the Law's institution of the Sabbath. It will be recalled[11] that the word means the last day of the week, our Saturday. But when he said it, a Jew knew very well that it also had a far finer, far richer meaning, that it referred to a sacred custom which was Israel's pride, and that it provided one of the unquestionable proofs of the presence of Yahweh among His people. An indication of the importance of the Sabbath in Jewish life is the frequency with which the Gospels speak of it: the word occurs nearly seventy times.

What exactly was the Sabbath? The Bible answers this in many places: 'It is a token between us' – between God and His people – a day set apart for God, that Israel was to observe 'through all the ages which lie before you' by refraining from work of any kind, by 'resting from all labours'[12] as God Himself had rested on the seventh day of creation. In communicating this divine commandment to his people, Moses added that any violation of the Sabbath was to be punished by death, and indeed the Book of Numbers recounts how, when the Israelites were passing through the desert, a man was found gathering firewood on the Sabbath day, and how he was in fact, stoned to death.[13]

There were many beautiful accounts of the origin of the Sabbath and of its importance, several of which have been preserved in the Talmud. Mankind's first song was a Sabbath hymn, which Adam sang on the seventh day when he learnt that God had forgiven him: some held that this was Psalm 91. Others were even better informed, and stated that it was exactly at the moment when the first Sabbath began that man was created; and that it was upon a Sabbath that Israel traversed the Red Sea in the escape from Egypt. And as everyone knew, Yahweh Himself continued to observe the Sabbath, as if He created the world anew each week: it was for this reason that a very well-known rabbinical axiom stated: 'The Sabbath, like circumcision, is anterior to the Law.'

Where, in fact, did the Sabbath come from? 'There are strong presumptions in favour of heathen origins,' says Jankélévitch,[14] who relates it to that belief in fortunate and unfortunate days which is to be found among 'all primitive nations and even those who have attained a high degree of civilization'. Baron and Lods seek its origin in the astronomy of the Babylonians; but the rigidly hebdomadal aspect of the Sabbath at the time of Christ proves that there must at least have been a reaction against any Mesopotamian astral usage, since lunar months do not necessarily have twenty-eight days, but sometimes twenty-nine or even thirty. In any case, it was during the exile that the Sabbath took on the very great importance that is so well known: the Jews in Babylon, who no longer had any Temple in which they might pray to God, all met on that day and had 'joy in the Lord', as Isaiah says.[15] After the return to the Promised Land, not only did they continue to observe this pious custom but they continually strengthened the regulations that guaranteed that it should be observed. From the Maccabean period onwards, it was a very serious offence not to keep the Sabbath; and on the other hand, keeping it well was meritorious.

As the Jewish day began[16] the previous evening, the Sabbath started at twilight on Friday. Legally it began 'with the night': but when was the beginning of the night? When three stars appeared in the sky, replied the rabbis. Between 'the first and the third star', the *hazzan* went up on to the roof of the highest building in the neighbourhood, taking with him the 'trumpet of the Sabbath' from the place in the synagogue where it was kept. He was then to blow two notes three times (some said six times, but not everybody agreed with them): the first was to warn the workers in the fields to leave their tasks, the second to tell the merchants to close their shops, and the third meant that the moment for lighting the lamp had come; and as it was blown the little yellow flame sprang up in all the Jewish homes, a silent religious presence. There was a very pretty expression – 'The Sabbath has begun to shine'.

On Friday, which was in fact called 'the day of preparation', the house had been carefully cleaned, and the women had cooked all the dishes that were to be eaten on the holy day – eaten cold, of course, for no housework or cooking was allowed. It was a particular mark of the good housewife that she never forgot to fill the Sabbath lamp with oil or to supply the house with those hard, flat rounds of bread, with fish, dates and figs. People would take a bath, particularly if, like the tanners and leather-dressers, theirs was a dirty trade. As soon as the lamp was lit they would sit down to a meal in which wine and aromatic herbs were included, and upon which a special threefold blessing was invoked. But after this no one ate anything until after having been to the synagogue on Saturday morning: a fact which explains the hunger of our Lord's disciples when, on the Sabbath day, they plucked the ears of corn and ate them.[17] At the synagogue the people heard some passage of the Bible read and commented upon; then they went home for their mid-day meal, which was also blessed in a particular manner. In those places where there was a *Beth ha-Midrash*, a House of Learning, the rabbis and doctors of the Law would resort to it in the afternoon to discuss theological questions. The people would have their supper at about five o'clock, but not without having blessed the light, the wine and the herbs three times, and the evening would go on until the trumpet gave the sign that the Sabbath was over. Then, even if they were in the middle of eating, they would rise, wash their hands and offer thanks over a goblet of wine: the sacred interval in ordinary life, the consecrated rest, was over.

The Sabbath, then, was a day of prayer; but it was not a cheerless day. There was nothing to prevent the dishes from being very well prepared or the wine from being uncommonly good, and people were actually called upon to wear their best clothes. A man who had worked hard the whole week long could feel the pleasure that God Himself had felt when the creation was finished. It was for this reason that the Law and its commentators were so insistent that the rest should be scrupulously observed. Indeed, one even gets the impression that the truly spiritual significance of the Sabbath, its meaning as a time when men should be in the presence of God, the consecrated day of the week, was being obliterated by its legalistic and ritual aspect: the essence of the commandment concerning the Sabbath, in the eyes of some, was that part which said that one was to do no work.

The rules governing this rest and the conditions in which it was to be observed were most scrupulously worked out. The Bible itself did more than lay down the principle: it went into detail and specified a certain number of kinds of work or activity that were forbidden on the Sabbath – lighting a fire, for example, or walking

more than six stadia. Making deductions from these rules, the
rabbis worked out a code that is preserved for us in the tractate
Shabbath. There were thirty-nine kinds of forbidden activity:
this was used in Israel for the greatest possible figure, forty
meaning a boundless quantity.[18] The list ranged from sowing to
carrying an object, and it included tying or untying a knot,
seizing any prey and writing two letters of the alphabet. As well
as direct rulings there was also a whole corpus of advice and of
prohibitions which were sometimes argued, as we shall see,
with a subtlety that verged upon Byzantine excess, not to say
absurdity,[19] but which were nevertheless the sign of a deep
desire to conform to the will of God.

The keeping of the Sabbath became, indeed, so rigorous an
obligation that the wisest among the rabbis were forced to
distinguish between the different kinds of forbidden activity, in
order that the disastrous results of a too-passive obedience might
be avoided. For example, ever since the time of the Maccabees,
when a thousand Jews let themselves be killed by the Syrians
rather than take up arms and violate the Sabbath, and since the
time of Pompey's siege of Jerusalem, when the defenders left the
walls the moment the star of Sabbath appeared in the evening sky,
it had been agreed that it was legitimate to fight in self-defence
on the day of rest. In the same way it was admitted that the
observance of the Sabbath might yield to some higher religious
duty, such as circumcision or the celebration of certain great
feasts. It was also permitted that one might help a man in danger
of his life on the Sabbath, or even an animal: Christ speaks of this
concession.[20] But the more rigid Jews would have nothing of
these compromises with the Law, and this was a perpetual
source of argument between the different schools of doctors: in
the rule of the Essenes' community it is flatly stated that it is
better to let an animal or even a man drown, rather than violate
the Sabbath.[21] At the time of Christ a reaction against this
extreme rigidity had set in; and in a way it may be said that He
was the chief of this reaction: the liberal rabbis said, 'The Sabbath
has been given to you; but you have not been given to the
Sabbath';[22] but Jesus was more direct, and giving the consecrated
day back its true spiritual significance, He said, 'The Sabbath was
made for man, not man for the Sabbath'.[23]

However questionable the formalism of the rules concerning the
Sabbath may appear, in some of their aspects, it is nevertheless a

fact that this obligatory pause for prayer at the end of the week, this weekly confrontation with God, set a very particular mark upon the Chosen People. 'This day of the holy kingdom,' as the *Book of Jubilees* put it, 'when there is rest from all the weariness that work lays upon men': and the Jews were proud of being the only nation in the world who had knowledge of it. It was so obvious a fact of Jewish life that even the Romans were obliged to recognize it. They thought it ridiculous, of course, and Tacitus makes game of it: he says that this odd race 'lost the seventh part of their lives' by doing nothing whatever on one day in the week; and that this was all in honour of Saturn, which was clearly proved by the fact that on that day they ate nothing but cold meals, by reason of the frigidity of the said planet.[24] But if we are to believe Josephus, it was because of the law of the Sabbath that the Roman empire refrained from recruiting the Jews for the army, lest at the first sound of the *hazzan*'s trumpet they should throw down both sword and buckler.

THE CONSECRATION OF THE YEAR BY THE FEASTS

If the day was made holy by the triple prayer and the week by the Sabbath, the year was sanctified by the feasts, which were celebrated at dates fixed by the Law. There were several of them: one might even say a great many. On some occasions they followed one another with scarcely a pause for three weeks on end. In autumn, at the beginning of the month of *Tisri*, for example, the new year, the days of penitence and the Feast of Tabernacles all come in quick succession. These were not like the Sabbath: there is no text comparable to that from the *Book of Jubilees* that has just been quoted to show that the religious law-giver was thinking of men's rest. But in fact the liturgical calendar created legal holidays – holidays such as those our Middle Ages knew. Of course, the primary intention was entirely religious: at the Passover or the Feast of Weeks, at *Purim* or *Yom Kippur*, the people's essential purpose was to glorify, thank and entreat the Eternal, the One, the Almighty.

Some of these feasts were celebrated at home, in the family (that basic religious unit), among friends, or in the group formed by a master and his disciples, which is to be seen with Christ and the twelve apostles. But like so many aspects of Jewish life they all had a strongly marked 'communal' character. It was not so much the individual as the entire nation which turned towards God, their own God. Each of these feasts had public ceremonies that corresponded to their essential meaning. Many of them were the occasion for pilgrimages, in which the pious Jew would take part as often as he could.

The pilgrimages of Israel: Mecca or Benares, or Lourdes at the height of August, give an idea of what Jerusalem could be on the days of the great holidays, when countless hosts of people converged upon it. The pilgrims came from everywhere; not only from every corner of Palestine but also from all those distant countries in which the Dispersion had settled still-faithful colonies of Jews; and at the ports of Caesarea and Joppa (particularly Joppa, for Caesarea was too heathen) specialized agencies landed boat-loads of pilgrims, as we see them landed today at Jidda, the port for Mecca. It was usual to go on pilgrimage in little groups of relatives and friends: there was great good feeling among pilgrims, and although no doubt the wealthy saw to it that they travelled in the greatest possible comfort, it would have been quite impossible for anyone finding some poor, ragged fellow on the deck of the boat or upon the road to ask him what he thought he was doing there. At the approach of the feasts, all the roads that led to the holy gates were filled with almost uninterrupted strings of caravans which would meet, greet one another and go on in company. There was a continual singing, the sound of innumerable voices chanting the famous psalms of pilgrimage to the tune of popular songs: these were the 'songs of ascents' which the Bible has preserved for us, and the most famous were Psalms 83 and 119–133, which every Israelite was supposed to have 'engraved upon his heart'. The first spoke of the great desire for pilgrimage: 'For the courts of the Lord's house, my soul faints with longing. The living God! at his name my heart, my whole being thrills with joy.' Others were filled with joyful hope, and sang of the happiness of the sacred road: 'Welcome sound, when I heard them saying, We will go into the Lord's house!' When the pilgrims reached the 'valley of the nettle-trees'[25] and the holy city came in sight, they blessed Yahweh and praised the glory of the city, 'built as a city should be built that is one in fellowship'. And many of them, as they 'trod the threshold of the gates', prostrated themselves and kissed the sacred ground.

How many pilgrims were there, at the time of the great feasts? Josephus says that at the Passover one year Herod Agrippa ordered a kidney from each lamb sacrificed to be given to him, and that he received six hundred thousand of them. 'And counting ten pilgrims, upon an average, for each lamb,' says the historian, without a blush, 'this allows us to reckon the number of pilgrims at six millions.' Later the Talmud raised this to twelve millions. Some people, by working out the number the Temple could hold, have thought it possible to reduce the figure to a hundred and sixty thousand; but this is obviously too low, since the tractate *Pesahim* (Passover) states that because of the great crowds it was necessary to repeat the services three times. It may be said, then, that something like half a million pilgrims came to Jerusalem at the time of the great feasts – five times its normal population.

This is a characteristic of Jewish life whose importance cannot be exaggerated: this communal praying of a whole nation together had a very strong tendency to promote unity and cohesion. The ragged day-labourer, the hermit in his loincloth, the wealthy Alexandrian or Babylonian merchant in his fine linen, all felt that they were brothers during the days that they spent in the courts of the Temple. During the actual religious ceremonies they stood there shoulder to shoulder. Afterwards, in the crowded streets, they would 'Walk about Sion, make the round of her towers, and count the number of them; mark well the defences that are hers, pass all her strongholds in review',[27] so that they might be able to tell those who had stayed at home everything that there was to be seen and with them to praise the Almighty who had ordained all this.

These feasts, which held so great a place in the life of Israel, dated from the most remote antiquity. In the beginning, no doubt, they were natural feasts, dictated by the cycle of the year, and borrowed from the older civilisations of Babylonia or Canaan – feasts of the spring, the harvest and the sowing. But for hundreds and hundreds of years the historical character of the Chosen People's religion had been imposed upon them, and for a very great while they had been celebrated as reminders of the most important happenings in sacred history. Many of them had a markedly penitential nature; and this, too, had a sacred and historical derivation. As everyone knew, Israel had very often sinned against its God, and had earned the just punishments that He had inflicted upon the nation: there was no better nor more necessary act than begging for His mercy. The 'autumn gathering' which called the people together at the time when the new year of the Law began, called them for penitence, and its sole aim was to entreat the Almighty's clemency.[28]

The holidays and the public feasts which commemorated past
misfortunes made up between them a very full calendar, so full
that there was not a single month without a religious manifestation
of one kind or another. In this calendar there was a distinction
between the great and the lesser feasts: some of the second were
simple popular holidays – the shearing festival, for example, was
one of these; it is mentioned as early as Genesis,[29] and it consisted
of a very cheerful feast and a blessing of the flocks: it took place
at the beginning of the summer. Another very happy festival was
that of *Purim*, which was celebrated on the fourteenth day of *Adar*
almost as Europeans celebrate the Carnival, with decorated carts
and fancy-dress – this is still the case in the modern state of
Israel. It was a feast in memory of the great danger that the
Chosen People had undergone when Haman, Ahasuerus' evil
minister, determined to destroy them, and of their providential
delivery when Esther, advised by the prudent Mordecai, won over
the king, so that Haman was hanged by the neck. During this
feast the Book of Esther, which tells the history of these events,
was read aloud in the synagogue, and invariably the listeners
broke out into wild applause. On the day before, the thirteenth of
Adar, the particularly observant Jews celebrated another feast,
the feast of Nicanor, which recalled another victory, that of Judas
Maccabaeus over the Syrian general Nicanor:[30] a fire was lit at
Modine, the Asmoneans' home, and runners carried torches from
it to the four corners of the Promised Land.[31] The Dedication was
another feast that commemorated one of the events of the war of
liberation, and one which had a great place in Israel's memory.
Judas Maccabaeus purified and re-dedicated the Temple after it
had been profaned by Antiochus Epiphanes, and in memory of
this houses were lit up, people sang and danced in the streets and
played upon the harp and the cymbals: as the prophet Haggai, in
the second chapter of his book, had foretold a particular purification for the twenty-fourth day of the ninth month, this was the day
that was fixed upon for the feast: it corresponded, roughly, to the
twenty-fourth of December, Christmas Eve.

The great feasts gave rise to far more impressive ceremonies,
above all the 'three major feasts', the *shalosh regalim*, the Passover,
Pentecost and the Day of Atonement. The oldest was that of the
first-fruits or of the harvest, which was called the Feast of Weeks,
because Deuteronomy said: 'From the day when the sickle is
first put to thy crops, count seven whole weeks, and then keep the

Feast of Weeks, honouring the Lord thy God' who gives all.[32] But it was not only material gifts that He gave. For the Jews also celebrated (as no one who has read Racine is likely to forget) 'the famous day when upon Mount Sinai the Law was given us'.[33] As Moses had received the Law fifty days after the Jews left Egypt,[34] that is to say, almost exactly seven weeks, the two celebrations had naturally merged into one another; and from the Greek for 'fiftieth' the feast was often called Pentecost, when its Jewish name *Hasartha*, or gathering, was not used. For indeed this was one of the feasts when the people gathered in extraordinary numbers in Jerusalem. It was above all a happy feast, and it consisted primarily of offering bread and sacrifices; but it also induced pious minds to reflect upon the Mosaic revelation. And it was upon the day of Pentecost that Christ's apostles, gathered to speak together of another, even higher revelation, were witnesses of a miracle which they recognised as the work of the Holy Spirit: a violent wind, a terrible noise, and the appearance of tongues of fire over each of them. From that time onwards Pentecost was to be the feast of the birth of Christ's Church.[35]

The Feast of Weeks was the great spring-time holiday: in the autumn three feasts one after the other ran through the first twenty-two days of *Tisri*. It appears that during the course of time their order had varied, but by Christ's day they were fixed thus: the first day of the month was the Feast of the New Year, and then, as we have seen,[36] the religious year began again; on the tenth day there was *Yom Kippur*, the Day of Atonement; then, from the fifteenth onwards, the Feast of Tabernacles. The first lasted ten days, and it included some splendid ceremonies, particularly the first day: the Bible called it 'a day to be marked by a blast of trumpets'.[37] There was a solemn procession, which must have been reminiscent of those of former times, when the Israelites' forefathers followed the ark of the covenant, singing hymns to the Almighty: a young bull, a ram and seven unblemished lambs of the year were offered to the Lord; and to these was added a goat, a sign of repentance for the sins of all.

Repentance was the keynote of the following days, from the tenth of *Tisri* onwards. Pious Jews often prepared themselves for these moving ceremonies by fasting, praying, many ritual ablutions and even by making a retreat. The high priest, for his part, was obliged to retire into a special room in the Temple, to sanctify himself by prayer. The Day of Atonement, *Yom*

Kippur, was so important that if a man spoke simply of 'the day', everyone knew that he meant this particular day. Of course, all work had to stop and the people had to fast, under pain of death: the Acts refer to this period as 'the time of the great fast'.[38] But it was above all necessary to mortify the soul, that is, to become fully aware of one's wretched state, and the overwhelming burden of one's sins. The rites of this holy day, which the pilgrims followed with profound devotion, were beautiful and full of mystery. On this one single day in the year, the high priest went into the Holy of Holies of the Temple, to purify it with the mingled blood of a goat and a bull. Then there was the strange ceremony of the scapegoat. A goat was chosen by lot, a goat that was to be called Azazel, said the sixteenth chapter of Leviticus, the name of an evil spirit. The high priest 'put both hands on its head, confessing all the sins and transgressions and faults Israel has committed, and laying the guilt of them on its head'. The people repeated a prayer which is not unlike our act of contrition: 'My God, Thy people have committed many sins before Thee, many crimes; but as it is written in the Law of Thy servant Moses, grant forgiveness for all faults in Thy mercy on this day of atonement.' Then a man, appointed for the purpose, drove the goat away, chasing it with a whip into the desert, that is to say a few miles from Jerusalem, as far as a cliff where it was abandoned to its unhappy fate, without anyone being allowed to feed it or look after it. After this, the high priest having solemnly washed himself, the People of God were cleansed.

These dark days were followed by others of a completely different nature. This was the Feast of Tabernacles, of little huts or booths; *the* feast, as it was called by the country people who remembered that in former times it was the celebration of the grape and olive harvest. As we have seen,[39] it was usual to go and live in the olive-grove or the vineyard throughout the time of harvest, in tents or huts made of branches: at the Feast of Tabernacles, therefore, the whole neighbourhood surrounding Jerusalem was covered with booths and tents in which the pilgrims and even the citizens dwelt for eight days. The meaning of the rite was clear: it put the Jews in mind of the time when they were 'wanderers upon the earth', moving about in the desert before they reached the Promised Land. Every day those who were living in the tabernacles went to the Temple; there were sacrifices, and in the courts processions, while the people sang the wonderful hundred and seventeenth psalm, that thank-offering to God, the Deliverer who from 'the very stone which the builders rejected made the chief stone at the corner'. Every day the high priest, followed by the people, went to fetch water in a golden pitcher from the Pool of Siloam and returned to make a libation with it at the west end of the altar. And in the evening there was the extraordinary festivity at the Temple in the court of the women: four great ritual candlesticks were lit, the Levite musicians with their lutes and cymbals took up their places on the fifteen steps that led to the court of the men, and at the sound of a trumpet a torch-dance began, while the people sang, 'In this place our fathers worshipped the sun, but we turn our faces towards the Only God'.[40] It may have been during this festal night that Christ said, 'I am the light of the world. He who follows me can never walk in darkness; he will possess the light which is life.'[41]

But of all the feasts that were scattered through the Jewish year, the holiest and the most fervently celebrated was the Passover. It was undoubtedly a very ancient feast, the successor of those in which the Jews' forefathers offered to God the firstlings of their cattle and the unleavened bread made from the first ears of the harvest. But from the time of Moses it had taken on another meaning: it was the feast of the deliverance, of the miraculous liberation, the feast of the escape from Egyptian bondage. It was said by the people that its name, *Pesah* or *Pesahim*, meant 'a passing' or 'a going over'; it may be that the word had an Egyptian derivation and that it was connected with the idea of remembrance.

At the time of Christ, the Passover was celebrated on the fourteenth day of *Nisan*,[42] which corresponded to the full moon of the vernal equinox: it was a fixed date, therefore, unlike the Christian Easter, for the Jewish months were lunar.[43] The ceremonies lasted for a week, but the most important took place on the first and second days. Essentially the rites were those which are to be found in chapter twelve of Exodus, where it is recounted how Moses told his people what to do so that the angel of death should not strike them and so that they might be able to escape from the land of persecution. The paschal lamb was therefore still sacrificed and its blood scattered with a branch of hyssop upon the lintel and the jambs of the door, and the people still ate unleavened bread and the flesh of the lamb. But it is not certain that everyone still strictly observed the rule that the sacred meal was to be eaten standing, every man with his loins girt, sandals on his feet and his staff in his hand.

Yet the ceremony was laid down with great exactness. On the afternoon of the fourteenth of *Nisan* everything took place at the Temple. Each man had chosen and bought the unblemished yearling lamb which the Law required; it was given to the sacrificers who stood at the entrance of the court of the priests, and a trumpet blast gave the signal for each sacrifice. The priest collected the blood and poured it out before the altar: thence it flowed down the gutters towards the Kidron. This great slaughter was called 'preparing the Passover'.[44] The entrails and the fat were thrown into the fire, and so throughout the Passover week a foul stench of burning flesh floated over the city. After this the sacrificed lamb was taken away by those who had given it to be eaten at the ritual meal, which took place in the upper chamber of the house.

The tractate *Pesahim* gives us the most precise details of this meal. None of the lamb's bones was to be broken, and it was to be roasted, not boiled. When it was ready, they first dipped unleavened bread in a red sauce called *hasereth* and drank a first glass of wine with a blessing, then recited Psalm 113, which tells how the Chosen People left Egypt. Then they drank some drops of salt water, in memory of the tears their forefathers had shed, and afterwards began to eat the lamb, accompanied by 'bitter herbs', horse-radish, bay, thyme, marjoram and basil. Two more glasses of wine were drunk, passed from hand to hand, and the third, drunk with particular solemnity, was called the 'goblet of benediction'. At this point all the people sang the *Hallel*, the chant of thanks, which was made from the four psalms 112–117: 'Not to us, Lord, not to us the glory; let thy name alone be honoured; thine the merciful, thine the faithful.' At the singing of the verse 'Blessed is he who comes in the name of the Lord' the fourth, and ritually the last, glass of wine was passed. All this was obligatory, so much so that those who were too poor to be able to buy the lamb, the wine and the herbs were given them by the community. But the rich could go on eating and drinking, so long as they did not exceed five goblets.

The Passover was a very cheerful feast. 'It is as savoury as an olive,' said the Talmud, 'and the *Hallel* should burst through the roof of the house.' A gnostic apocryphal book called the *Acts of John*, goes so far as to describe Christ's disciples forming a ring round Him and dancing to the time of their song. But it was also a time of ardent meditation, when each believer could feel the mystic bond that linked him to his people, and that he himself was also to be made free, free in the only way that is of importance, with his soul delivered from the dominion of sin. It was not at all by chance that Christ, using the bread and the wine of the traditional rite, should, at the last paschal supper, have given His disciples the sign of the supreme liberation with the words: 'This is my body . . . this is my blood.'

THE SABBATICAL YEAR AND THE JUBILEE

The day was marked with the seal of God; so was the week and each month in the year; but still this was not enough. The sequence of the years, too, had to be marked by sacred intervals. These were arranged so as to agree with the Jews' delight in the science of numbers,[45] that is, they were based upon the figure seven, which was considered to be holy. There was one sacred pause every seven years, at the end of 'the week of years'; and another every seven 'weeks of years': seven times seven or seventy times seven conveyed the idea of infinity. A very important fact, and one that shows the Jewish Law in a most amiable light, is that both the one pause and the other had a markedly generous and charitable character.

Every seventh year, then, was a sabbatical year, a year set apart from the others. This was not so much because of the religious ceremonies that it contained, but because of the social, humanitarian and even economic measures that were then applied. For during the sabbatical year the Law required that Hebrew slaves should be set free, particularly those who had been obliged to sell themselves to pay their debts.[46] At the same time the Law commanded the Jew 'to be open-handed towards thy brother'; and some rabbis interpreted this as an obligation to cancel all debts, whereas others thought it only referred to interest. And then, still more surprisingly, the earth itself was to have twelve months of rest, complete rest: it was neither ploughed nor sown nor harvested; only the strict necessities of life were to be taken from it.[47] Even the fruits of the vine and the olive were left by their owners, though the poor and the farm animals had the right to eat them:[48] in this rule may be seen both a charitable intention and agricultural foresight. Further-more, the Bible promised that the sixth year, the year before the sabbatical year, would be plentiful, and that no one would lack anything. This obligation seems strange to a man of the present day, but it was respected: the Chosen People formally promised to obey it in the days of Nehemiah,[49] and even in difficult times they kept their word, as, for example, when the garrison of Bethsura was obliged to ask the enemy for a truce because 'it was a year when the land lay fallow'.[50] This was a most exceptional custom; indeed, it was unique in history, and the Jews were very proud of it, as Josephus says. He also asserts that even the emperor had been obliged to renounce the raising of taxes during the sabbatical year; but this is far from sure. The Romans, for their part, certainly did not revere it; and for Tacitus it was but another proof of the nation's ingrained idleness. Obviously an institution of this kind aroused controversy, and the wealth of decisions and legislation in the Talmud proves that its application was far from simple. But at least the principle of the liberation of the slaves and the resting of the earth had been laid down, and that was already a great deal.

As for the year of jubilee, that is to say, the year which followed seven 'weeks of years', it was even more emphatic in its require-ments. Every fifty years all the slaves without exception were to be set free: all property that the poor had sold to the rich to pay their debts was to be restored to them, at a price that was strictly regulated by the Law. The intention was very fine; and if it had been carried into effect it would have set Israel far in advance of all other nations of the time as regards the question of slavery and that of the monopolizing of land, which was so serious a problem for the Romans, with their *latifundia*.[51] But its application would have caused great social and economic difficulties, so great, indeed, that the Talmud gives us to under-stand that the commandment of Leviticus was scarcely carried out at all. Little more was done than to sound trumpets all through the land 'on the tenth day of the seventh month' of the forty-ninth year. Yet at least God's words were not forgotten: 'Do not take advantage of your own fellow-countryman; each of you has a divine vengeance to reckon with; the vengeance of the Lord, your God.'

CHAPTER TWO

THE DWELLINGS OF GOD

The Temple, the 'shrine of the glory of God' – The Temple as Christ knew it – The Temple: its services and its symbolism – The synagogue: in no way a Temple – The services at the synagogue.

THE TEMPLE, THE 'SHRINE OF THE GLORY OF GOD'

Let us follow the ardent pilgrims, go with them into Jerusalem and accompany them as far as that place which is the goal of their long journey, a goal which has been made plain by their songs – 'How well, Lord, I love the house where thou dwellest, the shrine of thy glory! . . . Willingly would I give a thousand of my days for one spent in thy courts! . . . One request I have ever made of the Lord, let me claim it still, to dwell in the Lord's house my whole life long.' These are words in which the Psalmist, a score of times and more, describes the beauty of the Temple and the love that every pious Hebrew felt for it. The splendid building stood at the very heart of Israel's most urgent spiritual needs, just as it stood in the heart of the most sacred part of the holy city. In every possible respect, it was one of the essential realities of the life of the People of God.

There was but one Temple. 'The Single God has a single Temple,' says Josephus, 'a Temple that is for all men, as God is the God of all men.'[1] The temple which the Samaritans had built on Mount Gerizim was a mere heretical erection, an abomination before the Lord,[2] and the insignificant sanctuary that Onias had built not long before at Leontopolis[3] (it remained standing until AD 73) was no more than a paltry imitation, grudgingly tolerated in order not to offend the powerful Jewish colony in Egypt. The only valid sacrifices were those which were offered up to God on Mount Moriah.

The Temple of the One God had stood there for a thousand years, there in the very place where David and Solomon wished to

359

glorify the Almighty, who had allowed them to make Jerusalem the capital of their recently established kingdom.[4] From Solomon's day onwards, the Temple was so intimately linked with every event in the life of Israel, fortunate or unfortunate, that a history of the Chosen People is almost the same as a history of their Temple. In very early times, when the question of building a dwelling for Yahweh first arose, there was a certain amount of resistance. Some men thought that there was no point in destroying heathen sanctuaries,[5] as the Lord commanded them, merely to build just such a thing themselves: indeed, the prophet Nathan warned David against committing this error.[6] 'Thus saith the Lord,' said Isaiah, much later, 'Heaven is my throne, earth the footstool under my feet. What home will you build for me, what place can be my resting-place?'[7] But by the time the Temple had stood for ten centuries, a national institution and the symbol of the Chosen People's greatness, this current of extremely rigorous opinion had scarcely any importance left. May there have been some remaining Rechabites, those fanatical reactionaries, to reject it still, as they rejected everything that had to do with cities?[8] It is also possible that the Essenes may not have revered it entirely: but it was to be the most daring Christians who said, 'Yet we are not to think that the Most High dwells in temples made by men's hands'.[9] And in the meantime, Jesus Himself, respecting the traditions of His people, went to the Temple to pray there to His Father, as any other pious Jew would have done.

THE TEMPLE AS CHRIST KNEW IT

The Temple in which He prayed was not that which Solomon had built, that Temple whose building and whose splendour is so exactly recounted in the Book of Kings.[10] Solomon's Temple, alas, was sacked by Nebuchadnezzar at the time of the first siege of Jerusalem,[11] and then, eleven years later, in 586 BC, it was utterly ruined.[12] Nor yet was it the 'second Temple' which the prophets Haggai and Zechariah urged Zerubbabel to build after the return from exile: this was less imposing than Solomon's masterpiece, but as a sign of the resurrection of the nation and as the centre of the nation's resistance to paganism, it was very dear to the hearts of the Jews. Judas Maccabaeus cleansed it after its profanation by Antiochus Epiphanes, and then restored it as best he could, without, however, succeeding in disguising its almost ruined state, nor its relative poverty. No: the Temple of the

Gospels was quite new, so new indeed that it was still being built. It was not finished until the year 64, long after the death of Christ, and but a few months before it was destroyed for ever.

It was the temple of Herod, the 'third Temple', by which the Idumaean despot intended to outdo Solomon himself. He had doubled the flat surface of Mount Moriah by building great platforms upheld by vast substructures; he mobilised an army of workers, whose numbers varied from ten to eighteen thousand, caused ton after ton of materials to be brought and hesitated at no expense, so that Haggai's prophecy, 'Bright this new temple shall be, he tells you, as never the first was',[13] should be fulfilled by him. At first the Jews had regarded the tyrant's undertaking with distrust, but in the end they came round: had he not had a thousand priests taught how to build so that they might work on the sacred parts? And had not his architects arranged the order of work so well that the service of the Lord had never been interrupted for a single day? As each part of the old building was destroyed, so the corresponding part of the new was built.[14]

We may form a lively idea of this immense structure from the enthusiastic description of Josephus and from those in the Talmud; and the general impression is one that is made up of several different factors. There was something Babylonian about it, with its prodigious foundations, its complex of courts, its various levels and the Antonia fortress that flanked it. But the sanctuary itself was in the Graeco-Roman style – more Roman, indeed, than Greek, and aiming at a sense of the colossal which was later to find its full expression at Baalbek and Palmyra. With its colonnade, capitals and triangular pediment, it is a Heraclion in the Oriental manner, with a rather showy splendour. The Asiatic influence of the Hellenistic rulers and the capitals of Syria and Anatolia was also apparent. A finely carved white marble balustrade ran right round the roof, which was covered with gilded sheets of metal all provided with gleaming upright spikes, to prevent birds from perching on it. 'When the rising sun strikes it,' says Josephus, 'you would think that it was snow sparkling there.'[15]

Generally speaking, the plan was the same as that of the Temple of Solomon, but Herod had directed his chief architect to re-read chapters forty to forty-three of Ezekiel: in these, the prophet describes the future temple with extraordinary exactitude, the Temple of Israel restored to its glory, as he was shown it in a vision by a strange messenger, 'a man whose look dazzled the eye like bronze; he stood there in the gateway, holding a flaxen cord and a measuring-rod'.[16]

The way in was through gates pierced in the immense wall, deep covered passages, closed by double gates at each end: there were four on the west, on the city side, one of which opened on to the bridge of the Tyropoeon; two on the south; a single heavily fortified gate on the north; and two on the east, one of which was called the Golden Gate – some remains of it are still to be seen walled into the ramparts of the old town: the shafts of pillars and acanthus-leaf capitals. It was by this, or by the Shushan Gate, that our Lord must have left the Temple, during the holy week, when He went to the Mount of Olives.

Once through the gates, one found oneself in an immense rectangular court – the present court of the Mosque of Omar – whose longest side measured no less than five hundred cubits, or nearly two hundred and fifty yards: this was the court of the Gentiles, so called because everybody might go into it, men and women of the *goyim*, the unbelievers, and even heretics, excommunicated persons, those in mourning and those who were in a state of ritual uncleanliness. This 'outer temple', as Josephus calls it, was in fact a public place, the equivalent of Rome's forum or the agora at Athens. People came here to talk about important things or merely to gossip, to stroll about, pass the time of day or do business: yet it was forbidden to enter carrying a stick, wearing dirty shoes or with 'unclean' money about one; it was also forbidden to spit on the ground. All along the walls there were porticos, walks sheltered from the sun and the rain. In general their columns were thirty-six feet high; their roofs were made of cedar and their pavements of coloured stone. These porticos were renowned for their beauty: the eastern colonnade, which was called Solomon's Porch, was a triple row of two hundred and sixty-eight pillars, and it gave on to a magnificent view of the Mount of Olives and the valley of the Kidron. That which lay to the south was called the Royal Porch, and it was composed of three aisles, with the central one rising to a height of ninety-two feet on splendid Corinthian columns: its inspiration was entirely Greek, and it was worthy of its origin. These were the famous courts of the Temple, which rang with the arguments of the doctors of the Law, the cry of the sellers of doves and sparrows for the sacrifice of women after childbirth or healed lepers, and of the money-changers, who offered the pilgrims ritually clean coins against their pagan currency. There was a continual din; and just at hand, by the gates, the sellers of sacrificial animals kept their lowing and bleating merchandise. Christ's anger at the sight of this spectacle on the very threshold of the house of God is very easy to understand.

For in the middle of this fairground there stood the sanctuary itself, running from east to west and standing several yards higher than the court of the Gentiles. There was an excellent idea behind the planning of this, the idea of an upward progress, an ascent to that which is more holy. There were many levels, and to proceed from one to another it was necessary to go up a flight of steps: the highest level of all was that of the Holy of Holies. Fifteen steps, then, stood between the court of the Gentiles and the outer wall of the sanctuary: here, set against a balustrade there was the repeated inscription (two examples have been found) in Latin and Greek solemnly forbidding the pagans to go any farther: 'Anyone who is taken shall be killed, and he alone shall be answerable for his death.' It was therefore for the Jews only that the thirteen gates opened into the Temple properly so called: they were all splendid, but there was one more splendid than the others, and its decoration had earned it the name of the Beautiful Gate.[17] But there were still distinctions to be made: the women had only the right to go into the first court – though indeed they had plenty of room there, since it was no less than sixty-five yards in length. It was here that were to be found the thirteen recipients for offerings, which were commonly called the 'trumpets' because of the shape of their mouths:[18] the people were asked to throw in their shekels for the expenses of the Temple – wood and incense, for example – or by way of thank-offerings. The poor widow who gave not out of what she had to spare but 'her whole livelihood'[19] whom Christ held up as an example, must have stood there. At the four corners of the court of the women there were four 'chambers', that is to say, little courts which were used by the Nazarites[20] and the healed lepers, and for the wood for the altar, the wine and the oil.

From this a splendid flight of fifteen low curved steps led up to the court of the men, or the court of the Israelites: the gate that opened into it was particularly magnificent – the famous Nicanor Gate, which an immensely wealthy Alexandrian Jew had given to the Temple because of a vow that he made during a shipwreck. It was made entirely of bronze, and it was so heavy that twenty men were needed to open it: the sound of its opening was the signal that day had begun for the people of Jerusalem. This court was a long, narrow strip of some five yards by sixty-five which could become most uncomfortably crowded during the great celebrations: its only real purpose was to separate the men from the women during the services and thus to mark the superiority of the male in religious matters. Raised above this strip by no more than three steps and divided from it by a thin balustrade was the court of the priests, the beginning of the truly sacred area. It was from the little flight of steps in the middle of the balustrade that the high priest blessed the people.

This was the last enclosure, and it was very large, some sixty-five yards by nearly ninety: at the far end of it stood the sacred building, with its lofty colonnade, its soaring pediment and high above, the gilded spikes of its roof. On the north and the south of this court there were various covered halls, particularly the famous Hall of Cut Stone in which the Sanhedrim met,[21] and that of the spring, from which the water for the ritual ablutions was drawn: there were others for storing wood and incense and some which were used as stables for the sacrificial animals – one was even called the slaughter-house. How remarkable an appearance this holy court must have had! Here, as in the Temple of Solomon, were to be seen the great laver and the altar of burnt-offering. This was an enormous square block, thirteen feet high and its sides forty-seven feet long: it was made of unhewn stone, with its corners rising in horns and a whole system of gutters for carry- ing off the blood of the sacrifices. They stood there, the animals offered to Yahweh, tied to the eight cedar pillars, waiting to be pushed up the ramp to the level at which the sacrificial knife awaited them. They lowed and bleated, jostling one another: sometimes they resisted. Once dead, they were carried to the marble tables where they were cut to pieces, while their entrails were thrown into a continually blazing fire. It is difficult for us to imagine a religious ceremony accompanied by the sight of such butchery, a service in which the smell of incense mingles with the foul reek of animals just disembowelled and the stench of burning fat.

But the Temple itself was in utter contrast with the bloody turmoil of the court of the priests. It stood at a still higher level, at the top of twelve more steps, so that altogether between the pavement of the Temple itself and that of the court of the Gentiles there was a difference of nearly fifty feet in height. The colonnade of the Temple was ninety-eight feet high and a hundred and forty-seven feet wide, or a hundred cubits. There was no door, but there was a porch, and it was above this porch that Herod had wished to place an eagle made of gold, an action that provoked a furious riot.[22] As soon as one was within the entrance of the Temple the noise outside died away; the dullest mind felt the nearness of the divine. Next came the great door of the sanctuary, a cedar door covered with gold, with that famous golden vine above it which made the Romans laugh and say that Bacchus was the real god of Israel. This door was open throughout the day, but a magnificent curtain, embroidered in the Babylonian manner, hid its opening: it was no doubt this curtain or veil that was torn from top to bottom at the moment of Christ's death, as it is recounted by Saint Matthew:[23] this, at least, was the opinion of Saint Jerome and of Origen. Only the officiating priests, those whose turn it was, had the right to draw the veil aside and go on into the sanctum.

The sanctum: the focus of the attention, the expectation and the thoughts of the faithful. It was quite simple: a kind of long gallery panelled with the incorruptible cedar and cypress, and surrounded by rooms, three storeys of them, offices and lodgings, thirty-eight in all. It was divided into two by another curtain, a second 'veil of the Temple', or rather by a system of overlapping curtains that frustrated any impious eye. The first part, which was well lit by grilled windows, was the *hekal*, the sanctum properly so called: here stood the table for the shew-bread, the famous seven-branched candlestick which the legions of Titus carried off as booty and which is to be seen carved on a triumphal arch in Rome, and the gold-covered incense-altar, where the incense was placed twice every day. The second, almost dark, perpetually silent, was the *debir*, the very sacred place which was traditionally called the *qadosh haqedoshim*, the Holy of Holies. It was, of course, completely empty, with no statue, no symbol, nothing but the plain bare rock, the 'navel of the world', upon which the high priest, with his heart beating at being face to face with the invisible presence, set the incense, on one single day in the year, the Day of Atonement.

Thus built, the Temple of the One God was certainly one of the most majestic pieces of architecture to be seen at that time, and among the Jews it aroused a limitless admiration. Christ's own disciples bear witness to this.[24] Josephus goes on almost interminably about its splendour; and *The Letter of Aristeas*, one of the Jewish apocryphal books of the time of our Lord, speaking about an embassy said to have been sent by Pharaoh to the high priest, concludes that the Temple was even finer than the Egyptian monuments. 'The man who has not seen the Temple of Herod', said a rabbi of Babylon, 'has no idea of what a really beautiful building is.'[25] Yet what more can be said than that which the Bible itself has said, words that remain eternally true. 'Folly it were to think that God has a dwelling-place on earth. If the very heavens, and the heavens that are above the heavens, cannot contain thee, what welcome can it offer thee, this house which I have built?'[26] But Solomon also prayed that the Almighty's eyes 'should ever be watching, night and day, over this temple of thine, the chosen sanctuary of thy name; be this the meeting-place where thou wilt listen to thy servant's prayer. Whatever requests I or thy people Israel make shall find audience here; thou wilt listen from thy dwelling-place in heaven, and listening, wilt forgive.' The place where God gives audience to men: what higher thing can be said of the Temple of Jerusalem?

THE TEMPLE: ITS SERVICES AND ITS SYMBOLISM

There were thousands of priests to be seen in this wonderful building, and in its courts there were tens of thousands of believers. What were they doing there? Why did they come? The psalter gives the answer. 'See, I come into thy house with burnt-offerings,' says Psalm 65, 'to pay thee all the vows these lips have framed, this mouth has uttered, when trouble came upon me. Fat burnt-offerings of sheep shall be thine, and the smoke of ram's flesh; bullocks and goats shall be thy sacrifice.' And Psalm 137: 'I bow down in worship towards thy sanctuary, praising thy name for thy mercy and faithfulness . . . My purposes the Lord will yet speed; thy mercy, Lord, endures for ever, and wilt thou abandon us, the creatures of thy own hands?' To sacrifice and to pray: those were the reasons for coming to the Temple. The Christian mass was to keep these two basic elements, but it was to render the still material aspect of Israel's holy sacrifice spiritual and supernatural.

It must be confessed that the least appealing side of the worship in the Temple, to us, consists just in this bloody sacrifice and holocaust: its most striking characteristic leaves us with the impression of prodigious slaughter and the ceaseless flow of the blood of animals. Yet in these sacrifices we may discern two very ancient meanings, or rather intentions: the sacrificer thanks God by offering Him part of those things which His kindness has given, or else he pays for a sin, redeems it, by voluntarily depriving himself of some of these good things. But at the same time the believer, or the believing nation, since there were collective sacrifices as well as personal sacrifices, shows his desire to be at one with the Divinity: the covenant, the alliance, between God and Abraham was confirmed by a sacrifice. There was therefore no great feast without its sacrifice; and it was obligatory to come and make one on countless occasions of ordinary life – to obtain forgiveness for a sin, to remove ritual uncleanliness, to return thanks. The sacrifices were all classified: there were those with blood and those without, and the first were graduated according to the market value of the creature to be sacrificed – pigeons or doves, lambs, goats and rams, and finally bulls. If it were an expiatory sacrifice, the greater part of the animal's flesh was left for the priests and Levites. Among the sacrifices without blood, which were usually associated with the others, the chief were offerings of flour, in the form of a cake kneaded up with oil, and scented offerings, a mixture of incense, onyx, storax and galbanum, which was burnt every day upon the incense-altar. As it might be expected, an extraordinarily exact ritual governed the sacrifices in their smallest details, the choice of the animals, their qualities, the making of the shew-bread and of the incense. A brown mark on a lamb's head rendered it unfit to be a burnt-offering: the dough of the flour-sacrifice had to be utterly devoid of yeast. There are a very great many of these rules in the Bible, and the rabbis had produced enormous commentaries upon them.

Does this mean that Jewish piety was content merely to observe forms? It would be a very superficial and unjust judgment that would reduce the religion of Israel to a kind of bargaining with God. No doubt there were Jews, as there are Christians, who supposed that their sacrifice gave them some kind of claim upon Providence; but the true meaning of the sacrifice was that it was a prayer and an entreaty. Throughout the centuries the greatest prophets all reiterated that the material side of the burnt-offering was of no importance to God; the terrible Isaiah even said that He detested it: the man whom God looked upon with favour was the humble man with a contrite heart, who trembled at his Maker's word. Was Jacob saved by his sacrifices, or by his penitence and his anguished prayers? That inward religion which had been making a continual progress in Israel for hundreds of years could not be separated from the sacrificial aspect of worship: it gave sacrifice its true meaning. The rabbis insisted upon this point. One went so far as to cry, 'Honesty and justice are dearer to me than the Temple!'[27]

Besides, there were many worshippers who came not merely to offer sacrifices but to pray: Renan is mistaken when he says that there was nothing of an oratory, of a place of prayer, about the Temple. However surprising it may appear, one must think of the Temple and its courts as a place where there might be seen pious believers standing, only a few paces from the tables of the money-changers and the sellers of unblemished lambs, deeply plunged in meditation or prayer, unconscious of their neighbours, with their lips murmuring, their arms raised, or their bodies bowed in prostration. The Pharisee and the publican in Luke,[28] and the aged Simeon whom Joseph and Mary met in the court when they came to the Temple for the young mother's purification, were of this kind; and there were a great many others. In the very early morning, as soon as the thunderous noise of the opening of the Nicanor Gate was heard, many worshippers would hurry to the Temple to recite the *Shema* facing the sanctum of the Lord. At nightfall many came again for the 'evening offering'. Besides, the priests themselves brought the people in, made them a part of the religious ceremonies: in the morning, after the daily sacrifice of a lamb, a priest would come on to the steps that stood above the court of the men of Israel, recite the *Shema* aloud and then read a passage of the Law. At three in the afternoon there was a brief service in the same place, during which a priest uttered a short and beautiful formula of blessing upon the people, taken from chapter six of Numbers: 'The Lord bless thee, and keep thee; the Lord smile on thee, and be merciful to thee; the Lord turn His regard towards thee, and give thee peace.'

The Temple, then, was the place of the public and private sacrifices of the Chosen People, and the centre where they prayed: but this was by no means all. It was also the seat of the Sanhedrim,[29] that religious, political and judicial administration, which was at the same time the repository of tradition and a college of theology. And it was the seat of the financial administration which managed the immense sums that were produced by the religious taxation[30] and the offerings of the people. One of the tractates in the Talmud asserts that the gold from the *Corban*, the sacred treasury, 'filled three very large vats hollowed out in the underground part of the Temple after each collection'.[31]

Yet was the importance of the Temple as great at the time of Christ as it had been formerly? Perhaps not. To be sure, the Temple was revered: by expelling the traders from its courts, Christ Himself showed clearly how much He respected His Father's house. The Temple had its own branch of theology, as the place of the divine presence and the proof of the choosing of God's own people, a branch much worked upon by the rabbis. There was even a symbolism that centred about the Temple, and the apocryphal literature, Josephus and Philo give us the general ideas of it: the Temple was the centre of the world; it was also the world's image, and its furnishings represented the attributes of God. To a large extent these theories were based upon the cosmic visions of Ezekiel. It has been very rightly said[32] that the 'Sign of the Temple was, together with the Covenant, one of the essential realities of the Scriptures, and one of those by which they could be understood'. The Jews of the time of Christ were aware of this fact, and they attached the greatest possible importance to it. This is perfectly evident from the fact that one of the most serious indictments against Jesus was that He should have presumed to say, 'Destroy this temple, and in three days I will raise it up again'[33] – words which, in His mouth, conveyed an even greater idea of the Temple than that which the Jews had already formed, for He was likening the splendid building to His own body, the far more evident dwelling-place of a divine spirit: but they were words in which His judges could see nothing but blasphemy.

Yet it has been asked whether, by the time of Christ, this reverence and affection for the Temple were not to some degree diminishing, even among the most orthodox Jews. All the outward forms of worship were still preserved: but had they still a great deal of meaning? When, later, the Temple was threatened, there were great numbers of the faithful who gave their lives to defend it: but did they stand for anything more than a past that was already fading? A day was to come when the Temple lay in ruins, but when for all that the Jewish religion lived on, almost without worship in the sense of organized services; a religion centred about the observation of the Law rather than about sacrifice, because during the previous centuries another religious organization had come into being, not opposed to the Temple, but parallel with it; an organization whose importance was thenceforward primordial.

Josephus, speaking of the strange signs and tokens that appeared before the destruction of Jerusalem, tells of one – Tacitus also alludes to it[34] – that is full of significance: 'And upon the feast day called Pentecost, at night the priests going into the inner Temple to offer their wonted sacrifice, at first felt the place to move and tremble, and afterwards they heard a voice which said, Let us depart hence. Thus the God of Israel, announcing his departure, told his people that from then onwards he would not allow walls built with stone to enclose him.'

THE SYNAGOGUE: IN NO WAY A TEMPLE

The religious organization that had taken on so great an importance was that meeting, that assembly (assembly is the meaning of the name by which it was ordinarily called), which we have already seen playing a considerable part in the administrative and judicial life of the Jews, and even in their education: the beth ha-keneseth, the synagogue.[35] But those were only its secondary functions: the synagogue certainly governed the daily life of its members, appointed the local magistrates, saw to the teaching of the children and even constituted in itself a little university for the people; but it did so because it was primarily a beth ha-tefillah, a house of prayer, where men met to hear God speak by means of the words of His Law.

What was the origin of the synagogue? The most usual view is that it began in Babylon during the exile, as a substitute for the worship at the Temple, and that Ezra brought it into Palestine after the return. Others think that it was invented by Ezra and Nehemiah to strengthen their government. According to some rabbis and to some recent scholars, however, the synagogue is far older, going back before the destruction of the Temple by Nebuchadnezzar to the reforms of Josiah or even to those 'missions of Levites and priests' who went out in the time of King Jehoshaphat to teach the Law in all the cities of Judah, as we read in the Bible.[36] At all events, there are papyri that prove the existence of synagogues in Egypt in the third century BC, and Josephus speaks of one in Antioch under the descendants of Antiochus Epiphanes.[37] It is therefore exceedingly probable that, by the time our Lord went into the synagogue of Capernaum to take part in the traditional prayers and readings, Palestine and the whole of the Diaspora had for centuries been accustomed to that institution which has given Judaism its particular physiognomy right up to the present day.

Each village had its own synagogue, and each town had several. Any Jew who chose might erect one or, if he preferred, turn his own house into a synagogue. The associations of men of the same trade or profession had theirs, just as in the Middle Ages the guilds had their particular churches and chapels. The Jews of the Diaspora built special synagogues for themselves in Jerusalem, and it was in these that they met when they came on pilgrimage. The Acts mention some of these, as the synagogue of the Freedmen, of the Cyreneans and Alexandrians, and of those who came from Cilicia and Asia[38] – very reminiscent of the foreigners' churches in Rome: the French church of Saint Louis, for example, or the Spaniards' Saint James. It was said that there were between four and five hundred synagogues in Jerusalem, some of them standing in rows: in the same way the mosques, in the Mohammedan world, often bear no proportion to the number of a town's inhabitants.

'Synagogue' stood for both congregation and its place of meeting: in just the same way the church, the *ecclesia* or assembly, sat in a religious building which took on the same name. As far as it was possible, the synagogue was situated high up in the town or village, for, as the rabbis said, 'no man should live higher than the synagogue'. At the same time they did their best to set it by a source of fresh water, to make the ritual ablutions easier. In the Acts we see Saint Paul at Philippi in Macedonia going 'out beyond the city gates, by the river side, a meeting-place, we were told, for prayer'.[39]

The architecture of the synagogue was plain and adapted to the local style. The building, in essence, consisted of a rectangular hall, with columns dividing it into three aisles and supporting a gallery that ran round it, no doubt reserved for the women. There were three doors into the building, and in front of them a flight of steps. The more important synagogues, such as that of Capernaum, for example, which has been excavated, but which is some two hundred years later than that which out Lord would have seen, had a covered portico running along one side, with water for the ablutions flowing into a basin in the middle of it. Leaning against the outside wall of the synagogue there would be the little rooms that were used for the school or for lodging pilgrims. The decoration of the synagogues was also of the simplest kind: there might be palms painted on the plaster or the stucco, the five- or six-pointed star, and the seven-branched candlestick: at the time of Christ, the Mosaic prohibition against the representation of animals or men was still observed, though later it fell into disuse.

As the synagogue was in no way a place of worship, in the strict sense of the priestly celebration of a cult, it (like a mosque) had no altar. In something like a very small chapel, shut off by a curtain, there was the holy chest or cupboard, the *tebah*, which also had the ancient biblical name of *aron*, the ark.[40] Here were kept the precious scrolls, the Law and the *Sepharim*, preserved in a leather case and wrapped in linen. Beside them stood the horns and trumpets that were used for proclaiming fasts and holidays; and before the ark there were lamps continually burning. There was a platform or a pulpit for the reader who, turned towards Jerusalem, would comment upon the holy text. The congregation had benches or stools, and there was a great deal of competition for those in the front row: 'Their heart is set on taking the chief places at table and the first seats in the synagogue,' said Christ, in scorn of the Pharisees.[41] People would come early to take them, and some would go so far as to oil the *hazzan*'s palm to have them reserved. Before the service it was usual to sprinkle the floor with an infusion of mint, to purify the air.

The meetings and the subsidiary activities of the synagogue were managed by a small committee. It was entirely democratic: a council of ten elders, traditionally called 'the founders', elected one 'ruler of the synagogue', or sometimes three.[42] In any case, there was one president, one real leader, like Jairus at Capernaum. This was the system that the primitive Church adopted. The leader and the council decided upon the admission of proselytes, looked to the financial administration of the community, appointed the local judges and schoolmasters and arbitrated in the case of dispute between members of the congregation. The *hazzan* was their factotum: servant, sexton, beadle, caretaker, the person who carried out their sentences, and even, if there were no appointed schoolmaster, teacher. He was an indispensable man and he was aware of it: he was a person of real standing in the community. The wealthy synagogues also had employees of a lower grade: teachers, alms-collectors, trumpeters. But generally speaking these tasks were undertaken by members of the congregation; and it was the congregation, also, that provided those who officiated at the services.

THE SERVICES AT THE SYNAGOGUE

The services, too, were marked by their simplicity. The synagogue opened three times a day for those who wished to come and pray; and the *Shema* and the *Shemoneh Esreh* were recited. On the second and the fifth days of the week (that is, our Monday and Thursday), which were market-days and days upon which the judges sat, there was a more important meeting, one at which the assembled men from the countryside were reminded of the truths of the Law. But it was the Sabbath that was the chief day, and all the healthy members of the community then came to the main service of the week. Three men, or even one alone, were enough on the other days, but the Sabbath service required seven to officiate; and these seven were called in turn by the *hazzan*. In all cases the presence of ten men of Israel in the congregation was required before a meeting was complete under the Law.

There was nothing, nothing whatever, in this service that was in any way reminiscent of the service of the Temple: it had nothing sacrificial about it. Custom had fixed the order of its performance, and this was quite invariable. It began with prayers: the congregation, standing and facing towards Jerusalem, recited the *Shema* and the *Shemoneh Esreh*; or rather one man, standing before the ark, recited them aloud while the congregation prayed silently and then in a loud voice responded with the *Amen* that marked their souls' participation in the sacred words and their agreement with them. Any one of the faithful might fulfil this important office once he had come of age according to the Law, once he had become a man from the point of view of religion at the age of thirteen;[43] and it may well have been that our Lord prayed thus among His own people. After the prayers came the essence of the service, the reading of the Law. The *hazzan* took the holy scroll first from the ark and then from its two wrappings, and offered it to the first of the seven readers. True reading was required, and it was forbidden to utter more than one verse by heart. The text was divided into just 153 parts, so that the whole of the Pentateuch was read through in a little less than three years. (It was only later, and in Babylon, that these divisions were made three times as long, in order that the entirety of the Law should be read in one year.) The *hazzan* stood by the reader, and if in reading he made a mistake, the *hazzan* corrected it: if the *hazzan* saw that a passage was coming that might shock the people or make them laugh, he stopped the reader. Each verse, as it was read in Hebrew, was translated into Aramaic, so that everybody should understand. All lectors were allowed to make a commentary upon the text they had just read; and for this they usually sat down. The comments might take the form of a homily or of an exposition, a *midrash* whose length would vary according to the speaker.[44] There were some commentators of great reputation, just as there are well-known preachers today, and they were much in request in the synagogues: Jesus, and later Saint Paul, would certainly have been among these.

Added to this central body of the services there were various elements that might differ from synagogue to synagogue: these were further readings and prayers, analogous to the last Gospel and the prayers below the altar that in the course of time have been added to the mass. One of the readers then read the 'last lesson', which was always taken from the prophets. The man who did this was said to be *maphtir*, or to perform *maphtir*: it was thus that our Lord, one day in the synagogue of Nazareth, performed *maphtir*.[45] The reader quoted three verses at the most, which he had chosen beforehand and meditated upon – our Lord took two – and then he spoke upon them. In the same way it is very usual, in a Christian pulpit, to begin a sermon by a scriptural text, which is subsequently developed and commented upon. In the synagogue the commentary upon the prophets was obligatorily made in Aramaic.

Lastly the man who had recited the first prayers returned to the place before the *tebah* to say the final prayer. This ended with a blessing, which had to be said without a pause and without drawing breath. It seems that in some synagogues at this stage the people sang from the Book of Psalms, that famous biblical collection having become the Jewish communities' book of religious songs, as it was to be that of the Christian Church.

On going out, each person gave alms to the collectors who were in charge of the poor, and since gifts in kind were taken as well as money, the doorway and the porch of the synagogue were littered with a diversity of goods. The whole service would have lasted about an hour.

The importance of the synagogue and what it stood for in the life of Israel at the time of Christ cannot be over-estimated. What the town-hall and the church were for the mediaeval town, the synagogue was for the Jews. Everybody, without exception, went to the synagogue, not only for the services, but also for all administrative and judicial business. To be expelled from the synagogue was a disgrace; and thus, as Saint John observes, when the spreading of belief in Christ began to worry the Jews they came 'to an agreement that anyone who acknowledged Jesus as the Christ should be forbidden the synagogue'.[46] Throughout the Diaspora, it was the synagogue that ensured the Jewish community's union, kept faith alive, and prevented the believers from being swallowed up in the mass of heathendom.

It has been said that the synagogue set itself up against the Temple as its rival. But it does not appear that this was true at the time of Christ. The synagogue was then rather the Temple's antechamber, and it replaced the Temple for those who were unable to go up to Jerusalem. Yet it is quite certain that the spirit of the two institutions was not the same: on the one hand we have a solemn liturgical ritual of sacrifices, a most complex ceremonial; and on the other nothing but plain reading and prayers. In a way, the Christian mass was to be a blending of the two, the Eucharist being spiritually linked with the idea of sacrifice and the rest of the service being made up of prayers and reading, as in the synagogue.

In reality, once the synagogue had taken its predominant place in Jewish life, Israel no longer needed the Temple. What is more, the future of Israel's religion was assured from that moment on; for it could live independently of any sacred building and any particular worship. It had become a religion based on the Word, a purely doctrinal religion. Besides, it was in the synagogues themselves, to a large extent, that the innumerable commentators formed the tradition that the Talmud was to enshrine. The Romans might destroy the Temple, but it was beyond their power to prevent the Jewish communities scattered throughout their empire from meeting on the Sabbath day to pray to God and to read His Law. The Jews were conquered and dispersed, but Judaism survived because from that time onwards each believer carried within him the true essence of his worship: wherever there were gathered ten believers in the One God, there Israel was in existence, and God was with Israel. The true religious life had become spiritual.

When the scribe Ezra accustomed his people to meeting regularly for prayer after the return from the Babylonian captivity, did he foresee the prodigious consequences of his act?

CHAPTER THREE

THE MEN OF GOD

The priests and Levites in the service of the Temple – The doctors in the service of the Law – The Pharisees and the Sadducees – The Nazarites' vows and retreats in the desert – The monks of the Dead Sea.

THE PRIESTS AND LEVITES IN THE SERVICE OF THE TEMPLE
There was a popular saying in Jerusalem to the effect that there were as many priests and Levites in the Temple as there were stones in its walls. Clearly, this was a figure of speech, but it is nevertheless quite certain that an organization as vast and complex as the Temple needed a very considerable number of men, a number that may reasonably be set at twenty thousand.[1] The priesthood was unknown in the days of the patriarchs; under Moses it came into existence; and under the kings, when the Temple had become a national institution, the priests took on a very real importance. They were the necessary intermediaries for the offering of sacrifices to Yahweh, the guardians of His worship, and indispensable members of the community. The importance of the priesthood became even greater after the return from exile, since from that time onwards it was religion that gave Israel its governors, its institutions and the meaning, the reason, of its life. But at the same time a split occurred within the priesthood, resulting in a difference of rank. As Moses had organized it, there was one tribe, the tribe of Levi, that was set aside for the service of religion,[2] and therefore the priests were Levites: at the same time however, Aaron, the leader's brother, kept some of the higher priestly functions for himself and his family. Later, one of his descendants, Zadok, was confirmed in this pre-eminent position by King David. At the time of Christ there was a complete separation: the true priests, who all claimed to be Zadokites, were the only ones who performed the sacred rites, and the Levites were no longer anything but their servants.

Yet it was not the whole of the true or supposed race of Aaron,

377

the first sacrificing priest, that officiated in the Temple. Many of these Zadokites were now no more than poor and unlettered rustics, who would have looked strangely out of place in the holy courts. The powerful officials of the Temple had no sort of intention of sharing the tithes and the offerings with them: the Sanhedrim, whose task it was to choose from among the Zadokites 'unblemished' priests, took care to appoint none but 'respectable' people, well-to-do and nearly always from the same small number of families. The priesthood had thus come to form an exclusive caste, very conscious of itself and full of contempt for others, a caste to which one had to belong, as we have seen,[3] before one could pride oneself, as Josephus says, on one's noble lineage – a caste, furthermore, that was often hated by the common people and the lower clergy.[4]

The priests had to be physically perfect: 'No descendant of thine [Aaron's] that has any blemish shall be allowed',[5] said the Lord; and the unfortunate Hyrcanus lost the high priesthood the day his ears were lacerated.[6] Once they were chosen, they had to be 'set apart', consecrated in a scrupulously regulated ceremony:[7] after a ritual bath, they were dressed in white linen and anointed with oil; then they made three sacrifices, of a bull and two rams, laying their hands upon the animals before they offered them up. The consecrating priest took some of the blood of the third sacrifice, mixed with oil, and anointed the postulant upon the right ear, the right thumb and the right foot; then he set upon his hands and thighs some of the ram's fat, some unleavened bread and a cake of flour and oil, which were afterwards burnt upon the altar. These rites were of immemorial antiquity, and they were obviously intended to transmit supernatural powers to the new priest. Once consecrated, the priest enjoyed all kinds of privileges, of which by no means the least was that of living in the Temple and eating the sacrifices and the shew-bread. Their wives and their descendants also had this privilege: Herodias, who came of a priestly family, did not fail to profit by it. But on the other hand the Law had special punishments for priests who were guilty of certain offences or, even more, of certain ritual uncleanlinesses; and if their wives or daughters behaved themselves improperly, they too were very severely punished.[8]

At the head of the hierarchy stood the high priest. We have seen how real a diminution of power this office had suffered and how the Romans used it for political ends; but we have also seen how great an importance and standing it still possessed in the eyes of the people.⁹ And indeed everything was done to emphazise the consequence and the ritual holiness of the high priest. The ceremonies of his consecration were infinitely more solemn than those for an ordinary priest. The oil with which they were anointed was made from the fruit of chosen olive-trees, and it was impregnated with the most costly scents: the sacrifices that were made according to the Law might last for seven days. The high priest was the prime guardian of ritual cleanliness, and he had to conform to very strict rules; he might not marry a widow, a divorced woman or a former whore; he was never to eat game or the flesh of any animal that happened to be found lying dead (and therefore not killed in the manner prescribed by the Law); nor was he to drink wine before services, or trim 'the corners of his beard'. And he was to wear magnificent robes.

The Bible had rigidly laid down what the priests were to wear, and their clothes had not changed since very early times. In everyday life the priest was simply dressed: he wore drawers or a loincloth, a white tunic with a wide sash going three times round his waist, and a cone-shaped hat. But when he was officiating he wore special clothes: these consisted of wide and probably puffed-out trousers, a tunic woven from a single piece of cloth, with a wide opening at the neck and strings to hold it on at the shoulders, a waist-band four fingers wide, and a turban. The high priest wore the same clothes, but of a richer material, and in addition he wore the badges of his office. Thus his turban had two wide ribbons, one of which was violet: over his tunic he had a sleeveless surplice, which was also violet; and the lower part of this surplice was embroidered with pomegranates, between which there hung little golden bells that served both to keep demons off and to warn the people of the wearer's approach. Above the surplice came the ephod, which was like a chasuble, but shorter, and which was made of gold thread and crimson cloth: it was attached by gold shoulder-pieces, made of two pieces of onyx upon which the names of the twelve tribes of Israel were engraved.¹⁰ And lastly on his breast, linked to the ephod by rings of gold, he wore the pectoral, a cloth case decorated on the outside with twelve precious stones and containing the urim and thummim, holy objects that may have been prophetic dice or symbolic badges,¹¹ but whose use and meaning is unknown. For great ceremonies, the high priest's turban was replaced by a golden diadem engraved with the words 'Glory to God': but on the Day of Atonement he officiated wearing only a white tunic. The Romans had taken possession of these splendid vestments and they kept them in the Antonia fortress, giving them out only on the great holidays. The emperor Claudius was extremely popular among the Jews for having stopped this practice for a while. It may be added that the linen robes which the priests wore when they officiated were never washed, but always burnt: and that within the sanctuary itself all priests had to walk barefoot upon the paving perpetually wet with the water of the ablutions and that which washed away the blood of the sacrifices, and that they therefore caught special diseases, so that as we have seen[12] the Temple had its own specialists in upset stomachs.

The priesthood was divided into twenty-four classes, and this division dated from the reign of David.[13] Each class officiated in turn throughout one week. At a given day, all those whose turn it was went up to Jerusalem from all the places in Palestine where they lived for the rest of the time: these were preferably those cities which were traditionally called 'the cities of the Levites'. They spent the first night, which was always that of a Sabbath, in the court of the Temple, and then met to draw lots for the 'thirteen offices', that is to say, to determine who would immolate, who would prepare, who would clean, who would burn the incense, sound the trumpets, bless the people and so on. The class whose turn it was to officiate during the week undertook the control of the courts, the management of the Temple's goods and even the judgment of cases of open crime within the sacred precincts. Naturally, the most favoured classes were those whose turns of office coincided with the great feasts, for then the offerings and the sacrifices increased enormously: of the twenty-four classes, then, some were of higher standing than others. The first chapter of Saint Luke mentions all these customs in speaking of Zacharias, who was to be John the Baptist's father: he had been appointed as the burner of the incense at the drawing of the lots, and he was at the incense-altar when he saw an angel standing to the right of it. He belonged to the class of Abia, one of the most highly respected. If a great holiday fell to be celebrated during their week of duty, the priests whose turn it was, of course, performed the necessary sacrifices and ceremonies. During the days of the kings there had been specialized priests who were always at the Temple, serving as musicians or police officers or as those 'doorkeepers of the

Temple' who are mentioned in the Bible,[14] but whose functions are not clearly understood; but it is doubtful whether these permanently serving priests continued to exist. It has not been shown that there were any at the time of Christ.

In any case, these particular duties were performed by the Levites, who did a great deal more besides: they helped the priests to sacrifice, they jointed the animals and skinned them, they made the shew-bread and took care of the storehouses and the holy vessels: in short, they were the vergers and sacristans as well as the secretaries of the Temple administration and the clerks and ushers of the Sanhedrim. The position was reasonably well paid: it is said that the Levites received about half the whole tithe; and in addition they were exempt from all taxation. Generally speaking, a man would act as a Levite from the age of twenty-five to fifty, and then he would retire – having made his fortune, according to the tattle of the ungodly. But they belonged to a distinctly inferior social rank. They too may have been truly men of God, men consecrated to the Almighty, the substitutes for those first-born sons that all families should have given up to the service of the Lord according to the Law; but for all that they were looked down upon. They were forbidden upon pain of death to go into the sanctuary or touch the altar, which is a convincing proof that these descendants of the tribe of Levi were no longer held in any very high consideration. The Talmud even asserts that the priests in charge of policing the courts, particularly the superintendent of the Temple, who is mentioned in the Acts,[15] were very severe to the Levites. 'When the superintendent of the Temple makes his round of inspection, escorted by torch-bearers, and finds one of the Levites on duty asleep, he gives him a sound thrashing, and may indeed set fire to his clothes. One day a roaring noise was heard in the court and someone asked, "What is that?" "It is nothing," they replied, "nothing at all: only a Levite being beaten." '[16]

THE DOCTORS IN THE SERVICE OF THE LAW

There existed another class of men who also belonged to God, but not in a priestly capacity. They had nothing to do with worship; their dress differed in no way from that of the other Israelites; they ate none of the sacrificial meat nor the shew-bread; and although they did in fact make up a caste, they had no claim to belong to the blood of Aaron nor to the tribe of Levi.

These were the scribes, the direct descendants of those who appeared in the Jewish community just after the exile, and who played an ever-increasing part in it, devoting themselves more and more to the study of religious questions, to such an extent that towards the time of Christ the expressions 'scribe' and 'doctor of the Law' were commonly bracketed together, although to be sure not all scribes were necessarily doctors of the Law. As Father de Grandmaison says, they constituted at the same time a 'holy league' and an aristocracy of intellect and piety. It is a type unique in history.[17]

If they had been asked where they came from and why they thought themselves of such importance in Israel, they would have replied by quoting the verses from the Book of Nehemiah[18] which speak of their first establishment by Ezra, himself a scribe. Before 'the Great Assembly' of all the people, their forebears had 'read out of the book of the Law, clear and plain to give the sense of it, so that all could understand the reading'. One of the later scribes even said, 'The Law was received by Moses on Sinai, handed on by him to Joshua, by Joshua to the elders, and by the elders to the prophets, who entrusted them to the men of the Great Assembly'.[19] They had in fact taken a predominant place in the community, above all since the Maccabean wars, the national struggle against the Greeks. They had 'built a hedge round the Law',[20] and in doing so they had done a very great deal towards the defence of its doctrines against paganism, in the face of which they 'raised a barrier of fire'. They thought of themselves, and the people thought of them, as the guardians of a sacred trust, as men who would fight to protect it. It has been shown over and over again that all the institutions of this nation were essentially religious: in this nation, therefore, the outstanding experts in religious matters necessarily played a decisive part. The doctors of the Law left the great standing and the privileges of the Temple to the priests: they also left political intrigue to the upper clergy, who had but too great an appetite for such employments, and used their influence in a less spectacular but more efficient way. As we have seen, it was they who provided the true intellectual life of the nation and moulded its thought; it was they who controlled education, and particularly the higher education; it was they who named the judges and who fixed the jurisprudence; it was they who uttered the commentaries upon the Law in the synagogues, and the importance of the synagogical form of worship had increased with the increasing importance of the doctors of the Law. They had become members of the Great Sanhedrim, and in it they had that influence which ability always exercises in an assembly. Thanks to them, the famous council was not only a governing body and a supreme court, but also a theological college, an academy for religious questions,[21] in which the most lofty spiritual problems were studied – and not these alone, but also very often the humble and mundane application of the divine precepts. Indeed, they had their word to say upon everything.

How did a man become a doctor of the Law? In rather the same manner that one now becomes a professor in a university. Any Israelite at all might set out to win this title, whether he were rich or poor, of high birth or a working man's son. It will be remembered that most of the rabbis worked with their hands.[22] If any man felt the vocation to devote himself to the study of the Law he would go and join one of the schools that surrounded the most famous doctors. For teaching was an obligation of which the masters were often reminded: it was their duty to 'gather disciples'. Many of these masters taught in the courts of the Temple, under one or another of its porches. The students, sitting round the rabbi, would listen to his lessons for several years on end, doing their best, by the aids to memory that have already been mentioned,[23] to retain the least of his words: they treated their master with the utmost respect, escorted him as he walked about and took his side in arguments with the leaders of other schools. It does not appear that there was any giving of an official degree or doctorate at the end of these studies: at some given moment the rabbi would judge that his pupil could now stand on his own feet and that now, in his turn, he could preach and make commentaries. But from then onwards, although the Holy Scriptures laid no particular duty or restriction upon the doctor, he was to live publicly according to the requirements of the Law that he taught. The rabbis were to be known by the austerity of their clothes, by their habit of almost invariably wearing phylacteries on their forehead and their hands – phylacteries that were larger than those for ordinary people – by their grave, meditative and often pithy manner of speaking, and, in principle, by their pure and honest lives. Some carried zeal very far: there were those who were known to fast for three hundred days in the year and to recite a hundred benedictions every day.

They lived in the Law, and for the Law. It is not nearly enough to say that they studied the Bible: they scrutinized it in its smallest parts and analysed it with the utmost earnestness, to draw from it all the messages that it contained: for these were the messages of life. There was nothing in the nature of a scientific interest here. The doctors' immense knowledge of the holy books had nothing in common with what we call erudition. They studied the Law in order that the people whom they guided might obey the commands of the Mosaic injunctions in every aspect of their lives – that the people might be specifically Jewish, that is to say, proof against all pagan influence, in even the most humble details, even those that were apparently quite trivial. It was for this reason that the doctors stated that 'the study of the Torah was a greater matter than the building of the Temple', and that loving the holy text was even more important than honouring one's father and mother.[24] From their point of view (and history has proved them right) it was the Torah that ensured the existence of Israel. What more need be said to justify the work of the doctors who devoted themselves to it?[25]

To a Western mind the work in question may appear of doubtful value: it may even appear eccentric and incomprehensible. The ways in which the rabbis scrutinized the sacred text are indeed as remote as possible from logical analysis and rational exposition. One must throw Descartes aside if one is to enter into the state of mind of men for whom the immediate, concrete meaning of a text was very much less important and revealing than its metaphorical and supernatural sense, men for whom no occurrence or word had any real bearing except as a manifestation of the divine.

The often very fine-spun commentary of the *midrash*, the never-ending dialectic of the *pipul*, the expositions by 'the letter, the allegory, the homily and the mystery', which were called 'exegeses of Paradise', the commentaries according to the 'seven operations' laid down by Rabbi Hillel, and all the rest, can only be understood in this context. The same applies to the rabbis' minuteness, which sometimes seems astonishing. In a universe in which everything is sacred, everything is subject to the will of God: for this reason the doctors of the Law paid attention to details of human behaviour that are scarcely ever mentioned in theological treatises.[26]

We are well acquainted with the teaching of the doctors: it

forms the body of the Talmud – 'the Instruction' or 'the Recitation'. This extraordinary work, extraordinary both in its size and its contents, is made up of two great divisions: the first is the Mishnah, which is in classical Hebrew; it is the basic canonical legal code, and its sixty-three tractates cover the whole field of human activity. The second is the Gemara, an immense commentary upon the Mishnah; it was written in Aramaic, because of changes in time and place; and it exists in two recensions, that of Jerusalem and that of Babylon. The Midrash, a homiletic commentary upon the Bible, whose very particular method of production has already been mentioned,[27] was also considered part of the Talmudic literature. In its present form the Talmud is considerably later than the time of Christ, for the Mishnah was codified by Rabbi Judah the Prince in the latter part of the second century, the Gemara was drawn up in the fourth century, and the Midrash came into existence between about AD 350 and 1200. But there is no sort of doubt that the matter of the Talmud is far older. In the Mishnah there are gathered the teachings of the great Rabbi Hillel, whom Jesus might have seen in Jerusalem when He was a child, for Hillel did not die until the year 10 of our era, being then more than a hundred. The Gemara which is called that of Jerusalem was drawn up very shortly after the ruin of the holy city in AD 70 by the doctors of the Law who had taken refuge in the neighbourhood of the Sea of Galilee. The Talmudists assign teaching to one of two headings; they recognize two quite separate methods: the *Halachah*, dogmatic pronouncement or instruction, and the *Aggadah*, which is teaching by parable, figure, anecdote, historical reference or legend. Both these forms are to be seen in the teachings of the rabbis of the time of Christ; and indeed they are to be found in His own. Bearing in mind the great importance of memory in Jewish life,[28] one may say without much risk of error that all the information contained in the Talmud, with the possible exception of that which is directly connected with particular customs, shows us the thought of the doctors of the Law as it was transmitted by oral tradition for two centuries and more before Christ and as it was preserved long after His time.

We know many of these doctors who were contemporaries of our Lord. The two greatest rabbis of the first century before our era, Hillel and Shammai (those bitter opponents), were dead before the public ministry of our Lord began, but many of their disciples and competitors were very well known. Hillel's grandson Gamaliel was certainly teaching when Christ came to the Temple: he was a gentle, moderate man, whose weak constitution in no way diminished his holy zeal. His rival was the fierce Jochanan ben Zakkai: he was seventy, but he was to live on for another fifty years, filling his hearers with the most passionate enthusiasm and piety. There was also Rabbi Eleazar ben Asaria, a descendant of Ezra, who from being a priest had become a scribe: it was said that he was able to improvise three hundred amplifications of any given scriptural theme. There was Rabbi Joshua ben Chanania, who, as a very small child, had carried his cradle into the synagogue so that he might hear the Word. And then again, living on a mountain above the lake of Tiberias, there was Rabbi Yossi the Galilean, a famous interpreter of the prophets.

An over-hasty reading of the Gospel might easily induce Christians to judge these doctors harshly. One has a tendency to confuset hem with those Pharisees of the worst kind whom our Lord so often criticized; but this is not quite fair, since a doctor of the Law was not necessarily a Pharisee. It may undoubtedly be held that most of them were Christ's enemies at His trial because their spiritual attitude was utterly opposed to His, yet it is not certain that this was true of all. That Nicodemus whom Saint John shows as so candid and well-intentioned was a member of the Sanhedrim, and it certainly appears that he was a doctor of the Law.[29] And even among the Pharisaic doctors we find a Gamaliel. They were virtuous, profoundly religious men, and they formed an *élite* without the Chosen People could never have been what it was in the years that were to come.

For the part played by the doctors of the Law was to prove of the very first importance in the history of Israel. Their teaching brought into existence a 'Palestine of the spirit'; and from that time onwards any Jew, even if he were forced to leave the Holy Land, could send down his roots into this spiritual country. The Talmud was the product of their labours: and 'the greatest benefit that the Talmud conferred upon the Jewish people was to make them understand that the end of the Temple did not mean the end of their religion'.[30]

THE PHARISEES AND THE SADDUCEES

Both the priests of the Temple and the doctors of the Law were in differing ways, yet both in the full meaning of the words, men of God: but all the Israelites, from the highest to the lowest, also thought of themselves as men of God, in some degree. For they all belonged to God's own people, and they were all partners in the covenant and keepers of it. It is only by taking this all-embracing religious conception of life into account that one can understand the very well-known divisions of the Jews of the time of Christ into two groups, the Pharisees and the Sadducees.

Were these sects? In a way they were: the members of each group stood by one another, and were violently opposed, after the manner of sectaries, to those who belonged to the other. Yet neither group detached itself from the community; and this detachment is a necessary characteristic of a sect. Were they parties? Again, in a way they were, for they had very distinct political attitudes; yet political interests were not of the first importance for either the one or the other – and in this they differed from the group called the Herodians, whose whole conduct was dictated by their collaboration with the Romans and their hangers-on. Was it a question of different schools of theology? This is certainly arguable, since a difference in their concepts of religion and its defence was at the basis of their opposition to one another: but these schools extended their differences to matters that were entirely outside theology, and the differences affected the great body of the people, to whom the Pharisees and the Sadducees represented the two main currents of opinion. The two groups were at the same time sects, parties and religious movements.

Let us look back to the second century BC, to the time when the Jews united under the Maccabees to oppose the Seleucids' threat of paganization. When it had been a question of preventing the Greeks from imposing their idolatry upon the People of God, all the Jews had been in complete agreement. But when victory was won, two trends of thought became apparent. Although the Asmonean kings and high priests, the descendants of the Maccabees, had their origins in the 'resistance', they felt the Graeco-Roman world hemming in their little community on all sides, and they thought that the most prudent course was to maintain relations with it, at the same time yielding to it in no essential point whatever, and firmly maintaining the principles that ensured Israel's safeguard. This attitude was primarily concerned with the preservation of the Jewish community, whose existence might have been jeopardised by another war: but the mass of the people, who had provided the great majority of the fighting-men in the war of liberation and the *hasidim*, the 'pious men' of the time of the Maccabees, were utterly opposed to it. They said that it was impossible to defend the faith if one allowed any intercourse whatever with the heathens: a man was to live as a Jew, among other Jews, and to cast away as unclean and irreligious everything that was not Judaic. This was neither an illogical attitude nor one devoid of elevation of mind. The true believer was to separate himself from all pagans and from all those who were suspected of allowing themselves to be contaminated by paganism; and those who held by this harsh refusal derived their name from it – *perushim*, the separated, and hence the Pharisees. Their opponents, the Sadducees, had first been so called by way of a nickname, which may perhaps have meant 'the righteous', or possibly 'the sons of Zadok', after Solomon's high priest, because the upper clergy belonged to this party; and the nickname had become part of the language.

The essential difference between these two groups, therefore, lay in their response to the vital question, 'How, in the midst of a pagan world, are the People of God to be preserved?' 'By intelligence, diplomacy and prudence,' replied the Sadducees. 'By being absolute, downright and ready to risk everything,' said the Pharisees. But this was not all. They were also in disagreement upon what it was that they had to guard – upon the nature of their sacred trust. 'Let us keep to what is essential', said the Sadducees, 'to the written Law that Moses gave us, and to its six hundred and thirteen great principles: and where it is mute, let us act according to the requirements of the time.' 'Not at all,' cried the Pharisees. 'We must cause the laws of religion to permeate the whole of human life, and to do this we must complete the written Law with the tradition, the oral Law, that the scribes have been continually formulating since the return from exile.' An attitude, by the way, which explains the fact that most of the doctors of the Law were Pharisees.

It may be said, then, that in religious matters the Sadducees were more conservative than the Pharisees, since they rejected all additions to the written Law; but that in political matters they were less conservative. The Pharisees have often been called traditionalists; but for this to make sense the word 'tradition' must be understood as referring to the oral Law.

At the time of Christ, it appears that the Sadducees drew their members chiefly from the well-to-do class, the higher officials, wealthy merchants, land-owners and priests. They were in possession of the Temple and they controlled the Temple worship and the sacrifices; at the same time they were in command of the tithes and therefore of the financial system. It was from among the Sadducees that the statesmen and the diplomats were chosen – the men who maintained the essential relationships with the occupying authorities, relationships without which the country could not have carried on. Would it be fair to term them assimilated Jews? No doubt some of them, and particularly the most wealthy, members of the very powerful royal families, allowed themselves to be more or less won over by pagan influence; but there is nothing whatever to lead one to think that these formed the majority. From the political point of view, it would be equally unjust to confuse them, as their opponents were very apt to do, with vulgar collaborators or traitors. In their hearts they were opposed to the pagans, but for the good of the country they wanted to make the best of the situation that had been brought about by the coming of the Romans. The same considerations had led them to support Judas Maccabaeus when he wished to call in the Romans to help him against the Greeks, a measure that the *hasidim* opposed.[31] Furthermore, it must be observed that the Sadducean attitude had as its theological basis the universal aspect of the Jewish faith, that universalism whose early expression is to be found in such biblical books as those of Jonah and Tobit. And did not the spread of the Diaspora necessarily call for peaceful coexistence with the pagans?

In the strictly religious sphere the Sadducees held by the written Law alone; and some even insisted upon the Pentateuch and nothing more: they therefore rejected everything that was not formally laid down therein, everything that appeared to them a superaddition. As we have seen,[32] they considered the idea of resurrection as a dangerous novelty, and they thought the same of the beliefs concerning angels and demons that had come to have so much importance in religion and that fanatical Messianism which had gone to so many heads. In certain very remarkable passages Josephus states that they did not believe that God intervened in human affairs (they therefore rejected grace); that for them 'the choice between good and evil depended upon man's free will'; and that according to each man's choice so his soul would be rewarded and survive or be punished and disappear.[33]

From this the Sadducees would appear to be the ancestors both of the Pelagian heretics and of the rationalists. Perhaps it would be better to say that they were orthodox Jews, very little inclined to mysticism and even, indeed, somewhat indifferent.

Their behaviour in the life of the community was generally censured. This was not because they were more reactionary and conservative than their opponents: far from it, since as upholders of the ancient beliefs they called, for example, for the strict application of the rules of the sabbatical year,[34] the liberation of slaves and the cancellation of debts, whereas the Pharisaic rabbis, even the great Hillel, were so conscious of the difficulties that would arise from this that they allowed various compromises with the principle. But according to Josephus they were blamed for 'their harsh conduct' and for being haughty and even brutal towards the common people – at least, that was what the common people said.[35] And their contemptuous, disillusioned kind of wisdom also earned them dislike. It may be that as their influence had declined, so they had progressively grown harder: under such rulers as John Hyrcanus and Alexander Jannaeus, when the Jewish state had been expanding, they had been all-powerful; but since the conquest of Palestine by Pompey they had been continually losing ground, and the people's hatred for the Romans steadily strengthened their adversaries. They were in agreement with the Pharisees, no doubt, in taking up a hostile attitude with regard to Jesus, and this for many reasons: His message broke with the unalterable written Law; they were utterly opposed to His Messianism; and there was a danger that His movement might disturb their relationships with Rome. But afterwards they lost all influence, and they were reduced to helplessly watching their people's progress towards a disaster that their shrewd policy would undoubtedly have avoided.

As early as the time of Christ, the Pharisees were far more important than their rivals. There had been a period when the Asmonean princes tried to break their strength, and Alexander Jannaeus had crucified eight hundred Pharisees at once;[36] but those days were long past, and now their influence was continually increasing. Their organization may be quite fairly compared with that of a political party in a modern democratic state. The true Pharisees, those who were really 'separated', or as we should say the party-members, did not number more than between five and perhaps ten thousand: Josephus reckons that those who refused to take the oath to the emperor amounted to six thousand.[37] But a large part of the Jewish people, and particularly the poorer members of it, shared their point of view, and as we should say 'voted Pharisee': this allowed the Pharisees to make the somewhat exaggerated claim that they represented the whole nation. The party-leaders were recruited from among the scribes and the doctors of the Law; but this does not mean that all scribes and doctors of the Law were Pharisees, although, reading the Gospel, one might be tempted to suppose that this was the case. The chiefs of the Pharisees even counted some priests among their numbers. Of course, on the other hand, not all Pharisees were scribes and doctors of the Law either: the vast majority did not possess the necessary religious learning. But they were all convinced that they represented the finest part of the Chosen People, that they alone possessed the truth, and that they alone were true to the Covenant. From this arose their excessive pride and their ostentatious contempt for all who did not follow the 'party-line', and even more, for the wretched *am-ha-arez*, who did not possess the true faith.[38]

In politics, they were fiercely opposed to the pagan occupiers and to the petty rulers the Romans had set over the Chosen People. But since theirs was an essentially religious opposition, it took a violent form only when religion was threatened: for example, when Herod had his sacrilegious eagle placed over the Temple gate, they raised a riot against him to have it taken down. On several occasions they sent delegations to Rome to ask the conquerors to administer the country directly, so that the Jews should not have to suffer the rule of the Asmoneans, won over to the Sadducees, or that of the imperfectly circumcised Idumaean kinglets. It would be a mistake to think of them as a kind of organized resistance, prepared for violent direct action. There certainly was such a movement, that of the Zealots,[39] whom one might describe as forming the extreme left wing of Pharisaism, and who, coming under the domination of those fanatical killers the *sicarii* some time after the death of Christ, were to push matters on and on until they reached the last violent outbreak. At the time of Christ these people, this section of opinion, were of very little importance, and they were very far from carrying with them the whole mass of the Pharisees and their sympathizers. The Pharisees did not attack the Romans: they ignored them. They behaved exactly as the 'Guardians of the Gates', the *Natourci*

Karla and the *Shomre Hahomoth*, do in Israel today, who, since they do not recognize the Jewish state, suspecting it of over-much kindness for the *goyim*, refuse to have identity-cards and rarely leave the Mea Shearim district, where they all live together.[40] Besides, under Herod and then under the Roman procurators, no opposition could be anything but verbal or theoretical: it was only later that the movement was to take on such proportions and culminate in the revolts that were the nation's final ruin. And yet as early as the time of our Lord, if a Pharisee had been obliged to choose between the salvation of the Jewish state and that of Israel's religion, it was more than likely that he would have chosen the latter.

The Pharisees undoubtedly possessed a deep, firm and exacting faith – a faith that would not compromise. The word 'Pharisee' is often used as if it meant the same as 'Tartuffe' or 'hypocrite', but this is utterly mistaken. The doctrine which the doctors had taught them, and which they accepted, was that religion should inform and govern everything in Jewish life, so that the entirety of that life should remain specifically Jewish. A legal system, a jurisprudence, was drawn from the Law, a system that was to be obeyed in all circumstances, in the practices of daily life as well as in all civil, judicial and social relations. The Pharisees, then, granted that the religious Law was in a state of continuous development: although they were exceedingly strict about doctrine, they were at the same time progressive in the application of it; and it was for this reason that they went so far as to say that tradition, the product of the doctors' thought, was of greater importance than the priesthood or the kingship, and that it was as sacred as the text of the Torah itself. Tradition, thus understood, naturally embodied the more recent beliefs that the evolution of doctrine had brought into existence: the resurrection of the flesh, punishment after death, the intervention of good or wicked angels in the life of men, and an ardent Messianism which for many, no doubt, had a narrowly mundane application. Josephus says that 'they threw themselves upon Providence', or as we should say they acknowledged the part that divine grace plays in human life. Josephus also granted that they had 'kindly feelings and a wish for good mutual understanding', in other words, a true charity.

Yet it must be observed that within the Pharisaism of the time of Christ there were sharply opposed currents of opinion. In Pharisaism, as in all highly developed movements, a right and a left wing had come into being, the one interpreting the Pharisaic principles rigidly, the other in a more liberal manner. At the time when Christ came into the world, the leaders of the two schools of thought were the famous doctors Shammai and Hillel. Whenever there was any question of the application of the Law, these two were in utter disagreement: indeed, three hundred points upon which they were opposed had been recorded. Breadth of mind was the mark of the *Beth Hillel*; rigid exactitude that of the *Beth Shammai*. There is an anecdote that shows the difference between the two very clearly: one day a pagan came to see Rabbi Shammai and said, not without some degree of irony, that he would become a Jew if the rabbi were capable of explaining the Law to him while he, the pagan, could stand there balancing upon one leg; the severe doctor's reply to this strange request was a sharp blow with a ruler. The pagan went on to Hillel, and Hillel answered him, 'What is unpleasant to thyself that do not to thy neighbour: this is the whole Law'.[41] It seems that as early as the time of Christ the school of Hillel was tending to prevail over that of Shammai, and according to the Talmud this tendency later became more pronounced.

But although Pharisaism had grown to such proportions, it was nevertheless going through a crisis; or perhaps it would be more exact to say that it was for this very reason, that it was because it had become a numerous party, that it was going through this crisis – a party that had admitted members of a dubious integrity, who had joined for reasons that had nothing to do with the faith. In an apocryphal Jewish book of the first century AD called the *Testament* or the *Assumption of Moses*,[42] a strict and disillusioned Pharisee denounces 'these vile and impure men who claim to be the only pure, the only righteous beings, but who are nothing but monsters of pride': it is quite clear that he is referring to those who were called 'dyed Pharisees'. There was a proverb which the Talmud has preserved and which said, 'There are seven kinds of Pharisee: the "what do I get out of it?" Pharisee; the "I look the part" Pharisee; the "oh my poor head" Pharisee, who walks along the street with his head down so as not to see the women and who bangs against the wall; the pestle-Pharisee, who goes about so bent that he looks like a pestle in a mortar; the "what is my duty so that I may do it?" Pharisee; the "I do one good deed every day" Pharisee; and lastly the only real Pharisee, the one who is a Pharisee from fear of God and out of love for Him'.[43] It is an amusing piece of satire, and it brings the characters thoroughly to life. It also gives one a clearer understanding of our Lord's criticisms.

As everyone knows, the Gospel devotes a considerable amount of space to the Pharisees. Christ often came into contact with them, and He often speaks of them. Every Christian will remember the terrible words of chapter twenty-three of Matthew: 'Woe upon you, scribes and Pharisees, you hypocrites that shut the door of the kingdom of heaven in men's faces . . . Woe upon you, blind leaders . . . Serpents that you are, brood of vipers, how should you escape from the award of hell?' The denunciation goes on for two pages. What does He charge them with? Essentially with three things: with being liars, 'whited sepulchres', men who lay burdens upon others' shoulders that they did not carry themselves. Yet it may reasonably be held that his criticism was levelled at the 'dyed Pharisees', those who belonged to the first six kinds of Pharisee in the proverb, and not against the last. Christ's next reproach is more serious, and it is aimed at the Pharisees' pride (it does indeed appear that this fault was shared by all the members of the group), their love for the first seats in the synagogue and their claim to be the guides and the spiritual masters of Israel. Lastly, and above all, He charges them with being ritualists, with busying themselves with foolish trifles like the tithe of the dill or the cummin and with neglecting the essential, the living faith, the love of God and one's neighbour – in short, with being just what they were, men for whom the tradition counted more than the spirit. And this criticism went to the heart of the matter, to that which was inevitably to arouse an implacable enmity between the Pharisees of the first six categories and our Lord.

Yet the relationships of Christ with the 'separated men' were not confined merely to this antagonism. He Himself acknowledged the learning of the Pharisaic doctors;[44] and He would hold discussions with them, even when He knew that there were hidden traps in their questions.[45] More than this, He even had friendly contacts with some of their number,[46] and accepted their invitations to eat with them.[47] That Nicodemus who behaved as a secret supporter of our Lord was one of the leading Pharisees, and a member of the Sanhedrim.[48] Still more, when Herod Antipas, uneasy at Christ's preaching in his country, thought of making away with Him, it was some of the Pharisees who came to warn Him of the danger,[49] an action which in any case was quite in agreement with their general opposition to the Romans and their tools. It is perfectly clear that at the time of Christ's trial the Pharisees were His most bitter enemies; and yet once He was dead, many of them sympathized with the new doctrine. Everyone knows that the greatest of the Gospel-bearers was, together with the apostles, Saint Paul, and that he, as he said himself,[50] was a Pharisee and his fathers were Pharisees before him: and everyone will remember that striking passage in the Acts[51] where the Rabbi Gamaliel, 'who was held in esteem by all the people', and who had been the master of the man who was to become the apostle Paul, took up the defence of the Christians before the Sanhedrim with the most unusual courage.

The relationships between Pharisaism and Christianity are therefore far more complex than is commonly supposed. The Talmud records many sayings of Pharisaic rabbis, particularly those who followed Hillel, which are remarkably like some that are to be found in the Gospel; but there is no argument whatever to be founded on this, since no one can show that they are not later than Christ's teaching. Yet it cannot be denied that among the Pharisees there were men for whom the life of the spirit was something quite other than a mechanical obedience to precepts; and that even among the others (apart from the 'dyed Pharisees' and other 'whited sepulchres') there were certainly many sincere believers whose piety was respectable, even though they were unable to understand in time the great message that gave the lie to their narrow traditionalism, their formalism and their ritualism:[52] for 'the written law inflicts death, whereas the spiritual law brings life'.

THE NAZARITES' VOWS AND RETREATS IN THE DESERT
A deep piety and a wish to devote oneself to God could take other forms than joining the Pharisees or becoming a priest. Many Israelites, both men and women, made vows, just as Christians make them still, in order to obtain a favour or by way of giving thanks for a grace received. Generally speaking, these vows, which were made with far from disinterested motives, consisted of promising some offering or sacrifice. The vow of the *corban*, which is mentioned in the Gospel,[53] required that the person who took the vow should give the Temple some possession, such as a house, and this had the effect of preventing it from being

put to its ordinary use and from being given to another person, even to one's own parents if they were in need of it: one was allowed, however, to 'redeem the vow of the *corban*'. The Law had laid down rules concerning vows, and the doctors had dealt with all the cases in which vows might or might not be considered valid: a girl, a boy who was a minor, or a married woman, for example, could not take any vow whatever without the express consent of the father of the family.

There were other vows that were more concerned with the realities of the spirit. The person who took these would promise to behave according to certain requirements, at least for a given time. The Book of Numbers[54] had provided for the case of those men or women 'that would be set aside for the Lord'. These had a particular name: they were called Nazarites, which is derived from a Hebrew root that has both the sense of abstaining and of consecrating oneself. The custom was of great antiquity in Israel – it is mentioned as early as Amos[55] – and there were certainly Nazarites at the time of Christ, since one of the little courts in the corner of the great court of the Temple was reserved for them.[56] A whole tractate of the Mishnah is given up to them. Usually the Nazarites took their vows for a limited period of time: the doctors said that one month was the least that could be allowed. They had to take a threefold oath; that of abstaining from wine and any intoxicating drink, even wine-vinegar, from grape-juice, fresh or dried grapes and even 'the pips and the skins'; that of not 'passing any razor over his head until his consecration to the Lord has been completed; the growth of his hair is a sign of dedication', and lastly that of not going near any dead body, even that of his 'father or mother, brother or sister'. The Nazarite's consecration to God therefore included both the practice of certain abstinences and the promise of ritual cleanliness, a curious mixture which shows the custom's ancient origin: for Samson's strength had been in his hair, which was also a sign of his fidelity to Yahweh, and when Delilah had cut it off, he was helpless.[57] At the time of Christ, the rabbis who followed Hillel allowed that a Nazarite might, if there were no one else available, bury a body that the Law required to be buried, as, for example, that of an executed man upon a cross, for it was not to be left hanging overnight.[58] Why did the Nazarites take their vows? To win some particular grace or favour? Perhaps. To preserve a bodily integrity for the service of God? No doubt this too was a motive. But sometimes they did so from asceticism and from truly spiritual motives. Thus the tractate *Nedarim*[59] tells the touching story of a wonderfully beautiful young shepherd who, having gazed at himself like Narcissus in a pool, felt himself beset by passion, and 'not wishing to take pride in a flesh fated to turn to worms and creeping things', ran to the Temple to have his hair cut off and to make his vows.

Women could take the three Nazarite oaths: the Book of Numbers is absolutely clear upon this point. In the year AD 66, just at the time when the great revolt was on the point of bursting out, we find Queen Berenice with her hair cut off, staying at Jerusalem, abstaining from wine and praying a great deal at the Temple, because at that period, for some reason unknown to us, she had taken a Nazarite's vow.[60] It is probable that some young women even took an oath of virginity, either for life or for a certain time. Our Lady's reply to the angel of the Lord[61] has often been interpreted as meaning that the future mother of Christ had made a promise of this kind. And there was a Christian tradition, preserved in the apocryphal gospels, which represented Mary as a consecrated virgin staying in the Temple as a person under religious vows, spinning, weaving and embroidering the liturgical vestments.[62]

There was also another form of religious devotion that men and women could practise, for profoundly spiritual reasons, without making any such vows, and this was making a retreat in the 'desert'. The word 'desert' did not necessarily mean a Sahara or an Arabia Petraea, but rather an exceedingly solitary place, favourable to meditation and self-communion. The famous words of Saint Luke, 'The word of God came upon John . . . in the desert',[63] are understood by many as referring more to a spiritually empty place than one that was literally a waste. We also collect from the Gospel that the 'retreat in the desert' was to last for forty days, no doubt in memory of Moses' forty days upon Sinai or those during which Elijah went to Horeb: this was the length of the retreat that Jesus made before He took up His public ministry, and the place where, according to tradition, He stayed, is still called Jebel Qarantal, the Mountain of the Forty Days.[64] What did the person making the retreat do during this time? He fasted and prayed, living there before the face of God. It appears to have been a fairly usual custom, and we find Saint Paul, for example, retiring into the desert after what had happened to him at Damascus, before starting upon his apostolate.[65] Did these periods of staying in the desert then have the nature of a retreat 'in a centre of prayer'?[66] Perhaps they did; and in that case perhaps these retreats should also be related to the existence of a group of men of God in Israel who were in no way like the others: those men who were called the Essenes.

THE MONKS OF THE DEAD SEA

Both Josephus and Philo of Alexandria speak, not without enthusiasm, of a Jewish religious group of a particular kind; and the Elder Pliny, whether he had read of them in Philo or learnt about them himself in Palestine, honours these Jews with a long paragraph in the fifth chapter of his *Naturalis Historia*. It was common knowledge, then, that this group, this 'third school of Jewish philosophy', as Josephus calls it, the other two being the Sadducees and the Pharisees, had its geographical centre in the region of En Geddi, near the Dead Sea, and that there, joined in communities of prayer, 'without women, without love, without money, with only palm-trees for company', there lived men who subjected themselves to an exceedingly severe discipline and who were indifferent to all but that which had to do with God.

The name by which these men were called varied according to the author who wrote about them. Philo used the word *Essaioi*, Esseans, seeing in this an equivalent to *hosioi*, or pious men. Josephus wrote *Essenoi*, Essenes; and the etymologists argued as to whether the expression was derived from *esah*, a party, or from *hasid*, *hasidim*, the pious, who were none other than the ancestors of the Pharisees. The name Essenes prevailed; and following Frederick II and Voltaire, Renan adopted it. But no one knew much about the men to whom the name was applied.

Since 1947 all this has changed, and the Essenes have become by far the most famous of all the groups, bodies or sects into which the Jewish community was divided. In the spring of that year, a Bedouin of the Ta'amireh tribe was looking for a kid that had strayed – this has very much the air of the Gospel – and it so happened that he made his way into one of the many caves that open on the face of the cliff above the Dead Sea, the cave of 'Ain Feshkha. He was astonished to find several jars there – eleven, to be exact – some whole and some broken; and he was even more astonished to find that inside these jars there were cloth-wrapped leather scrolls, with incomprehensible writing upon them. These scrolls were bought by dealers in antiquities who, after negotiations as complex as the plot of any detective story, sold them to various customers: it was then discovered that they were of the very highest scientific interest – it was a question of a positive religious library, containing exceedingly ancient copies of certain biblical books as well as some works that do not form part of the canon of the Old Testament. Systematic researches in all the cliff caves during 1951 confirmed the very great importance of the discovery. From as early as 1948 it was suggested that this might very well be a library that had belonged to the Essenes.

Now between the foot of the cliff and the shore of the sinister lake there is a narrow plateau, much cut by terrible ravines, or rather a spur; and upon this spur stood a huddle of ruins, which had been known for a very long time under the name of Khirbet Qumrân but which had never been more than casually excavated or looked into. It was thought to be a commonplace Roman fortification. In 1951 a more careful excavation revealed a group of large buildings beneath the fortress: one of these was a hundred and twenty-one feet by ninety-eight; another still contained a writing-table sixteen feet long; and others were obviously storerooms and workshops, especially one potters' workshop with its kiln. There were also some immense bathing-pools. The description alone of such a group brought the idea of a monastery, of a religious community, most strongly to mind; and there was no doubt that Qumrân had in fact been a monastery once the archeologists discovered a cemetery of a thousand graves, in which the skeletons were carefully aligned. The connection between this and the community of En Geddi that Philo and Josephus spoke of was self-evident. At present there are very few who refuse to admit[67] that the astonishing discoveries in the neighbourhood of the Dead Sea put us into immediate touch with the Essenes.

The interest of these finds is clearly of the very highest order, and it has been said that it goes beyond that of Champollion's deciphering of the hieroglyphics or Schliemann's discovery of Troy. The Dead Sea scrolls, in providing copies of several biblical books that cannot, as we shall see, be later than AD 68, yield information of the most remarkable value for textual criticism. Furthermore, they have revealed parts of the literature of the Jews that were hitherto quite unknown, some of which – certain psalms, for example – are very nearly akin to the Bible, while others are quite unlike. It should also be added that some texts which were already known, but which seemed ill-placed or difficult to account for in the Jewish tradition, now fall into place in a logically established framework: the *Damascus Document*, a work that was found in 1896 in the *Genizah*, the book-cemetery of a synagogue in Old Cairo, is one of them. But above all these discoveries allow us to reconstruct the history of the Essenes, to form a far more exact picture of their life, to understand the spiritual quality that was peculiar to them, and to estimate the part they played in the Jewish community. In about the year 150 BC, when it became apparent that the resistance to Hellenism which had raised up the Chosen People against the Seleucids no longer had the character of a holy war, and that the descendants of the Maccabees, the Asmonean king-priests, were letting themselves slide towards compromise, a certain number of the *hasidim*, the pious, found that the doctrinal and almost passive opposition to which the Pharisees confined themselves was not enough. They resolved to break all ties with the régime and go back to 'the desert', that is to say, to Israel's holy origins. This chosen band of ardent men, which in the first place was made up of priests, 'the sons of Zadok, the guardians of the covenant', obeyed a mysterious person called the Master of Justice. These 'chosen of God' took refuge in the solitudes of the Dead Sea, and they devoted their whole lives to study and to the observance and the defence of His Law. It is obvious that the mere fact of their existence was a condemnation of the Temple's priesthood and of its government. A violent crisis therefore arose, at some date that cannot be determined, between official Judaism and the Essenian monks: a Master of Justice was put to death, perhaps by John Hyrcanus, perhaps later, and the members of the group fled to Damascus. They came back to Qumrân when the Roman occupation of Palestine under Pompey, in 63 BC, made their enemies no longer dangerous to them. There they were to stay for some hundred and thirty years, until that time during the Jewish revolt of AD 66–70, the spring of 68, to be exact, when the Gauls and the Germans of Titus' Tenth Legion carried out a terrible sweep through the region of the Dead Sea. The monastery was partly destroyed and then occupied by the soldiers: the monks fled or were massacred, but not before they had found time to hide their most precious treasures, their sacred books, in the caves of the nearby cliff. When Jesus was upon earth and uttering His message, therefore, there were Essenes at Qumrân, and no doubt in other places as well.

They kept themselves resolutely apart from the rest of the Chosen People: they formed monastic communities that wished to know nothing whatever of the outside world, and they were utterly indifferent to all political questions. Qumrân was most probably the mother-house of this species of religious order, but in many other places in Palestine, and perhaps beyond Palestine, there were smaller groups, each of ten men at least – ten, which was also the figure necessary for the constitution of a synagogue – under the direction of a priest.

A man would join 'the Community' (this was the term used by the Essenes themselves) after an examination and a double period of probation, first of one, then of two years. The new member gave up all his possessions to the Community, swore obedience 'to the rule and to his superiors', declared his intention 'to separate himself from the men of iniquity' and to live in truth, justice and charity. When he was accepted as a member he was obliged to practice several daily ablutions, wear a white linen robe, eat nothing but vegetables, observe the rites of ritual cleanliness even more scrupulously than the Pharisees, perhaps to speak in Hebrew and not in Aramaic, and finally to bury his excrement. But above all he was to take part in the communal meals of all the brethren, and to pray with them at regular hours and upon the holy feast-days.

The Essenian communities were divided into three ranks, priests, levites and laymen; they were under the direction of a leader, a president, the *Mebagger*, under whom a central council, a kind of chapter with twelve members, dealt with all important matters, particularly the punishment of those members who disobeyed the rule; and their supreme head was the Master of Justice. Women were not admitted – 'No one was born among the Essenes' – but it does seem likely that there were some female communities who obeyed the same rule: women's skeletons have been found at Qumrân.

Postulants' children might be taken in, and they would be given a special education. Outside the true communities there were probably solitary Essenes who carried their asceticism further, as we still see hermits on Mount Athos in Greece living in caves near coenobitic monasteries until they die. Josephus speaks of one of them, called Banous, who 'dwelt in the desert, dressed in loin-cloths supplied by the trees and living on what he could gather'.[68] This description inevitably brings Saint John the Baptist to mind; and as the place of his apostolate, the ford of Bethabara on the lower Jordan, was within a few hours' walk of Qumrân, it is possible that he too was one of these free-lance Essenes. Farther from the Dead Sea, there were undoubtedly sympathizers with Essenianism, possibly a sort of third order of Essenes, who lived in the world but who conformed to the rule as closely as they could. It appears that the sect of Therapeutae in Egypt, spoken of by Philo, may have been formed by those who copied the Essenes, or who were associated with them.

Essenianism was a creed of high spiritual quality. It is known to us from several works that were found among the scrolls: the *Rule of the Community* and the *Manual of Discipline* are primarily concerned with laying down the group's regulations, but the *Psalms of the New Covenant*, the strange and wonderful *War of the Sons of Light and the Sons of Darkness* and some commentaries upon certain passages in the Bible, particularly from Habakkuk and Micah, give us a clear understanding of the Essenes' teaching. It follows the strictest Mosaic line: there is only one way of seeking God, and that is the Law. God requires an absolute obedience to the Torah from the members of the Community, in virtue of a 'new covenant', which is a divine grace. It is therefore the duty of the Sons of Light to struggle against the wicked, the upholders of evil, the Sons of Darkness. It is their duty, moreover, because two antagonistic spirits have always divided sin-perverted mankind between them. For the Essenes, the soul is immortal, since it exists before the body comes into being and since after the body's death it goes back to that transcendent place from which it came. At the end of time, there will be a Last Judgment, when the men of perdition shall be destroyed and the predestinate, headed by the members of the Community, enter into the glory of God.

It is difficult to form an exact opinion of the importance of the Essenes in the religious life of the Jews: some say that they counted for very little indeed; others think that they had considerable weight.

Essenianism had grown up within a specifically Jewish frame-work and in a priestly *milieu*, among men who claimed to be the guardians of the pure tradition of Israel. Yet it is clear, never-theless, that it had taken in some religious elements that were not

Jewish. Josephus says that Essenianism had been influenced by the beliefs of the Pythagoreans and by the doctrine of the 'two spirits', which is precisely that of the Persian dualism, with its struggle between Ormuzd, the spirit of goodness, and Ahriman, the spirit of evil. The Essenes disagreed with a great part of the priestly system and with many of the official rites: they particularly refused to have anything to do with the 'sacrifice of blood', and would only make flour-offerings. At the time of the great feasts they sent representatives to the Temple, but they kept themselves markedly apart, probably staying in the little courtyard reserved for the ritually pure Nazarites. There is no sort of doubt that their manner of life was opposed to the basic tenets of Judaism. A rabbinical axiom, often quoted in the Talmud, said, 'A man must follow the paths of the world'; but for their part the Essenes would not follow the world's path; they did not share in the collective destiny of their people; and their claim that they alone constituted the true Israel, the Israel of Grace, was a complete break with that fundamental idea of the Jewish tradition according to which every believer was to find his salvation within the context of the Chosen People, within it, by it and together with it. No doubt the Master of Justice was one of the great religious figures in the history of mankind, and no doubt the teaching of the Essenes was one of the most noble that ever arose from Jewish thought: but it may well be asked whether these cloistered men, these solitaries, were able to exert any strong influence upon their contemporaries and upon the fate of the world.

Unless indeed – (for it would be wrong not to mention a hypothesis which, if the texts and the facts were to support it, would show the Essenes as the most important religious group, that which had the future for it) – unless indeed the Essenes were Christians as it were before Christianity. Or unless indeed the Christians were a kind of Essenes. As early as the eighteenth century Frederick II said that he was sure that this was the case; and later Renan defined Christianity as 'an Essenism that succeeded'. The hypothesis has often been propounded again since the discoveries in the caves and at Qumrân; and on occasion it has been flatly stated as a fact. According to some the Master of Justice was one of Christ's predecessors, unless Christ was Himself a Master of Justice, put to death by the priests as His forerunner had been.

This hypothesis is primarily based upon textual similarities that no one would attempt to deny. Saint John the Baptist, in saying, 'There is a voice of one crying: In the wilderness. . .', was using a quotation from Isaiah that was very usual among the Essenes. And from the mouth of Christ Himself we have phrases of a distinctly Essenian ring: He speaks, for example, of 'the new covenant' and of 'the Children of Light'. The idea of the creating Word in the Gospels, particularly Saint John's, comes very close to what the Essenian *Manual of Discipline* has to say upon God's thought, which from the void brought the world into being. In Saint Paul we find Essenian expressions repeated word for word,[69] and we meet with the dualism itself again in a Christian form in two of the writings of the early Church, the *Didache* and the *Epistle of Barnabas*, to say nothing of Saint Augustine and, much later, Saint Ignatius Loyola.[70] There are other arguments that can also be brought to support this thesis. Neither John the Baptist nor our Lord ever attack the Essenes, although they both deal severely with the Pharisees and the Sadducees. Better still, the evangelists never mention them at all, just as though they were of their number and as if they were speaking in their name. Finally, after the tumult of the years AD 66–70, the Essenes completely vanish from the scene: history does not mention them again. Does not this show that they simply became Christians? True Christians or perhaps heretics, like those Ebionites against whom Saint Irenaeus struggled, heretics who called themselves the 'Poor Men' and who explained everything by the contest between the 'two parts of God', Christ and the devil.

The hypothesis is in fact unsound. It goes against the evidence. Essenism was essentially a priestly movement, begun by priests and guided by priests: it had nothing in common with Christianity, which was a great people's movement from the beginning and which became more and more so as it went on. Essenism was based upon the most exact observance of the Law, so strict and rigid, indeed, that it appeared to out-Pharisee the Pharisees; and we may be very sure that an Essene would never have agreed with our Lord upon the keeping of the Sabbath or upon ritual cleanliness. Essenism certainly expected a Messiah; but a priestly Messiah, a Messiah of Aaron, a high priest who would be the holy one: the Christian concept of the Messiah is utterly opposed to this, just as the Church of Christ, open at once to all men, even the unclean and the sinners, is utterly opposed to anything in the nature of an exclusive sect – the Church which holds that the grace of the 'new covenant' is not reserved for a little group of monks and tertiaries, but is there for the benefit of all upright men.

Essenism, then, was a link between Judaism and Christianity; but it was not the only one. It was natural that there should be others as well, since Christ was born a Jew, lived as a Jew and spoke as a Jew. But none of these clear marks of kinship prevail against the fact of that immense and decisive advance which was the result of Christ's coming into the world.

CHAPTER FOUR

THE FAITH OF ISRAEL AND THE COMING OF THE MESSIAH

The first commandment of all – Was God withdrawing Himself from man? – 'And the second, its like' – Chosen People or universalism? – Was the letter to kill the spirit? – The Messiah. Who and when?

THE FIRST COMMANDMENT OF ALL

Such, then, was the frame within which the Jews led their religious life at the time when the coming of Christ into the world was to call it all in question. What remains to be shown is the nature of this life; that is to say, how the soul then lived its religion. And, since every religion evolves with the society which is its context, and is faced with new problems in each succeeding generation, we must also show what problems confronted the Jews of the first century, what new problems brought them to adopt new attitudes.

Everyone will remember the dialogue in the Gospel when a scribe asked our Lord, 'Which is the first commandment of all?' Jesus replied by quoting the opening verse of the *Shema*, the daily prayer: 'Listen, Israel; there is no God but the Lord thy God.'[1] He then went on to make an admirable commentary upon this quotation. The reply was pertinent: no Jew could have made any other. At almost the same period the apocryphal *Letter of Aristeas* said, 'The first teaching is that there is but one God alone'.[2] And this was indeed the basis of the faith of Israel, an absolute and uncompromising monotheism which would not admit even the slightest hint of idolatry: in the last analysis the entire religion had as its source the axiom, 'There is but one God'.

At the opening of the new era, this monotheistic faith was still as strongly rooted in the conscience of the people as it had been in the days when Judith proclaimed it before the elders of the besieged city, before making her exceedingly dangerous approach to Holofernes: 'It is something that we have not followed the evil example of our forefathers, who forsook their own God and worshipped alien Gods instead . . . At least we acknowledge one God, and Him only.'[3] The rabbis upheld it in all times and places. 'The condemnation of idolatry alone', said one of them, 'is of greater importance than all the precepts of the Torah.'[4] Another observed, 'The man who, by idolatry, takes God's yoke from off his neck, at the same time denies all His commandments'.[5] No Jew might compromise with this principle: the tractate *Sanhedrin* allowed that it was admissible, in the case of mortal danger, to violate the direct commandments of the Torah, but stated that there was no case whatever in which a man might yield to idolatry.[6] In the account of the martyred Rabbi Akiba's sublime death some time later, we are told how, when he knew that his tortured body was near its end, he recited the *Shema*, drawing out its last word *shad*, 'one' in the sense 'the Lord is one' – drawing it out until life left him.[7]

Were all Jews ready to show this kind of heroism? Would they all imitate those Maccabee brothers who chose rather to die than to yield to idolatry, even to the smallest degree? At all events it seems that direct unfaithfulness, formal apostasy, was very rare, even in rich and fashionable circles, where the way of life was more than three parts pagan. Once the uniqueness, the singleness, of God was in question, even people like Berenice or Herod Agrippa knew where their duty lay, and they spoke straight out to Rome. As for the populace, it was enough to wave the spectre of idolatry before them to produce an instant reaction of pious horror – a reaction against Herod the Great, for example, when he had his gold eagle placed on the pediment of the Temple, or against Pilate, when his troops entered Jerusalem with their standards showing. The Jews knew that what set them apart and what gave them their reason for existence was that they were the People of the One God – so much so, indeed, that according to the teaching of the doctors, 'Any man who repudiates idolatry is considered as a Jew'.[8] And pagans, such as Juvenal, Tacitus and Pliny, seeing how little the Jews welcomed the members of their various pantheons, paid them the compliment of calling them atheists.

The Jew believed in this single God, this one, invisible and immaterial Deity, the creator and the master of the world, all-powerful and all-knowing, not by any mental operation of reasoning or logical deduction, but in virtue of a revelation. For the Jew his God was indeed the very reverse of that 'God of the philosophers and the learned' of whom Pascal speaks; and his God imposed Himself upon his awareness with as much force as an object that might be touched or an animate being that might be seen. The Old Testament, the apocryphal books and the Gospels are filled with expressions that assert this unhesitating faith, for which the doctrine of monotheism is so apparent that it occurs to nobody to demonstrate its truth. The Lord is there, omnipresent, in the empty Holy of Holies in the heart of the Temple, but also manifest in all nature, which is His work and His 'foot-stool', as well as in the heart of the upright men who believe in Him. To deny this obvious fact was – and the Bible repeated it in several places – literally to be a *nabal*, a fool, a 'reckless heart'.[9] Not that this means that there were not evil men who behaved as though God did not exist: but there was nobody who professed a direct atheism, a doctrinal negation. In any case, there is no text that gives any evidence of such a thing happening.

It is this great idea of an omnipresent God, compelling recognition as the most undeniable of facts, that gives its real meaning to this whole vast network of rules and precepts in which, as we have seen, the life of the Jews was so rigidly enclosed. In a consecrated life everything is holy, since everything is obedient to God; and (to borrow one of Léon Bloy's most beautiful phrases) 'everything that happens is worthy of being worshipped'.[10] The trust in God and Providence which is so often taught in the Gospel was also one of the axioms of the teaching of the rabbis. This was so much the case that to say of a certain man that he was a true believer, a man of faith, meant that he was one who under all circumstances set his whole trust in God. The contrary expression, 'men of little faith', is used in both the Talmud and the Gospel as a qualification for those who are excessively concerned with the future. That famous Hebrew adverb *amen*, which the Christians repeat mechanically every day, expressed an act of faith and at the same time an act of submission to God and to His intentions. And do not the two translations which the Christians give to the word today correspond to these two meanings? 'So be it', we translate at the end of a prayer; but we render Christ's phrase *'amen dico vobis'* as 'verily, I say unto you'.

It certainly appears that a deep, sincere piety filled a great many Jewish souls: the strict rules and precepts fixed the framework of life, but they did not necessarily impede its spiritual impulses. It was not merely to obey the requirements of the Law that men prayed three times a day, that they went up frequently to the Temple and that they regularly fasted. One has but to open the Gospel to be conscious of the all-pervading atmosphere of prayer: again and again our Lord would 'steal away from them into the desert and pray there'; His disciples say, 'Lord, teach us how to pray'; and before the mystery that was to change, overturn and disrupt her whole life, a sublime prayer at once sprang from Our Lady's lips. The later Jewish apocryphal books and the tractates of the Talmud are no less rich in proofs of this universality of prayer. 'The Almighty', said the rabbis, 'earnestly desires to receive the prayers of upright men.' And they wisely added that even the man 'who feels himself an unworthy sinner should pray'; and again, 'even he who feels that he has not been heard should still pray'. For 'prayer is above sacrifice: it is even above good deeds'.[11]

This prayer might be, and indeed it often was, made from interested motives: people would pray that God and His Providence might give them eminently material favours, that they might be healed, helped to succeed, protected in voyages and so on. Yet the *Pirke Aboth*, the 'Sayings of the Fathers', said, 'Do not be like those servants who are always waiting for a present. Serve God without a reward.'[12] The most heartfelt of Israel's prayers, the prayer which best expresses a wholly disinterested, unselfish faith, is that which is continually to be heard from the Chosen People's saints and learned men: 'Blessed be the glory of God!' It is the same prayer as Christ's: 'Not to me, Lord, but to Thee alone the glory.'

WAS GOD WITHDRAWING HIMSELF FROM MAN?
In this Jewish religion of the time of Christ – a religion that it would be most unjust to call a soulless legalism and nothing more – there was one thing that astonishes us: God was never named. Is it possible to imagine a Christian who never says either 'Jesus' or 'Christ'? Or a Mohammedan who never calls upon Allah? And yet this was indeed the case. God's own name, the name that He had revealed to Moses on Sinai as a pledge of his mercy, was Yahweh: or rather, since vowels did not exist

in Hebrew, it was the sacred tetragrammaton, the four consonants YHWH. But gradually, over a period of about three hundred years, there had grown up a custom of never pronouncing it. At first there had been substituted the word *Adonai*, which the Seventy translated by the Greek *Kyrios*, Lord; but even this was only very rarely used, and then only in a few traditional prayers. The expressions *El* and *Elohim*, which were used in Genesis for God, were also avoided. The use of the holiest name of all, Yahweh, was practically confined to the high priest as he officiated in the Temple. But Rabbi Tarphon tells how, having slipped in among the priests during a ceremony and having listened attentively, he heard that the high priest 'swallowed' the name.[13] This tendency was carried so far that one rabbi taught: 'Whoever pronounces the Name may be sentenced to death.'[14]

If they might not name Him, how then did they refer to God? At *Yom Kippur* the high priest said, 'Oh Name, I have sinned before Thee'. It was usual to substitute 'Heaven' for the divine names, as we do today: 'May Heaven bless you', 'May Heaven be with you.' There were some stranger expressions: the 'Place', the 'Abode', the 'Indwelling' – the last, the *Shechinah*, also had a beautiful spiritual meaning, not unlike 'presence', or 'immanence'. 'Glory', 'Majesty', 'Power', were also usual terms, and even more usual, 'the Highest', 'the Holy One', 'the Merciful' and, of course, 'the Eternal'.

The explanation of this custom obviously lies in the uncompromising monotheism of the Jewish faith. Could the Chosen People, in daily contact with the pagans, call their God by His name, as if it were a question of some mere Jupiter, Adonis or Mithras? Yet this also corresponded to a change in the relationship between God and man. The world was obviously very far removed from the ancient ways: the sacred name of God was not yet known to Abraham, but he invited the Almighty and His angels to eat with him. Moses and the kings and the prophets had had astonishing confrontations with Him; but the world was no longer at that stage.

For the Jews it was an article of faith to know that the relationship between God and man was laid down by the covenant,[15] the pact between the Almighty and Abraham which was confirmed upon Mount Sinai. Israel, the people chosen by God as the witnesses of the monotheistic truth, knew and believed with all its strength that it had the privilege of an entirely special relationship with Him, that the right hand of the Almighty rested upon Israel's head; and it was in the light of this conviction that the Jews resolved the apparent contradiction between the two attributes that they recognised in God, justice and mercifulness. He was a completely just God, the Judge who weighed men's actions with undeviating weights; but at the same time he was the God of mercy. And this was fortunate, for were He to judge with rigid justice 'who', asks the Psalmist, 'has strength to bear it?' The Chosen People, reflecting upon their history, found in it the proof that the Lord had never exercised His justice in all its strictness, and that He had always granted forgiveness.

Yet there still remained the difficulty of reconciling fear of God with love of God, dread of His justice with hope for His merciful kindness: and this problem posed itself all the more urgently for the Jews of the time of Christ because at that period they felt oppressed and threatened, at the bottom of one of the great depressions in their history. One has the impression that at that time there were two currents, the one inducing the soul to draw nearer to God in a trustful impulse, the other imposing dread and reverence upon it. Both are to be seen in the Jewish faith of the time of Christ, and it is over-simplifying matters by far to say (as many people do) that the religion of the Old Testament is a religion of fear, and that of the New a religion of love.

By reason of the covenant, the Israelites had always thought of themselves as God's children, the sons of Yahweh. The expression 'Our Father' is often to be found in the Old Testament, but in a collective sense. God is the Father of Israel because He created the People of Israel, chose the nation and loaded it with favours. All Jews remembered the great voice of Isaiah and those chapters sixty-three and sixty-four which record his splendid trust. Most of the doctors of the Law followed this line of thought: thus the rabbi Ben Zakkai speaks of 'the stones of the altar which made peace between Israel and their Father who is in heaven'. But in the meantime another and more personal tendency was developing. In the Book of Wisdom the just man 'boasts of a divine parentage'.[16]* In a well-turned phrase, Rabbi Ben Shetah said,

*This is the Knox Version: the Vulgate reads, '*gloriatur patrem se habere Deum*'; and the Authorized Version, 'makes his boast that God is his father'.

'One must not behave like a spoilt child towards God the Father'; and Rabbi Ben Azaria advised men 'to do the will of Our Father who is in heaven'. There are even some Talmudic apologues in which God sends for His sinful son with the words, 'Can a son be ashamed to come back to his father?' It may then be said that there did exist a tendency that urged the soul to come nearer to God, to feel that He was infinitely good, that He reciprocated love and that He was always ready to answer man's appeal. But this was not the strongest current: the texts that show its existence are few, and it is not sure that some may not be later than the time of Christ. It was certainly another current of thought that was the most important.

It was dread; the same tendency that had, out of an excessive care for respect, brought about the disuse of the divine names. There is no sort of doubt that in the Old Testament fear of God had a more important place and was of a wider extent than love for Him. The prophet Isaiah, indeed, went so very far as to speak of his deepest joy being the fear of the Lord.[17] A famous proverb said: 'True wisdom is founded on fear of the Lord.'[18] And 'A blessed man is he, who fears the Lord', said the Psalmist.[19] This was certainly the dominant feeling in the religion of the Jews at the time of Christ. Those pagans who sympathized with the Jewish faith and who lived according to the Law were called 'God-fearing men'; and in several of the apocryphal books and in countless Talmudic texts the expression is synonymous with 'just' or 'righteous man'. Well before the time of our Lord, the rabbi Antigonus of Socco greeted his friends and ended his speeches with the words, 'And may the fear of God be upon you'.[20] Even though some rabbis taught that 'the love of God was more valuable than the fear of God', it may be supposed that this love was presented rather as the highest kind of ideal than as any immediate reality. That scribe in the Gospel who declared his agreement with Christ when our Lord had spoken on the first commandment of all was doubtless not an exception; but it is equally doubtless that the majority of the doctors would not have commented upon the verse of Deuteronomy (6, 5) which is quoted in the *Shema* in those well-known and admirable words, 'Thou shalt love the Lord thy God with the love of thy whole heart, and thy whole soul, and thy whole strength':[21] they would certainly have said, 'Thou shalt fear the Almighty'.

Was there no reaction among the believers at this withdrawal of God? There are signs which appear to show that there was. Several of the Old Testament books had spoken of wisdom,[22] treating it as an outward mark or evidence of the faith. The doctors had reacted violently: for them wisdom formed part of the same entity as the Law; it blended with the holy Torah and with their tradition.[23] But there was also a school that refused to identify wisdom, in the sense of a mystic knowledge of God and a trusting submission to His will, with any written text or formal precepts; for them wisdom was something near a hypostasis, almost the very substance of the Deity. The Book of Wisdom, which appears in the Septuagint, belonged to this school: the strict rabbis therefore refused to admit it to the canon. Many apocryphal books show the same tendency, particularly the *Book of Enoch*, which gave wisdom a personality, making it a kind of intermediary between God and man – observing at the same time that as wisdom had found no place for itself upon earth it had gone to dwell among the angels.

The considerable extension of the belief in angels also formed part of this same tendency: it was a belief that dated from the earliest days of the Chosen People – Abraham comes to mind, and the angels who were his guests, and Jacob wrestling at the ford of Jabbok – but since the return from exile, perhaps because of Persian influence, it had assumed a very great importance in the faith of the common people. The Sadducees, as it is stated in the Acts, would not believe in them at all:[24] Josephus says that the Essenes classed angelology among those branches of knowledge that were to be kept secret.[25] In the apocryphal books and the Talmud angels are of the greatest consequence, and in the Gospels, particularly that of Saint Luke, they are also given a very important part, being closely associated with the wonderful adventure of the Incarnation. People often spoke about angels: their characters were discussed, their ranks laid down, their armies numbered; even their names were known – Michael, Gabriel, Raphael, Raguel, Phanuel, Saraquiel. And naturally everyone was aware that although there were good angels there were also evil ones, with Satan at their head.

If God seemed to have withdrawn Himself, mediators were necessary: in this we see what was certainly a typical characteristic of Jewish religious life; and in this, too, Messianism was to find some of its sustenance.

'AND THE SECOND, ITS LIKE'

One of the poles of Judaism was its monotheistic faith: but it had
another, and this was its moral law. Here again was a point in
which it was radically different from Graeco-Roman paganism;
for whereas the Olympians were anything but models for decent
behaviour, the religion of Israel imposed upon man an ethical
just as much as a metaphysical rule. This had been the decisive
contribution of Moses, when, in the smoke of Sinai, he had heard
the almighty voice bidding him write the ten commandments.
After him, and in spite of innumerable backslidings, the result of
man's original sin, the faithful generations had continually
tightened and multiplied the connections between ethics and
belief. The Mosaic revelation amounted to the laying down of
natural moral law; but the prophets, especially, had gone far
beyond these precepts in their admirable attempt at making
religion more a matter of the innermost life of a man. And
since the return from exile the greatest part of the work of the
doctors of the Law had been the establishment of a legal code
based on the Torah which would allow men to behave according to
God's will in all circumstances. This rabbinical teaching may be
called excessively scrupulous and minute: but however that may
be, it is none the less wonderful to see a whole nation – not
merely a school of philosophy, as among the Greeks, but an
entire people – declare the pre-eminence of the moral law and
(at least officially) its desire to conduct itself in accordance with
that law's requirements.

At the time when Jesus came into the world, there is no
possible doubt that His people's moral monotheism had reached a
very high level. All the rabbis laid down the principle that the
first tribute that God claimed from man was holiness of life.
'You must be set apart, the servants of a God who is set apart',
said the Bible.[26]* Imitation of the divine holiness, therefore, was
the ideal that was set up before every man who wished to be true
to his faith. This principle was the source of an ethical teaching
which has been described as 'the loftiest and the most beautiful
part of the whole Jewish doctrine, superior to all the moral
doctrines of the Ancient World'.[27]

It is not our purpose to show the precepts of this doctrine in
detail here: besides, they are the same as those of the Christian

---

*This is the Knox Version: the Vulgate reads, *'sancti estote, quia ego
sanctus sum'*; and the Authorized Version, 'ye shall be holy; for I am holy'.

teaching. They do not confine themselves to prohibitions – do not kill, do not steal, do not lie. The virtues that the rabbis invariably extolled were uprightness, sincerity, chastity and humility. And at least for the best, it was not only a question of submitting to the requirements of the Law and of its interpreters, but of living truly in the sight of God, and of adapting oneself to Him. It is even certain that several rabbis were already teaching that doctrine to which our Lord was to give its final form, the doctrine that one should not act merely in obedience to moral imperatives, but also clean one's soul within. Christ's famous words: 'He who casts his eyes on a woman so as to lust after her has already committed adultery with her in his heart'[28] most strikingly express an idea that Rabbi Simeon ben Yochai had in his mind when he spoke of 'the sins of the eye', and of the 'unclean thoughts that lead to fornication'.[29]

Among the more original features of the Jewish moral teaching there are two that should be particularly pointed out. The first is the importance given to the virtue of chastity. Basing themselves upon the Mosaic commandment which forbade adultery, the inspired men who drew up the Bible and the rabbis who commented upon it had elaborated a whole ethic of sexuality, a system to which Christianity (except, as we have seen, in the question of marriage[30]) was to add nothing. Everything which moral theology forbids today was already forbidden then by the rabbis, and exactly forbidden – irregular conjugal relationships just as much as homosexuality. Sexual licentiousness was strongly disapproved of, and there were punishments laid down for the more serious cases of it. Josephus bears witness to this ideal of purity: 'We, the sons of the Hebrews, obey excellent laws. Whereas the other nations let boys of fourteen lie with whores and others who make a trade of their bodies, we do not allow a single prostitute to live in our country: the women who follow this calling are condemned to death. Before it is permitted by the law, we do not have any commerce with any woman: we are married as virgins; and we marry not with the idea of pleasure, but with that of begetting children.'[31] Josephus is not an entirely reliable witness, and it is likely that he is exaggerating somewhat: after all, we have seen[32] that prostitution certainly did exist in Israel. Yet still the proclamation of the ideal of purity and chastity is a great thing, above all at a time when the whole pagan world, and Roman society in particular, the society of Petronius'

Satiricon, was providing so many unfortunate examples of sexual depravity.

The second, and perhaps even more striking feature of the Jewish ethical doctrine was its insistence upon the virtues of kindness, fraternity and charity. If we go back to the dialogue in the Gospel between our Lord and the scribe, it will be seen that these virtues are so highly esteemed that the practice of them is put on an equal footing with the virtue of monotheistic faith. 'And the second, its like, is this, Thou shalt love thy neighbour as thyself.'[33] The commandment itself comes from Leviticus (19, 18). But in order to have spoken thus, and to have won the scribe's approval, our Lord must necessarily have been interpreting the most generally accepted feelings of His people.

It has been observed that the moral intention of the Mosaic precepts is entirely altruistic: it is less concerned with the perfection of the individual than with the elimination of all causes of strife, all ill relations between men. The Law forbade the injuring of one's neighbour by the theft of his goods or his wife, or by fraud; it forbade one to kill him. The inspired books, particularly Job, Psalms and Ecclesiasticus, and the prophets, with the rabbis after them, had developed a host of positive commandments from these prohibitions, and their tendency was to bring into being a general atmosphere of brotherliness among the Chosen People. In the Holy Scriptures there are countless precepts whose charitable intention is quite obvious: in the course of the present book we have seen several of these – that, for example, which required the creditor who had taken a cloak as a pledge to let the debtor have it back for the night, or that which forbade the harvesting of the corn round the edges or in the corners of the field, so that the poor might come and find something to help their poverty. The sabbatical year, too, was the outcome of the same kind of charitable intention.

Alms-giving was obligatory, required by the Law. 'Redeem thy sins in giving to the poor', repeated the doctors of the Law; and again, 'Give the poor man what belongs to him, for all that thou hast comes from God and belongs to all'. Everybody was to give alms, 'even the beggar who himself lives on them'. To be openhanded was to win merit in the eyes of God, for 'the poor man does more for the rich than the rich for the poor'. It was even an article of popular belief that in order to have sons it was essential to give handsome sums of money among the poor. There was also the parable of the two sheep who wanted to swim across a river: one sheep had given up its wool, and it crossed without coming to harm; the other had kept its wool, and this so weighed it down that it sank to the bottom.[34] Josephus says that the refusal of a request for alms was a very serious transgression: 'even graver than idolatry', asserts Rabbi Joshua ben Gorba. And there are many texts in the Talmud which show that the doctors of Israel, in requiring the faithful to give alms, desired that it should be done decently, kindly, and without wounding those who received it. 'It is better to throw yourself into a fiery furnace', said Rabbi Simeon ben Yochai, 'than to offer your poor neighbour a public insult.'[35] When the publican Zacchaeus, in the Gospel, said that he gave half of what he had to the poor,[36] was he exaggerating? Perhaps he was not.

One certainly comes away with the impression that in the Judaism of the time of Christ there were two tendencies upon the ethical plane as well as the metaphysical. The one was traditionalist, adhering strictly to the letter of the Law, maintaining the principles of rigid legality, of that retributive justice whose severity we have seen in an earlier chapter.[37] The second, on the other hand, tempered the rigours of the law with kindness, charity and brotherly love. It would appear, indeed, that this feeling of brotherliness had grown stronger among the Jews since the sufferings of the exile and those of Israel's subjection to the pagans who had occupied the land from that time onwards. The great Rabbi Hillel taught the second commandment, 'the like of the first', with unwearying zeal, and after him his disciple Akiba took up the teaching, in terms identical with those of our Lord. Clearly, all this does not mean that among the Jews there was no violence, no injustice, no cruelty, no monstrous social wickedness: a glance at the New Testament will show evil rich men, unjust employers and pitiless wealth. But the principle had already been laid down, and that was a great deal – the principle of charity which Jesus was to carry to its highest point.

CHOSEN PEOPLE OR UNIVERSALISM?

It was within the limits of the Jewish community that these brotherly feelings came into play. The duty of charity was defined in these terms: 'The helping of the unfortunate and unhappy Israelite, either directly or by means of one's money, and the comforting of him in his afflictions.'[38] The word

'Israelite' should be emphasized. Was kindness then only to be used towards members of the Chosen Race? Was the 'neighbour' whom one was to love 'as oneself' the pagan too, or did this refer only to one's fellow-Jew? Christ summed up the Jewish moral teaching upon this point in the words: 'Thou shalt love thy neighbour and hate thy enemy.'[39] And there are countless texts in the Talmud which show how well this observation was founded.

Here we have the crux of the second problem that faced the Jewish community. The doctrine of the covenant, which was, as we have seen, of such fundamental importance in Israel's conception of itself and of the part it had to play, gave rise to a certain attitude towards the heathen, towards all those who did not share the Chosen People's monotheistic faith. And, as we have also seen[40] the fact of having been chosen by the Almighty inflamed an extraordinary national pride. We may be certain that at the time of Christ this pride had not diminished by so much as an inch. On the contrary: it had grown even greater by reason of the complex of reactions to humiliation and resentment. For a conquered people, with their country occupied by foreigners, how great a consolation it must have been to read in the Book of Books such phrases as these: 'Who is like thee among the powers, oh people of Israel?', 'Is there a single nation, says God, who is like thee, oh my people of Israel?'; 'Thou art the glory of my power'; 'It is in thee that I have glorified myself.'[41] Certain rabbinical circles even advanced the extreme claim that it was not God who had chosen Israel but Israel that had chosen God, thus naturally coming under His protection. There was also a tradition, less theologically adventurous but no more modest, that before choosing His people, God had surveyed all the other nations, and that He had found the first wicked, the next shameless, the next given to lying. By this ingenious means the most outstanding virtues were attributed to Israel, and at the same time it was made clear that Israel alone possessed them.

The consequence of this national pride was to carry Israel towards exclusivism; and it must be admitted that this exclusivism seemed to be justified by the historical circumstances of Israel's life. This very small nation was surrounded by great hordes of pagans who by their very being threatened the most sacred part of the treasure of the Jews, their faith: it was therefore natural to adopt an attitude of distrust and even of hostility towards all strangers. The Jew had good reason to believe that in every pagan he saw a potential enemy. The rabbis in their teaching often put these words into the mouth of God: 'With you alone I have joined my name: I am not the God of the idolaters, but the God of Israel only.' There were many scriptural texts upon which they could easily make commentaries to show that the heathen were proud, lecherous men, given to unnatural vices, that they were violent and criminal, and that consequently there was not one of them who would share in the kingdom of God. There were also dreadful accounts of the idol-worshippers' behaviour: they told the tale, for example, of a pagan who wished to be rid of his old father, and who therefore tied him up and set a dog upon him.[42] By the time of Christ, Rabbi Ben Zakkai had not yet uttered his atrocious words: 'The best of the unbelievers, kill him!' This was not to be said until the persecution of Hadrian, when the rabbi had seen his beloved master, Rabbi Akiba, die a martyr's death under the hooks of the Roman executioners. It may not have reflected the whole of the ethical teaching of the rabbis, but this maxim certainly interpreted the feelings of the more violent men among the Jews: the others did not seek to kill the *goyim*, but merely to flee them like the plague and to spit in front of their idols when the chance offered.

And yet for a long while there had also been an entirely different tendency discernible in the Jewish mind. 'God also loves the nations', said some; and in this resides the principle of the Jewish universalism – a universalism about which we may also learn from the Bible. There were believers for whom the promise made to Abraham were not light words: 'In thee all the races of the world shall find a blessing.' Had not the elder Tobit said that God had given the Israelites the mission of making His name known to all nations?[43] Had not Jonah, amazed, heard the Lord pardon even the infamous inhabitants of Nineveh? Had not Jeremiah foretold that when the Messiah came, all nations would be brothers? And Malachi that the whole earth should share in salvation? Did not the pious Jew hear the Psalms sing of the boundless mercy that is shown to all creatures, and of the love 'whose wings shelter the sons of all men'? A current of universalism was in existence, then, and Hillel was one of its chief advocates: 'Love your companions on the earth,' he said, 'love all created beings, and bring them with you to the Law.'[44]

'Bring them with you . . .' There he put his finger upon the problem that confronted the Jewish community of his time –

which was also, as it will be remembered, the time of our Lord. The little nation of the faithful was not only surrounded by the heathen on all sides, it was also mixed with them. In Palestine itself there were pagans with whom the Jews were utterly obliged to enter into relations; and how much more so was this the case with the Jews of the Diaspora, scattered in an entirely heathen world? Was it possible to maintain a systematic exclusivism? Only with difficulty: more especially as some of the heathen showed a real sympathy for Judaism, living in the Jewish manner and accepting the 'seven chief commandments', also known as the 'commandments of the sons of Noah' – men, that is to say, who could increase the numbers of the little community of the faithful. By their mere existence, the proselytes, the 'God-fearing men', gave the upholders of universalism the better of their argument against those who believed in exclusivism. From what Saint Luke says in the second chapter of the Acts, it appears that there were many of these proselytes, a very great many.[45]

This, then, was one of the most serious questions that faced Israel in the time of Christ: which was right, the 'closed' or the 'open' conception of religion? Was it right to let Israel's faith run the risk of contamination by allowing contacts with the heathen in order to win them over? The doctors of the Law argued hotly over it, both sides basing themselves upon Deuteronomy 33, 3. Most of them thought that in this place the holy text meant only the peoples of God, that is to say the twelve tribes: but others produced another biblical text, Levitivus 18, 5: 'It is my laws my decrees you must keep; they give life to the man who lives by them . . .', which clearly did not 'close Yahweh's gate' against anyone. Rabbi Meir even went so far as to say, 'The *goy* who practises the Law is the equal of the high priest'.[46] How was this problem to be resolved? When the scribe asked Christ, 'And who is my neighbour?'[47] there was surely a note of deep anxiety in his voice. It was a question that many Jews must then have been asking themselves.

WAS THE LETTER TO KILL THE SPIRIT?
There was also a third problem, and this was even more serious than the other two, since it called the validity of the religious life itself into question. It was a problem that arose from the immense importance that the Torah had acquired – not only the written Law, contained in the Bible, but also the oral Law, or the whole

body of exegetical commentaries and judicial decisions that the rabbis had added to the Holy Writ. The intrusion of religious regulations into the remotest corners of daily life and behaviour was justified on the plea of safeguarding faith and morals. The only wish of the doctors, as they multiplied the rules and requirements, prohibitions and observances, was 'to raise a hedge around the Law',[48] to protect the revealed truth by imposing a religious control over everything. But was there not a risk that the hedge, growing continually thicker and higher, should eventually stifle the plant that it was intended to protect?

Not that this submission to all the precepts of the Torah was without its grandeur. To obey the Torah was to accomplish the will of God, which was clearly set down in it; and was not every man's, and above all every Israelite's, reason for existence the accomplishment of God's will? A pious Jew was certain, if he scrupulously obeyed all the precepts that his masters taught him, that he would be saved. He would have rejected with horror the attitude of the man of today, with his love of independence and his intense dislike for all authoritatively imposed forms of spiritual discipline. For the pious Jew, obedience was the first act of faith.

It must be admitted that the Torah laid down a very great number of precepts, and the rabbis were continually adding to them. They were not only concerned with the requirements of the moral law, nor with the needs of the spiritual life: there were countless observances in which it would have been exceedingly difficult to find any real religious meaning whatever – we have come across a fair number of them in the course of this present book. The doctors claimed that they were entitled to insist upon an obedience to their scrupulous legislation as exact as that which was due to the commandments of the divine and the natural law. 'It is only Satan and man's evil nature', they said, 'that raise up any objections against the teachings of the wise.' And according to them the violation of the least important of the precepts was the same as 'rejecting the Law, thrusting off God's yoke and denying the faith's foundation'.[49]

The great upholders of these meticulous requirements were the Pharisees, who, as we have seen,[50] were experts in the Torah and very much in favour of the strict interpretation of it. There was perhaps no single aspect of human behaviour for which they would not have found a biblical text upon which a decision could be based. This could not be done without the raising of a great many difficulties, but these the Pharisees surmounted with a dialectical virtuosity that compelled admiration. It must be added that they were not all in agreement upon the interpretation of the sacred texts, as we know, and from this there arose some remarkable variations in their jurisprudence: upon a single question the Talmud recorded contradictory opinions, since it was upon this vast mass of rabbinical teaching that its tractates were based. The subjects that attracted the doctors' chief attention were the Sabbath rest, ritual cleanliness, the regulations concerning food and circumcision. Upon each of these they had built up a staggering mass of casuistry, so extraordinary that it is difficult to believe that a whole nation can have taken it seriously.

Examples of its absurdity have been quoted so often that there is no point in repeating the details. One has but to look into the tractate *Shabbath*[51] to make an anthology of them; but several of the other tractates are just as rich. Everyone knows that some of the Pharisees went right over the edge into the ridiculous in their commentaries upon the commandment that prohibited all work upon the Sabbath day. Was it allowable to eat an egg laid upon that day, since the hen had broken the Law by working? The slaughter of an animal was forbidden: but if the animal in question was a louse, might one kill it? The rigorous doctors were utterly against this shocking profanation of the Lord's day; but the more liberal minds allowed that the louse might be deprived of its legs. There were the same scruples with regard to offerings and to purification. If a peasant had lodged a wheat-offering in his granary, had he the right to put 'profane' wheat there afterwards? How many strokes of the broom was he to give in order that his act might be legal? Another, carrying his tithe of asparagus, had dropped some on the ground: might he eat the asparagus that they had produced by seeding themselves there? If, among his other vows, a pious Nazarite had taken that of abstaining from any mashed-up or gruel-like food, might he eat certain onions that he had inadvertently crushed? Thousands of cases of this kind might be cited, all gravely settled by the learned, and all the occasions for erudite argument between the schools of Shammai and Hillel.

The dangers of such an attitude are quite obvious. Formalism or ritualism can empty a religion of its substance and reduce it to a mechanical observance of merely formal precepts. In Saint Paul's famous words, it is 'the written law [that] inflicts death', as opposed to the 'spiritual law [that] brings life'.[52]* Jewish thinkers and theologians have subsequently maintained that 'at no time were there any Jews of any authority to be found who declared that it was enough to satisfy the letter of the Law'.[53] No doubt this is true. But it is also none the less true that human nature being what it is, the trammelling effect of all these requirements and interdictions induced the faithful to practise evasion. The greatest gave the example: there was Hillel himself who, in order to get round the commandment that required all debts to be cancelled every seven years, invented the *prosbol*, a document which ensured the repayment of moneys owing.[54] The people followed the example. For example, since on the Sabbath one might only go a 'Sabbath day's journey', a fictitious domicile would be invented, so that from that point it was within the Law to start off on another six stadia. It was certainly excusable in the practising Jew to dodge the precepts in this way, for Saint Peter, though he was a believer and a humble man, admitted that the yoke was 'such as we and our fathers have been too weak to bear'.[55] But on the other hand the trickery does make our Lord's fierce denunciation of the Pharisees understandable – those 'hypocrites that will award to God his tithe, though it be of mint or dill or cummin, and have forgotten the weightier commandments of the Law, justice, mercy and honour', and who 'scour the outward part of the cup and dish, while all within is running with avarice and incontinence'.[56]

Here, then, was a problem of the utmost gravity; and there is no sort of doubt that some rabbis were perfectly aware of it. Some said that although it might look as though they were evading and tricking the precepts of the Law, they did so solely to make them more bearable for the people, so that they might observe them better. But there were others who were certainly conscious of the great damage that an excessive legalism might inflict upon the inner life of the soul. As we have seen,[57] some of them had come so far as to admit that 'it was not man who was committed to the Sabbath, but the Sabbath that was committed to man', a saying very close indeed to the words of our Lord Himself.[58] Was this understanding attitude widely spread? Did not the great majority of the masters stand out for strict obedience? Who can tell? If

---

*This is the Knox Version: the Vulgate reads, '*littera enim occidit, spiritus autem vivificat*'; and the Authorized Version, 'for the letter killeth, but the spirit giveth life'.

the whole of rabbinical thought had been frozen in ritualism and literalism it is difficult to see how the Jewish religion was able to survive the coming of Christianity instead of fading away and dying, or why, furthermore, it has been able, right up to the present day, to provide the spiritual nourishment of noble minds. But everything goes to show that the most usual attitude was that of plain and simple obedience to the precepts and observances. The problem of the letter and the spirit was still far from that solution which Christ was to give it.

THE MESSIAH. WHO AND WHEN?

And yet there was another problem with which the Jewish people were even more concerned, a problem in which each man felt that the nation's whole destiny was engaged: the problem of the Messiah. This too was one of the essential bases of Israel's religion, as much part of it as its monotheism and the doctrine of the covenant, to which, moreover, it was closely linked; it was one of the most striking characteristics of Judaism, and one of those which set it apart from all the other religions of antiquity. The Jews, instead of setting their golden age in the remote night of the distant past, looked forward to its coming in the future. This expectation of a happier age than the present had crystallized about the imposing image of a heaven-sent being charged with the mission of making the hope a reality. Towards the approach of the Christian era, it was usual to call this being by the title which the Holy Scriptures used for those providential men whom God had particularly employed to serve His purposes, kings of Israel, high priests and even foreign rulers who, like Cyrus the Persian, had been benefactors of the Chosen People, the title 'the Lord's anointed' – *meshiah* in Aramaic and *christos* in Greek. A great and fervent current of hope flowed towards this mysterious figure, an immense hope that had lifted the hearts of generation after generation of believers.[59]

This hope had never been so much alive, so vivid, nor its fulfilment so urgently awaited, than it was in this time of sadness and of deep, tormenting anxiety. This people had lived for centuries with and upon the divine promise: how then could it fail to believe, and believe with all its strength, that the Almighty was to cause Israel to triumph, that He would revenge their enemies' malignance, and that at the same time He would restore the Jews to their rights and their glory? The salvation was close at hand, and that for the very reason that the nation was now humiliated, and subjected to the rule of strangers. There are a thousand signs which show how keenly and with how much longing the Messiah was awaited at the time when Christ was born. 'The deliverance of Israel', in the words of Saint Luke[60]: would it come tomorrow?

The Gospel bears witness to the intensity of this expectation. There is all the hope of the nation in the question to John the Baptist, 'Who art thou?' – that is to say, 'Art thou the Messiah?'[61] It is there in the utterly simple answer of the Samaritan woman, 'I know that Messiah (that is, the Christ) is to come';[62] in the message that the Baptist sent to Jesus, 'Is it thy coming that was foretold, or are we yet waiting for some other?';[63] in the pilgrims' impatient questioning of our Lord at the Temple, 'How long wilt thou go on keeping us in suspense? If thou art the Christ, tell us openly';[64] as well as in the acclamations of the crowd when Jesus entered Jerusalem in triumph on Palm Sunday.[65] The feeling was indeed so overwhelmingly strong that our Lord was obliged to calm the people's extreme enthusiasm, for they meant to make a king of him, the Messiah of Israel.[66]

The apocryphal books, which, as it will be remembered, formed the literature of the Jews outside the Holy Scriptures, are no less revealing. The *Book of Enoch*, the *Testament of the Twelve Patriarchs* and the *Psalms of Solomon* all speak of the Messiah, and, the better to mark his superhuman nature, they nearly always mingle a great many wonders with their account of him.[67] The Messiah also enters into the apocalypses, those strange works that deal with the end of the world, and tell what it will be like: there was no strong division, furthermore, between the reign of the Messiah and that 'age to come' which was to behold the triumph of God – some thought that the reign of the Messiah was to have a given duration (from sixty to a thousand years, according to the school of thought), whereas others thought that it would merge with eternity or with Paradise. The Messiah, then, was the centre of a vast mass of confused, involved and even contradictory notions, from which there arose a few certainties that were acknowledged by all: the reign of the Messiah would begin a time of perfect happiness; the fulness of Israel's glory would be restored; God's justice would rule the world.

There were sceptics, however, people who laughed at the popular tales that told how, once the Messiah had come, there would no longer be any need even to harvest the corn or the grapes in order to have a perpetual abundance of wheat and wine, and that the grains in the ears would all be the size of a bullock's kidneys. 'When the Messiah comes' was a popular expression that corresponded roughly to our, 'When pigs have wings': another version was, 'When Elijah comes back'. A disillusioned Pharisee said, 'If you are taking a cutting from a plant and they hurry out to tell you that the Messiah has come, get on with your cutting and finish it: you will have plenty of time to go and meet him'. Yet it was the Sadducees, more than any others, who were thought to be half-hearted about the Messiah. Generally speaking, it seems that the common people awaited the Messiah with a much greater ardour than the learned and the rich: the Talmud does not contain a single rabbinical dictum upon the subject that can certainly be dated as early as the lifetime of Christ; they are all later than the year 70.

But among the common people the expectancy was strong, and even feverish. God had appeared to be silent for hundreds of years. 'The days drag on,' Ezekiel had said, 'and every vision faileth.' Five hundred years had passed since the death of Zechariah, and no great voice announcing the divine Word had been heard from that time on. People repeated the words of the Psalmist, 'There are no prophets left now, none can tell us how long we must endure'.[68] When, indeed, would he come, the Saviour, Israel's Redeemer? Anxiously they scrutinized the texts to find an answer, subjecting them to complicated forms of calculation based upon the numerical value of the words – calculations like those which are used today by the interpreters of the Book of Revelation, the Apocalypse of Saint John, who wish to prove that the end of the world is at hand. Josephus, although he takes care not to offend his Roman friends by explaining the messianic doctrines, often speaks of adventurers who obtained a following among the Jewish people by pretending to be the Messiah; and he observes that 'there was an ambiguous prophecy in the Holy Scriptures which told the Jews that in those times a man of their nation would become the master of the world'.[69]

There was a great deal of discussion upon the conditions in which the Messiah would come, and there was quite as much upon his nature; but all the Jews were agreed in holding that the place of his glorious return could only be Jerusalem, that city holy above all others, and a wonderfully renewed Promised Land in which, as the *Apocalypse of Baruch* put it, inexhaustible manna would feed mankind until the end of time. Yet minds were far less clear upon the subject of the supernatural manner of the Messiah's advent – or, which amounts to much the same thing, upon the subject of his personality. There were many things known about him, to be sure, for the Bible contained some exact information: he would be born 'from the stock of Jesse', a descendant of David, as Isaiah had said in that eleventh chapter in which he spoke so splendidly of the future king. Others asserted, and the tradition is preserved in the Talmud,[70] that he would be the 'son of Joseph', because 'the house of Joseph was a flame'. The 'Son of God' would also be a 'son of man', as anyone who had read Daniel knew very well. Would he be called Emmanuel, following the words of Isaiah, or rather, as Jeremiah said, *Yahweh sidqenou*, which, being shortened, is Yeshua, 'the Lord vindicates us', or, 'Yahweh saves us'? There were so many fascinating questions for this nation that was so given to meditating upon problems of this sort. Some, reading the Bible in the Greek version of the Septuagint, may very well have asked themselves whether the fourteenth verse of the seventh chapter of Isaiah did not mean that he would be born, miraculously, by a virgin.

But how would he set up his kingdom? It must be admitted that upon this point the vast majority of documents reflect an image that is quite remarkably unlike that which the Christians are accustomed to recognize as that of the Messiah. The seventeenth of the apocryphal *Psalms of Solomon* draws the picture at full length: this king, a son of David, raised up by God to 'purge Jerusalem of the heathen', sinless and endowed with all wisdom, entrusted with the almighty power, 'would break the pride of sinners like so many pots', and at the same time he 'would gather the holy nation and lead it with justice, in peace and equality'. This was a noble figure indeed, although national pride had left its mark upon it. But there were far more savage passages in the other apocryphal books: they emphasized the warlike character of the messianic king and dwelt upon the destruction of the heathen nations, the crushed heads, the piled-up bodies, the sharp arrows struck into the hearts of enemies. The *Fourth Book of Ezra* likens him to a devouring lion; the *Apocalypse of Baruch* compares his coming to an earthquake followed by a fire and then by a famine, for all the nations other than the Chosen People. These reactions are only too understandable: humiliated Israel awaited an avenger, or at all events a liberator who would give the nation back its place in the world. That, for the Jews, was the natural order of events; so much so, indeed, that even Christ's disciples retained this image and on several occasions asked Him whether He would not at last set up His kingdom upon earth, and whether He would not allow them to take part in His glorious reign.

And yet a closer reading of the Scriptures would have shown another image, one infinitely more touching. It was that of a sorrowful Messiah, taking men's afflictions and their distress upon himself and offering up his life for the expiation of their sins. Isaiah had shown him as 'one despised, left out of all human reckoning; bowed with misery and no stranger to weakness . . . for our sins he was wounded', and as an innocent lamb led to the slaughter.[71] Zechariah, too, had spoken of one, 'whom they had pierced through. Lament for him they must, and grieve bitterly . . . great shall be the mourning in Jerusalem';[72] and the last of the Old Testament books, rejected by the rabbis, the Book of Wisdom, which expressed one of the most living currents of Jewish spiritual life, showed the sacrifice of the 'just man' and his shameful death winning its victory over evil and over 'the devil's envy [that] brought death into the world.'[73] But few indeed would have been the Jews who were thinking of those prophetic verses in the holy books at the moment when, as Micah had foretold, there was born, far from home, in Bethlehem, 'least . . . among all the clans of Juda',[74] the child of a humble carpenter.

JESUS AMONG HIS PEOPLE AND IN HIS TIME

Jesus of Nazareth, a Jew among Jews – 'Christ has superseded the law' – The Jewish people and Jesus.

JESUS OF NAZARETH, A JEW AMONG JEWS

What kind of man was He, whose coming was to mark the greatest date in the history of the world, whose advent renewed, once and for all, the revelation made to Israel? How did He, as a man, fit into the pattern of this nation whose characteristics we have endeavoured to describe? What were the reasons, arising both from His nature and from that of His people, that were to force the break between them and bring about the bitter drama in which the message that He bore was to be delivered in all its fulness? No book upon life in Palestine at the time of Christ can close without having considered these questions.

A single phrase provides the answer, the phrase that Péguy addressed to 'the people of the Jews': 'He was a Jew, a plain Jew, a Jew like you, a Jew among you . . .'[1] All this is the undeniable fact, a fact that too many Christians have for too long a time tended to forget, but one which the most recent historical and exegetical work continually makes more and more evident. 'Jesus Christ, whom the Christians worship as God but [whom they hold to be] also truly man', was a Jew, a Palestinian Jew of the time of Augustus and Herod: He was not only a Jew by His origins, the manner of His everyday life and His habit of mind, but His spiritual message had its deep roots in the Jewish soil of Israel – 'A fact', writes Father Lagrange, 'which for us in no way takes away from its divine origin'.[2]

The New Testament texts could not be more categorical. Saint Paul, proudly stating that the Israelites were his 'own kinsmen by race', also recalls, as a self-evident truth, that 'theirs is the human stock from which Christ came'.[3] 'Our Lord took his origin from

Juda, that is certain',[4] adds the Epistle to the Hebrews; and in his usual symbolic manner Saint John repeats this statement in the Apocalypse.[5] The evangelists continually write of our Lord as the 'son of David', and two of them, Matthew and Luke, even give the genealogy of this remote descendant of the kings who had been the glory of the Chosen People.[6]

Jesus, 'born under the Law',[7] was at once taken into the Jewish community, according to the rules that we have already spoken of.[8] On the eighth day He was circumcised,[9] and this most characteristic of Jewish rites is still commemorated in the Christian Church on January 1st. His parents obeyed all the requirements of the Law, both for themselves and for Him: His mother performed the observances laid down in the Torah for women after childbirth, and He Himself was presented at the Temple, consecrated to the Lord and redeemed by the offering of two doves, like any other first-born son of a Jewish family.[10]

The name that was given Him, Yeshua, or Jesus, of which Joshua is another form, was a very old Jewish name, a God-bearing name meaning, 'Yahweh is salvation', or, 'Yahweh saves us', often to be found in the Bible, not only as the name of that famous Judge of Israel who stopped the sun in its course, but also as that by which the author of Ecclesiasticus signed his book, almost at the end – Jesus, the son of Sirach. It was a name that was born by four high priests between the years 37 BC and AD 70; and, according to Saint Luke, it was the name of one of our Lord's ancestors.[11] His parents' names, too, were thoroughly Jewish: Joseph was the name of that famous patriarch who was Pharaoh's chief minister and who settled Israel in Egypt; and Mary was one of the most usual women's names of that time, among the Jews.[12] And all the names of His relatives were Jewish: John (Yohanan) his cousin, who was to be the Baptist; John's parents, Zacharias and Elizabeth; and those whom the Gospel does not mention but who are to be found in the apocryphal writings as well as the tradition of the Church – Anne and Joachim, His maternal grandparents.

As a child, Jesus was certainly brought up in the Jewish way; that is to say, He received a religious education, learning to read in the Holy Scriptures at the *Beth ha-Sefer*, the school-house of His little town, and His parents taught Him to be a pious Israelite, taking Him with them when He was very young on their pilgrimages to Jerusalem. The episode of the Child among the doctors of the Law, debating with them in the Temple, tells us a great deal about the biblical instruction that He received: however supernatural His gifts in the theological sciences may have been, it is reasonable to suppose that a little boy of twelve must have been well schooled in order to fill the rabbis with 'amazement' at his knowledge.[13]

He certainly learnt His father's trade, that of a carpenter,[14] and when He was grown up, Jesus, like most of the Jews of His time, worked with His hands, making ploughs and yokes for oxen: there is a tradition, which Justin Martyr recorded in the second century, that preserves the memory of His labours. His contemporaries saw Him, then, wearing a wood shaving behind the ear, that being the particular mark of the wood-workers; and they saw Him smoothing wood with a plane and striking it with a mallet. The house where He lived in Nazareth, before He began His mission and had 'nowhere to lay His head', was no doubt one of those humble cube-like dwellings such as the peasants of Palestine have built from that day till this: it may have been in part a cave. And to sleep there, when night fell, He laid out the matting that served as a bed for the common people, and wrapped Himself in a rug or in His cloak.

His physical appearance, which thousands of painters were to dream about in the centuries to come, was that of a practising Jew of His time. He had long hair, not necessarily a beard, but certainly those curling side-locks which are the continuation of the hair at the temples and which the Law made obligatory.[15] His clothes were those that everybody wore: the Gospel speaks of His 'cloak without a seam',[16] and from the episode of the woman with an issue of blood it is clear that He did not omit to put those four tassels of wool required by Deuteronomy at the corners of His cloak – those *tzitzith* that symbolically remind the wearer of the Almighty's commandments.[17] And on His feet He wore sandals, as did most of His companions.

His food, as we see it in the texts, was the ordinary food of His country. He would rarely have eaten meat: in the Gospel the fatted calf is killed only upon an extraordinary occasion; and lamb is scarcely to be seen on the table except at the Passover supper. Fish, on the other hand, which, as we know, had an important place in the Jewish diet, is often mentioned: to prove to His disciples that He was not a spirit, the risen Christ ate a piece of roast fish with them, on the shores of the Sea of Galilee.[18]

The Gospel also speaks frequently of another of the Jews' chief forms of food, bread – that bread which our Lord was to raise to the rank of a sacramental symbol. And the wedding at Cana alone is enough to show that Christ undoubtedly drank that dark, thick wine that has to be mingled with water before it is served, wine which was also to be made part of the revelation of the Eucharist. The eating customs to which the Gospel refers are all of a very sober kind. As we have seen, Jewish cookery, at least among the poor, knew nothing of the elaborate Roman ways; but for all that, the family would be regaled with rich dishes on feast days; and in the Gospel we often see our Lord sharing in these banquets with His friends.

All these customs, as we see them in the four Gospels, show us Jesus as a Jewish man, different in no way from the other men of His race. The language that He spoke was that of his fellow-countrymen, the Aramaic which Saint Mark does not hesitate to quote, sprinkling his Greek text with its words, some of them being spoken by our Lord Himself.[19] As for Hebrew, the liturgical language, the language of the Bible, there is no doubt that He knew it too, since He was able to read a scriptural passage aloud in the synagogues and then comment upon it to His hearers.

When He began His ministry, in what context did He do so, and who were His helpers, His collaborators? The physical context was that of the Jewish land, that Palestine which He practically never left in all His many journeys. His disciples, the twelve apostles, were all Jews, most of them peasants and fishermen from Galilee: their names alone show this – Simon, John, Jude and Judas, Levi, who was to be Matthew, and the others. When He spoke, his style was so impregnated with the Jewish manner of expression that the rhythms, the balanced repetitions and the alliterations of Hebrew poetry[20] are to be felt even in the Greek of the Gospels, just as in His parables we are aware of the same manner of thought as that which produced the *midrash* of Israel. To say that He had an excellent knowledge of the Bible is quite inadequate: the sacred text formed part of His very mind; He was continually quoting from it, and even when He did not take the exact words of the Bible, how very often He referred to it, and how very often He set one part in agreement with another! Some of His most strikingly original sayings are nothing other than biblical quotations lit with another light.[21] It is clear that this was a habit of mind that He owed to His Jewish upbringing, if one

432

remembers how His mother Mary, in improvising the Magnificat, wove it almost from one end to the other out of memories of the Book, to such a degree that this splendid hymn appears to sum up all the great themes of the hope of the Jews.

But it was not only by birth, breeding, manner of life, friendship and means of expression that Jesus, as a man, was a Jew and so wholly a Jew that everything that has been said about the daily life of His people applies to Him and allows one to form a concrete image of Him, in His time and among His people. He was also a Jew in that He recognized that His people had a particular mission and a destiny entirely of their own. He, like all His countrymen, was a son of the covenant. And here again there is no doubt that we can see the influence of His mother's education: the whole of the end of the Magnificat glorifies 'the promise which He made to our forefathers, Abraham and his posterity for evermore'. 'Salvation, after all, is to come from the Jews', said Jesus to the Samaritan woman, as though this were a matter of course.[22] And it would even seem that at least at the beginning of His ministry He wished to limit the revelation of His message, 'to the lost sheep that belong to the house of Israel',[23] and not to, 'take the children's bread and throw it to the dogs';[24] as if He intended to root His teaching thoroughly in the Jewish earth before giving it that universal character that it was to have in the later period, when He bade His disciples go and preach 'all over the world, so that all nations may hear the truth'.

Jesus, a son of the covenant, behaved as an ardently religious practising Jew. The Gospel often mentions His going into synagogues to teach and pray – one feels that there He was at home – and when He was at Jerusalem He went up to the Temple to pray to His Father. His respect for the sacred building, the centre of Jewish religious life, is clear from His indignation against those 'who bought and sold in the Temple', who turned the 'house of prayer' into a 'den of thieves'.[25] He did not fail to celebrate the great feasts that stood like milestones in the year, sanctifying it: He celebrated the Feast of Tabernacles and that of the Dedication;[26] and only a few days before His death He told two of His disciples to make the arrangements for the Passover, so that He might celebrate it with them.[27] It is too widely supposed, and mistakenly, that He rejected and condemned all the observances of the Mosaic Law. He did nothing of the kind: as a well-known passage in Saint Matthew states formally,

'Believe me, heaven and earth must disappear sooner than one jot, one flourish disappear from the Law; it must all be accomplished. Whoever, then, sets aside one of these commandments, though it were the least, and teaches men to do the like, will be of least account in the kingdom of heaven.'[28] He referred with great respect to the Sabbath, that touchstone of Jewish observance: for example, when He spoke of the end of the world, He said, 'You must pray that your flight may not be . . . on the Sabbath day',[29] because it was forbidden, on that day, to travel more than a Sabbath day's journey or to carry away one's goods. One of the 'unrecorded sayings' found on a papyrus even attributes to our Lord the words: 'If you do not keep the Sabbath, you shall not see the Father.'[30] And if in fact He did take up a position against observances and against the Sabbath it was because of the excessive importance that the doctors gave to these ritualistic practices, and not because He was in disagreement with the underlying principle. His attitude is defined in the famous words, 'Do not think I have come to set aside the Law and the prophets; I have not come to set them aside, but to bring them to perfection'.[31]

All the essential themes of the Jewish faith are to be found in the teaching of Christ. In the very first place, there is that absolute and imperative monotheism, that reaching up towards the One God which was Israel's pride. For Jesus, God was always 'the first to be served', as Joan of Arc was to say. For Him, as we have said before, the 'first commandment of all' was that of loving God; and it was by no mere chance that in answer to the scribe He replied by reciting the *Shema*: 'Listen, Israel, there is no Lord but the Lord our God.'[32] But we have seen that the great evangelical principle, 'Thou shalt love thy neighbour as thyself', the 'second commandment',[33] also had its roots in the Jewish tradition. Christ's moral teaching, too, stemmed from the doctrine founded by Moses and developed by the prophets, by Job, the Psalmist and Jesus the son of Sirach, with the same design of making the spiritual life more inward and of preventing it from becoming a mechanical obedience to given commands. How many prophets, from Isaiah to Joel, had already said that fasting and spectacular penitence were not enough! Christian universalism itself is linked to a current of Jewish thought which, although it may not have been the most widely accepted, nevertheless possessed a very real strength.[34]

While it is true that our Lord cannot be held to have been a member of any of the religious sects that divided the Jewish community between them, there is no sort of doubt that His thought agreed with the teachings now of one group, now of another – even with the doctrine of those Pharisees who, from a superficial reading of the Gospel, seem to have been His enemies, men rejected by Him out of hand. Renan exaggerates when he says that, 'the Rabbi Hillel was the true master of Jesus'; but on many fundamental issues, such as the part played by Providence in the world and by Grace in man, our Lord's thought is in agreement with that of the Pharisees. In the same way we have seen[35] how many similarities may be pointed out between His doctrine and His manner of expressing it, and that of the Essenes, as it has been revealed by the Dead Sea scrolls. There are even some typically Christian rites that may be related, though only to a limited extent, to the customs of the monks of Qumrân: for example, there were those lustrations that remind one of John's baptism of Christ, and those meals of the whole community together which foreshadow the Last Supper, and in relation to which the Essenian texts speak of bread and wine.[36] All this situates Jesus and His message in a framework that is so clearly Jewish that any consideration of His thought and His personality which does not take account of the Jewish roots of both is bound to be mistaken.

In coming into the world, the Son of Mary assumed the function of that Messiah upon whom the hopes of Israel had centred for hundreds of years; and it was in the context of the 'redemption of Israel'[37] that He first made known the salvation that He brought mankind. Would this sublime concept of the Redeemer ever have been accessible unless a long tradition had brought it into existence and had developed it in the consciousness of the nation which had been entrusted with the expressed will of God? One must be deeply aware of the multifarious links that bound Jesus to His people, and thoroughly recognize His racial, intellectual, moral and spiritual attachment to the nation of the covenant in order to measure the extent to which He surpassed its fundamental ideas, and to understand why He was not the Messiah that Israel awaited.

'CHRIST HAS SUPERSEDED THE LAW'

For He was not. Broadly speaking, Israel did not acknowledge Jesus as the long-awaited Messiah: only a small group followed

Him. And from this refusal there resulted the bitter drama in which the short earthly ministry of the young Galilean who had taught His disciples a more perfect manner of knowing and serving God came to its end.

The reasons that one may assign to this refusal and its outcome are also related to the basic assumptions of the Jewish people, just as much as they are to the fundamental originality of His message. With Israel in the state it was at the time of our Lord's coming, was it possible for the Jews to accept a teaching which, although it was deeply rooted in their tradition, went far beyond its ordinary expression, and which even ran directly counter to their beliefs in some matters that might reasonably be thought to be of vital importance?

We have just seen Jesus, in many parts of His teaching, as the heir of Jewish thought. The heir to the whole of this thought? No. But to all that was purest in it, to all that was highest and which answered spiritual requirements best. And in the great body of rabbinical teaching, in the people's way of thinking, what did these higher elements stand for? There were doctors of the Law who were capable of holding up the great conception of God as a Father against the idea of an Almighty lost in mystery, a dreadful and a terrifying Judge, just as our Lord did so fully; but how many of them were there? There were some rabbis among the Pharisees and some theologians among the Essenes who maintained the doctrine of the gifts of Grace, so 'repugnant to the Jewish mind',[38] which was one of the chief themes of the teaching of Christ and of His interpreter, Saint Paul. The Talmud, as we know, gathered admirable texts upon charity, the love of one's neighbour and brotherly forgiveness of offence: but did these prevail against the hard-heartedness of the 'stiff-necked people', and against the famous 'eye for an eye, tooth for a tooth'? And although it is true that there were both scriptural texts and rabbinical precepts that taught a more heart-felt moral conduct in which it was not enough 'to cleanse the outward part of the cup' – a teaching in agreement with Christ's – there are many signs to show that they had less influence among the faithful than those which insisted upon a mechanical obedience to formal commands. Jesus may very well stand in the direct line of the great spiritual teachers of His people, but it is quite clear that He belonged to that small minority that made up its spiritual aristocracy, the forerunners, who are rarely in agreement with the main body.

And yet even in this limited group He stands out as a non-conformist. Jesus carried the implications of some of the rabbis' traditions to their ultimate extent, and in doing so He went infinitely beyond them. What rabbi, speaking of the Temple, that central point of religious life, would ever have dared to say that there could be 'one greater than the Temple',[39] or that 'the time is coming, nay, has already come, when true worshippers will worship the Father in spirit and in truth'?[40] What Jewish spiritual leader, laying down the rule of love for one's neighbour, would have dared utter the sublime paradox upon which the Christian doctrine is founded: 'But I tell you, Love your enemies',[41] even one as magnanimous as Hillel? There is in these words not only a fulfilment, but also a going beyond, a transcendence. A transcendence, furthermore, that is also to be seen in many other fields – in that of rites, for example. The two chief Christian rites, baptism and the eucharist, do appear to be related to certain Jewish ceremonies; but in fact the resemblance is only superficial. The Temple priests and the monks of Qumrân often bathed ritually, and John the Baptist took the penitents who came to him into the water of the river; but Christian baptism was to be something quite other than a lustration, even one made with the purpose of a symbolic cleansing; and as we are told in the Acts,[42] it was not even to be a 'baptism of repentance' like John's. The Essenes, too, had a communal meal in which the bread and the wine were blessed, but there is no text that leads one to suppose that there was any intention beyond that of establishing brotherliness. Instead of a ceremony, the Christians were to have a sacrament; and in the sacrament the believer's soul was to share in the life of God. Here we have left the traditions quite behind.

What, then, is the meaning of those words of our Lord's that have just been quoted: 'Do not think I have come to set aside the law and the prophets; I have not come to set them aside, but to bring them to perfection'? The words, 'bring them to perfection' have been much discussed. Our Lord certainly used an Aramaic expression, but as we do not know what it was, we are obliged to scrutinize the Greek of Saint Matthew, *plerosai*, which may mean 'to fulfil', 'to crown' or 'to perfect' just as well as 'to bring to fruition' or 'to bring to an end'. Historians and commentators have differed in their choice of translation; some have interpreted the words as meaning that Christ's message only carried on the tradition of Israel, others as meaning that it put a term to it.[43] But may not Christ's thought in fact have embraced both meanings, so that both are true? He 'brought the law to perfection', that is, He realised all the potentialities that it contained; but at that point the function of this Law came to an end – it was accomplished. Saint Paul, too, uses an ambiguous expression with very much the same meaning when he writes: 'Christ has superseded the law.'[44]*

It cannot be denied that upon certain questions – questions that were, as we know, of the utmost importance in Jewish eyes – Jesus left the traditions of His race and took up positions that could not but shock His people. It is here that we come into contact with the underlying causes of the drama.

This was a nation that had been fighting in the defence of its religion, and with it the reason for its own existence, for hundreds of years, a nation which, as it happens, was then under the rule and occupation of idol-worshipping pagans; and from long experience the Jews knew very well that the pagan could turn into a persecuting enemy. Defence of the faith, then, was a matter of life or death, and it was for this reason that the nation cast out heretics and schismatics with such horror, and so despised those who were unfaithful to the precepts of religion. But what was Christ's attitude? He went very much further than the most universalist of rabbis, seeing a brother in the uncircumcised pagan, the open sinner and the unbeliever. He did not in the least share the anti-Roman feelings of His more violent countrymen; in His famous reply, 'Give back to Caesar what is Caesar's', He made it perfectly clear that He was in no way whatever concerned with political questions; and He went so far as to hold up the faith of the pagan centurion of Capernaum as an example.[45] He treated Samaritans in the same way, those heretics whose 'bread was worse than swine's flesh'; for He would willingly talk with them, and He used them, too, as examples of gratitude and charity.[46] His gentleness reached out also to notorious sinners, the despised publicans, loose women and those *am-ha-arez* who were supposed to have no knowledge of the Law. There was here a reversal of all that was customary so complete that it could not appear as anything but scandalous.

*This is the Knox Version of Rom. 10, 4, and its unambiguity does not very happily render the French, which is: *'La fin de la Loi, c'est le Christ.'* The Vulgate reads: *'finis enim legis, Christus'*, and the Authorized Version: 'for Christ is the end of the law'.

This was a nation that, for the better defence of its faith, had for hundreds of years unceasingly armoured it with formal precepts which were to ensure the invariable observance of the great principles of religion. The tendency of the whole of the teaching of the rabbis was to see to it that in all the circumstances of his life a man should have a commandment that he might apply in the knowledge that by doing so he was acting in accordance with religion. For them the system's true protection, the 'hedge' of the Pharisees, was indeed the letter of the Law: but Jesus was against this rigidity. There were two questions which preoccupied the rabbis' minds: the observance of the Sabbath, and ritual uncleanliness. On both, Jesus took up positions that set public opinion at defiance. He might say that the Sabbath was made for man, and not man for the Sabbath without giving much offence: there were some doctors who were of the same opinion. But at the same time that He said that the day was to be respected, He spoke of Himself as 'master of the Sabbath'; He approved of His disciples' inattention to the rabbinical prohibitions;[47] and, if we are to follow the *Codex Bezae*, He even said to a man who was working on the holy day, 'If thou knowest what thou dost, blessed art thou'.[48] His attitude towards ritual uncleanliness was the same. By stating that 'it is not what goes into a man's mouth that makes him unclean',[49] Jesus reduced those precepts to which the rabbis attributed a capital importance to their true proportion. He went further still; for His teaching, which Saint Paul expresses in the words: 'The written law inflicts death, whereas the spiritual law brings life', proclaimed the vanity of all mere observance. This was to run directly against official teaching and against public opinion: it was to provoke an open breach.

But even if there had not been these two serious causes of disagreement, Jesus, as He was, had scarcely any chance of being acknowledged as the Messiah. The reasons are clear: as it is natural in a humiliated nation, the great majority of the Jews expected that the man sent by Providence should give them their revenge, and from this there had arisen the very widely spread image of the Messiah as a war-leader, a glorious king, the terror of his enemies, Israel's avenger. Did the son of the carpenter of Nazareth really answer to this description? It is significant that our Lord should Himself have told His disciples of the temptations that He had undergone and rejected during His retreat in the wilderness – and He must have done so, for they could have learnt of them from no other source. It is as though He had wished them to understand quite clearly, from the beginning, that His kingdom would not be of this world. And yet the idea of an entirely earthly Messiah was so firmly rooted that even His disciples ingenuously referred to it, that in their simplicity they asked Him whether it was in that time that He was going to set up the kingdom in Israel, and that they were astonished at His end. As for that image of a suffering Messiah, sacrificed for the salvation of the world, which might have been formed from a few short passages in the Bible, we must say again that it was 'completely foreign to the Judaism of the period towards the Christian era'. More than that, the public opinion of this proud nation would have found something scandalous in such a concept, for defeat had never appeared to them a mark of God. That is why no movement of pity aroused the watching crowd at the sight of this man, scourged, dripping with blood and the spittle of contempt. This ridiculous Messiah was fit for the cross.

There is no possible doubt that Jesus Himself was perfectly aware that He and His message ran against the feelings of His people. Such expressions as, 'and they had no confidence in Him', 'stumbling-block', and 'you give me no welcome' show His mind very clearly. As He said, speaking from the fulness of His knowledge, the 'new wine' that He brought was not to be put into 'old skins'. It was a truly new teaching that He meant to bring, even at the risk of breaking with those who held by the ancient doctrine.

Israel's refusal to accept the Messiah arose from a logical process that history is bound to acknowledge. It would be going beyond the scope of the present book to say that from the Christian point of view this refusal can only be fully understood in the light of its providential meaning, since a kind of necessity links it with the mystery of the redeeming sacrifice of the Cross. Yet it must be pointed out that this refusal set the seal upon another mystery, that of the wonderfully strange, the unique destiny of the people to whom the divine revelation had been entrusted, the people who had borne God within them.

THE JEWISH PEOPLE AND JESUS

One last question remains: was the refusal of Israel that of the whole nation? Were all Christ's countrymen aware of His mission and His message? Did they all know that He had proclaimed

Himself the Messiah, and were they capable of distinguishing that which might make Him a 'sign of contradiction'?

In order to answer this, one would have to know exactly what importance our Lord's earthly progress had in the life of His people, how widely His teaching and His miracles were known, and how many there were who believed in Him. This is a matter of great difficulty. There are no documents other than the Christian records – Josephus does not speak of our Lord at all[50] – and the four Gospels are our only source of information. But as everybody knows, inspired writers are not concerned with historical documentation, and those questions which would seem to a historian to be of capital importance never so much as enter their minds. The information they provide is therefore far from clear, and sometimes it even appears to be contradictory.

However, when one has read them, one comes away with the impression that the immediate repercussions of our Lord's ministry were not extensive. The three synoptic Gospels all agree that Galilee was the scene of the chief part of His teaching,[51] particularly the region of the lake and the neighbourhood of Capernaum. Now Galilee was a remote province, far from the centre, and it was one little esteemed by the Jews of Judaea, true defenders of the traditions of Israel. In Galilee itself, once the police of Herod Antipas grew busy, Jesus' activity became more discreet, and when He travelled He 'would not let anyone know of His passage'.[52] As well as the Galileans who listened to Him, there were no doubt others who came from elsewhere:[53] does this mean that there were very large numbers gathered together? At the time of the two miracles of the loaves and the fishes, five and four thousand men were fed: this is certainly a great many, but it is very far from being a whole nation, and a merely local assembly could account for such figures. In spite of the time that He passed in Judaea – one or two short periods in three years, according to the synoptic Gospels – it is quite clear from Saint Matthew that Jesus was not known in that part of the country when He went there in the last phase of His mission, for on Palm Sunday, the day of the Messiah's entry into Jerusalem, the bystanders asked, 'Who is this?'[54] And even if His ministry in Judaea did last as long as Saint John says, He still would not have been very widely known, since as the evangelist himself tells us, Jesus often kept Himself hidden.[55]

It therefore seems that Christ's message had considerable

influence and was generally known in Galilee, but that in the rest of Palestine its repercussions must have been very limited. The Jews of the Diaspora can only have heard of Him casually from pilgrims returning from Jerusalem; but quite apart from them, the great mass of the Jewish people were probably as ignorant of the Nazarene prophet's words as most Frenchmen of the Middle Ages would have been of the activities of some obscure agitator in Brittany or the Auvergne who finally came up to Paris, only to be hanged at the end of five days. It is certain that public opinion was not much stirred; and even those who did know what was going on may not have taken this tale of a people's prophet, an alleged Messiah, very seriously. Self-styled Messiahs were common enough: there were half a dozen between Christ's birth and the fall of Jerusalem. Besides, nobody had forgotten that Master of Justice of the Essenes who had quarrelled with the priesthood of Jerusalem, still less Judas of Gamala, who had been put to death in AD 6. These crises had not disturbed the public order for long. His better-informed countrymen would no doubt have regarded the human career of Jesus as something more than an ordinary piece of news, a *fait divers*, but as much less than an event of national importance.

Did His message at once cause a hostile reaction? It seems that for a long time there was sympathy for Him among the common people, and even enthusiasm. When Saint Luke says that, 'all the people hung upon his lips',[56] he certainly means the crowd, the populace, as opposed to the ruling class. There is a great deal of evidence to prove that up until the Sunday of His triumphal entry into Jerusalem, and including that day, popular feeling was in favour of Jesus. Besides, could those parts of His teaching which seem to us to be against the most settled Jewish traditions have seriously offended His hearers? The Galilean peasants and fishermen would scarcely have been very indignant when the young prophet treated the cumbrous, wearisome rabbinical regulations with no undue respect; and if He made game of the excessive scrupulosity of the tithe, from which they were the first sufferers, would that have vexed them very much?

His messianic character, so unlike that which was expected, might have caused a rapidly growing dissension; but He seems to have done His utmost to keep this in the background. It was only to the Samaritan woman, an unimportant foreigner, that He ever proclaimed Himself the Messiah; and every time His divinity was revealed to the apostles, as by His transfiguration, for example, or His miracles, He always required them to be silent. The only exception that He ever made to this rule was to accept the 'triumph' of His entry into Jerusalem on Palm Sunday; and even so it seems that this triumph was but a modest one. As for His miracles, Father Lagrange has very rightly observed that, however extraordinary they may have been, they were in no way a proof, in the eyes of the people, that He was the Messiah – still less that He made any such claim. For had not certain prophets, as Elijah and Elisha, raised up the dead?[57]

The roots of the conflict that came to its terrible end in April of the year 30 are not to be found in the spontaneous hostility of the people. Who, then, did bring it about? Saint James, that apostle who, in his Epistle, shows himself so profoundly Jewish, has no hesitation in replying that it was the rich and the powerful[58] – in short, Israel's ruling class. From the earliest days of Christ's ministry the doctors of the Law and the Pharisees, with a very few exceptions, were mistrustful of Him, and we see them setting Him questions that were merely traps and plotting against Him: it is clear that for their part they understood that the new revelation could not but clash with their traditional teaching. And the Sadducees' natural reaction when, at the end of His mission, our Lord taught in Judaea, was at first distrust and then hostility. Theirs was a policy designed to avoid difficulties, a policy of keeping on good terms with the Roman authorities, who detested these agitators who called themselves the Messiah or the King of Israel and who stirred up trouble. It was easy, then, for the two great religious parties to come to an agreement, and the very great majority of the Sanhedrim that judged Him on that tragic night from Thursday to Good Friday was against Him. As for the crowd (and crowds are notoriously fickle) it was easy enough to turn their approval into indignation by quoting some of His sayings, out of context, garbled and given a false meaning – sayings such as that in which He spoke of Himself as the Son of God, for example, or said that He could raise up the Temple again in three days. Love of conformity did the rest, and the people followed the authorities.

So on Friday, April 7th, in the year 30, a man was to be seen, a pitiful sight with His marked and blood-stained face, carrying a heavy beam on His shoulders and staggering under its weight as

He went down the stepped streets of Jerusalem from the judgment-hall of the Antonia fortress and then climbed towards the Gate of Ephraim. A troop of Roman auxiliaries escorted him, and with Him there went a few of His followers, mostly women. Did the crowd, the housewives on their way to the upper market for their Passover shopping, the craftsmen, the worshippers going up to the Temple, the ass-drivers, pay much attention to this procession? A condemned man being led to the place of execution was no very uncommon spectacle. And when all was over, when the three crosses, the Cross of Christ and those of the two thieves, stood upon the bare mound of Golgotha, that haunt of wandering dogs and vultures, how many of the travellers on the road to Jaffa stopped to gaze at those poor remnants of humanity, to read an inscription placed on the central cross and to ask the soldiers as they played at knuckle-bones, 'Who is it?' In the daily life of the Jewish people, may not the most important event in the history of the world have passed unnoticed?

BIBLIOGRAPHICAL NOTES

The documents that form the basis of the present book fall under four main headings: the Bible; the apocryphal books of the Old and the New Testaments; Josephus; and the Talmud.

Among recent editions of the Holy Book, two are outstandingly useful: *La Sainte Bible*, edited by L. Pirot and A. Clamer (in course of publication), whose notes are so extensive that some amount to positive articles; and the *Bible de Jérusalem*, whose publication in parts was finished in 1958, and which is crowded with valuable information. A great deal is also to be learnt from M. Zadoc Kahn's edition of the Old Testament – *La Bible traduite du texte original par les membres du Rabbinat français* (2 vols., Paris, 1957–58). For a concise introduction, see *What is the Bible?* by Daniel-Rops (Faith and Facts, 1958).

The apocryphal books (in the Catholic meaning of the expression) are to be found in *La Bible apocryphe: I, En marge de l'Ancien Testament*, by J. Bonsirven (Paris, 1953), and *II, Evangiles apocryphes*, by F. Amiot (Paris, 1952). There is also W. J. Ferrar's *The Uncanonical Jewish Books* (Translation of Early Documents, 1918), as well as many works, particularly in the Jewish Apocryphal Literature Series, on the separate books. For the New Testament Apocrypha we have J. Hervieux's *Apocryphal Gospels* (Faith and Facts, 1960), and *The Apocryphal New Testament* by M. R. James (1953).

Josephus, a Jewish historian somewhat later than the time of Christ, gives a considerable amount of information. His *Works* have been edited and translated by H. Thackeray and R. Marcus in the Loeb Classical Library (4 vols., London, 1925–30).

The reader will see, upon referring to pp. 384 and 385, why the Talmud may be used as a source, and with what reservations it is to be consulted. There are the thirty-six volumes of *The Babylonian Talmud in English*, edited by Rabbi Dr I. Epstein (London, Soncino Press, 1935–53), the one-volume *Everyman's Talmud* by A. Cohen, and Maurice Schwab's French version, which gives the whole of the Jerusalem Talmud together with the tractate *Berakoth* from the Babylonian Talmud (Paris, 1960). The tractate *Shabbath* has been translated into English by W. O. E. Oesterley, and in German there is the well-known *Kommentar zum Neuen Testament aus Talmud und Midrash* of H. Strack and P. Billerbeck (Munich, 1934). Another valuable book is J. Bonsirven's *Textes rabbiniques des deux premiers siècles chrétiens* (Rome, 1955).

Some of the dictionaries and the more important handbooks are exceedingly useful. Among the best is *A Dictionary of Life in Bible Times*, by W. Corswant, a Protestant: it is a book that is filled with knowledge, and it is admirably clear. The five fat volumes of Vigouroux's *Dictionnaire encyclopédique de la Bible* (1895–1912) contain a very great deal of information, and a *Supplément* to it has been appearing in parts since 1920, under the direction of Pirot and Robert.

Brepols published the valuable *Dictionnaire encyclopédique de la Bible* in 1960: other useful works are *Christus*, an encyclopedia edited by J. Huby (Paris, 1916), and *Catholicisme*, which is now being brought out by G. Jacquemet. The recently finished *Jewish Encyclopedia* is an essential book, and so is the re-cast *Initiation biblique* of Robert and Tricot (Paris, 1954). Lastly, four archaeological works, very different in size but all excellent: A. G. Barrois, *Archéologie biblique* (2 vols., Paris, 1939–53); W. F. Albright, *Archeology and the Religion of Israel* (1954); M. du Buit, *Archéologie du Peuple d'Israël* (Paris, 1958); and R. de Vaux, *Les Institutions de l'Ancien Testament* (Paris, 1960).

The subject of this present book has often been dealt with by other authors, with varying degrees of success. A. C. Bouquet, in his *Everyday Life in New Testament Times* (1953), tells us in fact very little about Jewish manners and customs, but continually refers to those of the Greeks and Romans of that period. Two earlier works are far richer: *La Palestine au temps de Jésus-Christ* (3rd edition, Paris, 1885) by Edmond Stapfer, a Protestant; and *La Vie privée du peuple juif à l'époque de Jésus-Christ* (Paris, 1910), by M.-B. Schwalm, a Dominican, which is particularly well documented upon social questions. There is also A. Edersheim's *The Temple, its Ministry and Services as they were in the Time of Christ*; and in *Les Années obscures de Jésus-Christ* (Paris, 1960), Robert Aron has dealt with certain aspects of our subject.

Obviously, one must also read the histories of Israel: for the general picture the classic work is G. Ricciotti's book, translated into French by Auvray under the title *Histoire d'Israël* (new edition, 1948); and the *Social and Religious History of the Jews* of the American professor S. W. Baron, a very recent book, is a mine of information. Our own *Israel and the Ancient World*, a much lighter work, is not without its usefulness as a general view. For particular questions and periods, one may consult: A. Lods, *The Prophets and the Rise of Judaism* (1950); C. Guignebert, *The Jewish World in the Time of Jesus* (1939); J. Bonsirven, *Les Idées juives au temps de Notre-Seigneur* (Paris, 1934); M.-J. Lagrange, *Le Judaïsme avant Jésus-Christ* (Paris, 1934); Stewart Perowne, *The Life and Times of Herod the Great* (1956); F. O. Busch, *Au Temps du Christ* (French translation by Diehl, Paris, 1957) – a book with a misleading title, for in fact it deals with Herod and his descendants; J. Juster, *Les Juifs dans l'Empire romain* (Paris, 1914); Marcel Simon, *Les sectes juives au temps de Jésus* (Paris, 1960); H. Regnault, *Une Province procuratorienne* (Paris, 1909); Paul Demann, *Les Juifs, Foi et Destinée* (Paris, 1960). Almost all these books have bibliographies that complete our own.

There are uncountable books on Jesus: we will only mention those which have a bearing upon our subject – that is to say, which deal to some extent with the everyday life. Catholic works: G. Ricciotti, *Vie de Jésus-Christ* (French translation by Vaussard, Paris, 1947); Daniel-Rops, *Jesus in His Time* (2nd edition, 1956); F. M. Willam, *La Vie de Jésus dans le pays et le peuple d'Israël* (French translation by Gautier,

Mulhouse, 1947); M. Marnas, *Quel est donc cet homme?* (Paris, 1927); M.-J. Lagrange, *L'Evangile de Jésus-Christ* (Paris, 1928); Jean Guitton, *Jésus* (Paris, 1956). Protestant works: H. Monnier, *La Mission historique de Jésus* (Paris, 1914); A. Réville, *Jésus de Nazareth* (Paris, 1906). Jewish works: J. Klausner, *Jésus de Nazareth* (Paris, 1933); Montefiore, *La Vie et l'Enseignement de Jésus-Christ* (Paris, 1931). Agnostic works: C. Guignebert, *Jésus* (Paris, 1938) and *Le Christ* (Paris, 1943); P.-L. Couchoud, *Le Dieu Jésus* (Paris, 1949). The moving plea of Jules Isaac, *Jésus et Israël* (latest edition Paris, 1959), deserves a separate mention: our 'Finale' owes a great deal to this book.

Lastly, for particular questions, we have turned to other works, which are often mentioned in the notes – for example, in those dealing with the geography of Palestine or the Dead Sea scrolls. Among these is Jean Daniélou's excellent book on Philo of Alexandria (Paris, 1958), R. Travers Hereford on the Pharisees, the *Langues sacrées* of Aufray, Poulain and Blaise (Paris, 1957), and lastly the admirable little book on *Le Monde gréco-romain au temps de Notre-Seigneur* by A. Festugière and P. Fabvre (Paris, 1935).

447

CHRONOLOGICAL TABLES

TABLE I

Date BC	Israel	Pagan Nations
2000(?)	Abraham	Hammurabi in Babylon: in Egypt, the XIIIth dynasty: the first palace of Cnossus in Crete
1800(?)	Jacob	The Hyksos in Egypt
1700(?)	Joseph in Egypt	Liberation of Egypt by
1600(?)		the Pharaohs of the XVIIIth dynasty (1580)
1440 or 1225	The Exodus	The revolutionary Pharaoh Amenophis IV (1375–1360). Rameses II (1290–1225)
1180	Joshua makes his way into the Land of Canaan	The Trojan war: Ulysses' wanderings
about 1100	Israel's struggle against the Philistines	Philistines upon the coast of Palestine
twelfth and eleventh centuries	The Judges (Deborah, Gideon, Jephthah, Samson): about 1080, Samuel	Beginning of the Aramaeans' pressure. Tyre in Phoenicia
end eleventh century		Terrible wave of Aryan invasion: the Dorians
1040–1012	Saul, King of Israel	
1012–975	David, King of Israel	The Phoenician maritime empire
975–935	The great king Solomon	Hiram, King of Tyre
935	Israel is split into two kingdoms, Israel and Judah	
ninth century	Omri rebuilds Samaria (about 880)	
eighth century	The prophets: Amos, Hosea, Isaiah	Foundation of Rome, 753
	Fall of Samaria and of the northern kingdom, 722	Sargon II, King of Assyria (722–705)
seventh century	Hezekiah (718–689): the prophet Micah: Josiah: the 'discovery' of the Law (639–609): the prophets Zephaniah, Habakkuk and Jeremiah	Zoroaster in Persia. Assurbanipal in Assyria (669–626)
586	Fall of Jerusalem	Nebuchadnezzar (604–562)
	The Jews exiled to Babylon	Buddha in India: Solon in Athens

448

Date BC	Israel	Pagan Nations
about 570	Tobit	Empires of Carthage, Marseilles and of the Etruscans
552		Cyrus founds the Persian empire
538	Cyrus allows the Jews to go back to their own country. Palestine a part of the Persian empire. Rebuilding of the Temple	Cyrus takes Babylon, 539. Peisistratus in Greece. Darius I (522–485). At Rome, the Tarquins and the revolution of 509
fifth century	Judith (?)	First Persian war
		Marathon, 490. Xerxes (485–465)
	The prophet Malachi	Second Persian war. Salamis, 480
445	Nehemiah rebuilds the walls of Jerusalem	In Rome, the code of the XII Tables: in Athens, the Parthenon. The Peloponnesian war and the ruin of Athens (431–404)
fourth century	Ezra and the compilation of the Bible	Death of Socrates, 399
		Spartan domination of Greece
		Philip of Macedon, and then Alexander
332	Alexander occupies Palestine	Death of Alexander: his empire is divided between his generals
third century	Palestine under the Ptolemies of Egypt	First Punic war (264–241)
200	The Seleucids take Palestine from the Ptolemies	Second Punic war (218–201)
		The Romans defeat the Seleucid Antiochus III
	The revolt of the Maccabees	Antiochus IV 'Epiphanes' (175–163)
166–165	Mattathius	
165–160	Judas Maccabaeus	Greece a Roman province (149–146)
		Third Punic war and the end of Carthage, 146
134–104	John Hyrcanus	The Gracchi in Rome (133–123)
103–76	Alexander Jannaeus	Marius and Sulla (Sulla dictator, 82)
76–67	Salome Alexandra	Pompey defeats Mithridates
63	Pompey takes Jerusalem	First triumvirate, 60

449

Date BC	Israel	Pagan Nations
63–40	Hyrcanus II	Caesar passes the Rubicon, 50; and is assassinated, 44
40–37	Antigonus	
37	Herod the Great begins his reign	Battle of Actium:Augustus emperor

TABLE II

FROM THE ACCESSION OF HEROD TO THE FALL OF JERUSALEM

Date	Life of Jesus and of the Church	Rome	Palestine
37 B.C.			Accession of Herod the Great
27 B.C.		Augustus emperor. Quirinus legate of Syria, 8 BC– 2 BC (first holding of the office)	
6 B.C.	Birth of Jesus		
4 B.C.			Death of Herod the Great. His realm is divided between his sons Archelaus, Antipas and Philip
0	Beginning of the Christian era		
6 AD	Jesus among the doctors of the Law		Simon, son of Boethos, high priest. Archelaus deposed. Coponius procurator. Annas high priest (6–15)
9			Ambivius procurator
12			Rufus procurator
14		Death of Augustus, accession of Tiberius	
15			Gratus procurator
18			Caiaphas high priest (18–36)
26			Pontius Pilate procurator

Date	Life of Jesus and of the Church	Rome	Palestine
27	Beginning of Christ's ministry		
28	Jesus preaches, principally in Galilee		
29	Martyrdom of Saint John the Baptist		
	Christ comes to Jerusalem		
30 (April)	Christ's trial and His Passion		
33	Martyrdom of Saint Stephen		
35	Conversion of Saint Paul		
36			Marcellus procurator
37		Death of Tiberius Caligula succeeds	Marullus procurator
41		Death of Caligula Claudius succeeds	Agrippa I (41–44) reconstitutes the Palestinian kingdom
42	Saint Paul begins his missions		
44			Cuspius Fadus procurator
48			Cumanus procurator
50	Saint Matthew writes his Gospel in Aramaic		
52			Felix procurator
54		Death of Claudius Nero succeeds	
59			Porcius Festus procurator
62			Albinus procurator
63	Saint Luke writes the Acts of the Apostles		
64			Florus procurator
67	Death of Saint Paul and Saint Peter		
68		Death of Nero Crisis of 68	The great rebellion, the 'Jewish war'
70		Galba, Otto, Vitellius	The fall of Jerusalem

Note.—for the Herods, see the table on page 66.

451

ABBREVIATIONS USED IN NOTES

All the biblical references are to the Knox Version; the Catholic and Protestant Bibles differ somewhat, but it should be easy to find the texts by the use of the following table.

CATHOLIC USAGE	ABBREVIATION	PROTESTANT USAGE
Genesis	Gen.	Genesis
Exodus	Ex.	Exodus
Leviticus	Lev.	Leviticus
Numbers	Num.	Numbers
Deuteronomy	Deut.	Deuteronomy
Josue	Jos.	Joshua
Judges	Jg.	Judges
Ruth	Ruth	Ruth
1 Kings	1 Kg.	I Samuel
2 Kings	2 Kg.	II Samuel
3 Kings	3 Kg.	I Kings
4 Kings	4 Kg.	II Kings
1 Paralipomena	1 Par.	I Chronicles
2 Paralipomena	2 Par.	II Chronicles
1 Esdras	1 Esd.	Ezra
2 Esdras (or Nehemias)	2 Esd.	Nehemiah
Tobias	Tob.	Tobit (in the Apocrypha)
Judith	Jdt.	Judith (in the Apocrypha)
Esther	Est.	Esther
Job	Job	Job
Psalms	Ps.	Psalms
Proverbs	Prov.	Proverbs
Ecclesiastes	Eccl.	Ecclesiastes
Song of Songs (or Canticle of Canticles)	Cant.	Song of Songs
Wisdom	Wis.	Wisdom (in the Apocrypha)
Ecclesiasticus	Ecclus.	Ecclesiasticus (in the Apocrypha)
Isaias	Is.	Isaiah
Jeremias	Jer.	Jeremiah
Lamentations	Lam.	Lamentations
Baruch	Bar.	Baruch (in the Apocrypha)
Ezechiel	Ez.	Ezekiel
Daniel	Dan.	Daniel
Osee	Os.	Hosea
Joel	Jl.	Joel
Amos	Am.	Amos
Abdias	Abd.	Obadiah
Jonas	Jon.	Jonah

CATHOLIC USAGE	ABBREVIATION	PROTESTANT USAGE
Micheas	Mic.	Micah
Nahum	Nah.	Nahum
Habacuc	Hab.	Habakkuk
Sophonias	Soph.	Zephaniah
Aggeus (or Aggaeus)	Agg.	Haggai
Zacharias	Zach.	Zechariah
Malachias	Mal.	Malachi
1 Machabees	1 Mac.	I Maccabees (in the Apocrypha)
2 Machabees	2 Mac.	II Maccabees (in the Apocrypha)

The arrangement of the books of the New Testament and their names are the same in both Bibles, except that the Catholics call the last book the Apocalypse (Apoc.), whereas the Protestants say Revelation.

There is a difference, too, in the numbering of the Psalms: at the end of verse 21 of Psalm 9, the Protestant Bible begins Psalm 10, making two psalms of it. From this point until verse 11 of Psalm 146, therefore, one must be added to the reference to find the place in the Protestant psalter. From verse 11 of Psalm 146 onwards, the remaining numbers coincide.

The works of Josephus are often quoted, and in the notes the references are abbreviated thus: The Antiquities of the Jews – Antiquities; The Life of Josephus written by Himself – Autobiography; The Wars of the Jews – Wars.

NOTES

PART I

CHAPTER ONE, THE GEOGRAPHICAL CONTEXT

1. See map

2. Gen. 21. 33, 34; 26. 1, 8, 14; Ex. 23. 31; 1 Par. 10. 1; Ez. 16. 27, 57; 25. 15, 16; Jl. 4. 4; Am. 6. 2; 9. 7

3. On the Philistines, see Daniel-Rops: *Histoire sainte, le Peuple de la Bible*

4. Ninety-eight exactly from Gen. 9. 18 to Acts 13. 19

5. See the words *Canaan* and *Cananéens* in the index of *Histoire sainte*

6. Gen. 9. 18

7. Heb. 11. 9

8. Zach. 2. 16

9. Matt. 2. 20

10. Babylonian Talmud, *Gittin*, folio 8

11. See *Paddan Aram* in the index of *Histoire sainte*

12. Cf. *Histoire sainte*, p. 324, and the chronological table at the end of this book, p. 448

13. See these two names in the index of *Histoire sainte*

14. Babylonian Talmud, *Sotah*, 49

15. Letter to Dardanus (*Epist.*, CXXIX, 4)

16. Ps. 41. 7

17. Ps. 136. 1, 5, 6

18. On the geology and geography of Palestine, see M. du Buit: *Géographie de la Terre sainte* (2 vol., 1959), F.-M. Abel: *Géographie de la Palestine* (Paris, 1938), G. S. Blake: *Geology and water resources in Palestine* (Jerusalem, 1928). A. Keller's *Biblio-*

graphie géologique et géographique (Paris, 1933), and *Le Pays Biblique* of Legendre (Paris, 1928) give a general view of the country's geography. This section owes a great deal to Raoul Blanchard's excellent chapter in vol. 8, *Asie occidentale*, of the *Géographie universelle* of Vidal de la Blache and L. Gallois (Paris, 1929)

19. Is. 35. 2

20. Jg. 15. 4, 5

21. Jg. 4. 14 et seq.

22. Jos. 11. 17

23. '*Nec Jordanes pelago accipitur, sed unum atque alterum lacum integer perfluit, tertio retinetur.*' (*Hist.* V, 6)

24. Jos. 11. 6 et seq.

25. *Histoire sainte*, p. 43

26. *Histoire sainte*, p. 121

27. *Histoire sainte*, p. 44

28. Dan., 3. 52 et seq.

29. It snows at Jerusalem every four or five years

30. *Histoire sainte*, p. 185

31. Mk. 14. 67

32. *Kilayim*, 9

33. Matt. 8. 23–27

34. Matt. 7. 27

35. See *Histoire sainte*, p. 302, and Num. 21. 18

36. Ez. 47. 8

37. See Daniel-Rops, *Jésus en son temps*, p. 503

38. Deut. 11. 10

39. On the flora of Palestine see Immanuel Loev's definitive work, *Die Flora der Juden* (Vienna, 1934); the series of articles on

the plants of the Bible signed P.F. which began to appear in *L'Ami du Clergé* in 1955 and which are still being published, at irregular intervals; the *Flora of Syria and Palestine* of Post (Beyrouth, 1942); and *From Cedar to Hyssop* by Crowfoot and Baldensperger (London, 1932)

40. It must be observed that the identification of some plants mentioned in the Bible or the Talmud is very difficult, and that it often gives rise to disagreement. For example, some authors hold that the apricot, the chestnut, the citron, the saffron-crocus and the privet only appear in the biblical flora because of mistakes in translation. (Cf. these five examples in W. Corswant's *Dictionary*)

41. Tomato in Arabic is *dama-dura*, which comes from the Italian *pomodoro* – a proof of its recent introduction

42. Ps. 91. 13–15

43. 3 Kg. 6. 15, 34

44. Gen. 13. 18

45. By the neck and not by the hair: 2 Kg. 18. 9–14

46. Lk. 15. 16

47. Eccl. 12. 5

48. Matt. 13. 32; Mk. 4. 32; Lk. 13. 19.

49. Matt. 17. 20; Lk. 17. 6

50. Is. 28. 27

51. Cant. 1. 13; 3. 16, etc.

52. Matt. 2. 11

53. Is. 35. 1

54. The Song of Songs speaks of the lily some ten times as the flower esteemed above all others. 2. 1, 2, 16; 6. 2, etc. It is also mentioned in Isaiah and Hosea and others

55. Matt. 6. 28; Lk. 12. 27

56. Pliny 13. 11

57. This was suggested by Bovel in his *Voyage en Terre sainte* (1861), p. 426 et seq.

58. Cant. 2. 1; Is. 30. 1

59. Ecclus. 24. 18; 39. 17; Wis. 2. 8

60. Acts 12. 13. Rhoda means rose

61. 3 Kg. 6. 23

62. See particularly Is. 41. 19; Ps. 127; Prov. 21. 20; Deut. 33. 24, or Ps. 44 or 132 and many other places in the Bible

63. Jg. 9. 7 et seq.

64. Jn. 1. 48

65. Which is not really a fruit but a receptacle of male and female flowers

66. *Shabbath* 5: the tractate *Orlah* speaks of figs in March

67. Matt. 21. 20; Mk. 11. 21

68. Matt. 7. 16; Lk. 6. 44; Jas. 3. 12

69. It needed two men with a pole to carry one bunch: Num. 13. 23

70. Is. 5. 2–7

71. This so alarmed the Romans that Diocletian put out an edict ordering a certain proportion of the vineyards of Gaul to be rooted up, a measure which was never thought necessary in Palestine. (See Roger Dion: *Histoire de la Vigne et du Vin en France* (Paris, 1959), p. 129 et seq.)

72. For example, Ps. 78. 8, 15.

73. Jn. 15. 1, 18

74. It was called 'The Watcher', *saqed*, from *saqad*, to watch

75. Cant. 4. 3 and 6. 7

76. The columns at the entrance of the Temple were adorned with pomegranates and the sacred robe of the high priest was embroidered with them

77. Gen. 27. 28
78. For life in the country, see p. 231
79. Gen. 25. 29–34
80. Ecclus. 24. 12 et seq.
81. Ps. 103. 18; Prov. 30. 26
82. Lev. 11. 5; Deut. 14. 7
83. 1 Pet. 5. 8
84. Cf. P. Dhorme: *Le Livre de Job*, p. 562; and *L'Ami du Clergé* for October 27th, 1955
85. Job 38. 36
86. *Shabbath* 24 and 18
87. Matt. 17. 24–27
88. Ex. 8. 20 et seq.
89. Cf. below, p. 202
90. Jl. 1 and 2
91. Lk. 14. 5
92. Job 39
93. Num. 19. 9, 22; 31. 23

94. Lev. 11. 7; Deut. 14. 8; Ex. 65. 4 and 66. 17, etc.
95. 2 Mac. 6. 18 and 7. 1
96. Matt. 8. 30; Mk. 5. 11; Lk. 8. 32
97. 1 Esd. 2. 67; 2 Esd. 7. 68
98. There is only the one allusion to a curb in James 3. 3, and the symbolic descriptions in the Apocalypse (6. 2; 9. 16, etc.)
99. Matt. 19. 24; Mk. 10. 25; Lk. 18. 25
100. Matt. 23. 24
101. Matt. 15. 26; Mk. 7. 27
102. Matt. 7. 6
103. According to the title of this section: Ps. 144. 16
104. On the fauna of Palestine, see Rodinheimer: *Die Tierwelt Palaestinas* (Leipzig, 1920)

CHAPTER TWO, THE HUMAN CONTEXT

1. Ps. 89. 4; Heb. 7. 24
2. Gen. 12. 1–2: for this whole section see *Histoire sainte*, ch. 1
3. Gen. 17. 9 et seq.
4. Jg. 5. 7–8
5. Acts 7
6. Acts 2. 15
7. Particularly Acts 13 and the Epistle to the Hebrews
8. See *Histoire sainte*, part 2, ch. 1 and 2
9. 4 Kg. 7. 16; 23. 1–3; Ps. 88. 4
10. Os. 6. 7; 8. 1
11. Rom. 2. 29
12. 2 Cor. 11. 22
13. Gen. 10. 25
14. See below, p. 350
15. Gen. 32. 29
16. Rimbaud
17. 2 Mac. 6. 6: it will be remembered that Maccabees are the last historic books of the Bible

18. Gen. 49. 8 et seq.
19. Deut. 26. 5
20. For all these different events, see the first part of our *Histoire sainte*
21. Gen. 10. 22
22. For these events, see *Histoire sainte*, part 3, ch. 3, section 'The idolatrous queens'
23. See below, p. 266, for the Aramaic language
24. Gen. 19. 30
25. Deut. 7. 1
26. On the Hittites, see the book by L. Delaporte (Paris, 1936)
27. The tablets of Ras-Shamra (Ugarit-Syria), which date from the fourteenth century BC, are known as proto-Phoenician: they were discovered from 1928 onwards, and they are of the highest possible interest for the beginnings of Scripture
28. See *Histoire sainte*, part 2,

ch. 1, section 'A problem of dates'

29. As we know, it was from his accent that Saint Peter was identified as one of the disciples of the Galilean Jesus in the high priest's courtyard (Matt. 26. 73)

30. There are still 'Jews' by religion, who are not 'Jews', known today; since the sixteenth century of our era at least there have been Chinese Jews, for example. In the state of Israel there is a village of Italians who originally came from San Nicando, near Bari; they were formerly Catholics and were converted to Judaism by one Donato Manduzio, a biblical fanatic, and taken by him to the Holy Land. They are thought of as full Jews. At present they are governed by a woman, Deborah Bonfito (see Henri Amouroux: *J'ai vu vivre Israël*, p. 71, (Paris, 1958)

31. Lk. 19

32. It is entirely possible that this is only meant as an expression of humility; although it is generally admitted that Saint Paul was small, weak and sickly

33. See below, p. 419

34. This was a difficult point in the earliest days of the Christian church. Whereas Saint Paul wished to admit pagans into the community of the children of God without obliging them to accept the Jewish observances, Saint Peter and the Judaizing members were hesitant. The difficulty was not overcome until the council at Jerusalem in 49–50. See the first two chapters of Daniel-Rops' *The Church of the Apostles and Martyrs* (1960)

35. Esd. 4. 4

36. *Tanahim*, 17. 4

37. *The Antiquities of the Jews*, 11. 8

38. Now Sebushieh

39. Jn. 4. 20

40. Guignebert: *Le Monde juif vers le temps de Jésus*, p. 253

41. To this day a group of Samaritans, about a hundred of them, still live at Nablus as their ancestors did: they pray on Mount Gerizim, and they have a very ancient copy of the Pentateuch which they are quite willing to have photographed

42. The Bible speaks of 'the cities' of Samaria and of the people who inhabit Samaria, but never of a Samaritan people

43. *Schebiith*, 8. 10

44. Such as S. W. Baron, professor at Columbia University, whose book is mentioned in the bibliographical notes

45. Is. 49. 1

46. Rom. 2. 20

47. The expression 'dispersion' or 'Diaspora' was common in the Judaism of the Hellenistic period: cf. 2 Mac. 1. 27; Jn. 7. 35; Jdt. 5. 23; Jas. 1. 1; 1 Peter 1. 1. On the Diaspora apart from the general works mentioned in the bibliographical notes (particularly Bonsirven and Guignebert) see J. Juster: *Les Juifs dans l'Empire romain*

48. *Sibylline Oracles* 3. 27

49. Josephus, *Antiquities* 14. 7

50. Philo: *Legatio ad Gaium* 36

51. *Antiquities* 17. 11; *Wars of the Jews* 2. 6

52. *Antiquities* 18. 3; Tacitus: *Annals* 2. 85; Suetonius: *Tiberius* 36

53. Dio Cassius 68. 32

54. That of S. W. Baron
55. S. Collon: *Remarques sur les quartiers juifs de la Rome antique* (*Mélange de l'Ecole française de Rome*, LVII, 72, 94)
56. See below, p. 60
57. On Philo, see *The Church of the Apostles and Martyrs*, and Jean Daniélou's excellent book (Paris, 1958)
58. Tob. 13. 4
59. This version, frequently quoted during the last two thousand years, is far from being faultless
60. *Contra Apionem* 2. 29
61. *Wars of the Jews* 2. 20. The question of Jewish proselytism will be treated more thoroughly in the fifth part of this book, p. 47

62. Quoted by Saint Augustine in *The City of God* 6. 11
63. *Pro Flacco* 28. 69
64. *Epigrams* 12. 57
65. Emile Mireaux has wisely remarked that as a result of this lack of central organization the fate of all the Jews in the world was delivered into the hands of the extremists in Palestine, who by stirring up three great risings against the Romans between 66 and 135 provoked reprisals and massacres throughout the empire. The impetus of Judaism, which was in full development at the time of Christ was completely halted; and this left the field clear for Christianity (*La Reine Bérénice*, p. 62). See also S. W. Baron, *op. cit.*, p. 287 et seq.

CHAPTER THREE, THE POLITICAL CONTEXT

1. Mk. 12. 13–17
2. See the judicious observations of S. W. Baron, *op. cit.*, p. 23 and 319
3. Fichte: *Sämtliche Werke* 7. 572
4. *Contra Apionem* 2. 16
5. Num. 11. 16.
6. *Antiquities* 12. 3
7. 1 Mac. 12. 6; 2 Mac. 1. 10; 4. 44; 11. 27
8. *Psalms of Solomon* 17. 48 (cf. *La Bible apocryphe*, J. Bonsirven, p. 169)
9. It will be remembered that until Pope John XXIII the Catholic Church kept this number for its cardinals
10. *Sanhedrin* 4. 2.
11. *Antiquities* 20. 9.
12. Particularly Acts 5. 17; 7. 1; 9. 1, etc.
13. Tractates *Hagigah* 2. 2;

Horayoth 2. 5 and 3. 1; *Eduyyoth* 5. 6; *Pesahim* 6. 33; *Shabbath*, etc.
14. See below, section on Justice, p. 166 et seq.
15. This idea is discussed by Büchler: *Das Synhedrium in Jerusalem und das Grosse Bet Din*
16. This name came from a little-known ancestor of the Maccabees: cf. the Merovingians, descendants of the obscure Mérovée
17. See the prohibition in Lev. 21. 13.
18. Josephus: *Antiquities* 12. 14; *Wars* 1. 4
19. See below, p. 386 et seq.
20. *Taanith*, 23 A
21. *History* 5. 9
22. This is the Herod, therefore, of whom the synoptic Gospels speak in relation to the

coming of the Magi and the massacre of the innocents. 'Some thirty-odd years': is it necessary to recall that Jesus was not born in the year 1 of our era, but probably in 6 BC? The date was erroneously calculated in the first place by a sixth-century monk, Dionysius Exiguus (cf. *Jesus in His time*, section 'At what date was Jesus born?')

23. For Herod's reign the source is, of course Josephus, particularly in the *Antiquities* 15 and 17. The historian claims to have used Herod's own memoirs

24. *Wars* 5. 6

25. On the Temple see below, p. 359

26. For example, he forced a hedgehog's skin over Rabbi Baba's head and face as far as his chin, so that the spines blinded the unfortunate man and lacerated him

27. The parable in Lk. 19. 12 was perhaps inspired by this incident

28. Strabo 16. 2, 45

29. Lk. 13. 32

30. Lk. 3. 19; Matt. 14. 3; Mk. 6. 17

31. Lk. 23. 7

32. Dio Cassius 59. 8

33. Strabo 16. 17

34. Another tetrarch mentioned by Saint Luke in the phrase quoted above, Lysanias, is absolutely unknown, so much so that some have doubted his existence, but it has been confirmed by two inscriptions found at Avila (see R. Savignac, *Revue biblique*, 1912, p. 533). Abilene is a district in the Anti-Lebanon, to the west of Damascus, that is to say at the extreme northern limit of Palestine. As for this Lysanias, he was

perhaps a son of one of the last marriages of Herod the Great

35. A list of the procurators is given in the chronological table on p. 450

36. Lk. 13. 1

37. For all the incidents concerning Pilate, see *Jesus in His time*, referring to the index

38. *Church History* 2. 7

39. Caligula was a nickname that the soldiers gave to the young Caius: a *caliga* was a military boot

40. *Antiquities* 19. 6

41. Acts 12. 1–3

42. *Saturnales* 6. 156

43. Acts 26. 27

44. Suetonius, *Titus* 7

45. Upon the dynasty of the Herods as a whole, see F. O. Busch's book, *Was begab sich aber zu der Zeit*. On Berenice, see the book of E. Mireaux already mentioned

46. See below, p. 159

47. Philo, *Legatio ad Gaium*, 23. 40

48. See below, p. 192

49. See the section on the Temple and the priests, pp. 359 and 377

50. Lk. 2. 1

51. For the census see the article by Father Lagrange in the *Revue biblique*, 1911, p. 67 et seq. For the Egyptian census see Grenfell and Hunt, *Oxyrinchus papyri* 2. 207

52. Jn. 8. 33

53. Tractate *Ohaloth* 18. 7

54. Jn. 18. 28

55. Acts 10. 28

56. *History* 5. 5

57. See Father J. Bonsirven's *La Bible Apocryphe* already mentioned: for example, pp. 193 and 200

NOTES

58. Rom. 13. 1, 5; 1 Tim. 2. 1, 4

59. Something of the same kind is to be seen in the Catholicism of today: the 'integrists' who are most rigid in matters of doctrine usually belong to the right wing, whereas the 'progressives', the left-wing Catholics, are usually more liberal in interpretation

60. They will be treated in the last part of this book, p. 386

61. Mk. 12. 13 also speaks of 'Herod's party'; this must have been a Sadducean group especially linked with the Idumaean dynasty

62. One of Christ's disciples, Simon the Zealot, belonged to this party (Lk. 6. 15; Acts 1. 13); Matt. 10. 4 and Mk. 3. 18 call him Simon the Canaanite, because of a confusion with the Aramaic word *qanana* which means 'zealous'. Some have thought that Judas may also have belonged to it, as Iscariot could mean 'one who resists'

63. *Antiquities* 18. 9. Josephus speaks of the Essenes as the representatives of one of the four schools of thought into which he divides his countrymen. But their activity was upon the religious plane alone (see below, p. 398). As for the Zealots, Josephus contradicts himself (ch. 23) asserting 'that they agreed in everything with the opinions of the Pharisees'

64. Josephus, *Wars* 2. 118

65. Acts 23. 14. et seq.

66. Saint Paul was mistaken for this Egyptian (Acts 21. 38)

67. Matt. 24; Mk. 13; Lk. 21

68. Tob. 13. 11, 13

CHAPTER FOUR, JERUSALEM

1. Ps. 121
2. Ps. 136
3. Is. 65. 19
4. Is. 44. 26
5. 2 Par. 6. 6
6. 1 Esd. 1. 3
7. Tob. 13. 17, 18
8. Kidron means 'cloudy torrent' (see Strack-Billerbeck, 2, p. 567)
9. 2 Par. 32. 30
10. Lk. 24. 50; Acts 1. 9
11. 3 Kg. 11. 4 et seq.
12. Ps. 75. 3
13. Gen. 14. 18
14. *Beresch, Rabbi,* 9
15. See the books on biblical archeology mentioned in the bibliographical notes, and Lemaire and Vincent's excellent chapter in the *Initiation biblique*
16. Gen. 11 and 12
17. On the events of the siege see 2 Kg. 5; 3 Kg. 1; 1 Par. 11
18. 2 Kg. 22
19. 3 Kg. 9. 15
20. 3 Kg. 3. 1
21. 4 Kg. 14. 13
22. 2 Par. 2–9
23. Soph. 1. 10
24. 2 Esd. 3. 16
25. See *Histoire sainte*, ch. *Le Royaume divisé contre soi-même*
26. Jer. 7. 3
27. Lam. 5
28. 4 Kg. 25
29. 2 Esd. 2 et seq.
30. See the beginning of 1 Mac.
31. 1 Mac. 12. 36
32. The Bible says nothing about the period that followed the war of the Maccabees, and Jose-

460

phus is our authority (*Antiquities* 15, and *Wars* 5)

33. *Ad Atticum*, 2. 9

34. Bar. 4. 34 and Josephus *Contra Apionem* 1. 72

35. J. Carcopino, *La Vie quotidienne à Rome*, p. 33

36. Diodorus 17. 52

37. See above, p. 45

38. Lam. 2. 15

39. Tractate *Sukkah*, 51. 6

40. Matt. 4. 5

41. Jl. 4. 2, 12

42. 4 Kg. 23. 10

43. Is. 66. 24

44. A faint echo of this terrible word still reaches us in the pretty French '*gêne*'

45. *History*, 5. 11

46. Jn. 10. 7

47. The various details come chiefly from the Talmud, particularly from the tractates *Erubin* 10; *Baba Mesia* 16; *Baba Kamma* 82; *Zebahim* 96; and *Megillah* 73

48. M. Du Buit, work mentioned in the bibliographical notes, p. 34

49. Mk. 2. 4

50. 3 Kg. 1. 9

51. Jn. 9

52. Jn. 5. 1–9

53. One of these columns is to be seen at the house of the White Fathers

54. Lk. 23. 7–12

55. *Wars* 1. 21

56. See the chapter 'The trial of Jesus' in *Jesus in His time*

57. Saint Paul was saved from the fury of the Jews by the guards of the Antonia fortress: Acts 21. 32

58. Jn. 19. 13

59. Cf. *La Forteresse Antonia à Jérusalem et la Question du prétoire*, a thesis for the doctorate of letters sustained by Sister Marie-Aline of Sion at Paris in May, 1955

60. See the section devoted to it below, p. 359

61. Ps. 41. 5

62. *Baba Kamma* 82, b

63. *Zebahim* 96, a

64. *Baba Kamma* 82, b

65. *Baba Mesia* 26, a

PART II

CHAPTER ONE, A CHILD OF ISRAEL

1. Is. 9. 5

2. Ps. 126 and 127

3. Lk. 1. 25

4. Talmudic commentary on Genesis, 71. 6

5. For the sin of Onan, see below, p. 121

6. Gen. 16. 2 and 30. 3

7. Unlike the Romans, the Jews do not seem to have practised adoption except in the case of children borne by a maid-servant, which the legitimate wife took as

her own (Gen. 16. 2). The very obvious cases of adoption in the Bible always concern foreigners: the daughter of Pharaoh, for example, who adopted Moses (Ex. 2. 10). As for Esther, she was already Mordecai's cousin before he adopted her (Esther 2. 7)

8. Ex. 1. 19

9. Gen. 35. 17; 38. 28; Ex. 1. 15

10. Lk. 2. 7. Obviously this birth must not be likened to

that of ordinary men: Catholic theologians tell us that Mary was virgin *ante partum, in partu, post partum*

11. *Shabbath* 18. 3
12. *Yebamoth* 12. 6
13. Jer. 20. 15
14. Gen. 50. 23
15. Ezekiel refers to this: Ez. 16. 4
16. Talmudic commentary upon Numbers: R. 11. 5
17. Ezekiel refers to this, 16. 5
18. *Oxyrinchus papyri*, 4, 744
19. See Havet, *Le Judaïsme*, p. 437
20. Lk. 2. 7
21. *Demonax*, 29
22. Gen. 49. 3
23. Gen. 24. 50; 37. 22; 43. 33
24. Formerly the birthright might be transferred to another son by the father, as we see in the famous case of Esau (Gen. 25. 29–34). But at the time of Christ the law that was applied laid down that the first-born could not be deprived of his right even if he were the child of a wife whom his father disliked intensely (Deut. 21. 15–17)
25. Gen. 28. 28
26. *Kethuboth* 64. 9
27. Gen. 21. 8
28. Gen. 17. 9–14; 21. 4; Lev. 12. 3
29. Jn. 7. 23
30. *Shabbath* 19
31. Bonsirven, *La Bible apocryphe*, p. 95
32. Gen. 17. 10 (cf. Jn. 7. 22 and Acts 7. 8)
33. Ex. 4. 24 (it appears from the biblical text that Moses was himself uncircumcised)
34. Jos. 5. 2–9

35. See the two foregoing citations
36. Gen. 17. 23
37. Ex. 4. 25; 1 Mac. 1. 63
38. *Shabbath* 19. 6
39. 1 Mac. 1. 63 and 2. 46
40. 1 Mac. 1. 15. 40a Lk. 2. 21
41. Deut. 10. 16 and 30. 6; Jer. 4. 4 and 9. 25
42. Lev. 12. 1–8
43. Ex. 13. 2–12; 34. 29; Num. 18. 15, etc.
44. Deut. 12. 31
45. Ex. 34. 19
46. Ex. 11 and 13. 14
47. It was the father who had to pay the redemption, but whether or not the offering was required depended upon the mother. A man who married a widow who had already had a son was not required to redeem a son that he might have subsequently
48. Lk. 2. 22–39
49. Ex. 3
50. *Rosh Hashanah* 16. 6
51. For example, Gen. 4. 26; 5. 3; 5. 29; 21. 3; 40. 51; 2 Kg. 12. 24, etc.
52. Lk. 1. 59–68
53. Gen. 4. 25, or 29. 32, or 38. 4, etc.
54. The 'house' to which one belonged was also sometimes mentioned (cf. below, p. 126)
55. Cf. Ricciotti: *Vie de Jésus-Christ*, p. 232 note 1
56. See *Histoire sainte*, p. 354
57. Cf. S. W. Baron, *op. cit.*, pp. 527–528
58. *Idem*, p. 520
59. Matt. 21. 28
60. Lk. 15. 29
61. For these observations and others, see A. Cohen's extracts from the Talmud

62. Prov. 13. 24; 29. 13; 24. 17; 22. 15, etc.

63. Ecclus. 22. 6; 23. 2; 30. 1

64. Prov. 22. 6

65. Deut. 6. 7; see also Prov. 4. 1

66. Ex. 13. 8; see also Deut. 4. 10; 11. 19; Jos. 4. 6 and 21; Ps. 77. 5

67. Babylonian *Shabbath* 119. 6

68. 1 Par. 16. 22

69. *Kethuboth* 8. 11

70. This law on education was only in existence for six years before the ruin of Jerusalem, so it was no doubt scarcely applied at all in Palestine; but the Jewish communities of the Diaspora retained it. Gamala's work is known to us through the Babylonian Talmud (*Baba Bathra* 21, a)

71. Some rabbis even asserted that learning word by word was a duty under the Law

72. See below, p. 269

73. Lk. 7. 31–32

74. *Baba Bathra* 21. 9

75. Josephus *Antiquities* 4. 8–12; *Contra Apionem* 2. 25

76. 2 Tim. 3. 15

77. *Sotah* 9, a

78. Lk. 1. 47–55

79. Zach. 8. 5

80. Matt. 11. 16–17

81. Job 40. 24

82. Cf. F. Amiot, *Les Evangiles apocryphes*

83. On this kind of rabbinical seminary, see below, p. 155 and p. 381 et seq.

84. *Pirke Aboth* 5. 21. It is very striking to note how Saint Luke's Gospel shows our Lord's growth by the gradation of the terms which refer to him: Saint Luke first speaks of 'the babe' (2. 16) then of 'the little child' (2. 40), then of 'the child Jesus' (2. 43) and lastly of 'Jesus' alone (2. 52) [this is the author's translation, not the Knox Version]

85. Lk. 2. 40 et seq.

86. Talmudic commentary on Ecclesiasticus, R, 1. 2. It is interesting to compare the methods of education in Israel with those of the pagan world, and then those of Christianity. See H. Marou's classic work, *Histoire de l'Education dans l'Antiquité* (Paris, 1948)

1. Gen. 29. 14

CHAPTER TWO, FAMILY, 'MY OWN FLESH AND BLOOD'

2. Ex. 12. 3; 13. 8

3. Jn. 4. 53; Acts 16. 34; 18. 8

4. Gen. 13. 8

5. 1 Par. 23. 21–22

6. The well-known arguments about the 'brothers' of Jesus, whose existence would destroy the Christian tradition of Mary's perpetual virginity, arose from the ambiguity of this term (cf. *Jesus in His time*, index to disputed questions)

7. Gen. 4. 9

8. See the whole of the end of Genesis

9. Gen. 1. 28

10. Commentary on Genesis, 5. 2

11. Matt. 19. 12

12. See below, p. 398

13. See below, p. 395–398

14. 1 Cor. 7. Later he was to modify his point of view: Eph. 5. 25

15. Matt. 8. 14; Mk. 1. 30; Lk. 4. 38; 1 Cor. 9. 5

16. Jg. 8. 30; 2 Kg. 1. 2; 2. 13; 3 Kg. 11. 1

17. 1 Kg. 1. 2

18. Is. 54. 6

19. *Yebamoth* 65, a, and 44, a

20. Koran 4. 3

21. Gen. 2. 21–24. The play on words is in verse 23

22. Gen. 4. 19

23. Jer. 2. 2; Ez. 16. 8; Os. 2. 9; Mal. 2. 14

24. *Yoma* 13, a

25. Saint Paul's statements (1 Tim. 3. 2; Tit. 1. 6) that a bishop and a deacon may only have one wife have sometimes been quoted to prove polygamy among the early Christians. These texts in fact forbid the remarriage of widowers

26. *Kiddushin* 29. 6

27. *Sanhedrin* 76. 6; *Bekoroth* 45. 6

28. Gen. 26. 34

29. Willam: *Marie, Mère de Jésus*, p. 147

30. *Yebamoth* 43, a

31. Ex. 34. 15–16

32. 2 Esd. 13. 23 et seq.

33. Gen. 16. 15; Ex. 2. 21; Num. 12. 1, etc.

34. Lev. 18. 6

35. Lev. 18. 7; Deut. 27. 20, etc.

36. Lev. 20. 11 and 14

37. Deut. 25. 7–10

38. Gen. 38. 9 (Onan's sin was not, as it is commonly supposed and as the dictionaries assert, masturbation)

39. Matt. 22. 23; Mk. 12. 18; Lk. 20. 27 (see Deut. 25. 6 and Ruth 4. 10)

40. Deut. 20. 7

41. Matt. 1. 20

42. Num. 5. 11–31

43. See Daniel-Rops: *Les Evangiles de la Vierge*, p. 143

44. Gen. 34. 12; 1 Kg. 18. 25; see also Ex. 22. 16

45. Ex. 22. 15

46. Deut. 22. 27

47. Gen. 29. 15

48. On these questions see Millar Burrows, *The Basis of Israelite Marriage*, and E. Neufeld, *Ancient Hebrew Marriage Laws*

49. Jn. 2. 2

50. Is. 61. 10

51. Cant. 3. 11

52. Jn. 3. 29

53. Tractate *Sotah*, 10

54. Cant. 3. 6

55. Gen. 24. 60; Tob. 9. 11; Ruth 4. 11

56. Jl. 2. 16; Ps. 18. 6

57. Cant. 1. 2 and 2. 13

58. In an enquiry entitled *Paysans en communauté de Bousrah*, Le Play has already gone into the question of these 'enlarged families'

59. On the rights of the father in the earliest period, see particularly Gen. 22; Jg. 11. 34; 1 Kg. 1; Ex. 21; Gen. 38, etc.

60. Deut. 21. 19

61. Ex. 20. 12

62. Unless God Himself took care of this. Example: Absolom. Ex. 21. 15

63. Lev. 20. 9

64. Matt. 19. 19

65. Eph. 6. 2

66. Ecclus. 3. 1–16

67. See the anecdotes of this kind in Cohen's extracts from the Talmud

68. Matt. 15. 4–5

69. Ex. 20. 17 and Deut. 5. 21

70. Ex. 21. 3

71. Gen. 12. 10–20

72. *Menahoth* 43, b

73. Jg. 5. 28; Cant. 2. 9

74. 1 Kg. 1. 12

75. Jn. 4. 27
76. Ex. 21. 10
77. Ez. 16. 10
78. Lev. 19. 3
79. Prov. 31. 16
80. *Kiddushin* 1. 7
81. *Baba Kamma* 15, a
82. For the preparation of the Last Supper Jesus said to his disciples, 'Go into the city, and there a man will meet you, carrying a jar of water' (Mk. 14. 13): this alone was a sufficiently distinctive sign
83. *Shabbath* 2. 6
84. For example, Is. 3. 16 and 47. 1–8; Am. 4. 1; Jer. 3. 1; Ez. 16. 1
85. Bonsirven, *Bible apocryphe*, p. 117
86. There are many citations of this kind in Cohen's extracts from the Talmud
87. *Ibid*
88. Gen. 2. 23
89. Gen. 2. 24 and Matt. 19. 5
90. Prov. 7. 4; 8
91. This figure is suggested by Proverbs 8. 22–31; and the same text together with Gen. 3. 15 is interpreted by Christianity as foretelling the role of the Virgin Mary
92. Ecclus. 26. 1–4

93. See Daniel-Rops, *De l'Amour humain dans la Bible*
94. Ecclus. 25. 13
95. Prov. 18. 22; Ecclus. 7. 28
96. Ex. 20. 14 and Deut. 5. 18
97. Job 24. 15
98. Commentary on Lev., R. 23. 12
99. Ecclus. 23. 22–23
100. Num. 5. 11, 31
101. Deut. 22. 22; Lev. 20. 21; Jn. 8. 5
102. Strack-Billerbeck, 2, p. 519
103. Ecclus. 23. 24–26
104. Deut. 22. 27
105. Lev. 19. 20
106. Deut. 24. 1
107. *Kethuboth* 3. 5
108. *Gittin* (Talmudic tractate on divorce) 9. 10
109. All these cases are cited by Cohen
110. Os. 2. 2
111. Is. 9. 1; Jer. 3. 8; Matt. 5. 31; Deut. 24. 1
112. Is. 104. 6
113. Deut. 24. 1–4; Jer. 3. 1
114. J. Carcopino, *La Vie quotidienne à Rome*
115. Mal. 2. 13
116. Matt. 19; Mk. 10; Lk. 16
117. 1 Cor. 7. 12–16

CHAPTER THREE, HIGH AND LOW, RICH AND POOR

1. 1 Kg. 1. 21
2. Gen. 49
3. See below, p. 377
4. Acts 26. 6
5. Apoc. 8. 2
6. *Vie de Jésus*, 1. 1
7. *Taanith* 4. 5
8. 2 Cor. 11. 22
9. Ecclus. 5. 1
10. Deut. 15. 7
11. Ps. 112. 7–8

12. Job 36. 6
13. Ps. 108. 16
14. Matt. 5 and Lk. 6
15. Lk. 152
16. Matt. 10. 24; 20. 27; 24. 45; Lk. 12. 35; 37. 7; Jn. 8. 35, etc.
17. Willam, *Vie de Jésus*, p. 128
18. On slavery in the Roman empire it is profitable to consult J. Carcopino, the book of Festugière and Fabre which is mentioned in

the bibliographical notes, and Ugo Enrico Paoli's *Vita Romana*

19. Ecclus. 33. 25–28

20. *Pirke Aboth* 2. 7; *Yadayim* 4. 7, etc.

21. Ecclus.33. 30-33. Obviously Ben Sirach, who is a practical man, justifies this kindness by saying, 'Because you need him, and if he is unhappy he will run away'. But for all that the words were still said

22. Job 31. 15

23. *Berakoth* 2. 7

24. Ex. 20. 10; 23. 12

25. Deut. 23. 16

26. *Yebamoth* 46, b

27. Lev. 22. 10–13

28. On the Hebrew slaves, see Ex. 21

29. It was contradicted, however, by Lev. 25. 39

30. Ex. 22. 3

31. Ex. 21. 5

32. Lev. 25. 40

33. *Arakin* 8. 5; *Kiddushin* 20, a

34. See below, 'The Age of God', p. 341

35. Ex. 21. 1

36. Lev. 25. 40

37. *Miroir des Lois* 2. 18. For the whole of this subject see R. Salomon, *L'Esclavage en droit comparé juif et romain*

38. Matt. 10. 24–25; 20. 27; 24. 45–47; Lk. 12. 37; 17. 7; Jn. 8. 35

39. Eph. 6. 5; Col. 3. 22; Tit. 2. 9

40. See *The Church of the Apostles and Martyrs* (index)

41. Ecclus. 7. 16

42. Gen. 3. 17–19

43. *Pesahim* 118, a

44. 2 Thes. 3. 10

45. Deut. 30. 19

46. 2 Thes. 3. 8 and Acts 20.

34

47. *Nedarim* 49. 6

48. Deut. 24. 14

49. Matt. 20. 1, 16

50. Mal. 3. 5

51. To form an idea of these very numerous texts, see Cohen's extracts from the Talmud

52. See the very interesting article by I. Mendelsohn, *Guilds in Ancient Palestine* in the *Bulletin de l'Ecole américaine pour les Recherches orientales*, 1940, Number 80

53. Mk. 1. 20

54. On the word and the fact, see the study by E. Würtheim, published in 1936 in *Beiträge zur Wissenschaft vom Alten und Neuen Testament* (Stuttgart)

55. Gen. 23. 7

56. 4 Kg. 11. 20

57. See above, p. 37 et seq.

58. Jn. 7. 49

59. *Berakoth* 47, b

60. See above, p. 38

61. Lk. 15. 8

62. Matt. 18. 28

63. Matt. 20. 2, (parable of the labourers)

64. Lk. 10. 35 (parable of the good Samaritan)

65. *Nedarim* 9. 10

66. Lk. 16. 19

67. Jas. 2. 2

68. Am. 4. 1–2

69. Nicanor was the object of a study by P. Roussel in the *Revue des Etudes grecques*, 37, p. 79 et seq.

70. Is. 5. 8

71. Mic. 2. 1

72. Lk. 16. 1

73. See below, p. 248 et seq.

74. See the observation quoted on p. 246

75. *Yebamoth* 50. 3, a

76. Jas. 4. 13

77. Upon banking techniques see below, p. 248
78. Upon the farming of taxes see below, p. 162 et seq.
79. *Antiquities* 17. 8 and 11
80. See above, p. 541
81. See *Histoire sainte*, p. 298 and p. 385
82. 1 Esd. 7. 11
83. Example 2 Esd. 8. 1, 4, 9, 13, 18
84. Above, p. 69 et seq.
85. See below, p. 370
86. Lk. 10. 25; Acts 5. 34
87. Matt. 23. 7
88. See above, p. 113
89. On the purely religious

function of the doctors of the Law, see below, p. 381
90. Matt. 13. 52
91. Lk. 5. 17
92. *Sanhedrin* 38, a
93. Ecclus. 13. 2
94. Upon this kind of writing, see the section on literature, p. 285–286
95. *Assumption of Moses*, 7. 30
96. *Menahoth* 13 and *Pesahim* 57
97. Always ready to draw up unjust decrees
98. *Pesahim* 49. b
99. *Ibid*
100. See below, p. 309 et seq.

CHAPTER FOUR, SOCIETY'S IMPERATIVE COMMANDS

1. *Antiquities* 14. 10
2. Jg. 5
3. See above, p. 74
4. Acts 10. 1 et seq.
5. From his name it would seem that he belonged either to the *gens Cornelia* or else to a family of freedmen of this illustrious house. Perhaps there was a *cohors italica* in garrison at Caesarea: in Syria there have been found some inscriptions of the *cohors italica II*. In any case there is no question of the famous *Legio italica*, for this was only raised later, by Nero. (Dio Cassius, *Roman History*, 55. 24.) 5 Acts 27. 1–12. Upon the *evocati Augusti*, see Cagnat, *Dictionnaire des Antiquités grecques et romaines*, 2. 867
6. Matt. 26. 51; Mk. 14. 47; Lk. 22. 50; Jn. 18. 10. The rule of the Essenian monks laid down that they were to carry nothing when they travelled except a

weapon to defend themselves against the brigands
7. Jg. 20. 16
8. 1 Mac. 3. 2
9. 2 Mac. 11. 6
10. See below, p. 398
11. Upon this idea of 'the holy war', see the exceedingly original pages of Father R. de Vaux in *Les Institutions de l'Ancien Testament*, 2, pp. 73–86
12. Saint Paul also speaks of 'the armour of light' (Rom. 13. 12)
13. Deut. 33. 29
14. 3 Kg. 4. 7 and 5. 27
15. 4 Kg. 15. 20
16. 4 Kg. 23. 35
17. 1 Esd. 4. 13; 2 Esd. 5. 4
18 *Annals* 12. 54
19. Rom. 13. 7
20. Matt. 22. 17; Mk. 12. 14; Lk. 20. 22
21. Matt. 9. 9
22. Lk. 19. 2
23. Lk. 3. 13
24. *Shebuoth* 39. 9

25. Lk. 18. 13
26. Gen. 14. 20
27. Josephus, *Antiquities* 16. 6
28. Ex. 30. 13
29. Matt. 17. 23
30. Deut. 26
31. Matt. 23. 23
32. Tractates *Bikkurim* 1 and *Besah* 3
33. Saint Paul, brought before the procurator Festus but fearing to be taken back to a Jewish court, said, 'I appeal to Caesar', that is to say to the emperor's tribunal sitting at Rome; and his request was granted. Acts 25. 1–12
34. Ex. 18. 16
35. 2 Esd. 8
36. Lev. 19. 2
37. *Makkoth* 23. 6
38. Is. 64. 5. The usual translation is 'filthy rag' or 'dirty linen'. The Hebrew was stronger, and some Italian versions have kept its coarseness in '*panna di mestrui*'
39. See above, p. 54
40. Acts 22 and 23
41. *Antiquities* 14. 5
42. 2 Cor. 11. 24
43. *Pirke Aboth* 4. 11
44. *Sanhedrin* 5, a
45. *Sanhedrin* 4. 2
46. *Sanhedrin* 17, a
47. *Sanhedrin* 36. 6
48. *Bekoroth* 4. 5
49. Matt. 5. 25
50. A great number of details given here are taken from this tractate: it is scarcely useful to give all the references. See principally its chapters 4, 7 and 8
51. Dan. 13. The precept was laid down by Deut. 19. 16–21
52. Num. 35. 30; Deut. 17. 6 and 19. 15; Jn. 8. 17, etc.
53. Deut. 17. 7
54. Deut. 19. 16–21. In fact it seems that this rule was only applied if the accused had been put to death and the false witnesses detected after the accusation. That in any case was the opinion of the less rigorous rabbis; their stricter colleagues held that the very intention should be punished
55. Ps. 26. 12; 34. 11; Pro. 6. 19; 12. 17; 14. 5, etc. Acts 6. 13
56. Matt. 5. 33
57. *Jérusalem*, May–June 1933, p. 464
58. *Wars* 4. 335
59. See above, pp. 115 and 119
60. Ex. 22. 20; 23. 9
61. Deut. 24. 17; 27. 19
62. Lev. 24. 22
63. *Contra Apionem* 2. 28
64. Rom. 10. 12; Gal. 3. 28
65. Gal. 3. 21; see also Heb. 9. 16
66. Deut. 21. 17
67. Lk. 15. 12
68. See below, p. 357
69. Ex. 21 and 22
70. Ex. 22. 12
71. Here it would be necessary to give so many biblical references that the list would be long and wearisome. These are only a few of those that are available: sin of idolatry, Ex. 22. 9; of blasphemy, Lev. 24. 16 (cf. Matt. 26. 65); of necromancy and divination, Lev. 20. 6; of breaking the Sabbath, Ex. 31. 14; of breaking the Passover, Num. 9. 13; of violating the law of circumcision, Gen. 17. 14, etc. On the prohibition of coming near to a menstruating woman, see Lev. 20. 18
72. See above, pp. 133 and 134
73. *Sanhedrin* 18, a
74. Ex. 21. 23; Lev. 24. 19; Deut. 19. 21

75. Gen. 4. 23

76. Matt. 5. 38, et seq. Here is a typical passage of the Talmud against the *lex talionis* ' "An eye for an eye": that means a payment in money. "In money," you say, "but perhaps it means putting out the eye (of the guilty man)". "Suppose that the eye that was lost was large and the other small: how then can we apply the *eye for an eye* according to the Scripture? Or suppose that a blind man has put another man's eye out, that a one-armed man has cut off another's arm, or that a cripple has crippled his neighbour: how then can we apply the law of an eye for an eye? Now the Torah says that *you shall have the same law*, a law equal for all." ' (*Baba Kamma* 836)

77. Gen. 9. 6

78. Ex. 21. 12; Deut. 19. 3

79. Deut. 24. 16

80. There are a very great many biblical texts upon these subjects: for example, Ex. 22, Deut. 21, Lev. 11, etc. and the three *Baba* tractates of the Talmud comment upon them in detail

81. Deut. 25. 16

82. Lev. 24. 12; Num. 15. 34

83. 3 Kg. 22. 27; 2 Par. 16. 10, etc. The prophet Jeremiah was also thrown into prison several times. Jer. 20. 2; 32. 2; 33. 1, etc.

84. 1 Esd. 7. 26; 2 Esd. 3. 25

85. For example, Matt. 5. 25;

14. 3; 18. 30, etc., Acts 4. 3; 5. 18; 8. 3, etc.

86. Acts 16. 24

87. Lev. 18. 29. According to the tractate *Makkoth* there were towns specially for these banished men as today some sentences carry enforced residence in given places

88. See for example Josephus, *Wars* 5 and 11

89. 2 Cor. 11. 24

90. See Chap. 10 of *Jesus in His Time*

91. Deut. 17. 7

92. Deut. 21. 22; 2 Kg. 4. 12. In *La Passion de Jésus, fait d'histoire ou objet de croyance*, (Paris, 1959), Marc Stéphane claims to prove that Jesus was not crucified but 'hung on the gibbet'

93. See above, p. 57

94. For all details of the Crucifixion see Chap. 11 of *Jesus in His Time*

95. Deut. 21. 23

96. A Sanhedrim which had eleven condemned men executed in seven years was considered unusually severe. Rabbi Eleazar ben Azania says eleven in seventy years. Rabbi Tarphon and Rabbi Akiba said, 'If we were members of a Sanhedrim nobody would ever be put to death'. (*Makkoth* 1. 10.)

97. Prov. 31. 6

98. Jesus refused the narcotic (Mk. 15. 23) or at least scarcely touched it (Matt. 27. 34)

CHAPTER FIVE, THE TABLETS OF HEAVEN AND HUMAN CALCULATIONS

1. Cf. Bonsirven, *Bible apocryphe*, p. 25. The *Book of Enoch* is one of those very visionary apocryphas which became more and more usual in Israel during this latest period. The sayings, prophecies and messages in it are attributed to 'The seventh patriarch after Adam', who was thought, from Gen. 5. 24, to have

been taken up to Heaven. Ecclus. 44. 16, speaks of him as a saint. The Ethiopian Bible includes the *Book of Enoch* in its canon

2. Ecclus. 43. 6

3. *Bible apocryphe*, p. 89

4. Deut. 34. 8. Periods of ten days are also often mentioned, and occurrences dated by the 10th day of the month, which seems rather to be a reference to a solar calendar. The Greeks, who used a calendar not unlike that of the Hebrews, were also acquainted with this division by tens, however. (For example, Gen. 24. 55; Num. 29. 7; Jos. 4. 19, etc.)

5. The year 29, in which our Lord travelled throughout Galilee, was one of these

6. G. Dalman, *Aramaïsche Dialektproben*, p. 3

7. *Sanhedrin* 1. 2

8. 23. 16; 34. 22. But Moses had also said that the year should begin with the Passover! Ex. 12. 2

9. 'It was on 1 *Tisri* that the world was created,' said Rabbi Eliezir, 'that the patriarchs were born and died, that Sarah, Rachel and Anne became pregnant, and that Joseph came out of prison'

10. Am. 1. 1

11. 1 Mac. 13. 41

12. Perhaps . . . But perhaps it may also have been a device for counting, or perhaps a game like solitaire. Yet in Egypt these tablets have thirty holes, which makes one think of the Egyptian solar month

13. 3 Kg. 6. 1, 37

14. If this could be proved as a fact it would solve the very difficult exegetical problem of the exact date of the Passover and of our Lord's celebration of the Last Supper (cf. *Jesus in His Time*, index of disputed questions). The synoptic Gospels fix 14 *Nisan* as the date of the Last Supper, but for Saint John it took place on the 13th and the Crucifixion on the 14th. It would be an important argument for those who believe that they can detect an Essenian influence working upon our Lord (cf. Jean Daniélou, *Les Manuscrits de la Mer morte et les Origines du Christianisme*, p. 26, commenting upon Jaubert, *La Date de la dernière Cène* in *Revue de l'Histoire des Religions*, 1954, pp. 140–176)

15. Some fragments of the *Enuma Elis* are given by Dhorme in his valuable *Choix de Textes religieux assyro-babyloniens*, p. 60

16. Ez. 20. 12. On the importance of the Sabbath, see the chapter devoted to it, p. 345

17. Lev. 23. 15

18. Jg. 8. 6; Mk. 15. 42

19. Matt. 27. 62

20. Dio Cassius 37. 18

21. For example, Ex. 12. 8; Lev. 23. 32; Ps. 54. 18, etc.

22. The Samaritans prayed between sunset and the end of twilight; the Jews between the going-down of the sun, about 3 p.m., and its vanishing

23. Dan. 3. 5; 4. 16

24. Num. 28. 4; 3 Kg. 18. 29–36

25. Matt. 20. 1, 16

26. Jn. 4. 6

27. Mk. 15. 25 and 34; cf. Matt. 27. 46

28. See the table of hours in J. Carcopino's *La Vie quotidienne à Rome*, p. 178

29. Matt. 26. 40; Mk. 14. 37

30. 4 Kg. 20. 9–11; Is. 38. 8

31. Ps. 89. 4

32. Matt. 14. 25
33. Mk. 13. 35
34. 1 Par. 23. 29
35. Matt. 6. 27; Lk. 12. 25
36. Based principally upon the 1,200 cubits of Hezekiah's aqueduct-tunnel (see above, p. 84) which has been found and measured: but was there not some bombast in this figure of 1,200?
37. Gen. 21. 16
38. Gen. 30. 36; 31. 23; Ex. 3. 18; Jon. 3. 3
39. Acts 1. 12
40. Matt. 5. (Many translations give one *mile*, but here it is not a question of the Roman mile, which was of 1,000 *double* paces)
41. Lk. 24. 13; Jn. 6. 19; 11. 18; Acts 14. 20; 21. 16
42. Acts 27. 28
43. Ez. 40
44. The exact translation of verse 6 of Psalm 15 is not to the effect that 'I have a piece of land in the place of delight' but rather that 'the cord has marked me out a place'
45. Matt. 5. 15; Mk. 4. 21; Lk. 11. 33
46. Jn. 2. 6
47. Jn. 12. 3
48. Jn. 19. 39
49. Prov. 16. 11
50. Gen. 23. 16
51. 1 Esd. 8. 27
52. See above, p. 162
53. Lk. 15. 8
54. Matt. 22. 19; Mk. 12. 15; Lk. 20. 24
55. Matt. 10. 29; Lk. 12. 6
56. See the article by J. Babelon, 'Monnaies', in the *Supplément Dictionnaire biblique*, vol. 5 with detailed bibliography
57. Ex. 20. 4
58. See above, p. 151

CHAPTER SIX, BED AND BOARD

1. Ps. 64. 11
2. Ps. 103. 27 and 144. 16. We know that this admirable hymn to creation reproduces almost word for word the revolutionary Pharaoh Akhenaton's (Amenophis IV) hymn to his God; but one cannot say from which direction the influence came. See Daniel-Rops, *Le Roi ivre de Dieu*
3. A notion particularly dear to that great theologian Father Chenu
4. Gen. 14. 18
5. Deut. 8. 12
6. Matt. 26. 30; *Berakoth* 7
7. Deut. 6. 4–9 and 11. 13–10
8. The word originally meant the jambs and lintels of the door, the holy place upon which the blood of the paschal lamb was sprinkled
9. See below, the section on clothes, p. 211
10. Prov. 30. 8
11. See Chap. 1, sections upon flora and fauna
12. Is. 58. 7; Lam. 4. 4; Matt. 14. 19; 15. 36; 26. 26; Lk. 24. 30; Acts 20. 11
13. Jn. 6. 13
14. Ex. 12. 34
15. Matt. 16. 6; Mk. 8. 15; Lk. 12. 1
16. Lev. 26. 26
17. Lev. 23. 14; Ruth 2. 14, etc.
18. A painting in the tomb of Rameses III shows pastry-cooks in the act of preparing these wonders

19. Ex. 3. 8–17; 13. 5, etc.
20. Prov. 30. 33
21. See above, p. 82
22. Prov. 16. 24; 24. 13
23. This is in the words upon the efficacy of prayer (Lk. 11. 12 and Matt. 7. 9). We shall return to this subject
24. Is. 1. 8; Jer. 10. 5
25. Num. 11. 5
26. Places cited in note 23
27. Jn. 21. 9 et seq.
28. *Shabbath* 22. 2
29. Matt. 3. 4, etc. In the Dead Sea scrolls a passage in the Rule of the Community speaks of the manner of eating grilled locusts
30. *Taanith* 69. 2
31. Apoc. 18. 13
32. Lev. 11. 7; Deut. 14. 8; Is. 65. 4; 66. 17
33. Deut. 14. 4–7 and Lev. 11. 6
34. Lev. 17. 13
35. Ex. 23. 19; 34. 26; Deut. 14. 21
36. Ecclus. 31. 27
37. Prov. 31. 6, 7
38. Gen. 49. 11; Deut. 32. 14
39. Matt. 9. 17
40. Cant. 7. 3
41. See below, p. 395
42. On the events at Mamre see *Histoire sainte* (index)
43. Matt. 22. 3 and Lk. 14. 16
44. Matt. 22. 11
45. Lk. 7. 45
46. Lk. 7. 44; Jn. 13. 5
47. Matt. 15. 2; Mk. 7. 3; Lk. 11. 38
48. See below, p. 398
49. Lk. 11. 38
50. Ps. 22. 5; 44. 8; 103. 15; Ez. 23. 41; Am. 6. 6; and also Lk. 7. 46; Jn. 12. 3
51. *Gittin* 70, a
52. For example, Jg. 19. 6

53. Mk. 14. 3; Jn. 13. 25
54. As in all this the customs were more Roman than Jewish, see the already-mentioned book by J. Carcopino, p. 304, etc.
55. See Father Prat: *Les Places d'honneur chez les Juifs contemporains du Christ* in *Recherches*, 1925, p. 512 et seq.
56. Ecclus. 31. 12 et seq.
57. Jn. 13. 26
58. Matt. 26. 29
59. Acts 2. 46; 1 Cor. 11. 17, etc.; Jude 12
60. See below, p. 349 et seq.
61. We refer the reader, so that he may be thoroughly disgusted, to J. Carcopino's incomparable description in *op. cit.*, p. 304 et seq.
62. Macrobius, *Saturnales*, 2. 9
63. Ex. 29. 22; Lev. 3. 9 and 9. 19
64. Ecclus. 31 and 37, *passim*
65. Lk. 6. 29
66. For priestly vestments, see part 3, p. 377: also for the phylacteries, fringes, etc., of the ordinary people
67. See M. du Buit, *Archéologie du Peuple d'Israël*, p. 91
68. Jn. 13. 4
69. The Old Testament often speaks of the *saq* (for example: Gen. 37. 34; Ps. 34. 13; Jer. 4. 8, etc.). It is also often referred to in the New Testament: Matt. 11. 21; Lk. 10. 13, etc. and Apoc. 11. 3
70. Jn. 19. 23
71. Ex. 22. 26; Deut. 24. 12
72. Matt. 21. 7–8
73. Dan. 10. 5; Apoc. 1. 13
74. Lk. 6. 38 and Is. 40. 11; Prov. 21. 14, etc.
75. Jg. 14. 12
76. Deut. 22. 5

77. Deut. 22. 11; Lev. 19. 19
78. Apoc. 18. 12
79. Lk. 16. 19
80. Matt. 19. 24.
81. Prov. 25. 12
82. Prov. 11. 22
83. 1 Tim. 2. 9
84. See above, p. 138 et seq.
85. Du Buit, *op cit.*, p. 76
86. Acts 9. 11
87. Prov. 19. 13
88. Deut. 22. 8
89. Prov. 11. 9 and 25. 24
90. Matt. 24. 17; Mk. 13. 15, etc.
91. Matt. 10. 27; Lk. 12. 2.
92. Matt. 14. 15; Lk. 22. 12
93. Lk. 24. 33; Acts 1. 13; 2. 2
94. *Shabbath* 11. 2
95. Prov. 5. 16, etc.
96. See above, p. 95 et seq.
97. Jn. 19. 41
98. See above, p. 22
99. See above, p. 93 et seq.
100. See above, p. 63 et seq.
101. See above, p. 67 et seq.

102. Matt. 6. 19; 24. 43; cf. also Job 24. 16, or Ez. 12. 5
103. Matt. 21. 42
104. Matt. 7. 24 and Lk. 6. 47
105. Is. 27. 9
106. Matt. 23. 27
107. Acts 23. 3
108. Lk. 5. 19 and Mk. 2. 4
109. *Moed Katon* 25
110. Matt. 7 and 13
111. Prov. 17. 13
112. Prov. 26. 14
113. Matt. 16. 19
114. See above, p. 16 et seq.
115. *Berakoth* 55
116. Mk. 14. 67
117. *Shabbath* 13. 1–2
118. Lk. 15. 8
119. Matt. 5. 15; Mk. 421; Lk. 11. 33
120. See above, p. 188 et seq.
121. Matt. 15. 27; Mk. 7. 28; Lk. 16. 21
122. *Nedarim* 37. 6
123. Prov. 7. 16
124. Is. 14. 11

CHAPTER SEVEN, 'BY THE SWEAT OF THY BROW'

1. See above, p. 146
2. See above, p. 148
3. Ecclus. 7. 15
4. Deut. 11. 14
5. *Berakoth* 58, a
6. Ps. 67. 14
7. Prov. 27. 23
8. Of course, among these herdsmen one group was universally despised – the swineherds. Yet herds of the unclean creatures certainly existed, and they were numerous, some even amounting to 2,000 head; they were to be found in the north-eastern part of the country, beyond the Sea of Galilee, in a half-paganized region. The fact that the Prodigal Son kept swine showed that he had sunk to the very bottom
9. *Shebiith* 1
10. Gen. 31. 40
11. Matt. 21. 33; Mk. 12. 1
12. Jg. 5. 7
13. See the very interesting works of Elian J. Finbert upon sheep and the life of the shepherds
14. Father Janssen, in his book on Nablus, has studied the names of sheep
15. Among the finest references in the Gospels, we have: Matt. 9. 36; 10. 6; 25. 32; Lk. 15. 3–6; Jn. 10. 2; 21. 15, etc.
16. See above, p. 6 et seq.
17. Lk. 13. 9

18. See above, p. 17
19. Deut. 11. 10
20. Is. 2. 4. Other translators give 'plough-shares', but the same word occurs in 1 Kg. 13. 20 where it obviously means a tool, so the translation 'mattock' seems better
21. Deut. 22. 10
22. Prov. 14. 4
23. Lk. 14. 19
24. Lk. 9. 62
25. Willam, *op. cit.*, p. 225
26. On the various cereals mentioned, see above, p. 23
27. Jn. 4. 35
28. Matt. 12. 1; Lk. 6. 1
29. Mk. 4. 29
30. Ruth 2; Lev. 19. 9 and 23. 22
31. Deut. 24. 19
32. Lev. 19. 9; 23. 22
33. Deut. 25. 4. Saint Paul alludes to this prohibition in his first Epistle to the Corinthians 9. 9
34. Ecclus. 5. 11
35. Matt. 3. 12
36. Matt. 13. 24–30
37. *Kethuboth* 111
38. *Peah* 7
39. Ps. 64. 10–14
40. S. W. Baron, *op. cit.*, p. 341
41. It is impossible to give all the places in the Gospel that refer to fishing and fishermen: here are a few, Matt. 4. 13. 17; Mk. 1; Lk. 5; Jn. 21., etc.
42. See above, p. 202
43. Strabo, *Geographica* 16. 2–45

44. Am. 4. 2. Some translations give 'fish-hooks'; the Hebrew says 'fishing thorns'
45. See on the one hand Matt. 4. 18–21; Mk. 1. 9, 16; Lk. 5. 2; Jn. 21. 6; and on the other Matt. 13. 47
46. Dom Biever, *Conférences de Saint-Etienne*, vol. 2, 302
47. Lev. 11. 10–12
48. Matt. 13. 48
49. Lk. 5. 7–10
50. Mk. 3. 17
51. Father Braun's edition of Saint Matthew's Gospel, p. 303
52. Matt. 4. 19; Mk. 1. 17
53. Jer. 25. 10; Apoc. 17. 22
54. Prov. 31. 13–19, 22–24
55. Ecclus. 38. 24–34
56. *Shabbath* 1. 3
57. For example, Is. 64. 7
58. Mk. 6. 3
59. Lev. 14. 45; Ecclus. 22. 16
60. Matt. 7. 4 Lk. 6. 42
61. *Baba Kamma* 3. 5
62. 2 Kg. 5. 11; 3 Kg. 5. 18, etc.
63. 4 Kg. 12. 12
64. Is. 44. 13–17
65. J. Carcopino, *Le Mystère d'un Symbole chrétien* (Paris, 1955)
66. *Dammai* 2. 4; 3. 4
67. *Baba Mesia* 38. 6
68. See the description of Babylon, the Scarlet Woman, Apoc. 17. 4
69. Mk. 9. 3
70. 2 Esd. 3. 8, 31
71. *Yebamoth* 63. 9

CHAPTER EIGHT, FROM TRADERS TO BRIGANDS

1. *Contra Apionem* 1. 12
2. See the judicious remarks of Corswant, in his book mentioned in the bibliographical notes, p. 445
3. For example, Prov. 31. 24
4. Am. 8. 5; Os. 12. 8

5. *Baba Kamma* 10. 9
6. *Baba Mesia* 5. 6
7. *Id.* 5. 9, and also *Baba Kamma* 9. 6
8. 3 Kg. 20. 34
9. See above, p. 41 et seq.

10. Unclean, because it was partly situated upon a burial-ground
11. See what is said concerning money, above, p. 192
12. Lk. 6. 38
13. 2 Kg. 5. 11; 3 Kg. 5. 11; 2 Par. 2. 10; and on the other hand 3 Kg. 10. 22, etc.
14. Jas. 4. 13
15. Upon this wholesale trade see the tractates *Dammai* 5 and *Baba Bathra* 5
16. Matt. 25. 9
17. This is the reason why the Jewish quarter in Rome was near the Tiber, where the cargoes of wheat arrived
18. Strabo, *Geographica*
19. Pliny, *Naturalis Historia* 12. 54
20. Clement of Alexandria, *Stromater* 1. 28; and Saint Paul, 1 Thess. 5. 22
21. Matt. 25. 27; see also Lk. 19. 23
22. *Baba Mesia* 6. 5
23. Deut. 15. 6
24. Ecclus. 26. 29
25. Ez. 26
26. Lev. 19. 11–35; 2 Kg. 24. 21; Prov. 11. 1; 16. 11, etc.
27. See what has been said upon civil and criminal law above, p. 172
28. Lev. 19. 36; Deut. 25. 13; Prov. 11. 1; 16. 11; Ez. 45. 10, etc.
29. Deut. 23. 19–20
30. Lk. 7. 36–41
31. *Baba Mesia* 5. 13
32. Philo, *In Flaccum* 7
33. Deut. 15. 3
34. *Baba Kamma* 7. 7
35. See above, p. 143
36. Matt. 23. 21–35
37. Lk. 16. 19–31

38. Matt. 6. 24; Lk. 16. 13. But Tob. 4. 7 and Ecclus. 4. 1 had already said things of the same nature
39. Wealth of iniquity: see the Unfaithful Steward in the Gospel (Lk. 16 1 et seq.)
40. Gen. 49. 13
41. Deut. 33. 19
42. Jg. 5. 17
43. On the 'ships of Tarshish' see Ps. 47. 8; Is. 2. 16; 23. 1; 60. 9, etc.
44. 3 Kg. 9 and 10; 2 Par. 8 and 9
45. Ecclus. 43. 26
46. Job 28. 14
47. I *Wars* 21. 5
48. 1 Mac. 15. 5
49. See *Histoire sainte* chap. *La Majesté royale*, section *Le Roi diplomate et commerçant*
50. III *Wars* 9. 2
51. See Daniel-Rops, *Saint Paul conquérant du Christ*, particularly chaps. 4 and 5
52. A. Poidebard, *La Trace de Rome dans le Désert de Syrie* (Paris, 1934). For a general view of the Romans' road system see the books of Carcopino and Paoli that have already been mentioned, and that of Festugière and Fabre which is given in the bibliographical notes
53. Ecclus. 34. 9–16
54. Strabo 17. 1 (807–812)
55. Lk. 2. 41 et seq.
56. On the Sabbath day's journey see above, p. 190
57. Lk. 12. 35
58. Matt. 10. 9
59. *Yebamoth* 16.
60. Matt. 10. 10 and Mk. and Lk.
61. See above, p. 215
62. *Shabbath* 17. 6

63. *Baba Mesia* 6. 3
64. *Shabbath* 5. 1
65. Acts 8. 26 et seq.
66. The hard harness collar bearing on the shoulders was not invented until about the year AD 1000 in the West: it was a positive revolution. See the classic work of Major Lefebvre des Noëttes
67. Lk. 2. 44
68. Lk. 10. 30
69. *Antiquities* 15. 10
70. *Id.* 20. 8.

CHAPTER NINE, THE SPOKEN AND THE WRITTEN WORD

1. The little book of Paul Auvray, Pierre Poulain and Albert Blaise, *Les Langues sacrées* (Paris, 1957), contains all that it is essential to know on the languages spoken and written at the time of Christ
2. They found the word *Sibboleth* particularly difficult to pronounce properly
3. Lk. 4. 16
4. On the Aramaeans see above, p. 36
5. 4 Kg. 18. 26
6. Matt. 26. 74
7. See particularly Mk. 14. 36; Acts 1. 19; Jn. 19. 13; Matt. 27. 33; Matt. 6. 24, etc.
8. Mk. 5. 41
9. Matt. 27. 46 and Mk. and Lk.
10. On the Aramaic Saint Matthew see the introduction to *Jesus in His Time*
11. On the religious use of Aramaic see below, p. 374
12. Louise Weiss, *La Syrie* (Paris, 1953)
13. Lk. 23. 38 and Jn. 19. 10
14. *Antiquities* 14. 10 and 12
15. *Sotah* 9. 14 and *Antiquities* 20. 11
16. Acts 22. 2
17. See Daniel-Rops, *What is the Bible?*
18. The German school of *Formgeschichte* strongly emphasizes oral transmission. See the excellent summary of Father J. van der Ploeg, *Le Rôle de la Tradition orale dans la Transmission du Texte de l'Ancien Testament* in *Revue Biblique* (January, 1947). See also the first chap. of *La Tradition et les Traditions*, by Father Y. Congar, (Paris, 1960)
19. *Gittin* 60, a
20. Preface to the tractate *Shabbath* by W. O. E. Oesterley, p. 54
21. See *What is the Bible?* and the introduction to *Jesus in His Time*
22. *Pirke Aboth* 3. 8
23. *Pirke Aboth* 4. 8
24. Quoted by Father Jousse: see below, note 28
25. See above, the chap. on education, p. 109
26. Lk. 6. 20–26
27. Lk. 1. 46–55
28. On this whole question the fundamental books are those of Father Marcel Jousse, particularly his *Le Style oral rythmique et mnémotechnique chez les verbomoteurs* (Paris, 1925); *Les Rabbins d'Israël, Les Récitatifs rythmiques parallèles* (Paris, 1930), and the great number of articles provoked by these works, particularly in the *Cahiers juifs*, 1934
29. On the scribes, see above, p. 154 et seq.

30. See *Histoire sainte*, chap. *Moïse et Canaan*, section *Ecris cela!*

31. The preceeding pages owe everything to the admirably clear account by Father Auvray in *Langues sacrées* (see note 1). We say nothing of the system of vocalization of Hebrew by the use of pointed vowels, which was invented much later and made usual in literary Hebrew at a time when spoken Hebrew was no longer used, by those rabbis who, between AD 500 and 1100 fixed the text of the Bible and at the same time added those commentaries which are known as *Masora* (*masoreth*)

32. *Initiation biblique*, p. 108

33. 2 Cor. 3. 3

34. Job 19. 24. (some translators of the Bible speak of a 'graver of iron and of lead', which makes no sense, since lead, which is a soft metal, could not possibly be used as an engraving-tool. It was melted into the grooves)

35. Job 19. 23

36. Apoc. 3. 5

37. Diodorus 2. 32; Herodotus 5. 58

38. 2 Tim. 4. 13

39. *Shabbath* 8. 2

40. 2 Cor. 3. 3

41. Apoc. 6. 14

42. On the Essenes see below, p. 398

43. See above, p. 155

44. H. E. del Medico maintains that the MSS found near Qumrân were those of a *Genizah* (cf. *L'Enigme des Manuscrits de la Mer morte*, Paris, 1957)

45. Paper was a Chinese invention spread by the Arabs when they came to a knowledge of it after taking Samarcand in 704. It was therefore unknown to the Jews at the time of Christ

46. Ex. 28. 11–36; 39. 14

47. Jer. 17. 1

48. Job 38. 14

49. Rom. 4. 11

50. Jn. 3. 33

51. Apoc. 5. 1

52. See Paoli's *Vita Romana*, mentioned above, p. 300 et seq.

53. *Shabbath* 10. 4

54. Acts 28. 21

55. Bouquet, work mentioned in the bibliography, p. 123

56. Bouquet, p. 129. The author does not give his sources and it is impossible for us to find the confirmation of this statement in the 'rabbinical archives'

CHAPTER TEN, LETTERS, ARTS AND SCIENCE

1. *Contra Apionem* 1. 8

2. *Et tout le reste est littérature* . . . (Verlaine)

3. The library of the caves of the Dead Sea did not contain a single work which was not religious. To be sure, if it was in fact the library of a monastery that would be quite natural

4. On the problem of forms of literary expression, see our observations in *What is the Bible?* and particularly A. Robert's account in the *Initiation Biblique*, p. 282 et seq.

5. Among the Dead Sea scrolls there is a commentary upon Habakkuk

6. On the Talmud, see below, p. 375 and bibliography, p. 445

7. See above, p. 367

8. Mk. 15. 34

9. We have a whole Targum of the Torah, called the Targum of Onkelios, and another of the prophets called that of Jonathan: they date from the fifth century, but are certainly based upon much older texts

10. 'To fulfil what is written...' This formula often recurs in the Gospels in one form or another: for example, Saint John, telling how the legs of the dead Christ were not broken but how a soldier opened His side with a spear, twice repeats, 'This was so ordained to fulfil what is written' – a passage of the Scriptures that he quotes. (John 19. 36.) This, exactly, was making a *pesher*

11. Upon the Jewish canon of the Scriptures, see *What is the Bible?*

12. On the 'sign of Jonah', cf. particularly Matt. 12. 40; Lk. 11. 32; Jon. 1. 7 and 2. 11

13. See *What is the Bible?* What the Protestants call apocryphal are, on the one hand, those books which the Jewish canon rejected but which the Catholic canon, fixed at the Council of Trent, admitted (they are sometimes called deutero-canonical); and on the other, that mass of more or less frenzied works which are called apocryphal by the Catholics

14. *Fourth Book of Esdras*, 14. 37–48

15. Gen. 5. 21–24

16. See Bonsirven, *La Bible apocryphe: En marge de l'Ancien Testament* (Paris, 1953)

17. The Apocalypse which closes the New Testament, the Apocalypse of Saint John, belongs to the same literary form; but it has been recognized by the Church as inspired

18. The Christians, too, had their apocryphas, usually written in a more popular style (see R. Tamisier, *Evangiles apocryphes*, Paris, 1952)

19. See above, p. 268

20. *Sanhedrin* 7. 2; *Yoma* 82. 2; Matt. 10. 27

21. On Saint Paul's lack of success at Athens, see Acts 17. 22–34

22. 'I am the voice that cries: "In the wilderness. . ."' is the reading of Isaiah. Note the right punctuation, which is usually changed to, 'that cries in the wilderness'. [This is the author's translation, not that of the Knox Version]

23. Jean Cocteau

24. These various forms are to be found in Num. 21. 27; Num. 23. 7; Is. 14. 4; Ez. 17. 2; 1 Kg. 10. 12, etc.

25. Lk. 4. 23

26. Matt. 15. 11

27. On the *Mashal*, see the remarks of Robert and Tricot in the pages of their excellent *Initiation Biblique* (p. 298 et seq.), and also the account in the *Ami du Clergé*, March 31, 1960, p. 194

28. These well-considered observations come from Mgr. Ricciotti's *Vie de Jésus-Christ*, par. 361

29. Ecclus. 32. 3

30. Gen. 4. 21

31. For example, Elisha asking for the services of a musician (4 Kg. 3. 15); or again, the messengers sent to meet Saul (1 Kg. 10)

32. 1 Kg. 16. 10

33. Barrois, *op. cit.*, 2. 193

34. On banquets, see above, p. 207 et seq.

35. Is. 23. 16

36. Matt. 9. 23

37. A very great many references, such as Ps. 46. 6; 97. 6; 150. 3; or again, 67. 26; 80. 3; 149. 3, etc.

38. 1 Par. 25. 1; 2 Par. 29. 30, or 35. 15

39. 1 Esd. 7. 24; 2 Esd. 11. 23

40. Col. 3. 16 (see also Eph. and Jas.)

41. In *Tu es Pierre*, Philippe Agostini filmed the village dances during a wedding at Cana

42. Cf. *Jesus in His Time*, chap. 'The Seed of the Church', section 'The Death of the Forerunner'

43. Corswant, *op. cit.*, p. 37

44. For example, S. W. Baron, *op. cit.*, p. 18.

45. Ex. 35. 31 et seq.

46. Ex. 20. 4; Deut. 5. 4

47. On dwellings, see above, p. 218

48. On money, see above, p. 192

49. Mosaics of the signs of the Zodiac have been found in various synagogues (for example, at Noara and Beth Alfa); they are all much later than the time of Christ

50. Prov. 8. 22

51. See chap. 3 of Cohen's extracts from the Talmud

52. Job 38. 31–32

53. Job 38. 33

54. *Pirke Aboth* 3. 23

55. *Berakoth* 11. 2

56. On the 'seven heavens' of Saint Paul, see Cohen, *op. cit.*

57. We are acquainted with the theory that the earth is made up of three layers: SI-AL, SI-MA, NI-FE

58. *Yoma* 54. 6

59. Is. 34. 11

60. 'The circle of the earth', Is. 40. 22

61. *Erubin* 22, b

62. Prov. 8. 26

63. On the ant, see Prov. 6. 8

64. See the list of animals in Job 39 and 40

65. Gen. 1. 21

66. Gen. 10. 11

67. Plato, *Republic* 10, and particularly *Timaeus*

68. The Cabala has been edited by Henri Sérouya (Grasset, Paris, 1947); see also Paul Vulliaud's translation (Paris, 1923 and 1930). Raymond Abellio has recently, and with a great many arguments, sustained the thesis of *La Bible, document chiffré* (Paris, 1950)

69. A. Cohen, *op. cit.*

CHAPTER ELEVEN, HABITS AND CUSTOMS; PERSONAL CLEANLINESS; AMUSEMENTS

1. Lk. 11. 27, see below, p. 308

2. *Essai sur l'Accélération de l'Histoire*

3. *Shabbath* 6. 5, see below, p. 304

4. A. Cohen, *op. cit.*

5. Lev. 11. 44

6. *Kiddushin* 66, a

7. *Hullin* 24, b

8. 9. 30

10. Matt. 27. 48, and Mk. and Lk.

11. *Shabbath* 9. 6

12. On the Nazarites, see below, p. 395

13. Num. 6. 5; Jg. 13. 5; 16. 17, and the case of the young Samuel, 1 Kg. 1. 2

14. Num. 8. 7

15. 2 Kg. 19. 25

16. Jer. 41. 5, etc.

17. 2 Kg. 10. 5; Is. 50. 6

18. Jer. 9. 25; 25. 23; 49. 32

19. Lev. 21. 5

20. Lev. 19. 28

21. Is. 44. 5

22. Apoc. 14. 9 and 7. 2–3

23. Absalom, who took so much care of his hair, 2 Kg. 14. 26

24. Cant. 5. 11

25. 1 Cor. 11. 14

26. See above, p. 000

27. Matt. 6. 17; 26. 7; Lk. 7. 46

28. Ex. 38. 8; see also Job 37. 18; Is. 3. 23

29. 1 Tim. 2. 9

30. Job 42. 14

31. For example, Cant. 1. 14

32. Ecclus. 24. 15 et seq.

33. The Gospel often alludes to scent. For example: Matt. 26. 6; Lk. 7. 36; Mk. 14. 3; Jn. 12. 1, etc.

34. Gen. 18

35. Matt. 10. 40; 25. 35, etc.

36. Matt. 10. 11

37. Rom. 12. 13

38. 1 Pet. 4. 9

39. Heb. 13. 2

40. 1 Kg. 18 and 20

41. Prov. 17. 17

42. Ecclus. 6. 5–17

43. See above, p. 207

44. It is impossible to give all the references to kissing in the Bible. Here are a few: kissing a guest, Gen. 29. 11; parents and children, Gen. 31. 28; Ruth 1. 14; Lk. 7. 45; Acts 20. 37; lovers, Prov. 5. 20; Cant. 1. 2; a superior, Lk. 7. 38; the kiss of Judas, Matt. 26. 49; of peace, Rom. 16. 16, etc.

45. Jas. 1. 1; Acts 15. 24 and Lk. 24. 36; Jn. 21. 26

46. Lk. 11. 27

47. On Jerusalem, see p. 96

48. Cf. A. Cohen, *op. cit.*

49. Acts 3. 1–3

50. Matt. 25. 35–40

51. Job 31. 19, 22

52. Deut. 23. 25

53. Lev. 29, 23 and 33. 22

54. Matt. 12. 27; Mk. etc.; see also Acts 19. 13

55. These are the seven cases of casting out of devils: the demoniac of Capernaum (Mk. 1. 21); the dumb blind man (Matt. 12. 22); the men possessed with devils among the Gergesene tombs (Matt. 8. 28); the dumb man in Matt. 9. 32; the daughter of the Canaanite woman (Mk. 7. 25); the epileptic child (Matt. 17. 14); and the woman who was healed on the Sabbath day (Lk. 13. 11)

56. Matt. 10. 1 and Mk. 3. 15

57. As we cannot, in the following pages, give all the references to the Talmudic tractates, we refer the reader to the book of Rabbi A. Cohen, which has already been mentioned, chap. 9. Our examples are all taken from him

58. 2 Mac. 12. 40

59. Is. 47. 12, etc.

60. Gen. 41. 45

61. On superstition in Rome, see Paoli's book, chap. 14

62. On the subject of education and the technique of memorizing by repetition in chorus, see above, p. 269, and Matt. 11. 16 and Lk. 7. 32

63. On childrens' games, see above, p. 112

64. Job 40. 29
65. Lk. 11. 51; 21. 34; Rom. 11. 9; 1 Tim. 3. 7; 2 Tim. 2. 26, etc.
66. Lev. 17. 13
67. Deut. 22. 6–7
68. Bouquet, *op. cit.*, p. 221
69. See the drawing in *Jesus in His Time*, chap. 10, section 'The Flagellation and the Crowning with Thorns', and also the photographs in the album 'Scenes and Documents' for *Jesus in His Time*
70. 1 Kg. 20. 20
71. Jg. 20. 16
72. Is. 22. 18 (some translations give *pelote* [ball or clew of wool] which would lead one to suppose that the ball was made of wool
73. 2 Mac. 4. 7–19
74. 1 Cor. 9. 24
75. Deut. 23. 17–18
76. Jn. 4. 18
77. Matt. 21. 31
78. Ez. 16. 30 speaks of real brothels: whores are mentioned in Jos. 2. 1; 6. 17; 3 Kg. 3. 16; Jer. 5. 7
79. 1 Cor. 6. 16
80. *Bible apocryphe*, p. 195
81. Lev. 19. 29
82. Lev. 21. 9
83. Lev. 21. 7
84. To be done with these unsavoury topics, we may note that castration, which all Israel's neighbours practised (guards were needed for harems), was certainly known to the Jews in the days of the Kings; and it cannot have disappeared at the time of Christ since He alludes to it in a famous passage (Matt. 19. 12) as a fact known to everyone. The Queen of Ethiopia's eunuch, who was converted by Philip the deacon (Acts 8. 27), was perhaps only a high official who had that title without having had to pay so very high a price for it. It will be remembered that Potiphar, Pharaoh's 'eunuch', was married (Gen. 39. 1–7)

CHAPTER TWELVE, WHEN THE BIRD-SONG DIES AWAY

1. Gen. 3. 19
2. Is. 38. 18 and Ps. 87. 5
3. A. Cohen, *op. cit.*
4. On cleanliness, see above, p. 301
5. Commentary on Leviticus, 34. 3
6. Acts 10. 14
7. Deut. 33. 12–14
8. *Baba Bathra* 2. 8
9. Lev. 14. 33–53 and 13. 47–55
10. See above, p. 225
11. *Berakoth* 25, a, and 60, b
12. See above, p. 211
13. See above, p. 211
14. William, *Vie de Jésus*, p. 133
15. p. 258; Lk. 4. 38
16. Jn. 4. 47
17. Acts 28. 6
18. Matt. 12. 10; Mk. 3. 1; Lk. 6. 6
19. Jn. 5. 5
20. Matt. 9. 2 and Mk. and Lk.
21. Matt. 8. 8
22. Baron, *op. cit.* Cf. A. Bloom, *La Lèpre dans l'ancienne Egypte et chez les anciens Hébreux*
23. Lk. 17. 12
24. 4 Kg. 5. 7
25. Ecclus. 38. 1–15
26. Jn. 9. 1–3
27. Ex. 15. 26
28. Ecclus. 38

29. *Sanhedrin* 17, b and p; and *Kiddushin* 66, d

30. *Kiddushin* 82, a

31. Lk. 10. 34

32. On the mandrake, see Cant. 7. 14; Gen. 30. 14

33. *Op. cit.*

34. *Shebuoth* 15. 6

35. All the foregoing details come from the Talmud: it has scarcely seemed worth while to give all the references to these picturesque texts.

36. Ez. 39. 12

37. Deut. 21. 23

38. Is. 14. 19

39. Gen. 46. 4

40. Gen. 50. 1

41. Acts 9. 37

42. *Shabbath* 23, 5

43. Jn. 19. 38

44. Matt. 27. 59; Mk. 15. 46; Lk. 24. 1; Jn. 19. 40

45. Jn. 11. 44; 20. 7

46. Jn. 11. 44

47. *Gittin* 56. 6

48. Jer. 9. 17

49. Matt. 9. 23

50. *Kethuboth* 4. 6; *Baba Mesia* 6. 1

51. F. Amiot, *Evangiles apocryphes*, p. 110

52. R. Aron, *op. cit.*

53. See above, p. 89

54. Jn. 11. 38

55. Jn. 20. 5

56. Mk. 16. 3

57. On the Herodium, see above, p. 64

58. Os. 9. 4; Ez. 24. 17

59. *Berakoth* 6. 1

60. On the *saq*, see p. 212

61. Matt. 23. 27; Lk. 11. 44

62. Matt. 8. 22

63. 1 Thess. 4. 13

64. 1 Kg. 28

65. Job 14. 13

66. Is. 38. 18

67. Ecclus. 41. 4

68. In the book that we have already mentioned, Robert Aron maintains that the *ruach*, the spirit, soul or breath of a man rejoins 'the breath of the Universe, leaving upon earth or in Sheol the material or psychic remnants of his personality'. From this he goes on to say that 'the essence of death lies not in an annihilation but in a kind of escape from the ordinary framework of life'. The spirit 'thus returns to a kind of spiritual reservoir in which the various souls accumulate'. Is the poet's idea Jewish, or Hindu, or theosophical? Or is it inspired by certain passages of Father Teilhard de Chardin? One cannot see what biblical or talmudic texts it could be based on

69. Cf. also Robert Aron

70. *Bible apocryphe*, pp. 56–62

71. *Id.*, p. 45

72. *Id.*, p. 240

73. Parable of the evil rich man and the beggar Lazarus

74. Episode of the good thief, Lk. 23. 43

75. Ecclus. 7. 40

76. Deut. 31. 16

77. Is. 36. 19; Ez. 38

78. Dan. 12. 2

79. *Bible apocryphe*: see the word 'resurrection' in the index

80. *Berakoth* 60, b

81. Matt. 22. 23 and Mk. and Lk.

82. Jn. 11. 21–27

83. Place cited, note 81

84. 1 Cor. the whole of the end of chap. 15

PART III

CHAPTER ONE, THE AGE OF GOD

1. Ps. 1. 2
2. Strack-Billerbeck, p. 390
3. Ps. 54. 18; Acts 10. 9
4. Upon the numerical equivalents, see above, p. 298
5. Ex. 13. 1–10 and 11–16; Deut. 6. 4, 9 and 11. 13–21 (on the phylacteries, see above, p. 343)
6. Dan. 3. 11
7. Lk. 18. 13. There are many passages in the Talmud which state that this attitude was obligatory (e.g. *Peah* 5)
8. Deut. 6. 4–7; 11. 13–21
9. Acts 3. 1
10. *Berakoth* 4. 4
11. On the days of the week, see above, p. 183
12. Ex. 31. 13–17
13. Num. 15. 32, 36
14. Jankélévitch's preface to the French edition of Oesterley's edition of the tractate *Shabbath*, p. 39
15. Is. 58. 13–14
16. See above, p. 185
17. Matt. 12. 2 and Mk. and Lk.
18. It will be remembered (p. 177) that a man condemned to flogging was only to have forty strokes less one
19. See below, for the whimsicalities of the legislation on the Sabbath, p. 420
20. Lk. 14. 5
21. See Daniélou, *Les Manuscrits de la Mer Morte et les Origines du Christianisme*, p. 34
22. Quoted by Stapfer, p. 344
23. Mk. 2. 27

24. Tacitus, *History*, 5. 2–4
25. Ps. 83. 6–8
26. *Wars*, 2. 14 and 6. 9
27. Ps. 47. 13–14
28. Cf. Daniel Barouki's *La Convocation d'Automne* (1960)
29. Gen. 31. 19 and 38. 12
30. 1 Mac. 7 and 2 Mac. 15
31. Today they light an immense seven-branched candlestick made from seven pipes from which gushes the oil from the wells at Heletz
32. Deut. 16. 9
33. First verses of *Athalie*
34. Ex. 19. 1–16
35. Acts 2
36. On the year, see above, p. 179 et seq.
37. Num. 29. 1
38. Acts 27. 9
39. On the harvest and the vintage, see above, pp. 233, 235
40. *Sukkah*, devoted to the Feast of Tabernacles
41. Jn. 8. 12
42. Num. 28. 16
43. See *Jesus in His Time*, ch. 9, section 'The Holy Week', last note
44. Lk. 22. 13 and Matt. and Mk.
45. See above, p. 296
46. On slaves, see above, p. 144. Cf. Ex. 21. 7–11 and Deut. 15. 12
47. Lev. 25. 4
48. Ex. 23. 10–11
49. 2 Eds. 10. 32
50. 1 Mac. 6. 49
51. Lev. 25. 8–17

CHAPTER TWO, THE DWELLINGS OF GOD

1. *Antiquities* 3. 6
2. On the Samaritans, see p. 39 et seq.
3. On the Temple of Egypt, see p. 44
4. See our chapter on Jerusalem, p. 80 et seq.
5. Deut. 12. 2, 9
6. 2 Kg. 7. 5–7
7. Is. 66. 1
8. Jer. 35. 2
9. Acts 7. 48: the words of the deacon Stephen
10. 3 Kg. 5. 6. 7 and 8
11. 4 Kg. 24
12. 4 Kg. 25
13. Agg. 2. 10
14. On Herod and the Temple, see above, pp. 64 and 87
15. Josephus: see particularly ch. 5 of *Wars*
16. Ez. 40. 3
17. Acts 3. 2
18. *Wars* 5. 14
19. Mk. 12. 41
20. On the Nazarites, see below, p. 295
21. On the Sanhedrim, see above, p. 53 et seq.
22. On Herod's eagle, see above, p. 63
23. Matt. 27. 51
24. Mk. 13. 1–2
25. *Sukkah* 51. 6
26. 3 Kg. 8. 27
27. There are many passages in the Old Testament upon this concept of an inner religion superior to all sacrifices: for example, Is. 43 and 66; Jer. 6. The rabbinical text is to be found in the Talmudic commentary upon Deuteronomy, 5. 3
28. Lk. 18. 10
29. On the Sanhedrim, see above, p. 53 et seq.
30. See above, p. 164
31. *Shekalim* 6, a
32. Jean Daniélou, *Le Signe du Temple* (Paris, 1943)
33. Upon these words, see the profound commentary of Father Dubarle in *Revue biblique* (January, 1939)
34. *Wars* 6 and Tacitus, *History* 5. 13
35. On the synagogue and its role in education, see p. 111
36. 2 Par. 17. 7–9
37. *Wars* 7. 3
38. Acts 6. 9
39. Acts 16. 13
40. The tractates *Megillah* and *Taanith* give all the details upon the synagogue
41. Matt. 23. 7
42. Acts 13. 15; Mk. 5. 22
43. See above, p. 113
44. Lk. 4. 20
45. Lk. 4. 16
46. Jn. 9. 22 (see also 12. 42; 19. 38)

CHAPTER THREE, THE MEN OF GOD

1. In his book *Jérusalem* Jérémias suggests 18,000; Büchler, 25,000 in his *Die Priester und der Cultus im letzten Jahrzeit des jerusalemischen Tempels*
2. See *Histoire sainte*, p. 133
3. Upon the nobility, see above, p. 139
4. Upon the hatred of the priestly class, see above, p. 157
5. Lev. 21. 16, etc.
6. See above, p. 62

7. Lev. 8 and Ex. 29

8. On the penalty of death by burning for the daughters of the high priest who prostituted themselves, see p. 176

9. On the office of the high priest, see above, p. 55; on the various high priests at the time of Christ, p. 55

10. Ex. 28

11. Ex. 28. 30

12. Temple physician, see above, p. 325

13. 1 Par. 24. 7–19

14. 4 Kg. 23. 4; 25. 18; Jer. 52. 24

15. Acts 4. 1

16. *Middoth* 1. 2

17. On the scribes as a social class, see p. 154 et seq.

18. 2 Esd. 8

19. *Pirke Aboth* 1. 1

20. It is found very frequently in the Talmud, particularly in *Pirke Aboth* 1. 1

21. Büchler in his book on the Sanhedrim, (quoted above, p. 54, note 15) particularly emphasises this role and he is followed by Lauterbach and Bickermann

22. See above, p. 147

23. Upon the ways of memorizing, see p. 271

24. *Megillah* 16. 6

25. Something of the same kind is known in our day, in the Communist world: Marxist thought must permeate the whole of life and govern it; everything in human behaviour must be specifically Marxist

26. Details of health and hygiene, for example, see p. 319 et seq.

27. On the *Midrash*, see above, p. 284

28. Upon memory, see above, p. 269

29. Jn. 3

30. Rabbi A. Cohen, *op. cit.*

31. 1 Mac. 8

32. On resurrection, see p. 334

33. *Wars* 2; *Antiquities* 13. 17 and 18

34. See the sabbatical year, p. 357

35. See the feeling against the priestly families, p. 157

36. See the struggle of the Asmoneans against the Pharisees, p. 57

37. *Antiquities* 17. 2

38. On the *Am-ha-arez*, see above, p. 149 et seq.

39. On the Zealots and the *Sicarii*, see above, p. 78

40. See Henri Amouroux, *J'ai vu vivre Israël*, p. 240

41. *Shabbath* 30, a

42. *Bible apocryphe*, p. 240

43. *Sotah* 13, b, Bar

44. Matt. 15. 5

45. Mk. 12. 28; Lk. 10. 25; Jn. 23. 2

46. Jn. 3. 1, etc.

47. Lk. 7. 36; 11. 37

48. Jn. 3. 1 and 7. 50

49. Lk. 13. 21

50. Acts 23 and 26; Phil. 3

51. Acts 5. 36–40

52. Upon the ritualism of the Pharisees, see below, p. 439

53. Mk. 7. 11; cf. Matt. 15. 5

54. Num. 6. 2

55. Am. 2. 11

56. Upon the court of the Nazarites in the Temple, see above, p. 363

57. Jg. 16. 17

58. *Siphra Nombres*, 26. 9, a

59. *Nedarim* 9. 6

60. Cf. Mireaux, *La Reine Bérénice*, p. 127

61. Lk. 1. 34
62. See R. Tamisier, *Evangiles apocryphes*, and Daniel-Rops, *Les Evangiles de la Vierge*
63. Lk. 3. 2
64. See *Jesus in His Time*, ch. 4
65. On Saint Paul's stay in the desert, see Daniel-Rops, *Saint Paul*, ch. 2
66. Father Daniélou, *Les Manuscrits de la Mer Morte*, p. 25
67. Cf. des Medico, work quoted, note 70
68. Josephus, *Autobiography* 11
69. See Daniélou, *op. cit.*, p. 95
70. There is an enormous bibliography on the Dead Sea scrolls. We will limit ourselves to mentioning a few books. There are so many works that the *Bibliographie zu den Handschriften*

vom Toten Meer of C. Burchard which came out in 1957 at Berlin is already out of date. Géza Vermes, *Les Manuscrits du Désert de Juda* (Paris, 1953); A. Dupont-Sommer, *Les Ecrits esséniens découverts pres de la mer Morte* (Paris, 1960); Millar Burrows, *The Dead Sea Scrolls* and *More Light on the Dead Sea Scrolls* (1956 and 1958); A. Vincent, *Les Manuscrits hébreux du désert de Juda* (Paris, 1953) (with selected texts) Jean Daniélou, *Les Manuscrits de la Mer Morte et les Origines du Christianisme* (Paris, 1957). Finally let us mention the two books in which H. E. del Medico argues against the 'Essenian thesis': *The Riddle of the Scrolls* (1958) and *Le Mythe des Esséniens* (Paris, 1958)

CHAPTER FOUR, THE FAITH OF ISRAEL AND THE COMING OF THE MESSIAH

1. Mk. 12. 28; Lk. 10. 25
2. Letter of Aristeas 132
3. Jg. 8. 18
4. *Horayoth* 8. 9
5. Commentary on Numbers 111
6. *Sanhedrin* 74, a
7. *Berakoth* 61, b
8. *Megillah* 13, a
9. Ps. 13 and 52: see also Ps. 9–10 and Jer. 5. 13
10. Léon Bloy, *La Femme pauvre* (1897)
11. These quotations are taken from various parts of the tractate *Berakoth*
12. *Pirke Aboth* 1. 3
13. *Jer-Yoma* 7. 40, d
14. *Pesikta* 148, a
15. Upon the importance of the covenant, see above, p. 29 et seq.

16. Wis. 2. 16; 5. 5; 14. 3, etc.
17. Is. 11. 2
18. Prov. 1. 7
19. Ps. 111. 1
20. *Pirke Aboth* 1. 3
21. See the references in note 1 and Deut. 6. 5
22. On Wisdom, see particularly Ecclus. 1. 1
23. Cf. *Pirke Aboth* 3
24. Acts 23. 8
25. *Wars* 2. 8
26. Lev. 11. 44; 19. 2; 20. 26; 21. 6, etc.
27. Bonsirven, *op. cit.*, p. 134
28. Matt. 5. 28
29. *Mekhilta* on Ex. 20. 4, p. 110
30. On marriage, see above, p. 116 et seq.

31. Josephus, *Autobiography* 9. 42 et seq.

32. See above, p. 316

33. Matt. 22. 39 and Mk. and Lk. in the places given in note 1

34. Various quotations from *Gittin* 7

35. *Kethuboth* 57, b

36. Lk. 19. 8

37. On the Law, see above, p. 165 et seq.

38. *Peah* 1. 1

39. Matt. 5. 43

40. On the national pride of the Jews, see above, p. 40

41. There are innumerable quotations to this effect in the Bible, for example: 1 Par. 17. 21; Ps. 88; Is. 49. 3; and innumerable Talmudic commentaries

42. See the citations and the references in Bonsirven's *Les Idées juives* p. 77

43. On the Diaspora, see above, p. 43 et seq.

44. *Pirke Aboth* 1. 12

45. Acts 2. 9–11

46. *Siphra* 56. 6

47. Lk. 10. 28

48. *Pirke Aboth* 1. 1

49. Several texts in Talmudic literature develop this idea; for example, *Siphra Nombres* 15. 22

50. On the Pharisees, see above, p. 386

51. There is a separate translation of the tractate *Shabbath*: see bibliography

52. 2 Cor. 3. 6

53. S. W. Baron, *op. cit.*

54. *Shebiith* 10. 3

55. Acts 15. 10

56. Matt. 23–25

57. On the Sabbath, see p. 345

58. Mk. 2. 23–28

59. On the origins and the evolution of messianism, see the last chapter of our *Histoire sainte*, and also the chapter in Father Bonsirven's *Idées juives*

60. Lk. 1. 68; 2. 38; 24. 21

61. Jn. 1. 29

62. Jn. 4. 25

63. Lk. 7. 19

64. Jn. 10. 24

65. Mk. 11. 10

66. Jn. 6. 15

67. See the word *Messie* in the index of *Bible apocryphe*.

68. Ps. 73. 9

69. *Wars* 6. 5

70. *Sukkah* 51, a, and *Baba Bathra* 73. 6.

71. Is. 53. 2–10 (see also 50. 4–9 and 52. 13)

72. Zach. 12. 10

73. Wis. 2. 10

74. Mic. 5. 1 (A. Lods writes, 'The idea of a suffering Messiah appears to have been completely foreign to the Judaism of about the time of Christ'. *La Bible* (Paris, 1937), p. 41). Father Lagrange and many Christian commentators are of the same opinion

FINALE: JESUS AMONG HIS PEOPLE AND IN HIS TIME

1. Péguy: *Le Mystère de la Charité de Jeanne d'Arc*, in *Cahiers de la Quinzaine* (January, 1910). The moving book of Jules Isaac, *Jésus et Israël* (Paris, 1948) develops this statement with a great wealth of argument and reference

2. M. J. Lagrange, *Le Judaïsme avant Jésus-Christ*, p. 9

3. Rom. 9. 3–6

4. Heb. 7. 14

5. Apoc. 5. 5
6. Matt. 1–17 and Lk. 3. 23–38
7. Col. 4. 4
8. Upon the rites at the time of a birth, see above, p. 101 et seq.
9. Lk. 2, 21
10. Lk. 2. 22–24
11. Jesus, son of Eliezer: Lk. 3. 29
12. On the name of Mary, see above, p. 108
13. Lk. 2. 41–50
14. Matt. 13. 54–57
15. Upon hair, see above, p. 303
16. On the cloak without a seam, see above, p. 213
17. Deut. 22. 1. Cf. Matt. 9. 20; Lk. 8. 43
18. Lk. 24. 42; Jn. 21. 9–14
19. On Christ's Aramaic, see above, p. 266
20. Upon the manner of expression, see above, p. 269
21. For example, the famous 'If a man strikes thee on thy right cheek, turn the other cheek also towards him' (Matt. 5. 39) arises from a verse in Lamentations (3. 30)
22. Jn. 4. 21–27
23. Matt. 10. 6
24. Mk. 7
25. Mk. 11. 15–17
26. For example, Jn. 7. 14; Jn. 10. 12, etc.
27. Mk. 14. 13; Lk. 22. 7; Matt. 26. 17
28. Matt. 5. 17–19
29. Matt. 24. 20
30. H. Pernot, *Pages choisies des Evangiles*, p. 11
31. Matt. 5. 17–20

32. See above, p. 406
33. See above, p. 414
34. See above, p. 419
35. See the section on the Essenes, p. 398
36. Daniélou, *op. cit.*, p. 28
37. Lk. 1. 68; 2. 38; 24. 21
38. J. Bonsirven, *op. cit.*, p. 211
39. Matt. 12. 6
40. Jn. 4. 21–23
41. 'Love your enemies', cf. p. 393
42. Acts 13. 24
43. Cf. J. Isaac, *op. cit.*, pp. 118–119
44. Rom. 10. 4
45. 'I have not found faith like this, even in Israel'
46. On Christ and the Samaritans, see p. 41
47. Mk. 2. 23–28; Matt. 12. 1–8; Lk. 6. 1–5
48. That which Théodore de Bèze sent to Cambridge, cf. *Jesus in His Time*, introduction and section 'The opposing Elements' in Chap. 8
49. Matt. 15. 11; Mk. 7. 15
50. See the introduction to *Jesus in His Time*, section 'The Silence of Flavius Josephus', particularly what is said about the interpolated passage
51. For example, Matt. 4; Mk. 1; Lk. 8
52. Mk. 9. 30
53. Matt. 4. 25; Mk. 3. 9; Lk. 6. 17
54. Matt. 21. 10
55. Jn. 7. 1, 10; 11. 54
56. Lk. 19. 48
57. Father Lagrange, *L'Evangile de Jésus-Christ*, p. 153
58. Jas. 5. 6

INDEX